The Officia
to CorelDRAW!™ 6
for Windows 95

About the Authors...

Martin Matthews and Carole Boggs Matthews are experts in graphic design and desktop publishing. They are also the authors of over 30 computer books, including *CorelDRAW!™ 4 Made Easy*, *CorelDRAW!™ 5 Made Easy*, *Using Pagemaker 5 for Windows*, and *Networking Windows for Workgroups*.

The Official Guide to CorelDRAW!™ 6 for Windows 95

Martin Matthews
Carole Boggs Matthews

Osborne **McGraw-Hill**

Berkeley New York St. Louis San Francisco Auckland Bogotá Hamburg London Madrid Mexico City Milan Montreal New Delhi Panama City Paris São Paulo Singapore Sydney Tokyo Toronto

Osborne **McGraw-Hill**
2600 Tenth Street
Berkeley, California 94710
U.S.A.

For information on translations or book distributors outside the U.S.A., or to arrange bulk purchase discounts for sales promotions, premiums, or fundraisers, please contact Osborne **McGraw-Hill** at the above address.

The Official Guide to CorelDRAW!™ 6 for Windows 95

1234567890 DOC 99876

ISBN 0-07-882168-1

Publisher: Larry Levitsky
Aquisitions Editor: Scott Rogers
Project Editor: Mark Karmendy
Copy Editor: Dennis Weaver
Computer Designer: Jani Beckwith
Cover Designer: TMA

Cover art, *Radio 3*, by Theodor Ushev, Grand Prize recipient for Page Layout and Design, Corel World Design Contest, 1995

CONTENTS AT A GLANCE

CONTENTS

FOREWORD

The Official Guide to CorelDRAW!™ 6 for Windows 95 represents the first in a series of books dedicated to the users of Corel software. The launch of this series gives users the ability to understand the depth of the software product they have purchased. The authors, along with staff at Corel, have spent many hours working on the accuracy and features included in this book.

This publication will provide an in-depth overview of Corel's first Windows 95™ product offering. New users, as well as those who have purchased upgrades, will find significant value in these pages. The "CorelDRAW! in Action" boxes will help improve your ability to make excellent use of CorelDRAW. The publication will also reveal tips and tricks which have been developed over several versions of CorelDRAW by the most experienced users.

The "Official Guide to Corel products" series represents a giant step in the ability of Corel to disseminate information to our users through the help of Osborne/McGraw-Hill and the fine authors involved in the series. Congratulations to the team at Osborne who have created an excellent book.

Dr. Michael C.J. Cowpland
President & CEO
Corel Corporation

ACKNOWLEDGMENTS

This book is the first from the new CorelPRESS imprint and is the inspiration of Dr. Michael Cowpland and Michael Bellefeuille of Corel Corporation, and Larry Levitsky and Scott Rogers of Osborne/McGraw-Hill. They had the determination to make it happen and the fortitude to see it through. This book and the press behind it are their creation.

A number of other people at Corel Corporation, at Osborne, and elsewhere provided much appreciated assistance in producing *The Official Guide to CorelDRAW!™ 6 for Windows 95*.

The Corel Corporation team, ably lead by Michael Bellefeuille, had Kim Connerty as the most capable point person who also is the most knowledgable person on Draw. Throughout the project Kim always had ready answers or quickly got us in contact with the person who did. Among other knowledgable people that Kim pointed us to were Ann Covan and Denise Zutruen on PRESENTS, Jean-Louis Marin on DREAM, David Garrett on PAINT, and John Sevez and Rus Miller for printing.

The team assembled by Osborne/McGraw-Hill was superbly lead by Scott Rogers with invaluable support from Daniela Dell'Orco. The Osborne editorial team was lead by Mark Karmendy who, with Dennis Weaver as copy editor, made sure the book was readable. A special thanks also to Julia Woods for helping make the project a reality.

Erik Paulsen is responsible for much of the excellent work of bringing this book up to the CorelDRAW!™ 6 release. Erik put in many long hours fighting inoperable betas and impossible schedules. Bruce Dobson ably reviewed the book for technical accuracy.

All of these people put out a considerable amount of effort in a short period of time along with more than a little of themselves to produce an excellent product. Their effort and the results are greatly appreciated.

INTRODUCTION

Since its initial release in January of 1989, CorelDRAW!™ has become the most talked-about graphics software package for IBM-compatible PCs. It is easy to understand why the program has received many major industry awards and so much favorable attention. Quite simply, no other drawing package offers so many powerful drawing, text-handling, autotracing, color separation, and special effects capabilities in a single package. CorelDRAW!™ 6 continues this tradition by adding an enhanced user interface, a new Corel PRESENTS™, CorelDREAM 3D™, Corel MOTION 3D™, as well as a large number of other enhancements to its existing applicaitons and utilities.

Uniquely Corel + Osborne

Unlike all other books on CorelDRAW!™, *The Official Guide to CorelDRAW!™ 6 for Windows 95* brings together the people at Corel Corporation who have the technical expertise you can only get from creating the product, with the book production and distribution expertise of the people at Osborne/McGraw-Hill. Every chapter of this book was read and commented on by people within Corel who are involved daily with the creation of the product. This dialog was invaluable in providing detail insights into the product and tips on how to use it.

About This Book

The Official Guide to CorelDRAW!™ 6 for Windows 95 is a step-by-step guide to CorelDRAW!™ that leads you from elementary skills to more complex ones. Each chapter contains hands-on exercises that are richly and clearly illustrated, against which you can match the results on your computer screen.

This book makes few assumptions about your graphics experience or computer background. If you have never used a mouse or worked with a drawing package, you can begin with the exercises in the early chapters and move forward as you master each skill. On the other hand, if you have experience in desktop publishing, graphic design, or technical illustration, you can concentrate on the chapters that cover more advanced features or features that are new to you. Even the basic chapters contain exercises that stimulate your creativity, so it is worth your while to browse through each chapter in order to gain new knowledge and ideas.

How This Book Is Organized

The Official Guide to CorelDRAW!™ 6 for Windows 95 is designed to let you learn by doing, regardless of whether you are a new, intermediate, or advanced user of CorelDRAW!. You begin to draw right away and as the book proceeds, you continue to build on the skills you have learned in previous chapters.

The organization of this book is based on the philosophy that knowing how to perform a particular task is more important than simply knowing the location of a tool or menu command. The body of the book, therefore, contains step-by-step exercises that begin with basic drawing skills and then progress to advanced skills that combine multiple techniques.

The organization of each chapter will help you quickly locate any information that you need to learn. Each section within a chapter begins with an overview of a particular skill and its importance in the context of other CorelDRAW!™ functions. In most chapters, every section contains one or more hands-on exercises that allow you to practice the skill being taught.

Conventions Used in This Book

The Official Guide to CorelDRAW!™ 6 for Windows 95 uses several conventions designed to help you locate information quickly. The most important of these are listed here:

- Terms essential to the operation of CorelDRAW!™ or the understanding of this book appear in italics the first time they are introduced.
- The first time an icon or tool in the CorelDRAW! toolbox or interface is discussed, it often appears as a small graphic in the margin beside the text.
- You can locate the steps of any exercise quickly by looking for the numbered paragraphs that are indented from the left margin.
- Names of keys on the keyboard appear in small capital letters, which set them off from the regular text, for example, ENTER.
- Text or information that you must enter using the keyboard appears in boldface.

Getting Acquainted with CorelDRAW! 6

1

Welcome to CorelDRAW! 6. You have selected one of the most innovative and advanced graphics tools available for the PC. Coreldraw will sharpen your creative edge by allowing you to create and edit any line, shape, or character with ease and precision; fit text to a curve; autotrace existing artwork; create custom color separations and moving animation presentations; produce desktop publishing documents; and accomplish many other tasks. You can combine Coreldraw's features to achieve many different special effects, such as placing a line of text or an object in perspective; folding, contouring, rotating, or extruding a line of text or an object; blending two lines of text or two objects; and creating mirror images, masks, and 3-D simulations. CorelDRAW! 6 for Windows 95 makes these and other capabilities work for you at speeds far surpassing those of other graphics programs.

NOTE: *CorelDRAW! 6 will only run under Windows 95. If you are using a previous version of Windows you will need to upgrade to Windows 95. Previous versions of Coreldraw will run under both older versions of Windows and Windows 95, but will not take advantage of all of Windows 95 advanced features.*

The CorelDRAW! 6 Package

When you buy the CorelDRAW! 6 package you get much more than a program for drawing and illustration. There are actually four major products or applications within the package, in addition to six utilities. These products and their functions are listed in the following table.

Product	Function
CorelDRAW!	Drawing and illustration with text handling
Corel PHOTO-PAINT	Painting and photo retouching with image enhancement
Corel FONT MASTER	Font management utility for organizing TrueType and Type1 fonts
CorelDEPTH	Creating 3D text and graphics
Corel PRESENTS	Creating presentations using other Corel objects, charts, and animations
CorelDREAM 3D	Creating three-dimensional images
Corel MOTION 3D	Creating animations using three-dimensional objects
Corel OCR-TRACE	Converting bitmapped images to vector graphics and printed text to editable text (Optical Character Recognition)
Corel MULTIMEDIA MANAGER	Organizing and accessing multimedia files (graphic images, animations, sound files, etc.)
Corel CAPTURE	Capturing screen images
Corel SCRIPT Dialog Editor	Creating custom dialog boxes
Corel SCRIPT	Creating scripts for automating tasks

In addition to the applications and utilities, this CorelDRAW! 6 package also includes 1,000 fonts and over 25,000 pieces of clip art to support your creative and technical endeavors. Your software also contains many symbols that you can use as you would text characters, as well as 1000 high-resolution photographs and a library of animations and cartoon figures to use in Corel PRESENTS.

This book will show you how to use and master each of the Corel applications in a hands-on approach that allows you to follow along on your computer.

Starting Coreldraw

To start Coreldraw, first turn on your computer. When Windows 95 has completed loading, your screen should appear similar to Figure 1-1.

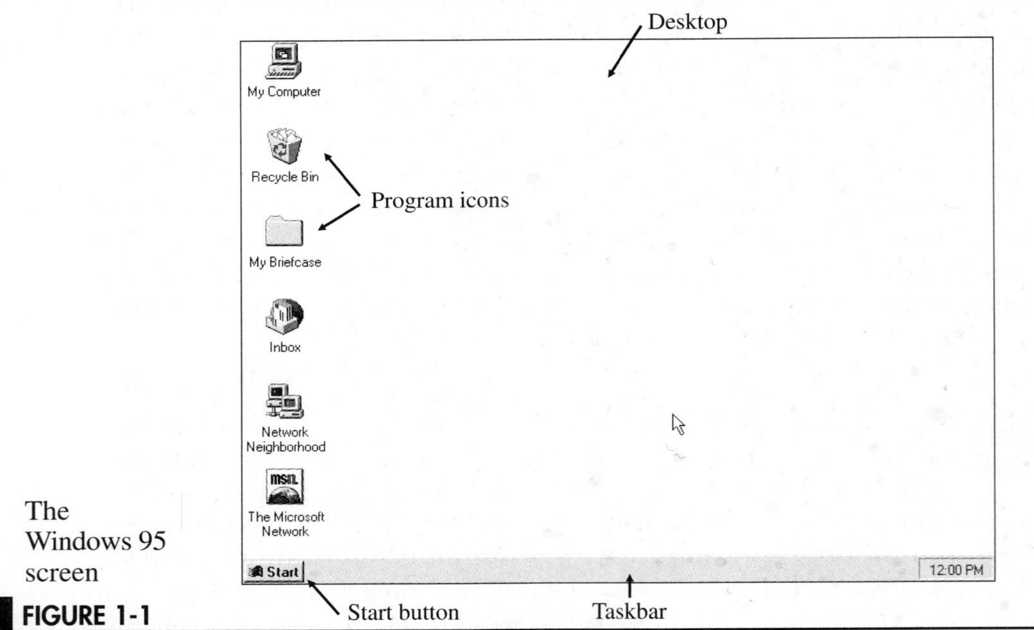

The Windows 95 screen

FIGURE 1-1

Across the bottom of the screen is the Windows 95 *Taskbar*. The Taskbar is where you start a program, switch among programs already running, and access Windows 95 applications and utilities. You can move the Taskbar to any of the four sides of the screen, hide it, or have it displayed on top of or behind another window. You will use the Start menu on the Taskbar to start Coreldraw.

1. Click on the Start button on the Taskbar (with your mouse, place the mouse pointer on top of the button labeled "Start" and press and release the left mouse button) to display the Start menu, shown here:

The Start menu contains commands for opening Windows 95 utilities (Shut Down, Run, Help, Find, and Settings) and your programs. The Windows 95 utilities can be started by clicking on the appropriate Start menu icon or name. Selecting a command with an arrow (Find, Settings, Documents, and Programs) opens a *flyout* submenu containing additional choices. The Find command opens a dialog box for locating files stored on your hard drives or, if you are connected to a network, files on other network drives. You can also open applications and documents in Windows 95 using *shortcuts*. A shortcut is an icon that can be placed on the Start menu. Clicking on the icon will then start the application. Shortcuts can also be placed directly on the desktop, as shown in Figure 1-1. When you install a program, Windows 95 will place the program group only in the Programs menu.

Customize IT! *You can add shortcuts to your applications on the Start menu by opening the Start menu and clicking on Settings. In the Settings flyout menu, click on Taskbar, then click on the Start Menu Programs tab. Click on Add, then click on Browse. Locate the program you want to add to the Start menu and double-click on it. (CorelDRAW! 6 is located in the C:\Corel6\Programs folder if you accepted the default folder name during installation.) Click on Next, then double-click on the menu you want to add the program to. Type the name you want for the program and click on Finish. You can also add a program to the top of the Start menu by dragging its icon from Windows Explorer onto the Start button.*

2. In the Start menu, point on Programs, then point on Corel Graphics. (If you chose a different name for the Coreldraw program group during installation, point on the name you used.) The Corel applications menu will be displayed, as shown here.

AUTION: *If you don't see "Corel Graphics" (or the name for the Corel program group you chose) in the Programs menu, you need to install Coreldraw.*

3. Click on CorelDRW! 6.

After a moment, a copyright and information screen is displayed, then the Welcome to CorelDRAW window shown in Figure 1-2 will be displayed. The Welcome screen provides a quick way to start a new drawing, open a previously saved drawing, open the last drawing you worked on, open a template, or start the Coreldraw tutorial. If you don't want the Welcome window displayed when you start Coreldraw, click on the checkbox (the small square box with the check mark in it) at the bottom of the window.

Click on the Start a New CorelDRAW Graphic icon (the top button in the window). After a moment a new, blank page will be displayed.

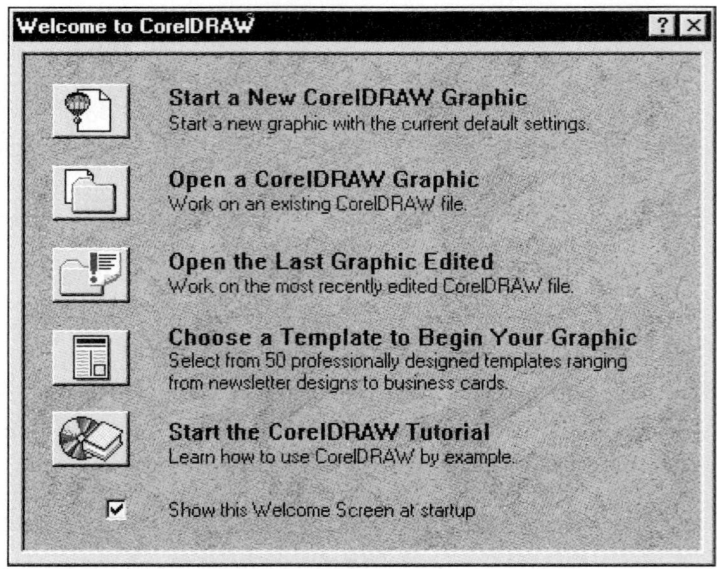

Welcome to CorelDRAW window

FIGURE 1-2

The CorelDRAW Screen

You will see references to the various screen components of Coreldraw many times throughout this book. Take a moment now to familiarize yourself with these terms and their functions within the program. Figure 1-3 shows the location of each screen component.

CORELDRAW WINDOW The Coreldraw application window contains the Coreldraw menus and tools and the workspace for multiple document windows.

DOCUMENT WINDOW The document window contains the drawing you are working on and is at the heart of the *Multiple Document Interface* (MDI)—a new feature in CorelDRAW! 6. This allows you to work on more than one drawing at a time by opening additional document windows. MDI also gives you an easy method for combining elements from separate drawings or working with multiple views of the same drawing. For example, one window could contain a full-page view of your drawing while you work on the same drawing in a magnified view in another window. When you start Coreldraw, only one document window is opened and it is

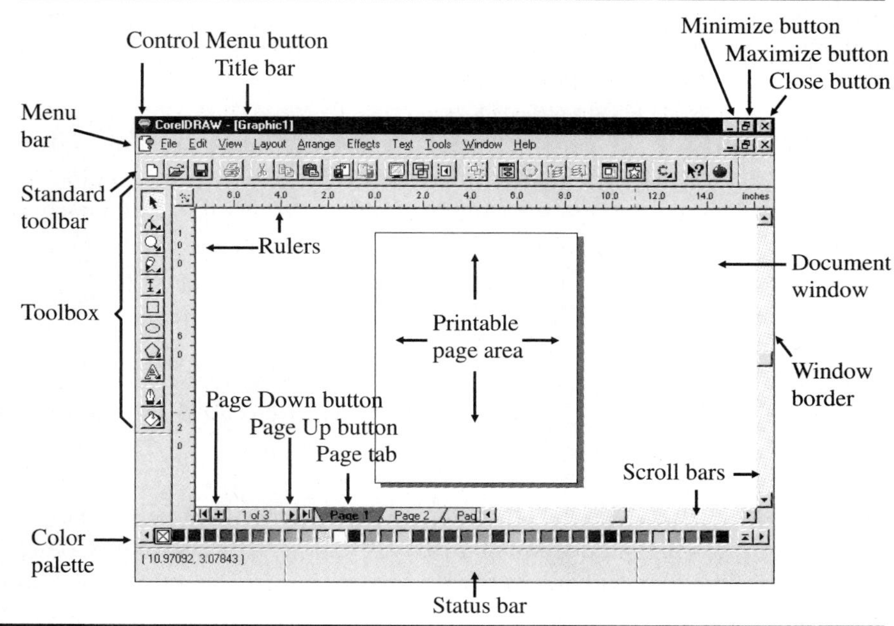

FIGURE 1-3 The Coreldraw window

maximized by default. You will learn how to work with multiple document windows in the section "Working With Multiple Views" later in this chapter.

WINDOW BORDER The Window border marks the boundaries of the Coreldraw application and document windows. By placing your mouse pointer on and dragging the border, you can change the size of the window either vertically or horizontally; or, when you point on a corner, you can change both dimensions at the same time. If the application or document windows are maximized (full screen display), they cannot be resized.

TITLE BAR The Title bar, at the top of the Coreldraw application and document windows, shows the name of the program you are working in and the name of the currently loaded image. When you first load Coreldraw, the document hasn't been saved yet, so the title bar reads "Graphic1." After you save a file, the file extension .cdr will appear after the filename. (All files in Coreldraw format have the file extension .cdr directly after the filename.) When a document window is maximized, as shown in Figure 1-3, only the Coreldraw application window Title bar is visible.

MINIMIZE BUTTON The Minimize button is in the Title bar at the upper-right corner of both windows, the third button from the right. Click on this button to decrease the size of the window so you only see the task on the Taskbar. When running minimized within Windows 95, Coreldraw frees up memory that you can use to run another application. To restore Coreldraw to its previous size, position the mouse over the Coreldraw task button on the Taskbar and click.

MAXIMIZE BUTTON If you want to make the Coreldraw window fill the entire screen, or the document window fill the entire workspace, click on the Maximize button located to the right of the Minimize button. When the window is maximized this button then turns into the Restore button, as shown in the margin. You can return the Coreldraw window, or a document window, to its previous size by clicking on the Restore button.

CLOSE BUTTON When you want to exit Coreldraw, or close a document window, you can click on the Close button, located to the right of the Maximize button on the far right of the Title bar.

CONTROL MENU BUTTON The Control Menu button on the far left of the Title bar of both the program and document windows provides access to the Control menu, which is another way to move, minimize, maximize, or otherwise change the

Coreldraw program or document windows. To use the Control menu, simply click on the icon, or press ALT-SPACEBAR for the program window or ALT-HYPHEN for the document window, and the Control menu will open. Select the option you want by clicking on it or typing the underlined letter. When you have finished, click anywhere outside the Control menu or press ESC to close it. The Control menu is a Windows feature that is seldom used in Coreldraw.

MENU BAR The menu bar contains ten menus that you open or pull down by clicking on one of the menu names. See the section "Coreldraw Menus" later in this chapter for a brief summary of the command options in each menu.

STANDARD TOOLBAR The Standard toolbar, immediately below the Menu bar, contains a set of buttons that allows you to carry out a number of menu commands with a single click on a button. See the section "Toolbar Buttons" later in this chapter for an explanation of each button. CorelDRAW! 6 can display a number of different toolbars. To turn toolbars on or off, click on any toolbar border with the right mouse button. The Toolbar *pop-up* menu will be displayed, as shown here.

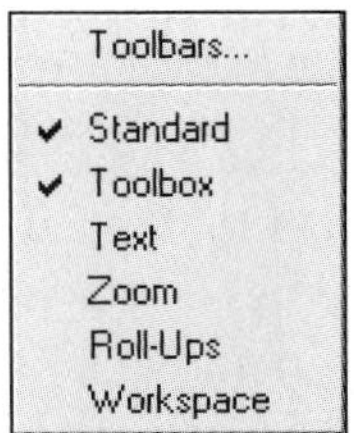

Toolbars with a check mark are turned on (displayed). To *toggle* a toolbar on or off, click on the toolbar name. Toolbars can also be displayed by clicking on the Toolbar option, which opens the Toolbars dialog box, shown here.

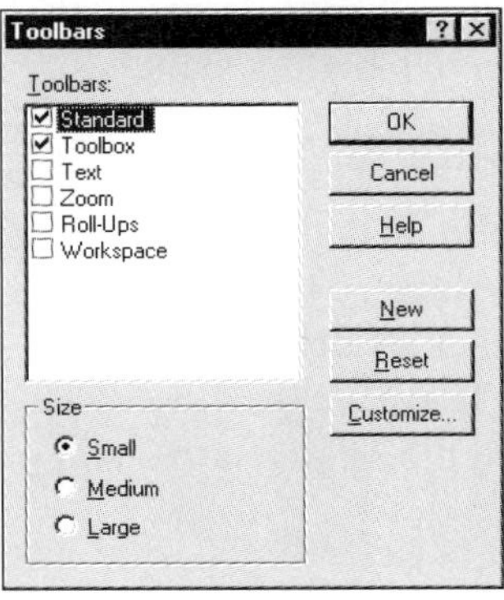

With the Toolbars dialog box you can also change the size of the buttons on he toolbars. Clicking on the Customize button opens the Toolbars tab of the Customize dialog box where you can create your own toolbar containing the tools you use most often. Customizing Coreldraw's interface is covered in Chapter 14, "Combining Coreldraw Features."

NOTE: *Corel also refers to the Standard toolbar as the "ribbon bar." However, the name toolbar is generally used by Windows applications. Throughout this book the Standard toolbar will be referred to simply as the toolbar, and the other toolbars will be referred to by their full names. For example, the Text toolbar.*

PRINTABLE PAGE AREA The printable page area is the rectangle in the center of the document window where your Coreldraw images are created. The exact size of the page depends on the settings you choose through the Page Setup command in the Layout menu. When you first load Coreldraw, the screen displays the total printable page area. Once you learn about magnification later in this chapter, you can adjust the area of the page that is visible at any one time.

SCROLL BARS The scroll bars on the right and bottom-right of the document window are most useful when you are looking at a magnified view of the page. Use the horizontal scroll bar to move to the left or right of the currently visible area of the page; use the vertical scroll bar to move to an area of the page that is above or below the currently visible area.

PAGE UP/DOWN BUTTONS To move through the pages in your document in sequence, click on either the Page Up button (to see the next page) or Page Down button (to view the previous page). To switch to the first page of your document, click on the First Page button to the left of the Page Down button. The Last Page button, to the right of the Page Up button, switches to the last page.

RULERS The horizontal and vertical rulers that appear in Figure 1-3 might not be on your screen. These are optional and must be specifically turned on by selecting Rulers from the View menu. A dashed line in each ruler shows you where the mouse pointer is. You can see such lines at about 11 inches on the horizontal ruler and about 3 inches on the vertical ruler. These are the same as the coordinates in the Status bar. The rulers allow you to judge the relative sizes and placements of objects quickly and accurately.

TOOLBOX The Toolbox contains tools that carry out the majority of the drawing and editing functions in Coreldraw. Click on a tool button to select it. The selected tool button will have a light gray background. Other changes to the screen or to a selected object may also occur, depending on which tool you have selected. For a brief explanation of the function of each tool, see the section, "The Coreldraw Toolbox," later in this chapter. The Toolbox can be left fixed on the left side of the Coreldraw window or can be made into a floating toolbox that you can drag around the screen. By having the Toolbox float, you allow your drawing to take up the extra half-inch of the screen that was occupied by the Toolbox.

COLOR PALETTE The Color palette at the bottom of the Coreldraw window in Figure 1-3 allows you to apply shades of gray and colors to the objects you create. Like the rulers, the Color palette can be turned on or off in the View menu and you can also select the type of colors you want displayed. In Coreldraw, shading and color can be applied to either a character's or an object's outline or body.

STATUS BAR The Status bar, which in CorelDRAW! 6 appears by default at the bottom of the screen, contains a rich source of information about the image you have on your screen. When you first load Coreldraw, this bar contains only a pair of numbers: the coordinates of the mouse pointer. When you are drawing or editing images, however, it displays information such as number, type, and dimensions of objects you select and the distance you travel when moving these objects. The exact nature of the information displayed depends on what you are doing at the time. The Status bar is an invaluable aid to technical illustration or to any work that requires precision. The Status bar may be moved below the Menu bar at the top of the application window, reduced to a single line of text, or turned off altogether to provide a larger drawing area. The information displayed on the Status bar can also be customized. To customize the Status bar, click on it with the right mouse button. The Status Bar pop-up menu, shown here, is displayed.

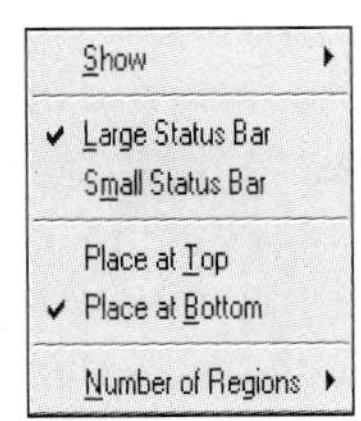

The Status Bar pop-up menu lets you select what will be displayed on the Status bar, how many lines will be displayed, where the Status bar will be displayed, the number of regions the Status bar will have (selectable from two to six), and the size of each region.

With a basic understanding of the screen elements, you can get around the Coreldraw program and document windows easily. The next four sections of this chapter explore the primary interface elements—menus, dialog boxes, buttons, and tools—in greater depth.

Coreldraw Menus

When you open or *pull down* a menu, some commands appear in boldface while others appear dimmer, in gray. You can select any command that appears in boldface, but commands in gray are not available to you at the moment. Commands become available for selection depending on the objects you are working with and the actions you apply to them.

You'll learn to use the menus by working with particular functions of Coreldraw, but the following sections will briefly describe the major purposes of each. Open each menu by clicking on it and look at the menu as you are reading about it.

THE FILE MENU The File menu allows you to start a new drawing, to save a drawing as a *file* on a disk, and to reopen a drawing you have previously saved. You can also import and export parts or all of a drawing, print a drawing, and exit from Coreldraw. The four most recent files you have worked with are listed at the bottom of the menu and can be easily opened by clicking on the filename. You can also access Microsoft Exchange, part of the Windows 95 package, to send Coreldraw files as either electronic mail (e-mail) or as a fax.

THE EDIT MENU The Edit menu allows you to undo, redo, or repeat the last action you performed; to cut, copy, and paste objects or images; to delete, duplicate, or *clone* (duplicate where the copy also receives any modifications made to the original) objects; to select all the objects in a drawing; to select text in multiple text frames; to copy properties from one object to another; to locate objects by their properties using the Find by Properties roll-up; and to insert objects from and manage links with other applications. With Coreldraw's Insert Memo option you can attach a "note" to a Coreldraw document, or a document created in another application. Your note can include bitmapped graphics. You can also create barcodes for your documents.

The Edit and other menus contain options that open "roll-ups," which is short for "roll-up window." A roll-up window is a dialog box that can remain on the screen either at its normal size or "rolled up" with just its title bar showing. Roll-ups will be fully discussed in the next major section, "Dialog Boxes."

THE VIEW MENU The View menu has one major function: to help you customize the user interface and make Coreldraw work the way you want it to. Use the commands in this menu to customize your screen tools; to set the properties of Tools, Objects and Styles; to display or hide the Rulers, Status bar, Toolbox, and Color Palette; to set the screen for Wireframe or Full-screen previews of your images; and to determine how you want bitmaps and colors displayed.

THE LAYOUT MENU The Layout menu allows you to control the layout of pages. You can insert or delete pages, go from one page to another, set margins and page sizes, show the page border, show facing pages, add a page frame, specify the paper color and layout, and work with layers that allow you to construct your drawing in multiple overlays. You can manage styles and the scale assigned to drawings and set attributes for the grid and for guidelines. Finally, you can turn on or off the property of an object *snapping to* the grid, guidelines, or another object as you move the first object. These options are discussed throughout the book.

THE ARRANGE MENU The Arrange menu deals with the relative placement of objects within an image. Select the commands in this menu to align or order a selected object or group of objects; to combine, group, ungroup, or break apart selected objects; and to weld, intersect, trim, or separate objects. You can also convert text and objects like rectangles to curves. The Transform roll-up allows you to position, rotate, scale and mirror, size, and skew a selection. You can also clear (remove) transformations. You will find more details about the Arrange menu commands in Chapter 5.

THE EFFECTS MENU The Effects menu allows you to open a number of roll-ups, with which you can create special effects with text and objects that transform their images. The Add Perspective command allows you to create a perspective view of an object, as if it was stretching towards an imaginary vanishing point, which gives a three-dimensional effect. Among the roll-ups available are Envelope, where you can place text or an object in an envelope and then shape that envelope to change the appearance of an object; Blend, which allows you to combine two lines of text or two objects; Extrude and Contour, which give a three-dimensional effect to an image; PowerLine, which draws lines that look like they were created with traditional artist tools; and Lens, which creates the effect of looking at an object through a lens, as in magnification. You can also select areas of imported bitmaps by color and combine objects to create irregular-shaped borders around bitmaps. Also with the Effects menu, you can copy or clone the effects from one object to another. Special effects are discussed in more detail in Chapter 13.

THE TEXT MENU The Text menu provides features for formatting and handling text, including changing the character, frame, and paragraph attributes; finding and replacing text; checking spelling and grammar; and locating synonyms. You can also fit text to a path, straighten it back out, or align it to a baseline. If you are doing a lot of typing, you can enter shortcuts in the Type Assist dialog box to, among other things, automatically capitalize the first letter of a sentence, correct two initial capital letters, and replace something you type, like "cdr," with a word you have specified, like "Coreldraw." Finally, you can open an Edit Text dialog box with the currently selected text and change both the text and its character and paragraph attributes.

THE TOOLS MENU The Tools menu is used to customize Coreldraw's menus, toolbars, and other tools; and for miscellaneous functions not found in other menus. The Options command provides for the fine-tuning of many different program parameters. These options are discussed throughout the book. The Customize command opens the Customize dialog box shown in Figure 1-4. You can customize keyboard shortcuts, menus, color palettes, roll-ups, and toolbars by adding or removing functions. The Customize dialog box functions are covered in Chapter 14. The View Manager allows you to create a list of views of your document. Each view has a specific magnification and area allowing you to switch quickly between close-up and overall views of your work. The Color Manager allows you to calibrate your monitor, scanner, and printer to accurately display and reproduce colors. You can open the Symbol and Presets roll-ups, where you can select text symbols and *presets* (frequently used actions for creating objects that have been recorded and stored). The Object Data roll-up allows you to create a database of information linked to a particular object. For example, you can attach a part number to a technical drawing along with the cost and any other information related to it. With the Dimensions roll-up you set the formatting for dimension lines (explained in the section "The Coreldraw Toolbox" later in this chapter) and numeric formats. The

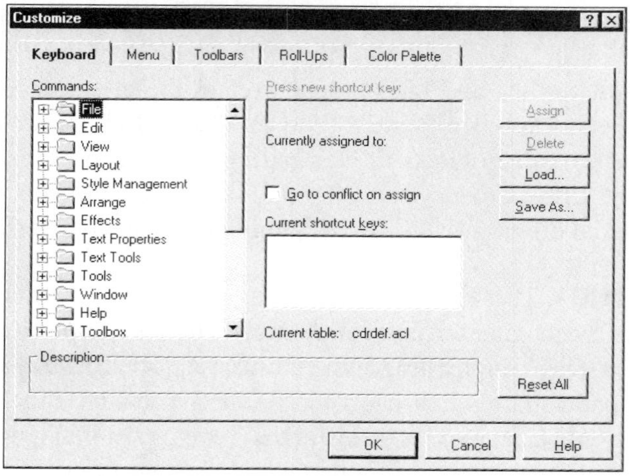

Customize dialog box

FIGURE 1-4

Tools menu also allows you to create patterns out of a selected object, attach line endings or arrows to the end of a line, create an outline style, and create symbols from a selected object. You can extract text as an ASCII string for editing, and then merge it back into a drawing. The Scripts command opens Corel SCRIPT EDITOR, an application for creating and running *scripts*, preset actions that you define to automate frequently used tasks, replacing a number of steps with a single step. See Chapter 14 for information on using Corel SCRIPT EDITOR.

THE WINDOW MENU The new Multiple Document Interface with Coreldraw 6 is controlled with the Window menu. You use the Window menu to open additional document windows for multiple views of a drawing, to arrange nonmaximized document windows in the Coreldraw workspace, and to switch between open document windows.

THE HELP MENU The Help menu allows you to access a wealth of online help features, including a tutorial and a tour of Coreldraw's features. The Help Topics command opens the CorelDRAW Help dialog box where you can choose help topics that cover the screen, menus, tools, and keyboard shortcuts and that also explain how to perform certain functions; find information about a specific command; and search the Help files for a specific word or phrase. What's This will display the Help file relating to a tool or menu command that you select. You can also run a tutorial on Coreldraw and get technical support. The final option on the Help menu, About Coreldraw, displays information on the current version of Coreldraw and other useful information on the number of objects and groups that are open, system resources, and the available disk space on your hard drives.

There are other ways in which you can get help. First, by pressing F1, the Help Contents dialog box is displayed; pressing and holding down SHIFT while pressing F1, or clicking on the second from the right button in the toolbar provide the same *context-sensitive* help, where the mouse pointer changes to a question mark and arrow, shown here.

You can then click this question mark on a menu command or screen item and a help window will be displayed, providing information on that particular subject.

Dialog Boxes

Some menu commands are automatic: Click on them and Coreldraw performs the action immediately. Other commands are followed by three dots (an ellipsis), indicating that you must enter additional information before Coreldraw can execute the command. You enter this additional information through dialog boxes that pop up on the screen when you click on the command. This section introduces you to the look and feel of typical dialog boxes. Also, much of what is said here applies to roll-ups, which are very similar to dialog boxes.

Dialog boxes contain several kinds of controls and other ways for you to enter information. Compare the following descriptions with the dialog box elements in Figures 1-5 and 1-6 to familiarize yourself with operations in a dialog box. Look at Figure 1-5 first.

OPTION BUTTONS Round option buttons like those in Figure 1-5 present you with mutually exclusive choices. In a group of option buttons, you can select only one at a time. When you click on an option button to select it, the interior becomes dark.

CHECK BOXES Square check boxes offer you choices that are not mutually exclusive, so you can select more than one option simultaneously. Check boxes, which are shown in Figure 1-5, behave like light switches: you turn them on or off when you click to select or deselect them. When you turn on or enable an option in a check box, a check mark fills it. When you turn off or disable the option, the check mark disappears.

COMMAND BUTTONS The larger buttons in a dialog box are command buttons, which are also shown in Figure 1-5. When selected, a command button is highlighted temporarily, and usually Coreldraw performs the command instantly. When you click on a command button that has a label followed by an ellipsis, you open another dialog box that is nested within it.

SPINNER, OR NUMERIC ENTRY BOX A rectangle that contains numeric entries and that has a pair of up and down scroll arrows is a spinner, or a numeric entry box (shown in Figure 1-5). You can change the numeric values in four ways. To increase or decrease the value by a single increment, click on the up or down arrow, respectively. To increase or decrease the value by a large amount, press and hold the mouse button over one of the scroll arrows or position the mouse pointer between the arrows and then drag the mouse up or down to change the number. You can also double-click on the value itself to select it and then type in a new number.

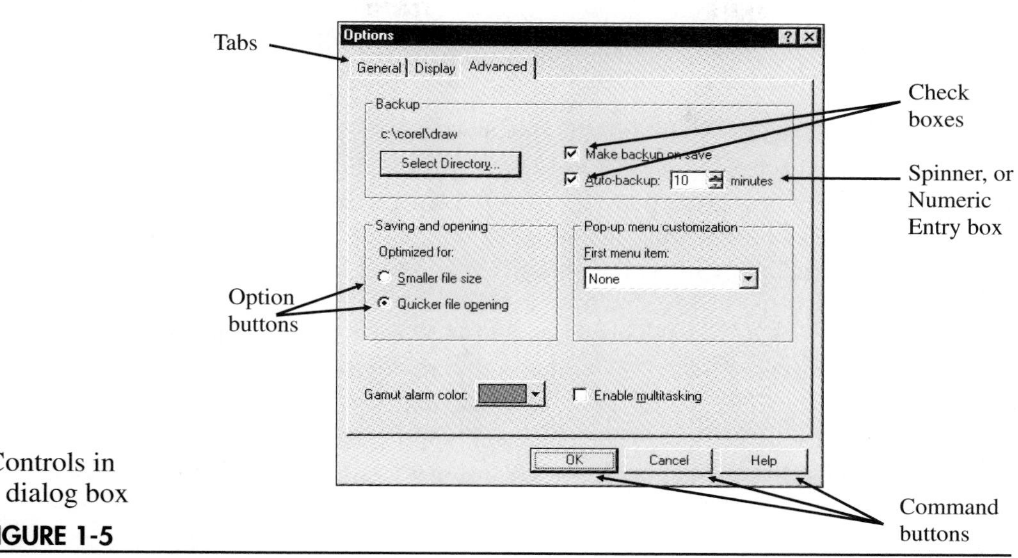

Controls in a dialog box

FIGURE 1-5

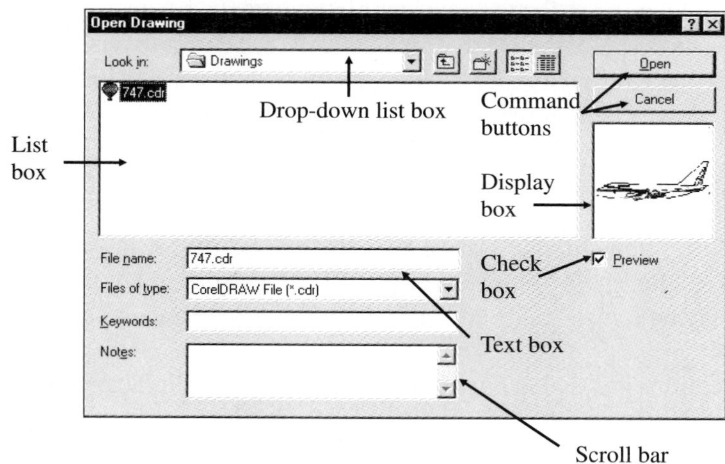

Additional dialog box controls

FIGURE 1-6

TABS Some dialog boxes, like the one shown in Figure 1-5, actually contain several dialog boxes in one. You select which dialog box you want to work on by clicking on one of the tabs at the top of the dialog box. The dialog box contents changes according to which tab has been selected.

DROP-DOWN LIST BOX Rectangles with a downward pointing arrow on the right are drop-down list boxes, as shown in Figure 1-6. By clicking on the arrow, a list drops down (or in a few cases, pops up) from which you can select an option. When a drop-down list is opened, you can choose an option by clicking on it or by typing enough letters to uniquely select the option.

TEXT BOX Text boxes, like the one shown in Figure 1-6, are used in some dialog boxes to enter strings of text. Depending on the dialog box involved, text strings might represent filenames, path names, or text to appear in an image. To enter new text where none exists, click in the text box and type the text. To edit an existing text string, click on the string, then use the keyboard to erase or add text or double-click on the text to select it, then type the new text. You will become familiar with the specific keys to use as you learn about each type of text box.

LIST BOX List boxes list the names of choices available to the user, such as filenames, folder and drive names, or typestyle names. Click on a name in the list box to select it. List boxes (see Figure 1-6) are open all the time, but are otherwise similar to drop-down list boxes.

Many list boxes and drop-down list boxes have scroll bars on their right side in order to display more of the list than is initially displayed. You can use the scroll bar to access the portions of the list that are outside of the currently visible area. To move up or down one name at a time, click on the up or down arrows on the scroll bar. To move up or down continuously, press and hold the mouse button over the up or down arrow of the scroll bar. Alternatively, you can click on the scroll bar itself, drag the scroll box, or press PGUP or PGDN to move up or down the list box in large increments.

DISPLAY BOX Some dialog boxes, such as the one shown in Figure 1-6, contain display boxes that show you your current selection. You cannot perform any action in the display box; instead, its contents change as you change your selections in the dialog box.

Some options in a dialog box may appear dim or gray, indicating that you cannot select them at the moment. There may also be a command button within a dialog box that appears in boldface or has a bold outline around it. This command button represents the default selection. You can simply press ENTER to accept the default selection. (The OK command button is normally the default.) You can leave most dialog boxes without changing any settings by clicking on the Cancel button or pressing ESC.

You will learn more about operating within dialog boxes and about specific dialog boxes as you read the other chapters in this book.

Roll-Up Windows

Roll-up windows are a special form of dialog box that you can keep on the screen to allow faster access to the features provided in the window. Once you've opened a roll-up, you can choose any of the offered features and watch them take effect while the roll-up stays open on the screen. You can also move the roll-up by dragging its Title bar. After you've completed a task, you then have the choice of either keeping the roll-up on the screen in its full size, shown here on the left, or rolling it up to its minimized size by clicking on the arrow in the upper-right corner, to the left of the Close button, shown here on the right.

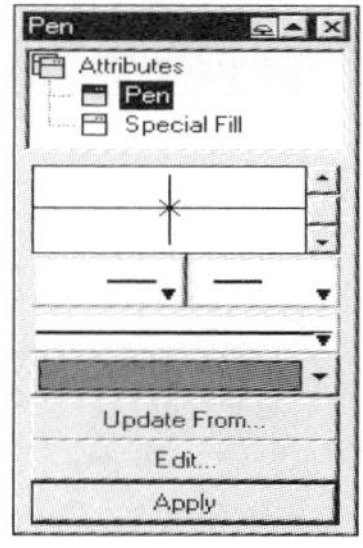

You can also have a roll-up close after you've used it (instead of having it remain on the screen) by clicking on the *Tack* button. When the Tack button is in the pin-up mode, as shown here, the roll-up behaves like a dialog box; once you have made a selection the roll-up closes.

Many of Coreldraw's roll-ups have a list box at the top of the roll-up that allows you to change the function of the roll-up. In the illustration above you can have the roll-up display the options for either the outline pen or special fills. (The outline pen is covered in Chapter 6 and fills are covered in Chapter 7.) Simply click on the function you want to work with.

You can create your own custom roll-ups by pressing CTRL *and then dragging an icon from one roll-up to another. Both roll-ups need to open (displayed on the screen) at the time.*

More than one roll-up can be kept on your screen at a time. You can also remove any roll-up from the screen by clicking on its Close button.

Toolbar Buttons

As handy as menu options are, some require as many as three or four steps to carry them out. For that reason, CorelDRAW! 6 has a toolbar with 22 buttons on it that carry out 22 different menu options by simply clicking on a button. The toolbar is shown here and the buttons and the functions they perform are described in Table 1-1.

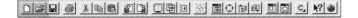

The CoreldrawToolbox

One of the features that makes Coreldraw so easy to work with is the economy of the screen. The number of tools in the Coreldraw Toolbox (see Figure 1-7) is deceptively small. Several of the tools have more than one function, and nested submenus *fly out* when you select them. This method of organization reduces screen clutter and keeps related functions together.

The tools in the Coreldraw Toolbox perform three different kinds of functions. Some allow you to draw objects, others let you edit the objects you have drawn, and a third group permits you to alter the appearance of the screen so that you can work more efficiently. This section describes each tool briefly in the context of its respective function.

Button	Function Performed	Button	Function Performed
	Create a new drawing		Display drawing as a wireframe
	Open a drawing		Snap selection to guidelines
	Save active drawing		Group selected objects
	Print active drawing		Open the Align and Distribute dialog box
	Cut selection to clipboard		Convert text or an object to curves
	Copy selection to clipboard		Move selection to the top layer
	Paste contents of clipboard		Move selection to bottom layer
	Import text or object		Open the Transform roll-up
	Export selection to another format		Open the Symbol roll-up Launch Corel applications
	Display drawing in full-screen preview		Initiate context-sensitive help Open Tutor Notes

Toolbar buttons and their functions

TABLE 1-1

Drawing Tools

Coreldraw allows you to create or work with nine different types of objects, as shown in Figure 1-8. Because you use the same tools and techniques for some of the objects,

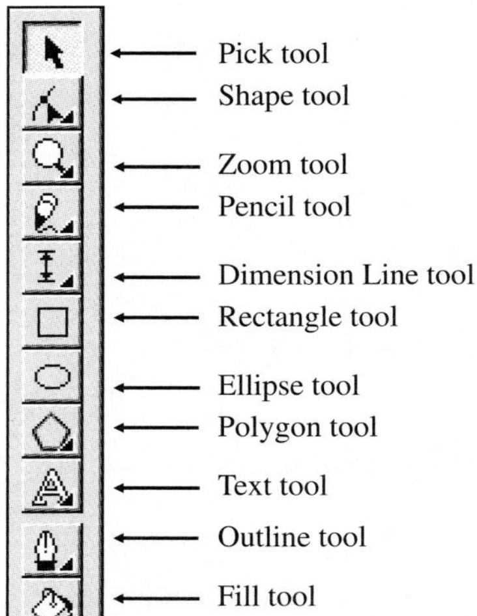

Coreldraw Toolbox icons

FIGURE 1-7

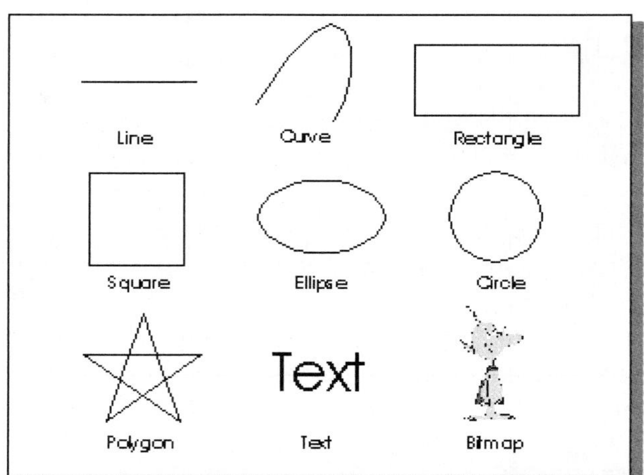

The nine types of objects

FIGURE 1-8

however, there are actually only six different *classes* of objects. These classes, and the kinds of objects you can design in each, are

- Lines and curves
- Rectangles and squares
- Ellipses and circles
- Polygons
- Text
- Bitmap (pixel-based) images imported from a scanner or paint program

Does nine seem like a small number? Professional artists and graphic designers know that basic geometrical shapes are the building blocks on which more elaborate images are constructed. After you "build" an object using one of the drawing tools, you can use one or more of the editing tools in the Coreldraw Toolbox to reshape, rearrange, color, and outline it.

The five creating tools—the Pencil tool, the Rectangle tool, the Ellipse tool, the Polygon tool, and the Text tool—are all you need to create eight of the nine object types in Coreldraw. You work with the last object type, a bitmap image, after importing it. (See Chapters 7 and 17 for a more complete discussion of this subject.)

THE PENCIL TOOL The Pencil tool, the top icon shown in the margin, is the most basic drawing tool in the Coreldraw Toolbox. This single tool allows you to create lines, curves, and curved objects. The Pencil tool can be changed from Freehand drawing to a more sophisticated multimode instrument (the rightmost icon shown on the flyout in the margin) using Bézier (pronounced "be-zee-aye," with a soft sound on the "be," as in "bear") lines and curves. Freehand mode is the default and is used for less precise work. Bézier mode is selected from the flyout menu. Click on the Pencil tool, hold the mouse button down, and two icons, one for each drawing mode, are displayed, as shown on the left. Bézier mode is used for smooth, precise curves, which remain so even when magnified or distorted.

Chapter 2 guides you through a series of exercises that teach you the basic Coreldraw skills for using this tool in both modes. You can select one of the Pencil tools by pressing F5 or clicking on the Pencil icon. When a Pencil tool is selected, the mouse pointer becomes a crosshair, like the one shown here:

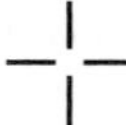

THE DIMENSION TOOL The six Dimension Lines modes, the icons of which are shown here, are used to place lines that show dimensions between two objects or locations, create *callouts* to identify an object, and measure the angle between two lines, as you would use in technical drawings. In Chapter 2, you will also learn how to use dimension lines.

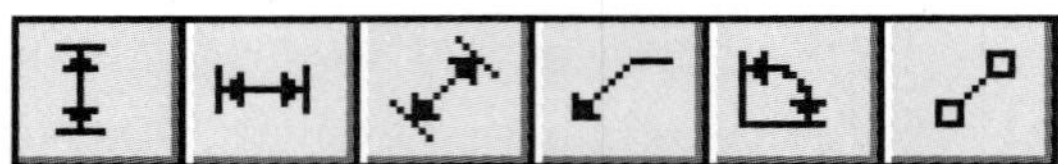

THE RECTANGLE TOOL The Rectangle tool lets you draw rectangles and squares. You'll create your own rectangles and squares in Chapter 3. To round the corners of a rectangle, however, you need to use the Shape tool, one of the editing tools in the Coreldraw Toolbox. To select the Rectangle tool, press F6 or click on the Rectangle button. The mouse pointer becomes a crosshair.

THE ELLIPSE TOOL The Ellipse tool allows you to create ellipses and perfect circles. You will learn more about using the Ellipse tool in Chapter 3. To select the Ellipse tool, press F7 or click on the Ellipse button. The mouse pointer becomes a crosshair.

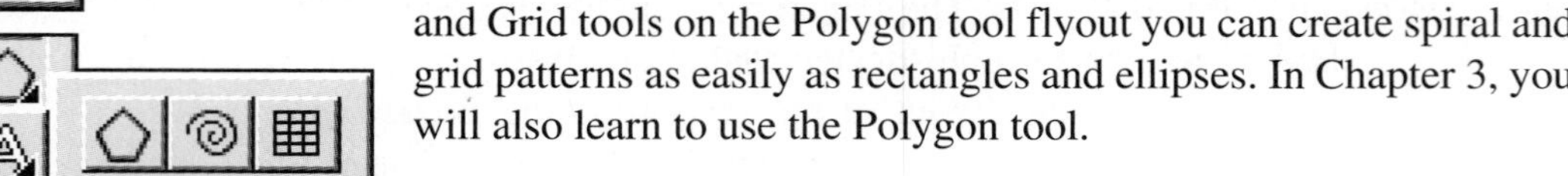

THE POLYGON TOOL The Polygon tool, which is new in CorelDRAW! 6, allows you to create multisided shapes as simply as rectangles and ellipses. With the Spiral and Grid tools on the Polygon tool flyout you can create spiral and grid patterns as easily as rectangles and ellipses. In Chapter 3, you will also learn to use the Polygon tool.

THE TEXT TOOL The Text tool contains a flyout menu with two icons (shown in the margin) for choosing between artistic text (left) and paragraph text (right). Artistic text is a simple string of characters as might appear on a poster. Paragraph text is longer and has more spacing attributes; the text in a brochure is an example of paragraph text. Either form of the text tool gives you access to the many Corel Systems fonts and to thousands of other commercial fonts as well. Besides alphabetic characters, Coreldraw includes an extensive symbol library that you can also access with the Text tool. Chapter 4 teaches you how to work with text in Coreldraw.

To select the Artistic Text tool, press F8 or click on the Artistic Text button. The mouse pointer becomes a crosshair.

If you "scribbled" on the page while trying out any of the drawing tools, clear the screen before proceeding. To do this, select the Edit menu and click on the Select All command. Then press DEL.

Editing Tools

Once you have created objects on a page with the drawing or text tools, you use a different group of tools to move, arrange, shape, and manipulate the objects. The editing tools include the Pick tool, the Shape tool, the Outline tool, and the Fill tool.

THE PICK TOOL The Pick tool is really two tools in one, varying according to the mode. In the *select mode,* you can select objects in order to move, arrange, group, or combine them. In the *transformation mode,* you can use the Pick tool to rotate, skew, stretch, reflect, move, or scale a selected object. This tool does not let you change the basic shape of an object, however. Chapters 5 and 8 introduce you to all the functions of the Pick tool.

THE SHAPE TOOL The Shape tool allows you to modify the shape of an object. Use this tool to smooth or distort any shape, add rounded corners to rectangles, convert a circle into a wedge or arc, modify a curve, or kern individual characters in a text string. You can select the Shape tool by clicking on it or by pressing F10. The Knife and Eraser tools on the Shape tool flyout allow you to "cut" and erase lines, curves, and objects. Chapters 9 and 10 cover the basics of using these tools.

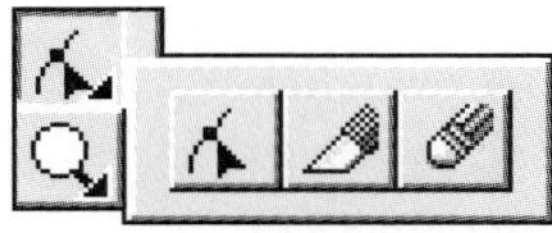

THE OUTLINE TOOL The Outline tool, like the Pick tool, functions in more than one way. Use the Outline tool and its associated flyout menu or roll-up to choose a standard or custom outline color or to create a custom outline "pen" for a selected object. Chapters 6 and 7 instruct you in the use of this tool.

THE FILL TOOL Use the Fill tool and its associated flyout menu or roll-up to select a standard or custom fill color for selected objects or text. As you'll learn in Chapter 7, your options include custom colors, PostScript screens, patterns, fountain and texture fills, and PostScript textures.

Tools for Customizing the Coreldraw Screen

The third group of tools help you customize the Coreldraw interface so that it works the way you want it to. Only one of these tools, the Zoom tool, is visible on the Coreldraw Toolbox. The Zoom tool lets you control just how much of your drawing you will view at one time. Use this tool when you need to work on a smaller area in fine detail, or when you need to zoom in or out of a picture. When the Zoom tool is selected, clicking the right mouse button will open the Zoom pop-up menu, allowing you to select a preset magnification or view. You will be using the Zoom tool throughout this book.

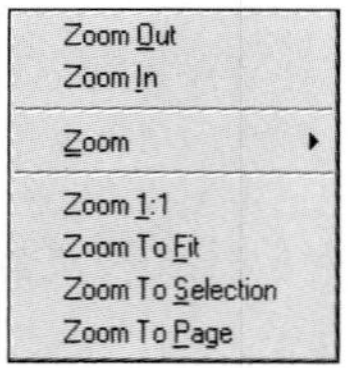

Customize IT! *The function of the right mouse button when using the Zoom tool can be changed using the Zoom Tool Properties dialog box. The dialog box is opened by clicking on the Zoom tool with the right mouse button and then selecting Properties from the pop-up menu. You can set the right mouse button to zoom out by selecting the Zoom Out option button on the dialog box. You can also have a flyout with all the Zoom tool options displayed when you select the Zoom tool by way of the Use traditional zoom flyout check box on the dialog box.*

The Zoom tool resembles a small magnifying glass and is really a view adjustment tool because it allows you to zoom in or out of the viewing area in a variety of different ways. Because the Zoom tool gives you complete control over the content of the viewing area, it can enhance every object you draw and increases the usefulness of every tool in the Coreldraw Toolbox.

When you start Coreldraw or open a new file, Zoom To Page view is the default view of the page in the document window. This view has obvious limitations if you need to edit images or do fine detail work. The Zoom tool can customize the viewing

area of your screen any way you wish. As you become familiar with this tool, you will experience greater drawing convenience and ease in editing.

The Panning tool is also on the Zoom tool flyout. The Panning tool allows you to scroll the viewable area of your drawing, in much the same way as you would use the scroll bars. The advantage of using the Panning tool is that you can move the viewable area both horizontally and vertically at one time. When the Panning tool is selected, the mouse pointer turns into a hand holding a crosshair. To pan your viewable area, select the Panning tool, click on a point and then drag the pointer in the direction you want to move your viewable area, and click again. Your drawing will scroll so that the first point you selected moves to the second point you selected.

You can also use the Zoom toolbar to adjust your viewable area. The Zoom toolbar contains seven separate tools. You display the Zoom toolbar using either the Toolbar pop-up menu (opened by clicking on any toolbar border with the right mouse button) or by selecting Toolbars from the View menu.

ZOOM IN The Zoom In tool allows you to zoom in on any area of a drawing that you select by drawing a rectangle with the Zoom In tool around the area you want.

ZOOM OUT The Zoom Out tool either zooms out of your current image by a factor of two or, if your screen currently shows a zoom-in view, returns you to the previous view.

ZOOM ACTUAL SIZE The Zoom Actual Size tool lets you see your drawing in the actual size it will be printed.

ZOOM TO SELECTED The Zoom To Selected tool zooms in on the selected objects in your drawing so they fill the drawing area.

ZOOM TO ALL OBJECTS The Zoom To All Objects tool lets you see all of the current drawing—everything you have placed on the page—in the active document window.

ZOOM TO PAGE The Zoom To Page tool returns you to the default full-page view of your graphic.

Using Magnification and View Selection

Adjusting the view on your screen (in particular, adjusting the magnification) is critical to being able to draw with precision. Therefore, the remainder of this chapter is spent learning to use the various Zoom tools to change the view presented on the screen and to work with multiple-document windows.

In order to have something to magnify, open any piece of clip art that you wish. The file Usa_t.cmx was used here. It was imported off the fourth Coreldraw CD-ROM with these steps.

1. Select Import from the File menu. The Import dialog box shown in Figure 1-9 will be displayed.
2. Select your CD-ROM drive in the Look in drop-down list box. Double-click on the Clipart folder, double-click on the Map folder, and then double-click on the Nthamer folder (use the horizontal scroll bar to locate the folders).
3. In the Nthamer folder, locate the file Usa_t.cmx and double-click on it. The file will be imported into the active document window.

You also need to open the Zoom toolbar for the following exercises.

4. Select the View menu and then click on Toolbars. In the Toolbars dialog box, select the Zoom checkbox and click on OK.

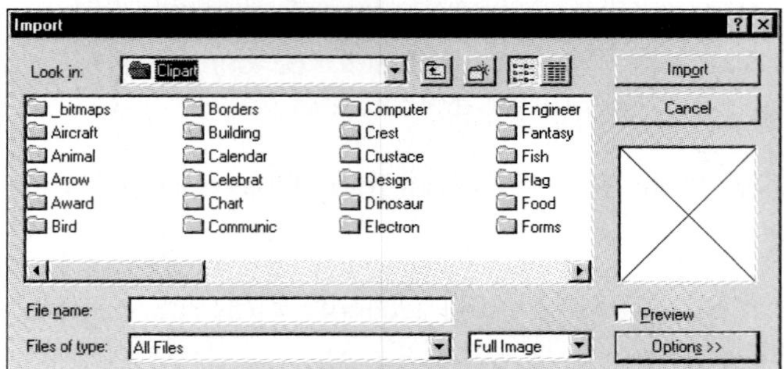

Import dialog box

FIGURE 1-9

Floating toolbars can be resized in the same way you resize windows: by dragging on the toolbar borders.

1

When you have a picture and the Zoom toolbar on your screen, you are ready to try the exercises in the next section. You can select the Zoom tools using either the mouse or your keyboard. To select a tool using the mouse, simply click on it. To select a tool using the keyboard, you must use individual function keys for each of the Zoom tools. (The Actual Size tool is not available through the keyboard.) The function keys and the Zoom tools they activate are

- **F2** Zoom In
- **F3** Zoom Out
- **SHIFT-F2** Zoom To Selected
- **F4** Zoom To All Objects
- **SHIFT-F4** Zoom To Page

All of the Zoom tools except the Zoom In and Panning tools perform their functions automatically when you select them. The following sections discuss each Zoom tool and present hands-on exercises for you to practice using them.

The Zoom In Tool

The Zoom In tool is the most versatile of the six Zoom tools because it lets you define precisely how much of your picture you want to view at once. It is invaluable for drawing fine details or editing small areas of a picture.

Defining the Viewing Area

To magnify an area of a drawing with the Zoom In tool you have to define the zoom-in area through a series of four general steps. Try this yourself now on the map or the piece of clip art you are using:

1. Select the Zoom In tool by clicking on it on the Zoom toolbar or by pressing F2. The mouse pointer changes to an image of a magnifying glass containing a plus sign.

2. Position the mouse pointer at any corner of the area you want to magnify; usually it is most convenient to start at the upper-left corner.
3. Press and hold the mouse button at that corner and then drag the mouse diagonally toward the opposite corner of the area on which you want to zoom in. A dotted rectangle (a *marquee*) will follow your mouse pointer and "lasso" the zoom-in area, as in the example in Figure 1-10.
4. When you have surrounded the area on which you want to zoom in, release the mouse button. The screen redraws, as in Figure 1-11, and the document window now contains a close-up view of only the objects you selected.

You can zoom in on successively finer areas of the screen using the Zoom In tool. You must reselect the Zoom In tool each time you wish to magnify further, however, for as soon as the screen is redrawn, Coreldraw automatically returns to the Pick tool. Simply select the Zoom In tool again and select another area, as shown in Figure 1-11. The number of times you can zoom in depends on the type of monitor and display adapter you use. Try zooming in on progressively smaller areas; eventually, you reach a point where you are unable to zoom in any further. When

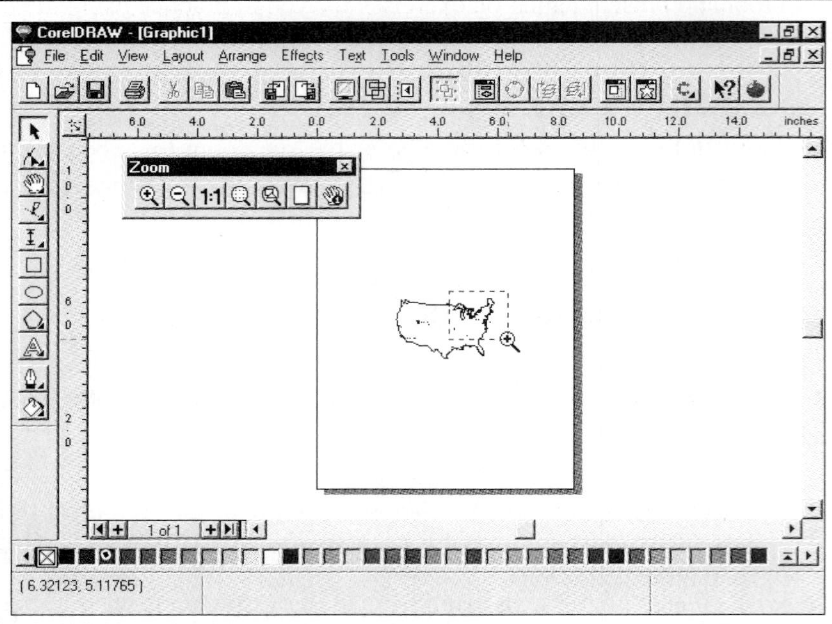

Selecting an area with the marquee

FIGURE 1-10

this occurs, you have reached the maximum magnification possible for your monitor and display adapter. At that point, you must use another Zoom tool first before you can use the Zoom In tool again.

The Zoom Out Tool

The Zoom Out tool looks like the main Zoom tool, except that it has a minus sign. As soon as you select this tool, it defines the zoom-out area for you automatically in one of two ways:

- If you are currently in Actual Size, Zoom To All Objects, or Zoom To Page viewing mode, selecting the Zoom Out tool causes your current viewing area to zoom out (expand) by a factor of two.
- If you are currently in a Zoom In viewing magnification, selecting the Zoom Out tool causes you to return to the previously selected view. You can therefore use the Zoom Out tool to back out of successive zoom ins one step at a time.

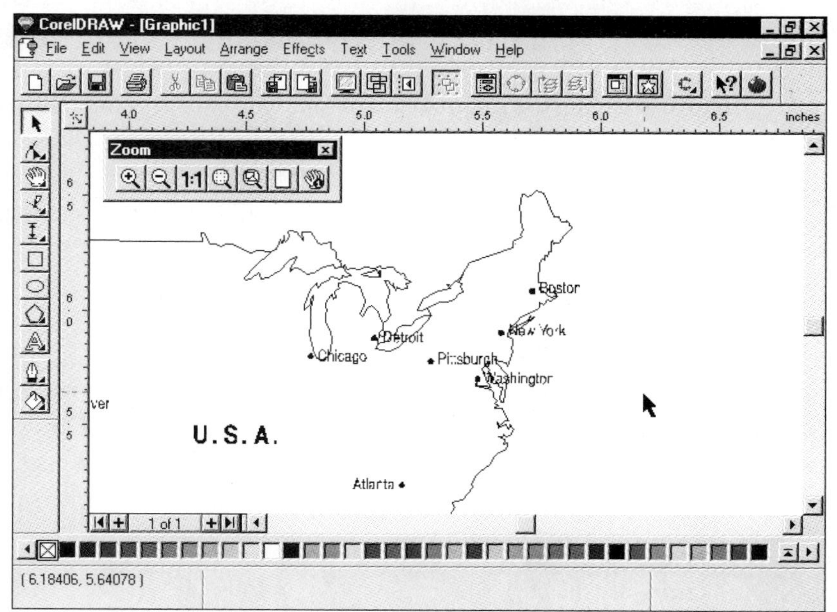

A close-up view of the selected area

FIGURE 1-11

The maximum zoom out you can achieve is a view that allows you to see one side of a 150 by 150-foot drawing.

To use the Zoom Out tool click on the Zoom Out button or press F3. The mouse pointer does not change shape when you select this tool, but the screen redraws according to the preceding rules.

In the following simple exercise, you will practice using the Zoom Out tool on the map or clip art that you opened and used above. (Your screen should be at one greater stage of magnification than that shown in Figure 1-11.)

1. Click on the Zoom Out tool or press F3. The screen redraws to the previous level of magnification, as shown in Figure 1-11.
2. Click on the Zoom Out tool again. Your screen should now look like Figure 1-10, which is at Zoom To Page view where you started.
3. Select the Zoom Out tool a third time. You can still see the full page, but it now appears at half size, as in Figure 1-12.

NOTE: *Figure 1-13 also shows another of Coreldraw's help features. When you point on a tool, and leave the pointer on the tool for a few seconds, a box displaying the function of the tool will be displayed. In this case, it identifies the Zoom Out tool.*

4. Continue selecting the Zoom Out tool until you cannot zoom out any further.

You have seen how the Zoom In and Zoom Out tools work well together when you are interested in editing a picture in minute detail. In the next section, you will learn how to achieve the kind of view that is useful when you want to print your image.

Viewing at Actual Size

When you want to see approximately how your image will look when printed, use the Zoom Actual Size tool. At a 1:1 viewing magnification, 1 inch on your screen corresponds to about 1 inch on the printed page. The amount of the page you see at this magnification may vary, depending on your monitor, video adapter, and the way Microsoft Windows 95 works with your monitor.

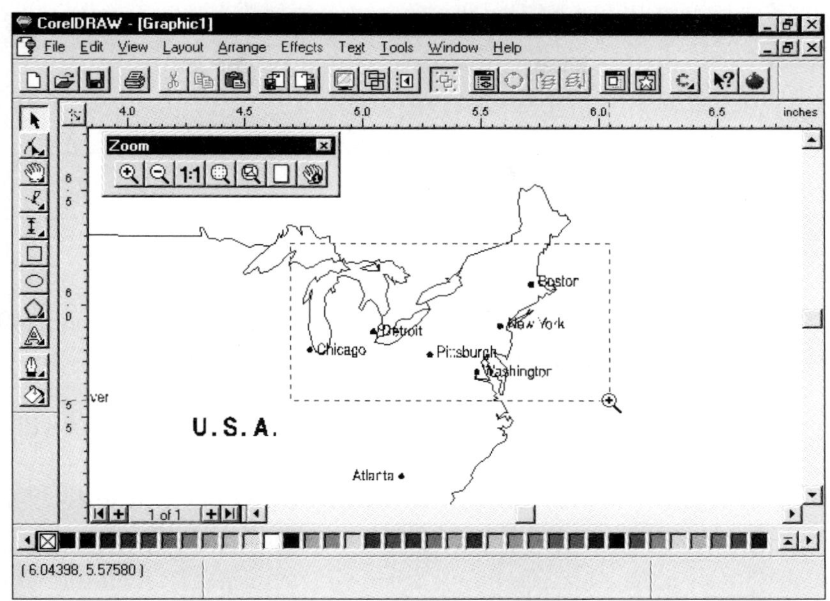

Zooming in a second time

FIGURE 1-12

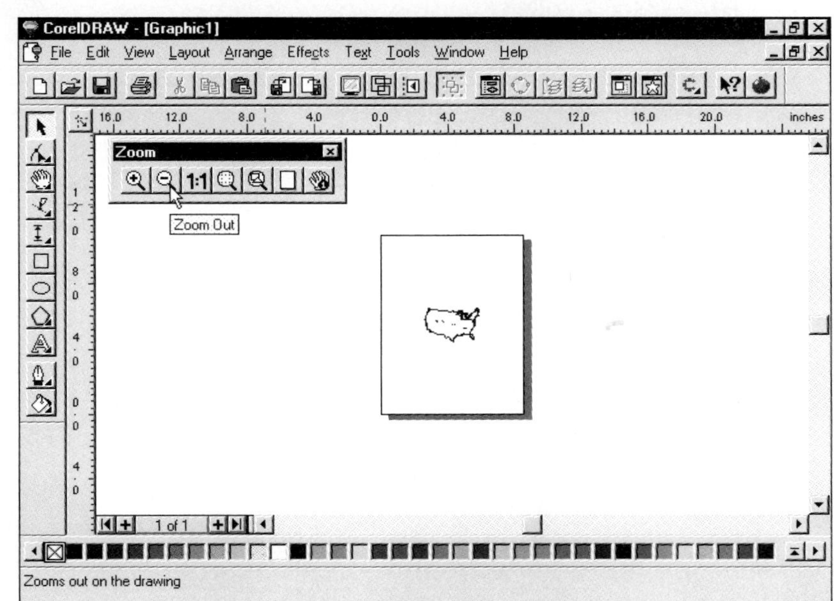

Zooming out to a 50-percent page view

FIGURE 1-13

Customize IT! *You can calibrate Coreldraw so that one inch on your screen will be exactly one inch on the printed page. Open the Zoom Tool Properties dialog box by selecting the Zoom tool on the toolbox and then clicking the right mouse button while pointing on the tool. Select Properties from the pop-up menu. When the Zoom Tool Properties dialog box is displayed, click on the Edit Resolution command button. Your screen will display horizontal and vertical rulers and two spinners (numeric entry boxes) where you can set the number of pixels (the smallest point on your monitor display) that will equal one foot.*

To achieve actual-size viewing magnification, click on the Zoom Actual Size tool. You can practice using this tool on the map that you used earlier.

1. Select the Zoom Actual Size (1:1) tool. The screen redraws to display an area of your image similar to Figure 1-14. The actual area may vary because of the variety of monitors and display adapters available. At this viewing magnification, your text still appears small.
2. Click on the Zoom Out tool. Since you were in a 1:1 view previously, you zoom out by a factor of 2.

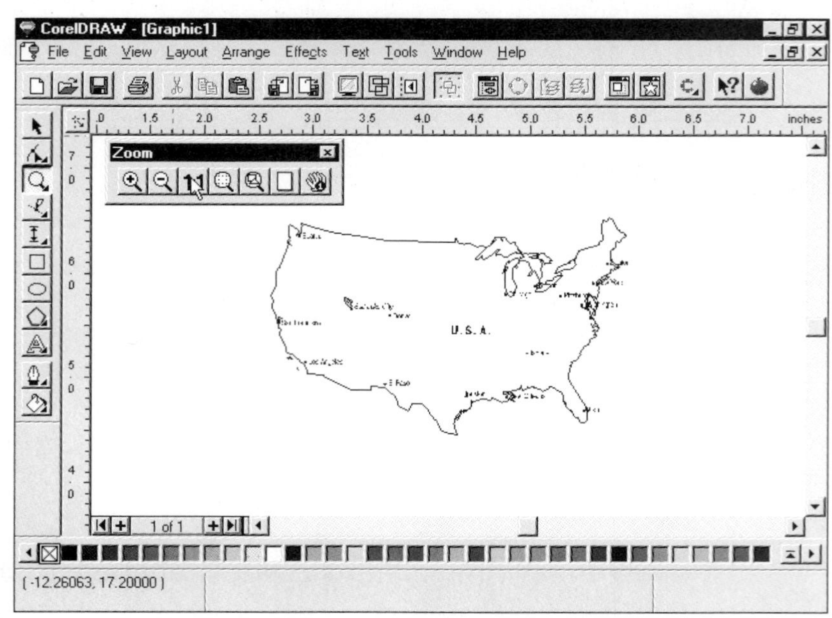

Viewing an image at actual size

FIGURE 1-14

The next two sections show you how to fit either a selected part of or an entire image within the document window. This is different from a specific level of magnification.

Viewing a Selected Object

Often you want to look at just one part of an object. As you have already seen, you can lasso that part with the Zoom In tool and display it that way. You can also select an object and zoom in on just that selected object with the Zoom To Selected tool. This is simpler than lassoing and is useful for odd-shaped objects.

See how this works with the map or piece of clip art on your screen by following these instructions (the image on your screen should be zoomed out to show some or all of the page edges).

1. Click on the map or the object on your screen with the Pick tool to select it. The object should have eight *selection boxes* (small black squares in each corner and the middle of each side) around it.
2. Click on the Zoom To Selected tool. The object on your screen should enlarge until it just fills the viewing window, as you can see in Figure 1-15.
3. Clear the screen by clicking on Select All from the Edit menu, and then pressing DEL.

Fitting a Graphic in a Window

When the pictures you draw extend all the way to the edge of the page, they already fit within the viewing window. The Zoom To All Objects tool is not of much use to you in such cases. When some blank space exists, however, you can use the Zoom To All Objects tool to view everything you have drawn, but no more. This can be especially useful for drawings that occupy only a small area of a page.

To select Zoom To All Objects view, click on the Zoom To All Objects tool or press F4. The screen redraws to fill the entire viewing area with the graphic image. Practice using this tool on one of the sample Coreldraw files in the following exercise.

1. Click on the Zoom To Page tool and import another clip art file. Pelican3.cmx from the \Clipart\Bird\ folder on the fourth CD-ROM is

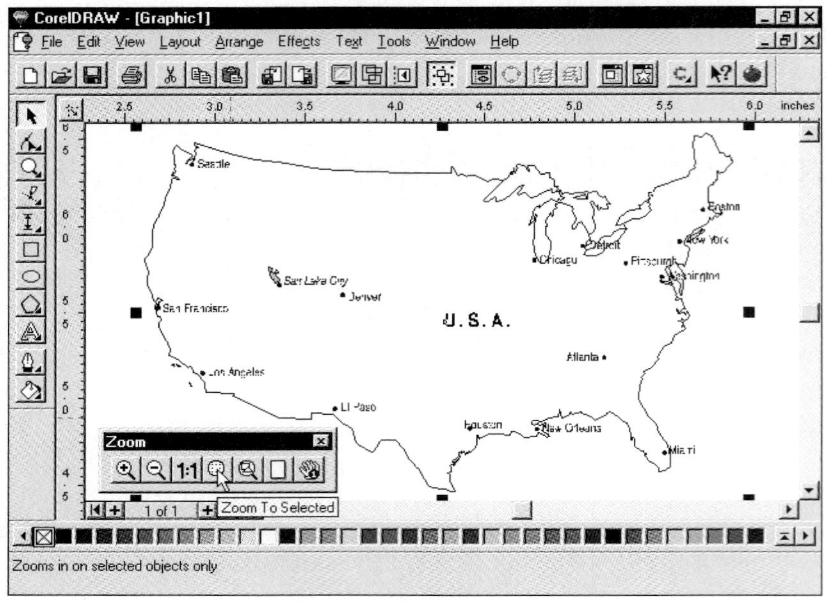

The selected object fills the screen

FIGURE 1-15

used here. Note that there is some blank or "white" space at both the bottom and top of the page, as seen in Figure 1-16.

OTE: *In Figure 1-16, the Zoom toolbar has been resized to a vertical layout. You can resize any toolbar by dragging on any of the toolbar borders.*

2. Select the Zoom To All Objects view by clicking on the Zoom To All Objects tool. Now you see only the pelican, as shown in Figure 1-17.

Viewing an Entire Page

The Zoom To Page view is the default view when you load Coreldraw or open a drawing. It is easy to return to this view from any other view you have selected. Simply click on the Zoom To Page tool or press SHIFT-F4.

You have now mastered all of the zooming tools, but there is still another method, called *panning,* that you can use to control your viewing area.

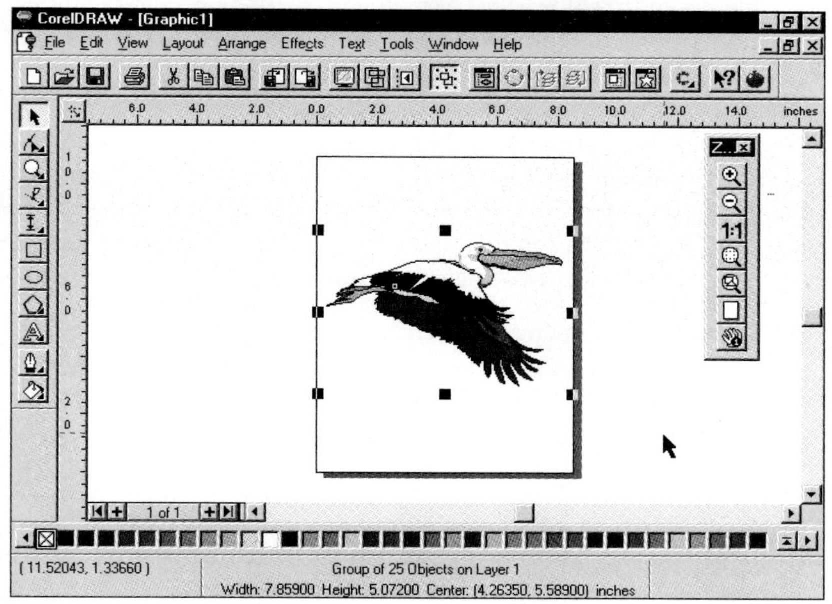

Image with blank space at top and bottom

FIGURE 1-16

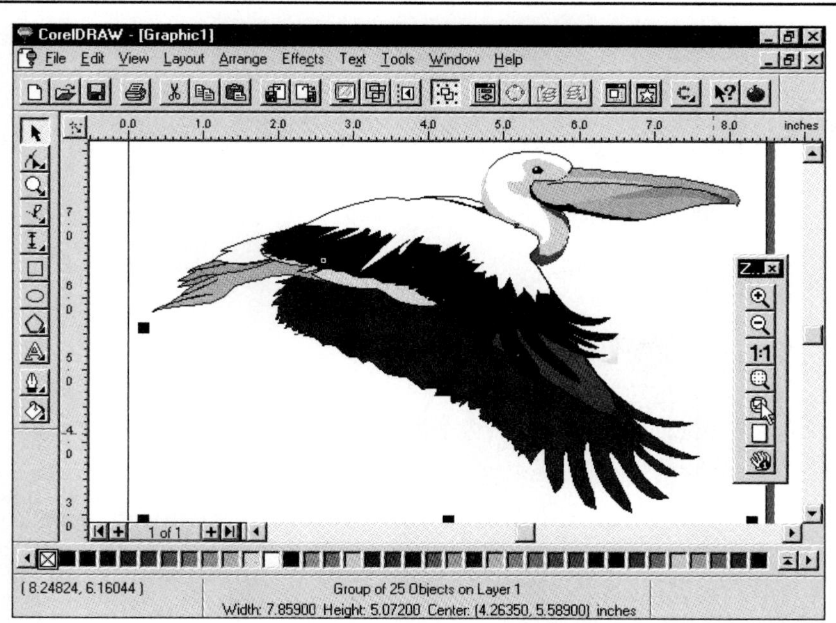

Fitting the image within the viewing area

FIGURE 1-17

Use the Zoom In tool to select a small portion of the pelican, as shown in Figure 1-18. That portion will fill the viewing area, and even though you see only the selected part, the whole drawing has been expanded.

Regardless of which view you are in, you can always move beyond your current viewing area to see what lies beyond it. This operation is called panning and moves the image around on the screen so you can see different parts of it. You can use either the Panning tool on the Zoom toolbar and the Zoom flyout, or the horizontal and vertical scroll bars at the bottom and right sides of your screen to pan a picture. Figure 1-18 shows the three different parts of the scroll bars you can use for panning.

- To pan in small increments, click on a scroll arrow. The size of the increment varies, depending on your monitor and display adapter combination. If you click on the right-horizontal scroll arrow, the image in the viewing window appears to move to the left. If you click on the left-horizontal arrow, the image appears to move to the right. This is an excellent method to use when you need to edit an image in fine detail.
- To pan in large increments, click on the scroll bar on either side of the scroll box, located in the middle of the horizontal and vertical scroll bars. Once again, the image appears to move in the opposite direction from

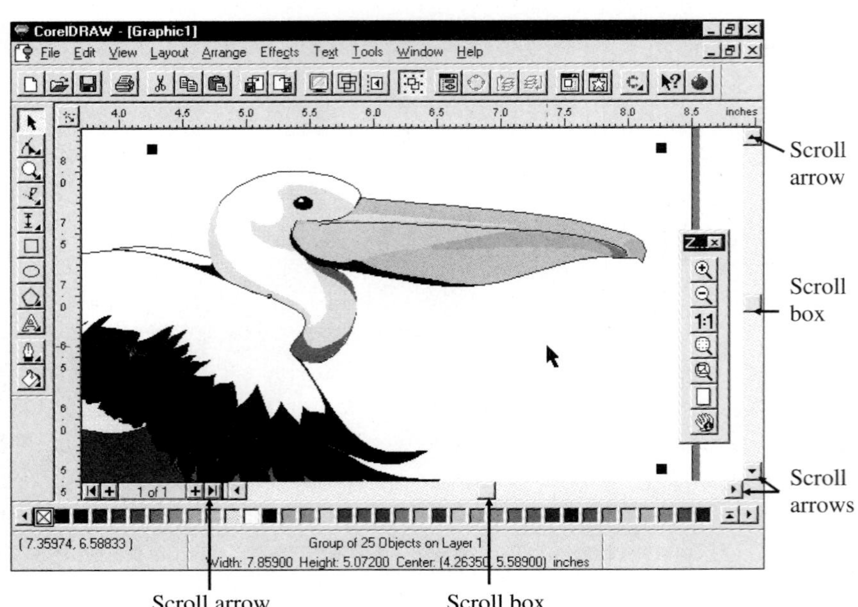

Using the parts of the scroll bar to pan a drawing

FIGURE 1-18

where you clicked. This method has only limited usefulness for editing because the movement of the screen is rather jumpy and unpredictable.

- To control the exact distance that you pan, position the mouse pointer over the scroll box and drag it across the scroll bar in the direction that you want to pan. Release the mouse button when you reach the desired area.

CAUTION: *Panning with the scroll box can result in very large movements of your image, moving it completely out of view. If you get lost, click on the Zoom To All Objects or Zoom To Page buttons to bring your image back to the center of the screen.*

The Panning tool simplifies the panning process by enabling you to move the area of your drawing being displayed both horizontally and vertically at one time. The next exercise demonstrates how the Panning tool works.

1. Click on the Panning tool on the Zoom toolbar. The pointer changes to a hand holding a crosshair.
2. With the Panning tool, click on the eye of the pelican.
3. Drag the hand towards the center of the screen. As you drag the pointer, a line extends from the first point you selected to the mouse pointer, as shown in Figure 1-19.
4. Release the mouse button and the first point you selected (the pelican's eye) moves to the point where you released the mouse button.

Using the View Manager

As you work with more complicated drawings you may find yourself needing to work with a number of different views of the drawing: a full page view to see the entire drawing as well as magnified views to make precise changes to small sections of the drawing. With multipage documents you may need to switch back and forth between pages, also. The View Manager roll-up, a new feature of CorelDRAW! 6, enables you to build a library of views of your drawing. To switch between views you use the View Manager roll-up, opened from the Tools menu, shown in Figure 1-20.

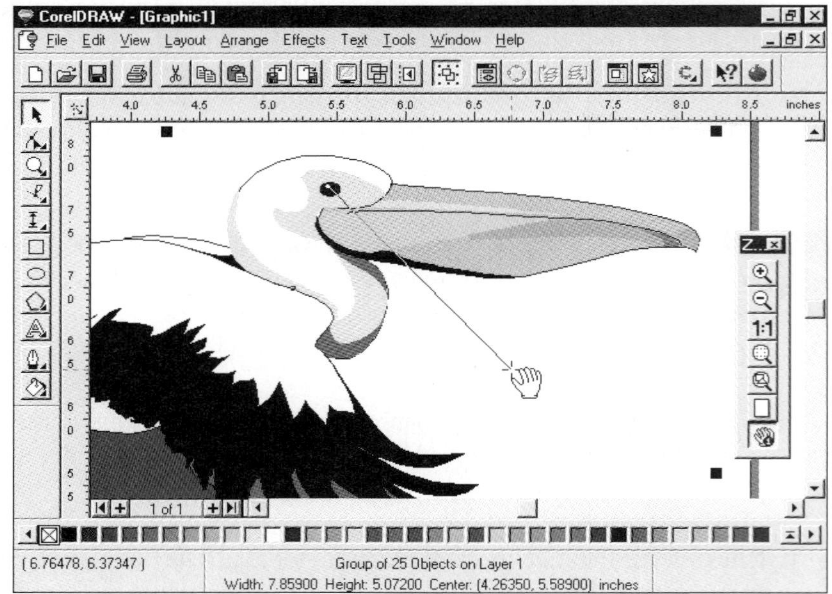

Panning the image with the Panning tool

FIGURE 1-19

The View Manager contains a list box displaying the defined views of your drawing. Each view has a name (which you can change), the page the view is applied to, and the magnification of the view. The magnifying glass icon is used to turn the view on or off; when a view is turned off (the magnifying glass icon is grayed out) it cannot be applied to the document. The page icon selects whether or not the view can be applied to all pages, or to just the page included in the view definition. When

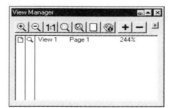

View Manager roll-up

FIGURE 1-20

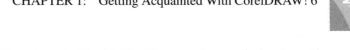

the page icon is selected (it appears in black), the view can be applied only to the defined page. When the page icon is deselected (it appears in gray), the view will be applied to the current page. To change between settings, click on the page or magnifying glass icons.

The View Manager options are contained on a pop-up menu you open by clicking on the small arrow in the upper-right corner of the roll-up. Switch to View switches to the currently selected view in the View Manager. New, Delete, and Rename allow you to add, remove, or rename the selected view. The Zoom Tools option turns the Zoom tool buttons displayed on the View Manager on or off. Choosing the What's This? option opens the Help topic for the item you select.

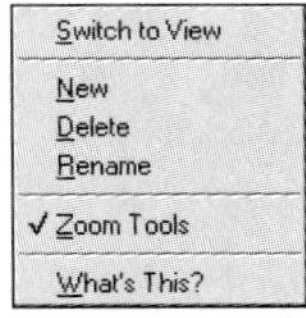

When Zoom Tools is selected, the familiar zoom tool buttons are displayed along with New (the button with the "+" sign) and Delete (the button with the "-" sign) buttons. These buttons have the same effect as the New and Delete commands on the View Manager pop-up menu.

IP: *You can also use the View Manager to place bookmarks in your document. By defining a view for a specific page (the page icon is selected), switching to that view will make that page the active (selected) page. You can use this feature to quickly switch between pages in a multipage document.*

In the next exercise you will learn how to add, rename, delete, and switch between views.

1. Switch to Zoom To Page view by clicking on the Zoom To Page tool. From the Tools menu, select View Manager. Click on the Add button and the View Manager list box will display "View 1, Page 1, 100%."

2. Click on the Zoom to All Objects button on the Zoom toolbar, then click on the Add button on the View Manager. A new view, "View 2, Page 1, 128%," is displayed in the list box.

3. Switch back to the original, full page, view by clicking on "View 1" in the list box, clicking the right mouse button, and selecting Switch to View from the pop-up menu. Your drawing reverts to Zoom to Page view.
4. Select "View 2" by clicking on it. Click the right mouse button to display the pop-up menu and select Rename. "View 2" becomes highlighted and the text cursor is placed at the end of the phrase.
5. Type **All Objects** and press ENTER. "View 2" is renamed "All Objects."
6. With All Objects view still selected, click on the small arrow in the upper-right corner of the View Manager roll-up to display the pop-up menu.
7. Select Delete from the pop-up menu. The All Objects view is removed from the View Manager list box. Close the View Manager by clicking on the Close button in the upper-right corner of the roll-up.

TIP: *You can also switch between views by double-clicking quickly on the name of the view. If you double-click more slowly you can rename the view. Experiment with how fast you have to double-click to activate the view, and how much slower you have to double-click in order to rename the view.*

Now that you are familiar with all of the means for adjusting the viewable area of your work, you have complete control over the portion of your drawing that you display at any one time. In Chapters 5 and 8, you will put this new skill to work to help you select, arrange, and move objects and text.

Working with Multiple Views

You can also work with multiple views of a drawing using the Multiple Document Interface. The Window menu provides the options you use to open and arrange multiple document windows. In the next exercise you will learn how to use this new feature of Coreldraw 6. The drawing you used in the previous exercise should still be displayed.

1. Reduce the size of the document window by clicking on the Restore button located on the right side of the menu bar (not the Title bar). Your screen should look similar to Figure 1-21. You can now resize the

document window by pointing on the document window border and dragging.

2. Select New Window from the Window menu. A new document window is opened.
3. Select Tile Vertically from the Window menu. Your screen should appear similar to Figure 1-22.
4. Select the Zoom In tool from the Zoom toolbox and zoom in on the pelican in one of the windows, as shown in Figure 1-23.

By opening multiple document windows, you can work on a small area in one window while observing the changes to the entire drawing or a larger selected area. You can also have multiple drawings open at the same time, allowing you to easily exchange objects between drawings.

In addition to tiling the windows vertically, you can tile them horizontally or *cascade* them. Cascaded windows are layered on top of each other with each window offset slightly down and to the right of the window beneath it.

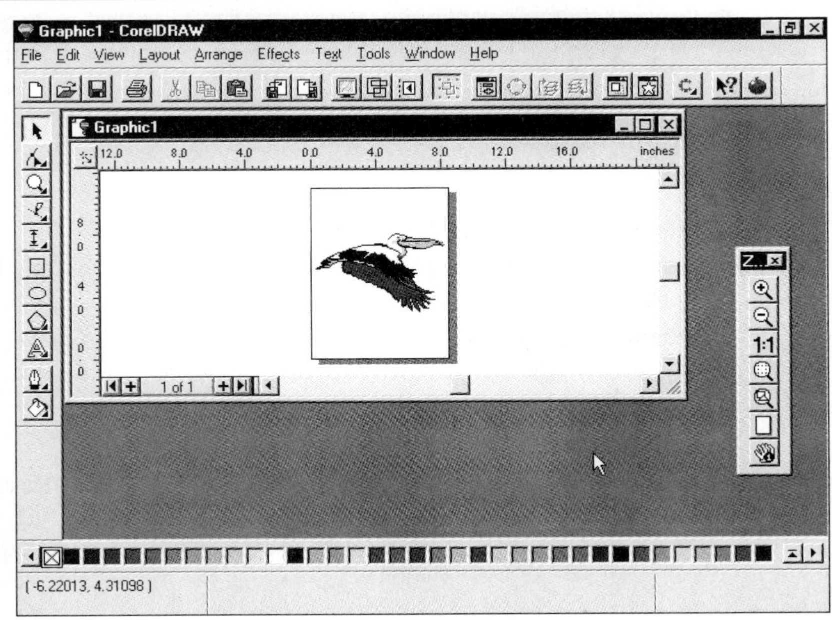

Document window reduced in size

FIGURE 1-21

Document windows tiled vertically

FIGURE 1-22

Document windows with different levels of magnification

FIGURE 1-23

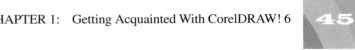

Quitting Coreldraw

Now that you are familiar with the screen components, exit Coreldraw and return to the Windows 95 Desktop. You can use the mouse, the keyboard and mouse, or the keyboard alone to quit Coreldraw.

Using the mouse, click on the Close button in the upper-right corner, or double-click on the Control menu box in the upper-left corner. You can use the File menu to quit Coreldraw by selecting the File menu and then clicking on Exit.

Using the keyboard alone, you can either press ALT-F to display the File menu and then press X, or press ALT-F4.

IP: *If you have attempted to draw during this session, you will get a message like: Save changes to Graphic 1?" Click on the No command button to abandon your changes.*

If you are like most Coreldraw users, you will want to begin drawing immediately. This book encourages you to draw. In Chapter 2, you will use the Pencil tool to begin drawing lines and curves.

COREL DRAW!™ 6 in action

***Evolution of the Species*—Stephen Arscott**

Stephen Arscott used many of Coreldraw's tools to create this award-winning poster for Corel's World Design Contest. With the exercises in this book you will learn how to use these tools to create dynamic graphics.

Stephen Arscott, who has won several awards in Corel's World Design Contest, lives and works in Mississauaga, Ontario, Canada. He can be reached at (905) 896-4664.

Drawing and Working with Lines and Curves

The Pencil tool is the most versatile tool in the Coreldraw toolbox. By using this tool in its two modes, Freehand and Bézier you can create both straight and curved lines, and from these simple building blocks you can construct an almost infinite variety of irregular and polygon shapes. The Dimension Line tool, another type of pencil tool, allows you to place vertical, horizontal, and slanted dimension lines, measure the angle between two lines; link objects with lines that move with the objects; and place callouts on drawings. Work through the exercises in this chapter to become thoroughly familiar with these most basic Coreldraw tools.

Freehand Versus Bézier Mode

The Pencil tool has two modes of drawing: Freehand, where curves mirror the movements of your hand on a mouse, and Bézier (pronounced "be-zee-aye," with a soft sound on the "be," as in "bear") mode, where curves are precisely placed between two or more points you identify. Drawing straight lines is very similar in the two modes, but drawing curves is very different. In the remaining sections of this chapter, Freehand mode, the default, will be discussed first, and then Bézier mode. Dimension Lines and Callouts are discussed after the first two drawing modes.

NOTE: *The term Pencil tool describes both the Freehand tool and Bézier tool on the toolbox. The exercises in this book will generally instruct you to select either tool by its name, rather than the Pencil tool. When the term Pencil tool is used it refers to whichever tool is displayed on the toolbox. The tool button displayed on the toolbox is the tool you used last; the default is the Freehand tool.*

Drawing Straight Lines

In the language of Coreldraw, *line* refers to any straight line, while *curve* refers to curved lines, irregular lines, and closed objects you create with such lines. Drawing a straight line requires that you work with the mouse in a different way than when you draw a curved or irregular line. To draw a straight line in Coreldraw, follow these steps:

1. Load Coreldraw if it isn't running already.
2. Position the mouse pointer over the Freehand tool button and click once. The pointer changes to a crosshair as you move it off the button, and the button becomes lighter.
3. Position the crosshair pointer where you want a line to begin. This can be anywhere inside the printable page area.
4. Press *and immediately release (click)* the left mouse button, and then move the crosshair pointer toward the point where you want to end the line. A straight line appears and extends as far as you move the crosshair pointer, as shown here. You can move the line in any direction, or make the segment longer or shorter.

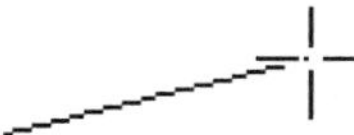

5. When you have established the length and direction you want, complete the line by clicking the mouse button again. As shown here, a small square *node* appears at each end of the line to show that the line is complete and can be selected for further work.

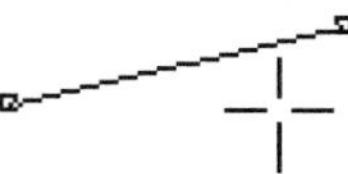

Press DEL to clear the line from the screen.

IP: *When you begin to draw a line, be sure to release the mouse button immediately after you press it. If you continue to hold down the mouse button while moving the crosshair pointer, you create a curve instead of a straight line.*

Using the Status Bar to Improve Precision

Chapter 1 introduced you briefly to the Status bar and its potential for helping you draw with precision and accuracy. In the next exercise, pay attention to the useful information that appears on the Status bar.

1. If the rulers are not displayed on your screen, open the Layout menu and click on Rulers to display them.
2. With the Freehand tool still selected, begin another line by clicking the mouse button at a point about halfway down the left side of the page. The coordinates on the left side of the Status bar should be *about* 1.0, 5.5 inches (absolute precision is not important).
3. Move the mouse toward the right side of the page. Don't click a second time yet.
4. Notice that as soon as you clicked once and began to move the mouse, a message appeared on the Status bar, as shown here:

(4.33454, 6.68954) | DX:1.52172 DY:0.59477 inches Distance: 1.63382 Angle: 21 Start: (4.25000, 5.50000) End: (5.77172, 6.09477) | Outline: 0.00300 ir

Look more closely at the Status bar. It includes information about the line you are drawing. The codes in the Status bar and their meanings are discussed next. (Your measurements may be different. Also, the measurements may be set as millimeters, inches, picas, points, ciceros, or didots. If your screen does not show the same measurement units as this book, you can change the setting by selecting Grid and Ruler Setup from the Layout menu, selecting the Ruler tab on the Grid & Ruler Setup dialog box, and then setting both Units drop-down list boxes to inches.)

DX The *DX* code refers to the *x*-coordinate or horizontal location of your line on the page relative to the starting point. The number following this code identifies how far your line has traveled (in other words, its distance) from that starting point along the x or horizontal axis. A positive number (one with no minus sign in front of it) indicates that you are extending the line to the right of the starting point, while a negative number indicates the reverse.

DY The *DY* code refers to the *y*-coordinate or vertical location of your line on the page relative to the starting point. The number following this code identifies how far your line has traveled (its distance) above or below that starting point along the y or vertical axis. A positive number indicates that you are extending the line above the starting point, while a negative number indicates that you are extending it below the starting point.

INCHES The unit of measurement for the current *DX* and *DY* position indicators appears on the Status bar as well. The Coreldraw default is inches, but you can change it using the Grid and Ruler Setup dialog box opened from the Layout menu. You'll gain experience with the grid later in this chapter.

DISTANCE The number following this text indicates the length of your line relative to the starting point. Unlike the *DX* and *DY* values, which reflect the horizontal and vertical distance between the start and end points, Distance reflects the total length of the line.

ANGLE The number following this text indicates the angle of the line relative to an imaginary compass, where 0 degrees is at the three o'clock position, 90 degrees is at the twelve o'clock position, 180 degrees is at the nine o'clock position, and -90 degrees is at the six o'clock position.

START AND END The pairs of numbers following each of these items represent the x and y coordinates of the start and end points of the line.

Continue the preceding exercise with these steps:

1. Choose an end point for the line and click again to freeze the line in place. Note that the Status bar indicators disappear as soon as you complete the line.
2. Press DEL to delete the line before going further.

Customizing the Status bar

With CorelDRAW! 6, you can customize the information displayed as well as the placement on the Status bar. You customize the Status bar with the Status bar pop-up menu, shown here, opened by clicking on the Status bar with the right mouse button.

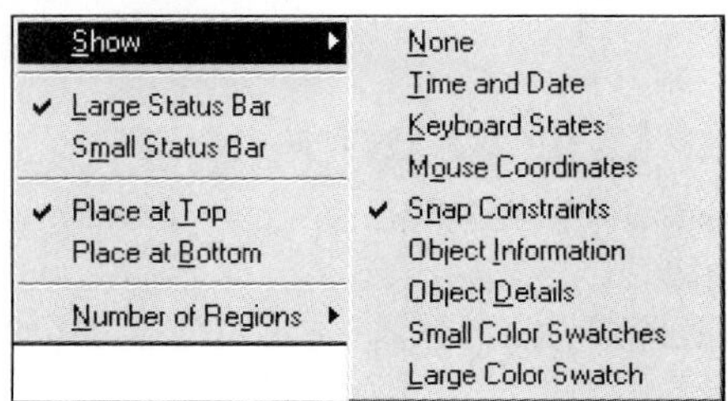

Selecting the Show option displays a flyout listing the information that can be displayed. You can also set the number of lines displayed; where the Status bar is placed; and the number of *regions*, or sections, the Status bar is divided into. Move the Status bar to the top of the screen by selecting Place at Top.

Customize IT! *You can resize the Status bar by pointing on the top border (the pointer will change to a double-headed arrow) and dragging. To change the width of a region, point on one of the vertical lines on the Status bar. When the pointer changes to a two-headed arrow, drag the line to its new location.*

Information appears on the Status bar only when you are performing some action on an object. This information makes Coreldraw especially useful for applications requiring great precision, such as technical illustration.

Erasing Portions of a Line

In the following exercise, you'll practice erasing part of a line that you have extended but not completed. You can always backtrack and shorten a line in Coreldraw, as long as you have not clicked a second time to complete it.

1. With the Freehand tool still selected, choose a starting point for another line.
2. Move the pointer downward and to the right until the *DX* indicator reads about 5.00 inches and the *DY* indicator reads about -1.00 inches (again, measurements need only be approximate), as shown in Figure 2-1.
3. Without clicking the mouse button a second time, shorten the line until the *DX* indicator reads about 4.00 inches. Notice that the line you have drawn behaves flexibly and becomes shorter as you move the mouse backward.
4. Click a second time to freeze the line at about *DX* 4.00 inches.
5. Before going any further, delete the line by pressing DEL.

Constraining a Line to an Angle

You need not rely on the Status bar alone to control the precision of your drawing. You can also use the CTRL key while drawing to *constrain* (force) a line to an angle in increments of 15 degrees. In the following exercise, you'll create a series of seven straight lines this way.

1. With the Freehand tool still selected, press and hold CTRL and click the mouse button to choose a starting point for the line.

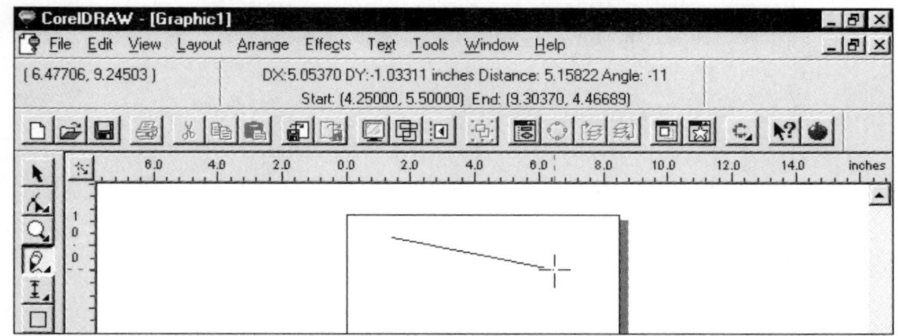

Extending a line using the Status bar indicator

FIGURE 2-1

2. Release the mouse button, but continue holding CTRL as you extend the line outward and downward from the starting point. Try moving the line to different angles in a clockwise direction. As the angle indicator in the Status bar shows, the line does not move smoothly but instead "jumps" in increments of 15 degrees.
3. Now, extend the line straight outward, so that the angle indicator on the Status bar reads 0 degrees. While still holding down CTRL, click the mouse button a second time to freeze the line at this angle.
4. Release CTRL. (Remember always to release the mouse button *before* you release CTRL. If you release CTRL first, the line isn't necessarily constrained to a set angle.)
5. Draw six more lines in the same way, each sharing a common starting point. Extend the second line at an angle of 15 degrees, the third at an angle of 30 degrees, the fourth at an angle of 45 degrees, the fifth at an angle of 60 degrees, the sixth at an angle of 75 degrees, and the seventh at an angle of 90 degrees. When you are finished, your lines should match the pattern shown in Figure 2-2.

Clearing the Screen

Before going any further, clear the screen of the lines you have created so far.

1. Click on the Edit menu to open it.
2. Click on Select All.
3. Press DEL.

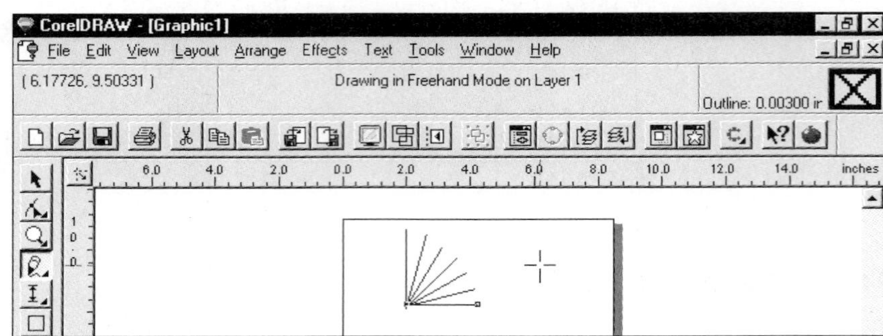

Constraining lines to angles in 15-degree increments

FIGURE 2-2

Drawing Multisegment Lines

With Coreldraw, you can easily draw several straight lines in sequence so that each begins where the previous one left off. Use this technique both for drawing open-ended line figures and for constructing polygon shapes. In the present exercise, you will construct a series of peaks and valleys. The Freehand tool should still be selected; if it isn't, select it using a shortcut—press the F5 function key.

1. Click to choose a line starting point. Extend a line upward and to the right.
2. When you reach the desired end point for the line, freeze it in place with a double-click rather than a single click of the mouse button. Use the CTRL key if you want to constrain your lines to 15 degree increments.
3. Move the mouse downward and to the right, without clicking again. The flexible line follows the crosshair pointer automatically.
4. Double-click again to freeze the second line in place.
5. Continue zigzagging in this way until you have created several peaks and valleys similar to those in Figure 2-3.
6. When you reach the last valley, click once instead of twice to end the multisegment line.
7. Press DEL to clear the screen before proceeding.

IP: *After the final click, if you make a mistake drawing, you can erase the last line segment you completed in one of two ways. You either press* ALT-BACKSPACE *to delete individual line segments, or select the Undo Curve Append command from the Edit menu. (You can also recreate deleted line segments with Redo Curve Append.) Don't press* DEL *when drawing a multisegment line, or you will erase all of the segments you have drawn so far.*

Drawing a Polygon Shape

A polygon is a closed two-dimensional figure bounded by straight lines. One of CorelDRAW! 6's new features is the Polygon tool, which allows you create polygons as easily as rectangles and ellipses. Creating these objects will be covered in Chapter 3. You can also create polygon shapes in Coreldraw by drawing multisegment lines and then connecting the end point to the starting point. In the following exercise, you'll create a polygon figure like the one shown here:

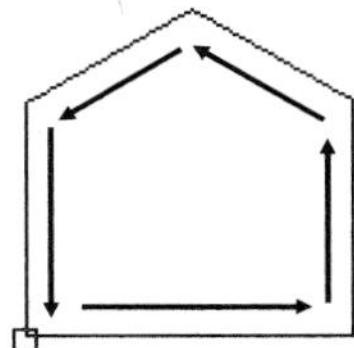

IP: *The polygon may be easier to draw if you use the* CTRL *key to constrain the angles of the lines while you draw them.*

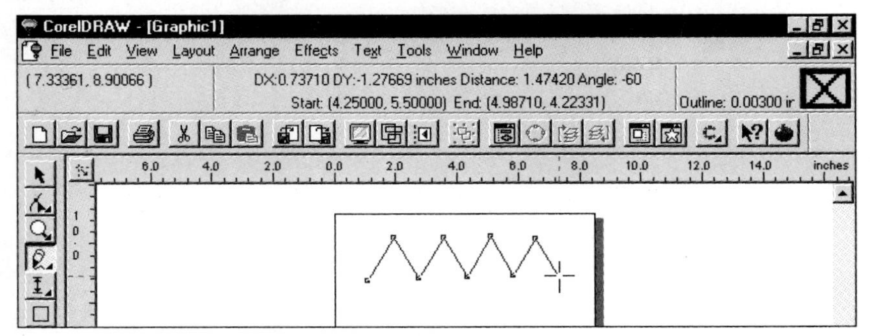

Drawing multisegment lines

FIGURE 2-3

1. Draw the first line, double-clicking at the line end point so that you can continue drawing without interruption.
2. Draw four additional lines in the same way, following the pattern shown above. End the last line segment with a single click at the point where the first line segment began.

OTE: *In Coreldraw a polygon is an object that has certain properties. You can create a polygon shape using the either Pencil tool, but it will not have the properties of a polygon object. Polygons are covered in Chapter 3.*

Did your last line segment "snap" to the beginning of the first? Or does a small gap remain between them? If you can still see a small gap, don't worry. In the section "Joining Lines and Curves Automatically," later in this chapter, you'll learn how to adjust the level of sensitivity at which one line will join automatically to another. If your lines did snap together to form an enclosed polygon shape, it may fill with a solid black color if a black fill is selected. For now, clear the screen and begin the next exercise.

Straight Lines In Bézier Mode

The Bézier mode of drawing identifies end points or nodes and places lines or curves between them. Therefore, drawing straight lines in Bézier mode is very similar to drawing straight lines in Freehand mode. Try it next using the following steps and see for yourself.

1. Select Bézier mode by pointing on the Pencil tool and pressing and holding the mouse button down until the Pencil flyout appears, like this:

2. Click on the Bézier tool, the button on the right of the flyout.

Your Status bar should now include the words "Drawing in Bézier Mode..."

Drawing Single Lines in Bézier Mode

Now draw a single line segment as you did earlier in Freehand mode.

1. Click on a starting point in the middle-left of the page, immediately release the mouse button (if you hold down the mouse button, Coreldraw will think you are drawing a curve), and move the mouse pointer to the upper-right of the page.

   Notice that the starting point is a solid black square. This starting point is a *node*, a point on a line that is used to define the line. When you start the line, the starting point is selected and is therefore black. Also, there is no line connecting the starting point and the mouse pointer and no information in the Status bar except the coordinates of the mouse pointer. A line does not appear and there is no information in the Status bar because a Bézier line is not defined until you have placed at least two nodes.

2. Click to place an end node. A straight line is drawn between the two nodes, as shown below. Information about the line is displayed in the Status bar: "Curve on Layer 1" and "Number of nodes: 2." (In Coreldraw, a Bézier straight line is a special type of curve.)

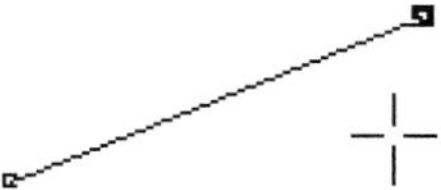

Drawing a Polygon in Bézier Mode

Unlike Freehand mode, you can continue to add line segments after clicking on an end node only once in Bézier mode. Do that next to build a polygon shape (your screen should still be as you left it after drawing the first Bézier line segment).

1. Click on two more nodes, first one straight down toward the lower right and the other toward the lower left. Lines will be added connecting the nodes.

2. Position the mouse pointer on top of the original starting node and click one final time. The result is a four-sided polygon shape like the one shown in Figure 2-4. If your sides join to form a polygon (that is, not an

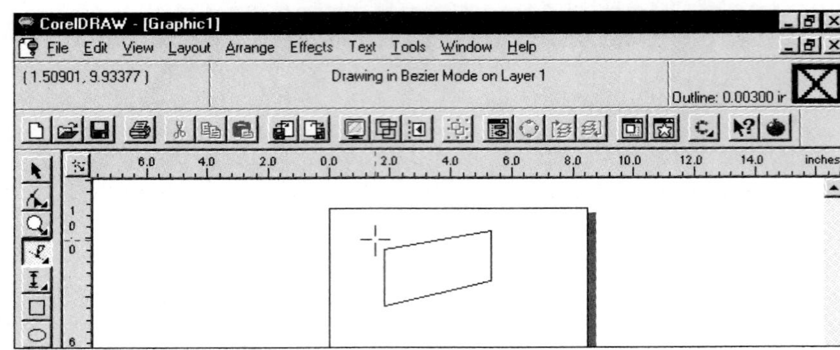

Bézier polygon

FIGURE 2-4

open shape) and you are using a fill pattern, your polygon will fill with the pattern defined as the default, such as a solid black color. Chapter 7 discusses this in more detail.

As you can see, there are many mechanical similarities between Freehand and Bézier drawing of straight lines. The results are virtually the same, but the screen looks very different during the creation of the lines. For straight lines, there is little reason to use Bézier over Freehand.

3. Press DEL to clear your screen.

IP: *As in Freehand, in Bézier mode you can move the mouse pointer in any direction, including backward, over the path already traveled to "erase" the object before clicking on a node. After clicking on a node, you can use Undo (either ALT-BACKSPACE or choose Undo from the Edit menu) to erase the previous line (or curve) segment. If you want to delete the entire object while it is still selected (you can see all of the nodes), press DEL.*

IP: *If you want to draw two or more Bézier line segments that are not connected, draw the first line, press the SPACEBAR twice, then draw your second line.*

In the next exercise you will use the Freehand tool again. To select the Freehand tool, click on the Bézier tool button and hold the mouse button until the flyout appears. Release the mouse button and click on the Freehand tool. You are returned to your drawing in Freehand mode, ready to begin working with curves.

Customize IT! *When you are working with both Pencil tools, there is an easier way to switch between them. You can tear off the Pencil flyout and place it anywhere on your screen. To tear off the flyout point on the Pencil tool and hold the mouse button until the flyout appears. Release the mouse button and point on the border of the flyout menu. Drag (hold the mouse button down and move the mouse pointer) the Pencil tool flyout away from the toolbox. The Pencil tools are now in ir own window with a Title bar and Close button. Drag the Pencil tools flyout to onvenient location using its Title bar. You can use this method to tear off any of flyouts in the toolbox.*

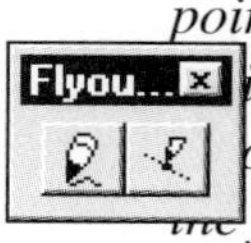

Flyou...

Drawing Curves in Freehand Mode

The Freehand tool has a twofold purpose in Coreldraw: you can use it to draw curved or irregular lines as well as straight lines. This section introduces you to the basics of drawing a simple curve, closing the path of a curve to form a closed curve object, and erasing unwanted portions of a curve as you draw.

Use the following steps to draw a simple curve.

1. Select the Freehand tool if it is not still selected.
2. Position the crosshair pointer at the point on the page where you want a curve to begin and then press and hold the mouse button. The Start and End coordinates appear on the Status bar.
3. Continue to hold the mouse button and drag the mouse along the path where you want the curve to continue. Follow the example in Figure 2-5.
4. Upon completing the curve, release the mouse button. The curve disappears momentarily while Coreldraw calculates exactly where it should go. Then the curve reappears with many small square nodes, as in Figure 2-5. Note that when you have finished, the words "Curve on Layer 1" and the number of nodes appear in the middle of the Status bar, and the message "Open Path" appears at the right side of the Status bar. "Open Path" indicates that you have drawn a curved line, not a closed figure.

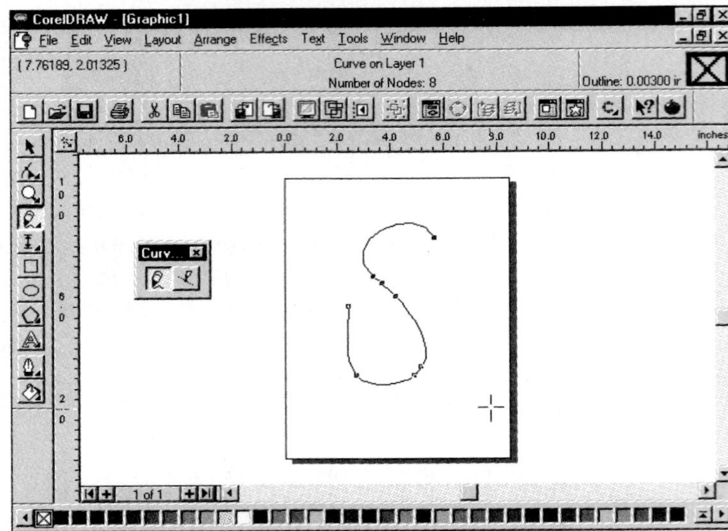

Drawing a curve with the Freehand tool

FIGURE 2-5

5. Press DEL or select the Undo command from the Edit menu to clear the curve you have just drawn.

IP: *To draw a straight line, click and release the mouse button. To draw a curve, press and hold the mouse button and drag the mouse along the desired path.*

Erasing Portions of a Curve

Should you make a mistake while drawing a curve, you can backtrack and erase what you have drawn, as long as you have not yet released the mouse button. You use SHIFT to erase the portion of a curve that you no longer want.

1. Begin another curve by placing the pointer at the point you want the curve to start, then pressing and holding the mouse button.
2. Drag the mouse as desired. Do not release the mouse button yet.
3. While still holding down the mouse button, press and hold SHIFT and backtrack over as much of the curve as you wish to erase.

4. After you have erased a portion of the curve, release SHIFT and continue to draw by dragging the mouse in the desired direction.
5. Release the mouse button to finalize the curve. Delete the curve by pressing DEL.

Drawing Multisegment Curves

Just as you drew multisegment lines, you can also draw multisegment curves. You can join two successive curves together automatically if the starting point of the second curve is within a few pixels of the end point of the first curve.

1. Select a starting point for the first curve and begin dragging the mouse.
2. Complete the curve by releasing the mouse button. Do not move the pointer from the point at which your first curve ends.
3. Draw the second curve and complete it. The second curve should "snap" to the first.

If the two curved lines didn't snap together, you moved the pointer farther than five pixels away before starting the second curve. Don't worry about it at this point. Coreldraw has a default value of five pixels distance for automatic joining of lines and curves. In the "Joining Lines and Curves Automatically" section of this chapter, you will learn how to adjust the sensitivity of this AutoJoin feature.

Closing an Open Path

When you drew your first curve, the message "Open Path" appeared at the right side of the Status bar. This message indicates that your curved line is not a closed object and, therefore, that you cannot fill it with a color or pattern (see Chapter 7). You can create a closed curve object with the Freehand tool, however. Refer to Figure 2-6 to create a closed outline of any shape for this exercise. You'll draw this shape as a single curve.

Before beginning the exercise, choose Select All from the Edit menu and press DEL to clear the screen.

You may at this point want to set an option to fill a closed shape with a color or pattern. To do this, you can click on the Fill button (the bottom tool button on the toolbox) and click on the black color square on the flyout. A Uniform Fill default dialog box will be displayed as shown here. Confirm that the Graphic check box is

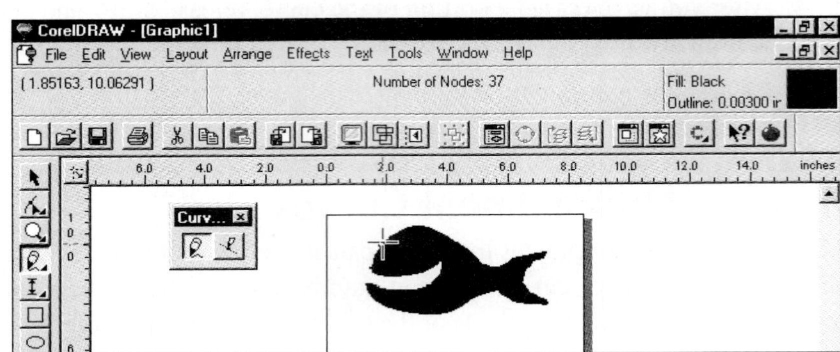

Drawing a closed curve object

FIGURE 2-6

selected (it should have a check mark in it) and click on OK. Coreldraw's extensive fill options are covered in Chapter 7.

1. Select the Freehand tool.
2. Start the curve wherever you wish.
3. Continue dragging the mouse to create the closed shape. Your drawing doesn't have to look exactly like the one in Figure 2-6. If you make a mistake, press SHIFT and backtrack to erase the portions of the curve that you do not want.
4. When you return to the point at which you began, make sure you are over your starting point and then release the mouse button. After a second, the object reappears as a solid black shape (if you have a black fill selected).

Note that the message in the middle of the Status bar now reads "Curve" and the number of nodes. At the right side of the Status bar, the message "Fill:Black" appears, followed by a representation of a solid black color. This indicates that you now have a closed curve object and that it is filled with the default color, black.

Editable Preview Versus Wireframe Modes

In the last exercise it was noted that the polygon would fill with solid black color when and if the polygon was closed and if a solid black fill was selected as the default. You can see the full color of an object as you are working on it in Coreldraw's Editable Preview mode. Occasionally you may wish to work in *Wireframe mode*, where you can see only an object's outline and therefore not its color. Although by default all work is done in Editable Preview mode, you can switch to Wireframe mode when it is beneficial to work with an object's outline. You do this by choosing Wireframe from the View menu. You can return to Editable Preview mode by again choosing Wireframe to turn it off. Try this with the current drawing.

IP: *You can also switch between Wireframe and Editable Preview modes by clicking on the Wireframe button on the toolbar, shown here, or by pressing SHIFT-F9.*

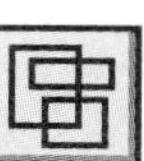

Drawing Curves In Bézier Mode

If you are like most people, drawing smooth curves in Freehand mode is very difficult, if not impossible. Of course, as you'll see in Chapter 9, Coreldraw's Shape tool allows you to clean up messy artwork very quickly. As an alternative, though, the Bézier mode of drawing allows you to draw smooth curves to start with—after a little practice.

The principle of Bézier drawing is that you place a node, set a pair of control points that determine the slope and height or depth of the curve, and then place the next node. The method is to place the crosshair where you want a node, press and hold the mouse button while you drag the control points until you are satisfied with their positioning, release the mouse button, and go on and do the same thing for the next node. When you have two or more nodes, curves appear between them, reflecting your settings. This is very different from Freehand mode drawing and will take some getting used to. Dragging the mouse with the button depressed moves the control points in two dimensions and only indirectly identifies the path of the curve. Understanding how to handle control points, though, will help you use the Shape tool in Chapter 9.

The only way to really understand Bézier drawing is to try it.

1. Clear your screen by deleting your drawing.
2. Click on the Bézier tool button in the Pencil tools flyout.
3. Move the mouse pointer to where you want to start the curve and press and hold the mouse button.
4. Move the mouse in any direction while continuing to press the mouse button, and you should see the *control points* appear—two small black boxes and dashed lines connecting them to the larger node, as shown here:

   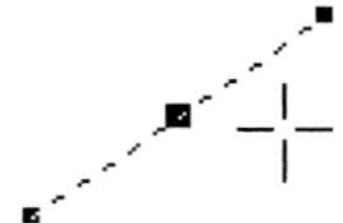

   There are three principles involved in moving the mouse to set the control points:

   - Begin by dragging a control point in the direction that you want the curve to leave the node.
   - Drag the control point away from the node to increase the height or depth of the curve, and drag the control point toward the node to decrease the height or depth.
   - Rotate the control points about the node to change the slope of the curve. The slope follows the rotational increment of the control point.

5. Drag the control point out away from the node toward two o'clock and swing it in an arc about the node. Notice how the two points move in opposite directions. Continue to hold the left mouse button.
6. Drag the control point in toward the node until it is about a half inch away from the node and swing it until the control point that you clicked on is pointing at two o'clock. Your node should look like this:

7. Release the mouse button and move the pointer to where you want the second node to be—about two inches to the right and in line with the first node.
8. Again press and hold the left mouse button to set the node. A curve segment is drawn between the two nodes.
9. Drag the control point toward five o'clock so it is about a half inch away from the node.
10. Release the mouse button. Your curve segment should now look like this:

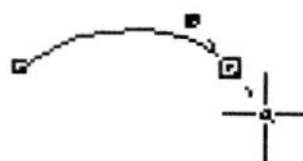

11. Move the pointer and press and hold the mouse button to set a third node about one inch below and in the middle of the first two nodes. A second curve segment will appear.
12. Drag the control point so it is about a quarter of an inch to the left of the node, at ten o'clock.
13. Release the mouse button. Your drawing should look similar to this:

14. Move the mouse pointer until it is on top of the first node you set and press and hold the mouse button. A third curve segment should appear.
15. Drag the control points until they are about a half inch away from the node and the top control point is aimed at twelve o'clock, like this:

16. Release the mouse button. This completes your curved triangle, which will be filled with solid black in Editable Preview.

OTE: *If your curved triangle does not fill with solid black, it is probably because you need to turn off Wireframe mode in the View menu.*

Practice drawing other Bézier objects. Notice how moving the control points both in and out from the node and in an arc around the node can radically change the curve segment to its left (behind the node) and to the right (ahead of the node). Also, notice how the number of nodes can effect the finished object. As a general rule, the fewer nodes the better, but there are some minimums.

A continuous curve like a circle should have a node every 120 degrees or three nodes on a circle like this:

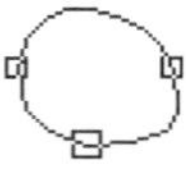

A curve that changes direction, such as a sine wave, needs a node for every two changes in direction, as shown here:

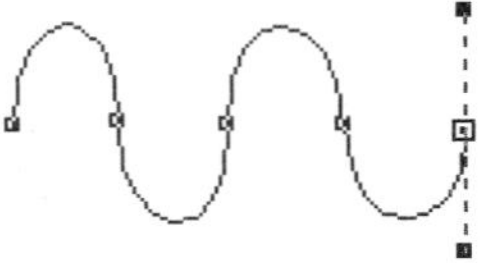

A curve that changes direction in a sharp point (called a cusp) needs a node for every change in direction, like this:

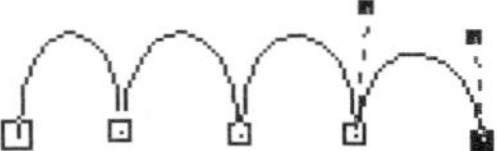

Using the Shape tool to modify an object using its nodes, and how to create the different types of nodes, will be covered in Chapter 9.

Clear the screen by clicking on Select All from the Edit menu and pressing DEL.

The Dimension Line Tools

Dimension lines can be used to display measurements; sizes of objects; distances between them; or measure angles, as you might need in technical drawings. You can also attach labels to objects and link separate objects with lines that move with the objects.

Coreldraw offers four Dimension Line tools for adding measurements:

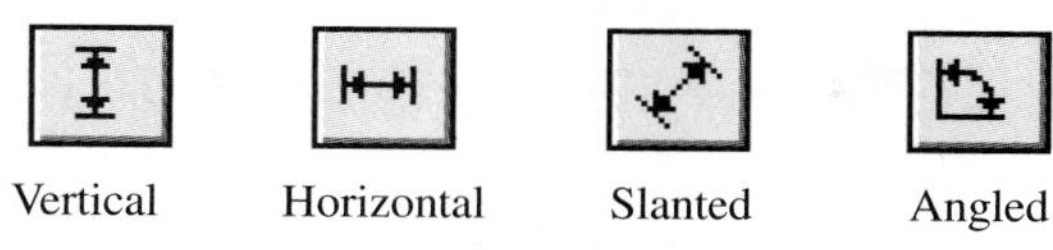

Figure 2-7 shows examples of how these four tools may be used.

Setting the Drawing Scale

Technical drawings and illustrations are usually created at something other than actual size. For example, an illustration of a desk might be scaled so that one inch on the drawing equals one foot in the real world so the drawing will fit on a standard sheet of paper when printed. The drawing scale is set from the Grid & Ruler Setup dialog box, which you open by selecting Grid and Ruler Setup from the Layout

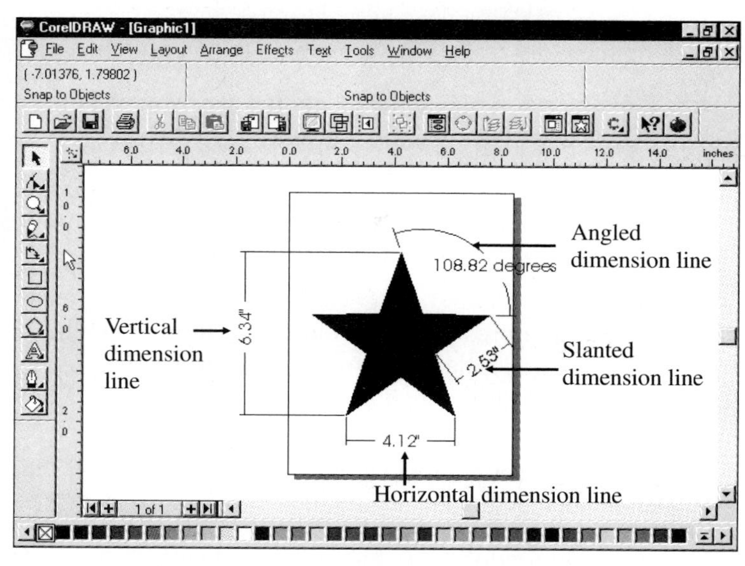

Examples of Dimension Lines

FIGURE 2-7

menu. When the Grid & Rulers dialog box is displayed, select the Ruler tab and click on Edit Scale. The Drawing Scale dialog box will be displayed, as shown here:

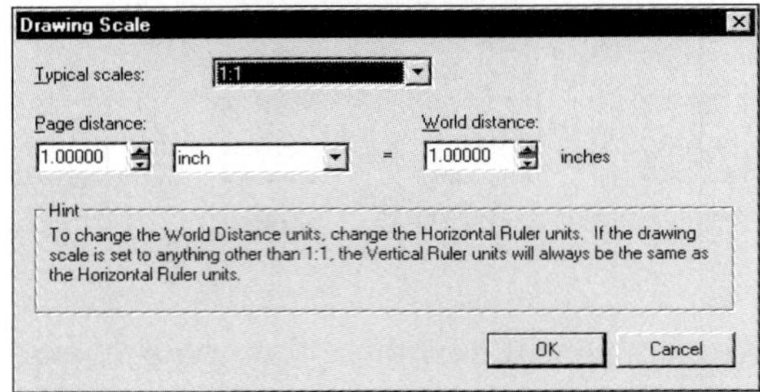

In it you equate a number of units on the page to "real world" equivalents. For example, to measure the scale of an airplane, you might set inches on a page equivalent to feet of an airplane (the world), or the number of millimeters on a blueprint to meters of an object. Close the Edit Scale dialog box without making any changes by clicking on Cancel before proceeding.

Using Dimension Lines

Since the four Dimension Line tools operate similarly, you will experiment with just three of the tools. There are three steps to drawing a dimension line:

1. Click on the point of the drawing where the measurement is to begin.
2. Drag the dimension line to the location where you want the ending point to be placed and click again to place it.
3. Move the pointer, moving the dimension line and the label rectangle, to where you want the dimension line extended and the label placed, and then click again to place the line and label.

In the following exercises you will be using most of the Dimension Line tools. Tearing off the Dimension Line flyout from the toolbox will speed up your work by making it easier to switch between tools.

1. Hold the mouse button while clicking on the Dimension Line tool to open the flyout.
2. Point on the border of the flyout and drag it away from the toolbox. The Dimension Line flyout is placed in a new window.

You can also resize the Dimension Line flyout by dragging on its border.

1. Point on the border of the Dimension Line flyout. The mouse pointer will change to a double-headed arrow.
2. Drag the arrow down until the border changes shape, like this:

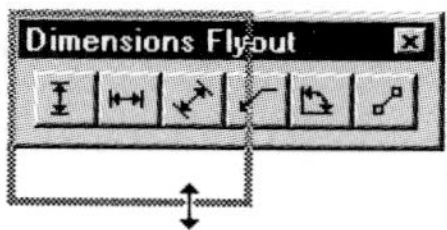

3. Release the mouse button. The Dimension Line flyout should now have two rows rather than one row of buttons.

To see how to draw and position a dimension line, follow these steps:

1. Select the Freehand tool and draw two boxes, something like what is shown in Figure 2-8, which shows the completed drawing with three dimension lines. You measure this drawing first with the Horizontal Dimension tool.
2. Select Snap To Objects from the Layout menu. When Snap To Objects is selected, there will be a check mark to the left of the command on the menu.

OTE: *Snap To Objects must be turned on (selected) for dimension lines to stay with the source object as it is moved or resized.*

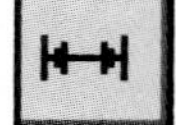

3. Select the Horizontal Dimension tool. The pointer will change into a crosshair.
4. Move the pointer to the bottom-left corner of the drawing and click the mouse button to anchor the beginning point, as shown here:

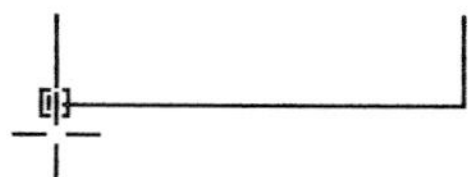

5. Experiment with moving the dimension line by moving the pointer left and right, up and down. Move the pointer off the page as well. You'll see how the horizontal dimension line can be positioned left or right, shortened, or lengthened by moving the pointer. When you have seen what to expect in the horizontal line movement, move the pointer to the bottom-right corner of the drawing, and click again.
6. Experiment again by moving the horizontal line up and down. See how you can position it in exact locations. A small rectangle surrounds the pointer as you move it. This identifies the location of the dimension label.

Pull the line down slightly and place the pointer somewhere near the middle of the horizontal line, then click the mouse button. The dimension value replaces the small rectangular box on the line.

Figure 2-8, displayed earlier, shows what your screen may look like (your font and point size may differ). You can see the dimension label has been placed approximately where you clicked the final time.

You can change the format, unit of measurement, and placement of the dimension label by changing the settings in the Dimensions roll-up, opened from

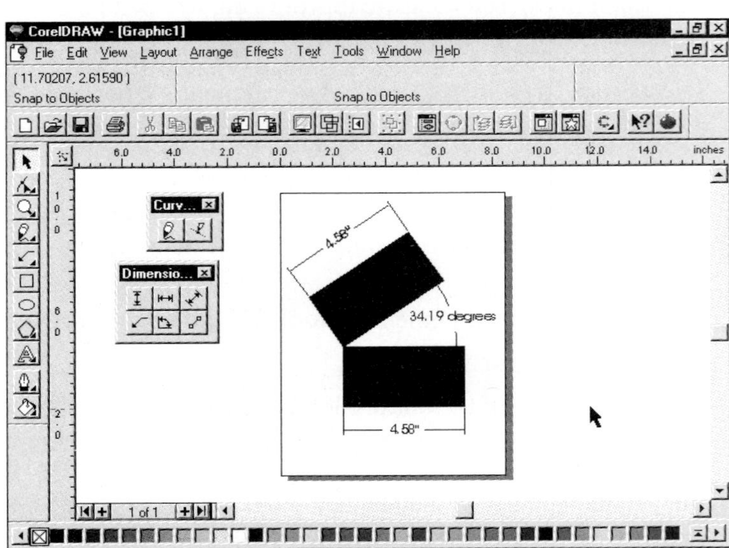

Drawing measured with three dimension lines

FIGURE 2-8

the Tools menu, or by pressing ALT-F2. To open the Dimensions roll-up from the Tools menu, open the Tools menu and select Dimensions. A flyout menu appears with two choices: Linear and Angular. Click on Linear to display the roll-up shown in Figure 1-9.

At the top of the roll-up is a list box that displays the possible functions of the roll-up. In this case, you can select between Linear or Angular dimension line attributes. The Units tab (the leftmost tab) controls the Style (Decimal, Fractional, US Architectural, and US Engineering), Precision (from 1 inch to 0.0000000001 inch), and Units of measurement (all standard English and metric units from inch and millimeter to miles and kilometers, as well as points, picas, ciceros, and didots). The Dynamic dimensioning check box determines whether or not the dimension line will be automatically updated as the dimensioned object is resized.

The Label tab (the rightmost tab) controls the placement of the dimension label in relation to the dimension line. The label can be placed above, below, or in the middle of the dimension line. The text in the dimension label for slanted dimension lines can be rotated with the line or placed horizontally. You can also add a prefix and suffix to the dimension line text.

Close the Dimensions roll-up by clicking on its Close button.

Try this second method of placing a dimension line. You are going to measure the distance from the upper-left corner to the upper-right corner of the upper box in the drawing with a slanted dimension line.

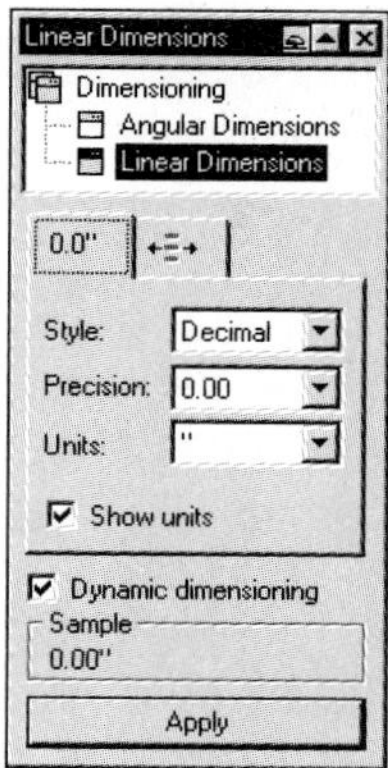

Linear Dimensions roll-up

FIGURE 2-9

1. Select the Slanted Dimension tool from the flyout. Place the pointer on the top-left corner of the upper box and click once as before to begin the measurement.
2. Move the pointer diagonally to the top right of the upper box and click to identify the end point.
3. Move the pointer to the left, dragging the dimension line away from the drawing, as shown in Figure 2-8. Move the rectangle near the center of the diagonal line and click to place the dimension label.

A new feature of CorelDRAW! 6 is the Angled Dimension Line tool, used to measure the angle between three points on the drawing. The next exercise will demonstrate how this works.

1. Select the Angled Dimension Line tool from the flyout.
2. Click on the point where the two boxes touch. This is the *apex* of the triangle you are measuring.
3. Click on the upper-right corner of the lower box, directly to the right of the apex.
4. Point on the lower-right corner of the upper box. Notice that, as you move the pointer, a curved line (actually, an arc of a circle) connects the second point selected and the pointer.
5. Click on the lower-right corner of the upper box. You have now defined the three points of the triangle needed to measure the angle of the apex.
6. Click once more to place the label.

Figure 2-8 again shows how the resulting lines differ. Depending on the requirements of the drawings, you can use vertical, horizontal, slanted, or angled Dimension tools to produce a dimension line shaped the way you need it.

IP: When drawing with the Slanted Dimension Line tool, you can constrain the lines to 15-degree increments by holding down CTRL simultaneously.

Using Callouts

Another tool on the Dimension Lines toolbar is for creating callouts. A *callout* is used to identify or emphasize an area or point on a drawing, as shown here:

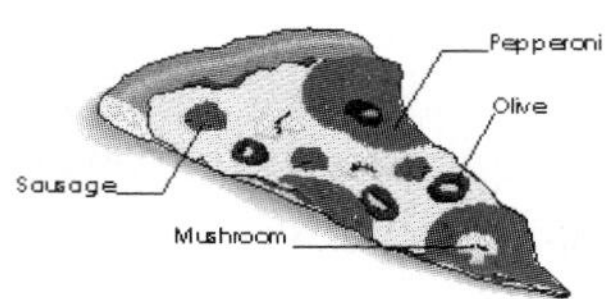

Using the figure just drawn with the dimension lines, you will create two callouts: the first is a two-segment line that requires three clicks of the mouse button. The second is a one-segment line requiring one single click and one double-click. Figure 2-10 shows the results.

1. Select the Callout tool.
2. To identify the starting point, click on the right side of the upper box. Move the pointer up slightly and to the right and click again. This ends

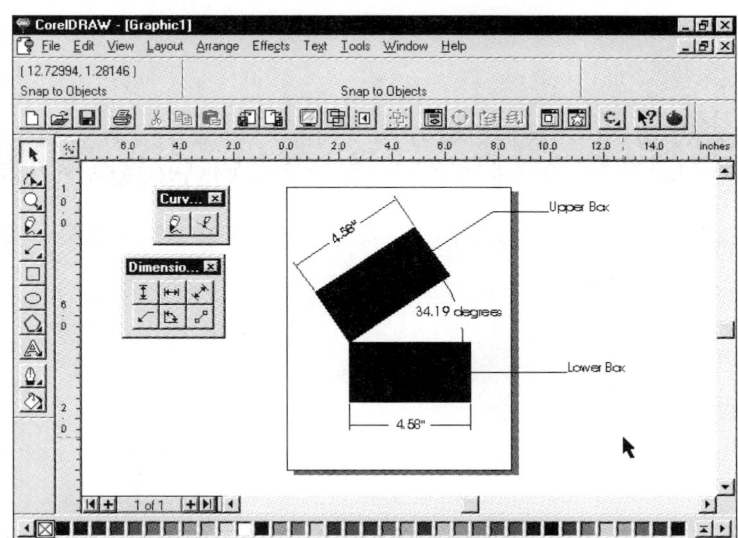

Drawing with callouts

FIGURE 2-10

the first line segment. Move the pointer to the right until you are satisfied with the second line segment and click again. At this point, the pointer turns into an I-beam icon for entering text for the callout. Type **Upper Box**.

The process is very similar to that for creating a one-segment line, except that a double-click replaces the last two clicks.

1. Move the pointer to the right side of the lower box and click once to anchor the line and begin the line segment. Move the line to the right and double-click when the line is the length you want. Type **Lower Box**. Your drawing should look something like Figure 2-10. Delete the drawing to prepare for the next section.

Connector Lines

Connector lines are similar to callouts—both connect two objects and move as the objects are moved. While callouts link an object and a text label, connector lines can link any two objects. This exercise demonstrates how connector lines work. Before beginning the exercise confirm that Snap To Objects is selected on the View menu.

1. Turn on Wireframe view by selecting Wireframe from the View menu, or by pressing SHIFT-F9, or by clicking on the Wireframe button on the toolbar.
2. Select the Freehand tool and draw a triangle and a box, similar to Figure 2-11 (without the connector line).

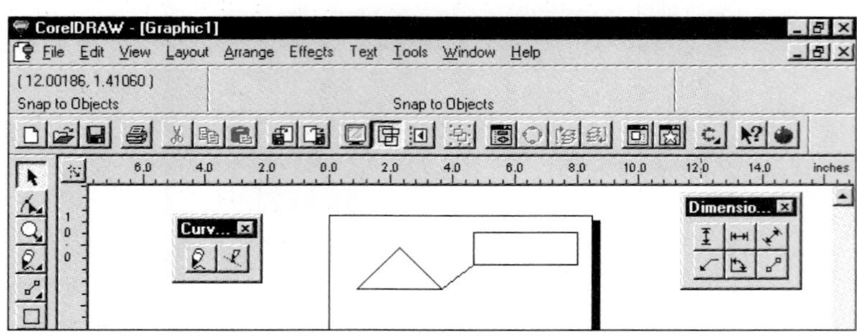

Two objects linked with a connector line

FIGURE 2-11

3. Select the Connector line tool (the bottom-right tool in the Dimension Lines window if you resized it to two rows).
4. Point on a corner of the triangle. A hollow box will be placed around the node, as shown here.

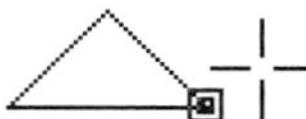

5. Click on the corner of the triangle, then click on one of the corners of the box you drew.

The two objects are now linked with the connector line. Select the Pick tool (the first tool in the toolbox), point on the border of either object, then press the mouse button and drag the object to confirm that the line stays connected as the objects are moved. (Using the Pick tool to move objects is explained fully in Chapter 5.) Delete your drawing, then close the Dimension Lines flyout by clicking on its Close button (in the upper-left corner of the flyout) to prepare for the next section on how to increase precision.

Increasing Precision

In addition to the mouse pointer coordinates and the other line and curve data displayed in the Status bar, Coreldraw has three features that aid in precision drawing. These are an adjustable grid that underlies the drawing surface and assists in aligning points and objects, a pair of rulers to give you a visual reference to where you are, and the ability to place nonprinting guidelines on the page for purposes of alignment.

TIP: When the objects are moved, you can control whether the Connector lines snap to the closest node or the original node using the Connector Tool Properties dialog box. To open the dialog box, select the Connector Line tool, then click the right mouse button and select Properties from the flyout.

The grid, the guidelines, and objects can optionally be given a magnet-like property that causes points or objects that are placed near them to be drawn to them. These are called Snap To Grid, Snap To Guidelines, Snap To Objects, Snap to All, and Snap to None. The Snap To property can be turned on and off, like the rulers, from the Layout menu. You can also turn Snap To Grid on and off by pressing CTRL-Y. In addition, the Layout menu provides access to setup dialog boxes for grids and guidelines. The Grid & Ruler Setup dialog box allows you to display the grid on the screen (as a series of faint dots) and to determine the horizontal and vertical spacing of the grid. The Grid & Ruler Setup dialog box also allows you to turn the Snap To Grid property on and off by clicking on its check box. With the Guidelines Setup dialog box, you can place guidelines with a very high degree of precision. You can also place guidelines by dragging them from either ruler and placing them by visually aligning them in the opposite ruler.

This section shows you how to use the rulers and the grid to draw with greater precision. Guidelines will be used and discussed further in a later section.

Setting the Grid and Displaying Rulers

You will next make several changes to the settings for the grid and turn on the Snap To property. Then you will turn on the display of both the grid and the rulers.

1. Select Grid Setup from the Layout menu. The dialog box in Figure 2-12 appears. The settings in yours may be different from the ones in the figure.

The Ruler tab controls the units of measurement displayed on the rulers and the origin, or zero points, of the rulers. The default is the lower-left corner of the printable page, represented by Vertical and Horizontal Origins of zero inches. The Edit Scale command button opens the Edit Scale dialog box, as you saw previously, which controls the scale of your drawing. The Grid tab allows you to set the

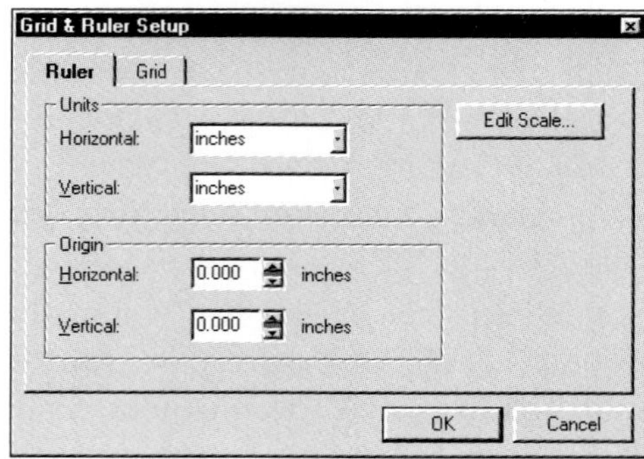

Grid & Ruler Setup dialog box

FIGURE 2-12

Horizontal and Vertical Frequency of the grid (the number of points per unit selected from the Ruler tab), turn the display of the grid on or off, and activate the Snap To Grid attribute. When Snap To Grid is activated, objects will snap to the grid whether or not it is displayed.

1. Adjust both horizontal and vertical grid frequencies to 16.00 per inch, if necessary. First select inches from both Units' drop-down list boxes on the Ruler tab, if necessary, then set the Vertical Origin to 11 inches and the Horizontal Origin to zero inches. This moves the rulers' zero points to the upper-left corner of the page.
2. Click on the Grid tab and set both Frequency spinners to 16.00. To change the value in the spinner, point on the up or down scroll arrow and press the mouse button until the number changes to 16.00. Alternatively, you can highlight on the numeric value itself and type in the new number.
3. Look at the Show Grid check box. If no check mark appears in it, select it to make the grid visible. If a check mark already appears in front of it, you don't need to do anything. Also click on the Snap to Grid check box if it's not already selected. Click on OK to save these settings and close the dialog box.
4. Reopen the Layout menu and notice that Snap To Grid now has a check mark in front of it, showing the feature is turned on. Click on Snap to objects to turn it off.
5. If there is not already a check mark by it, select Rulers from the View menu. Since you have set the grid units to inches, the rulers will also display in inches, as in Figure 2-13. Notice that the zero point for both the horizontal and vertical rulers begins at the upper-left corner of the page, as shown in the figure. This is a convenient way to set the rulers so that you can measure everything relative to that corner.

Joining Lines and Curves Automatically

Coreldraw has a feature called Auto-join that causes lines and curves to snap together automatically when their end points are separated by a preset number of *pixels* (the smallest element on a screen—the "dots" with which everything is displayed). You can adjust the Auto-join value, the threshold number of pixels, through the General

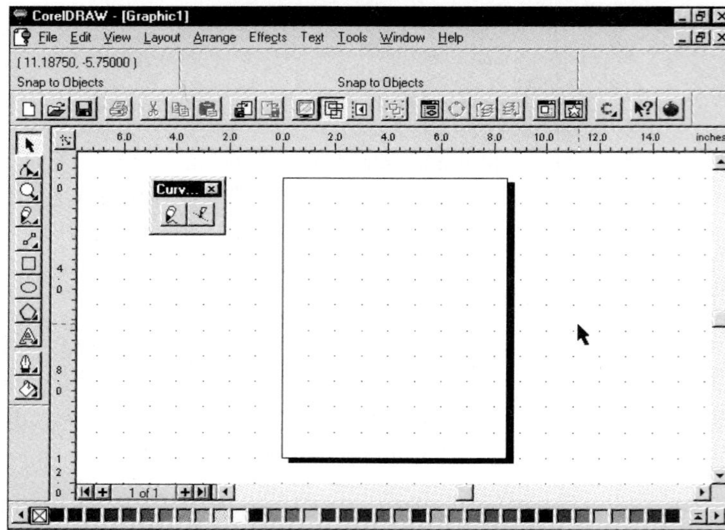

Displaying the grid

FIGURE 2-13

tab on the Curves, Bézier Tool Properties dialog box opened by selecting either Pencil tool, clicking the right mouse button, and selecting Properties.

Literal joining of two end points is important because Coreldraw classifies an object as being either open or closed. If an object is open, you cannot fill it with a color or pattern. Try out the Auto-join feature and then change the Auto-join threshold to see the effect with these steps.

1. Select the Freehand tool, then move the crosshair to a point 1 inch to the right of the zero point on the horizontal ruler and 2 inches below the zero point on the vertical ruler. Notice that as you move the mouse, dotted "shadow" lines in each ruler show you the exact location of your pointer.
2. Click once at this point to begin drawing a line. The parameters appear on the Status bar.
3. Using the rulers and Status bar to help you, extend the line 4 inches to the right. The *DX* and Distance parameters on the Status bar should read 4.0 inches. Click a second time to freeze the line in position. Notice how both the grid display and the grid's Snap To feature help you do this.

4. Move the crosshair exactly 1/4 inch to the right of the end point of the line. Use the rulers to help you.
5. Press and hold the mouse button at this point and drag the mouse to form a squiggling curve, as shown here:

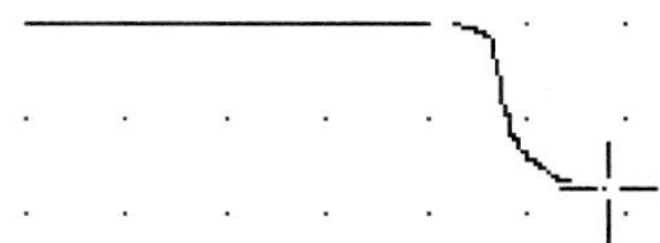

6. Release the mouse button to complete the curve. If you began the curve 1/4 inch or more to the right of the line end point, the curve remains separate from the line and does not snap to it. In order to make a curve snap to a line automatically at this distance, you'll need to adjust the Auto-join threshold value in the Curve, Bézier Tool Properties dialog box. (You'll become familiar with this process in the next section.)

Adjusting the Auto-join Threshold

The Auto-join feature determines how far apart (in pixels) two Freehand or Bézier lines or curves have to be for them to join together automatically. If the setting in the Preferences-Curves dialog box is a small number, such as 3 or less, lines snap together only if you draw with a very exact hand. Use this lower setting when you want to *prevent* lines from joining accidentally. If your technique is less precise, you can set the AutoJoin threshold value to a number higher than 5 pixels so that lines will snap together even if you don't have a steady hand.

1. Select Properties from the View menu, then select Tool from the flyout. In the Tool Properties dialog box, select Curve, Bézier from the Tools drop-down list box on the General tab, as shown in Figure 2-14. The default setting for the features on this tab is 5 pixels. You'll use some of the other settings later on, when you learn skills for which these settings are useful. For now, concern yourself only with the Auto-join setting.
2. Set the Auto-join value to 10 pixels using the up scroll arrow. (10 pixels is the maximum value.)
3. Click on OK to save the new value and return to the drawing.

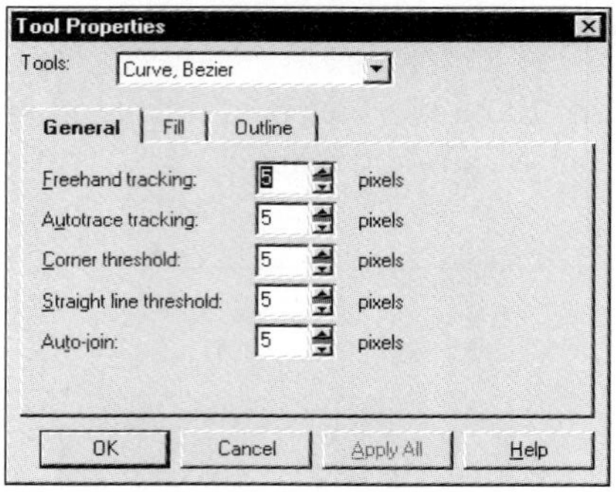

Tool Properties
Tools: Curve, Bezier
General | Fill | Outline
Freehand tracking: 5 pixels
Autotrace tracking: 5 pixels
Corner threshold: 5 pixels
Straight line threshold: 5 pixels
Auto-join: 5 pixels
OK | Cancel | Apply All | Help

Auto-join setting in the Preferences-Curves dialog box

FIGURE 2-14

4. Now you can redraw the line and make the curve snap to it. With the Freehand tool selected, redraw a straight line as you did in steps 1 through 3 of the previous section, except move the line down four inches on the vertical ruler.
5. Move the crosshair to a point 1/4 inch to the right of the end point of the line and then press and hold the mouse button to begin drawing a curve.
6. Drag the mouse and draw the squiggling curve as you did in step 5 of the previous section.
7. Release the mouse button. This time, the curve joins automatically to the line, as shown in Figure 2-15.

Delete your work to clear the screen before going further.

The AutoJoin feature has other uses besides allowing you to connect lines and curves. You can also use it to accomplish the following:

- Join lines to lines or curves to curves
- Add a curve or line to the end of an existing curve, line, or object that you have selected
- Create closed curve objects and polygons by starting and ending a curve (or a series of line segments) at the same point

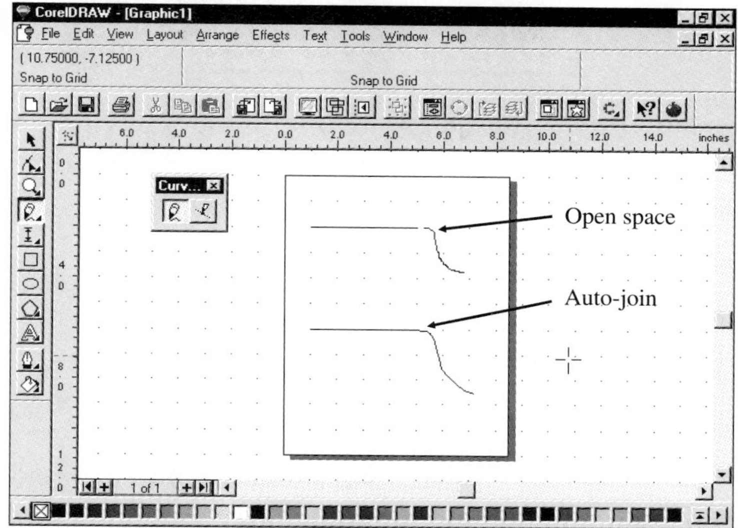

Before and after: curve snapping to a line (Auto-join value high)

FIGURE 2-15

Creating a Drawing Using Lines, Curves, and Polygons

You have learned how to create all of the simple objects—line, curve, closed curve, and polygon—that you can make with the Pencil tool. In this exercise, you'll bring together all of the skills you have learned by drawing a kite that consists of lines, curves, and a polygon. Use Figures 2-16 through 2-19 as a guide to help you position the start and end points of the lines and curves.

1. Turn on the rulers and show the grid (if they do not appear onscreen already) by selecting Rulers from the View menu and Show Grid from the Grid & Ruler Setup dialog box opened from the Layout menu. Select Wireframe view, if it's not already selected.
2. Also from the Layout menu, select Snap To Guidelines (if not already selected). You have now turned on most of Coreldraw's precision enhancement features.

   Guidelines, nonprinting lines placed on a drawing by either dragging on a ruler or with the Guideline Setup dialog box, are used like the grid to

COREL DRAW!™ 6 in action

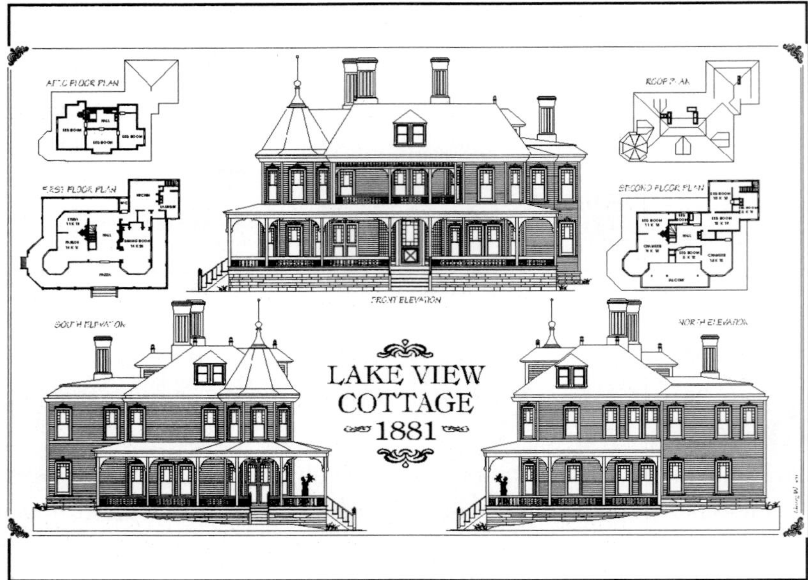

***Lake View Cottage 1881*—Gerry Wilson**

The drawing tools and aids (grids and guidelines) you've learned in this chapter may seem simple, but they are the building blocks of complex drawings, such as this drawing of a Victorian cottage. This drawing could be created using only the tools covered in this chapter (adding text will be covered in Chapter 4).

Lake View Cottage 1881 by Gerry Wilson was the December winner in the Technical Drawings and Charts category of Corel's fifth $1,000,000 World Design Contest. Gerry is from Brooklyn, N.Y. and can be reached at (718) 836-9181.

align objects in a drawing. Guidelines have two major benefits over the grid: they can be placed anywhere, not just on a ruler mark, and, since they are continuous dotted lines, they provide a better visual reference than the grid dots. When a guideline is near a grid line, the guideline always takes priority. This allows you to place a guideline very near a grid line and have objects on a drawing aligned to the guideline. One of CorelDRAW!S 6's new features is the ability to place diagonal guidelines. Previously, guidelines could only be horizontal or vertical.

2

Since the drawing you are doing here uses only major ruler coordinates, you could very easily do it without guidelines. Use the guidelines anyway to see how they work and to use them as a visual reference.

3. With any tool and from any point on the horizontal ruler at the top of the drawing area, drag a horizontal guideline down to 7 inches below the zero point on the vertical ruler. (Move the mouse pointer to the horizontal ruler; press and hold the left mouse button while moving the mouse pointer, along with the dotted line that appears, down to 7 inches; then release the mouse button.) You'll see that the Snap To Grid helps you

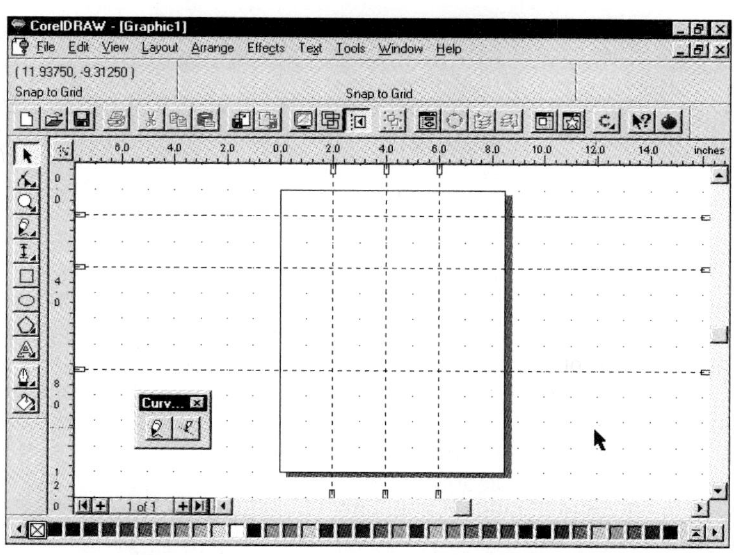

Guidelines in place

FIGURE 2-16

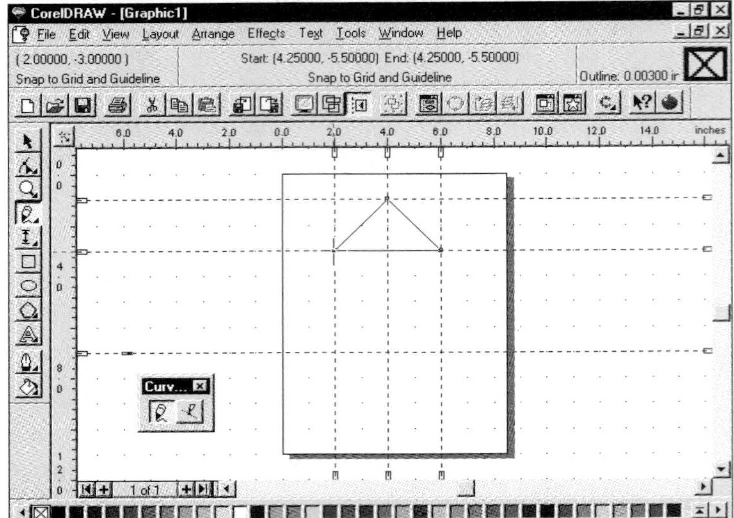

Drawing a kite: the first three line segments

FIGURE 2-17

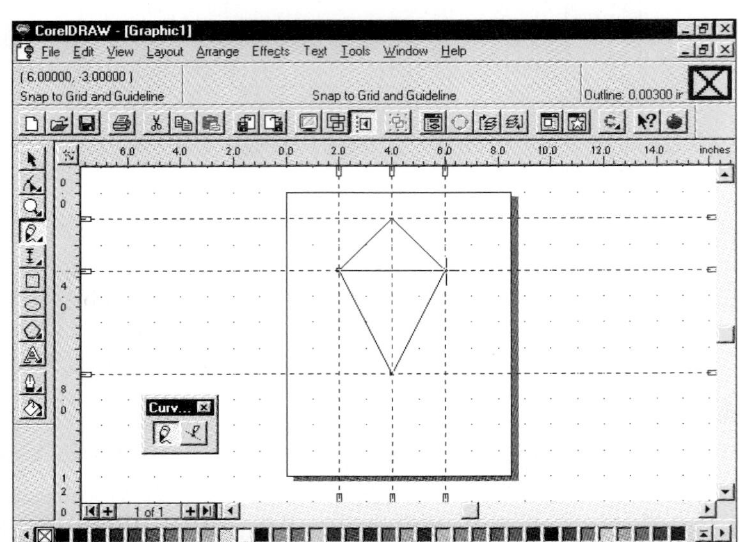

Completing the basic kite shape

FIGURE 2-18

align the guideline. Your screen should look like this as you are dragging the guideline:

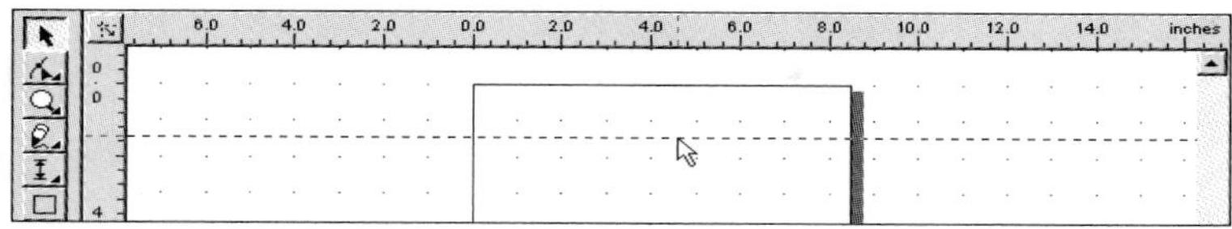

4. As you did in step 3, drag two more horizontal guidelines down to 3 inches and 1 inch below the zero point on the vertical ruler.

   If you misplace a guideline, move the mouse pointer to it, press the mouse button and a four-headed arrow appears. Drag the line into proper position. You can drag a guideline back to the ruler to get rid of it. Also, you can double-click on a guideline to open the Guideline Setup dialog box. From there you can place a guideline precisely or delete it.

5. Again as in step 3, drag three vertical guidelines to the right from the vertical ruler and place them at 6, 4, and 2 inches to the right of the zero point on the horizontal ruler.

   When you are done placing all of the guidelines, your screen should look like the one shown in Figure 2-16.

6. Select the Freehand tool. Your first task will be to form a triangular shape, as shown in Figure 2-17.

7. Move to a point 2 inches to the right of the zero point on the horizontal ruler and 3 inches below the zero point on the vertical ruler and then click once to start a line.

8. Extend the line upward and to the right until you reach a point 4 inches to the right of the horizontal zero point and 1 inch below the vertical zero point. Use the Status bar information to help you. Double-click and release the mouse button at this point. With the intersections of the guidelines at each of these points, the lines you are drawing jump to these points if you get anywhere near them.

9. Extend the next line segment downward and to the right until you reach a point 6 inches to the right of the horizontal zero point and 3 inches below the vertical zero point. Double-click at this point to add another line segment.

10. Extend another line segment horizontally to the left until you reach the starting point. Double-click at this point. The last line segment will connect to the first line segment and form a triangle, as shown in Figure 2-17.
11. From this point, extend another line segment downward and to the right until you reach a point 4 inches to the right of the horizontal zero point and 7 inches below the vertical zero point. Double-click at this point to complete this segment.
12. Now, extend a segment upward to the lower-right corner of the original triangle, as in Figure 2-18. Click just once to finish the line and complete the basic kite shape.
13. Next, add a vertical crosspiece to the kite. Since this line must be absolutely vertical, begin by pressing and holding CTRL and then clicking once at the top of the kite.
14. While holding CTRL, extend this new line to the base of the kite, as shown in Figure 2-19 of the completed kite, and then click once. Release CTRL. You are next going to attach a curve to this line.

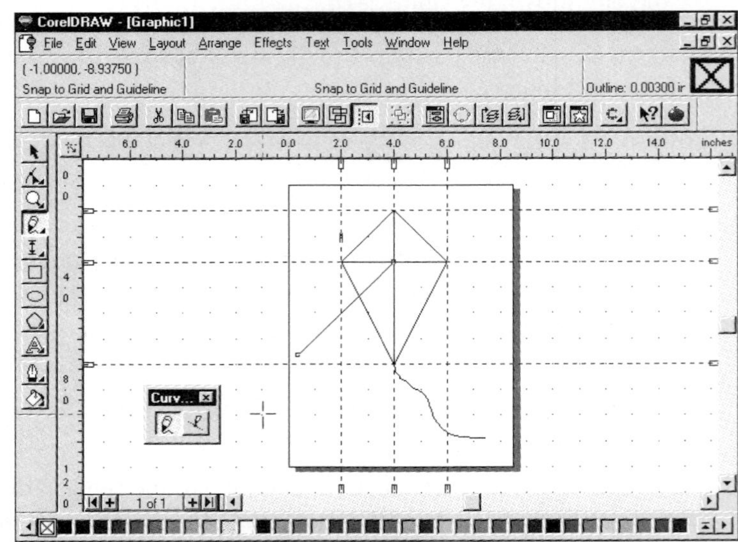

Adding a vertical crosspiece, a tail, and a string to complete the kite

FIGURE 2-19

15. To attach a curve to the line, press and hold the mouse button and then draw a kite tail similar to the one in Figure 2-19. Release the mouse button to complete the curve.

16. Finally, add a string to the kite. While pressing and holding CTRL, click on the point at which the crosspieces meet and extend a line diagonally downward and to the left until you reach the margin of the printable page area. Use Figure 2-19 as a guide. Click once to complete the line. Release CTRL.

17. Your kite should now look similar to the one in Figure 2-19. Leave the kite on your screen for the concluding section of this chapter.

18. To remove the grid lines, turn off the grid by selecting Grid and Ruler Setup from the Layout menu. Click on Show Grid on the Grid tab. The check mark will be removed. Click on OK.

Saving Your Work

As you work on your own drawings, save your work frequently during a session. If you don't save often enough, you could lose an image in the event of an unexpected power or hardware failure.

In order to save a new drawing, you must establish a filename for it. To save the kite you just drew, follow these steps:

1. Select the Save As command from the File menu to display the Save Drawing dialog box shown in Figure 2-20. The Save in text box should show that you are in the C:\Corel\Programs folder of your hard drive. (Path names may vary, depending on how and where you installed the software. In Figure 2-20, the folder \Drawings is used instead of \Programs.) You can see the complete path to the selected folder by clicking on the down arrow on the Save in drop-down list box.

IP: *When saving a drawing for the first time, a shortcut step to displaying the Save Drawing dialog box is to click on the Save button on the toolbar.*

2. If the path is different from what you want or if you want to save the drawing in a different drive and/or folder, for example, C:\Drawings, change to the correct drive and folder in the Save in drop-down list box.

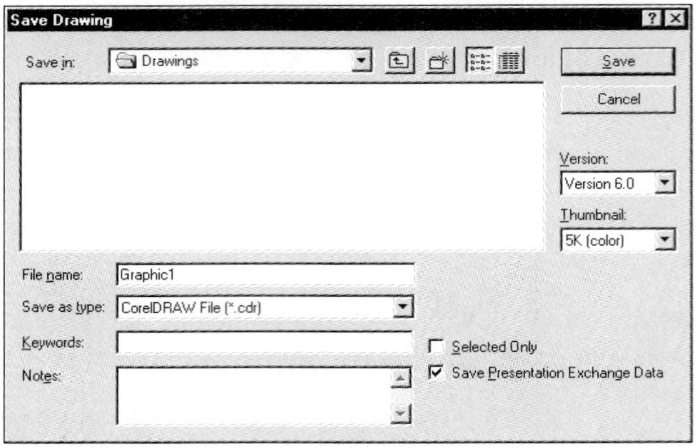

Save Drawing dialog box

FIGURE 2-20

If the drive or directory name you want is not visible in the Save in drop-down list box, position the pointer over the up or down arrow on the scroll bar, then press and hold the mouse button until the path name becomes visible. You can then select the drive or folder name.

3. Name the drawing by clicking in the File name text box and then typing the desired name of your file. Delete the default characters if they are not what you want. Coreldraw adds the .cdr extension for you when you select the OK command button. In this case, type **Kite**.
4. Save the file by clicking on the Save command button or pressing ENTER. Coreldraw adds the extension .cdr to the file, and you exit the Save Drawing dialog box and return to your drawing. Notice that the Title bar now contains the name of your drawing, Kite.CDR.
5. Select Close from the File menu to clear the screen before continuing. Since you have just saved a picture, the Save Changes warning box doesn't appear.

The foregoing procedure applies only the first time you save a drawing. To save a drawing that has already been saved,

6. Select Save from the File menu, or click on the Save icon, or press CTRL-S.

Customize IT! *Coreldraw will automatically save your work as you work on it. Open the Tools menu and select Options. On the Options dialog box, click on the Advanced tab. With the Backup options you can select the default folder for saving your work, whether or not to create a backup file when the drawing is saved, and the time interval for automatically saving your work. The default value is 10 minutes.*

2

Retrieving a File

To open a drawing that you have saved, use the following procedure. In this exercise, you'll open the Kite.CDR file you just saved.

1. Select Open from the File menu. The Open Drawing dialog box appears, as in Figure 2-21. Its layout is very similar to the Save Drawing dialog box.

IP: A shortcut step to displaying the Open Drawing dialog box is to click on the Open icon on the toolbar.

If you saved your file in a directory other than the default directory (the Draw directory):

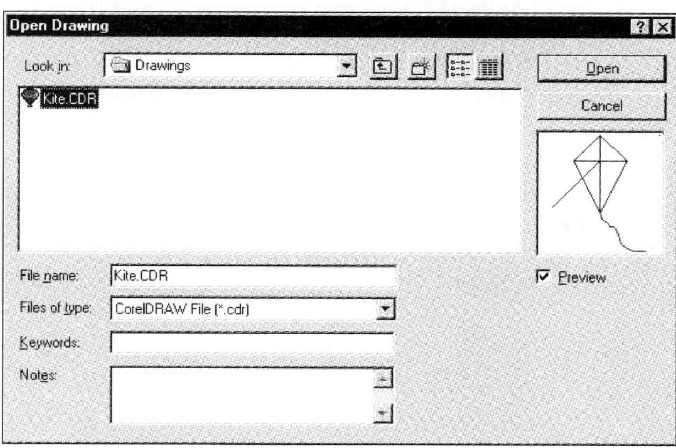

Open Drawing dialog box

FIGURE 2-21

1. Select the drive and/or folder name from the Look in drop-down list box. Use the scroll bar if necessary.
2. If you can't see the file Kite.CDR in the File Name list box, position the mouse pointer over the down arrow on the scroll bar and then press and hold it until the filename becomes visible.

IP: *Coreldraw keeps a list of your most recently opened files at the bottom of the File menu. You can open any of the files listed by selecting it from the File menu.*

3. Click once on the filename, Kite.CDR. The name appears in reverse video (white lettering on colored background—depending on the color options set) and displays in the File name text box. Also, you will see a miniature of the drawing in the Preview box if the Preview check box is selected.
4. To open the file, select the Open command or press ENTER. You may see a Conflicting Styles dialog box telling you that the styles in Kite.cdr are different from those in Coreldrw.cdt and asking whether you want the Coreldraw styles to prevail. For now, click on NO. After a moment, the file displays in the window and its name appears in the Title bar.
5. Exit Coreldraw by pressing ALT-F4, or by selecting Exit from the File menu.

IP: There's a shortcut to opening a file once you are in the Open Drawing dialog box. Instead of clicking once on the filename and then clicking on OK, you can simply double-click on the filename.

That's all there is to it. You have created a complete drawing using the various modes of the Pencil tool, saved it, and loaded it again. Along the way, you have learned how to do Freehand and Bézier drawings of both lines and curves and to use the dimension lines, callouts, rulers, grid, guidelines, and Status bar to help you work.

Drawing and Working with Rectangles, Ellipses, and Polygons

3

Rectangles, ellipses, and polygons are basic shapes that underlie many complex forms in nature or created by humans. In this chapter, you will learn to use the Coreldraw tools that simplify the creation of rectangles, squares, ellipses, circles, and polygons: the Rectangle, Ellipse, and Polygon tools. As you work your way through the exercises in later chapters, you will apply a host of Coreldraw special effects, fills, and shaping techniques to make these basic shapes come alive.

Drawing a Rectangle

Using the Rectangle tool on the Coreldraw toolbox, you can draw a rectangle from any of its four corners, as well as from the center outward. Having this freedom and control over the placement of rectangles saves you time and effort when you lay out your drawings.

Drawing a Rectangle from Any Corner

When you start a rectangle from one of its four corners, the corner that represents the starting point always remains fixed as you draw, while the rest of the outline expands or contracts as you move the pointer diagonally. The following exercise will help you become familiar with how Coreldraw works when you use different corners as starting points. Before drawing a rectangle, you will customize your Coreldraw workspace.

1. Load Coreldraw if you are not running it already.
2. Open the View menu and make sure Rulers, Status bar, Toolbox, and Wireframe are selected. There is a check mark in front of each option when it is selected. If not, click on the item to select it.
3. Point on the Status bar and press the right mouse button to display the Status bar pop-up menu. Then click on Place at Top to move the Status bar from its default position at the bottom of the screen to its alternate position below the Menu bar.

A lot of attention is placed on the Status bar in this and later chapters. You can customize the Status bar to work the way you want it to. If you prefer to keep the Status bar at the bottom of the screen, you can leave it there. You can also use the Status bar pop-up to customize the information displayed. The Status bar is divided into regions (two to six) with multiple rows per region. To change the information on a row, click on it with the right mouse button, and then click on Show from the pop-up. Select the information you want displayed in the selected row from the Show flyout. While working with these exercises, be sure Object Details and Object Information are displayed (the default is to display this information in the two rows of the center region).

4. Point on the border of the Toolbox, press the mouse button, and drag the Toolbox onto the workspace. Once again, this gives you a chance to try an alternate arrangement for the Toolbox. The figures and illustrations in this chapter reflect this alternative arrangement. If you don't like it, feel free to return to the default setting by dragging the Toolbox back to the side of the screen.

OTE: *In the rest of this book, the term drag will be used to indicate pressing the mouse button, moving the pointer, and then releasing the button.*

Next you will move the zero points on both rulers to the upper-left corner of the printable page area. Coreldraw's default is to place the zero points of the rulers at the lower-left corner of the printable page area. This is the standard method of measuring a page used by the printing industry. Many people find it easier to measure a page from the top down, as you will do in these exercises. However, using the upper-left corner as the zero point means that all vertical measurements are represented by negative numbers. In your own work, you can use whatever zero point works best for you. For these exercises, the measurements will be given measured from the upper-left corner.

1. Point on the button at the intersection of the vertical and horizontal rulers. Drag the ruler crosshair to the upper-left corner of the page, as shown here:

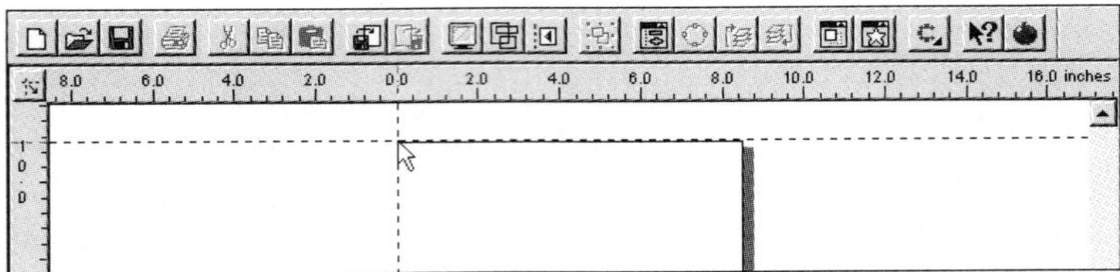

Notice that the lines snap to the corner grid point. Release the mouse button, and the zero point on the rulers will be aligned with the upper-left corner of the page.

2. Select the Rectangle tool and move the pointer onto the workspace. The mouse pointer changes to a crosshair.
3. Position the pointer near the upper-left corner of the printable page area and drag the pointer downward and to the right along a diagonal path, as shown in Figure 3-1. The Width and Height indicators in the status line will change as you move the pointer.
4. Experiment with different widths and heights until you achieve the shape you want. You can easily modify the shape of the rectangle by redirecting the movement of the mouse. Notice that the upper-left corner, which was your starting point, remains fixed.

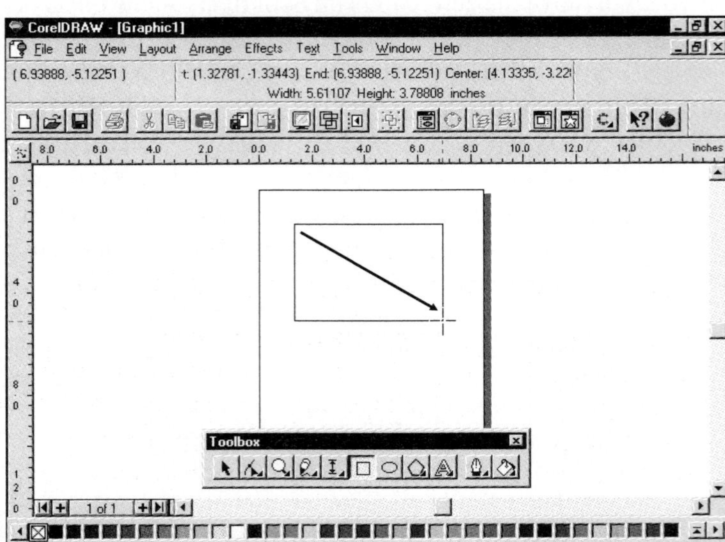

Drawing a rectangle

FIGURE 3-1

5. When the rectangle is the size and shape you want, release the mouse button. This action freezes the rectangle in place, and a node will appear at each of the four corners. The Status bar displays the message "Rectangle on Layer 1", as in Figure 3-2. Depending on your current Fill settings, "Fill: Black" followed by a black square, may also be displayed. The "Fill: Black" message indicates that the rectangle has a default interior color of black. If you do not have Wireframe selected in the View menu and Fill is set to Black, the rectangle you drew will be black. You will learn more about fills in Chapter 7.
6. Point on a new starting point and then drag along a diagonal path downward and to the left. Release the mouse button when the rectangle has the dimensions you want. Practice making several rectangles by starting at different corners.
7. While the last rectangle is still selected—has nodes at the corners—select Delete from the Edit menu or press DEL to remove it.
8. Clear the whole page by clicking on Select All from the Edit Menu and then pressing DEL.

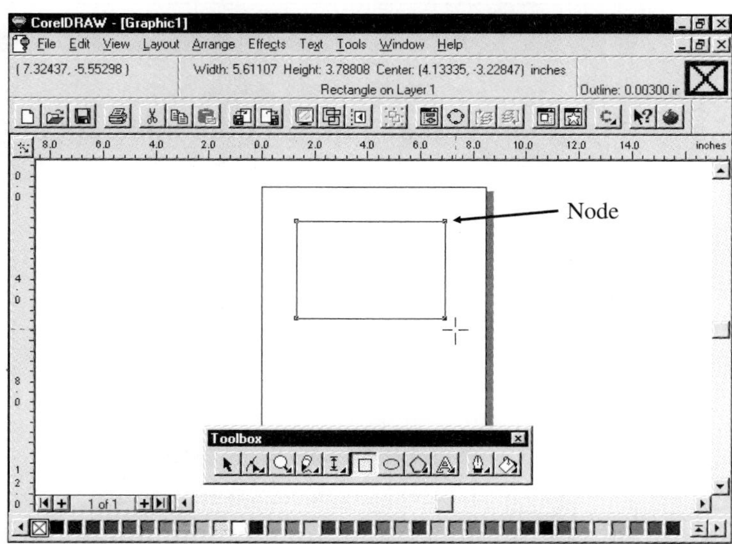

The completed rectangle

FIGURE 3-2

The type of information appearing in the Status bar reflects the kind of object you are drawing. When you create a line, the status line displays the *x* and *y* coordinates, the distance (*DX*, *DY*) traveled, and the angle of the line. When you create a rectangle, the status bar displays the width, height, start, end, and center. After the mouse button is released, the start and end are no longer shown.

Drawing a Rectangle from the Center Outward

Coreldraw also allows you to draw a rectangle from the center outward. Using this technique, you can place rectangular shapes more precisely within a graphic without having to pay close attention to rulers or grid spacing (for example, to draw a frame around a group of objects). The width and height indicators display the exact dimensions of the rectangle as you draw. Draw a rectangle now, using the center as its starting point.

1. With the Rectangle tool still selected, point on the center of the printable page area then press and hold SHIFT. Keep SHIFT pressed as you drag the mouse. As with any rectangle, you can draw in any direction, as you see in Figure 3-3.

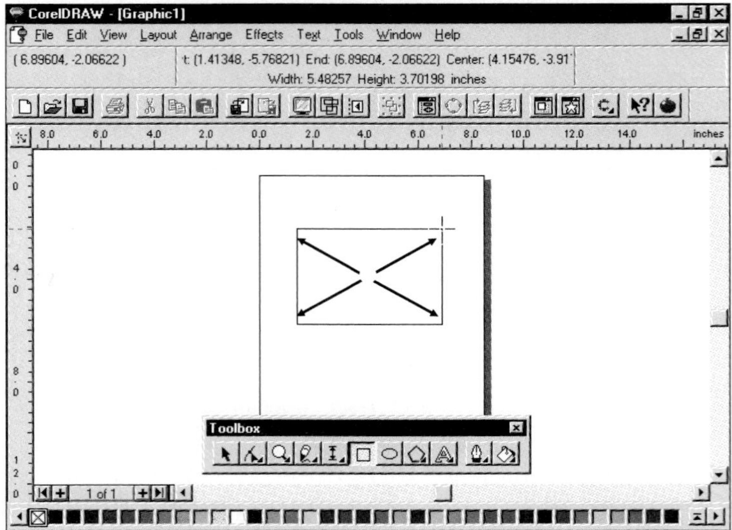

Drawing a rectangle from the center outward

FIGURE 3-3

2. Release the mouse button first and then the SHIFT key to complete the rectangle. If you release SHIFT first, the starting point of your rectangle will be one of the corners rather than the center.
3. Press DEL to clear the rectangle from the screen.

Drawing a Square

In Coreldraw, you use the same tool to produce both rectangles and perfect squares. The technique is similar, except that you use the CTRL key to constrain a rectangle to a square.

Drawing a Square from Any Corner

Follow these steps to draw a square. As with a rectangle, you can use any corner as your starting point.

1. With the Rectangle tool selected, position the pointer where you want to begin the square.
2. Press and hold CTRL, and then drag the pointer diagonally in any direction. Note that the status line indicators show that the width and height of the shape are equal, as in Figure 3-4.
3. To complete the square, release the mouse button first, and then release CTRL. If you release CTRL first, you might draw a rectangle with unequal sides rather than a square.
4. Press DEL to clear the square from the screen.

You can draw a square using the center as the starting point just as you did a rectangle. To do this, you must press both CTRL and SHIFT, as well as the mouse button.

Practicing with the Grid

If your work includes technical illustrations, architectural renderings, or graphic design, you might sometimes find it necessary to align your objects horizontally or

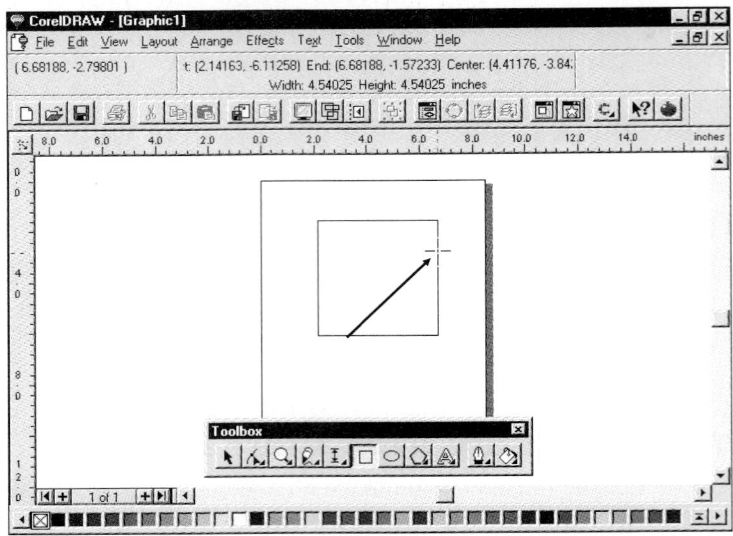

Drawing a square

FIGURE 3-4

vertically in fixed increments. In this section, you can practice aligning rectangles and squares *while* drawing them. Later in this book you will be introduced to techniques for aligning shapes *after* you have drawn them.

IP: *As you learned in the previous chapter, the grid in Coreldraw can either be invisible or a pattern of dots on the screen. Objects are aligned to the grid because of the Snap To feature, which is similar to a magnetic attraction.*

One way to align objects while drawing is to take advantage of the Grid and Ruler Setup and Snap To commands on the Layout menu. The process of aligning new objects to a grid consists of four steps.

- Adjusting the grid spacing
- Displaying the grid (optional)
- Displaying the rulers (optional)
- Enabling the Snap To Grid feature

Even though you don't have to display the grid or rulers to use the grid and the Snap To feature, having them on your screen will help align your work.

Follow these steps to practice using the grid.

1. Open the Layout menu and select Grid and Ruler Setup. The Grid & Ruler Setup dialog box shown in Figure 3-5 will be displayed.
2. Make sure inches is selected in both the Horizontal and Vertical Units drop-down list boxes. Notice that the Vertical Origin is set to 11 inches. This reflects your dragging the rulers' zero point to the upper-left corner of the page. If you prefer, you can adjust the zero point using the Grid & Ruler dialog box rather than dragging the rulers.
3. Select the Grid tab, as shown in Figure 3-6. Adjust both the Horizontal and Vertical Grid Frequency values to 2.000 per inch. You can use either the spinner scroll arrows or you can drag across the value to highlight it and type **2**. Pressing TAB will select the next drop-down list box or check box.
4. If they are not already selected, click on the Show Grid and Snap To Grid check boxes, then click on OK to save these settings and exit the dialog box.
5. If you didn't do it previously, turn on the rulers and Wireframe view by selecting both Rulers and Wireframe from the View menu. Check marks will appear next to both commands, indicating that they are now active.
6. Next, select the Rectangle tool and position the pointer at the 1-inch mark on the horizontal ruler and –1 inch on the vertical ruler. As long as the pointer is close to this position, the corner of the rectangle will align

3

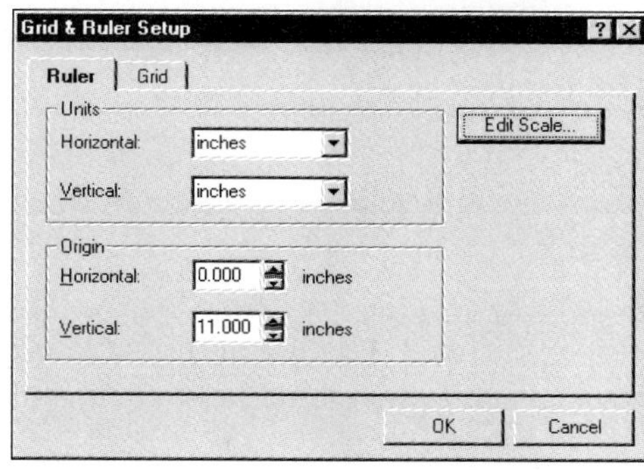

Grid & Ruler Setup dialog box

FIGURE 3-5

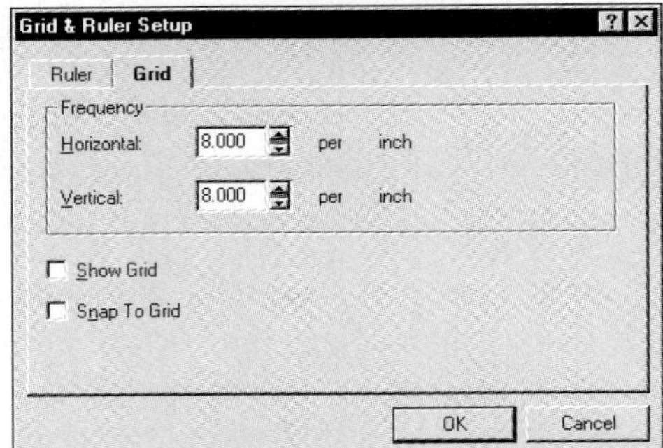

Adjusting Grid Frequency

FIGURE 3-6

perfectly to the 1-inch marks when you begin to draw. This is the Snap To feature in operation.

7. Drag the pointer downward and to the right to draw a rectangle 4 inches wide and 3 inches high. Use the information displayed in the Status bar to guide you.
8. Draw a second rectangle the same size as the first, beginning at a point 1/2 inch to the right and 1/2 inch below the starting point of the first. The extension of the mouse pointer in the rulers—a dotted line—should align exactly with the 1 1/2-inch marks on both rulers (the vertical ruler will display –1 1/2 inches). The grid setting prevents you from "missing the mark."
9. Draw a third rectangle from a starting point 1/2 inch below and 1/2 inch to the right of the starting point of the second. Your three rectangles should align like the ones in Figure 3-7.
10. Click on Select All from the Edit menu and press DEL to clear all of the rectangles from the screen.

IP: *You can also select all the objects in your drawing by double-clicking on the Pick Tool.*

Now that you have practiced drawing all possible types of rectangles, you are ready to build a drawing with rectangular and freehand elements.

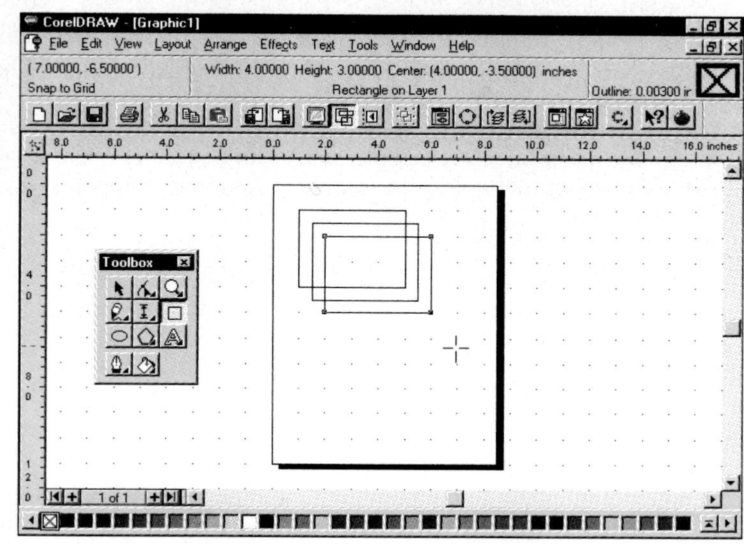

Drawing rectangles at 1/2-inch intervals

FIGURE 3-7

Creating a Drawing Using Rectangles and Squares

In the following exercise, you will integrate all the skills you have learned so far by creating a teacup that includes rectangles, squares, and freehand drawing elements. In the process, you will also learn how to adjust the relative smoothness of curved lines you draw with the Freehand tool. The adjustment involves a feature called Freehand Tracking, which controls how closely Coreldraw follows the movements of your mouse pointer when you draw curves.

To prepare for this exercise, select Grid and Ruler Setup from the Layout menu and adjust both the Horizontal and Vertical Grid Frequency to 8.00 per inch on the Grid tab of the Grid & Scale dialog box. Both Show Grid and Snap To Grid should still be selected, and Rulers should be displayed. Refer to the steps in the preceding section if necessary.

When you are ready to create the drawing, proceed through the following steps, using the numbers in Figure 3-8 as a guide. If you wish, use the rulers as an aid in laying out your work.

1. Draw a rectangle (1) to represent the body of the teacup. Place the pointer at 2 inches on the horizontal ruler and –4 inches on the vertical ruler, then drag the pointer to 6 inches on the horizontal ruler and –9 inches on the vertical ruler.
2. Position your pointer at the right side of this rectangle and attach a rectangular handle (2) to the body of the teacup. The handle should touch the edge of the teacup but not overlap it; the grid settings you have chosen will prevent overlapping.
3. Draw a smaller rectangle (3) inside the one you just created (2) to make the opening in the handle.
4. Now select the Freehand tool and add a straight line (4) to the base of the teacup. (Freehand mode should be selected, not Bézier. If you need to change the drawing mode, click on and hold the lower-right corner of the Pencil tool until the flyout appears, then click on the leftmost button.) This represents the top of the saucer. Remember to press and hold CTRL while drawing to ensure that the line remains perfectly horizontal; use the information in the Status bar if you need guidance.
5. Extend diagonal lines (5) and (6) down from each end of the top of the saucer. Check the status bar indicators as you draw. The angle for the diagonal line to the left (6) should read –45 degrees, while the angle for the diagonal line to the right (5) should read –135 degrees. Again, press and hold CTRL while drawing the line to ensure that the line remains on a 15-degree increment. Also, be sure to make both lines the same length.

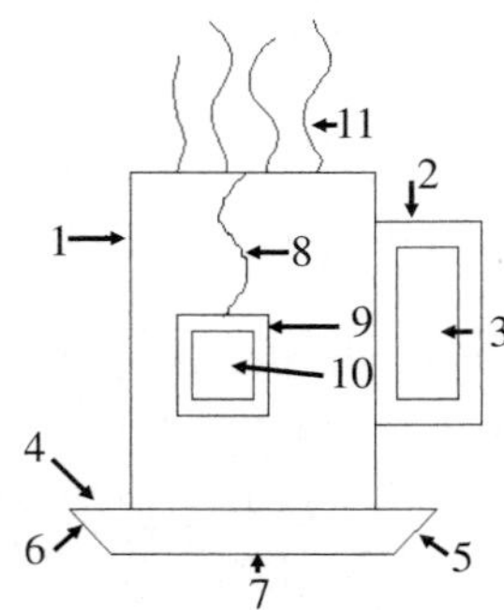

Drawing a teacup using rectangles, squares, and freehand elements

FIGURE 3-8

Each line snaps to the top of the saucer to form a multisegment line, as you learned in Chapter 2.

6. Now add another straight line (7) to form the bottom of the saucer. Remember to constrain the line using CTRL. Click on the lower node of the left diagonal line, then place the pointer on the lower node of the right line and click once. The saucer base snaps to the other line segments to form a single object, a polygon shape.
7. With the Freehand tool still selected, press and hold the mouse button and draw a curve (8) to represent the string of a tea bag. Does your string appear excessively jagged? If it does, you can adjust the Freehand Tracking setting in the next set of steps.
8. Before adjusting the Freehand Tracking value, erase the tea bag string you have just drawn by selecting Undo from the Edit menu.
9. Point on the Freehand tool and click the right mouse button. A pop-up menu appears with two commands: What's This? (to open the Help topic) and Properties. You will use the Tool Properties dialog box to adjust the Freehand Tracking. Select Properties from the pop-up to display the Curves, Bézier settings on the Tool Properties dialog box shown in Figure 3-9. You used this same dialog box in Chapter 2 to adjust the Auto-join values. The default value in the spinner next to Freehand Tracking is 5, but you are going to adjust it to a higher number to make smoother curves.
10. Adjust the Freehand Tracking sensitivity to 10 pixels. This is the highest number possible and causes Coreldraw to smooth your curved lines as

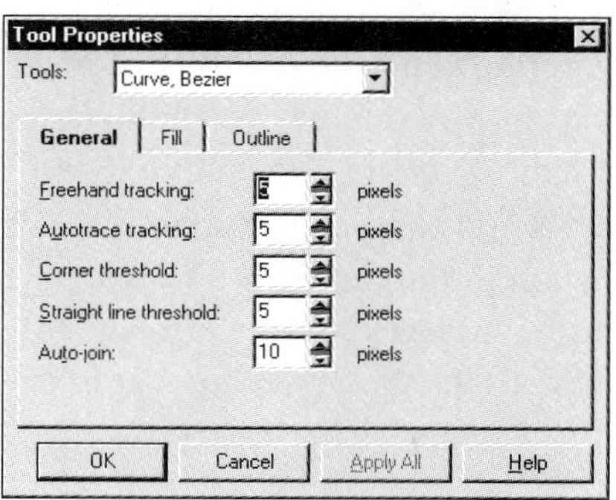

Adjusting the Freehand Tracking value for smoother curves

FIGURE 3-9

you draw. Lower numbers, on the other hand, cause the Pencil tool to track every little dip and rise as you move the mouse.

11. Select OK to exit the dialog box and save your setting.
12. Now draw the tea bag string a second time. Your curve should be somewhat smoother now, more like the one in Figure 3-8.
13. Next, attach a tag to the string. Select the Rectangle tool again, position the pointer about 3/4 inch below the bottom of the string, press and hold CTRL and SHIFT simultaneously, and draw a square (9) from the center outward.
14. To add a center label to the tag, create a smaller square (10) inside the first square. Remember to press and hold the CTRL key to constrain the object to a square.
15. To add a finishing touch to your drawing, create some steam (11) by selecting the Freehand tool and drawing some curves. Since you have set Freehand Tracking to a higher number of pixels, you can create more effective "steam."
16. Finally, save your drawing. Select the Save As command from the File menu and, after you select the folder you want to use, type **teacup**. When you click on OK, Coreldraw adds the extension .CDR automatically.
17. Select Close from the File menu to exit your drawing, then select New from the File menu and Document from the flyout to open a new document and prepare for a new drawing.

Drawing an Ellipse

The Ellipse tool in Coreldraw allows you to create both ellipses and perfect circles. Follow the exercises in this section to create ellipses and circles of many different shapes and sizes. In later chapters, you will expand your skills and apply a rich variety of special effects and shaping techniques to these basic geometrical forms.

Coreldraw allows you to start an ellipse from any point on the rim or to draw an ellipse from the center point outward by using the SHIFT key. This second method allows you to place ellipses precisely within a graphic.

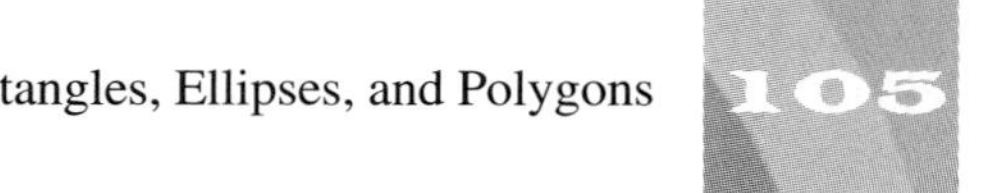

Using the Rim as a Starting Point for an Ellipse

You can initiate an ellipse from any point on its rim. This flexibility in choosing your starting point allows you to position an ellipse within a drawing without sacrificing precision. Although you cannot use a corner as a starting point for ellipses and circles, you can still use the width and height indicators as guides.

Coreldraw gives you an additional visual cue when you are drawing ellipses and circles. If your starting point is on the upper half of the rim, Coreldraw places the node at the uppermost point of the ellipse; if your starting point is on the lower half of the rim, Coreldraw places the node at the bottommost point of the ellipse. In the following exercises you will become familiar with how Coreldraw functions when you choose different points on the rim as starting points for an ellipse.

1. Click on the Ellipse tool and position the pointer anywhere on the printable page area, and drag the mouse downward and to the right along a diagonal path, as shown in Figure 3-10. The indicators on the status line display the width and height of the ellipse.

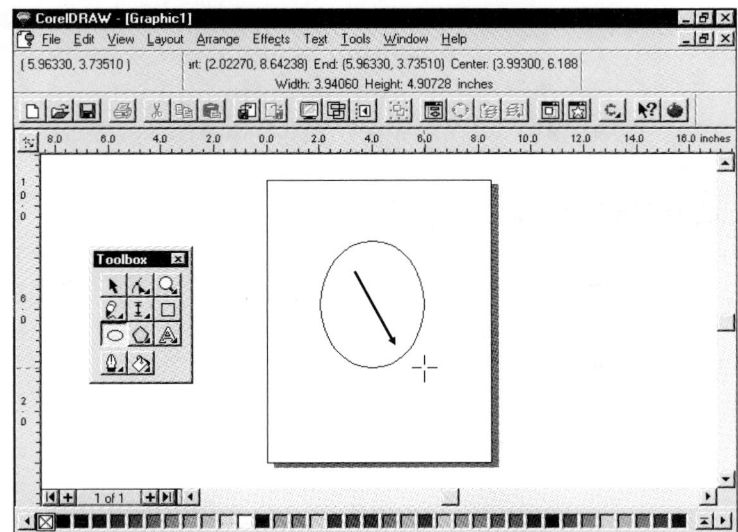

FIGURE 3-10 Drawing an ellipse from top to bottom

2. When the ellipse is the shape you want, release the mouse button. This action completes the ellipse and freezes it in place. As in Figure 3-11, a single node appears at the uppermost point of the ellipse, and the status line changes to display the messages "Ellipse on Layer 1." Press DEL to clear the page.
3. Choose a new starting point and draw an ellipse from bottom to top. Place the pointer at the desired starting point and then drag the pointer upward in a diagonal direction.
4. When the ellipse has the dimensions you want, release the mouse button. Note that the node is now at the bottom of the ellipse.
5. Press DEL to clear this ellipse from the screen.

Drawing an Ellipse from the Center Outward

Coreldraw allows you to draw an ellipse from the center outward, just as you did with rectangles and squares. This feature offers you a more precise method of placing

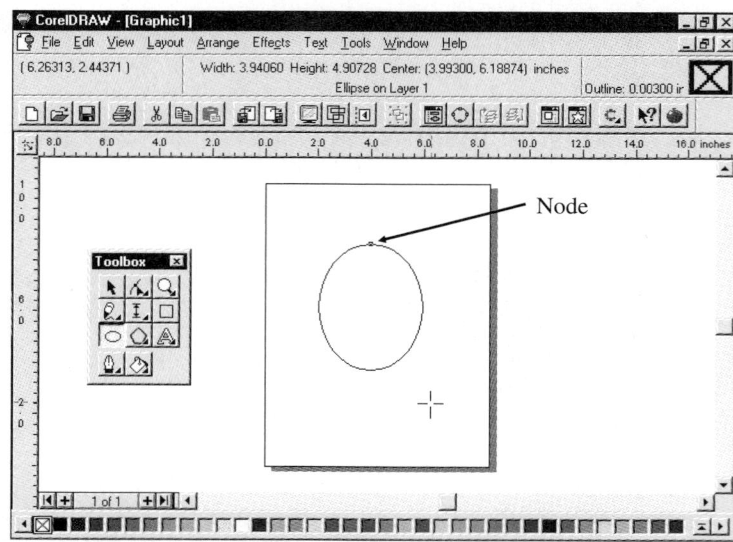

A completed ellipse showing the node at the top

FIGURE 3-11

an ellipse, especially when you are combining an ellipse with other objects. The width and height indicators continue to display the exact dimensions of the ellipse as you draw. Practice drawing an ellipse using the center as a starting point with the following steps.

1. With the Ellipse tool selected, press and hold SHIFT and place the pointer at the desired starting point. Keep SHIFT depressed as you drag the mouse. As with any ellipse, you can draw in whichever direction you choose, as you see in Figure 3-12, in which an ellipse was drawn from its center outward.
2. Release the mouse button and then release SHIFT to complete the ellipse.
3. Clear the ellipse from the screen by pressing DEL.

Drawing a Circle

In Coreldraw, you use a single tool to produce both ellipses and perfect circles, just as you use the same tool to produce rectangles and squares. The technique is similar: you use CTRL to constrain an ellipse to a circle. As with ellipses, you can choose either the rim or the center of the circle as a starting point.

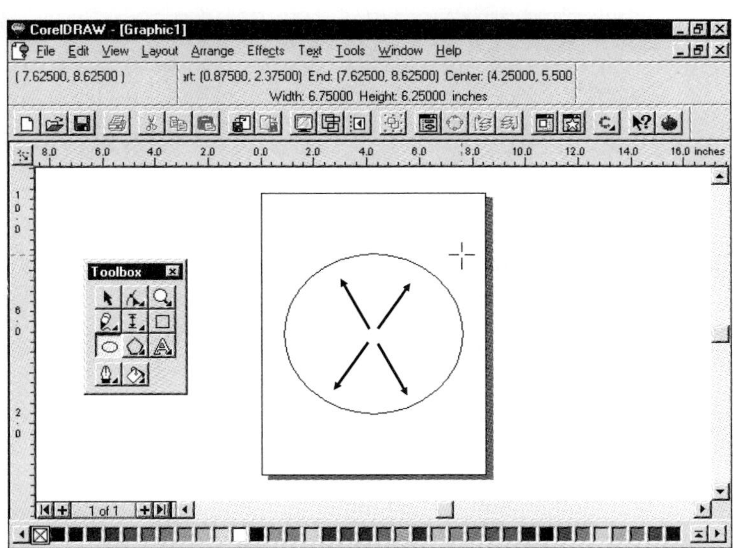

Drawing an ellipse from the center outward

FIGURE 3-12

Using the Rim as a Starting Point for a Circle

Perform the following exercise to create a perfect circle, starting from the circle's rim.

1. With the Ellipse tool selected, position the pointer at a desired starting point.
2. Press and hold CTRL, and then drag the pointer to draw diagonally in any direction. As you can see in Figure 3-13, the status line indicators show that both the width and the height of the shape are equal.
3. To complete the circle, release the mouse button and then CTRL.
4. Clear the circle from the screen by pressing DEL.

Because of the way Coreldraw works, you are actually creating an imaginary rectangle when you draw an ellipse or circle. That is why the status line indicator for a perfect circle displays width and height instead of diameter. The ellipse or circle

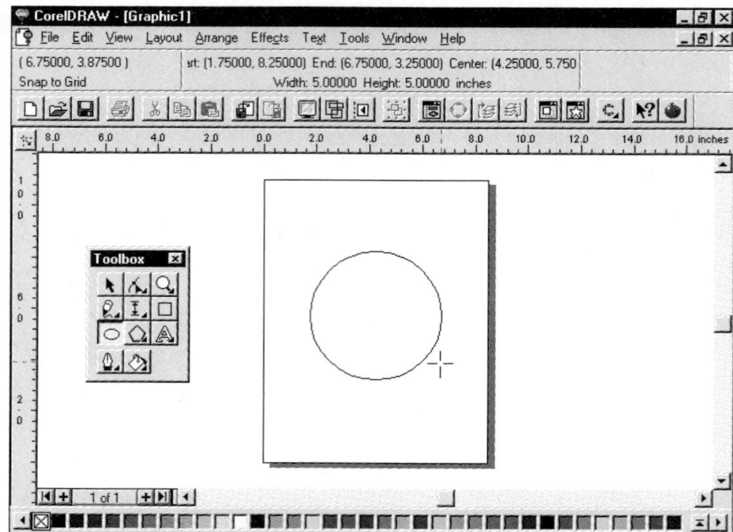

Drawing a circle using the CTRL key

FIGURE 3-13

fits inside the rectangle, as you will see more clearly when you begin to select objects later in Chapter 5.

As is true with other objects, you can draw a circle using the center as a starting point by pressing CTRL-SHIFT.

Drawing a Polygon

3

CorelDRAW! 6 has increased the speed and ease with which you can create objects with the addition of the Polygon tool. You use the Polygon tool in the same way you use the Rectangle and Ellipse tools. As shown here, you have three types of Polygon tools to choose from: the Polygon tool draws regular polygons, the Spiral tool creates a spiral curve, and the Grid tool creates rows and columns of boxes.

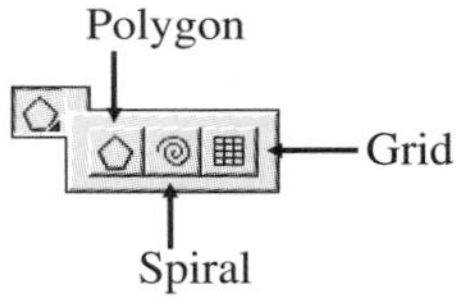

The default polygon shape is a pentagon (a five-sided polygon), but you can create many more shapes using the Polygon settings on the Tool Properties dialog box, shown in Figure 3-14. To open the Tool Properties dialog box for one of the Polygon tools, right click on the desired tool and select Properties from the pop-up. The polygon properties on the Tool Properties dialog box allow you to set the number of sides the polygon will have, with a maximum of 500; the Sharpness of the polygon (adjusts the angle at which lines are connected to the nodes of the polygon); and options for creating a star-shaped polygon. There is also a display box that allows you to preview the polygon settings. The Fill and Outline tabs allow you to set the fill and outline properties for the Polygon tool. Chapter 7 will explain how to work with fills and outlines.

IP: *You can open the Tool Properties dialog box for any drawing tool by either right-clicking on the Tool button or by double-clicking on the button.*

When the Polygon option button is selected, the nodes (points) of the polygon are connected by straight lines. The Star option button creates additional nodes between each point defined in the Number of points spinner. These are connected

Tool Properties dialog box for polygons

FIGURE 3-14

to the defined nodes to create a star shape. Click on the Star option button to see this effect in the display box. The final option button is Polygon As Star. This differs from the Star option button in how Coreldraw creates the polygon. When the Star option button is selected, the polygon is drawn as shown here:

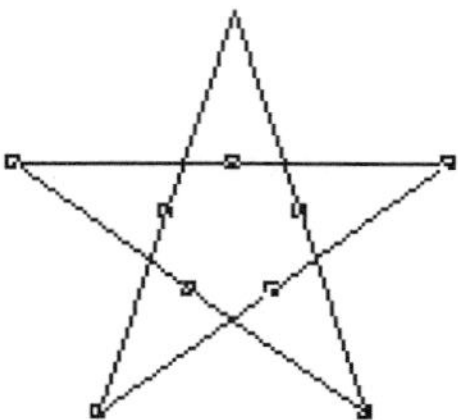

Notice that there is a node at each point of the star as well as in the middle of each line connecting the opposite points of the star. The same shape, this time created with the Polygon As Star option button selected, is shown here:

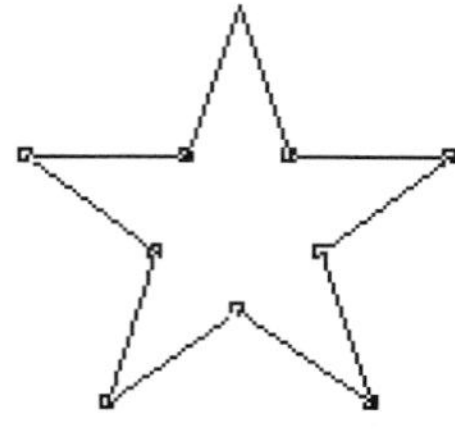

When the Polygon As Star option is selected, the lines do not connect directly to the opposite points. Rather, each outer node is connected to an inner node, and then the next node around the circumference. The Sharpness setting allows you to create "fat" or "skinny" stars in this mode, unlike the Star option, which has more limited Sharpness settings (the exact range depends on the number of points selected). This difference effects how the polygon behaves as it is modified. Experiment with the different settings by changing the options and observing the effect of each change in the display box. Try a larger number of points and vary the Sharpness setting with all three options: Polygon, Star, and Polygon As Star. As you can see, The Polygon tool is an extremely versatile method for creating complex shapes.

Select Spiral from the Tool drop-down list box to display the property options for Spiral polygons. The Number of Revolutions spinner allows you to set the number of revolutions the spiral will have (with a maximum of 100). Select Grids from the Tool drop-down list box to display the property options for grids. Both the number of rows and the number of columns can be defined (with a maximum of 50 rows and 50 columns). Close the Tool Properties dialog box before proceeding.

Previously you created polygon shapes using the Freehand and Bézier tools. These are different than the polygon objects you will create the Polygon tool. Polygons are "live" objects whose properties can be changed after they are created. While you can change some properties of both polygon shapes and objects (such as fill and outline), with polygon objects you can also change the number of points, sharpness, or any other property, and apply them to the object. With polygon shapes you have to either edit or redraw the shape to change the basic form. Also, with the Polygon tool you can create these complex objects much more easily.

Try out the Polygon tool with this exercise.

1. Double-click on the Polygon tool. The tool will be selected and the Polygon Tool Properties will be displayed. Set the Number of points to 5, and click on the Polygon option button to select it. Click on OK.
2. Place the pointer in the upper-left corner of the printable page area, at 1 inch on both the horizontal and vertical rulers. (The ruler zero points should be at the upper-left corner of the page.)
3. Drag the pointer to the right and down to 7 inches on the horizontal ruler and –5 inches on the vertical ruler. Release the mouse button.

   Your polygon should look similar to the top polygon shown in Figure 3-15.
4. Double-click on the Polygon tool again to display the Polygon Tool Properties dialog box. Click on the Polygon As Star option button and set the Sharpness to 50. Then click on OK.

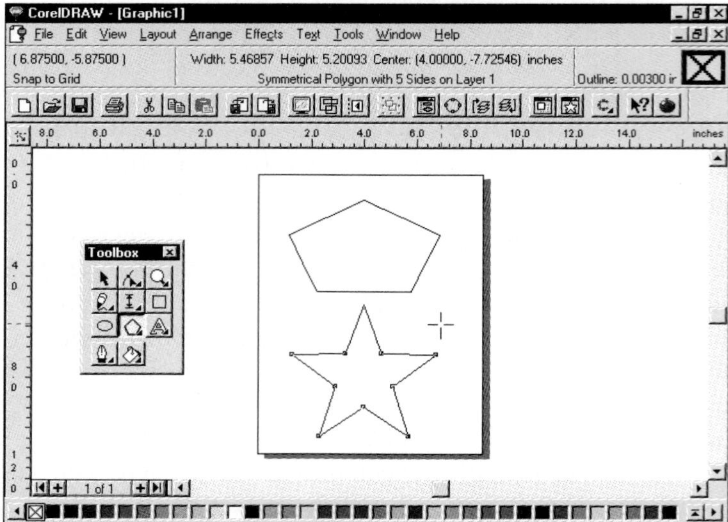

Polygons created with the Polygon tool

FIGURE 3-15

5. Place the crosshair below the first polygon, at 4 inches on the horizontal ruler and –8 inches on the vertical ruler.
6. Press both the SHIFT and CTRL keys and drag outward in any direction.
7. When your polygon is approximately as wide as the first polygon you drew release the mouse button and then the SHIFT and CTRL keys.

Your drawing should look similar to Figure 3-15. Next, you will see the effects of changing the properties of a polygon using the Object Properties dialog box.

1. Select the Pick tool and point on the border of the star polygon you just created, then click the right mouse button. A pop-up menu will appear containing options for editing the object.

   These options are also available from the different menus on the menu bar, but the pop-up menu groups them all in one place.

2. Select Properties (located at the bottom of the pop-up). The Object Properties dialog box shown in Figure 3-16 will be displayed.

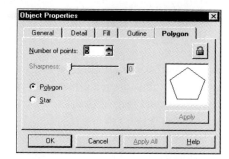

FIGURE 3-16 Object Properties dialog box

The Polygon tab contains the same options you saw in the Tool Properties dialog box. (If you had selected another type of object, the Polygon tab would be replaced by the tab for that type of object.) While the Tool Properties dialog box changes the properties for the tool (effecting the objects you then create with the tool), the Object Properties dialog box settings only effect the selected object. Additionally, the Object Properties dialog box contains a padlock button in the upper-left corner of the Polygon tab. Clicking on this button changes the image to a "locked" padlock and prevents the object from being modified until it is "unlocked."

1. Set the Number of points to 10 and click on the Star option button, then click on OK. Your polygon should now look like this:

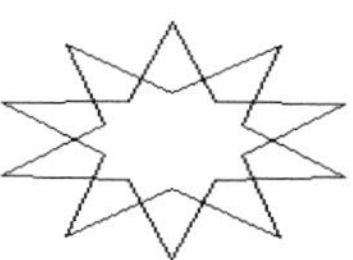

2. Select the Pick tool and right-click on the border of the polygon again, then select Properties from the pop-up. In the Object Properties dialog box, click on the Polygon option button on the Polygon tab. Click on OK.

   Your polygon should now look like this:

3. Clear the screen by choosing Select All from the Edit menu and pressing DEL.

As you have seen, the Polygon tool enables you to quickly and easily create and modify any number of complex objects.

Now that you have created some rectangles, ellipses, and polygons using all of the available techniques, you can integrate these shapes into an original drawing. Continue with the next section to consolidate your skills.

Creating a Drawing Using Rectangles, Ellipses, and Polygons

The following exercise brings together all the skills you have learned so far. You will create a drawing (of a Jack in the box) that will include ellipses, circles, rectangles, squares, polygons and freehand drawing elements. The grid can assist you with some of the geometrical elements of the drawing; other elements you can draw freehand. The first few steps get you into the habit of anticipating and preparing for your drawing needs before you actually begin to draw so that you can draw quickly and without interruption. Use the numbers in Figure 3-17 as a guide in creating your drawing.

1. To prepare for the geometrical portion of the drawing, select Grid and Ruler Setup from the Layout menu and adjust both the Horizontal and

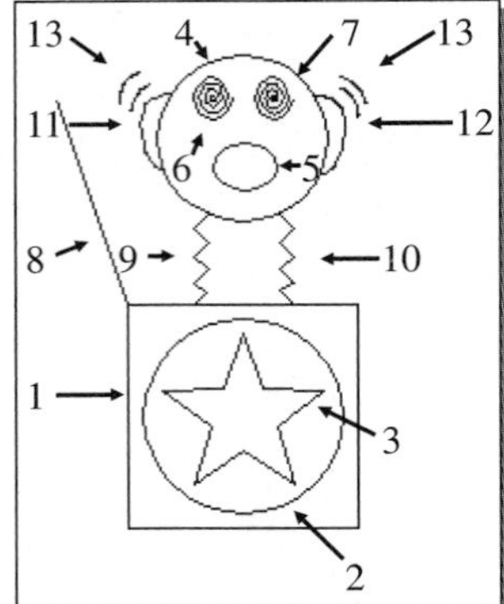

Jack in the box

FIGURE 3-17

Vertical Grid Frequencies to 4.00 per inch. Make sure Snap to Grid is selected. If you need help, refer to the "Practicing with the Grid" section of this chapter.

2. Select Properties from the View menu, then click on Tool from the pop-up menu that appears. The Tool Properties dialog box you've used previously is displayed. Select Curve, Bézier from the Tools drop-down list box. On the General tab that is displayed, set the Freehand Tracking to 10 pixels, and Auto-join to 5 pixels, if they are not already. Click on OK to exit the dialog box.

3. Select the Rectangle tool and position the pointer at the 4 inch mark on the horizontal ruler and the –7 1/2 inch mark on the vertical ruler. Draw a square from the center (press both CTRL and SHIFT) that extends from this point to the 6 inch mark on the horizontal ruler and to the –9 1/2 inch mark on the vertical ruler. This square will constitute the main element of the box (1).

IP: *You can drag a horizontal guideline to –9 1/2 inches and a vertical guideline to 6 inches to make it easier to draw the object.*

4. Click on the Ellipse tool and place a circle on the side of the box by pointing on the same place you started the square: 4 inches on the horizontal ruler and –7 1/2 inches on the vertical ruler. Press CTRL and SHIFT to draw the circle from the center. Release CTRL-SHIFT then the mouse button when the circle is slightly smaller than the square (2).

5. Double-click on the Polygon tool to select it and open the Tool Properties dialog box again. The General tab will display the Polygon options. Select the Polygon as Star option button, set the number of points to 5, and the Sharpness to 50. Click on OK.

6. Add a star to the box in the same way you added the circle: point on the center of the square (4 inches on the horizontal ruler and –7 1/2 inches on the vertical ruler), press CTRL-SHIFT, and drag until the star polygon is slightly smaller than the circle (3).

7. Select the Ellipse tool again to draw Jack's head. Place the pointer at 4 inches on the horizontal ruler and 2 1/2 inches on the vertical ruler and

3

draw a circle 3 inches in diameter from the center (4). Use the Status bar to determine the diameter of the circle as you draw it.

8. With the Ellipse tool still selected, you will draw Jack's mouth. Turn off the Snap To feature by opening the Layout menu and clicking on any Snap To options that are selected. (Remember that a menu item will have a checkmark in front of it when it is selected: none of the Snap To options should be checked.)

9. Draw Jack's mouth by pointing on the starting point and dragging the mouse (5). The mouth can be a circle or ellipse drawn from the rim or center, but it will be easier to place if drawn from the center. Use the Figure 3-17 as a guide.

The eyes are created by drawing two spiral polygons above and slightly to the left and right of the center of the circle you drew for Jack's head. The eyes will be easier to place by drawing from the center.

IP: *Use the Zoom tool to magnify the area you are working on. Press SHIFT-F4 to return to the full page view.*

10. Point on the Polygon tool and press the mouse button until the Polygon tool flyout appears, then select the Spiral tool.

11. Point on the place where you want to place the left eye, press SHIFT and drag down and to the right. Release SHIFT and the mouse button when the left eye is the size you want (6). If you do not like the eye after you draw it, press DEL immediately to erase it, then try again. Draw the right eye using the same technique (7).

12. In the next step, adding a lid to the box, you will use the Snap To Grid feature again. Turn on the Snap To Grid feature using the keyboard shortcut by pressing CTRL-Y. The Status bar now displays Snap To Grid.

13. Now add the lid to the box by selecting the Freehand tool and pointing on the upper-left corner of the box. Click on the corner to set the first node of the line, then move the pointer up and slightly to the left about 4 inches and click again to set the second node of the line (8). Remember to release the mouse button after setting the first node to create a straight line; if you drag with the button pressed, you will create a curve.

You will add the accordion folds that attach the head to the box in the next steps. Your grid settings of 4 per inch are too coarse for these objects, so you will change the grid settings before drawing them.

14. Select Grid and Ruler Setup from the Layout menu. On the Grid tab of the Grid & Ruler dialog box set the Horizontal and Vertical Grid Frequency values to 8 per inch. Click on OK.

15. Point on the lower-left edge of Jack's head to select the starting point for the first multisegment line. Press and hold CTRL to constrain the line segments to 15-degree increments, then click once to begin the line, and double-click to set each successive node. When your line reaches the edge of the box, click once to end the line (9).

16. Repeat the steps above, starting on the lower-right edge of Jack's head, to create the second multisegment line (10).

17. Now add an ear to each side of Jack's head. Point on the upper-left rim of Jack's head where you want the ear to begin, then drag the pointer in an arc that connects to the circle about 1 1/2 inches lower than the starting point (11). Repeat these steps for the right ear (12).

18. Your final step is to add two small freehand lines by each ear (13). These lines will add a feeling of movement to Jack's head, as if he had just sprung from the box. Use the Freehand tool to draw these lines as shown in Figure 3-17. (If you draw too close to the ears, or draw the lines too close together, the AutoJoin feature will snap your freehand curves to the ears or each other.)

19. Save your drawing by selecting the Save As command from the File menu. When the Save As dialog box appears, select the correct folder (the folder where you are storing your work), type **jack**, and click on OK.

20. Finally, if you want to leave Coreldraw for a while, choose Exit from the File menu to return to Windows 95. If you want to go on to Chapter 4 without leaving Coreldraw, select Close from the File menu to clear the screen. Then click on the New button (shown here) on the toolbar to open a new document.

Congratulations! You have mastered the Rectangle, Ellipse, and Polygon tools and created another masterpiece with Coreldraw.

Adding Text

The advanced text-handling features of Coreldraw let you turn text into a work of art. You can rotate, skew, reshape, and edit a single character or text *string* (a group of characters) just as you would any other object. You can perform these feats with the extensive library of fonts provided with Coreldraw or available from other manufacturers. The fonts provided with Coreldraw either are or look similar to standard industry fonts and will print on any Windows-compatible printer. Since the Corel fonts are in the Windows standard TrueType format, you can use them with all your Windows applications—a real bonus!

In this chapter, you will learn how to insert text into a drawing and select the font, style, point size, alignment, and spacing attributes of your text. You will also learn how to enter special foreign language or symbol characters. After you have completed the exercises in this chapter, you will be ready to tackle more advanced techniques for reshaping your text in Chapter 10.

Entering Text

The Text tool, the last of the six basic drawing tools in Coreldraw, is represented by the letter "A." You use the Text tool to insert text into your drawings, just as you use the Ellipse, Rectangle, or Polygon tool to insert geometrical objects. The process of inserting text into a drawing can involve up to seven steps.

1. Select either the Artistic Text or Paragraph Text tool.
2. Select an insertion point.
3. Enter text.
4. Select a Font and Style.
5. Choose the Size of your text.
6. Set the Alignment for the text.
7. Adjust the spacing between the letters, words, and lines of your text.

The sections that follow treat each of the preceding steps in greater detail. Since most of this chapter consists of exercises, however, the order in which you perform these steps may vary slightly from this list.

Selecting the Text Tool

You use the Text tool in Coreldraw to enter new text on a page. In the following brief exercise, you will first adjust the page format and then select the Text tool.

1. If the printable page area is in Portrait format (vertical instead of horizontal), select Page Setup from the Layout menu. When the Page Settings dialog box shown in Figure 4-1 is displayed, click on the Landscape option button to select the horizontal format. Then click on OK.

OTE: *Coreldraw always "remembers" the page setup you used the last time you created a drawing. New drawings will have the same settings as the last drawing you saved.*

2. If Wireframe mode is selected, turn it off by clicking on the Wireframe button on the toolbar. You can determine if Wireframe mode is selected

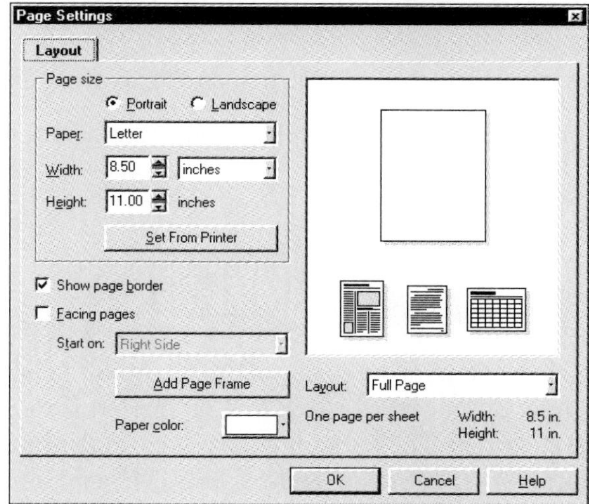

Page Settings dialog box

FIGURE 4-1

by opening the View menu and seeing if there is a check mark by Wireframe or by checking if the Wireframe button on the toolbar appears depressed (the face will be lighter).

3. Make sure you have a black fill selected by pressing on the Fill button on the toolbox (point on the Fill tool and press the mouse button) and selecting the solid black square on the flyout:

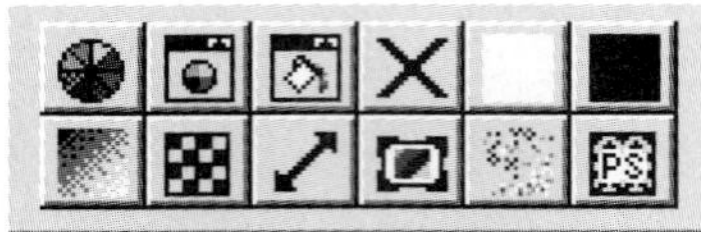

Since you have a new drawing without any objects selected, the Uniform Fill defaults dialog box shown here is displayed.

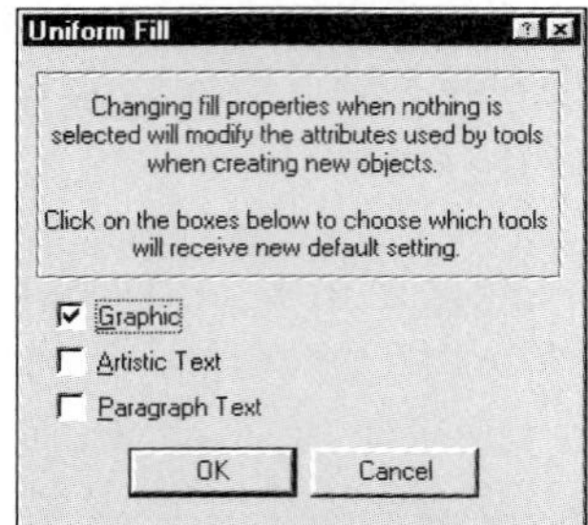

1. Click on the Graphic, Artistic Text and Paragraph Text check boxes, if they are not already selected. Click on OK to close the dialog box.

2. Press on the Text tool to open the flyout. A two-button flyout appears, as shown here:

The buttons represent the two uses of the Text tool: to enter artistic text and to enter paragraph text. The Artistic Text tool on the left is the default; you use it to enter shorter text strings. The Paragraph Text tool on the right allows you to work with larger blocks of text. The differences between artistic and paragraph text are explained in the next section.

Select the Artistic Text tool by clicking on the left button. The mouse pointer turns into a crosshair.

Artistic and Paragraph Text

Artistic text is designed for shorter text strings, such as titles, captions, and notes, that can be up to 32,000 characters long. Paragraph text is designed for larger blocks of text, such as copy for a brochure. Each paragraph can have up to 32,000 characters and each paragraph text file can have up to 32,000 paragraphs. Paragraph text is added in frames. Each frame is a rectangular area on a page that you define to hold the paragraph text.

To enter artistic text, you simply click the Artistic Text tool at the point on the page where you want text to begin. For a paragraph, you drag a *frame* (the box to contain the text) from where you want text to start to where you want text to end. Frames can be linked so that a paragraph text file will flow from frame to frame.

IP: *If you don't create a frame with the Paragraph Text tool first, clicking on the printable page area with the Paragraph Text tool will automatically create a frame that fills the entire page to the margins.*

Paragraph text behaves like text in a word processor: text will automatically wrap at the end of a line; text can be justified (aligned on the left and right), as well as left-aligned, right-aligned, and centered; text can be cut and pasted to and from the Clipboard; you can adjust the space between paragraphs in addition to adjusting the space between characters, words, and lines; you can set tabs and indents; and you can create up to eight columns with a gutter (space between columns) that you define. Bulleted lists can be created using any of the symbols included with Coreldraw as bullets. Paragraph text can also be wrapped around other objects. This means that the text will be aligned with the outline of an object, even when that outline is irregularly shaped. Also, you can import text files created with a word processor, such as Word for Windows or WordPerfect.

Selecting an Insertion Point

The insertion point is the point on the page where you want a new text string to begin. In Coreldraw, you can enter text directly on the page, or you can type it in a

4

special dialog box, where you also select its attributes. To select an insertion point and prepare for the other exercises in this chapter, follow these steps.

1. Select Grid and Ruler Setup from the Layout menu. In the Grid & Ruler Setup dialog box Ruler tab confirm inches are selected in both the Horizontal and Vertical Units drop-down list boxes, and set the Horizontal Origin to 0 and the Vertical Origin to 8.5 inches (the upper-left corner of the page). Tick Divisions should be set to 8 per tick. Select the Grid tab and make sure that Snap To Grid and Show Grid are selected, then set both the Horizontal and Vertical Grid Frequencies to 2.00 per unit (inches). Click on OK. If your screen does not already display rulers, also select Rulers from the View menu.

2. With the Artistic text tool still selected, position the mouse pointer at the top center of the page area at 5 1/2 inches horizontal and –1 1/2 inch vertical, click once, and type **Coreldraw**. Select Edit Text from the Text menu, or use the shortcut key combination CTRL-SHIFT-T. The Edit Text dialog box displays, as shown in Figure 4-2.

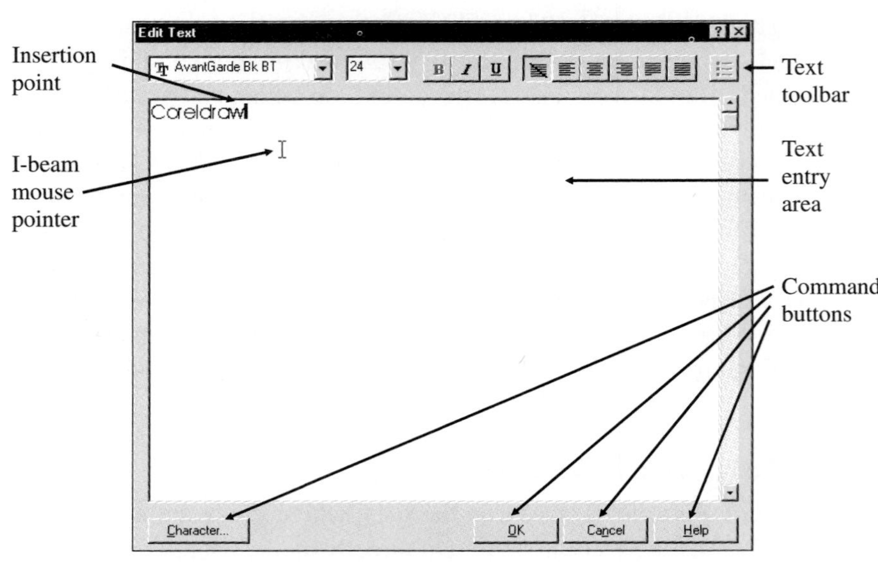

Edit Text dialog box

FIGURE 4-2

Edit Text Dialog Box

Using the Edit Text dialog box, you can enter text and then customize it in many different ways. Take a moment to become familiar with the layout of this dialog box and the way the keyboard functions within it.

The following paragraphs describe the components of the Edit Text dialog box and its respective functions. Figure 4-2 shows the major components. While this discussion is for Artistic Text, the Edit Text dialog box is the same for Paragraph Text.

INSERTION POINT An insertion point appears in the text entry area at the right end of the text string when you first open this dialog box. You can type or edit your text string, or series of characters, in this window. You can move the insertion point anywhere within the text string by using the arrow keys (including HOME and END) or by clicking the I-beam mouse pointer where you want the insertion point.

COMMAND BUTTONS The Character command button opens the Character Attributes dialog box, discussed next, that allows you to set character attributes. Both OK and Cancel close the Edit Text dialog box. OK saves the work you have done in the dialog box and displays it onscreen, and Cancel allows you to exit the Edit Text dialog box without saving any changes that have been made.

TEXT TOOLBAR The Text toolbar available on the Edit Text dialog box contains the major functions available on the full Text toolbar (which will be covered in the section "Using The Text Toolbar"). These are the font and size, alignment, and bulleted lists. These functions will be covered later in this chapter.

Character Attributes Dialog Box

Clicking on the Character command button in the Edit Text dialog box opens the Character Attributes dialog box shown in Figure 4-3. The Character Attributes dialog box allows you to do character formatting using the elements described in the following paragraphs. You can open the Character Attributes dialog box by selecting it from the Edit Text dialog box, by selecting Character from the Text menu, or by double-clicking on a text node with the Shape tool (although, the dialog box adds the shift and angle controls on the Alignment tab when opened this way).

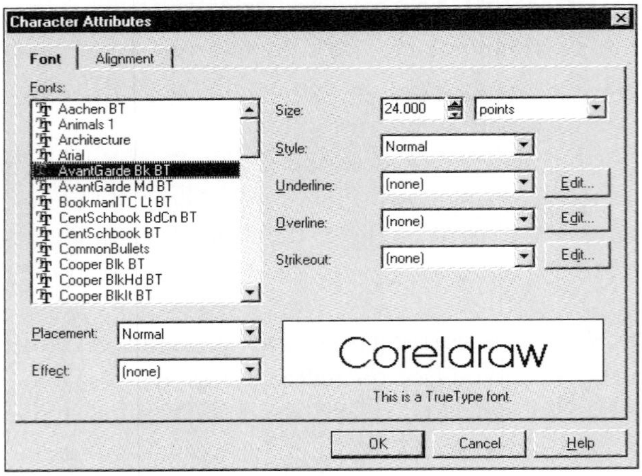

Character Attributes Font tab dialog box

FIGURE 4-3

FONTS LIST BOX The Fonts list box contains the names of all the fonts installed on your computer from which you can choose, including those provided by Coreldraw and any you may have from other sources.

SIZE SELECTION BOX Use the type size spinner to choose the size for the text you enter. The default setting for this attribute is 24 points, but you can change this value. (See "Selecting a Type Size" later in this chapter.)

TYPE SIZE UNITS DROP-DOWN LIST BOX Click on the arrow in the Size units box to change the unit of measuring type sizes from points (the default) to inches, millimeters, picas and points, points, ciceros and didots, or didots. (Cicero and didots are rarely encountered and will not be used in this book.) Points is the standard method of measuring type size in the printing industry, and will be used throughout this book.

IP: *You may find it easier to use inches or millimeters when working with large text sizes, as you might in a poster, for example. One inch is approximately equal to 72 points.*

STYLE DROP-DOWN LIST BOX Once you choose a font, use the Style list box to specify the style in which you want the font to appear. In Coreldraw, font refers to an entire character set that shares the same basic design (for example, Arial), regardless of the size (for example, 10 points) or weight (for example, bold or italic). A style is narrower in scope. One style includes only a single weight (normal, bold, italic, or bold-italic) for a particular font. Although there are usually four possible styles for any font, some fonts have fewer styles. The Style list box will display only the styles available for the selected font.

UNDERLINE, OVERLINE, AND STRIKEOUT DROP-DOWN LIST BOXES The Underline, Overline, and Strikeout drop-down list boxes let you add a single or double line of various thicknesses below, above, or through the middle of selected text. The thickness and position of the lines are selected using the Edit Underline dialog box, shown here. The same options are available for Overline and Strikeout lines.

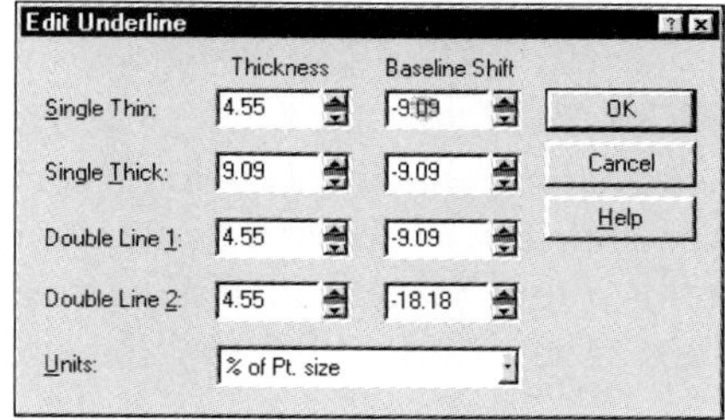

RANGE KERNING Kerning is the space between pairs of characters. For example, the letters AV require less space than EF to look good when printed. You will work with kerning in Chapter 10.

SAMPLE CHARACTERS DISPLAY BOX When you select a font, the Sample Characters display box will display in that font as much of your text as fits in the box. This gives you a true WYSIWYG (What You See Is What You Get) example of the font. Additionally, Coreldraw adds a statement below the display box that indicates whether the font is a TrueType font or another type of font, such as a Type 1 PostScript font.

PLACEMENT DROP-DOWN LIST BOX Use the Placement drop-down list box to subscript (a smaller character placed lower than the other characters) or superscript (a smaller character placed higher than the other characters) selected text.

EFFECTS The Effects drop-down list box allows you to format your text as either Small Caps (lower case characters are changed to upper case with the same height as the lower case version) or All Caps (all characters are converted to upper case). These effects are useful for headlines and titles.

Options for aligning your text are available using the Alignment tab, shown in Figure 4-4.

ALIGNMENT OPTION BUTTONS Use the Alignment option buttons to align your text relative to the insertion point. The default setting for artistic text is None, or unaligned. The choices of Left, Center, Right, Full Justify(right and left), Force Justify, or None are fully described under "Aligning Text" later in this chapter.

CHARACTER, WORD, AND LINE SPACING SELECTION BOXES The Spacing selection boxes allow you to specify the spacing between characters, words, and lines. See the "Adjusting Text Spacing" section in this chapter for detailed instructions on how to adjust spacing.

HORIZONTAL SHIFT, VERTICAL SHIFT, AND ANGLE The Horizontal Shift, Vertical Shift, and Angle options are only available when you open the Character Attributes dialog box using the Shape tool. The Horizontal Shift option moves the text right or left. The Vertical Shift option moves the text up or down relative to the baseline. The Angle option skews the text. These options are covered in Chapter 10.

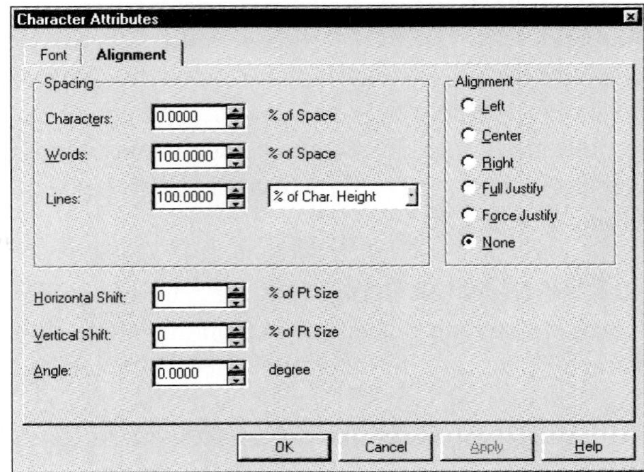

Character Attributes Alignment tab dialog box

FIGURE 4-4

Using the Keyboard and Mouse

You can use both the mouse and the keyboard to move among the attributes in the Character Attributes dialog box. If you are using a mouse to move around in this dialog box, you can select an attribute in three different ways: by clicking on an option or command button, by changing the value in a spinner (numeric entry box), or by choosing from a drop-down or regular list box. You work with option or command buttons to choose alignment and to close the dialog box; with list boxes to choose fonts; with drop-down list boxes to choose styles, units, types of lines, and placement of text, and with a spinner to choose from different font sizes and the spacing of text.

If you prefer to use the keyboard in the Character Attributes dialog box, you can select most attributes using TAB, SHIFT-TAB, and the arrow keys on your numeric pad. When you first enter the dialog box, the highlight appears in the upper left of the Font tab—the list of fonts. To move to the next attribute, press TAB, or press ALT along with the appropriate underlined letter. Continuing to press TAB moves you from one attribute to the next, while SHIFT-TAB moves you between attributes in the reverse order. CTRL-TAB selects the next tab on the dialog box and CTRL-SHIFT-TAB selects the previous tab. Pressing ENTER selects your choice.

Now you are familiar with the Edit Text and Character dialog boxes as they appear with Artistic Text. The only difference with paragraph text is that a Paragraph dialog box is available. This will be discussed in later sections in this chapter. In the following sections, you will learn how to set Artistic Text attributes for yourself.

Entering Text

Text can be entered either directly on the printable page area on the Coreldraw page or in the text entry area in the Edit Text dialog box. In the next section, you will become acquainted with the use of the Edit Text dialog box, followed by some of the unique properties of direct entry, including the use of the Text toolbar. The exercises on text entry and manipulation will use both methods to let you see for yourself when to use one over the other.

Entering Text in the Edit Text Dialog Box

When you first open the Edit Text dialog box, the text entry area is automatically selected, as you can see by the insertion point in Figure 4-2. If you are not in the

Edit Text dialog box, press CTRL-SHIFT-T now to return there. To enter text, simply begin typing. For this exercise, enter text in the following way.

1. Type **Coreldraw** at the insertion point if it's not there already.
2. Press ENTER to begin a new line, type **Made**, and press ENTER again.
3. On the third line, type **Easy**, and press ENTER again.

Your text entry area should now look like this:

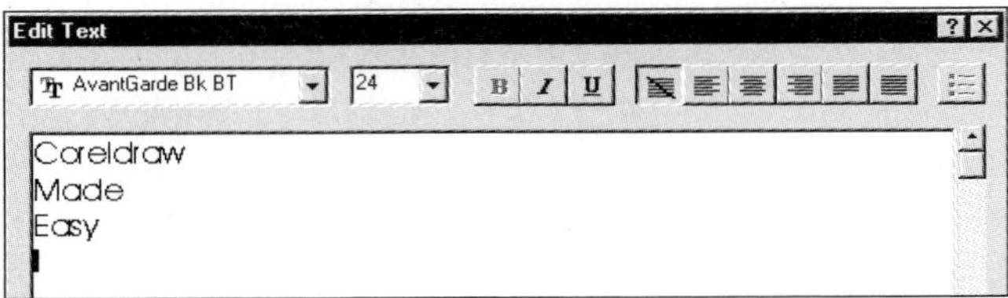

Using the Keyboard to Move Around

The way you use your keyboard to move around in the Coreldraw text entry area may differ from the way you use it in a word processor. Whenever you have several lines of text in the text entry area, you can use the following keyboard commands.

- Press ENTER to start a new line within the text entry area and begin entering text into it. The window will hold as many lines of text as you generate, as long as you do not exceed the 32,000-character limit.
- Press the DOWN ARROW key to move the insertion point down one line. (This does not apply if you are already on the last line of text.)
- Press PGDN to move the insertion point down to the right end of the last line of text.
- Press the UP ARROW key to move the insertion point up one line. (This has no effect if you are already on the top line of text.)
- Press PGUP to move the insertion point up to the first line of text.
- Press HOME to move the insertion point to the beginning of the current line.

- Press CTRL-HOME to move the insertion point to the beginning of the first line of text.
- Press END to move the insertion point to the end of the current line.
- Press CTRL-END to move to the end of the last line of text.
- Press the RIGHT ARROW key to move the insertion point one letter at a time to the right.
- Press the LEFT ARROW key to move the insertion point one letter at a time to the left.
- Press BACKSPACE to delete the character immediately preceding the insertion point.
- Press DEL to delete the character immediately following the insertion point.

Using the Mouse

You can also perform some text entry operations using the mouse.

- Use the scroll bar at the right side of the text entry area to locate a line of text that is not currently visible.
- If you want to insert text at a given point, click on that point.
- To select one or more characters in a text string, position the insertion point at the first character you want to select and then drag the mouse across the desired characters. The characters appear highlighted, as shown here:

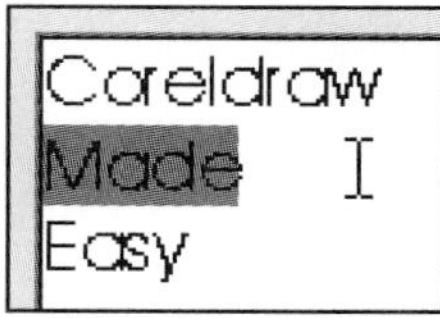

- You can delete a text string that you have selected in this way by pressing DEL.

Continue to experiment with the keyboard controls and the mouse until you feel comfortable with them. Entering text directly on the printable page area, you will find, uses the same text editing techniques.

Entering Text Directly on the Printable Page Area

Coreldraw allows you to type both Artistic and Paragraph Text directly on the printable page area with the attributes that you choose. The mechanics of entering the text here are the same as entering it in the text entry area of the Edit Text dialog box: you establish the insertion point by clicking the mouse, and you use the same navigating and editing keys as you do in the text entry area (HOME, END, BACKSPACE, DEL, and the arrow keys).

To change the attributes of the text you enter, you can use the Edit Text dialog box, directly open the Character Attributes dialog box from the Text menu, press its shortcut key CTRL-T, or use the Text toolbar that lets you access the more common attributes. The following exercise repeats the previous text entry, but this time directly in the printable page area.

1. Close the Edit Text Edit dialog box by clicking on the OK button.
2. Press DEL to delete the text you entered in the Edit Text dialog box.
3. Select the Artistic Text tool (if its not still selected) and place the insertion point at 5 1/2 inches horizontal and –1 1/2 inches vertical.
4. Type **Coreldraw**, press ENTER, type **Made**, press ENTER, and finally, type **Easy**, and press ENTER once more. You should be looking at the same text entry that you made earlier in the Edit Text dialog box.
5. Select Edit Text from the Text menu to verify this. When you are satisfied that it's the same, return to the printable page area by clicking the Cancel or OK button.

Now that you have a feel for both the Edit Text dialog box and direct-entry methods of adding text, the following section will introduce you to the Text toolbar.

Using the Text Toolbar

The Text toolbar lets you select the font, type size, type style, and alignment for your text. You can also create bulleted lists, set indents and columns, and display nonprinting formatting commands such as returns at the end of paragraphs, tabs, and spaces. To display the Text toolbar, open the View menu and select Toolbars, then select Text. The default position for the Text toolbar is at the top of your screen, below the Standard toolbar. Like the other toolbars, you can drag the Text toolbar anywhere on the screen and resize it. The Text toolbar is shown here and the buttons and their functions are described in Table 4-1. (The Text toolbar is shown floating and resized; in its default position all the options may not be visible, depending on your screen resolution.)

In the following exercises you will learn how to use the Text toolbar to apply formatting to your text.

Customize IT! *Feel free to customize the Text toolbar by making it floating (by pointing on the border of the toolbar and dragging onto your work area) and resizing it (pointing on the edge of the toolbar until the pointer turns into a two-headed arrow, and then dragging). You can do this with any Coreldraw toolbar.*

Aligning Text

The next exercise involves deciding how you want to align the text. You have five choices available on the Text toolbar with either artistic or paragraph text: None, Left, Center, Right, Full Justified, and Force Justified.

Left Alignment

When you choose this setting, the left edge of each line will be aligned vertically. (Your text should still be selected.)

1. If the Left alignment button (the second button from the left in the row of alignment buttons) is not selected, use the mouse to select it by clicking on it. The Left button lightens and appears depressed when you select it.

TABLE 4-1 Text Toolbar Buttons and Their Functions

Button	Function
Default Artistic Text	Selects preset text style
AvantGarde Bk BT	Selects font
24	Selects type size
B	Applies bold style
I	Applies italic style
U	Applies underline style
	Applies no alignment
	Applies left-justified alignment
	Applies center-justified alignment
	Applies right-justified alignment
	Applies full-justified alignment
	Applies force-justified alignment
	Indents paragraph text to the left
	Outdents paragraph text to the right
	Creates a bulleted list from selected paragraph text
¶	Displays nonprinting characters on screen

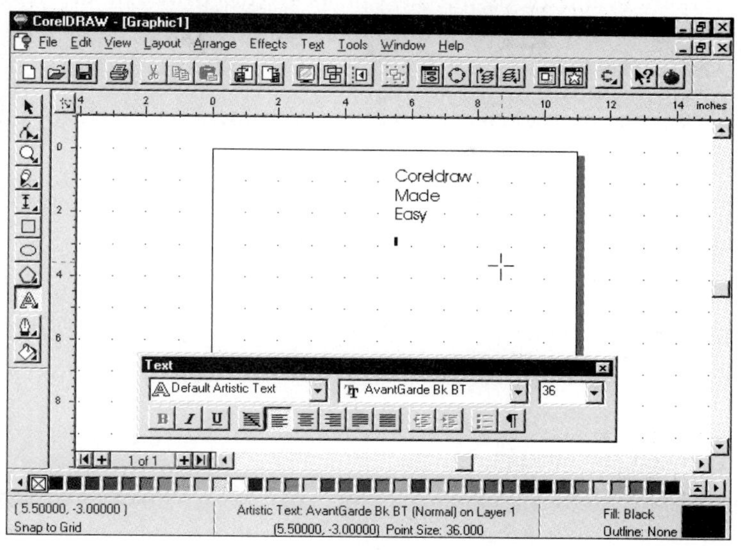

Left-justified text

FIGURE 4-5

2. The text that you entered displays on the page in the default font, left-aligned at the 5 1/2 inch mark, as in Figure 4-5. The text string has a default fill of black like other closed objects in Coreldraw.
3. Leave this text on the page and select another insertion point, at the 3 inch vertical mark and the 5 1/2 inch horizontal mark, just below the first text string.

NOTE: *The type size in Figures 4-5 and 4-6 looks larger than what appears on your screen. The size has been increased from the default 24 points to 36 points so you can better see the text and the effects of alignment selections. You will do the same on your screen when you use the Size attribute.*

Center Alignment

When you select Center alignment, the initial insertion point becomes the midpoint of any text string you type. Perform these steps to compare center alignment with left alignment.

1. Type **Coreldraw** on one line, press ENTER; **Made** on the next, press ENTER; and **Easy** on the third line, and press ENTER again, as you did in the last section.

2. Using the mouse, change to center alignment by clicking on the Center button (the third button from the left).
3. The text you entered appears in the default font, center-aligned with respect to the 5 1/2 inch mark.
4. Leave this text on the page. Select a third insertion point, this time at the –5 inch vertical mark and the 5 1/2 inch horizontal mark, just below the center-aligned text.

Right Alignment

When you select Right alignment, the right edge of each line will be aligned vertically. Follow these steps to compare right alignment with left and center alignment:

1. Again type **Coreldraw Made Easy** on three lines as you did in the previous exercises.

2. Using the mouse, change to right alignment by clicking on the Right button (the fourth button from the left).
3. The text you entered appears in the default font, right-aligned with respect to the 5 1/2 inch mark.
4. Leave this text on the page. Select a fourth insertion point, this time at the –7 inch vertical and 5 1/2 inch horizontal mark.

No Alignment

When you select no alignment, text displays on the page exactly as you enter it. This selection is useful when you want to add unusual spacing at the beginning of a line in a text string. Perform these steps to compare text with no alignment to text with left, center, and right alignment:

1. Type **Coreldraw** and press ENTER.
2. On the second line, indent two spaces, type **Made**, and press ENTER again.

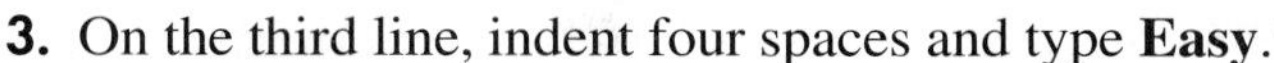

3. On the third line, indent four spaces and type **Easy**.

4. Using the mouse, change the alignment to None by clicking on the leftmost alignment button.
5. The text that you entered appears in the default font, with the spacing exactly as you typed it. Your page should now look like Figure 4-6.
6. Clear the page of text by choosing Select All from the Edit menu, and pressing DEL. Notice the Text toolbar remains on the screen.

Full-justified text is aligned on both the left and right and is created by the second button from the right. Force-justified text is similar to full-justified except that the last line of each paragraph is expanded to be equal in width to the rest of the paragraph. A paragraph is defined as all the text you enter until you press ENTER. In the previous examples you created three paragraphs, each one consisting of one word and ENTER. With text such as you have entered here, full-justified alignment will look just like left alignment because you pressed ENTER at the end of each line. Remember, force-justified has the same effect as full-justified except that the last line of each paragraph will be expanded to the full width of the paragraph. With Artistic text this is the width of the longest line in the text block, as shown here:

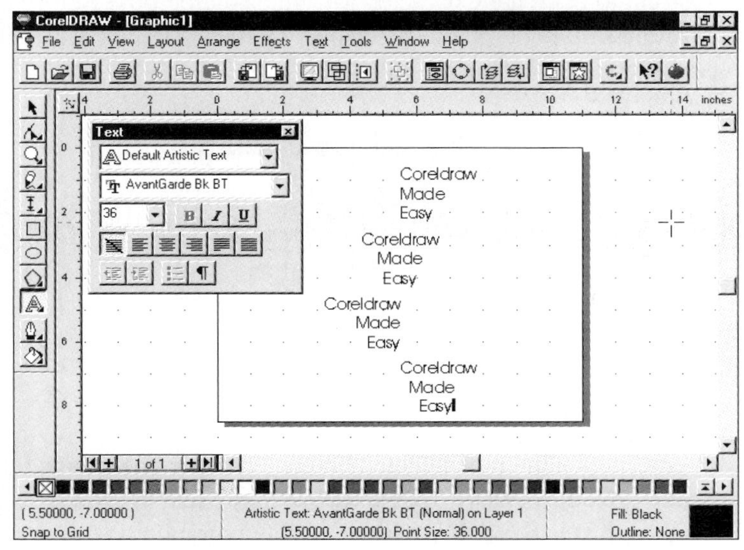

Center, right, and unaligned text added

FIGURE 4-6

CorelDRAW!
M a d e
E a s y

Selecting a Type Size

Normally, you will select alignment and font settings for a text string before you specify the type size, which is measured in points (approximately 72 points make up an inch). For this exercise, however, you will want to see results on the full page in a larger size than the default value of 24 points.

To change the default type size from 24 to 60 points using the mouse, follow these steps:

1. Make sure you have not placed an insertion point with either Text tool in the open document. If you have, select the Pick tool (the first tool on the Toolbox) and click anywhere on the page. To change a default text attribute, you cannot have any text selected, an insertion point placed, or an active paragraph text frame. If you do, your changes will only effect the selected text, not the default value.

2. Open the Text menu and select Character, or use the CTRL-T keyboard shortcut to open the Character Attributes dialog box. Before the Character Attributes dialog box will be displayed, the Character Attributes default dialog box will appear, as shown here:

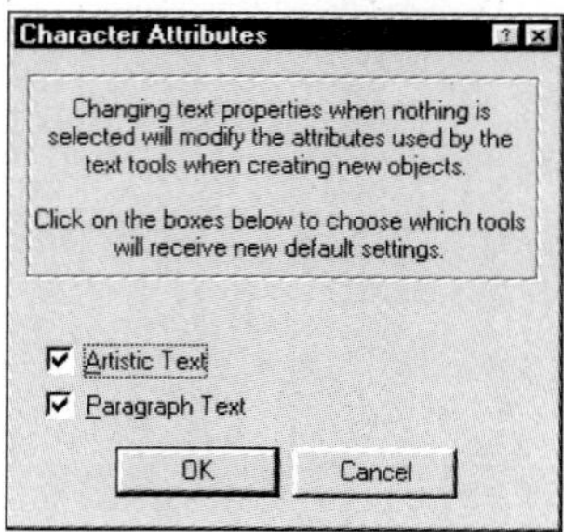

Depending on the tool selected before you open the Character Attributes dialog box, the Artistic Text and Paragraph Text check boxes might not be displayed. If either the Artistic text or Paragraph text tools are selected, the check boxes will not be displayed. Coreldraw assumes that you only want to change the defaults for the selected text tool. When the another tool is selected, the check boxes will be displayed to allow you to specify what type of text you want the new default values applied to.

3. Click on the Paragraph Text check box to turn it off (if it is displayed); only Artistic Text should be selected. Click on OK. The Character Attributes dialog box will now be displayed.
4. Double-click on the Size numeric entry box to select it, then type **60**. Click on OK. The default size for artistic text is now set to 60 points, while the default for paragraph text remains at 24 points.

IP: *Text defaults can also be set from the Text toolbar. Using the Character Attributes dialog box allows you to set defaults for properties that are not displayed on the Text toolbar (such as underlining).*

Selecting a Font

So far, you have used only the default font in Coreldraw. In this section, you will have the opportunity to experiment with some of the different fonts and styles supplied with your Coreldraw software.

Different Fonts

Many books and trade magazines offer guidelines for selecting an appropriate font. A thorough discussion of the subject is beyond the scope of this book; however, when choosing the font to use in a Coreldraw graphic, you should consider the tone and purpose of your work, as well as your intended audience. As an example, consider the two fonts shown here:

Brush Script

Futura Book

You probably would not choose an elaborate, script font such as Brush Script for a graphic that you would present to a meeting of civil engineers; a font such as Futura Book might prove a better choice.

NOTE: *The discussion of fonts in this and the following chapters talks about fonts that may or may not be available to you, depending on what fonts you have installed on your system. All of the fonts discussed are included with CorelDRAW! 6. Feel free to substitute other similar fonts if you do not have the specific fonts discussed here installed. You can preview your fonts with the Character Attributes dialog box.*

Practice selecting fonts in the following exercise (the Text toolbar should still be open on your screen).

1. Select the Artistic Text tool (if it's not still selected) and then, by clicking, place an insertion point at the 3 inch mark on the horizontal ruler and 1 inch on the vertical ruler.
2. Type **Avante Garde**. Press and hold SHIFT while pressing HOME to select the text you just typed.
3. Select the AvantGarde Bk font from the Font drop-down list box on the Text toolbar, if it's not already selected. (Avante Garde is the default Coreldraw font.) You select a font by:
   a) Clicking on the drop-down arrow on the right end of the Font drop-down list box;
   b) Using the scroll bar to scroll the list of fonts until you see the font you want;
   c) Clicking on the font you want.

NOTE: *The common name for a font will not always match the name of the actual font file you select in the Font drop-down list box. The filename will often use abbreviations. In these exercises, you will type the common name of the font before selecting it using the font filename.*

4. In your printable page area, you will see the Avante Garde text string with the selected attributes, as shown next:

Avante Garde

5. Select another insertion point at the 3 inch mark on the horizontal ruler and the 2 1/2 inch mark on the vertical ruler.

6. Type **Balloon** and press SHIFT-HOME to select the text.

7. Select the Balloon Bd font in the Fonts drop-down list box. You will see the Balloon text string beneath the Avante Garde text string, like this:

Avante Garde
BALLOON

OTE: *Balloon, like some other fonts designed for headlines, does not include lowercase characters.*

8. Select a third insertion point at the 3 inch mark on the horizontal ruler and the 4 inch mark on the vertical ruler.

9. Type **Franklin Gothic** and press SHIFT-HOME to select the text.

10. Select the FrnkGoth ITC Hv font from the drop-down list box. Your text strings should look like this:

Avante Garde
BALLOON
Franklin Gothic

11. Select a fourth insertion point at the 3 inch mark on the horizontal ruler and the 5 1/2 inch mark on the vertical ruler.

12. Type **Animals** and press SHIFT-HOME to select the text.

13. Select Animals 1 from the Font drop-down list box. Notice that nonalphabetic symbols, rather than letters, appear in the sample

characters window as you can see next. This font, like many others that come with Coreldraw, consists of symbols rather than letters.

Avante Garde

BALLOON

Franklin Gothic

 **OTE:** *Even though you have entered all of the text strings at the same point size, some appear larger than others. Each font has its own characteristic width and height.*

14. Clear the screen by selecting Select All from the Edit menu and pressing DEL.

Practice trying out different fonts. When you are ready for the next section, clear the screen by choosing Select All from the Edit menu and pressing DEL. You will now learn how to select different styles that are available for some fonts.

Selecting a Style

While you were experimenting with fonts in the foregoing exercise, you may have noticed that not all styles were offered for some fonts. This is because some fonts have only one or two styles available, while others have three or four.

Perform the following exercise to practice selecting available type styles for the Coreldraw fonts. This exercise uses the direct-entry method and the Text toolbar. The instructions are less descriptive since you should now have the ability to easily move through the menus.

1. With a new drawing and nothing selected on your screen, select the Artistic text tool (if it's not already selected), then open the Text menu and select the Character option. Since the Artistic text tool is already selected, the Character Attributes defaults dialog box will not be displayed.

2. In the Character Attributes dialog box, change the font to Times New Roman, the text size to 72 points, and the alignment to center, then click on OK.

3. Select the Artistic Text tool and then choose an insertion point that is at the 5 1/2 inch mark on the horizontal ruler and the 1 inch mark on the vertical ruler.

4. Type **Times New Roman**. This provides an example of the font in Normal style as you can see here:

Times New Roman

5. Select another insertion point at the 5 1/2 inch horizontal and 2 1/2 inch vertical ruler marks.

6. Type **Times New Roman**, highlight the text by dragging across it with the mouse, and click on the Italic button on the Text toolbar. The italic text is displayed, like this:

Times New Roman
Times New Roman

7. Select another insertion point at 5 1/2 inch horizontal and at 4 inch on the vertical ruler and type **Times New Roman**.

8. Select one more insertion point at 5 1/2 inch horizontal and 5 1/2 inch vertical and type **Times New Roman** again. Instead of highlighting either of the text strings by dragging or with the keyboard (SHIFT-HOME), you will use the Pick tool.

Chapter 5 provides an in-depth discussion on the use of the Pick tool, but it's necessary at this point to introduce the text-selecting properties of the tool.

For Coreldraw to change the attributes of a text string, the string must be selected. In simple cases, where there is only one string, some attributes can be changed without you doing the selecting because Coreldraw "knows" which text to change. As you increase the number of text strings, you must highlight the text by dragging; or, if Coreldraw does not accept the attribute change, select it with the Pick tool.

1. Select the Pick tool (the first tool on the Toolbar) and click on a letter in the first of the two new text strings you just typed. The words "Times New Roman" become surrounded by eight selection markers. The full use of these boxes is discussed in Chapter 5, but for the purposes here, they identify the text as being selected.

AUTION: *Double-clicking on text with the Pick tool invokes the Rotate and Skew feature. If you accidentally do this, just click on the text again to get the selection boxes back.*

2. In the Text toolbar, select the Bold button. The third text sample becomes bold.
3. Click on the last text string to select it, then click on both the Bold and Italic buttons. Click on a blank portion of the screen to remove the highlighting. The text strings on your screen should now look like this:

Times New Roman
Times New Roman
Times New Roman
Times New Roman

Take a few moments to practice selecting styles for other fonts. When you have finished, choose Select All from the Edit menu and press DEL to clear the screen. Continue with the next section to learn how to adjust spacing when you enter a new text string.

Adjusting Text Spacing

The settings for spacing in the Character Attributes dialog box allow you to control the space between characters, words, and lines of text and give you considerable control over how text looks.

In this chapter, you are working with attributes only as you enter text. However, Coreldraw also allows you to adjust text spacing interactively. This means that even after text displays on the page, you can change the spacing of one character, several characters, or an entire text string without going back to the dialog box. You will learn more about how to change spacing attributes for existing text in Chapter 10.

Setting Up the Exercise

In the following exercise, you will have the opportunity to review what you have learned thus far about setting text attributes.

1. With a new drawing and nothing selected on your screen, select the Pick tool, then open the Character Attributes dialog box. Click on OK in the Character Attributes defaults dialog box with both Artistic and Paragraph Text selected.
2. In the Character Attributes dialog box, change the font to Garmd ITC Bk BT (Garamond ITC Book), the style to Normal, and the text size to 48 points. Click on the Alignment tab, set the alignment to center, and click on OK.

TIP: *When the Fonts list box is selected (one of the font names is highlighted) you can type the first letter of the font name and the list will scroll automatically to the first font name that begins with the letter you typed. For example, if Avante Garde is the selected font and you want to change to Times New Roman, type **T**. The list will then scroll to and select the first font name that begins with T.*

3. Select the Artistic Text tool and select an insertion point near the top of the page at 5 1/2 inches on the horizontal ruler and –1 1/2 inches on the vertical ruler.
4. Enter four lines of text in the printable page area. Type your name on the first line, your address on the second, your city, state, and ZIP code on the third, and your telephone number on the fourth. It should look like Figure 4-7, except that the actual text in your printable page area will be your name and address as you have entered them.
5. Select a new insertion point at 5 1/2 inches on the horizontal ruler and –5 inches on the vertical ruler. Open the Character Attributes dialog box and click on the Alignment tab. Since you have an insertion point selected, the Character Attributes defaults dialog box will not be displayed and the

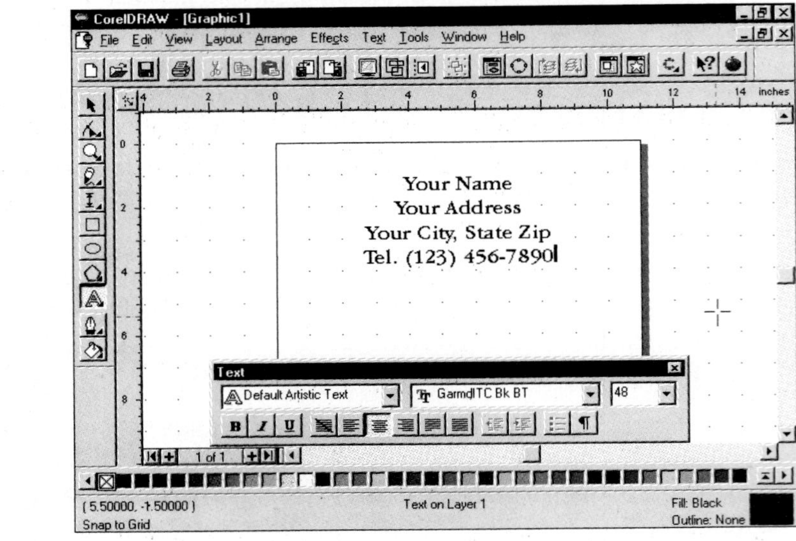

Initial text with Garamond ITC Book, Normal style, Center alignment, 48 points

FIGURE 4-7

changes you make will only effect the text you type from the insertion point, not the default values.

Spacing Options

The three options for adjusting spacing in the Character Attributes Alignment tab dialog box are Characters, Words, and Lines. You will change them in the next exercise, so take a moment to become familiar with the options.

CHARACTER The Character option controls spacing between characters within each word of the text. The default value is 0 percent of the normal space for a given font and size. In other words, as a default, Coreldraw uses only the normal spacing between characters that has been designed into a font unless you change that value. This measurement is relative, rather than absolute, so that your spacing will stay constant as you scale your text or change the font. You can adjust the value of intercharacter spacing in increments of whole percentage points using the scroll arrows or you can type in a value.

WORD The Word option controls spacing between each word of the text that you enter. The default value is 100 percent of a space "character" (pressing the SPACEBAR

once) in a given font and size. You can adjust the value of interword spacing in increments of whole percentage points using the scroll arrows or by typing in a value.

LINE When your text contains more than one line, the Line option controls the amount of space between each line. In the printing industry, this type of spacing is also known as leading (pronounced *led-ing*). The default value is 100 percent of the type size, which means that if your text size is 10 points, the total amount of space between two lines is exactly 10 points. (This is not the space between the top of the characters on one line and the bottom of the characters on the other; it is the space between the baselines of the characters on both lines. The baseline is an imaginary line the characters sit on.)

You can adjust the spacing values in two ways: by scrolling with the mouse or by using the keyboard.

To adjust values using the mouse only:

1. Position the mouse pointer on the up or down scroll arrow. If you want to increase the value, position it on the up arrow; if you want to decrease the value, position it on the down arrow.
2. Press and hold the mouse button until the value you want displays in the adjoining box and then release the mouse button.
3. Another way to use the mouse is to point on the line between the up and down scroll arrows. Hold the button until the pointer changes to a short line with arrows pointing up and down.
4. Drag the pointer up or down and the value will change as you drag the mouse.

To adjust values using the keyboard:

1. Use TAB or SHIFT-TAB to go from item to item in the dialog box. When you reach one of the spacing number boxes, the entire number will be highlighted. This means that if you type a new number, you will completely replace the original number.
2. Type in the value you want. To go to the next setting, press TAB or SHIFT-TAB.

Adjusting and Comparing Spacing

Now that you are acquainted with the way spacing works, you will create another text string, identical to the first except that its spacing values differ. You can then visually compare the results of your spacing adjustments.

1. The Character Attributes Alignment tab should still be displayed. Adjust the spacing in the Characters spinner to 50 percent, Words to 200 percent, and Lines to 130 percent of Character height. This means that the additional space between characters will equal half of the normal space, the space between words will equal twice the normal space, and the space between lines will equal 1.3 times the height of the font itself. Click on OK.
2. Type your name, street address, city, state, ZIP code, and telephone number on four separate lines.

   The second text string now displays the new settings, as you can see in Figure 4-8.
3. Choose Select All from the Edit menu and press DEL to clear the screen.

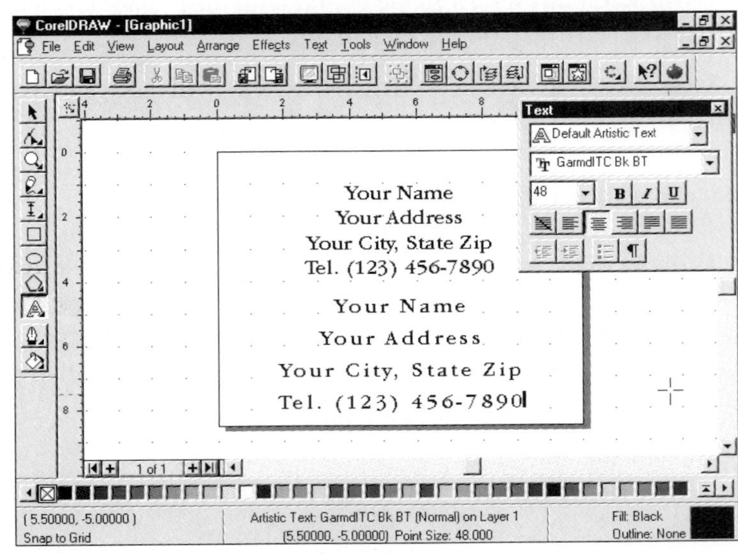

Comparison of default and custom spacing attributes

FIGURE 4-8

Working with Paragraphs

So far in this chapter, all of your work has been in Artistic Text mode. This is fine for titles, captions, and other pieces of text that are only a few short lines. If you are creating a brochure, a flyer, or other document where you need large blocks of text, you should use Paragraph Text mode. Paragraph Text offers several features that are valuable for large blocks of text and are not available with Artistic Text. Among these features are the following.

- An increase in the character limit from a total of 32,000 characters to 32,000 paragraphs of 32,000 characters each
- Automatic word wrap at the end of each line
- Variable line length controlled by a frame, or bounding box, whose dimensions and attributes can be changed
- The ability to define up to eight columns with variable column widths and intercolumn (gutter) spacing
- The ability to import text created with a word processor
- Adjustable interparagraph spacing
- The ability to control text hyphenation

As with Artistic Text, Paragraph Text can be entered directly on the printable page area, or you can open the Edit Text dialog box and use the text entry area.

Paragraph Attributes

Paragraph attributes are set using the Paragraph dialog box shown in Figure 4-9. You open this dialog box using the Paragraph command from the Text menu, or the Paragraph command button in the Edit Text dialog box. With the Paragraph dialog box, you can adjust spacing, alignment, hyphenation, tabs (left, right, center, and decimal), indents, and the symbol and its attributes used for bulleted lists.

Paragraph Spacing

The spacing options in the Paragraph dialog box are the same as those in the Character Attributes dialog box except for the Before and After paragraph options.

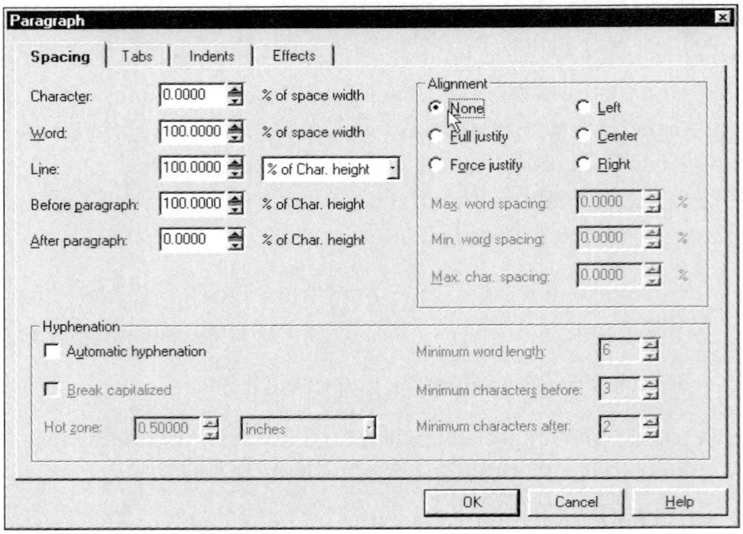

Paragraph dialog box

FIGURE 4-9

If you are in Paragraph mode and you have more than one paragraph, the Before and After paragraph options control the amount of space between each pair of paragraphs. The default values are 100 percent of the type size Before paragraph and 0 percent After paragraph. If your text size is 10 points, the space between paragraphs will be 10 points. You can adjust the interparagraph spacing by increments of 1/10 of 1 percent.

Try out Paragraph mode now with these steps.

1. Select Character from the Text menu, select Paragraph text and click on OK on the Character Attributes default dialog box, and select Bookman ITC Light as the font, Normal style, 24 points for the size, and full-justified for the alignment. Click on OK. 
2. Create a frame for your paragraph text by selecting the Paragraph Text tool (the rightmost button on the Text tool flyout) and placing the mouse pointer at 1 inch on the horizontal ruler and 1/2 inch on the vertical ruler.
3. Drag the mouse pointer to 10 inches on the horizontal ruler and 8 inches on the vertical ruler, as shown in Figure 4-10, and then release the mouse button. The frame dimensions of the paragraph will be set. After you

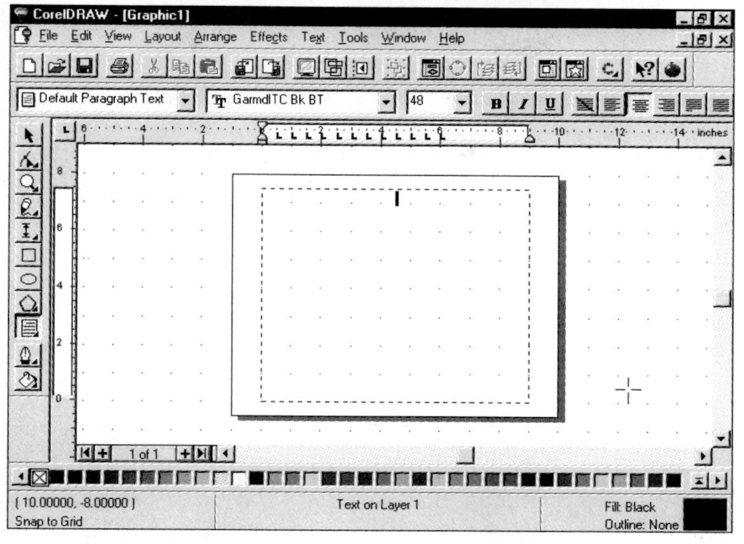

Forming the Paragraph text frame or bounding box

FIGURE 4-10

release the mouse button, the insertion point appears at the beginning of the frame. The Status bar will display "Text on Layer 1" and the rulers will display the preset tab stops.

4. Type several paragraphs, such as those shown following this step. It doesn't matter what you type as long as you have two or more paragraphs about as long as those shown. Press ENTER only at the end of each paragraph and let Coreldraw automatically wrap the text at the end of each line. Here are two sample paragraphs you can type:

   The advanced text-handling features of Coreldraw let you turn text into a work of art. You can rotate, skew, reshape, and edit a single character or text string (a group of characters) just as you would any other object.

   You can perform these feats with the extensive library of fonts provided with Coreldraw or available from other manufacturers. The fonts provided with Coreldraw either are or look similar to standard industry fonts and will print on any Windows-compatible printer. Since the Corel fonts are in the Windows standard TrueType format, you can use them with all your Windows applications—a real bonus!

5. Select both paragraphs by pressing CTRL-SHIFT-HOME.

6. Open the Text menu and select Paragraph to open the Paragraph dialog box, shown in Figure 4-9. Click on the Spacing tab, if it's not already selected, then change Line spacing to 120 percent and After Paragraph spacing to 200 percent.

7. Click on OK to close the dialog box and press END to remove the highlight. The text will appear within the frame, as shown in Figure 4-11. To preserve the typing you have done, save this file.

8. From the File menu, select Save As. If necessary, change to the folder containing your drawings, type **Paratext** in the filename text box, and press ENTER or click on Save.

Hyphenation

When enabled by clicking on the Automatic Hyphenation check box in the Paragraph dialog box, Coreldraw will hyphenate words at the end of a line if three conditions occur: they begin before the left edge of the Hot Zone, they continue beyond the right edge of the frame, and a valid hyphenation break occurs within the zone. The Hot Zone extends from the right side of the paragraph text frame toward the left,

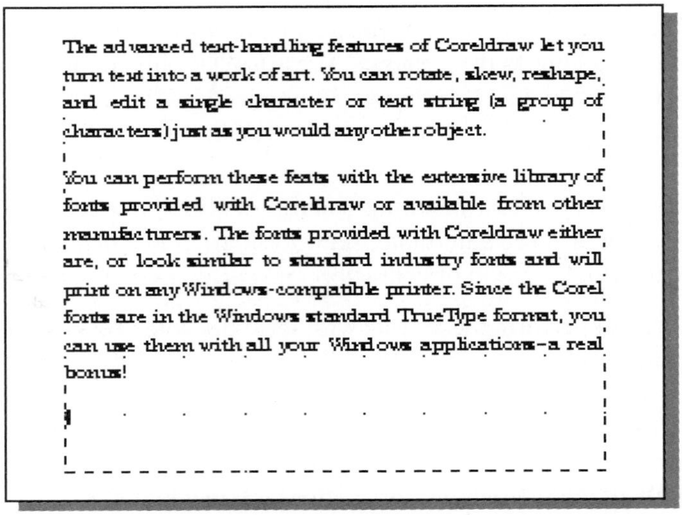

The advanced text-handling features of Coreldraw let you turn text into a work of art. You can rotate, skew, reshape, and edit a single character or text string (a group of characters) just as you would any other object.

You can perform these feats with the extensive library of fonts provided with Coreldraw or available from other manufacturers. The fonts provided with Coreldraw either are, or look similar to standard industry fonts and will print on any Windows-compatible printer. Since the Corel fonts are in the Windows standard TrueType format, you can use them with all your Windows applications—a real bonus!

Paragraph text as it is displayed on the page

FIGURE 4-11

according to the distance listed in the Hot Zone spinner. If a word begins in the hot zone and continues beyond the frame's right edge, it will wrap to the beginning of the next line.

Using the two paragraphs that are still on your screen, try Coreldraw's hyphenation capability with these steps.

1. Select the two paragraphs you entered previously. Select Paragraph from the Text menu to open the Paragraph dialog box.
2. Click on the Automatic Hyphenation check box. Leave the default 0.50 inches Hot Zone, and click on OK.
3. Press END to remove the selection highlighting. You can now see the hyphens that have been added. The word "characters" has been hyphenated in Figure 4-12.
4. Press CTRL-S to save your changes.

Extracting Text from Coreldraw

Coreldraw includes a feature that allows you to extract text from Coreldraw in a format that is usable in a word processing program. You can modify the text in the word processor and then merge the text back into Coreldraw, automatically

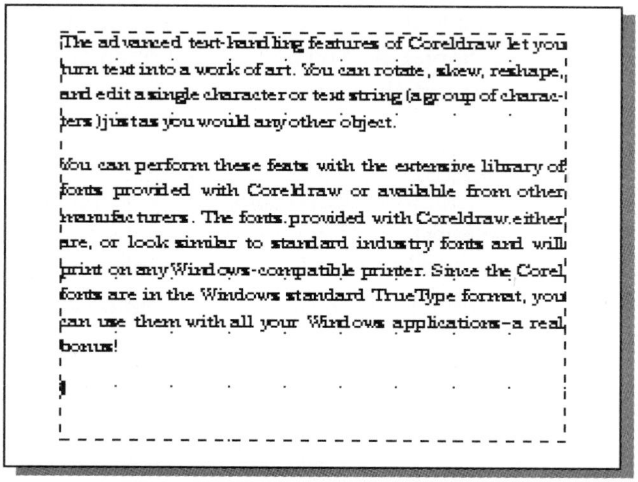

The advanced text-handling features of Coreldraw let you
turn text into a work of art. You can rotate, skew, reshape,
and edit a single character or text string (a group of characters) just as you would any other object.

You can perform these feats with the extensive library of
fonts provided with Coreldraw or available from other
manufacturers. The fonts provided with Coreldraw either
are, or look similar to standard industry fonts and will
print on any Windows-compatible printer. Since the Corel
fonts are in the Windows standard TrueType format, you
can use them with all your Windows applications—a real
bonus!

Hyphenated text

FIGURE 4-12

reattaching all of the formatting (such as font, size, and style) that was originally attached to the text. (In the word processing program, you will not see any of the formatting.)

In this section, you will extract the paragraph text you entered, bring that text into a word processor, modify it, save it, save it again as a plain text file, and place it on the Windows Clipboard. In the next section, you will bring each of these files back into Coreldraw.

Start by extracting the text from Coreldraw. The text you typed should still be on the screen, as shown in Figure 4-12. To extract it, you must select it with the Pick tool.

1. Select the Pick tool and click on the Paragraph frame to select the text.
2. From the Tools menu, select Extract. The Extract dialog box will open, as shown here:

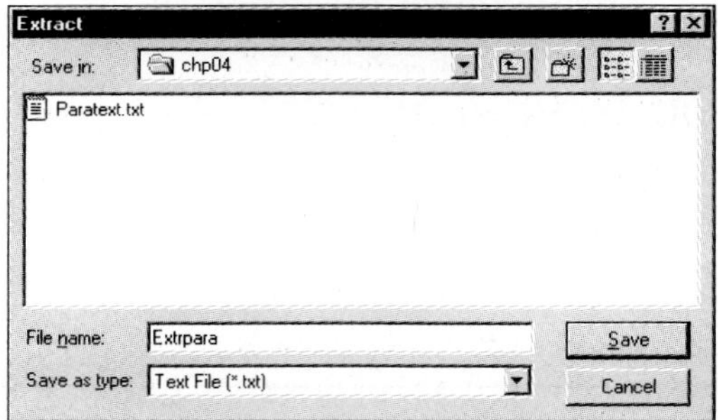

3. Make sure a suitable folder is selected, type **Extrpara** in the File name text box, and click on OK. You have now written an ANSI text file containing the paragraphs you entered.

In the following steps you will switch out of Coreldraw without closing it, open Windows WordPad, and edit that file. (Almost any word processor could be used in place of Windows WordPad.)

1. Click on the Minimize button (the leftmost button on the right side of the Title bar).
2. Click on the Start button on the Windows Taskbar to open the Start menu, point on Programs, then point on Accessories.

3. In the Accessories flyout menu, click on WordPad. The WordPad word processing program will open.
4. Select Open from the File menu. In the Look In list box, locate the folder where you extracted the Extrapara.txt file. In the Files of type list box, choose Text Documents (*.txt) and then click on *Extrpara.txt* in the files list box. The filename is displayed in the File name text box. Click on Open.

The text you entered in Coreldraw will appear on the Windows WordPad screen, as shown in Figure 4-13.

The first two lines and the last four lines of text (the last line is blank) are reserved for Coreldraw to use in merging the text back in. It is, therefore, very important that you do not change these six lines or the paragraph codes in front of each paragraph, or Coreldraw will not be able to merge this file. You can change all other parts of the file except the first two and last four lines, and the paragraph codes.

1. Modify any of the text you entered. In this exercise, it doesn't matter what you modify, as long as you can recognize the change when you get back to Coreldraw.

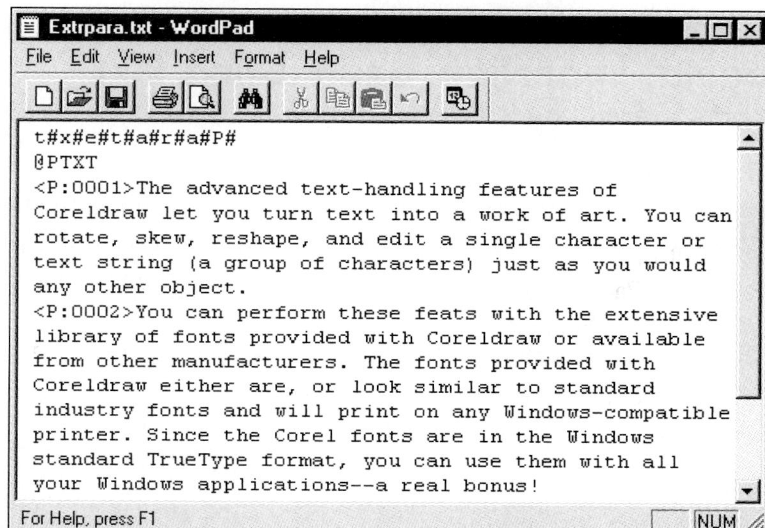

Paragraph text in WordPad

FIGURE 4-13

2. When you finish modifying the text, open the File menu and save the file under its original filename, Extrapara.txt. This is the file that will be used to merge back into your Coreldraw paratext.cdr file.

Now that you have saved the merge file, you can remove the first two and last four lines as well as the paragraph codes to make another text file that you can import into Coreldraw. Also, you will copy the remaining text to the Windows Clipboard and paste it into Coreldraw.

1. Delete the first two and last four lines of the file as well as the paragraph codes so you only have the text you entered (select the text by dragging over it with the mouse and press DEL).
2. From the File menu, select Save As, select your folder, then type **Import.txt**, and click on Save. This is the file you will import.
3. Select all of the text you entered and have now modified by dragging over it with the mouse, then select Copy from the Edit menu. This places a copy of the text on the Windows Clipboard.
4. Click on the Close button to exit WordPad.
5. Restore Coreldraw by clicking on the Coreldraw button on the Taskbar. Coreldraw will reappear on the screen.

Merging, Importing, and Pasting Text into Coreldraw

You now have four copies of the text you entered: the original file you saved in Paratext.cdr, the modified merge file Extrpara.txt, the clean text file Import.txt, and finally, the copy on the Windows Clipboard. Use each of the last three of these copies to see how Coreldraw merges, imports, and pastes text from outside Coreldraw.

1. From the Tools menu, select Merge-Back. The Merge-Back dialog box will open.

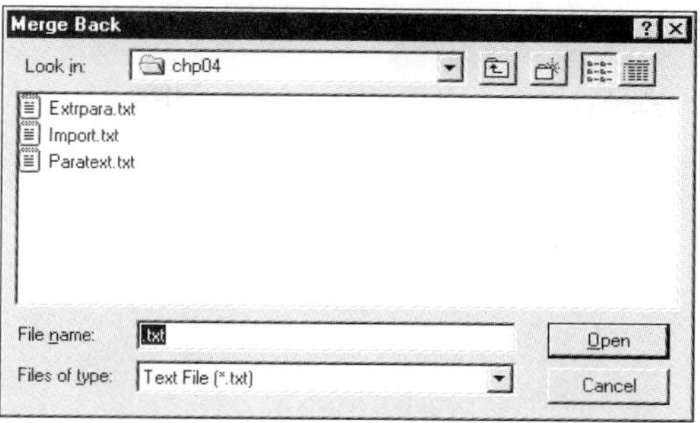

2. Double-click on extrpara.txt in the files list box. After a moment you will see the revised text displayed on the page. The copy of Paratext.cdr in memory has now been revised with the changes you made in Windows WordPad. All of the formatting in the original file has been maintained. You may need to zoom in on the text to see it. If you had some graphic elements in the file, they would also remain unchanged. Only the words and their positions have changed.
3. Save the revised file if you wish, then choose Select All from the Edit menu and press DEL to clear your screen.
4. Select the Paragraph Text tool and draw a paragraph bounding box from 1 inch on the horizontal and –1/2 inch on the vertical ruler to 10 inches on the horizontal and –8 inches on the vertical ruler.
5. Press CTRL-V or choose Paste from the Edit menu. The revised text will flow into the paragraph frame from the Windows Clipboard. The only difference is that now there is a carriage return at the end of each line.
6. Click on Cancel to throw away the imported text.
7. The frame that you established in step 4 returns to the screen.
8. Open the File menu, select Import, make sure you are in the correct folder, and then double-click on Import.txt. The revised text will be brought into the paragraph frame.

You have now seen how you get text out of Coreldraw and how you can bring text back into Coreldraw in three different ways. Now look at how you can use columns in Coreldraw.

Putting Text in Columns

Many brochures, flyers, and other documents appropriate for Coreldraw put text into multiple columns instead of one wider column in an effort to make the text easier to read. Try it here. You should still have the revised paragraphs you pasted into the paragraph frame on your screen and the insertion point should be at the end of the last line.

1. Press CTRL-SHIFT-HOME to select both of your paragraphs.
2. Open the Text menu and select Columns. The Column dialog box will open, as shown in Figure 4-14.
3. Make sure that the Equal Column Widths check box is checked, then enter 2 in the Number of columns spinner and press TAB. The default values for the column widths should be 4.25 inches with a .5 inch gutter (the space between the columns). If your settings are different, set the column widths to those values.
4. Click on OK to close the Columns dialog box, then press END to unselect your text. After a moment the text will appear in a two-column format, as shown in Figure 4-15.

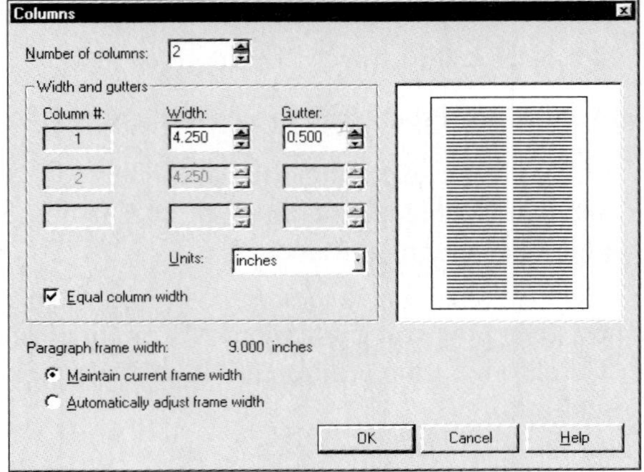

Column dialog box

FIGURE 4-14

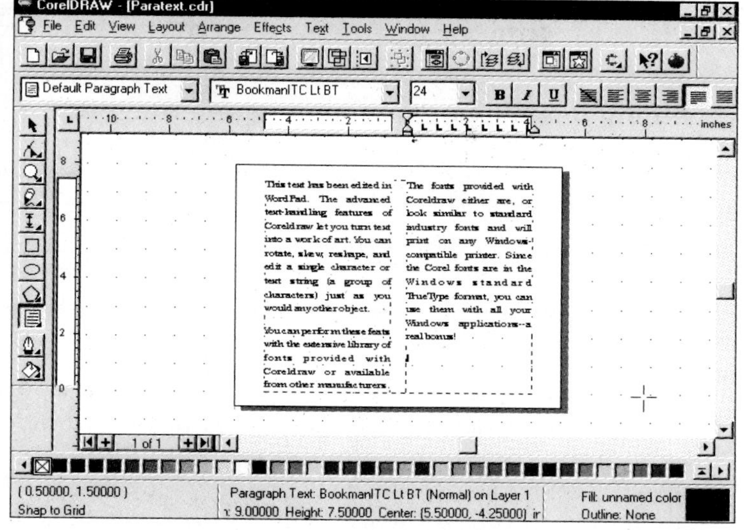

Paragraph text in two-column format

FIGURE 4-15

Using the Spelling Checker

Coreldraw allows you to spell check text in either Artistic or Paragraph Text mode. To use the spelling checker, you can either select the text to check, which can be one word or an entire block of text, or you can check the entire text file. You open the Spell Checking dialog box by selecting Proofreading from the Text menu, then selecting Spelling from the flyout. The Spell Checking dialog box is displayed as shown in Figure 4-16.

When the Spell Checking dialog box is opened the spell checking is started. If a word is found that is not among the words in the dictionary, it will be highlighted in the Sentence list box. Coreldraw will automatically offer spelling alternatives, which will appear in the Change To list box. If you select one of the alternatives in the list, that word replaces the highlighted word in your text. You can choose between replacing this particular occurrence or all occurrences of the word by clicking on either Change or Change All. If you don't want to replace the word with any of the suggested alternatives, you can ignore either one or all occurrences of the word by clicking on either Ignore or Ignore All. Finally, you can manually edit the word in the Sentence list box.

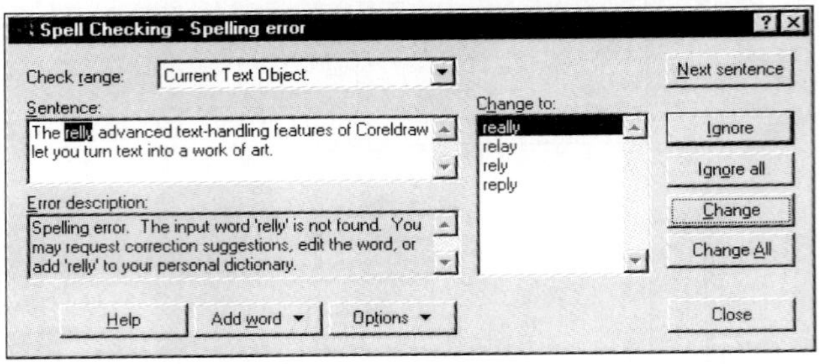

Spell Checking dialog box

FIGURE 4-16

You will check the spelling of the two paragraphs you currently have on your screen in the next exercise. Before beginning, add the misspelled word "relly" to the text.

1. Select the Pick tool to select the paragraphs, then select Proofreading from the Text menu and Spelling from the flyout. The Spell Checking dialog box will open.

   The spelling checker will begin checking the text. If nothing else, it will stop on the word "relly" as you can see in Figure 4-16.

2. To accept the suggested spelling, click on Change. If you think you made the same spelling mistake elsewhere in your document, click on Change All.

   If you use the a word that isn't included with the standard dictionary, but is spelled correctly, you may want to add that word to your Personal Dictionary. Do that next by continuing with these steps:

3. When the word that is not included in the standard dictionary is highlighted in the Sentence list box, click on the Add Word button. The word is added to USERPD, the default user Personal Dictionary.

4. If no other misspelled words are found, a message appears "Spell check complete." Click on OK to close the Spell Checking dialog box and return to your paragraph text.

Proofreading

You can accomplish both spell checking and grammar checking by selecting either Quick Proofreading or Full Proofreading from the Proofreading flyout. The Proofread dialog boxes are identical to the Spell Checking dialog box, except for the title bar. In addition to checking your spelling, proofreading will check for punctuation and grammar errors.

Thesaurus

Coreldraw's Thesaurus provides synonyms and definitions for selected or manually entered words. Simply highlight a word using the Text tool and open the Thesaurus from the Text menu, or open the Thesaurus, enter a word in the Look Up text box and click on Look Up. In either case, Coreldraw offers various definitions and synonyms. If you decide to replace the word you looked up, highlight the new word and click on Replace.

If you highlight the word "advanced" in your paragraph text and open the Thesaurus, the dialog box will look like Figure 4-17. You can then select a synonym like "modern" and click on Replace or select a different definition and get a different set of synonyms from which to choose. If you don't want any of the synonyms, click on Close.

Find and Replace

Find and Replace are two additional features to help you edit your text. The Find dialog box, shown next, is opened by choosing Find from the Text menu. A text

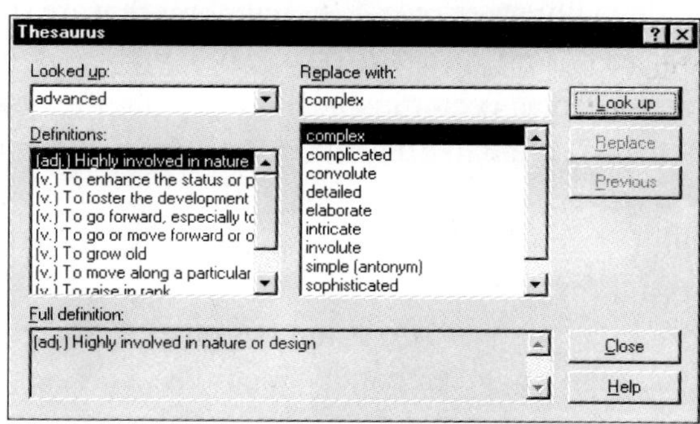

FIGURE 4-17 Thesaurus dialog box

string up to 100 characters long can be entered in the Find text box. Clicking on Find Next will move the highlight from its current location in the text to the next occurrence of the text string you entered. When the end of the document is reached, you will be prompted whether you want the search to continue from the beginning of the paragraph text. The Match Case option is used when you want an exact match, including upper and lowercase, of a text string.

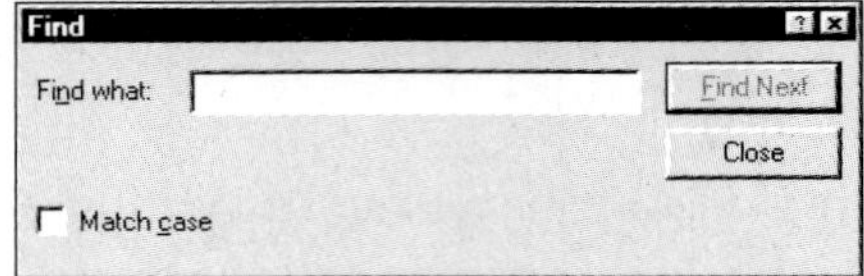

The Replace dialog box, shown next, is similar to Find and is also found on the Text menu. With Replace, you can replace the selected text with another text string. The Replace option can also match the case of the search string. You can replace single occurrences of the search string, with confirmation, or replace all the occurrences in the paragraph text without confirmation.

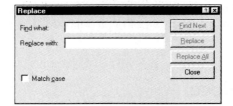

Using the Symbol Library

Coreldraw includes a library of over 5,000 symbols that are stored and retrieved like characters in a font, using the Text tool. The symbols are simple but effective drawings that are stored as vector images. As a result, the symbols can be enlarged, stretched, rotated, and edited like any other Coreldraw object without any loss in the quality of the image. Also, they take very little room to store. To use the symbols, you must install them on your hard disk. Coreldraw's Install program will do this for you when you install Coreldraw.

The symbols are organized into a number of categories; for example, Animals, Common Bullets, Sign Language, and Wingdings. These categories are like fonts. You first select a category, and then from that category you select a particular symbol.

The number of symbols in a category varies from 30 to over 200, with the average around 80. Corel includes with Coreldraw a catalog of all of the symbols, giving each a number within a category. If you know this number, once you have selected a category you can enter the number and get the symbol. Also, as you will see in a moment, you can select a symbol from a display box once you have decided on a category.

Try this feature now by selecting several symbols.

1. Click on the Symbols button on the ribbon bar (fourth button from the right). The Symbols roll-up opens, as shown in Figure 4-18.
2. Click on several categories in the drop-down list box at the top of the roll-up to view the symbols in each category.
3. Use the scroll arrows to see additional symbols in the selected category.
4. Repeat steps 2 and 3 to look at a number of symbols. Notice that below the scroll arrows there is a Size number box where you can specify the initial size of a symbol when it is placed on the page.
5. Change the size to 1 inch and then drag a symbol onto the printed page area.
6. Drag several more symbols at various sizes onto the printed page area.

The Symbol Library provides a good source of quick art that can be used for many purposes.

Symbols roll-up

FIGURE 4-18

CORELDRAW!™ 6 in action

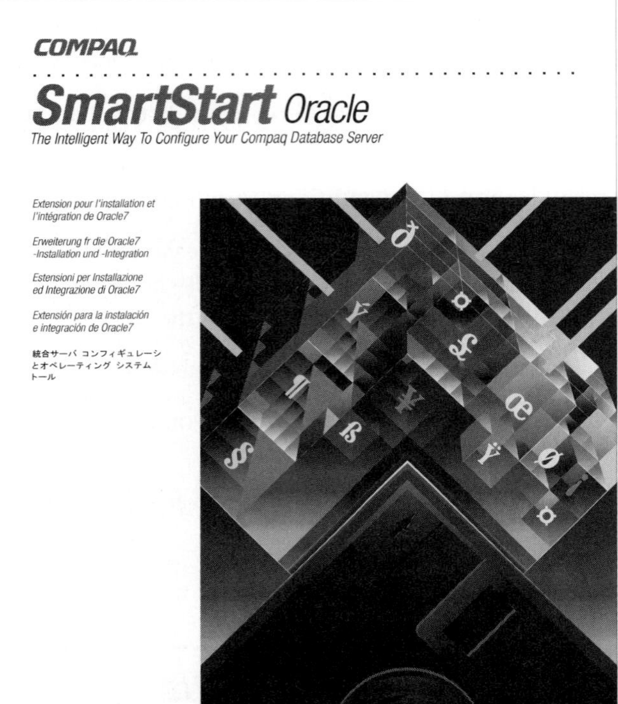

***Compaq SmartStart Oracle package*—Chris Purcell**

Chris Purcell used Coreldraw's text tools to put the finishing touches on this package design for Compaq Computers. Notice the special characters (various international monetary symbols and other characters) in the graphic design. This design illustrates how simple elements can be combined to create striking images.

Chris Purcell of Houston, Texas, has won several awards in Corel's World Design Contest. He can be reached at (713) 374-4679.

Entering Special Characters

Coreldraw includes several different proprietary character sets beyond the standard alphabet and characters that appear on your computer keyboard. You can enter special characters either on the drawing page or in the text entry area of the Edit Text dialog box, and you can adjust alignment, type size, and spacing for these special characters just as you can for alphabetic characters.

A complete listing of the contents of each character set appears on the Character Reference Chart provided with your software. Also, some of the character sets are available as symbols in the Symbol Library. Each of the fonts is a category in the list box, and each of the characters is a symbol.

No matter which of the character sets you are using, characters above ASCII 126 are not accessible by pressing a single key on your keyboard. To type one of these special characters, press and hold ALT and then type the appropriate number on your numeric keypad. Be sure to include the 0 that precedes each number. For example, to type an ellipsis (. . .) in the standard character set, type **0133**. Always refer to your Coreldraw Character Reference Chart when you are entering special characters.

You can also assign keyboard shortcuts, called *hot keys*, to insert extended characters you use often, using the CTRL key and a number key (for example, setting CTRL-1 to insert an ellipsis). Follow these steps to set a hot-key combination.

1. Select the character in your text that you want to assign a hot key to, then open the Layout menu and select the Styles Manager. The Styles roll-up shown in Figure 4-19 is displayed.

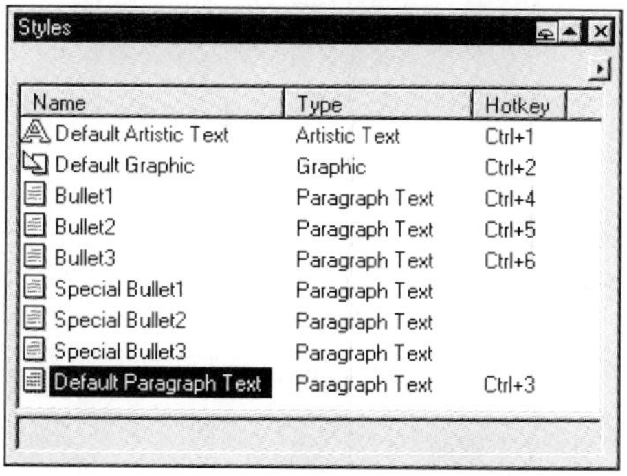

Styles

Name	Type	Hotkey
Default Artistic Text	Artistic Text	Ctrl+1
Default Graphic	Graphic	Ctrl+2
Bullet1	Paragraph Text	Ctrl+4
Bullet2	Paragraph Text	Ctrl+5
Bullet3	Paragraph Text	Ctrl+6
Special Bullet1	Paragraph Text	
Special Bullet2	Paragraph Text	
Special Bullet3	Paragraph Text	
Default Paragraph Text	Paragraph Text	Ctrl+3

Styles roll-up

FIGURE 4-19

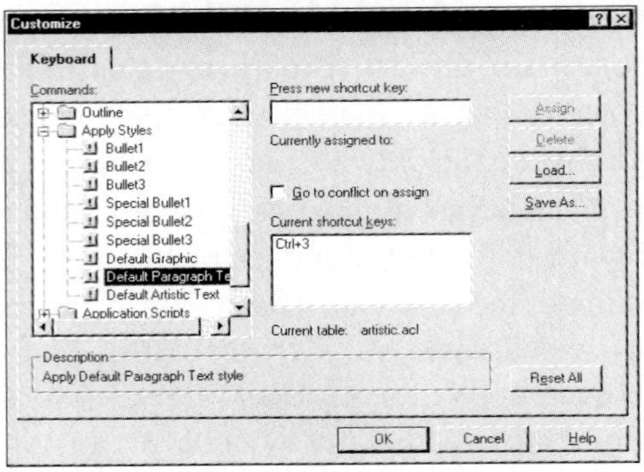

Set Hotkeys dialog box

FIGURE 4-20

2. Click on the right-pointing arrow on the side of the Style roll-up. In the menu that is displayed, select Edit Hot Key. The Customize dialog box, shown in Figure 4-20, is displayed.
3. Press a new key combination (one that is not already assigned).
4. Click on OK to exit the dialog box and save your new hot key.

Now that you have mastered the basics of working with text in Coreldraw, you are ready to work with Coreldraw's extensive features for arranging your objects.

Selecting, Moving, And Arranging Objects

5

In order to change the appearance or position of any object or text string, you must first select it. Once you have selected an object, you can move and rearrange it; stretch, scale, rotate, or skew it; give it a custom outline; or fill it with a color or pattern. Learning how to select an object is an important first step to mastering most of the skills in Coreldraw. Though you were introduced to the basics of text selection in Chapter 4, this chapter shows you the full capabilities of object and text selection.

You use the Pick tool, the first tool in the Coreldraw toolbox, to select objects and text. When you first load Coreldraw, the Pick tool is automatically active and remains active until you choose a different tool. If you are already working with one of the other tools, you can activate the Pick tool by clicking on the Pick tool button on the toolbox.

TIP: *Pressing the SPACEBAR once is an alternative way to reactivate the Pick tool when you are using one of the other tools. This shortcut allows you to switch back and forth between tools quickly. To reactivate the tool you were working with before you selected the Pick tool, press the SPACEBAR again. Use this shortcut when you want to draw objects, immediately move, rearrange, or transform them, and then continue drawing.*

The Pick tool performs more than one function; it has both a select mode and a transformation mode. The select mode includes all those functions—selecting, moving, and arranging—that do not require you to change the size or structure of the object. The transformation mode allows you to stretch, scale, rotate, skew, or reflect objects. This chapter covers the functions of the select mode; Chapter 8 will acquaint you with the use of the Pick tool in the transformation mode.

Selecting and Deselecting Objects

You can select objects only when the Pick tool is active. This tool is always active when you first open a drawing, when you begin a new drawing, and immediately after you save your work. To activate the Pick tool when you're using the Shape tool or one of the drawing tools, you either press the SPACEBAR or click on the Pick tool button once.

Once the Pick tool is active, you can select one or more objects by:

- Clicking on the outline of an object
- Holding down SHIFT while clicking on the outlines of several objects
- *Lassoing* several objects by drawing an imaginary line around them with the Pick tool

The technique you choose depends on the number of objects you are selecting, the placement of the objects within the graphic, and whether it's more convenient to select objects with the mouse or with the keyboard shortcuts.

The Coreldraw screen gives you three visual cues to let you know that an object is selected. First, a *selection box*, consisting of eight small rectangles called *handles*, surrounds the object. These markers allow you to stretch and scale the object, as you'll learn in Chapter 8. Second, one or more tiny hollow nodes appear on the outline of the object or group of objects. The number of nodes displayed depends on the type and number of objects selected. The nodes are the means by which you can change an object's shape, as you'll learn in Chapters 9 and 10. Finally, the Status bar tells you the type of object you have selected (rectangle, ellipse, polygon, curve, and so on) or the number of objects you have selected if you have selected more than one.

Single Objects

Any time you activate the Pick tool while working on a graphic, the Pick tool automatically selects the last object you were working on with another tool. If you want to select a different object, simply click once anywhere on the new object's outline. If you are using Wireframe mode or the object is unfilled, clicking on the inside of a rectangle or ellipse, or on an open space inside a letter, has no effect. If you are using Wireframe mode, you can select an object by clicking inside it if Treat all objects as filled is selected (checked) in the Pick Tool Properties dialog box. (To open the Pick Tool Properties dialog box, point on the Pick tool and click the right mouse button, then select Properties from the flyout.) Also, you must click on a point unique to that object; it cannot share that point with the outline of any other object. Only if an object is the same type and size as another object on top of it will it have no unique selection point available. For information on how to select superimposed objects without unique selection points, see the "Cycling Through Objects" section of this chapter.

To *deselect* an object or text string so that the tools or menu commands you use no longer effect it, click in any open area on the page. Alternatively, you can select a different object and thereby automatically deselect the previously selected object.

In the following exercise, you will practice selecting and deselecting objects in a piece of clip art. You will use the SPACEBAR to select objects that you have just drawn and the mouse to select other objects.

1. To work with this drawing, select Landscape mode and turn off Rulers to give you more room. Also, in the Grid & Ruler Setup dialog box, turn off Snap To Grid and Show Grid if they are turned on.
2. From the \Clipart\Animal\ folder on the fourth CD-ROM, import the Dolphin1.cmx file. If you do not have this available to you, open any simple black and white piece of clip-art you have. Save this as Dolphin1.cdr. Note that when the drawing is displayed on the screen, the Pick tool is already active, as shown in Figure 5-1.

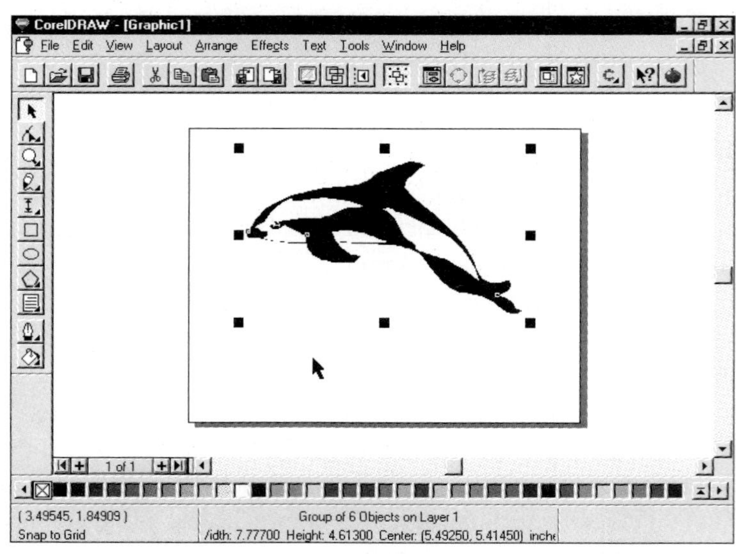

Dolphin1.cmx as imported with the Pick tool selected

FIGURE 5-1

OTE: *People from the Pacific Northwest may recognize that this is not a dolphin but an Orca, or Killer whale. In deference to its filename, though, it will continue to be called a dolphin.*

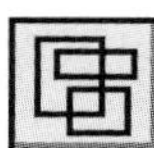

3. Turn on Wireframe in the View menu or by clicking on the Wireframe button on the toolbar, then press F4 to select Zoom To Fit view. The screen redraws to show a screen similar to what you see in Figure 5-2.

4. Select the Freehand tool and use it to draw a very simple little fish in the lower-left corner of the drawing. Be sure to connect the starting point to the end point so that the curve representing the fish becomes a closed path that you can fill later.
5. As soon as the fish appears, press the SPACEBAR to activate the Pick tool. Since the fish is the last object you drew, Coreldraw automatically selects it. A selection box surrounds the fish, and the Status bar indicates "Curve on Layer 1," as in Figure 5-3.

5

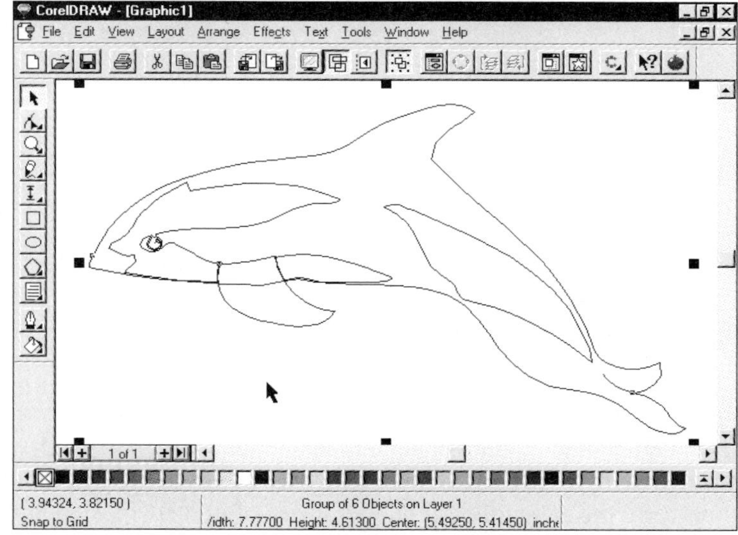

Magnifying Dolphin1.cdr in Wireframe view

FIGURE 5-2

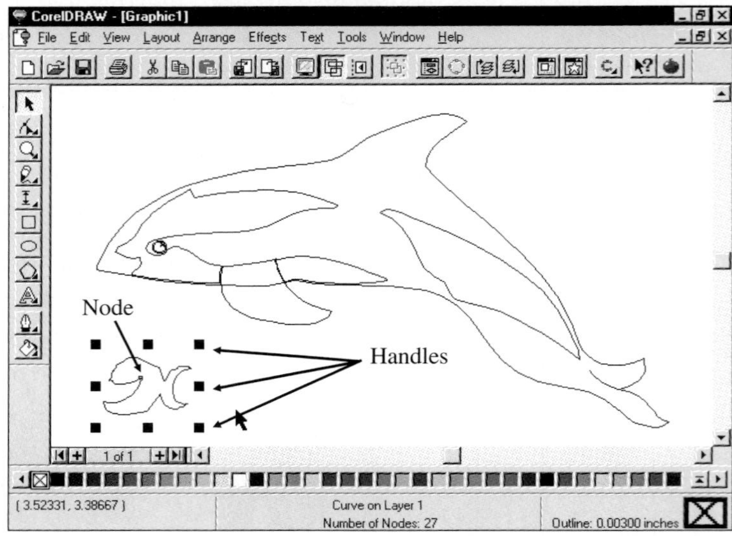

Using the SPACEBAR to select the last object drawn

FIGURE 5-3

6. Click on the outline of the fish. Black two-way arrows replace the handles of the selection box, as you can see here:

   Clicking on a selected object enables the rotate and skew functions of the Pick tool.

7. Click on the fish's outline again to toggle back to the Select mode. If the handles disappear, you missed the outline of the fish. Click on the outline again to select it.

Multiple Objects

It's often more convenient to perform an operation on several objects simultaneously than to perform the same operation on a series of objects individually. Assume, for example, that you want to move the dolphin and the fish together to another location within the drawing. Since these are two separate objects, moving each object individually would be tedious and might lead to inaccurate placement.

Coreldraw gives you three alternative solutions to this type of problem. The first solution, *jointly selecting* the objects, is appropriate when you want to keep multiple objects together only temporarily, without merging them into a single entity. For example, you might want to fill a certain number of objects in a drawing with the same color or pattern or move them all by the same distance. You can jointly select several objects by clicking on them while holding down the SHIFT key, by drawing a marquee around them, by using the Select All command in the Edit menu, or by double-clicking on the Pick tool. Your choice of technique depends on both the number of objects you want to select and their location within the graphic.

If the multiple objects you want to select are components of a larger object and should remain together at all times, you might choose to *group* them, as you will learn to do later in this chapter. Coreldraw will still remember that a grouped object is made up of separate smaller objects. If the multiple objects belong together and contain many curves, you can choose to *combine* them into a single object. Combining objects, unlike grouping them, reduces the amount of memory they require and also allows you to reshape the entire resulting object.

You will learn more about the uses of grouping and combining multiple objects in the "Arranging Objects" portion of this chapter. The following group of sections lets you practice common methods of selecting multiple objects.

Selecting with the SHIFT Key

When you want to select a few objects at a time, you can conveniently select them one after another by clicking on them while holding down the SHIFT key. The SHIFT key method is especially useful when the objects you want to select are not next to one another within the graphic. In the next exercise, you will practice selecting multiple objects using the following method:

- Select the first object by clicking on its outline.
- Depress and hold SHIFT and select the next object.
- Continue selecting objects in this way, holding down SHIFT continuously.
- When you have selected all desired objects, release SHIFT.

To deselect one or more of the objects you have selected in this way, hold down SHIFT and click again on that object's outline. This action affects only that object; other objects in the group remain selected. To deselect all of the selected objects simultaneously, click on any free space.

IP: *To deselect all the selected objects, press ESC. This is especially useful when your drawing contains very little white space to click on to deselect objects.*

Each time you select another object using SHIFT, the selection box expands to surround all the objects you have selected so far. Objects that you did not select also may fall within the boundaries of the selection box, making it difficult for you to see just which objects you have selected. The following exercise shows how you can use the Status bar information and the document window as aids in selecting multiple objects with SHIFT. The dolphin and the fish should still be on your screen.

1. Click on the fish if it is not already selected. A selection box surrounds the object, and the Status bar indicates that you have selected a curve.
2. Depress and hold SHIFT and click anywhere on the outlines of the dolphin. The message in the Status bar changes to "2 Objects Selected on Layer 1," and the selection box shown in Figure 5-4 surrounds both objects. Release SHIFT.

Selecting with the Marquee

If you need to select a large number of objects at once, using the mouse and SHIFT can be tedious. A shortcut is to draw a marquee around all of the desired objects with the Pick tool. The method for using a marquee is as follows.

1. Position the mouse pointer just above and to the left of the first object you want to select. (You can begin from any corner of the group of objects, but the upper-left corner is usually most convenient.)
2. Depress the mouse button and drag the mouse diagonally in the direction of the other objects you want to select. A dotted rectangle (the marquee) follows the pointer. Make sure that each object you want to select falls completely within this rectangle or Coreldraw will not select it.

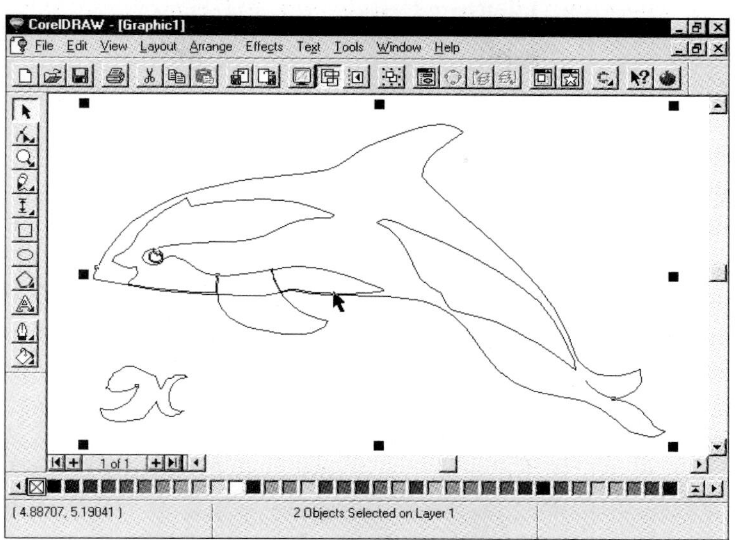

Selecting multiple objects using SHIFT

FIGURE 5-4

3. CorelDRAW! 6 has added a new method of using the marquee to select objects. If you hold down the ALT key while dragging, Coreldraw will select all the objects the marquee touches, even if the object is not completely surrounded. When selecting objects with the ALT key, be sure to release the mouse button before ALT.

4. When you have enclosed the last object you want to select within the marquee, release the mouse button. The selection box appears around all of the objects within the selected area.

If you want to exclude some of the objects that fall within the selected area, you can deselect them using SHIFT. Lasso the entire group of objects first, press and hold SHIFT, and click on a particular object's outline to deselect that object. You can also use the Status bar and document window as "quality control" aids to guide you in selecting exactly the objects you want.

Perform the following exercise to gain skill at selecting objects quickly with the marquee. Use the Zoom tool for magnification, the Status bar for information, and the document window to make the selection process more efficient. Use SHIFT to fine-tune your selection and add or subtract objects to or from the group you selected with the marquee.

1. Press SHIFT-F4 to switch to Zoom to Page view. Click on any white space outside of the fish and dolphin to deselect them.
2. Position the mouse pointer above and to the left of the dolphin. Drag the mouse downward and to the right until the marquee surrounds both the dolphin and the fish, like this:

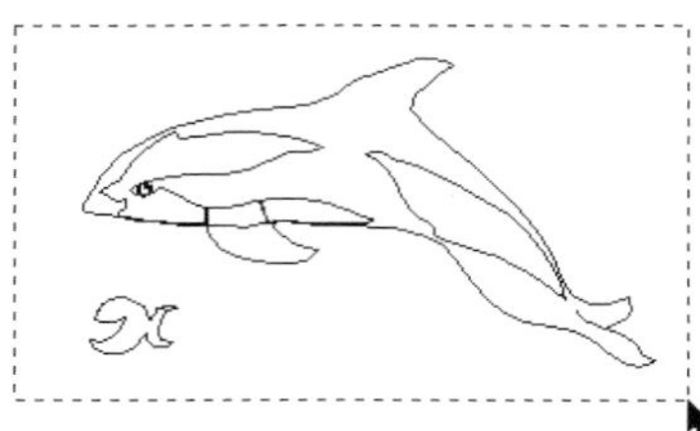

3. Release the mouse button. The selection box appears, and the Status bar indicates that two objects are selected.
4. Press and hold SHIFT and then click once anywhere on the outline of the fish. Coreldraw deselects it, and the Status bar shows that only the group of objects that make up the dolphin is selected.
5. Click on any white space to deselect the dolphin.

Selecting All Objects in a Graphic

If you want to perform an operation on all the objects in a graphic, you can select them by drawing a marquee. Two quicker ways to select all objects are simply to choose Select All from the Edit menu, or double-click on the Pick tool. Either method ensures that you haven't left any objects out.

You now know several methods for selecting single and multiple objects. Most of the time, selecting objects is a straightforward process in Coreldraw. However, what if your graphic contains many small objects or you want to select an object that may have several other layers of objects on top of it? The next section makes that process easy for you.

Cycling Through Objects

The object selection techniques you have learned so far in this chapter are adequate for many applications. However, when working with complex drawings containing many objects or superimposed objects, you may find it more convenient to cycle through the objects using TAB. The following steps summarize this technique.

1. Select an object near or on top of the object you want to select.
2. Press TAB. Coreldraw deselects the first object and selects the next object in the drawing. The "next" object is the one that was drawn just prior to the currently selected object. Each time you press TAB, Coreldraw cycles backward to another object. If you press TAB often enough, you eventually select the first object again, and the cycle begins once more.

The following sections show you two different situations in which you might choose to cycle through objects in a drawing. The first section provides an example of objects that have other objects superimposed on them. The second section demonstrates how to locate and select small objects in a complex drawing.

Cycling Through Superimposed Objects

You may recall that in order to select an object in Coreldraw, you must click on a unique point on its outline, a point not shared by any other object. This limitation does not exist when you have separate objects, because you can usually see separate outlines. The only exception is when two or more objects are the same size and shape and overlay one another exactly.

Why might you choose to create two identical overlapping objects? You can achieve desirable and interesting design effects by varying the color and thickness of the outlines and fills used in each object. In Chapters 6 and 7, you will learn more about outlines and fill colors. For now, you need only know that to select the object in the background, you first select the top object and then press TAB to select the object behind it. If there are more than two objects you simply keep pressing TAB to select them. The Status bar will inform you as to which object is selected.

Cycling Through Many Objects

There is another, more common use for TAB when selecting objects in Coreldraw. Clip art, technical illustrations, and other complex drawings often contain many small objects close together. Even in magnified view, trying to select one or more of these with the mouse can be difficult at best. To ease the process, you can select one object and then press TAB repeatedly until the minute detail you are looking for is selected. Coreldraw cycles backward through the objects, selecting them in the reverse order to which you drew them. To cycle forward through the objects in a drawing, press SHIFT-TAB. Perform the following brief exercise to gain a clearer understanding of how the TAB key method of selection works. The dolphin and fish should still be on your screen in Wireframe, full-page view.

1. Press F4 to switch to Zoom to Fit view. Also, click on the Wireframe button on the toolbar to turn it off so you can see the fill patterns.
2. Click on the dolphin to select it. The Status bar shows you that it is a group of six separate objects.
3. Press TAB. The fish you drew will be selected. Press TAB again and you will reselect the dolphin. You can see how TAB cycles through objects.
4. With the dolphin selected, select Ungroup from the Arrange menu. This breaks apart the dolphin into its six components. The Status bar now reads "6 Objects Selected on Layer 1." (You will learn more about the Group and Ungroup commands later in this chapter.)
5. Press TAB several times. On the first TAB, you will again go to the fish you drew. On the second and successive TABs, you will start cycling through the components of the dolphin. TAB all the way through the dolphin until you get to the fish again.
6. Press SHIFT-TAB several times. Now Coreldraw selects objects in the opposite order. See if you can identify all six components by a combination of the selection box handles and the information in the Status bar. For example, Figure 5-5 shows that the white of the dolphin's eye has been selected—you know this by the fill color and the selection box.

Now you are familiar with all of the available techniques for selecting any number of objects. In the next portion of this chapter, you will move selected objects to other areas within the drawing.

Moving Objects

Once you have selected an object, you can move it by positioning the pointer over any point on its outline (not on the selection box) and then dragging the mouse along with the object to the desired location. The Status bar provides you with precise,

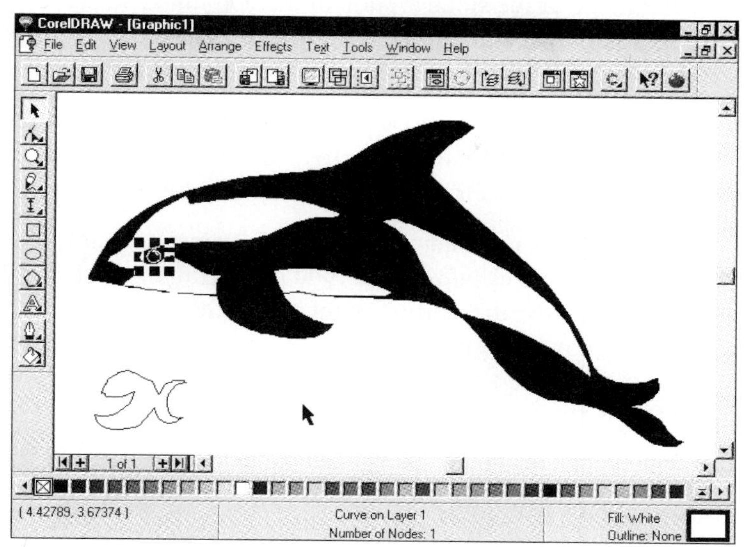

Using TAB to select just the white of the dolphin's eye

FIGURE 5-5

real-time information about the distance you are traveling, the x and y components of that distance, and the angle of movement. You can achieve precision worthy of the most demanding technical illustrations if you choose to work with the Status bar and grid.

Factors such as the number of objects you want to move, whether you want to constrain movement to a 90-degree angle, and whether you want to make a copy of the object determine your choice of technique.

Moving a Single Object

The appearance of an object undergoes several changes during the process of moving it. Try the following exercise to dissect the dolphin and become familiar with those changes. The dolphin and fish should still be on your screen.

1. Select the fish by clicking on its outline, then delete it by pressing DEL. (If you happen to delete one of the components of the dolphin in error, immediately press CTRL-Z or select Undo Delete from the Edit menu.)
2. Press SHIFT-F4 to switch to Zoom to Page view and select Wireframe on the toolbar to turn it back on.

3. Click on one of the smaller parts of the dolphin to select it—for example, the outline of one of the white areas, not the main outline. If you select the main outline, the Status bar will tell you the selected object has a black fill.

4. Move the mouse pointer to any point on the outline of the selected part of the dolphin, and begin dragging the mouse downward to separate the component you selected from the rest of the dolphin.

   The screen does not change immediately, because Coreldraw has a built-in, three-pixel safety zone; you must drag the mouse at least three pixels away from the starting point before the object begins to "move." As soon as you pass the three-pixel safety zone, the mouse pointer changes to a four-way arrow, and a dotted replica of the selection box follows the pointer, as shown in Figure 5-6. This dotted box represents the object while you are moving it; as you can see in the figure, the object itself seems to remain in its original position.

5. When you have dragged the dotted box below the dolphin, release the mouse button. The outline of the white areas disappears from its original position and reappears in the new location.

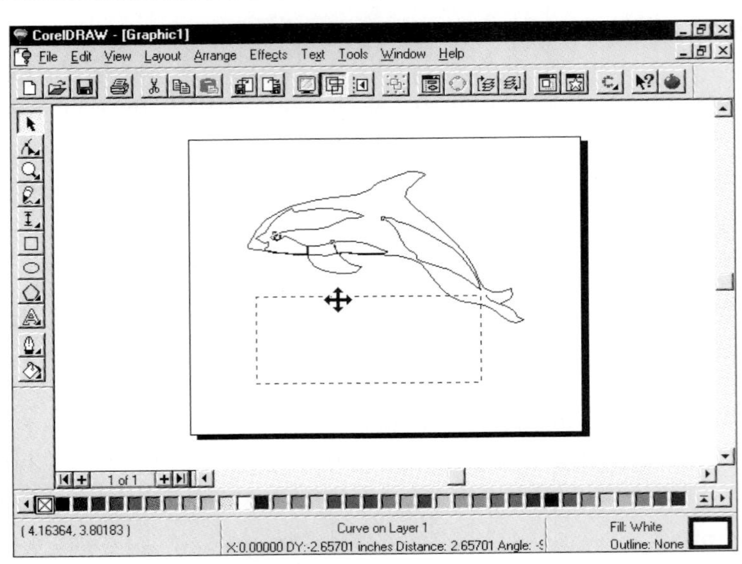

Dragging the dotted move box to move an object

FIGURE 5-6

NOTE: *You may find that moving one of the selected objects causes other objects to move. This is because the objects are still grouped. How grouped objects can be grouped and then grouped with other objects will be explained in the section "Grouping and Ungrouping Objects" later in this chapter.*

6. Press TAB to select the next object and drag it below the dolphin. Continue that process until all six components are separated as shown here:

These are the basic steps involved in moving an object, but Coreldraw offers you additional refinements for moving multiple objects, constraining an object to move at a 90-degree angle, and retaining a copy of an object while moving it.

Moving Multiple Objects

The technique for moving multiple, selected objects differs very little from the way you move single objects. When more than one object is selected, you simply press and hold the mouse button on the outline of any one of the objects within the selected group. The entire group moves together as you drag the mouse, as you can see in this simple exercise.

1. Press F4 to switch to Zoom To Fit view and draw a marquee to lasso the two components of the dolphin's eye. The Status bar should indicate that two objects are selected.
2. Position the mouse pointer over either of the outlines in the eye, and then drag the mouse until the dotted move box is back in the main outline of the dolphin, as shown in Figure 5-7.
3. Release the mouse button. The eye components disappear from their original location and reappear in the new location.

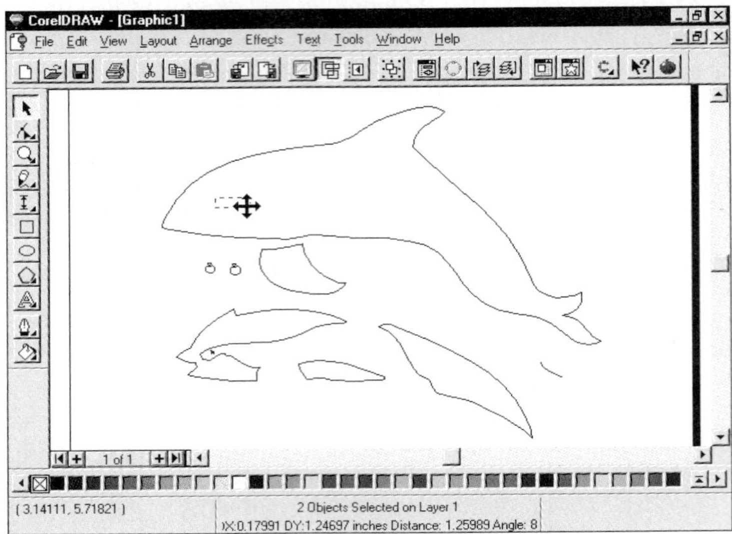

Moving multiple objects to a new location

FIGURE 5-7

Moving at a 90-Degree Angle

The techniques you have learned so far in this chapter apply to moving objects in any direction. But what if the nature of your drawing requires that you move objects straight up or down, or directly to the right or left? You could, of course, use the coordinates information in the Status bar to reposition the object precisely. However, Coreldraw also offers you a more intuitive method of moving objects at an exact 90-degree angle using CTRL. This is a convenient method for obtaining precision without slowing your drawing pace. Perform the following exercise to practice constraining the movement of objects vertically or horizontally. To prepare for the exercise, the two components of the eye need to be in line horizontally.

1. If the two eye components are not inline horizontally, select one of the components and move it up or down vertically until it is inline horizontally with the other.
2. Select one of the eye components, press and hold CTRL, and then drag the component towards the other component of the eye. Even if you don't have a steady hand, the component remains at exactly the same horizontal level of the drawing. The information on the Status bar verifies the

steadiness of your movement: the DY indicator remains at zero and the angle indicator either remains at zero or at 180 degrees, depending on which component you choose, as in the following illustration:

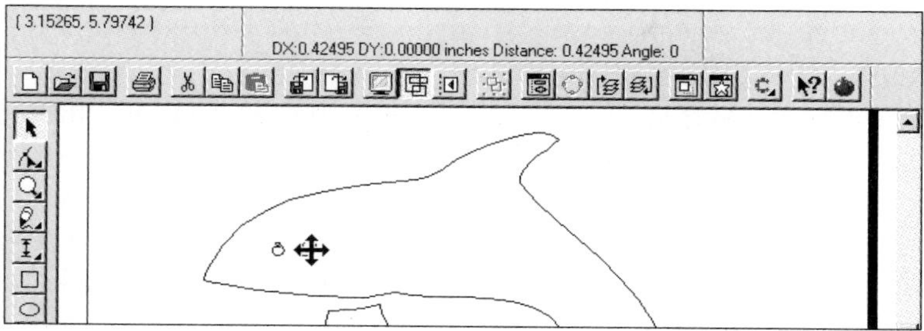

OTE: *In the illustrations, the Status bar has been moved to the top of the screen. You can place the Status bar wherever you wish using the Status bar popup (right-click on the Status bar).*

Release the mouse button first and then release CTRL to reposition the component at the new location. If you release CTRL first, the selected object is no longer constrained and can move up or down relative to the starting point.

3. Press and hold CTRL and the mouse button a second time. This time, drag the eye component above its current location. The component remains at the same vertical level, and the DX indicator remains at zero. This time the angle indicator displays 90 degrees:

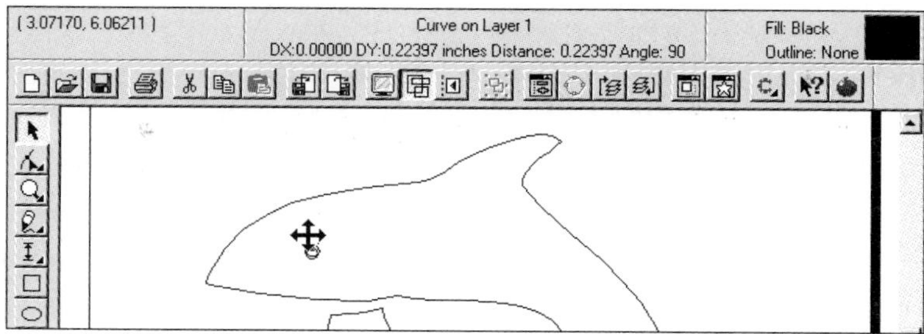

4. Release the mouse button and CTRL when you reach a satisfactory location.

Moving Objects with the Keyboard (Nudge)

As you moved objects in the preceding exercises, you probably found that it was difficult to move an object in very small increments with any precision—most people repeatedly overshoot the mark.

Coreldraw has a feature called Nudge, which allows you to use the arrow keys on your keyboard to move the selected object(s) by as little as 0.001 inch. The amount by which you move an object each time you press an arrow key, and the unit of measure, are determined in the Options dialog box opened from the Tools menu. The default increment is 0.10 inch. Also, since you only have arrow keys pointing in 90-degree increments, nudging is always constrained to 90-degree increments. Follow these steps to practice nudging by positioning the black part of the eye within the white part.

1. Look at the Status bar and determine whether you have the black part of the eye selected by looking at the fill indicator on the right. If it doesn't say "Black," press TAB until you have selected the black part.
2. Open the Options dialog box from the Tools menu and set the Nudge increment in the General tab to 0.01 inch. Click on OK to return to the drawing.
3. Press the arrow keys as necessary to move the black part of the eye until it is centered in the white part. When you think you have it aligned, turn off Wireframe from the View menu to see the black part in the white.

Practice this on your own for several minutes. Nudging can be very useful.

Positioning an Object Using Precise Measurements

If you wish to position an object an exact measured distance from its current location, or at a specific location using coordinates, use the Transform Position roll-up that you open from the Arrange menu. The Transform roll-up has five sets of options, selected from the list box at the top of the roll-up. The Position option allows you to enter horizontal and vertical measurements with which to position the selected object(s), as shown here:

Position
Transform
Position
Rotation
Position:
H: 0.00000 inches
V: 0.00000 inches
Relative Position
Apply To Duplicate
Apply

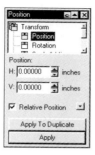

To move the object to the right horizontally or up vertically, enter a positive number; to move it to the left or down, enter a negative number. If the Relative Position check box is not checked, the horizontal and vertical measurements are absolute coordinates on the grid formed by the rulers. With Relative Position checked, the measurements are the distance you want to move the object from its current location. The down arrow in the lower right of the roll-up expands the roll-up to include a set of node check boxes that specify that part of the object you are moving is aligned to measurements entered, as shown here:

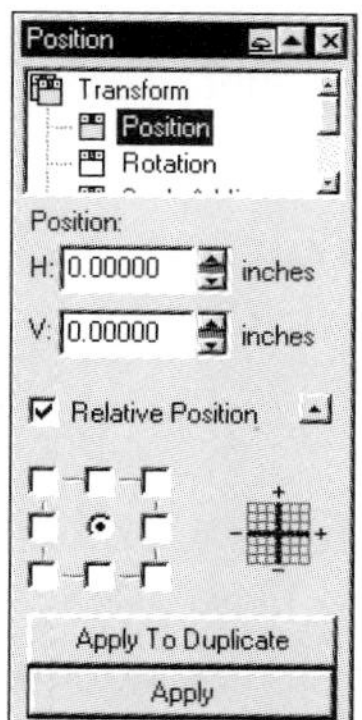

Follow these steps to move an object to precise coordinates (some part of the dolphin should still be selected).

1. Press SHIFT-F4 to switch to Zoom To Page view, then select Rulers from the View menu if they are not already on and drag the zero points of the rulers (the crosshair in the upper-left corner of the rulers) to the upper-left corner of the page to reset the ruler origins so that 0 appears on the upper-left corner of the page.

2. Select Transform from the Arrange menu. The Relative Position check box should not be selected.
3. Click on the down arrow to expand the roll-up and click on the center node, indicating that the center of the object should be aligned to the measurements you will enter.

NOTE: *The "node box" represents the parts of the object that are used to align, i.e., if you clicked the upper-left box, the upper-left "corner" of the object would align on the coordinates.*

4. Press TAB to cycle through the components of the dolphin until you reach the object that represents the main black area of the dolphin.
5. Enter **4.25** in the Horizontal Position spinner and **–2.5** in the Vertical Position spinner. Click on Apply. The black area will be relocated so that its center is aligned with the coordinates. You can also leave the original object in place and move a copy to the specific location by clicking on the Apply To Duplicate button.

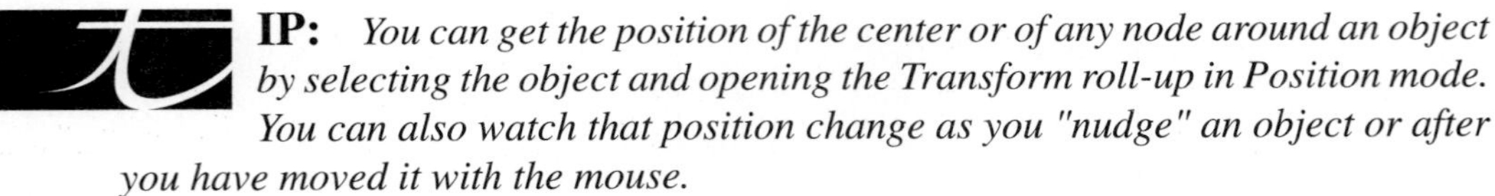

TIP: *You can get the position of the center or of any node around an object by selecting the object and opening the Transform roll-up in Position mode. You can also watch that position change as you "nudge" an object or after you have moved it with the mouse.*

6. Close your dolphin drawing by selecting Close from the File menu. Open a new document by selecting New from the File menu and then Document from the flyout. A new document window is displayed. Also, click on the Transform roll-up's Close button to close it.

Copying an Object While Moving It

You may recall that while you are moving an object, it seems to remain in place and you appear to be moving only a dotted rectangular substitute. Coreldraw lets you take this feature a step further: you can make an identical copy of the object as you move it. The copy remains at the initial location while you move the original to a new location. This handy technique has interesting design possibilities, as you can discover for yourself by performing the next exercise.

1. Select Grid and Ruler Setup from the Layout menu, on the Ruler tab set Vertical Grid Origin to 8.5 inches and Horizontal Grid Origin to 0. Both Units should be set to inches. On the Grid tab, set both the Horizontal and Vertical Grid Frequency to 2.0 per inch, and turn on Show Grid and Snap To Grid. Click on OK. Then, from the View menu, turn on the Rulers option if it is off and turn off Wireframe if it is on. Your page should still be in Landscape mode.
2. Select the Text tool and then select an insertion point at the 1 inch mark on the horizontal ruler and –1.5 inches on the vertical ruler. Type **Arrow** in lower case with a capital "A". Select the word by selecting the Pick tool, open the Text toolbar, and set the text attributes to Benguiat normal (or any font and style you choose) and 100 points. Close the Text toolbar.
3. Press and hold the mouse button over the outline of any letter and begin to drag downward and to the right. Since you have set grid spacing in large units, the dotted move box travels and snaps in visibly discrete increments.
4. Continue holding down the mouse button. When the upper-left corner of the dotted move box snaps to a point 1/2 inch below and to the right of the starting point (about midway down and across the letter "A"), press and release the + key in the numeric keypad. At the left of the Status bar, the message "Leave Original" appears, as shown in Figure 5-8. The + key in Coreldraw is also called the Leave Original key.
5. Release the mouse button. An exact copy of the object appears at the starting point and the original appears at the new location. (If nothing happens, press and release the + key more rapidly.)
6. Make four more copies of the text string in the same way, using the + key or right mouse button, and moving the text object in 1/2-inch increments downward and to the right. You must release the mouse button for each copy. You should now have a total of six identical text strings.
7. Change the direction in which you move the text object. Make five additional copies as you move the text object downward and to the left in 1/2-inch increments. When you are finished, 11 identical text strings form an arrowhead shape. Your screen should look like Figure 5-9.
8. Select Save As from the File menu and save this drawing under the name arrow1.cdr in the folder you are using for saving your work, then select

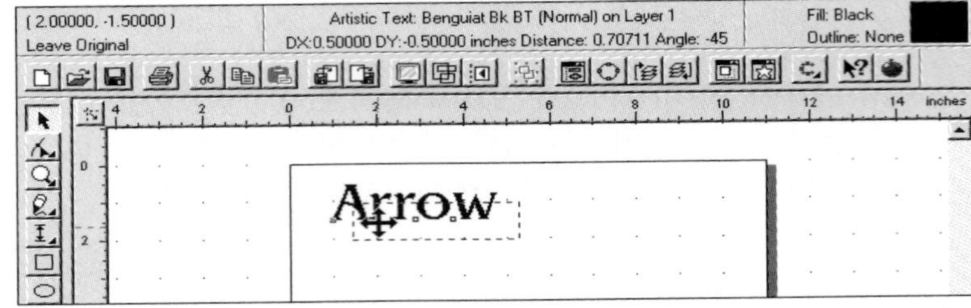

Copying an object while moving it

FIGURE 5-8

Close to close the drawing. Select New and then Document to open a new document window.

Using the preceding exercise as an example, you can probably think up additional design ideas for copying single or multiple objects as you move them. Go on to the next sections of this chapter to discover ways of changing the relative order of objects within a drawing.

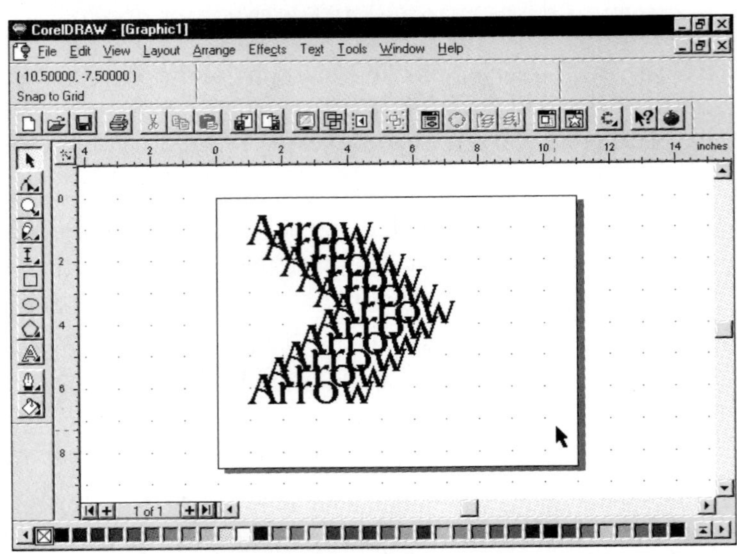

Completed arrow design

FIGURE 5-9

Arranging Objects

In Coreldraw, you can align objects relative to one another, change the order of superimposed objects, and group and combine separate objects. All of these techniques are ways of arranging objects on the page. The Arrange menu contains all of the commands you will use in this chapter, plus a few others that are discussed in later chapters. The next four sections demonstrate the most common methods of arranging selected objects.

Reordering Superimposed Objects

When you draw a series of objects, Coreldraw always places the object you drew *last* on top of all of the other objects. If you could look at the Arrow1.cdr file in 3-D, for example, you would see that the first text string you created is beneath all of the others you subsequently copied.

You can change the order of objects at any time by applying one of seven commands on the Order flyout of the Arrange menu to a selected object or group of objects. The seven commands—To Front, To Back, Forward One, Back One, Reverse Order, Before Object, and After Object—appear on a flyout menu, as shown here:

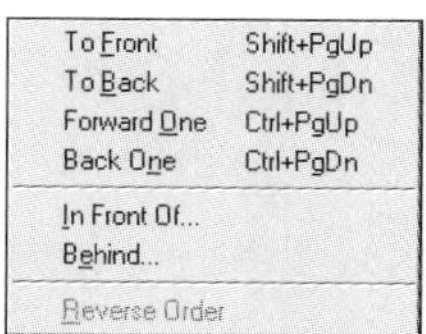

The To Front, To Back, Forward One, and Back One commands rearrange the selected objects relative to the other objects on the page, but they do not rearrange objects within a selected group. The Reverse Order command reverses the order of the selected objects relative to each other, but it does not alter the relationship between the selected objects and the other objects in the drawing. The Before and After Object commands rearrange the *sequence* of objects. You select the first object, then select Before or After Object and click on the other object.

OTE: *Once selected objects have been grouped, they cannot be reordered. You can, however, ungroup the objects, change the order of the objects, and then regroup the objects.*

Practice working with these commands now using a new piece of clip art, the CD-ROM file panda_b.cmx. If this is not available to you, use any piece of simple clip art you have available. Your page should still be in Portrait mode.

1. Open the Grid & Ruler Setup dialog box and turn off Snap to Grid and Show Grid. Turn off the rulers as well.
2. Select Import from the File menu and import the file panda_b.cmx in the \Clipart\Animal\ folder on the fourth CD-ROM.
3. Click anywhere on the drawing. When the drawing is selected, you'll see it's a group of eight objects.
4. Choose Ungroup from the Arrange menu to allow rearrangement of the individual objects.
5. Select (lasso) the eyes, nose, and mouth of the panda as shown here:

   Be sure to include both eyes, the nose, and the mouth, but not the ears or hind paw. You have selected everything you want if you have selected four objects.
6. Press F2 to select the Zoom tool and lasso just the face.
7. Open the Arrange menu and from the Order flyout select To Back. The eyes, nose, and mouth disappear behind the white of the face that had been in the background, as shown in Figure 5-10. When you apply this command to a group of objects, however, the relative order of the objects *within* the group does not change.
8. With the same group of objects still selected, select To Front from the Order flyout on the Arrange menu. Now the objects reappear in their original order, in front of the background objects.

Using the To Back command on selected objects

FIGURE 5-10

9. Leave these objects selected and select Back One from the Order flyout on the Arrange menu. This command moves the selected objects back behind the first layer (that is beneath them). Since the next layer back is transparent (only an outline), there is no effect in doing this. If you select Back One several more times, you will see that there are two transparent layers, then the eyes disappear under the third layer, and, finally, the nose and mouth disappear behind the fourth layer.
10. Select the To Front command to return the objects to their original order on the screen. Leave this drawing on the screen for the next exercise.

Grouping and Ungrouping Objects

Selecting multiple objects with the marquee or SHIFT key is fine if you want to apply certain commands or operations to them on a one-time basis only. However, most drawings contain subsets of objects that belong together, such as the elements of a logo on a business card. If you want the same set of objects to form a single entity at all times, consider *grouping* them instead of merely selecting them.

To group multiple objects, you first select them and then apply the Group command from the Arrange menu. Thereafter, the group responds to any operation collectively. You can move, align, color, and outline them together, without individually selecting each component of the group. However, Coreldraw still "knows" that the component objects have separate identities. As a result, you cannot apply the Reverse Order command to a group or reshape the group using the Shape tool. You can also create groups within groups, and then use the Ungroup command to break them down into their component objects again.

TIP: *To select a single object in a group, press CTRL while clicking on the object. The selected object can then be moved, resized, or otherwise modified. The handles on the bounding box of the selected object will be small circles, rather the squares, indicating the selecting object is part of a group.*

In the last exercise, all objects in the panda_b.cmx file were selected and then ungrouped. Continue working with this file to become familiar with the basics of grouping and ungrouping objects.

1. The group made up of the parts of the face should still be selected. The Status bar should display the message "4 Objects Selected on Layer 1," as shown in Figure 5-11.

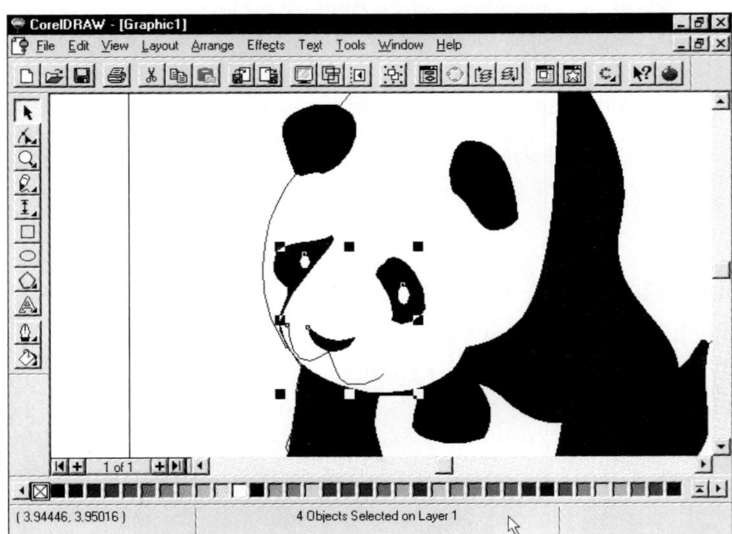

Grouping multiple objects

FIGURE 5-11

2. Select Group from the Arrange menu. The Status bar message changes immediately from "4 Objects Selected on Layer 1" to "Group of 4 Objects on Layer 1."
3. Open the Order flyout from the Arrange menu and notice that Reverse Order is dim—it isn't available, since the selected objects have been grouped. Select Ungroup and then select Reverse Order from the Order flyout. The four objects that used to form the group are now reversed in order—what was on top is now on the bottom relative to the other item in the group. You don't really see any change, though, because the only change is *within* the group.
4. Select Reverse Order again from the Order flyout. The original order returns.
5. Click on one of the black patches behind the eyes. This selects both black patches as well as both ears. Hold down SHIFT and then click on both eyes to select them. You will have three objects selected: the black objects and the eyes.
6. Select Reverse Order and now the eyes disappear behind the black patches. One final time, select Reverse Order to restore the original order.
7. Select Group from the Arrange menu. The message in the Status bar changes to "Group of 3 Objects on Layer 1."
8. Press F3 to zoom out and return to your previous view.
9. Press and hold the mouse button at any point along the outline of any of the selected objects and drag the selected objects to the bottom of the page. The entire group moves together and relocates when you release the mouse button, as shown in Figure 5-12.
10. Practice moving the group around, ungrouping, forming new groups, rearranging the groups, and moving various objects in relation to one another.

    Before and after grouping objects and text strings, look at the menus to see how grouping affects which commands you can and cannot select.
11. When you are done, select Close from the File menu to clear the screen. Do not save any changes to this drawing.

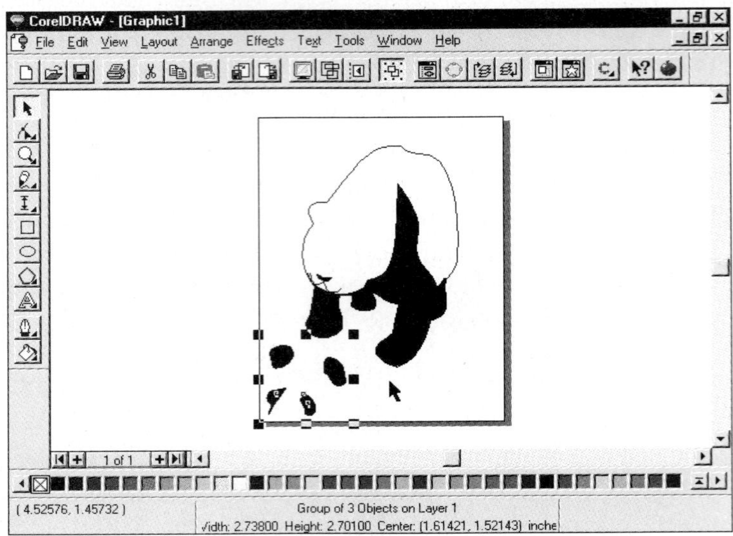

Moving the selected group

FIGURE 5-12

Combining and Breaking Objects Apart

The Arrange menu contains two sets of commands that seem almost identical in content, but are actually two different operations: Group/Ungroup and Combine/Break Apart. Grouping is used when you want to simply "handle" a group of objects as a single object; for example when you want to move, copy, or position them. Combining on the other hand, is a more complex operation that is used in the following situations.

- When you want multiple objects to become a single object that you can reshape with the Shape tool
- When the objects contain many nodes and curves and you want to reduce the total amount of memory they consume
- When you want to create special effects such as transparent masks, behind which you can place other objects

In these situations, simply grouping objects would not yield the desired results.

Later chapters, especially Chapter 14, contain several examples of creative uses for the Combine command. There is one interesting use of Combine, however, that you can try out in this chapter. If you combine objects with other objects contained within them, the net result is a reverse color effect that makes alternating objects transparent and creates contrast. For a clearer understanding of how this works, try the following exercise.

1. Open the teacup.cdr file. The window displays a solid black mass, as shown next, because you haven't yet applied different fill colors or outlines to separate objects. (If your tea cup does not fill with black, it could be for one of two reasons: Wireframe is still turned on in the View menu or No Fill is the active fill. In the latter case, select all of the tea cup and saucer, open the Fill flyout, and click on the black fill.)

2. Press SHIFT-F9 to go to Wireframe view and select both the larger rectangle that forms the outline of the handle and the inner rectangle. Use either the marquee or the SHIFT key method. When you are done, the Status bar should say "2 Objects Selected on Layer 1."
3. Select Combine from the Arrange menu. Press SHIFT-F9 again to turn off Wireframe, and the inside of the inner rectangle becomes transparent, as you can see here:

4. This "special effect" occurs because the Combine command causes all overlapping areas in a graphic to appear transparent. Notice that the Status bar now refers to the combined object as a single curve object. Because of the hollow areas you created when you selected the Combine command, you can now distinguish the handle from the rest of the cup.

5. Save this file under the new name Teacup2.cdr.
6. Select the newly combined handle, if it is not still selected, and then select the Break Apart command from the Arrange menu. All objects revert to their previous state and become black again.

7. Clear the screen by selecting Close. Do not save any changes. Then click on the New (leftmost) button on the toolbar.

Aligning Objects

Earlier in this chapter, you saw how you can move objects precisely using the CTRL key as a substitute for the grid. The Align and Distribute command from the Arrange menu offers you another quick and easy method for aligning selected objects without having to spend all of your drawing time measuring. To align objects, you simply select the objects, click on the Align and Distribute command, and then adjust the horizontal and vertical alignment settings in the Align & Distribute roll-up.

You could try to memorize the abstract effects of all 15 possible settings, but experiencing those settings for yourself might be more meaningful. In the following exercise, you will create a rectangle and pretend it's a billiard table. Then you will add a billiard ball and apply various alignment settings to the ball and the table.

1. Start with the page in Landscape orientation with the rulers and grid displayed, Snap To Grid turned on, the horizontal and vertical grid frequencies set to 16 per inch, the vertical grid origin set to 8.5, Horizontal Grid Origin set to 0, and Wireframe view turned on. Select the Rectangle tool and draw a rectangle 8 inches wide and 4 inches high. This rectangle represents the surface of the billiard table.
2. Select the Ellipse tool, press and hold both SHIFT and CTRL, and draw a perfectly circular "ball" of about 1/2-inch diameter from the center out in the middle of the table.
3. Press the SPACEBAR to switch to the Pick tool and select the ball. Next, press SHIFT and select the table, then select Align & Distribute from the Arrange menu. The Align & Distribute roll-up appears, shown in Figure 5-13.

The Align & Distribute roll-up contains two areas of option buttons. The settings in the horizontal row of the roll-up pertain to the relative *horizontal* alignment of the selected objects, while the settings in the vertical row of the roll-up pertain to

COREL DRAW!™ 6 in action

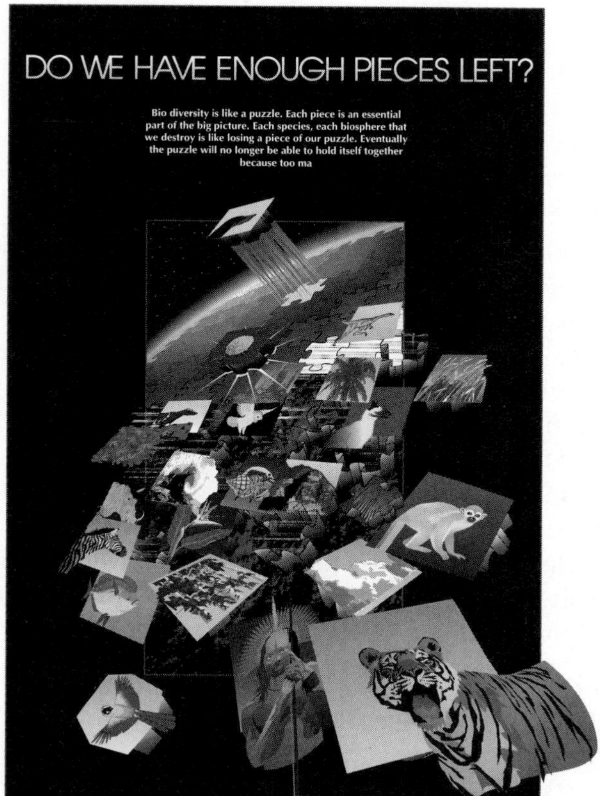

***Puzzle*—Stephen Arscott**

You can see how grouping objects helped artist Stephen Arscott create and arrange the puzzle pieces in this poster for the Friends of the Earth. You will learn some of the advanced techniques Stephen used (particularly Extrude and PowerClip) in later chapters.

Stephen Arscott lives and works in Mississauaga, Ontario, Canada. He can be reached at (905) 896-4664.

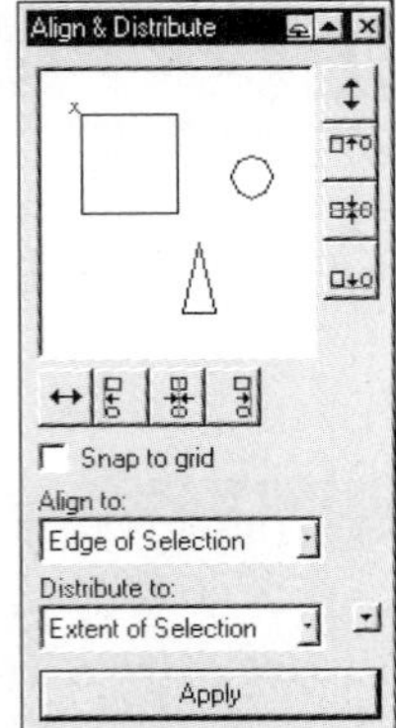

Align & Distribute roll-up

FIGURE 5-13

their relative *vertical* alignment. You can set horizontal and vertical alignment independently of each other or mix them, for a total of 15 possible settings. When multiple objects are selected and you choose the Horizontally Left, Horizontally Right, Vertically Top, or Vertically Bottom alignment option, Coreldraw repositions all but one of the objects. The object *last selected* remains in place. All other objects are moved to carry out the desired alignment. When you select Horizontally Center or Vertically Center alignment, however, Coreldraw repositions all of the selected objects, unless one of them is already in the desired location.

1. Select Horizontally Left in the Align & Distribute roll-up and then click on Apply. The billiard ball reappears in position 1 in Figure 5-14, aligned to the left edge of the table.

   If your screen does not look like Figure 5-14—you can see only half of your table, or your table moved and the ball stayed stationary—then you selected your table first and the ball last. The last object selected stays stationary, and previously selected items are moved the first time you do an alignment.

2. Select the Align & Distribute command repeatedly and choose each of the numbered settings in the following list, one at a time. As you select each setting, check the location of the billiard ball against the corresponding numbers in Figure 5-14.

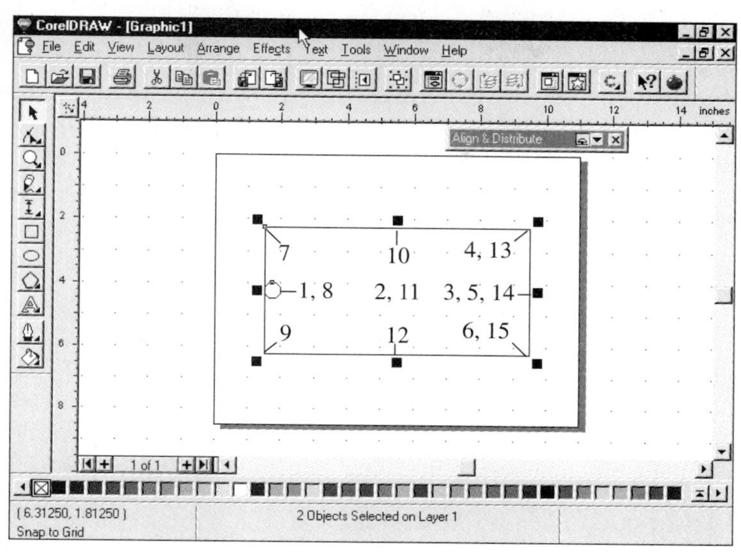

Results of Align & Distribute roll-up settings

FIGURE 5-14

5

(1) Horizontally Left
(2) Horizontally Center
(3) Horizontally Right
(4) Vertically Top
(5) Vertically Center
(6) Vertically Bottom
(7) Horizontally Left-Vertically Top
(8) Horizontally Left-Vertically Center
(9) Horizontally Left-Vertically Bottom
(10) Horizontally Center-Vertically Top
(11) Horizontally Center-Vertically Center
(12) Horizontally Center-Vertically Bottom
(13) Horizontally Right-Vertically Top
(14) Horizontally Right-Vertically Center
(15) Horizontally Right-Vertically Bottom

If you do the above alignments having selected the ball first and the table second, you will notice that the ball always moves and the table stays in one place, as you would expect.

The Align & Distribute dialog box has three additional options, Snap to Grid, and Align to and Distribute to drop-down list boxes. You are familiar with the Snap to option; the Align to drop-down list box offers three options for aligning objects: Edge of Selection, Center of Page, and Edge of Page. The selected option determines which anchor point is used to align the selected objects. The Distribute command is used to arrange the selected objects based on the distance between the objects. In other words, you can arrange the objects so they are spaced equally from each other, and set the amount of space between the objects. When any of these options are used, you want to set it before setting the horizontal and/or vertical alignments. Try the Snap to and Align to options now.

1. Open the Align & Distribute roll-up and select Center of Page from the Align to drop-down list box. Then select Horizontally Center and Vertically Center alignment. Click on Apply. The ball returns to the center of the table, and both objects are positioned in the center of the page.
2. Make sure Center of Page is still selected in the Align to drop-down list box, then click on Horizontally Left and Vertically Top, and click on OK. The ball moves to the upper-left corner of the table, and the upper-left corner of the table moves to the center of the page, as shown in Figure 5-15.

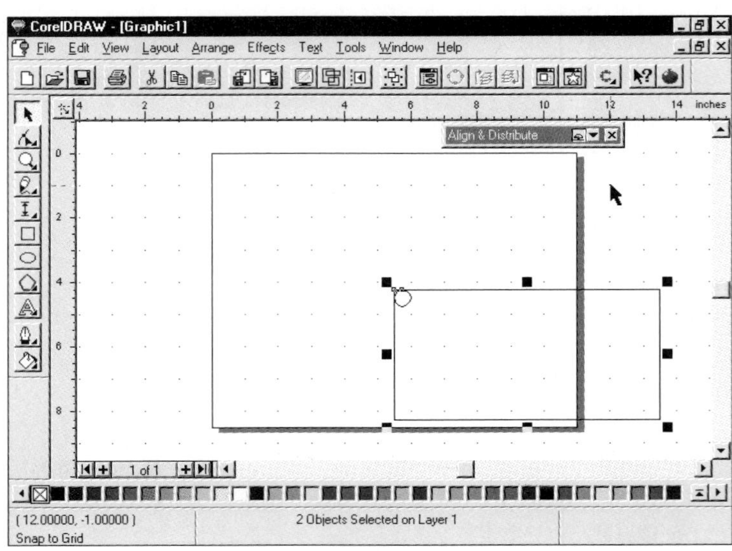

Upper-left corner aligned to center of page

FIGURE 5-15

In Align to Center of Page, the objects first position themselves in accordance with the horizontal and vertical alignment instructions, and then the common point of alignment is positioned in the center of the page.

1. Click on anything other than the ball or the table to deselect them both, then click on the table to select only it.
2. In the Grid Setup dialog box reached from the Layout menu, set both Horizontal and Vertical Grid Frequency to 2.
3. Using the arrow keys, nudge the table so that it is away from grid lines in both directions.
4. Open the Align & Distribute dialog box and click on Horizontally Left and Vertically Top and select Snap to Grid. Click on Apply. The table will move to the nearest grid point that is up and to the left of the table's original position.

5

The Align to Grid command does not position objects in relation to each other, but rather it individually aligns objects (all that are selected) in relation to the nearest grid point in the direction specified by the horizontal and vertical alignment commands.

Experiment on your own, perhaps with other objects in drawings you have already created. Other objects may align in a slightly different way, depending on the order in which you select alignment settings.

When you are through practicing using the Align feature, clear the screen by selecting the table and the ball and pressing DEL. Close the Align & Distribute roll-up by clicking on its Close button.

Layers

Coreldraw also allows you to create a drawing in different layers. Just as you can stack transparencies on an overhead projector, you can create a drawing in distinct layers so that you can hide certain objects, prevent certain objects from being changed, and control the printing of the drawing layer by layer. This last feature is important in more complex drawings where printing time is a factor.

You probably noticed in the examples throughout this book that the Status bar displays the current object followed by the words "on Layer 1." This is the layer assigned to all new drawings. You can have as many layers as you want, but new objects are placed only on the active layer.

Layering is controlled by the Layers roll-up (accessed by selecting Layers Manager from the Layout menu or by pressing CTRL-F3), which looks like this:

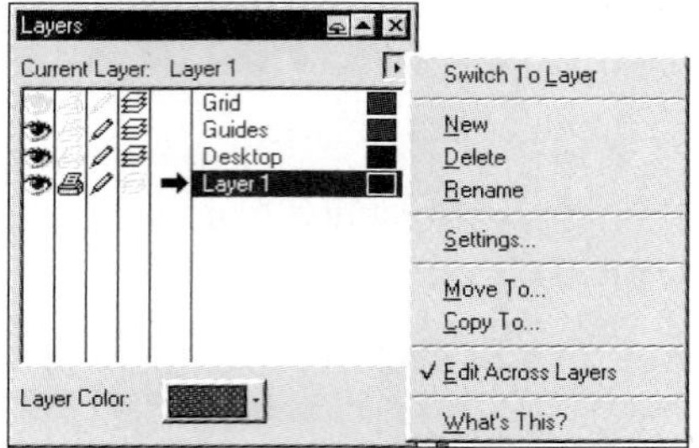

The four layers that appear in the Layers roll-up are Coreldraw's defaults: Grid, Guides, Desktop, and Layer 1. There are five possible icons to the left of each layer: an eye that says the layer is visible, a printer that tells you the layer is printable, a pencil that says a layer is unlocked so you can place objects on it, a stack of pages indicating whether the layer is a master layer, and a right-pointing arrow showing the current (active) layer. Master layers are layers that are automatically included on each page in a multipage document. For example, headers and footers could be added to a multipage document by creating a header/footer master layer. Layer 1 is the current layer, and all new objects and text will be on it. A layer becomes active when you select and highlight its name in the Layers roll-up. The Desktop is active when you have Edit Across Layers selected in the Layers pop-up menu, as you do in this default setup. Edit Across Layers has to be selected to work with multiple layers in Coreldraw.

The Guides layer contains any guidelines that you may choose. These are the same guidelines available from the Layout menu, and drawings made on other layers will snap to them. You can also draw on the Guides layer by making it the current layer. Whatever you draw can then be used as a guide when Snap to Guidelines is selected from the Layout menu. The Grid layer is similar to the Guides layer, except you cannot make the Grid layer the current layer. Consequently, it is a locked layer on which nothing can be drawn. The Grid layer is simply a series of points that can help you draw accurately in other layers.

Layer Features

Clicking on the right-pointing arrow below the Title bar of the Layers roll-up opens a flyout menu, which allows you to create a new layer or to edit, delete, copy, or

move existing layers. Additionally, you can change the stacking order of your layers or use multilayering to select objects across any layer, except for locked or hidden objects.

Editing a Layer

When you double-click on a layer in the Layers roll-up or choose Settings from the flyout, the Layer Settings dialog box opens, as shown here:

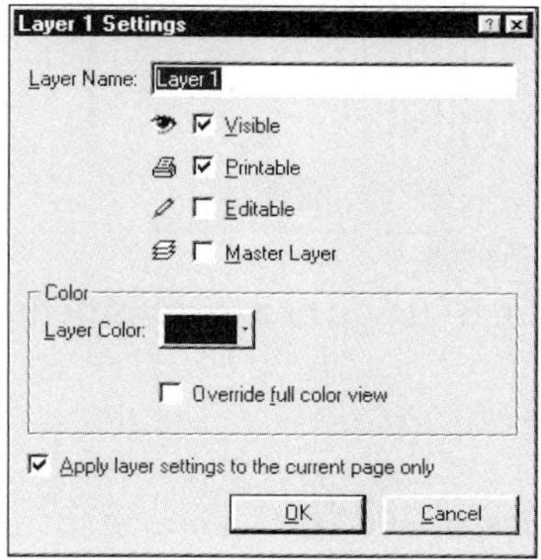

A text box identifies the name of the layer, which you can rename anything you want using up to 32 characters. The dialog box contains six check boxes. The first check box allows you to choose whether to make a layer visible or invisible on the screen, an option that is useful when trying to present objects on a complex graphic more clearly. A layer may be printable or unprintable. It may be locked, whereby a layer cannot be accidentally edited. You can make a layer a master layer so that it can be included on each page in a multipage document. If the Apply layer settings to the current page only check box is not checked, all objects on the master layer will be displayed on all pages of the document. You can also set Color Override, which determines whether you see your object as a color outline or a black solid on the screen. (The default is a black solid.) You can change the color of the outline by clicking on the down arrow in the color display button.

OTE: *The Layers Settings dialog box for Guides or Grid layers contains an added Setup button. Depending on which layer is current, the Guidelines Setup or Grid Setup dialog box will open when Setup is selected.*

Creating a Layer

If you choose New from the Layers flyout menu, a new layer is inserted in the Layers roll-up, like this:

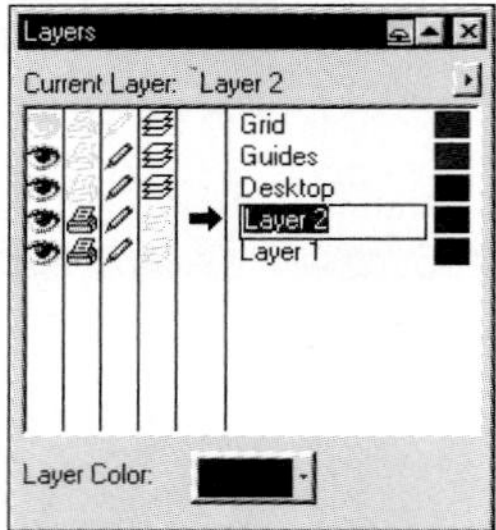

You use the Layers Settings dialog box to modify the new layer.

Deleting a Layer

To delete a layer, simply click on the layer name in the Layers roll-up window and then click on the right-pointing arrow. Choose Delete from the flyout and the layer and all of its objects are deleted. When you delete a layer, the layer below it on the list becomes the active layer.

Moving or Copying Objects or Text from One Layer to Another

The procedures are the same for both moving and copying objects and text from one layer to another. First, you must select the object you want to move or copy. You can tell which layer it is on by the displayed message on the Status bar. Next, from the Layers roll-up, click on the right-pointing arrow and choose either Move To or Copy To. A "To?" arrow appears. Finally, click the "To?" arrow on the new layer in the Layers roll-up window where you want the object located.

Editing Across Layers

Generally, in order to select an object, it must be on the active layer. By choosing the Edit Across Layers option from the Layers roll-up flyout menu, you can select and edit any object regardless of the layer on which it resides. There are two things to note about multilayering. First, locking a layer overrides the Edit Across Layers option's access to objects on that layer. Second, in order to perform the moving and copying features, Edit Across Layers must be active.

Changing the Layer Stacking Order

The order in which the layers are listed in the Layers roll-up window is the same order in which the layers are stacked in your drawing; the top layer being first in the list and the bottom layer last in the list. To change the existing order, drag the layer name you want to move from its present location in the Layers list box and place it on top of the name of the layer you want it to overlay in your drawing. When you release the mouse button, the list will be rearranged—as will the order of the layers in your drawing. You can get an understanding of layering with the following simple exercise.

1. Your page should be in Landscape orientation with rulers and Wireframe off, Grid off, and Snap to Grid on.
2. With the Rectangle tool, draw a rectangle roughly three inches square.
3. With the rectangle selected, open the Fill tool at the bottom of the toolbox and click on solid black.
4. With the Ellipse tool, draw an ellipse inside the rectangle and, with the Fill tool, make it white.
5. With the Text tool, type **Super** in the ellipse. Use the Text roll-up to adjust the size so it will fit inside the ellipse. You now have a stack of three objects, one on top of the other, all on Layer 1:

6. Open the Layers roll-up by selecting Layers Manager from the Layout menu.
7. From the Layers flyout, select New.

8. Click in the column to the left of Layer 1 to make it the current layer, click on the rectangle you drew (make sure you have not selected the ellipse), open the Layers flyout menu, choose Move To, and click on Layer 2. The black rectangle now covers the ellipse and text, proving that Layer 2 is on top of Layer 1, as shown next. (Click on Layer 1 to further clinch this proof.)

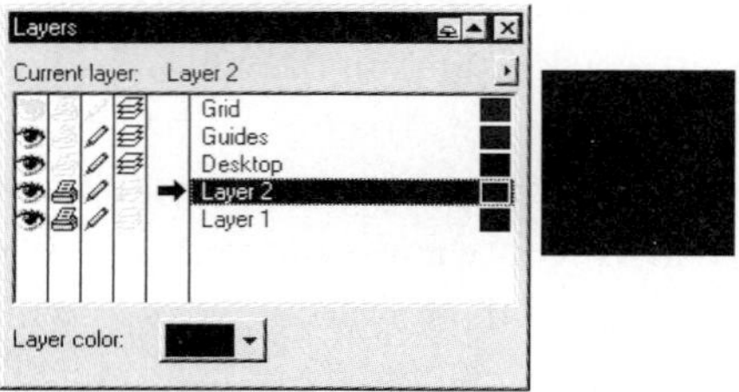

9. In the Layers roll-up window, drag Layer 1 up above Layer 2. Coreldraw switches the two layers to restore the original order of your drawing, like this:

10. Select all the objects and press DEL to clear the screen.

IP: *To select all the objects in your drawing, double-click on the Pick tool.*

Weld, Intersection, and Trim

In addition to Group and Combine, there are three additional ways to join two or more objects into one or more new objects that have a single fill and cannot be broken apart. These are Weld, Intersection, and Trim. Weld joins two or more overlapping

objects to create a resulting object with a border that is the sum of the original objects and with overlapping borders removed. Intersection joins two or more overlapping objects to create a resulting object that takes on the border of the intersection of the original objects. Trim creates a new object that is the part of the last selected object that is not common to other overlapping objects. In all three cases, the outline and fill features of the last object selected will be in effect for the new object(s). Try out these additional methods of joining objects with the following exercise.

1. Select Portrait orientation and turn on Wireframe mode.
2. Using the Ellipse tool, draw a circle in the upper-left portion of the page. Fill it with any color pattern by clicking on the Color palette at the bottom of the screen (you won't initially see the fill since you are in Wireframe mode). (Chapter 7 describes the Fill feature in depth.)
3. Using the Rectangle tool, draw a rectangle that overlaps the circle. Fill it with a different color.
4. With the Pick tool, lasso both objects to select them. From the Edit menu, choose Copy and then, again from the Edit menu, choose Paste twice. Three copies of the original two objects are now on top of each other, with the top copy selected.
5. Drag the selected copy to the bottom of the page and select the second copy (you need to click first on the ellipse and then the rectangle—you can't use marquee selection in this case or you would get both remaining copies) and drag it to the middle of the page. Your page should now look like Figure 5-16.
6. With the Pick tool, click on the top ellipse to select it.
7. From the Arrange menu, select Weld. The Weld roll-up is displayed as shown in Figure 5-17.
8. Click on the Weld To command button. The pointer changes to a thick arrow. Click on the top rectangle. The outline of the two objects becomes one and the common border is removed, as shown here:

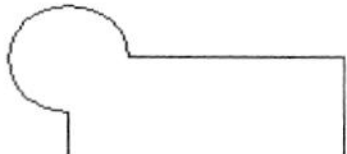

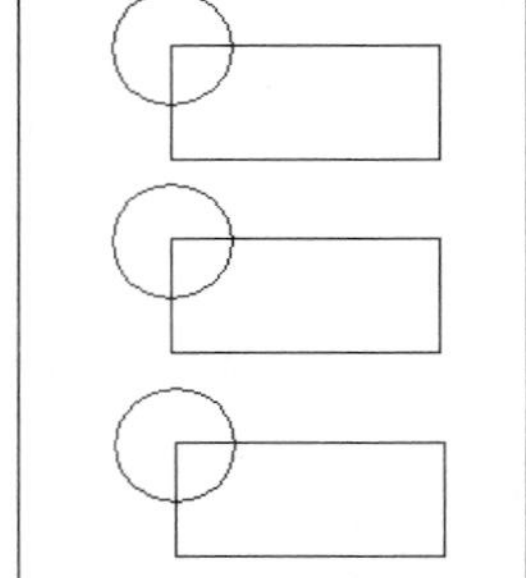

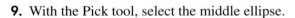

Separate objects ready for joining

FIGURE 5-16

9. With the Pick tool, select the middle ellipse.
10. Click on Intersect in the Weld roll-up. Then click on the Intersect With command button. The pointer changes to a thick arrow again. Click on the middle rectangle. In the middle is a new object formed by the intersection of the original objects, as you can see by dragging the objects apart:

11. Finally, click on the bottom ellipse.

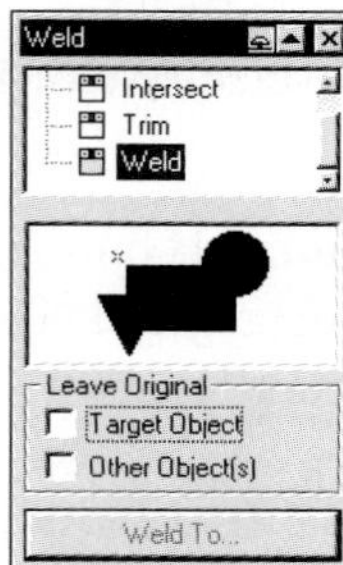

Weld roll-up

FIGURE 5-17

12. Click on Trim in the Weld roll-up, then click on the Trim command button. Click on the bottom rectangle with the thick arrow. Drag the ellipse to the left and what was the rectangle to the right. You can see the rectangle has a "bite" taken out of it where the ellipse was overlapping it like this:

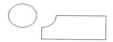

13. Turn off Wireframe in the View menu and you can see that the resulting fill of the newly created object is the fill of the last selected object, as shown in Figure 5-18.

14. Select all the objects and press DEL (the work shouldn't remain on the screen for the next chapter).

Now you have had an opportunity to practice all of the functions of the Pick tool that do not require you to change the size or structure of selected objects. In Chapter 8 you will explore the Transformation mode of the Pick tool and learn to stretch, scale, rotate, skew, and mirror a selected object or group of objects. First, though, in Chapters 6 and 7 you will get experience using the Outline and Fill tools and applying color.

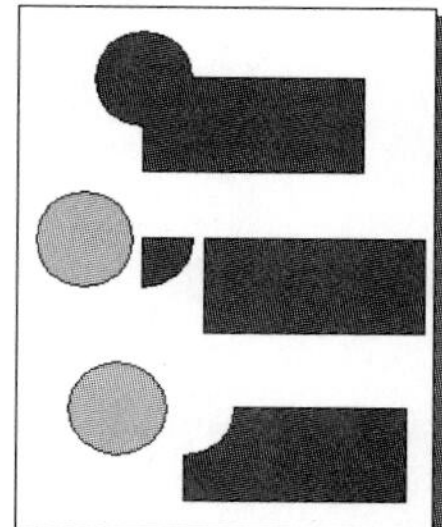

Joined objects take on the fill of the last selected object

FIGURE 5-18

Defining the Outline Pen

In Coreldraw, all objects have an outline width and color, and object fill properties. In addition, text has its own set of properties, as you will learn in Chapter 10. All of the objects you created and edited until now have had standard black fills and fixed-width black outlines. In this chapter, you will learn how to modify outline properties using the Coreldraw Outline Pen.

The Outline Pen is actually two tools in one. In order to create an outline for any object, you need to define the *Outline Pen* and the *outline color* in two separate steps. Think of the Outline Pen as a calligraphic pen capable of representing the shape of an almost infinite number of replaceable nibs and of emulating the possible ways you can slant your hand while drawing. The outline color, which you will learn about in Chapter 7, represents the ink and textures that flow from the pen.

When defining an Outline Pen for any object, you can vary the line width, line style, corner shape, line ending style, and nib shape of the pen. You can also control the placement of the outline relative to the object's fill color. Coreldraw allows you a great degree of control over the shape and appearance of your drawings. With your first try, you can create ornate calligraphic effects and simulate a hand-sketched look digitally.

Defining Outline Pen Properties

The method you use to define Outline Pen properties depends on whether you are editing properties for existing objects or altering the default outline settings. The default outline properties are applied when you create a new object. The following list summarizes the available possibilities.

- To edit Outline Pen properties for an existing object (including grouped or combined objects), activate the Pick tool, select the object, and then click on the Outline Tool to open the Outline Pen flyout.

- To begin setting new Outline Pen default properties, first make sure that no object is selected. Click on the Outline Tool to open the Outline Pen flyout.

Once you have selected the Outline Tool, you can choose between defining a custom Outline Pen or selecting a preset outline width from the Outline Pen flyout. In the remaining sections of this chapter, you will practice customizing Outline Pen properties and selecting preset Outline Pen widths for both planned and existing objects.

Using the Outline Pen

You have complete control over the properties of the Outline Pen in Coreldraw, thanks to a series of properties that can be modified. There are three ways to modify these properties.

- Directly from the Outline Pen flyout, as shown in the following illustration. You use the flyout to make quick standard changes to an outline. All three ways of changing properties start with this flyout menu.

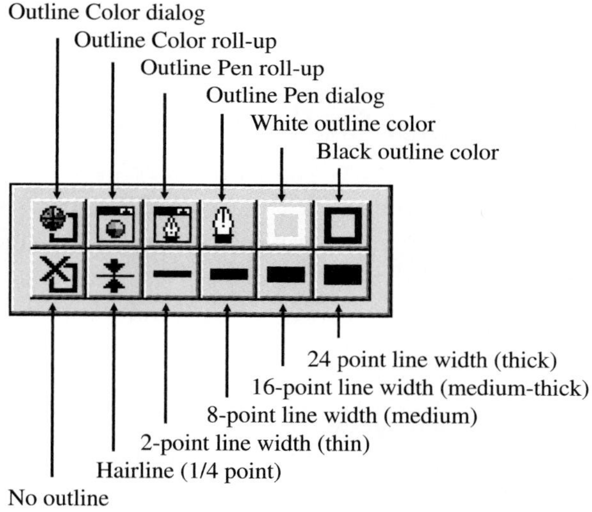

6

- From a dialog box that allows the properties to be modified with greater precision. The dialog box is displayed by clicking on the Outline Pen button, the fourth icon in the top row of the flyout menu (which is identical in appearance to the Outline Pen tool). By altering the settings in this dialog box, you can vary the outline's placement and width, change the shape of corners and line ending styles, design custom nibs, and create an array of calligraphic effects.

- From the Pen roll-up, shown in the following illustration. The Pen roll-up is displayed by clicking on the Pen Roll-Up button (shown in the margin), next to the Outline Pen button. The roll-up can be used once and closed or left on the screen, where it can be rolled up or down as needed.

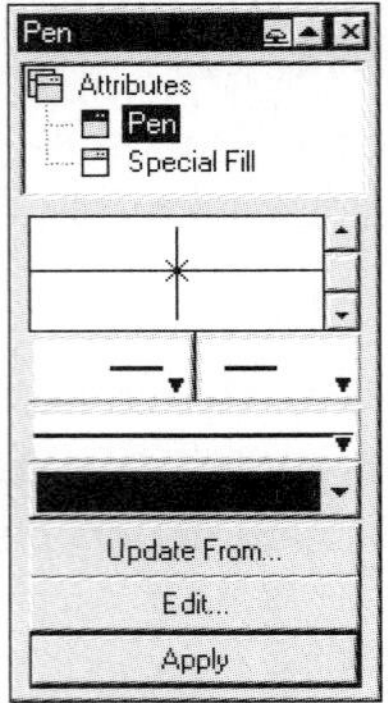

Selecting a Preset Outline Pen Width

Width is the Outline Pen property you will change most frequently, so Coreldraw offers shortcuts that save you time. The flyout that appears when you select the Outline Tool contains six preset outline widths from which you can choose (including no outline).

Button	Line Width
	No outline
	Hairline (1/4 point)
	2-point line
	8-point line
	16-point line
	24-point line

You can choose one of these options for a currently selected object or as a new default. When you choose a preset outline width for a selected object, you apply that width to the selected object only. When you click on one of these options without having first selected an object, however, Coreldraw assumes that you want to set the option as a new default width.

In the following exercises, you will create an object with default Outline Pen properties and become familiar with the settings in the Outline Pen dialog box and Pen roll-up. Then, you will edit Outline Pen properties for existing objects you will create. Finally, you will set up new default Outline Pen properties that will apply to objects you draw later.

Creating Objects with Default Properties

When you create a new object, Coreldraw applies the current default settings to it automatically. You can leave those settings as they are or edit them. When you edit Outline Pen settings for a newly created object, however, your changes apply only to that object. Other objects that you create keep the default Outline Pen properties until you set new defaults. You will change the defaults themselves in the section "Customizing Outline Pen Defaults," later in this chapter.

In the exercise that follows, you will create a text string, open the Outline Tool flyout to access the Outline Pen dialog box, and observe the default Outline Pen properties that are standard with Coreldraw.

1. Make sure that the Rulers, Show Grid, and Snap To Grid commands are turned off, then open the Zoom toolbar (from the View menu select Toolbars and then Zoom) and select Actual Size (1:1).

2. Activate the Artistic Text tool and select an insertion point near the upper-left edge of the page. Type **outline pen**.
3. Drag the text I-beam pointer over the text to select it, then open the Character Attributes dialog box by selecting the Character option from the Text menu.
4. Click on the Font tab, if it is not already selected, and set the text properties to a serif font such as Times New Roman, Century Schoolbook, or Garamond, Normal style, and 90 points. Your Character Attributes dialog box should look like Figure 6-1.

5. Select the Alignment tab, as shown in Figure 6-2, and then select the Left Alignment option button. Set Character Spacing to 10 percent and click on OK to apply the settings to your text. Select the Pick tool and your screen will look like Figure 6-3.

6. Assuming that Wireframe is turned off on the View menu (if it isn't, turn it off), the text string is displayed with the default outline and fill properties. For the purposes of this exercise, you want to remove the fill color to clearly view your outline. To do this, click on the X at the left end of the onscreen color palette (shown here) at the bottom of your window. (If your text seems to have vanished completely, you will find a solution in the next step.)

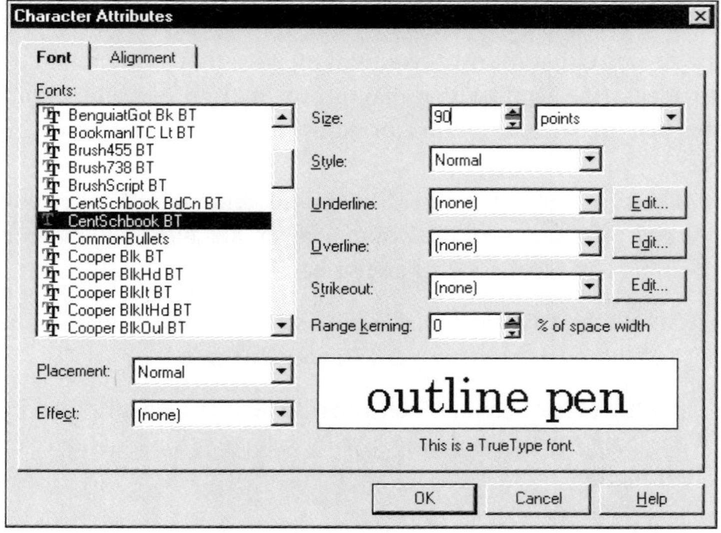

Font settings in the Character Attributes dialog box Font tab

FIGURE 6-1

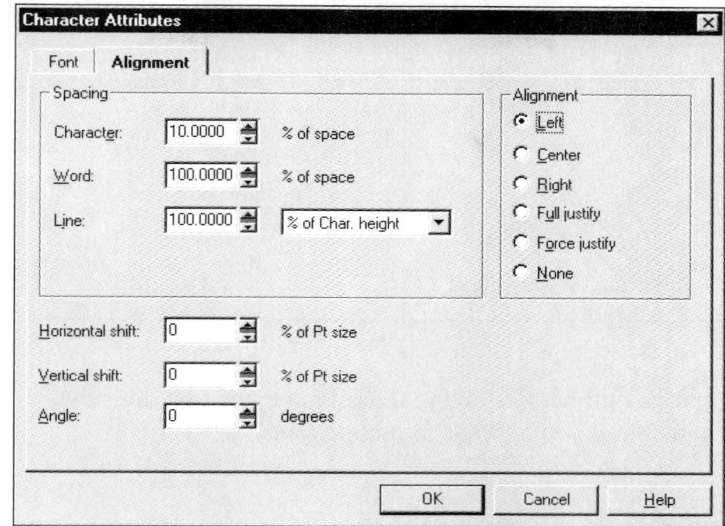

Alignment settings in the Character Attributes dialog box Alignment tab

FIGURE 6-2

7. Click on the Outline Tool to open the flyout. Click on the Hairline button, second from the left in the bottom row. The text string redisplays with a hairline outline and no fill, as shown in Figure 6-4. (Your text may have disappeared in step 6 because your text defaults were set for a solid fill

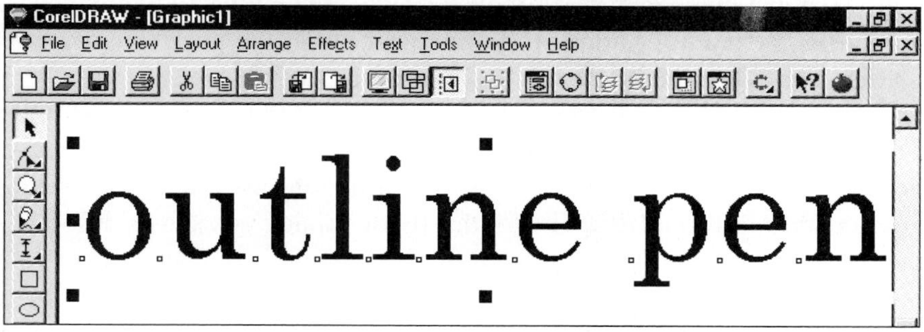

Text after Character settings applied

FIGURE 6-3

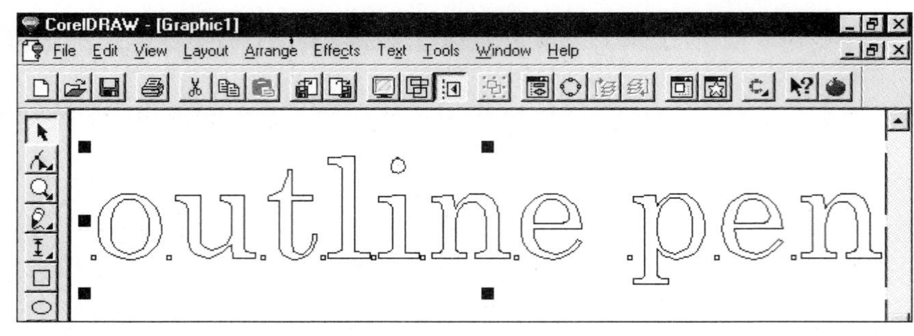

Text with fill removed and Hairline Outline Pen applied

FIGURE 6-4

and no outline. Removing the fill made the text invisible in full-color mode until you applied an outline to it.)

Outline Pen Properties

The Outline Tool flyout contains two types of options. The first type (the six icons in the second row plus the Pen Roll-Up and Outline Pen dialog box) consists of controls for the Outline Pen, which you will use throughout this chapter. The second type (the remaining four icons), which you will work with in Chapter 7, contain controls for the outline color.

While the Outline Tool flyout offers an easy method of applying preset line width and color properties, the Outline Pen dialog box allows you to change all the possible Outline Pen properties. To open the Outline Pen dialog box, click on the Outline Tool to open the flyout. Click on the fourth button in the first row, the Outline Pen button (shown in the margin). It looks just like the Outline Tool, but it has the more specialized function of allowing you to specify all the possible properties of the Outline Pen. The Outline Pen dialog box opens, as in Figure 6-5.

The Outline Pen dialog box contains controls for nine Outline Pen properties. The default settings on your screen should match the settings in Figure 6-5, unless you or another user altered them since installing the software. (One setting that is an exception and could differ is Width.) If your dialog box shows different settings, the following sections will explain how to adjust them to match the ones in Figure 6-5. Take a moment to become familiar with the properties and how they function.

COLOR A display box in the upper-left area of the dialog box shows you the current outline pen color. When you click on the Color display box, a Color palette is opened

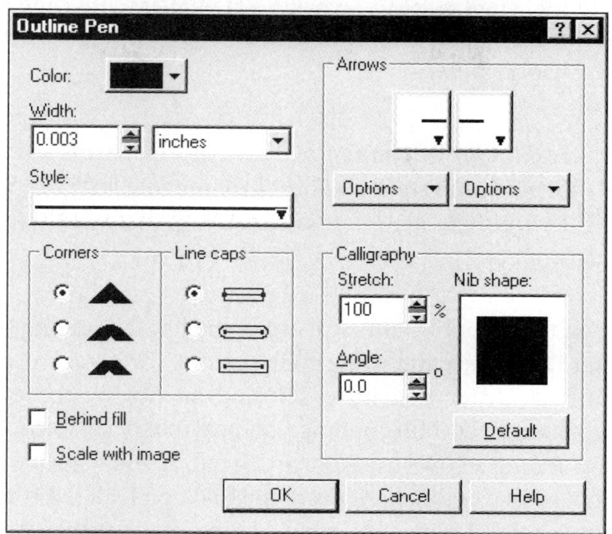

Outline Pen dialog box

FIGURE 6-5

that is identical to the normal onscreen palette except for the arrangement of the color choices. At the bottom of the Color palette is the Others button, which opens the Outline Color dialog box, giving you access to the full range of outline coloring. In Chapter 7, you will learn how these features are used.

ARROWS The pair of boxes next to the Color display box allow you to select or construct a line ending (such as an arrowhead) to go on either end of a line. These line endings are displayed in a flyout that you can open by clicking on either the left (line-beginning) or right (line-ending) Arrows display box, as shown here:

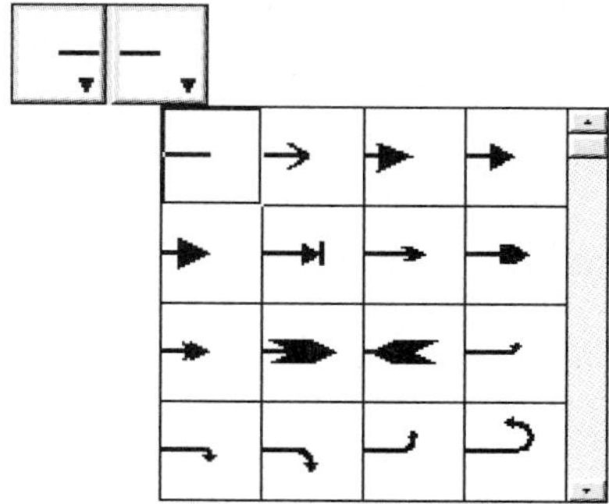

To select a line ending, scroll through the boxes of line endings until you see the one you want. Click on the line ending you want, and it will appear in its respective small Arrows display box.

IP: *To find the beginning of a line (normally the left end) or the end of a line (normally the right end) click on the line with the Shape tool and press* HOME *to highlight the beginning node. Pressing* END *will cause the ending node to be highlighted.*

Clicking on the Options button for either the line-beginning or line-ending arrow opens a menu that offers the same four options for each: None, Swap, Edit, and Delete From List. After you have selected an object, the options are enabled. Choosing None removes a line ending you previously selected. You can reverse the beginning and ending arrows by choosing Swap. If you want to remove a line ending from the flyout of line endings, select it and click on Delete From List. Selecting the Edit option opens the Arrowhead Editor dialog box shown here:

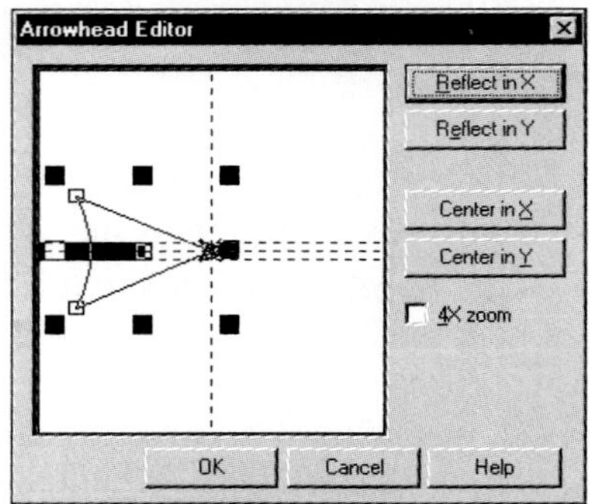

The Arrowhead Editor displays an enlarged arrowhead and allows you to move, scale, and stretch the arrowhead by dragging on it or one of its control boxes. You can center the arrowhead relative to the X in the middle of the Editor, either horizontally by selecting Center in X or vertically by selecting Center in Y. Also, you can flip or *reflect* the arrowhead relative to the center, either horizontally by selecting Reflect in X or vertically by selecting Reflect in Y. Finally, you can magnify the arrowhead image by clicking on 4X zoom.

LINE WIDTH Under the Color area of the Outline Pen dialog box are two boxes for controlling the current line width. You can change either the specific width number or the unit of measure (from inches to points, for example).

LINE STYLE A third box, under the line width, shows the current line style. The solid line shown in the Style box in Figure 6-5 is the default line style. Clicking on the Style display box opens a flyout that allows you to choose from a number of dotted and dashed line styles, as you can see here:

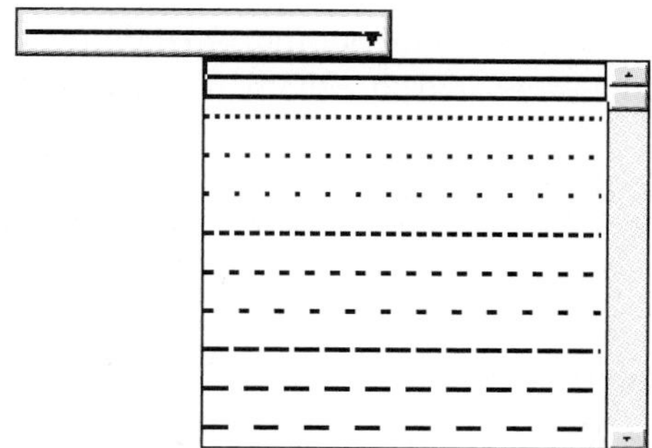

To choose a line style, use the scroll bar to display the style you want and click on that line style. You'll be returned to the Outline Pen dialog box and the line style you selected will now be in the display box.

CORNERS The Corners options have the most effect on objects that tend to have sharp corners: lines, open and closed curve objects, rectangles, and fonts in large sizes. The three option buttons in this area of the dialog box allow you to choose just how Coreldraw shapes those corners. The first (default) option shows a sharp or *miter* corner, where the outer edges of two joining lines or curve segments extend until they meet. By altering the Miter Limit setting in the Preferences dialog box, you can control the angle below which Coreldraw flattens or bevels the edge of a sharp curve. When you choose the second option button, Coreldraw rounds the corners where two lines or curve segments meet. When you choose the third (or *bevel* corner) option button, corners of joining curve or line segments are flattened. The results of the Corners settings are usually subtle, unless you magnify an object or combine Corners settings with Nib Shape properties for calligraphic effects.

LINE CAPS The Line Caps options apply to lines and open curves, but not to closed path objects such as rectangles, closed curves, or ellipses. These settings determine the ending styles of lines and curves. The first or default option is a *butt line* end style, where the line ends exactly at the end point. The second option gives you *rounded line* end points. When you choose either the second or the third (*square line*) end type, the line extends beyond the end point for a distance equal to half of the line thickness. When you select any of the line end caps, that style applies to both end points of the line or curve. If you have selected dashed lines as your line type for an object, each dash takes on the shape of the line end style you choose.

CALLIGRAPHY The remaining two Outline Pen properties—Stretch and Angle—help you define a custom pen shape, analogous to the *nib* or point of a calligraphic pen. With default values of 100 percent stretch and 0-degree angle, the pen shape is square, resulting in a plain outline. On their own, these settings will not create calligraphic effects. When you alter them in combination, however, they allow you to outline objects with varying thick and thin strokes at the angle of your choice. You can set the shape of the nib either interactively or by changing the values in the Stretch and Angle numeric spinners. Using the interactive method, you click and drag the mouse pointer inside the Nib Shape display box, where the pointer changes to a cross. The Stretch and Angle settings are automatically adjusted as you distort the nib shape. You can restore the default square nib by selecting the Default command button below the Nib Shape box. The Corners settings work with the Calligraphy settings to define the appearance of calligraphic strokes, as you will learn in "A Pen Shape for Calligraphic Effects," later in this chapter.

BEHIND FILL The Behind Fill check box lets you specify whether the outline of an object should appear in front of or behind the object's fill. The default setting is in front of the fill (empty check box), but if you create objects with thick outlines, you may want to activate Behind Fill. This is especially advisable with text, where thick outlines appearing in front of the fill can obliterate empty spaces and cause text to appear smudged, like this:

outline pen

When you place an outline behind the fill, only half of it is visible. The outline therefore appears to be only half as thick as specified.

SCALE WITH IMAGE When the Scale With Image check box is selected, the width and angle of the outline change proportionally as you resize, rotate, or skew the object. Coreldraw automatically updates the width and angle settings in the Outline Pen dialog box when Scale With Image is active. When the Scale With Image setting is *not* active, the width and angle of an object's outline do not change, no matter how you stretch, scale, rotate, or skew the object. This can lead to some interesting but unintended changes in appearance when you define a calligraphic pen nib for the object, as you will see in the "Scaling the Outline with the Image" section later in this chapter.

Now that you are familiar with the options in the Outline Pen dialog box, exit the dialog box by selecting Cancel. Clear the screen by selecting Select All from the Edit menu and pressing DEL before going on.

Customizing Outline Pen Defaults

Different artists have different styles, and you may prefer to create most of your objects with Outline Pen styles that differ from the standard settings. In the following exercise, you will learn how to customize Outline Pen defaults. Objects that you create after changing the default properties will then conform to the appearance that characterizes your working style.

Changing the default Outline Pen properties is a simple process: With no objects selected, you change the desired Outline Pen properties using the Outline Tool flyout, the Outline Pen dialog box, or Pen roll-up. When you create new objects, they will have the new default properties.

1. Start with a blank page. (If you are in an existing drawing and want to change default settings, make sure that no object is selected.) Then, select the Outline Tool and click on the Outline Pen button. Since no object is selected, the dialog box shown here appears.

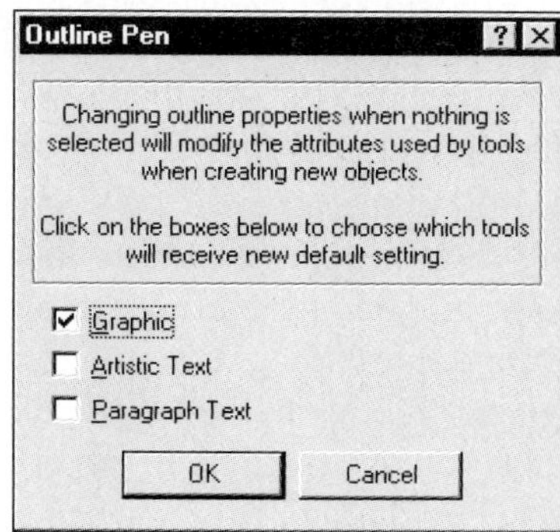

2. Click on the Artistic Text and Paragraph Text check boxes (Graphic should be already checked), so that all three have check marks, to have the defaults apply to all new objects. Then click on OK. The Outline Pen dialog box will be displayed.

3. The settings in your Outline Pen dialog box should be the same as those in Figure 6-5. Change the line width measurement units to points by selecting points from the units drop-down list box.

As you go through this chapter, you will exercise all of the options in this dialog box and become familiar with their effects and what your likes and dislikes are. When you are finished with the chapter, you can come back to the Outline Pen dialog box and set the defaults to what is right for you.

4. Click on OK to close the dialog box and save any changes you made.

It's that easy to alter default settings for the Outline Pen. As with almost every other Coreldraw feature, customization is the key word.

On the other hand, if you are involved in technical illustration or your normal Coreldraw tasks are relatively uncomplicated, you may seldom require calligraphy or other special options in the Outline Pen dialog box. The Pen roll-up provides another method of setting line width and color, line style, and line beginning and end styles.

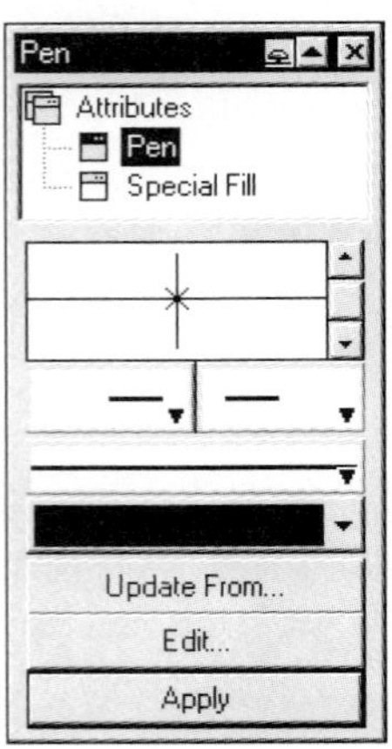

The Pen roll-up, shown here, is opened by clicking on the Pen Roll-Up button on the Outline Tool flyout.

The top option allows you to select which property you want to use. The next option in the Pen roll-up allows you to adjust the outline thickness. The default width that should appear is a hairline, shown by a thin line 1/4-point wide, met by two arrows. By clicking on the downward-pointing scroll arrow, you reduce the line thickness to zero, represented by an X through the box, signifying no outline. By clicking on the upward-pointing arrow, you can increase the line width, starting with the hairline, then a line 1-point wide, and then in .01-point increments. Below the outline thickness option are the familiar line ending, line style, and color options. To update the pen properties from a given object, click on Update From and the pointer will turn into a From arrow, which you use to click on the object. The properties of the object then update the Outline Pen dialog box. (You can then apply these properties to another selected object, or make them the defaults.) To open the Outline Pen dialog box, click on Edit. To apply the properties you have set in the Pen roll-up to a selected object, click on Apply.

Editing Outline Pen Properties of Existing Objects

To redefine Outline Pen properties for an existing (not newly created) object, you must select the object before you open the Outline Tool flyout. If you try to change any Outline Pen properties without having selected an object, Coreldraw assumes that you want to set new defaults for the Outline Pen and any changes you make in the Outline Pen dialog box will not affect existing objects.

When you define Outline Pen properties for an existing object that is selected, you are in effect *editing* the object's current outline style. The changes you make apply to that object only and have no effect on the default settings for objects you create later.

If you use the SHIFT method to select multiple objects in order to change their Outline Pen properties, the Outline Pen dialog box displays the settings for the last object that you selected in the group. If you use the marquee method to select the objects, the dialog box displays the settings for the last object that you drew. Any changes you make will apply to all of the selected objects, however, so be very careful about changing Outline Pen properties for more than one object at a time.

Each of the following sections concentrates on the effects of editing a specific property or related set of properties in the Outline Pen dialog box. You will work with simple files that best demonstrate how changes to a property can alter the overall design and mood of an image.

Adjusting Line Width

The line width you assign to an object's Outline Pen helps define the balance and weight of that object within a drawing. In the following exercise, you will alter the line width for several elements in a text object that you create and then observe how your changes affect it.

1. Open the Outline Pen dialog box and make sure both the Behind Fill and Scale With Image check boxes are unchecked. If either contains a check mark, click on the box to remove it. Close the dialog box.

2. Select the Artistic Text tool, click anywhere on the page, and type **Hot tips**. Select the words "Hot tips" using the Pick tool.
3. Open the Text toolbar by pointing on the border of toolbox and pressing the right mouse button and then selecting Text from the Toolbars popup menu.
4. Use the Text toolbar to set the text to 72 points, Bauhaus HV BT.
5. With the text still selected, magnify the area around the words with the Zoom-in tool. Your screen should now display an area similar to Figure 6-6.

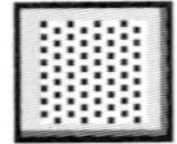

6. In the color palette at the bottom of your screen, click on the tenth button from the X on the left. This is the 10-percent black fill (look in the Status bar).

7. Open the Outline Tool flyout and click on the 2-point line button (the third button from the left in the second row). Click on the Pick tool. Now, the words "Hot tips" should look like this:

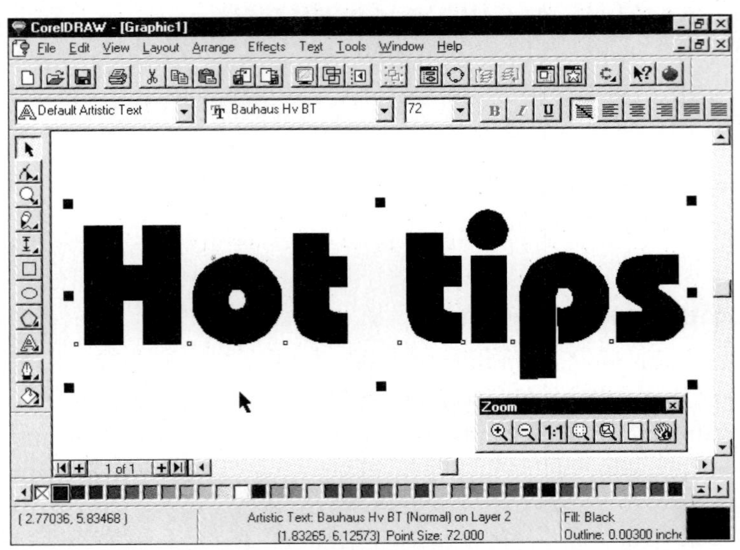

Magnified view of "Hot tips"

FIGURE 6-6

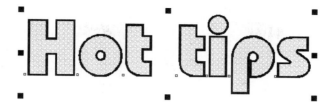

8. Open the Outline Tool flyout a third time and click on the 8-point line button (the fourth button from the left in the second row). "Hot tips" should now look like this:

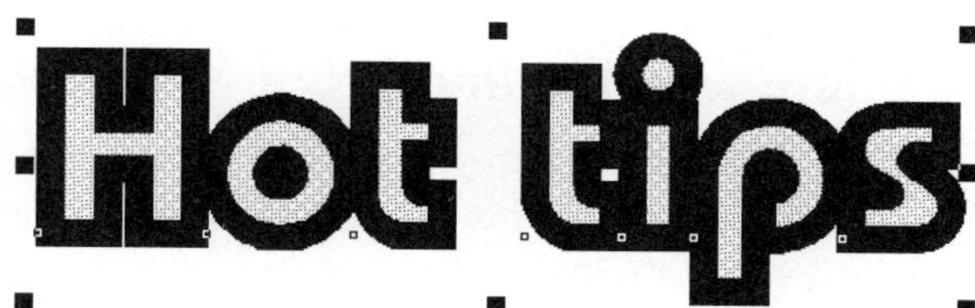

As you can see, the variation in line width makes a big difference in how an object looks, and you can vary the line width either by selecting one of the preset options on the flyout menu or by entering an exact width in the Outline Pen dialog box.

Leave the "Hot tips" text on your screen for further use. The next section explores the design possibilities of placing outlines of objects behind or in front of their fills.

Adjusting Placement of Outline and Fill

The Behind Fill setting in the Outline Pen dialog box determines whether the outline of a selected object is placed behind or in front of the object's fill. This property is most important when you are working with text. Thick outlines appearing in front of the fill can clog up the open spaces in letters, making the letters appear unclear, as you saw in the 8-point example in the last exercise. In the following exercise, you will adjust outline placement for the letters in the "Hot tips" text currently displayed.

1. Open the Outline Pen dialog box, click on the Behind Fill check box to select it and then select OK to exit the dialog box. The word reappears with a much thinner outline, as shown here:

Actually the outline is just as thick as before, but half of it is hidden behind the fill.

In the next section, you will observe how the Scale With Image setting affects the appearance of resized or transformed objects.

Scaling the Outline with the Image

A wide outline, such as the 8-point width you applied in the last exercise, may be appropriate for large letters, say 72 points and above. If you scale that large type down to 24 points, however, the wide border doesn't look good at all, as you can see here:

The Coreldraw Outline Pen dialog box has an option to scale an outline's properties with the image. If you select Scale With Image by clicking on the check box, an outline's properties will be appropriately scaled as you change the image. The default, though, is to not scale the properties, and you are likely to get something that looks like the last illustration.

1. With the "Hot tips" text still on the screen with an 8-point outline placed behind the fill, use the Text toolbar to scale the image to 24 points. You should get an image on your screen that looks like that shown in the last illustration.

2. Press ALT-BACKSPACE to return the text to its original size.
3. Open the Outline Pen dialog box. Click on the Scale With Image check box to select it, and click on OK.
4. Again, scale the text image to 24 points. You now get a much more usable image:

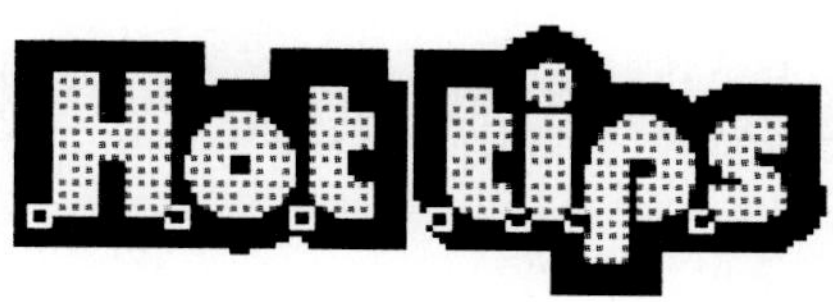

5. Clear the image from the screen by selecting Select All from the Edit menu and pressing DEL.

6

Setting Sharp (Miter), Rounded, or Beveled Outline Corners

The effect of changing corner properties of the Outline Pen is so subtle that it is almost unnoticeable—unless the selected object has a thick outline as well as sharp corners. A thick outline enables you to see the shape of the object change as you cycle through the Corners options. Perform the following exercise to practice altering Corners settings for the letter "E."

1. Press SHIFT-F4 to switch to Full-Page view, then select the Text tool, click anywhere on the page, and type **E**.
2. Select the letter "E" with the Pick tool and, from the Text toolbar, select AvantGarde MD BT and type in **204 points**.
3. Drag the letter "E" to the center of the printable page, then use the zoom-in tool to magnify the character until it fills the window.

4. With the letter still selected, Click on the Outline Tool, and select the 16-point line width button (the fifth button from the left). Next click on the X on the left end of the onscreen Color palette, to turn off the fill.

When you have completed the preceding steps, your screen should look like Figure 6-7. On the screen you see the outline of the letter "E" with 12 corners on which to test the three corner styles. The default (the sharp or miter corner) is currently displayed, and is shown in Figure 6-8a.

5. Open the Outline Pen dialog box, click on the rounded corner option button, and click on OK. You should see a distinct change in the corners, as shown in Figure 6-8b.
6. Again open the Outline Pen dialog box, select the beveled corner option, and click on OK. Once more, the corners change, as shown in Figure 6-8c.
7. Select Select All from the Edit menu, and press DEL to clear the screen.

In creating your own drawing, you will find the effects of the Corners options most dramatic when you assign thick outlines to objects that contain at least some cusp nodes. (Cusp nodes are used when a line changes direction sharply. Working

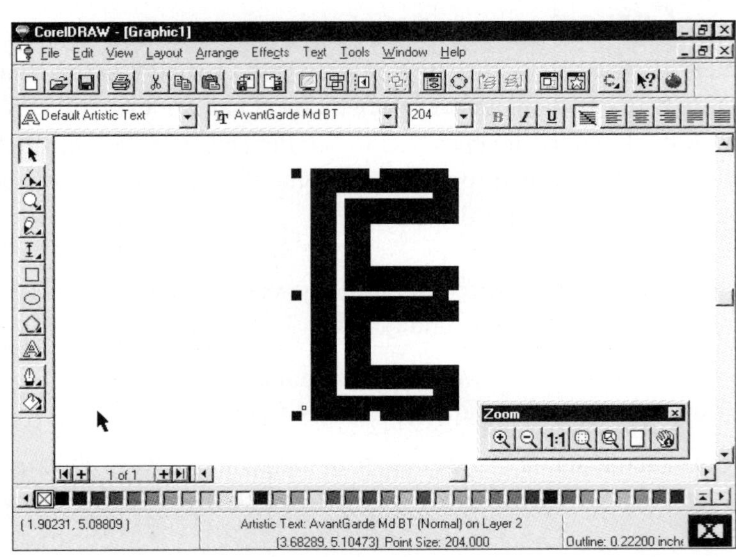

The letter "E" set up to display the types of corners

FIGURE 6-7

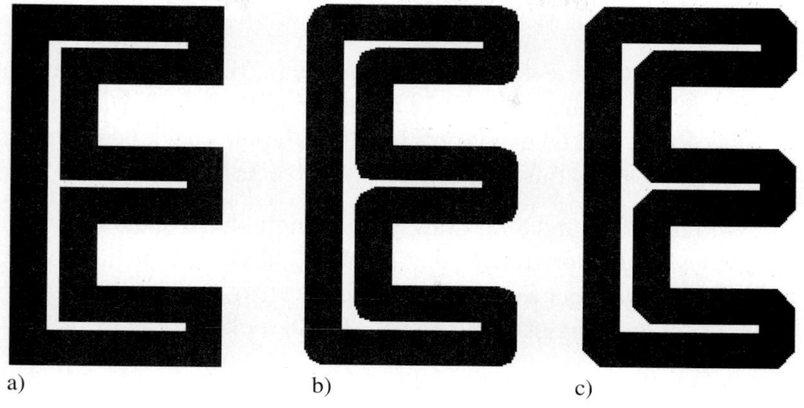

The letter "E" with (a) miter or sharp, (b) rounded, and (c) beveled corners

FIGURE 6-8

with the different types of nodes is covered in Chapter 9.) In the next section, you will explore when and how changes to the line end styles can alter an object's appearance.

Selecting Line End Caps

Line end options (*end caps*) apply only to straight lines and open-ended curves. It is difficult to see the difference between line end types unless you create very thick lines or magnify the line a lot—you'll do both here.

1. Switch to Zoom To Page view, then from the View menu, select Rulers. If the rulers zero point is not set to the upper-left corner of the page, drag the zero point from the point where the rulers meet to the upper-left corner of the page. From the Layout menu, select Snap To Guidelines if not already selected.
2. Drag vertical guidelines from the vertical ruler to 2 and 4 inches on the horizontal ruler.
3. Drag horizontal guidelines from the horizontal ruler to –2 1/2, –3, and –3 1/2 inches on the vertical ruler.

4. Zoom-in on the area from 1 inch on the horizontal ruler and 2 inches on the vertical ruler to 5 inches on the horizontal ruler and 4 inches on the vertical ruler.
5. Select the Outline Tool and click on the far right line width on the bottom row of the flyout, which is 24 points or .333 inch. The Outline Pen default dialog box will be displayed with the Graphic check box selected. Click on OK to apply this width to graphic objects.
6. With the Freehand tool, draw three straight, horizontal lines from 2 to 4 inches on the horizontal ruler at 2 1/2, 3, and 3 1/2 inches on the vertical ruler. (Remember that you can hold the CTRL key to constrain your lines to 15-degree angles.)Your screen should look like Figure 6-9.

The default line end cap, the *butt* end, is shown in Figure 6-9. The lines end exactly at the termination of the line and are squared off.

7. With the Pick tool, select the middle line, open the Outline Pen dialog box, select the middle or rounded line cap, and click on OK. The line endings on the middle line are now rounded and project beyond the termination of the line, as shown here:

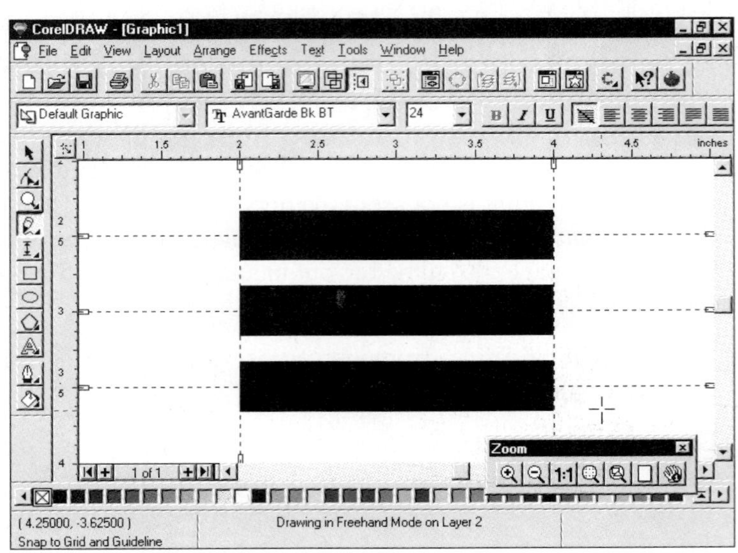

Lines ready for testing line end caps

FIGURE 6-9

8. Select the bottom horizontal line, open the Outline Pen dialog box, select the bottom or square line cap, and click on OK. The line endings on the bottom line are now square and project beyond the termination of the line by one-half of the line width. The three line end caps are shown here:

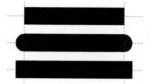

9. Clear the screen by selecting Select All from the Edit menu and pressing DEL. Remove the guidelines by dragging them onto the rulers or scrollbars.

If an image contains many open-ended curves, selecting rounded line end caps can soften the image, even if the lines are thin. Conversely, you can select butt or square line end styles to give an object a more rough-hewn, sharp appearance.

Using Different Line Styles

So far in this book, all the lines you have drawn, including the lines in the characters you have typed, have been solid lines. Coreldraw provides a list box full of line styles.

In the following exercise, you'll try out various line styles, look at them in various widths, and apply the different line end caps to them.

1. Open the Outline Pen default settings dialog box, and select both the Graphic and Artistic Text check boxes. Then, click on OK to apply a new default line width to these two types of objects.

2. When the Outline Pen dialog box opens, change the line width to 4 points and click on OK.

You are starting with a thicker line because a hairline (1/4 point) is too small for demonstrating the different types of lines. The dots in a dotted line are the same

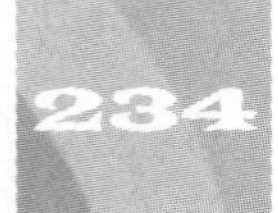

height as the line is wide. Therefore, a dotted hairline has dots that are .003-inch high—three thousandths of an inch! These will print on most laser and PostScript printers, but many other printers cannot print them, and the screen does not display them correctly without magnification.

3. Select Actual Size magnification (1:1) and, with the Freehand tool, draw four straight horizontal lines, each about 3 1/2 inches long, leaving 1/2 inch of vertical space between each line.
4. Click on the Text tool, click below the lines you just drew and type **Corel**, select it with the Pick tool, and use the Text toolbar to select Bauhaus Hv BT and 60 points.
5. While the text is still selected, click on the X at the left end of the onscreen palette to turn off the fill. Your screen should look like Figure 6-10.

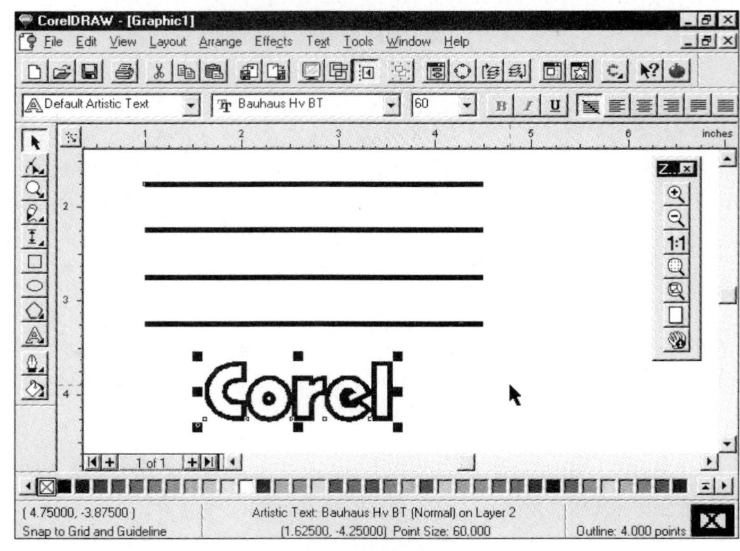

Lines and text prepared for testing line styles

FIGURE 6-10

6. With the Pick tool, click on the second horizontal line, open the Outline Pen dialog box, and click on the Style arrow. A dashed and dotted line styles list box will open, as shown here:

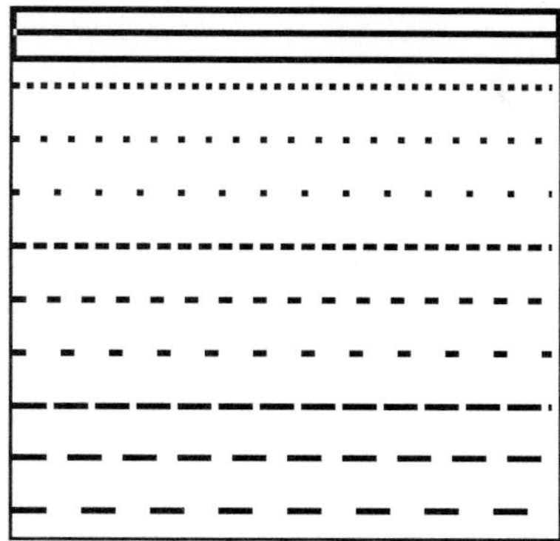

7. Select the second line type from the top. The list box closes, and a normal dotted line appears in the dialog box's line styles box. Click on OK.
8. Select the third horizontal line and then, from the same Outline Pen dialog box, click on the Styles list box, select a dashed line from further down the list. Click on OK.
9. Select the fourth horizontal line and, from the line styles list box, select the dash-dot line (use the scroll bars to find it). Again, click on OK.
10. Select the text and, from the line styles list box, select the first dotted line and click on OK. Your screen should now look like Figure 6-11.

Next, you can look at how dotted and dashed lines look at various line widths and with various line end caps. Try different combinations by repeating the steps above with different property settings.

11. When you are ready to proceed, double-click on the Pick tool and press DEL to clear the work area.

There is much variety in the styles, widths, and ends you can use with lines. In the next section, you will see how to further enhance a line with many different arrowheads and tail feathers.

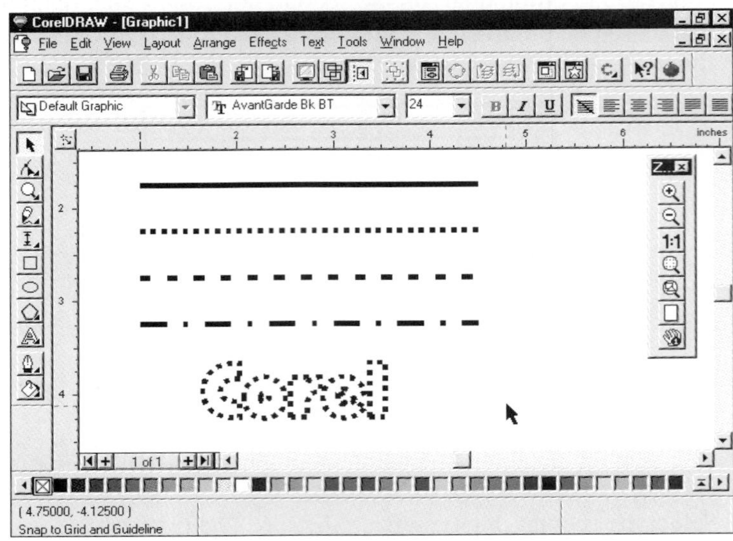

Using various line styles with 4-point lines

FIGURE 6-11

Adding and Editing Arrowheads

In the earlier section, "Selecting Line End Caps," you saw one technique for ending lines. There are, additionally, a number of arrowhead and tail feather options that you can place on the end of a line. You can also customize an existing arrowhead with the Arrowhead Editor, and add new arrowheads to the arrowhead display boxes. In the next two exercises, you will add some arrowheads and tail feathers and customize them using the Outline Pen dialog box, Pen roll-up, and Arrowhead Editor. You should still be in Actual Size view from the last exercise.

1. Select the Outline Tool, click on the 2-point button (third from the left on the flyout). Click on Artistic Text, and Paragraph Text (keep Graphic checked) in the Outline Pen default settings dialog box, and then OK to apply this to all new objects.
2. With the Freehand tool, draw three horizontal lines about 3 inches long and one inch apart on the vertical ruler. Be sure to draw the lines from left to right so the left end is the beginning of the line. Use the scroll bars to center the three lines on your screen.

3. With the Shape tool (the second tool from the top of the toolbox), click on the first line and notice that the left end of the line has the larger node, as shown here:

The larger node marks the beginning of the line, the default position for the feathers, while the smaller node marks the end of the line, where the arrowhead will be placed.

4. Change to the Pick tool. The first line should automatically be selected.
5. From the Outline Pen dialog box, click on the Arrows line-ending (right) display box. An arrowhead selection display box will open.

To put an arrowhead on the right end of this line,

1. Click on the second arrowhead from the right on the top row.
2. To add some tail feathers on the left end of the line, click on the Arrows line-beginning (left) display box, scroll the set of arrowhead display boxes by pressing the down scroll arrow three times, and then click on the last set of tail feathers on the right end of the bottom row, as shown here:

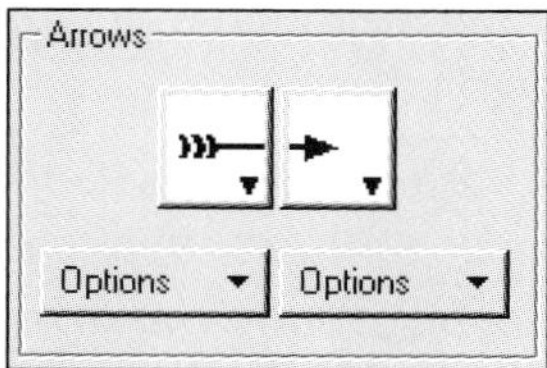

3. Click on OK to return to your drawing, and click on a blank area of the screen. Your arrow should look like this:

4. Use the Pen roll-up to place line endings of your choice on the second and third lines. Click on the next line and then open the Pen roll-up from the Pen Roll-Up button on the Outline Tool flyout if it's not already on your screen. The second field down (after the roll-up type selection box) contains line-beginning (left) and line-ending (right) display boxes identical to those

in the Outline Pen dialog box. Click on a box and make your selection, repeat this for the other end, and then click on Apply. (Note that the last line style used in the Pen roll-up will be the one now used. For example, if you last selected a dotted line from the Pen roll-up, your lines will become dotted when you click on Apply.) One possible set of choices is shown here:

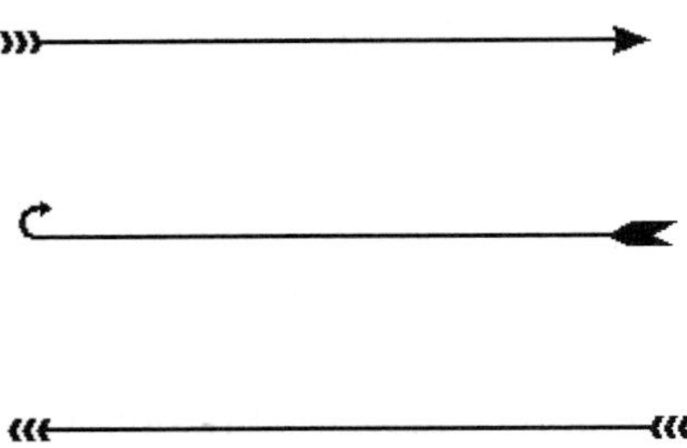

5. With the Pick tool, draw a marquee around the three lines and set the line width to 8 points (you can use the sixth button from the left on the Outline Tool flyout). Notice how the size of the line endings changes with the size of the line.
6. Select Select All from the Edit menu and press DEL to clear the work area.

Next, use the Arrowhead Editor to modify an existing arrowhead.

CAUTION: *If you close the Arrowhead Editor after modifying an arrowhead, you will have permanently modified the arrowhead you were working on. You can again modify the arrowhead to try to re-create the original, but you may not get it exactly the way it was.*

TIP: *To prevent permanently modifying your arrowhead file, backup the CORELDRW.END file by making a copy of it. Open Windows Explorer from the Start menu on the Taskbar, then select the drive and directory where you have installed CorelDRAW! (C:\COREL\ is the default) and open the CUSTOM subdirectory. Select the CORELDRW.END file and select Copy from the Edit menu, then select Paste. A copy of the file named Copy of CORELDRW.END will be added to the directory. To restore the original file, delete the CORELDRW.END file you have changed, and then rename the copy of the file to CORELDRW.END. Then you can modify arrowheads as you wish and, when you are done, restore the original arrowheads.*

1. At actual-size magnification, draw a horizontal line in the middle of the page.
2. Using the Pen roll-up, click on Edit to open the Outline Pen dialog box.
3. Select the Arrows line-ending (right) box and click on the second arrowhead from the right on the top row. Click on the right Options button and choose the Edit option.
4. By clicking and dragging on the eight boundary markers, you can modify the arrowhead, stretch out both the left and right ends, and reduce the height. In the latter operation, it is likely that the arrowhead will get off center vertically. Use the Center in Y command button to correct this. Try Reflect in X to see the effect of this, and use it to return the arrowhead to its original orientation. When you are done, your dialog box should look like this:

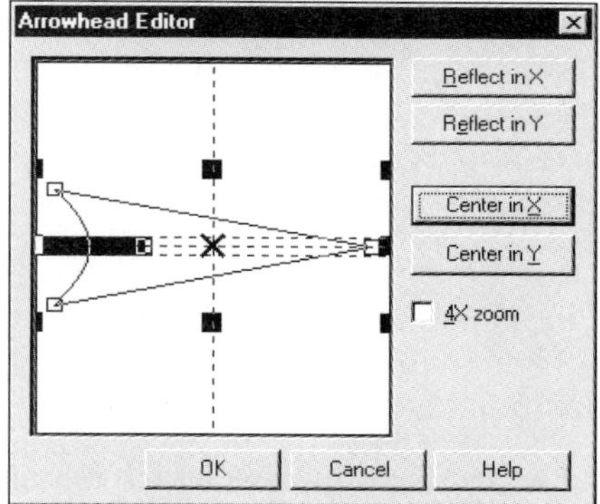

6

CAUTION: *If you click on OK and close the Arrowhead Editor, you will permanently modify this arrowhead in the Arrows display box. You can come back and move everything back to its original position (see the illustration in the "Arrows" section in the early part of this chapter to see how this should look) or follow the procedures in the previous tip. However, unless you want to do that, choose Cancel to exit the Arrowhead Editor.*

Select Select All from the Edit menu and press DEL to clear the work area.

The Arrowhead Editor is used to stretch, scale, and position an existing arrowhead in relation to the line it will be applied to. If you want to create a new arrowhead, do so in Coreldraw as you would any other object (if you build an arrowhead with multiple objects, select them all and use Combine from the Arrange menu to make one object out of them). Then, use the Create Arrow command in the Tools menu to save the new arrowhead at the end of the list of arrowheads. It does not matter if you have the relative size of the new arrowhead correct because you can modify this with the Arrowhead Editor.

In the next section, you will begin working with the pen shapes—Width, Angle, and Stretch—that make calligraphic effects possible in Coreldraw.

A Pen Shape for Calligraphic Effects

The Stretch and Angle settings in the Outline Pen dialog box are in a separate enclosed area subtitled "Calligraphy." The Calligraphy option allows you to create variable calligraphic nibs that can be highly effective with freehand drawings and text. If you adjust both the Stretch and Angle settings in various combinations, you can approximate a freehand style of drawing.

In the following exercise, you will experiment with the Nib Shape settings, using some curves you will draw, to achieve both hand-sketched and comic strip-style looks. You will create three copies of certain drawings and then modify each with different settings.

1. At Actual Size magnification, and with the rulers turned off, set your pen width to 8 points in the Outline Pen dialog box. Draw an approximation of the objects shown here:
2. With the Pick tool, select the drawings with a marquee box. After selecting all the objects, group them using the Group command in the Arrange menu. Turn off their fill by clicking on the X at the left end of the onscreen palette.
3. From the Edit menu, select Duplicate. Drag the highlighted copy to one side of the original. Repeat the Duplicate operation by pressing CTRL-D. Your screen will look something like Figure 6-12. (You may have to decrease your magnification.)
4. Save this image by opening the File menu and selecting Save As. Name the file Curves.
5. Select the first group of drawings by clicking on it with the Pick tool, then open the Outline Pen dialog box. The current Calligraphy settings for this are 100 percent Stretch and 0.0 degrees Angle.

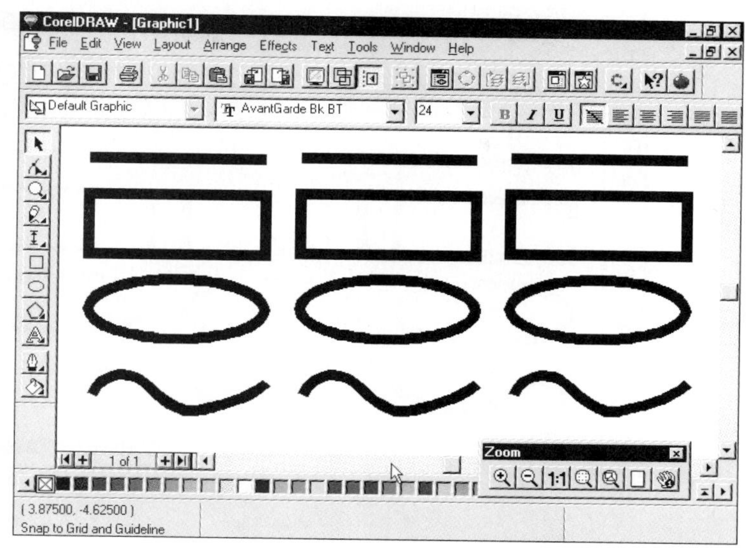

Drawings that will be modified to demonstrate calligraphic effects

FIGURE 6-12

6. Change the Stretch to 80 percent and the Angle to 10 degrees. This setting translates into a thicker outline and not much slant, with the pen "held" at a 10-degree angle. Click on OK. The effects are shown in outline (a) of Figure 6-13. Its look is not much different.
7. To vary line thickness, open the Outline Pen dialog box and experiment with the Stretch of the nib, expressed as a percentage of the nib width. Keep decreasing the Stretch value all the way to 2 percent, and then select OK. The vertical lines show the changes most clearly.

IP: *It is easier to use the numeric entry boxes to achieve exact Angle and Stretch settings. Interactively using the mouse pointer in the Nib Shape display box is better suited to nibs that can be approximately sized by eye.*

As the value in the Stretch numeric entry box decreases, you effectively flatten the nib in one direction; the black symbol representing a pen nib is broad in one dimension and extremely narrow in the other, which makes more extreme calligraphic effects possible. If you were to increase the Stretch value all the way to

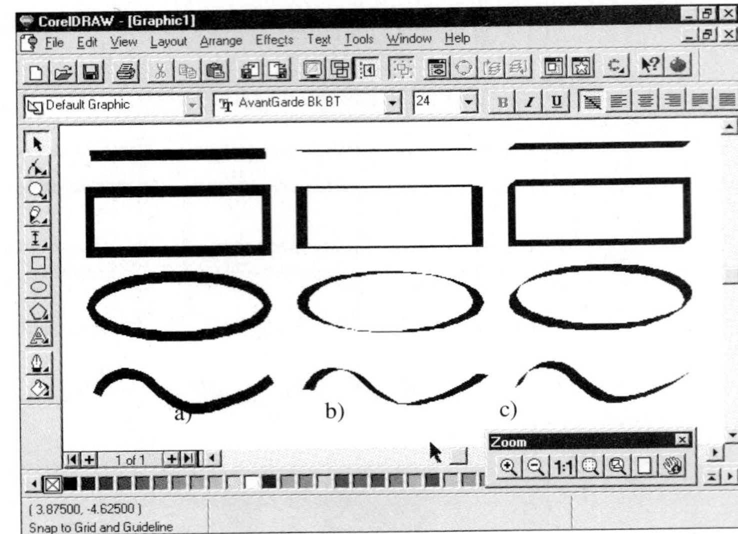

Outline (a) shows an Angle of 10 degrees, and Stretch of 80%; (b) an Angle of 80 degrees and Stretch of 10%; (c) an Angle of 130 degrees and Stretch of 10%

FIGURE 6-13

100 percent, the curves of the image would have the same thickness everywhere, and no calligraphic effects could result.

TIP: *The Stretch settings represent the relative squareness or roundness of the nib, with 100 percent representing a square nib and 1 percent representing a long and narrow nib. As the Stretch percentage value decreases, the variation in line thickness of a drawn object increases.*

8. Select the second group. Open the Outline Pen dialog box once more. Reverse the settings this time; set the Stretch to 10 percent, and adjust the Angle of the nib to 80 degrees. You will recall that the Angle setting is analogous to the way you hold a calligraphic pen in your hand (at a 0-degree setting, the Nib Shape display box alters to show you a perfectly vertical nib). Here the angle is quite pronounced.
9. Select OK to exit the dialog box. Now the areas that display the thickest and thinnest lines have shifted (by 70 degrees), as shown in outline (b) of Figure 6-13. Adjusting the Angle value is therefore a convenient way to control where thick and thin lines appear on any selected object.

10. Select the third group. Access the Outline Pen dialog box again and set Stretch to 10 and Angle to 130, and then select OK. The curves are redrawn with the thickness of the outline somewhat reversed from the previous setting. It is much like a cartoon drawing. See outline (c) of Figure 6-13.

IP: *In the Outline Pen dialog box, click on the Default button for Calligraphy. This resets the Stretch and Angle settings to the default values of 100 percent and 0 degrees, respectively—a square nib with no variations in thickness.*

Experiment with Stretch and Angle settings at different outline widths, too. To obtain greater variation in line thickness, set Stretch at a reduced value, such as 4 percent. To change the placement of the thinner segments of the curve, try different Angle settings.

11. Select Select All from the Edit menu and press DEL to clear the screen.

The possibilities for creating custom calligraphic nibs should spark your imagination. An interesting use for an image sketched faintly at 0.01-inch width might be as a background illustration in a newsletter, where the text overprints the image without obscuring it totally. You have probably seen applications like this involving outlines of scanned photographs. Chapter 17 will give you more information on how to outline bitmap and scanned images.

IP: *Avoid using 0.00-inch widths unless your draft printer is also the printer you will be using for your final output. As an outline Width setting, 0.00 inch represents the thinnest line your printer is capable of printing. For PostScript printers, this is 1 pixel or 0.03 inch, but for a Linotronic or other high-resolution imagesetter, 0.00 inch could represent something even thinner. Because of the variations among printers, this setting does not truly represent a fixed width, and the screen does not display a WYSIWYG representation of it.*

Angle settings are especially useful to help you fine-tune the exact location of thick and thin lines within a drawing. With precise, degree-by-degree control available, you can make sure that thinner areas of a selected curve are positioned exactly where you want them.

Outline Pen Hints

The range of choices available to you makes the Outline Tool one of the richer areas of Coreldraw. The following sections contain selected hints for making the most of your choices and coordinating your settings with the type of work you are doing.

Defining an Outline Pen for Text

Do you want text in your drawings to appear normally? Or are you aiming for exaggerated or stylized effects? For a clean-cut look, it's best to create text without an outline, using the X in the Outline Tool flyout menu. When text has a visible outline, some characters appear to be drawn thicker, with the result that spaces within letters (such as in a lowercase "a" or "e") are partially or wholly filled in. This is especially true when you create text in small point sizes.

If your design calls for outlined text, a good way to maintain readability in smaller point sizes is to activate the Behind Fill option in the Outline Pen dialog box. As mentioned earlier, Behind Fill causes the outline to appear half as thick as it really is, because the other half of the outline is hidden behind the object's fill.

In some cases, you may really prefer a slightly smudgy graphic look of text with thick outlines. Let the purpose and design of your illustration be your guide in choosing how to outline text.

Varying Your Calligraphic Style

Unless you have a background in calligraphy, the wealth of Width, Angle, Stretch, and Corners settings available to you in the Outline Pen dialog box can be confusing. The following hints should help put you on the right track if you know the effect you would like to achieve.

Desktop publishers can create faint background illustrations from original artwork or scanned photos and then overprint them with text. The result is a visible but not distracting piece of artwork that enhances the mood of an article or feature. Recommended settings for this kind of graphics effect are Width, 0.03 inch or less; Stretch, 14 percent or less; and a variable Angle according to your tastes. Keep in mind that if you reduce the outline Width setting below 0.02 inch (or 1.2 points), you will not be able to see an accurate representation of the calligraphy on your screen. The outline will still print according to your specifications, however.

Illustrators, cartoonists, and other artists seeking a traditional hand-sketched look should set Calligraphy options to achieve the desired variation in line thickness. For finer lines, Outline Pen width should be fairly thin, below 0.05 inch; and for blunter strokes, above 0.06 inch. Stretch should be set to 1 to 2 percent for the maximum variation in line thickness, and closer to 100 percent for minimal variation. The fine-tuning possible with Angle settings permits you to place thicker or thinner lines at exact locations.

For those who are interested in extremely broad calligraphic strokes, consider setting Stretch below 100 percent, removing the fill of an object, and then varying the Angle settings. The example text that follows has a three-dimensional look because it was created at a Width of 0.04 inch, at an Angle of 75 degrees, and with a Stretch of 10 percent:

TIP: *When the Angle field is 0.0, the pen is vertical. When the Angle is increased, the slant of the pen increases. When the Stretch is 100 percent (the maximum value allowed), the nib shape is a square. When the Stretch is reduced, the nib becomes thinner.*

Copying Outline Styles

You can imagine how useful the Copy Properties From command from the Edit menu can be when you need to copy Outline Pen styles to, or from, even larger blocks of text or groups of objects.

Follow these steps to use the Copy Properties From command.

1. Have both objects on the screen—those containing the properties to be copied and those to be copied to.
2. Click with the Pick tool on the object to be copied to.
3. Select Copy Properties From on the Edit menu. The Copy Properties dialog box is displayed:

4. Place a check mark beside the Outline Pen option. Click on OK. The pointer turns into an arrow.
5. Move the arrow to the object to copy from and click the pointer. Properties will be copied to the first selected object from the second.

In the next chapter, you will learn how to work with the colors and textures for the Outline Pen and for fills that can be applied to closed curves, text, and other objects.

Enviro—Chris Purcell

The Outline Pen and its many options played an important part in creating Chris Purcell's *Enviro*. Chris used his award-winning skills to combine a hard-edged electronic circuit board with an iridescent organic leaf.

Chris Purcell lives and works in Houston, TX, and is the winner of several awards in the Corel's World Design Contest. He can be reached at (713) 374-4679.

Defining Outline and Fill Color

To define an object's outline completely in Coreldraw, you must define both the Outline Pen shape and the Outline Color properties. You learned how to select properties for the Outline Pen in Chapter 6; in this chapter, you will become familiar with the tools and techniques used to define Outline and Fill Color. As you know, the Outline Pen allows you to draw with the characteristic style of a calligraphic pen, using "nibs" of various sizes. Outline Color represents the colors and textures that flow from the pen.

This chapter also introduces you to the Coreldraw Fill tool. The Fill tool, as its icon suggests, functions like a paint bucket with a limitless supply of paint, capable of filling the interior of any *closed* object. A closed object is any object that is a closed path; such objects include everything you create with the Rectangle and Ellipse tools as well as objects created with multiple straight and curved lines in which you made sure to close each intersection. If you draw a curve object in which the two end nodes do not join, the object remains an open path, and you cannot fill it. When you select such an object, the words "Open Path" appear on the Status bar. (You can close an open path by joining its end nodes with the Shape tool, as you will learn in Chapter 9.)

The Basics of Color

Coreldraw offers several methods for defining colors; the best method for you to use will depend on the ultimate use of your work. Coreldraw graphics can be printed on paper, using traditional printing methods; output to a film recorder to create photographic slides or negatives; printed on a desktop color printer, either to paper or overhead transparencies; output to video tape for a multimedia production; or your work may only be viewed on a monitor, for example, as a graphic on the World Wide Web (a graphical user interface to the Internet).

Each of these types of output has its own requirements that effect your choice of color model. To understand the differences between these systems, and how they relate to the colors you see on your monitor, you have to understand a little bit about color theory.

Additive and Subtractive Primary Colors

All the colors of the rainbow, and all their shades and tones, can be created using just three *primary* colors: red, green, and blue (RGB). These are the *additive* primary colors, because new colors are created by adding the primary colors together. For example, to create yellow, red and green are combined. The exact shade of yellow will be determined by the ratio of red to green. This is how colors are displayed on your computer monitor or television screen. If you look closely at either (a 30x magnifier helps), you can see that each color is made from red, green, and blue elements. (This is easier to see on a television because of the lower resolution.)

Colors can also be defined using the *subtractive primary* colors: cyan, magenta, and yellow. The subtractive primary colors are created by combining the additive primary colors. Yellow is the combination of red and green, magenta is the combination of red and blue, and cyan is the combination of blue and green. The main use of the subtractive primary colors is for process color (CMYK) printing (also called four-color printing).

Spot and Process Color Printing

For many Coreldraw users, their work is commercially printed using either *spot* or *process* colors. With spot colors, each color is produced using a separate ink. With process colors, each color is produced using a combination of four inks: cyan, magenta, yellow, and black.

When your output requirements include printing on paper or other surfaces, you have to determine whether to use spot or process colors in your design. Spot colors are usually used when a design has fewer than four colors in it, or when colors that cannot be reproduced with process color inks (such as metallic or iridescent colors) are desired. Process colors are used when a wide range of colors are desired, for example, when an image includes a scanned photograph. Commercial printers can use both spot and process colors in the same design during printing.

Spot and Process Color Inks

Spot color inks are opaque, so that the color you see is reflected off of the surface of the ink. This allows for very bright colors, as well as metallic and iridescent colors. Process color inks, on the other hand, are transparent, so the color you see is the light reflected off of the surface of the paper (or other medium) the inks have been applied to.

While a separate spot color ink exists for each spot color, there are only four process color inks: cyan, magenta, yellow, and black. (In theory, cyan, magenta, and yellow combine to make black. In reality, they produce a muddy brown, so black is needed to get true blacks and grays in process color printing.) Every other process color is created by combining various amounts of these four inks.

Since spot color inks reflect light from their surface, to produce a blue object on a page you would use a blue ink. The same is not true for process color inks—they work by absorbing parts of the color spectrum. As light passes through a process color ink, color is subtracted from it. For example, if you wanted an object to appear blue, you would apply cyan and magenta process color inks to the page. These would absorb (subtract) the red and green components of the light, leaving just the blue to be reflected. Both the Outline and Fill tools offer you a choice between spot color and process color.

Each color applied during printing requires a separate step during the printing process. Process color printing requires a minimum of four steps. Spot color printing requires as many steps as there are colors. More steps during printing increase the cost of the job, and increase the likelihood of registration errors (where the inks are not applied in exactly the right place because of paper shift). While process color printing is generally recommended when four or more colors are used (and spot color printing when fewer colors are needed), for special effects or precise color match, you may use more than four spot colors or combine spot colors with process colors.

Spot and Process Color Libraries

Accurately representing spot and process colors on a computer monitor is extremely difficult. There are several reasons for this; first, all colors on monitors are created using the additive primary colors—red, green, and blue. Because of the realities of applying ink to paper, not all process colors can be represented accurately this way. Each type of color reproduction model has its own *color space* or *gamut*. This is the range of colors that can be reproduced with that color model. While the color spaces of the different color models have areas of overlap with each other, they also have colors that cannot be reproduced using another color model.

Another problem is that monitors are affected by a number of factors, including the light in the room, the age of the monitor, and how the monitor is adjusted. (Appendix A explains how to adjust your monitor to give you the best representation of colors using Coreldraw's Color Manager.) To help you control the color in your final output, Coreldraw includes seven standard color-matching systems used in the printing industry, only one of which is spot color (although FOCOLTONE can simulate spot color):

FOCOLTONE Colors
PANTONE Spot Colors
PANTONE Process Colors
TRUMATCH Colors
SpectraMaster Colors
TOYO colors
DIC Colors

These color matching systems, or *palettes*, allow you to specify a color based on its actual printed appearance. Each library has a *swatch book* available, which contains the colors in the library printed on coated and uncoated paper. (The swatch books are available from the manufacturer, they are not included with Coreldraw.)

In addition to the four Color palettes, Coreldraw has nine other systems, or *models*, for specifying color:

CMY (Cyan, Magenta, and Yellow) color model
CMYK (Cyan, Magenta, Yellow, Black) color model
CMYK255 (Cyan, Magenta, Yellow, Black) color model
RGB (Red, Green, Blue) color model
HSB (Hue, Saturation, Brightness) color model
HLS (Hue, Lightness, Saturation) color model
L*a*b (Luminance and Chroma) color model
YIQ (Luminance and Chroma) color model
Grayscale

Selecting a Color Model

If accurate color is important in your finished design, you must select the appropriate color model, determined by the type of output needed, when you begin the project.

While you can use any of these systems for specifying a color, the results might not be what you expect. This is because of your monitor's ability to accurately reproduce colors, and color shifts that occur when a color is translated from one color model to another. If you specified all your colors using the RGB model, then printed your document using process (CMYK) colors, each RGB color would have to be translated to the closest CMYK color. It is very likely that some of your RGB colors would be impossible to translate because they are outside the CMYK color space, and that unwanted color shifts would also be introduced. On the other hand, if you are preparing a graphic for film output and used the CMYK color model you would have the same problem in reverse. This is because film recorders use the RGB color model, so all your CMYK colors would have to be translated to RGB, with the same translation problems.

CMY The CMY model uses the subtractive primaries cyan, magenta, and yellow. Colors are represented as a value between 0 and 255. Since black is not included with this color model, it is not the best choice for creating work to be printed with process colors.

CMYK AND CMYK255 Both of these systems create colors using cyan, magenta, yellow, and black. The CMYK model represents colors as a percentage (maximum yellow, for example, is 100), while CMYK255 represents each color as a value between 0 and 255 (maximum yellow would be 255). You should use either of these models when your work will printed using process colors.

RGB The red, green, blue model (the primary colors) is a good choice when your work will be displayed on a monitor, or output to a film recorder or video tape (as part of a multimedia presentation, for example). This is because these devices use the RGB color model.

HSB Hue, saturation, and brightness offer a more intuitive way of selecting colors than the RGB model. Hue is the basic color represented as part of a circle and identified by its position in the circle. Red is 0 or 360 degrees, yellow is 60 degrees, green is 120 degrees, cyan is 180 degrees, blue is 240 degrees, and magenta is 300 degrees.

Saturation is the amount of gray in the color. Decreasing saturation moves the color towards white and increasing it moves the color towards black. Brightness controls the intensity of the color—decreasing brightness moves the color towards black, while increasing it moves the color towards the pure hue.

You may find the HSB model the most comfortable to work with, and it can be used as an alternative to the RGB model.

HLS Hue, lightness, and saturation is similar to the HSB model. Again, the hue is represented by a circle, with each color represented by its position. Unlike HSB, the saturation of the color is measured from the center of the hue circle. As the saturation value is increased (that is, moved away from the center of the circle), the color moves towards its pure tone. As it is decreased, the color moves towards black. The lightness value determines the range of color values. A low value moves the color towards black, while a high value (255 is the maximum) moves the color towards white. A middle value (127, for example) gives you the widest range of available colors.

L*A*B* L*a*b* is an industry standard developed by the Commission Internationale de l'Eclairage, which was formed in the early 1900s to develop a standard for measuring color based upon how we perceive color. The L*a*b* model includes the color spaces of both the RGB and CMYK color models.

The lightness value determines the brightness of the color, while the a value describes the color along an axis that ranges from green to red, and the b axis ranges from blue to yellow. The lightness value can range from 0 to 100, while the a and b values range from –60 to 60.

YIQ YIQ is the color model used for television broadcasts (the North American video standard—NTSC). Y is the luminance value, and I and Q are the chromacity values. On a color television or monitor all three values are displayed; on a black and white TV or monitor only the Y value is displayed.

IP: *When you want to create a grayscale image, using only the Y component of the YIQ model will often produce better results than using the Convert To command from the Image menu in CorelPHOTO-PAINT.*

As you see, you have many ways to define a color in Coreldraw. If your output will be commercially printed using spot or process colors, you should use one of the color libraries to define your colors, relying on printed color samples to judge the final appearance. Custom process colors can be created using either the CMYK or CMYK255 color models.

If your output will be displayed electronically, or output to film, you can use either RGB or one of the similar models to define colors. Remember, though, to not trust your monitor unless you have calibrated it to your chosen output device. (Appendix A explains how to use Corel's Color Manager to calibrate for a system.)

Outline and Fill Textures

Your options for assigning outline and fill colors do not end with the choice of a variety of colors. Unlike a handheld pen, the Coreldraw pen not only dispenses "ink" in all colors of the rainbow, it can lay down an assortment of textures and halftone screens for PostScript printing. In addition, the Fill tool can dispense other types of fills that the Outline Color tool does not provide: fountain fills in any combination of colors, two-color and full-color pattern fills from the Coreldraw library, texture fills, and 52 different grayscale PostScript texture fills. You will learn more about these types of fills in "Custom Fountain Fills," "Bitmap and Vector Fill Patterns," and "PostScript Texture Fills" later in this chapter.

The exercises in this chapter give you practice in specifying color, gray shades, and PostScript halftone screen patterns for your object outlines and fills. The exercises also give you practice using fountain fills, bitmap fills, vector pattern fills, and PostScript texture fills for objects. The Coreldraw document window faithfully reproduces your settings unless you have chosen a PostScript halftone screen or texture fill. In CorelDRAW! 6, both PostScript and texture fills can be viewed in a preview display box, but not in the document window. To see the full effect of the PostScript or texture fills, you must print out your work on a PostScript printer. See Chapter 12 for assistance with printing.

Defining an Object's Outline Color Attributes

You define outline colors in Coreldraw using the Outline Color dialog box, shown in Figure 7-1, which you access from the Outline Pen flyout. This dialog box allows you to choose a color *model* as well as a color, and to select from among several options for other color attributes. The options available in the Outline Color dialog box are determined by whether a color model, palette, or mixer is selected, and the model selected in the Model drop-down list box. You will be using the Outline Color dialog box throughout this chapter; its features will be covered in detail as they are used.

IP: *If your Outline Color dialog box does not look like Figure 7-1, it has been previously used and left in another mode. You will see how to change this in a moment.*

Your first step in defining Outline Color properties is to determine whether you want to define the properties for existing objects or the default settings for new objects. (An existing object can be one that you have just drawn or one that you have saved previously.) When defining Outline Color properties for an existing object, you are in effect editing its current properties. The changes you make apply to that object only, not to additional objects you may create later.

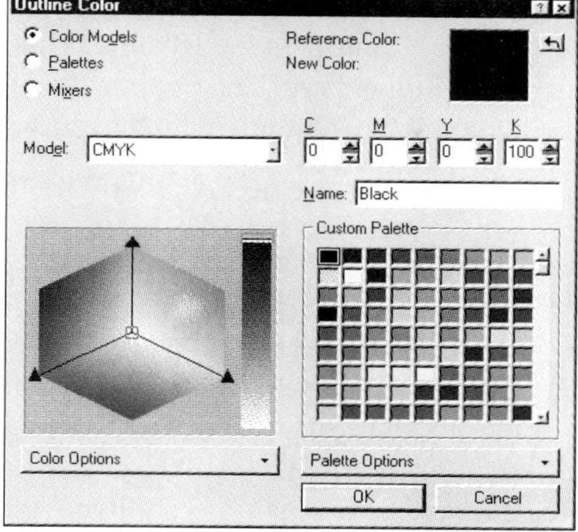

Outline Color dialog box

FIGURE 7-1

On the other hand, when you change an attribute without first selecting an object, Coreldraw assumes that you want to change the default properties for objects that you draw in the future. The object or series of objects that you draw next will automatically incorporate the newly defined default Outline Color properties.

IP: *Always work in full color mode when you alter Outline Color properties. Wireframe mode does not show you how the selected outline color looks. For most properties, full color mode lets you see the result of your changes instantly.*

Setting New Outline Spot Color Defaults

In the following exercise, you will define the default Outline Color properties using the Outline Color dialog box and then create objects with those defaults. To prepare for the exercise, you should be in Portrait page orientation, Wireframe should be turned off, and the grid should not be displayed. Select Actual Size (1:1) view from the Zoom toolbar. (Open the Tools menu and select Toolbars, then Zoom; when the Zoom toolbar is displayed, click on the 1:1 button.)

1. If necessary, clear the screen by deleting all objects and then click on the Outline Pen tool. When the Outline Pen flyout appears, select the Outline Color button, the first button on the left in the first row. It looks like a color wheel and is shown here. The Outline Color default dialog box appears, asking you which default settings you want to change.
2. Verify that Graphic is selected and click on OK. The Outline Color dialog box is displayed.
3. Click on the Palettes option button, then select spot color by clicking on the down arrow on the Type drop-down list box and selecting PANTONE Spot Colors. The Outline Color dialog box should now look like Figure 7-2. (Yours may not show the same color selected.)

There are some differences between the Outline Color dialog box with a spot color method selected (as shown in Figure 7-2) and the same dialog box with a process color method selected (as shown in Figure 7-1). These differences are largely a function of the color model and will be covered later in this chapter. Only the spot color dialog box allows you to adjust the percentage of tint and to select a PostScript halftone and its properties (see "Outlining with PostScript Halftone Screen Patterns"

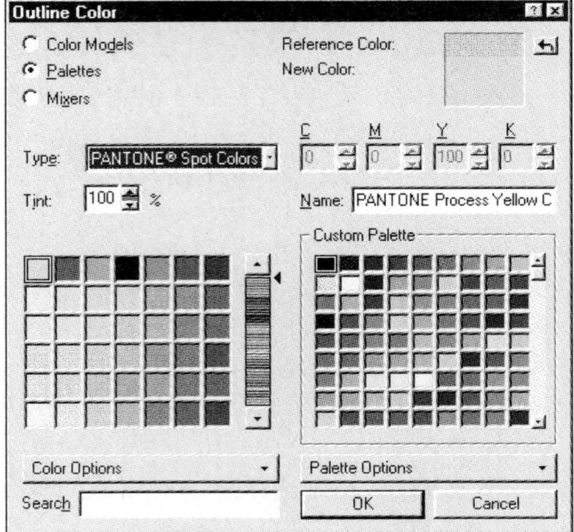

Outline Color dialog box for PANTONE Spot Colors

FIGURE 7-2

later in this chapter). All versions of the Outline Color dialog box have a Palette Options button located below the Custom Palette display box that opens the menu shown here:

Rename Color...
Delete Color...
New Palette
Open Palette...
Save Palette
Save As...

The Palette menu allows you to add colors to or delete colors from the current palette, and to load a custom palette from your hard disk or save it to disk.

The colors you select using spot colors are from the PANTONE Color Matching System. Since the colors that appear in the color display box are only approximations, you should use the PANTONE Color Reference Manual to evaluate your choice of colors before printing. In addition, you can specify a percentage of the tint of any spot colors you select. The effect of settings below 100 percent is to render a lighter shade of the selected color on your monitor or color printout.

Continue setting the Outline Color defaults with these steps.

4. Click on the middle color in the top row of the Color palette. The selected color, PANTONE Process Black CV, appears in a color display box in the upper-right corner of the dialog box. The % Tint spinner shows a value of 100 (the default value). The PANTONE identification name for this color displays in the Name text box. Click on OK to set the default Outline Color properties and exit the Outline Color dialog box. New objects that you create will now have the default outline color. Now create a new object with the defaults.

5. From the Outline Pen flyout, select the 2-point width (bottom row, third from the right), click on OK to have it apply to graphic objects, then, with the Freehand tool, draw several curves, as shown in Figure 7-3. (If your closed loop at the bottom is filled with black, open the Fill tool and click on the X button to turn off the fill.)

The curves are created with the default outline color and 2-point line width. In the next section, you will learn how to change the outline color for existing objects.

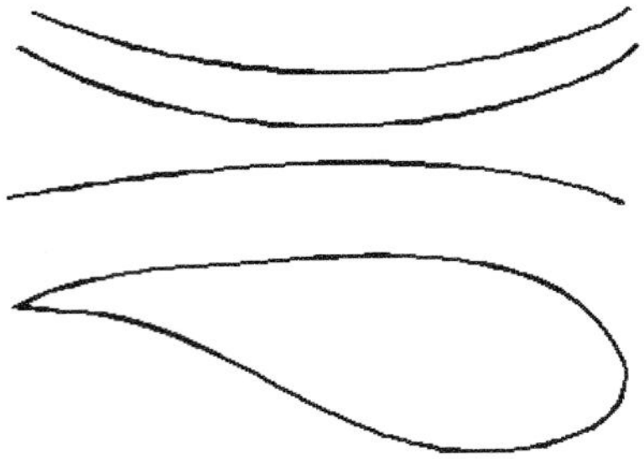

Curved shapes in PANTONE Process Black CV

FIGURE 7-3

Changing Spot Color Outlines

In the following exercise, you will assign spot colors and shades of gray to the outline of your existing Coreldraw objects (created in the previous exercise).

1. With the Pick tool, drag a marquee around all of the objects you created in the previous exercise to select them, then choose Group from the Arrange menu. By grouping the objects, any changes you make will be applied to all the objects in the group.
2. To begin editing the existing Outline Color properties, click on the Outline Pen and the Custom Outline Color button. The Outline Color dialog box appears.

IP: *If an item is selected, you can immediately open the Outline Color dialog box by pressing the shortcut keys SHIFT-F12.*

3. Select Palettes and PANTONE Spot colors, then click on the second color from the right in the top row of the Color palette. The PANTONE identification name and number for this color, "PANTONE Red 032 CV," displays in the color name text box. If you have the PANTONE Color Reference Manual, you can compare what you see on the screen with what you see in the manual. There probably is a difference since most color monitors are not perfectly calibrated.
4. Click on OK. Notice that the curves have changed to a red color.

5. Open the Outline Color dialog box again. Select Palettes and PANTONE Spot colors, if they are not still selected. Once more click on PANTONE Process Black (the middle color in the top row) and set the tint value to 50 percent. The color preview display box now displays a 50-percent gray shade in the lower part of the display box, which you can compare with the current color in the top of the window.
6. Click on OK. You will see an actual representation of a 50-percent gray shade in the drawing, as shown in Figure 7-4.
7. Open the Outline Color dialog box once more, choose Palettes and PANTONE Spot Colors, reselect PANTONE Red 032 CV (second color from the right in the top row), and then return the tint value to 50 percent. You have just selected a lighter tint of PANTONE Red.
8. Select OK to exit the dialog box with the new Outline Color setting.
9. Save this as Curves2 and clear the screen by selecting Close from the File menu. Open a new document by clicking on the New button on the toolbar.

Both the Outline Pen shape and color defaults must be set before creating an object. In the next section, you will set both defaults and use them with Artistic Text.

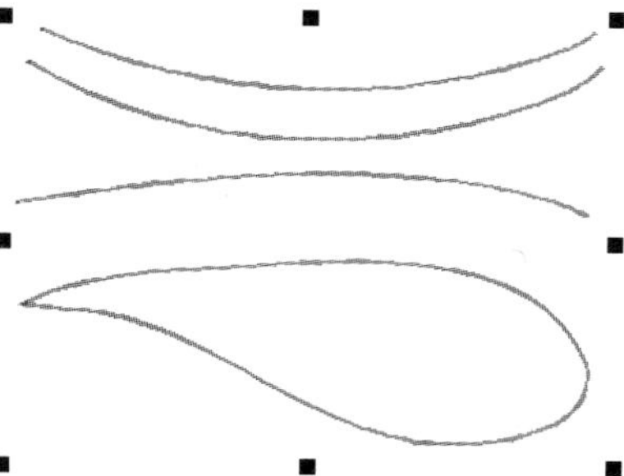

Curves at 50% gray shade

FIGURE 7-4

Setting New Spot Color Outline Pen Defaults

In this exercise, you will change defaults for both the Outline Pen and Spot Outline Color properties, and then create new objects that exhibit those defaults automatically.

1. Set the display magnification to Actual Size (1:1).
2. Without creating or selecting any objects, point and hold on the Outline Pen tool and then click on the Outline Pen dialog button, the third tool from the right on the first row of the flyout. In the Outline Pen default dialog box, select Artistic Text (you can leave Graphic selected in addition) and click on OK to open the Outline Pen dialog box.
3. When the Outline Pen dialog box appears, set the Outline Pen properties as follows: Width, 0.15 inch; Style, solid line; Corners, sharp (miter); Line Caps, butt (top option); Stretch, 10 percent; Angle,–45 degrees. Do not check either Behind Fill or Scale With Image.
4. Click on the Color button at the top-left section of the dialog box. The Color drop-down palette opens, as shown here:

This Color palette, although smaller, has the same colors to choose from as the Color palette in the Outline Color dialog box.

5. Click on the Others button at the bottom of the color palette. The Outline Color dialog box appears.
6. Verify that PANTONE Spot Colors is selected, then choose PANTONE Blue 072 CV color (first box on the right in the top row), and tint value of

100 percent. Select OK twice to save these settings and exit both the Outline Color and Outline Pen dialog boxes.

7. Activate Rulers, make sure Wireframe is off, and then click on the Text tool. Click in the lower-left section of your screen.
8. Open the Text toolbar and select the following text properties: no alignment, BrushScript BT, normal, 300 points, then press ENTER. Type a capital **A**, and select the Pick tool. The letter "A" should be selected. If you followed all the steps up to this point, the text should have a default fill of black. Your screen should look like Figure 7-5, except that the color of the outline is blue. Remember that *all* of the new Outline Pen and Color properties you have selected apply to the new object automatically.
9. Clear the screen by deleting all the objects. Do not save your work.

If you create the same kinds of images regularly in your work, you probably have strong personal preferences for what you would like default outlines to look like. If you wish, start a new drawing on your own, setting up the Outline Pen and Outline Color default properties that will apply to the basic elements in your

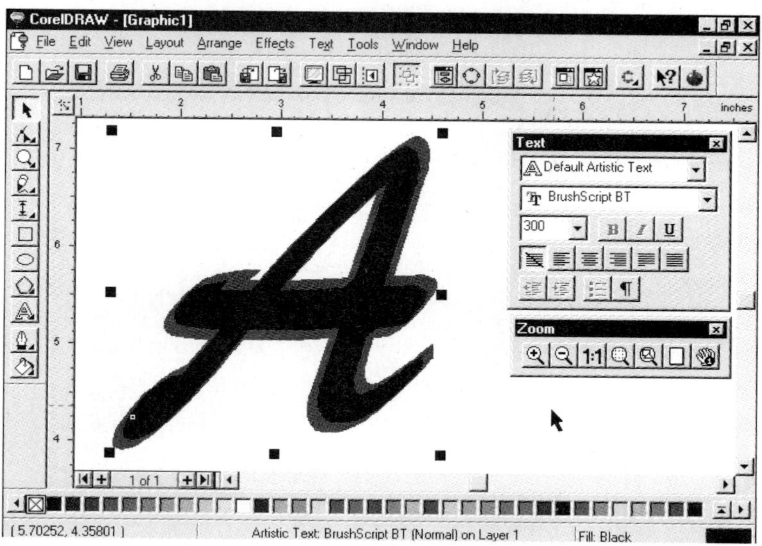

Letter created with the new default PANTONE spot color outline

FIGURE 7-5

drawing. You can edit settings for objects that should have different outline fills by selecting them after you draw them and accessing the appropriate dialog boxes. If you are not satisfied with the results of your Outline Pen or Outline Color attribute settings, you can make adjustments during the drawing process.

You may find selecting a particular spot color from the Color palette difficult—it can be hard to find a particular PANTONE color from the more than 700 that are shown. If you have a PANTONE Color Reference Manual or know the PANTONE name or number of a particular color, there is another way to select a spot color. Click on the Color Options command button, then select Show Color Names from the Color Options flyout, and a list of PANTONE color names, as shown in Figure 7-6, is provided. When you select a color on the list, it is displayed in the color display box to the right of the list. Also, you can enter a few characters of a PANTONE name or number in the Search text box, and that name or number will be highlighted in the list while the color is shown in the display box.

If you click on OK to leave the Outline Color dialog box, you are returned to your drawing. The next time you select the Outline Color button from the Outline Pen flyout menu, you will get the list of PANTONE colors that you just left (Figure 7-6), not the palette shown in Figure 7-2. If you want to return to the palette when you next select the Outline Color button, deselect Show Color Names from the Color Options flyout before leaving the Outline Color dialog box.

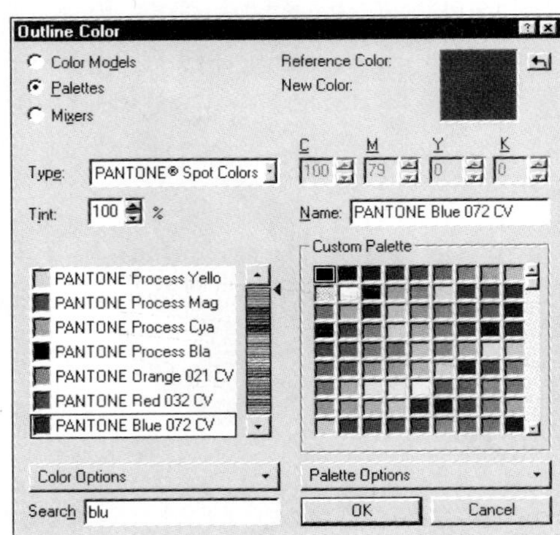

Outline Color dialog box listing spot colors by name

FIGURE 7-6

Using the Pen Roll-Up for Outline Color

The Pen roll-up, which you'll remember from Chapter 6, opens from the Outline Pen flyout (third button from the left in the top row). It provides two ways to select or change outline color.

The first is the color button (fourth bar up from the bottom), which opens the same Color palette you accessed from the Outline Pen dialog box. Clicking on a color in the Pen roll-up palette, and then clicking on Apply, will apply the color to the outline of the selected object. Clicking on Others will access the Select Color dialog box.

The second method of applying outline color from the Pen roll-up is to click on the Edit button (second from the bottom), which opens the full Outline Pen dialog box. Click on the Color button to open the Color palette and then click on Others to open the Outline Color dialog box. This is, of course, the same dialog box you get by clicking on the Outline Color button in the Outline Pen flyout or by pressing SHIFT-F12.

If you own or use a PostScript printer, go on to the next section to learn how to assign a PostScript halftone screen as an outline color. This option is available only when you choose a spot color library, and it takes effect only if you have a PostScript printer. Even if you don't own a PostScript printer, you can use PostScript halftone screens if your work will be output by a service bureau or commercial printer. While you cannot see PostScript patterns on the screen, you can preview them using the Preview display box on the PostScript dialog box.

7

Outlining with Postscript Halftone Screen Patterns

If you work with a PostScript printer, you can elect to fill an outline with a halftone screen pattern of the currently selected spot color. The Coreldraw window displays PostScript halftone screen patterns as solid colors only; to see the patterns, you must print the images on a PostScript printer.

The concept of a *halftone screen* is probably familiar to you already; it is a method of representing continuous tone or color by patterns of dots. Black and white and color photographs in newspapers and magazines are examples of halftone images that you see every day. When a black and white photograph is printed in a newspaper, only one color of ink (black) is used. Shades of gray are created by alternating black dots with the white of the paper. When viewed from a normal reading distance, the dots and white space combine to give the impression of gray tones. You can see this by looking closely at a photograph in a newspaper. CMYK color halftones are similar, except that four colors are used. Tints of spot colors are created in the same way. Since you cannot view the results of your selections on screen, this section does not feature any exercises. However, some guidelines for selecting halftone screen patterns, frequency, and angle are presented in the next section. Chapter 12 has more instructions on printing with PostScript printers.

Selecting Halftone Screen Patterns

To begin defining a halftone screen outline, make sure you have selected the spot color and tint in which you want to print your outline. Then, click on the Color Options command button at the bottom left of the Outline Color dialog box. Select PostScript Options from the Color Options flyout. The PostScript Options dialog box opens. This dialog box contains settings for Type, Frequency, and Angle properties of the PostScript halftone patterns, as shown here:

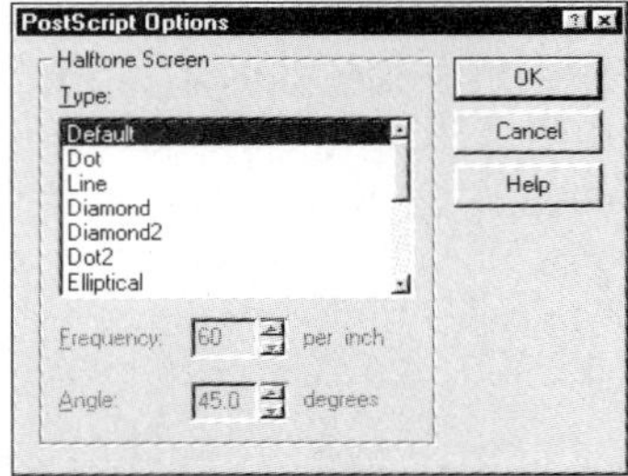

Selecting Halftone Screen Type

The Type option in the PostScript Options dialog box features 15 halftone patterns that are available for your Outline Color work. Your choices are Default, Dot, Line, Diamond, Diamond2, Dot2, Elliptical, Euclidean, Grid, Lines, MicroWaves, OutCircleBlk, OutCircleWhi, Rhomboid, and Star. (Default is a separate, plain or "constant" screen without a pattern in it.) To select a halftone screen type, scroll through the list until you see the name of the desired pattern and click on the name to select it.

Selecting Halftone Screen Frequency

The Frequency option in the PostScript Options dialog box allows you to determine how many times per inch the pattern should occur within the outline. The available range is from 0 to 1,500 per inch, and the default setting is 60. The number you select depends upon the resolution of your ultimate output device; refer to Chapter 12 for more details on frequency settings for PostScript halftone screens.

Setting Halftone Screen Angle

The third option in the PostScript Options dialog box allows you to specify the angle of the screen pattern when you print it. Keep in mind that the halftone screen angle remains constant, no matter how you transform an object. If you stretch, scale, rotate, or skew an object after assigning it a halftone screen outline, you could alter its appearance significantly. If you do not want this to happen, remember to change the screen angle after performing a transform operation to match the offset of the transformed object. You will achieve the best results by setting your screen angle at 0, 45, 90, or 180 degrees.

Outlining with Process Color

With the process color system, you specify color in terms of either a set of subtractive primary colors (cyan, magenta, yellow, and black) or select the colors from one of the process color palettes.

To specify process colors for an existing object, you select or create the object, click and hold on the Outline Pen tool, and click again on the Outline Color button in the flyout. When the Outline Color dialog box appears, you select one of the process color palettes to use in defining the color you want.

In the following exercise, you will specify both the Outline Pen and Process Outline Color for a text string.

1. At Actual Size (1:1) magnification with Wireframe turned off, select the Text tool, click in the middle of the left side, and type **CorelDRAW!**. Activate the Pick tool to select the text string.
2. Open the Text toolbar and select BrushScript BT Normal, 72-point type.

3. From the Fill tool flyout, click on X to turn off the fill. From the Outline Pen flyout, open the Outline Pen dialog box. Select rounded corners, set Width at 0.083 inch (6 points), Stretch at 14 percent, Angle at 0 degrees, and click on OK.

When you are back in the drawing, your screen should look like this:

Your settings resulted in a moderately thick text outline, and the calligraphic Nib Shape created an "artistic" look. The rounded corners setting adds a more polished look to the outlines of corners of angular letters. The current color does not do it justice, so you will change it now.

4. With the text string still selected, click on the Outline Pen once more. This time, select the Outline Color button (the first button on the left in the first row of the flyout) to open the Outline Color dialog box.
5. If necessary, select the CMYK Color Model to switch color selection methods. The options in the dialog box change instantly. Take a moment to again familiarize yourself with the Outline Color dialog box. Move the markers in each of the visual selector boxes and notice how the color changes in the color display box, and how the percentages in the numeric entry boxes change as well. Using the scroll arrows or your mouse and keyboard, set the following color mix: Cyan 60 percent, Magenta 80 percent, Yellow 0 percent, and Black (K) 20 percent. The color display box shows a real-time approximation of changes to the color as you scroll to or enter each specified value. When you have specified all of the values, the color display box shows a deep blue.
6. Click on OK to exit the dialog box. The text string's outline displays as a deep blue, providing a contrast to the light background.
7. Press SHIFT-F12 or click on the Outline Color button in the Outline Pen flyout.
8. In the Custom Palette display box, use the scroll arrow to bring the next to last row of colors into view (the last row has two color boxes). If you

click on the first box on the right in the next to last row, you'll see the name Deep Blue in the Name text box and that the color percentages are the same. The color is already defined.

Next, define your own color and add it to the Custom Color palette. Leave the Coreldraw text string on your screen and the Outline Color dialog box open. You can use the text string to test your new color.

Defining a New Color and Adding It to the Custom Palettes

The Custom Palettes in the Outline Color dialog box display 100 colors, including 10 shades of gray. You have seen how you can define a new color with this color selector when you want to apply it to an object. But if you want to use a color over and over, say a special corporate color you've defined, you will want to add this color to the Outline Color Custom Palettes.

In the following exercise, you will define a new color. In the last exercise, the color you entered was already on the palette and in the name list. The new color you will define is Deep Royal Blue.

1. Select CMYK from the Model drop-down list box.
2. Type in the numeric entry boxes, or use the spinners, to define a color mix of 100-percent cyan, 55-percent magenta, 0-percent yellow, and 45-percent black. The color display box will show the color, but the Name text box is empty because the color is not defined.
3. Click on the Name text box and type **Deep Royal Blue**. Your dialog box should look like that shown in Figure 7-7. (The squares may appear to be different because of the way the color combinations print in black and white.)
4. Click on OK to return to your drawing and see your new color. More important, clicking on OK defined your new color and added it to the Color palette and the name list. See for yourself with the next step.
5. Press SHIFT-F12 to reopen the Outline Color dialog box with your new color highlighted at the bottom of the palette and the name Deep Royal Blue in the Name text box.

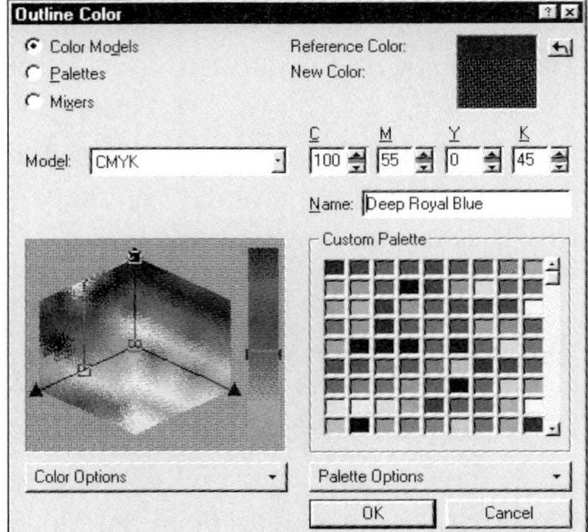

Deep Royal Blue being defined

FIGURE 7-7

While it is nice to have a new color in the palette, having it at the end of the list is not very handy. Coreldraw, though, allows you to rearrange colors by dragging them around the palette. You can drag a color to any existing location and release the mouse button, and all the existing colors shift to the right and down to accommodate the new color.

6. Point on the new color you just defined (the bottom, rightmost color), press and hold the mouse button while dragging the new color to the top of the palette. When you reach the top of the list box, the colors will automatically scroll until the first row is displayed. Drag the color up to the second row from the top and then over to the fourth color from the right. Now Deep Royal Blue (your new color) is between Blue and Cyan, as shown by the pointer in Figure 7-8.
7. Click on OK to close the dialog box and return to the drawing. Leave the text string on your screen to use in the next exercise.

In the next section of this chapter, you will learn a shortcut to specifying Outline Color that will be useful if you usually print to a black and white printer.

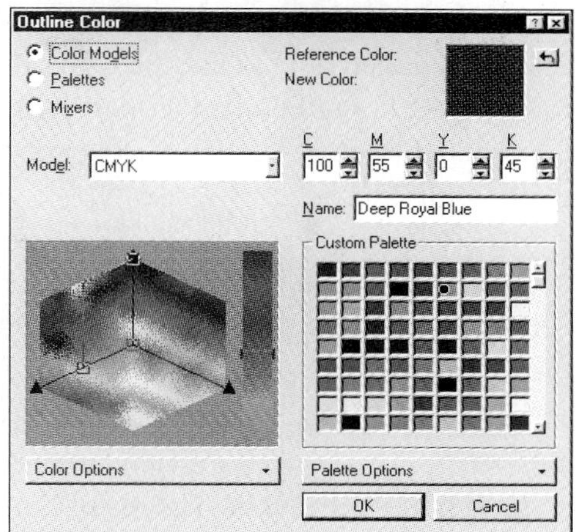

Result of dragging Deep Royal Blue between Blue and Cyan

FIGURE 7-8

Outlining with Black, White, or Gray

When you worked with the Outline Pen in Chapter 6, you saw how the second row of the Outline Pen flyout contained five preset outline widths that you could select simply by clicking on the desired button. You can also select a preset white or black outline from the Outline Pen flyout.

To select a preset Outline Color for an existing object, you select the object, open the Outline Pen flyout, and then click on the appropriate button. To select one of these options as the default outline color, click on the desired button in the Outline Pen flyout without first selecting an object.

You can use either the spot color or process color system to define other shades of gray. To define shades of gray using the spot color method, access the Outline Color dialog box and set shades of gray by clicking on black and setting % Tint in increments of 1 percent. To define custom shades of gray using the process color method, define a percentage for black only, leaving cyan, magenta, and yellow all at 0 percent.

Copying Outline Color and Pen Styles

In previous chapters, you learned how to use the Copy Properties From command in the Edit menu to copy text or Outline Pen properties from one object to another. You use the same command to copy Outline Color properties between objects, as you will see in the following exercise.

1. With the "CorelDRAW!" text string still on the screen from the previous exercise, zoom out to reduce the size enough to draw a rectangle around the string.
2. With the Rectangle tool, draw a rectangle around the word "CorelDRAW!"; then select the Pick tool. If your rectangle is filled, turn off the fill by clicking on the X in the Fill flyout. The result is a rectangle around the text string. The rectangle is selected, by default.
3. Select the Copy Properties From command from the Edit menu. When the Copy Properties dialog box appears, click on both the Outline Pen and the Outline Color check boxes, and then click on OK. The pointer turns into a thick arrow to use to point to the source object from which to copy its outline properties.
4. Click on the "CorelDRAW!" text string. The rectangle redisplays to show the same outline thickness and color as the text string, like this:

If your rectangle does not come out as you just saw, it could be that the specifications on your text have been changed. They should be a 6-point line width, with a 50-percent black outline color, and no fill.

5. Clear the screen by deleting all the objects.

For more practice with the Outline Color tool, you can go back to the Jack in the box file or any other drawing that you created and edited in earlier chapters. You can begin to differentiate objects by varying their outlines. You can give custom outlines to interior objects or copy outline styles to multiple objects at one time.

Defining Fill Color Properties

The final step in completing an object in Coreldraw is to define its fill properties. The Fill tool is similar to the Outline Color tool in that it can dispense spot color, process color, and PostScript halftone screen patterns. In addition, the Fill tool can apply various fountain, pattern, and texture fills.

The Fill tool flyout, shown in Figure 7-9, is accessed from the Fill tool button. The first, or leftmost, button in the top row of the Fill tool flyout is the Fill Color button. This button opens the Uniform Fill dialog box, which lets you define custom spot and process color fills and PostScript halftone screen patterns. The next button opens the Color roll-up, which gives you access to the color palettes. The next button opens the Special Fill roll-up where you can select and edit each of the types of fills. The last three buttons in the top row of the flyout let you set no fill, white fill, or black fill. The six buttons on the second row of the flyout allow you to edit and apply fountain fills, two-color bitmap patterns, vector patterns, full-color bitmap patterns, texture fills, and PostScript fills.

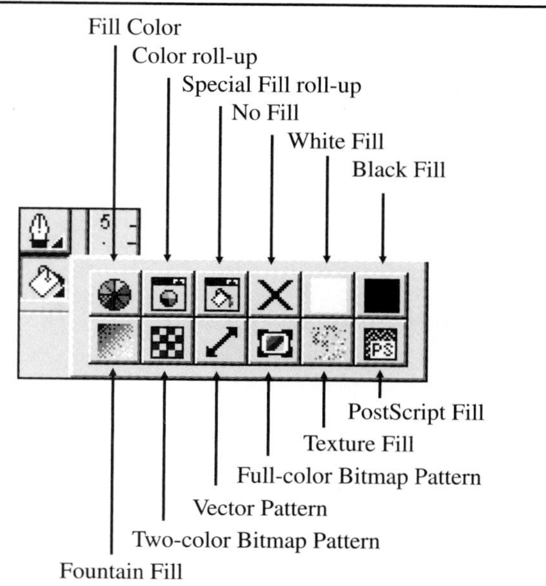

Buttons on the Fill tool flyout

FIGURE 7-9

Setting default fill properties is accomplished in the same manner as outline defaults; settings defined without any objects being selected become the new default fill properties. Objects you create in the future will be filled with the default fill properties automatically. When defining fill properties for an existing object, you are editing that object's current fill. The changes you make apply to that object only, not to additional objects you may create later.

The remaining sections in this chapter offer you practice in working with each dialog box and selecting fill properties for each of the major types of fills. Whether you are setting fill properties for selected objects or altering default properties for objects you haven't drawn yet, the main steps involved are similar.

Filling an Object with Uniform Spot Color

To fill an object with spot color, process color, or a PostScript halftone screen pattern, you use the settings in the Uniform Fill dialog box. This dialog box appears when you click on the Fill Color tool, the first button on the Fill tool flyout. Except for the title, the Uniform Fill dialog box is identical in appearance and function to the Outline Color dialog box you worked with previously. You can also open the Uniform Fill dialog box with the shortcut keys SHIFT-F11. The name "Uniform Fill" distinguishes this type of fill from fountain, pattern, texture, and PostScript fills, which involve multiple hues or patterns rather than a single color.

TIP: *You will recall that spot color is the preferred color system when an image contains fewer than four colors or if you want to use PostScript halftone screen patterns. If you do not have a PostScript printer at your disposal and your work does not require spot color or four-color printing, you can use any of the color models to specify fill colors.*

As mentioned previously, an object must be a closed path in order for you to fill it. However, a closed path does not assure a solid object. If you combine two or more objects, as you learned to do in Chapter 5, "holes" result where the combined objects overlap. You can then create interesting design effects by surrounding the holes with outline and fill colors. Perform the following exercise to create a logo with transparent text, outline it, and assign a uniform fill spot color to it. You will edit this logo throughout the rest of the chapter as you learn new ways to use the Fill tool flyout.

1. To prepare the screen, set magnification to Actual Size (1:1). In the Grid & Ruler Setup dialog box opened from the Layout menu, set both Horizontal and Vertical Grid Frequency units to picas, points; then set the Vertical Grid Origin to 66 picas and the Horizontal Grid Origin to 0 picas. On the Grid tab set the Frequency to 1 and select Snap To Grid; Click on OK. Activate both Wireframe and Rulers from the View menu; because of the grid settings, the rulers display in picas rather than inches. Close the Text toolbar and Zoom toolbar if they are open.
2. Before beginning to draw, set the default Outline Pen and Outline Color properties back to the original Coreldraw defaults. To do this, open the Outline Pen Dialog box from the Outline Pen flyout. When the Outline Pen defaults dialog box appears, select Graphic and Artistic Text and click on OK. Adjust settings in the Outline Pen dialog box as follows: black color; Width, 0.003 inch; Corners, sharp; Line Caps, butt (topmost); no Arrows; Style, solid line; Angle, 0 degrees; and Stretch, 100 percent. No check boxes should be selected. Click on OK to make these settings the default Outline Pen properties.
3. Select the Ellipse tool and position the pointer at the 24-pica mark on the horizontal ruler and the –33-pica mark on the vertical ruler. Draw a perfect circle from the center outward, starting from this point, by holding both the SHIFT and CTRL keys down while dragging the mouse. Make the circle 20 picas in diameter or the largest circle you can draw, using the information on the Status bar to help you. When the circle is drawn, click on Black fill on the onscreen Color palette (the leftmost color button).
4. Select the Text tool. Select an insertion point near the left edge of the circle, at the 18-pica mark on the horizontal ruler and the –26-pica mark on the vertical ruler. You do not have to position the pointer exactly, because you can align the text and circle later. Type **The World of Corel DRAW!**, one word per line. Then, select the text by selecting the Pick tool, and choose Character from the Text menu. Select the following text properties: Aachen BT bold (available on CD-ROM), 40 points, and center alignment. Set Character spacing to 20 percent and Line spacing to 80 percent, and then click on OK. Drag the text as necessary to center it vertically and horizontally within the circle, as shown in Figure 7-10.

Depending on the type of display and display adapter you have, the diameter of the circle and the point size you can fit in the circle may differ from what is described

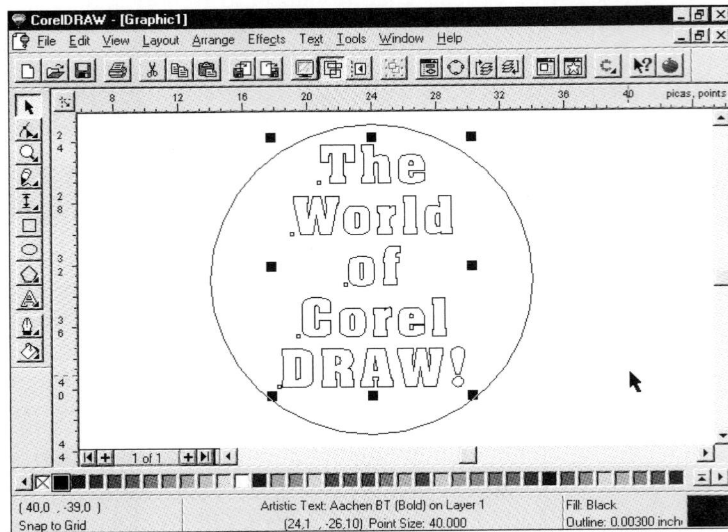

Centering the text string within the circle

FIGURE 7-10

and shown here. Draw the biggest circle and use the largest type size needed to fill your screen at actual size magnification.

5. Click on both Rulers and Wireframe from the View menu again to deactivate them. You cannot clearly distinguish the text from the circle now, because they have the same outline and fill colors.
6. Select Options from the Tools menu (or press CTRL-J). When the Options dialog box appears, on the General tab, adjust both the Horizontal and Vertical numeric settings for the Place Duplicate and Clones option to –2,0 picas, points. Make sure that you make it minus and that you place a comma rather than a period after the 2. Duplicate objects that you create with this setting are offset from the original by the specified amount (in this case, 2 picas below and to the left of the original). Click on OK.
7. If necessary, activate the Pick tool, select the circle, and then click on Duplicate from the Edit menu. A duplicate of the circle appears below and to the left of the original, and is selected immediately. Press SHIFT-PGDN to move the duplicate behind the original.

8. Change the fill of this duplicate circle to none by clicking on the X at the left of the color palette at the bottom of your screen.

9. Select both the original circle and the text string again using the SHIFT key, and select Combine from the Arrange menu. The message in the Status bar changes from "2 objects selected" to "Curve on Layer 1." The "Fill:" message at the right side of the Status bar displays a default fill of black, but the text now appears white, as shown in Figure 7-11. In combining the two objects, you have converted both the circle and the text string to curves. The area behind the text has become not white but transparent.

10. Select Save from the File menu. When the Save Drawing dialog box appears, select the folder where you are saving your drawings and type the name **Fill-1** in the File name text box, then click on Save.

11. With the combined circle and text still selected, open the Fill flyout and click on the Fill Color button (you can also press SHIFT-F11). The Uniform Fill dialog box appears. Select the Palettes option button, then select

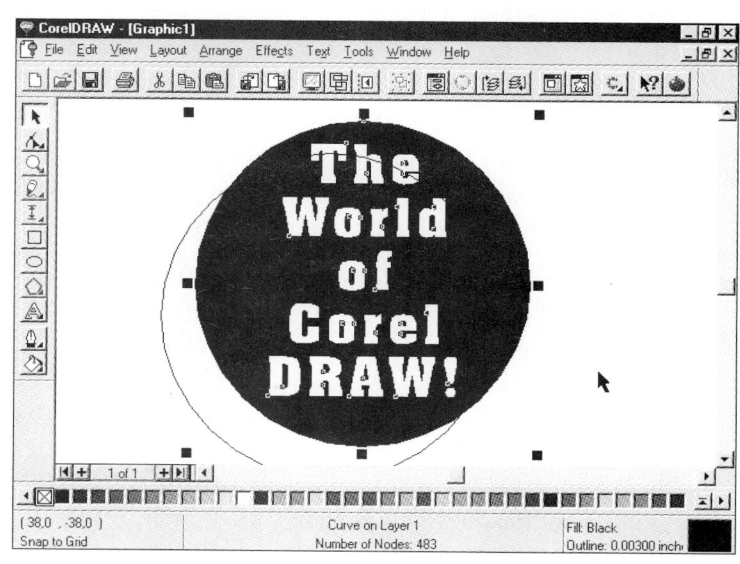

Combining two objects to form a curve object with transparent "holes"

FIGURE 7-11

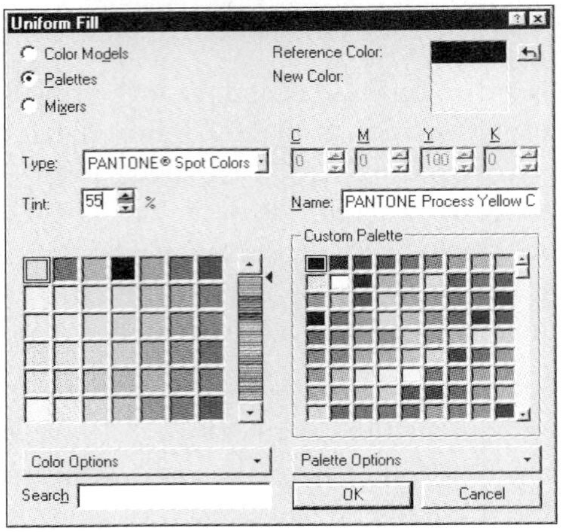

Setting for a spot color uniform fill

FIGURE 7-12

PANTONE Spot Colors from the Type drop-down list box, and deselect Show Color Names from the Color Options flyout if it is selected. Then, select the leftmost color in the top row of the palette, PANTONE Process Yellow CV, and set the tint to 55 percent. Your settings should match those in Figure 7-12.

12. Click on OK to exit the dialog box. Now you can see some contrast between the black outline and the fill colors. The text has the same outline style as the circular shape because Coreldraw treats the text curves as "holes" or edges within the single combined object. The outline is very thin, however, so you will thicken it in the next step.

13. With the curve object still selected, open the Outline Pen flyout. Click on the Outline Pen Dialog button to open the Outline Pen dialog box (or press F12). Change the Width setting for the Outline Pen to 5.0 points. (Notice not picas & points, just points.) Select the Behind Fill option and then click on OK to apply these settings to the object. Now you see a heavier outline around both the outer rim of the circle and the text, as shown in Figure 7-13. Because you activated the Behind Fill option, the "ink" of the outline doesn't completely clog up the transparent spaces in the text.

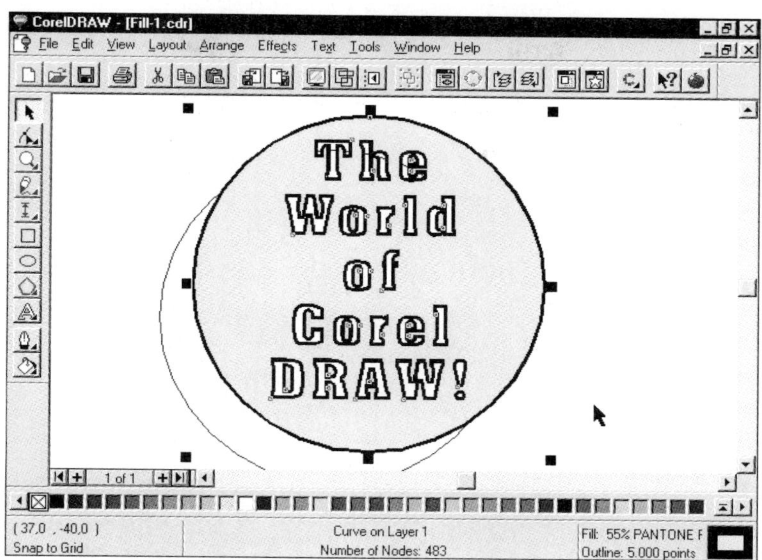

Outline appearing behind fill for clearer text appearance

FIGURE 7-13

14. You are ready to give the finishing touches to the curve object. Press SHIFT-F12 to access the Outline Color dialog box. If not already selected, select PANTONE Spot Colors to be the color palette. Type **293** in the Search text box to select PANTONE 293 CV as the color (a medium blue). Set the tint to 52 percent and click on OK to exit the dialog box.
15. Select the duplicate circle. Press SHIFT-F11 to access the Uniform Fill dialog box. Select PANTONE Spot Color and type **281** in the Search text box to select PANTONE 281 CV (a dark purplish blue), and leave the tint at 100 percent. Click on OK to select this setting and exit the dialog box.
16. The image redisplays to show the background circle creating a dramatic "shadow" effect behind the curve object. The alignment is not quite right yet, however; white space may be visible behind the upper portion of the word "The." To remedy this situation, deactivate the Snap To Grid command and adjust the position of the background circle slightly so that it fills the word "The" completely. Now all of the transparent spaces behind the letters in the curve object have fill behind them.

Combined object in Full-Screen preview

FIGURE 7-14

17. To see this apparent fill more closely, turn on Full-Screen preview by pressing F9. Your screen should look similar to Figure 7-14.
18. Press SPACEBAR to turn off Full Screen preview and then press CTRL-S to save the changes you have made to this graphic. Leave the graphic on the screen to use in the next exercise.

The kind of object you have just created makes an excellent specimen for outline and fill experiments of all kinds. In the next section, you will add an interesting design effect by specifying a PostScript halftone screen pattern for the background circle in Fill-1.cdr.

Filling an Object with Postscript Halftone Screen Patterns

When you choose the spot color rather than the process color system in the Uniform Fill dialog box, another set of fill specifications becomes available. If you work with a PostScript printer, you can fill an object with a halftone screen pattern of the currently selected spot color. You will recall from your work with Outline Color that the Coreldraw document window displays PostScript halftone screen patterns as

solid colors; to see how they actually look, you have to print them on a PostScript printer.

You define a PostScript halftone screen pattern by selecting the PostScript Options command from the Color Options flyout in the Uniform Fill dialog box. You can choose from 15 different screen options, and you can vary the frequency (number of occurrences per inch) and angle of any screen pattern to achieve dramatic differences in the appearance of a spot color fill.

In the following exercise, you will assign a PostScript halftone screen pattern of a specified angle and frequency to the combined circle-text foreground object in the Fill-1.cdr image and save the altered image under a new name. If you have a PostScript printer, you can print this image with the printing techniques covered in Chapter 12.

1. With Fill-1.cdr still on the screen, select the foreground curve and press SHIFT-F11.
2. When the Uniform Fill dialog box appears, make sure that the Type text box shows PANTONE Spot Colors, click on the Color Options command button, then select PostScript Options from the Color Options flyout. The PostScript Options dialog box appears.
3. Scroll through the Type list box until the MicroWaves halftone screen type is visible and then select it.

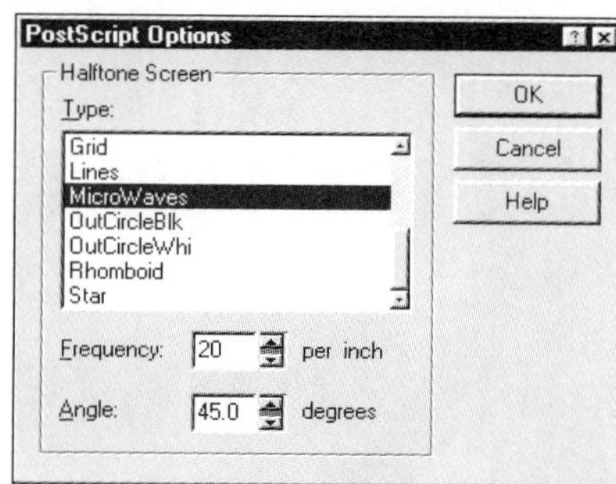

Defining a custom PostScript screen pattern

FIGURE 7-15

4. Adjust the Frequency setting to 20 per inch. This is a very low frequency (the minimum is 0, the maximum 1,500) and will display a dramatic pattern on a 600 dpi PostScript printer.
5. If necessary, use the scroll arrows to adjust the number in the Angle numeric entry box to 45 degrees. This will cause the screen pattern to tilt at a 45-degree angle.

When your settings match the ones in Figure 7-15, click on OK to exit the PostScript Options dialog box. Click on OK again to exit the Uniform Fill dialog box and return to the screen image. You will not notice anything different because the preview window cannot display PostScript patterns.

6. Select the Save As command in the File menu and type **Fill-2** in the File Name text box of the Save Drawing dialog box. Click on OK to save the file under this new name. After you complete Chapter 12, you can print this file to see the results of your settings if you have a PostScript printer. Your results should look like Figure 7-16.

When you assign PostScript halftone screen pattern fills to objects, base your choice of frequency on the resolution of the PostScript printer you will use. On any

Printed image of the PostScript halftone screen

FIGURE 7-16

TABLE 7-1 Printer Resolution and Number of Gray Levels for PostScript Halftone Screens

Selected Frequency	Number of Gray Levels		
	300 dpi	600 dpi	1,270 dpi
30 per inch	101	401	1,600
60 per inch	26	101	401
100 per inch	10	37	145
120 per inch	7	26	101

PostScript printer, low frequencies result in more dramatic pattern effects, while high frequencies result in the pattern being hardly visible. The resolution of the printer, not any absolute number, determines what constitutes a low or a high frequency. To achieve the same visual effect on different printers, you should vary the frequency assigned to a screen. For example, you should assign lower screen frequencies when the printer resolution is 300 dpi, higher frequencies for 600 dpi printers, and higher still for imagesetting equipment at resolutions of 1,270 dpi and above. Table 7-1 provides information on the number of visible gray levels for each printer resolution at a given screen frequency.

You can specify a PostScript halftone screen pattern as a default fill in the same way that you would specify a normal spot color. The next section will introduce you to one of the most creative types of fills, *fountain fills*, which can be used to effect smooth transitions of two different colors through the interior of an object.

Custom Fountain Fills

When you specify fill colors using the Uniform Fill dialog boxes, you are limited to one color per object. When you select the Fountain Fill button on the Fill tool flyout, however, you can define a fill that blends two different colors or shades of color. If you are familiar with state-of-the-art paint programs or business presentation slides, you have probably seen fountain fills used to make smooth transitions of two different colors or tints. Coreldraw makes the color drama of fountain fills available to you through the Fountain Fill dialog box.

By adjusting settings in the Fountain Fill dialog box, you can fill any object with two different colors or tints in such a way that the colors blend evenly from one extreme to the other. Coreldraw allows you to create four different types of fountain fills: linear, radial, conical, and square. In a *linear* fountain fill, the color transition occurs in one direction only, determined by the angle that you specify. In a *radial* fountain fill, the blend of start and end colors proceeds concentrically, from the center of the object outward or from the outer rim inward. In a *conical* fill, the blend of colors is made of wedge-shaped steps that radiate in clockwise and counter-clockwise directions. In a *square* fill, the blend of colors is in square rings. Whichever type of fountain fill you select, you can specify colors using either the spot color or process color system. If you choose spot color, you can also define PostScript halftone screen patterns to add an extra visual "punch" to your fountain fills.

The following exercises provide practice defining linear, radial, conical, and square fountain fills using spot color, PostScript halftone screen patterns, and process color.

Defining Linear Fountain Fills

When you specify a linear fountain fill, the start color begins at one edge of the object and the end color appears at the opposite side. In between, the colors blend smoothly along an imaginary line extending from one edge to the other. The direction of the color blend depends on the angle of the fill, over which you have complete control.

You can also control the speed and fineness of the display that defines the fountain fill in the Coreldraw window. You do this by choosing Options from the Tools menu, clicking on Display, and adjusting the Preview fountain steps settings. A low setting (2 is the lower limit) causes the fountain fill to display rapidly with a small number of circles. A high value (256 is the upper limit) causes the filled object to redraw very slowly on the screen, but it also results in a very finely graded transition of color. For all output devices except PostScript printers, the Fountain Steps setting also determines the resolution at which the fountain fill will print. You will have the opportunity to practice adjusting this setting and viewing the results on the screen in the "Fill Tool Hints" section of this chapter.

As with other outlines and fills, you can define a linear fountain fill for existing objects or you can set defaults for objects that you have not yet created. The exercises in the next few sections use existing objects as examples.

Spot Color Linear Fountain Fills

Theoretically, you can select any two colors as the start and end colors when you specify a linear fountain fill using the spot color system. In practice, however, it's best to select two tints of the *same* color if you intend to send color separations of the resulting image to a commercial printer. The reason for this has to do with the way spot color is physically reproduced, which makes it difficult to blend two discrete colors evenly.

In the following exercise, you will define a spot color linear fountain fill for the objects in the Fill-1.cdr file, which you created earlier in the chapter.

1. Close any open files, then open the original Fill-1.cdr file you set up earlier in this chapter (not one of the edited versions). Your screen displays a curve object containing a PANTONE Process Yellow CV spot color at 55-percent tint and a blue PANTONE 293 CV outline at a 52-percent tint. A darker blue fills a circle behind the object.

IP: *To check the current fill colors for an existing object at any time, just select the object, click on the Fill tool, and click on the Uniform Fill button to display the Uniform Fill dialog box.*

2. Adjust the viewing area to Zoom To All Objects magnification.
3. Deselect all objects and reselect the combined circle-text curve object alone.
4. Click on the Fill tool and then on the Fountain Fill button in the Fill tool flyout (first button from the left on the bottom row), or press F11. The Fountain Fill dialog box displays, as shown in Figure 7-17.

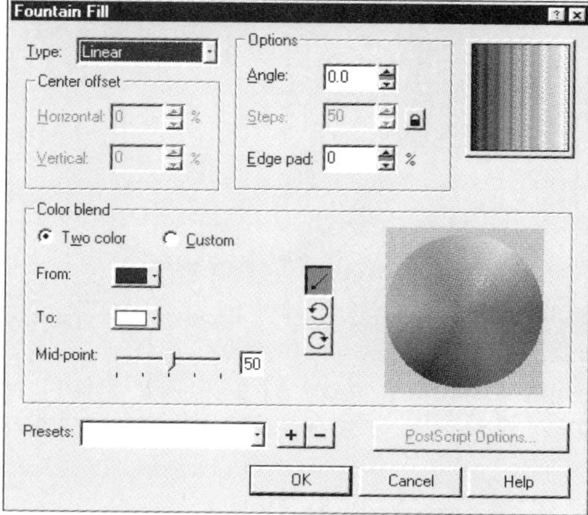

FIGURE 7-17 The (default) Fountain Fill dialog box

The Fountain Fill dialog box contains controls for the type of fountain fill (linear, radial, conical, or square); the angle, which determines the direction of the fill; and the From and To colors of the fill. A display box shows the current fill, and other controls for several fill options are available. The default settings are Type, Linear; Angle, 0 degrees; From color, black; and To color, white. These settings would result in a fill that is white on the right, blending gradually into solid black on the left.

5. Leave the Type setting at Linear. Click on the From color button and then click on Other. In the Fountain Fill dialog box, select PANTONE Spot Colors as the palette and PANTONE Process Yellow CV (first color in the list) at 100-percent tint. Click on OK. Similarly, set the To color to PANTONE Process Yellow CV, but at 0-percent tint, which will look virtually white. Remember that when you define color using the spot color method, both the start and end colors should be different tints of the same color.

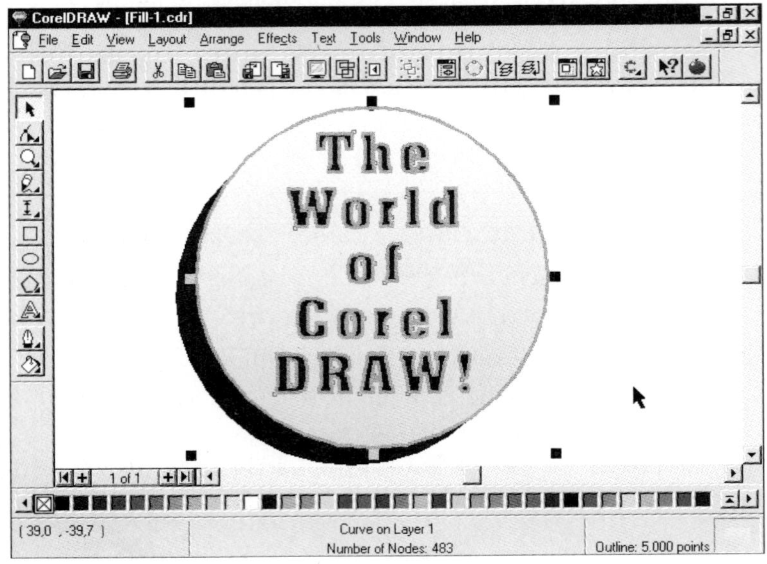

Spot color linear fountain fill at a 90-degree angle

FIGURE 7-18

6. Set the Angle to 90 and click on OK to exit the Fountain Fill dialog box with the new settings. The circle object now shows a darker yellow fill at the bottom, with a gradual transition to white at the top, as shown in Figure 7-18.

7. Access the Fountain Fill dialog box again (F11). This time, change the Angle setting to 45 degrees and then click on OK to exit the dialog box. Now, the combined circle-text redisplays with a fountain fill that is lighter at the upper right and darker at the lower left.

8. For an interesting enhancement, create a fountain fill for the background circle that runs in the opposite direction from the fill for the curve object. To do this, select the background circle and press F11. When the Fountain Fill dialog box appears, set the From color to PANTONE 281 (use the Search for text box) at a 100-percent tint. Click on OK.

9. Then set the To color to PANTONE 281 at a 30-percent tint. Change the Angle setting to minus 135 degrees, the exact opposite of the 45-degree setting you chose for the fill of the curve object. This setting will result in a fill running in the exact opposite direction from the fill for the foreground object.

10. Click on OK to exit the dialog box. When the objects are redrawn, you can see that the area behind the letters is a richer color at the upper right than at the lower left. This arrangement adds some visual tension to the mock logo.

11. Select the Save As command from the File menu. When the Save Drawing dialog box appears, type the filename **Fill-3** in the File Name text box, and then click on the OK command button to save the altered picture under this new name.

TIP: *If you plan to use a commercial printing process to reproduce images that contain spot color fountain fills, make sure the start and end colors are two tints of the same color. If you do not plan to reproduce your images by a commercial process, however, this restriction does not apply.*

When you select the spot color method of assigning start and end colors, you can create a fountain fill from black to white by specifying colors as 0 or 100-percent black. Spot color is especially useful for black and white linear fountain fills if you are interested in assigning a PostScript halftone screen pattern to the object at the same time. In the next section, you will review the process of specifying a PostScript halftone screen pattern with a linear fountain fill.

Spot Color Linear Fountain Fills with PostScript Halftone Screens

You will recall from your previous work with outline fill colors that the preview window cannot show you how a selected PostScript halftone screen pattern will look when printed. You must actually print the object with such a fill on a PostScript device in order to see the results. The same is true of PostScript halftone screens when you combine them with fountain fills, which is possible when you use the spot color system to specify start and end colors. Here are some tips that should help you achieve a better design on the first try.

- Set the angle of the PostScript halftone screen either at the same angle as the linear fountain fill or at an angle that complements it in a design sense. (You do not want the eye to travel in too many directions at once.) Sometimes, you can determine the best angle only by experimentation; varying the angle of the halftone screen from the angle of the fountain fill can produce unexpected results.
- If you want the halftone screen to be visible when you print it, use a low-frequency setting in the PostScript Options dialog box. This is most important if the Fountain Stripes setting in the Preferences dialog box, which controls the fineness of the fountain fill itself, is high.

Go on to the next set of sections to experiment with fountain fills that radiate from the center outward or from the rim inward.

Defining Radial Fountain Fills

When you specify a radial fountain fill, the start color appears all around the outer area of the object and the end color appears at its center, or vice versa. The blending of colors or tints occurs in concentric circles. Because color density in radial fountain fills changes gradually in a circular pattern, a 3-D look is easy to achieve.

You cannot specify an angle when you select a radial fountain fill, but you can control the location of the fill's apparent center. You'll see one way to change the center of a radial fountain fill in this chapter and two others in Chapters 13 and 14.

You can use either spot color or process color to define a radial fountain fill. When you use spot color, you have the additional option of selecting a PostScript halftone screen pattern. The tips contained in the previous section, "Spot Color Linear Fountain Fills with PostScript Halftone Screens," apply to radial fountain fills, too.

You can control both the speed and fineness of the display that defines the fountain fill in full-color mode by adjusting the Preview Fountain Steps setting in the Preferences dialog box, as discussed under "Defining Linear Fountain Fills," earlier in this chapter.

As with the linear fountain fill, you can define a radial fountain fill for existing objects or set defaults for objects that you haven't yet created. The exercises in the next few sections use existing objects as examples.

Spot Color Radial Fountain Fills

Here, you will define a black and white spot color radial fountain fill for the objects in the Fill-1.cdr file that you created earlier in the chapter.

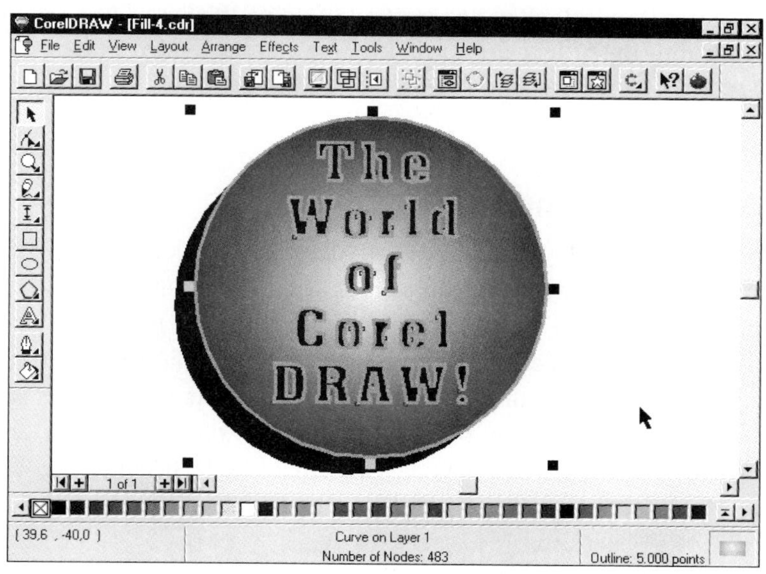

Spot color radial fountain fill with lighter shade at center

FIGURE 7-19

1. Close any open files and open the Fill-1.cdr file.
2. Adjust viewing magnification to fit-in-window. Select the combined circle-text and press F11 for the Fountain Fill Dialog box.
3. Set the type to Radial. Click on the From color button and then click on Other. Select PANTONE Spot Colors as the palette, PANTONE Process Black CV with 100-percent tint as the color, and then click on OK to return to the Fountain Fill dialog box. For the To color, also select PANTONE Process Black with 0-percent tint, and click on OK. Then, select OK again to exit the Fountain Fill dialog box. The circle-text object redisplays with a brighter area (the 0-percent black of the color range) in its center, as you can see in Figure 7-19. The apparent play of light you achieve with this kind of fill creates a 3-D effect, making the surface of the "globe" appear to curve.

Select Save As from the File menu. When the Save Drawing dialog box appears, type **Fill-4** in the File name text box and then press ENTER or click on OK.

As long as you choose the spot color method of specifying color, you can select a PostScript halftone screen pattern with a radial fountain fill. The added 3-D effect possible with radial fountain fills can lead to quite dramatic results when you add a halftone screen.

You can change the center of a radial fountain fill to create an off center highlight for the object. You'll look at one method of doing this next. Two other methods for accomplishing this effect are available; both are included among the techniques discussed in Chapter 14.

Edge Padding and Center Offset

The Fountain Fill dialog box allows you to add edge padding and to offset the center of a radial fill. You may have noticed that when Coreldraw creates a fountain fill, it is initially square, with sides equal to the longest side of the object's boundary box. When the creation process is complete, the excess is clipped off to fit the shape of the object; for example, the circles in this chapter. As a result, the starting and/or ending bands of the fill may be clipped off. *Edge padding* allows you to increase the percentage of an object's boundary box that is to be occupied by the starting and ending bands up to a maximum of 45 percent. Explore edge padding with the following brief exercise.

1. With Fill-4.cdr still on your screen and the circle-text object still selected, press F11 to open the Fountain Fill dialog box.
2. Type **20** in the Edge Pad numeric entry box and click on OK. Your drawing should look like Figure 7-20. Compare this with Figure 7-19 and you will see the impact of adding 20-percent edge padding.

The other function of the Fountain Fill dialog box is offsetting the center of a radial fill. Look at that next.

1. Again, press F11 to open the Fountain Fill dialog box. (Be sure the Radial Type is still selected.)
2. Type **20** in both the Horizontal and Vertical numeric entry boxes under Center offset and click on OK.
3. You should see the center of the radial fountain fill offset to the upper-right corner, as shown in Figure 7-21.
4. Save the current image as Fill-5.

Defining Conical and Square Fountain Fills

When you choose a conical fountain fill, the start color appears in a wedge shape from the outer edge to the center of the object. The end color is also a wedge shape from the outer edge to the center of the object on the side opposite from the start color. The blending of colors radiates in both clockwise and counterclockwise directions from the start color. Figure 7-22 shows a conical fountain fill with a 20-percent horizontal and vertical offset and a 20-degree angular rotation.

Square fountain fills are similar to radial fountain fills except that the bands are square instead of round. The From color is the outermost band and the To the innermost. The corners of the square provide a star effect, as you can see in Figure 7-23.

You can specify an angle and control the location of both a conical and square fill's apparent center when you select a conical or square fountain fill. A square fill can also have edge padding. You can use either spot or process color to define both conical and square fill as well as PostScript halftone screen patterns. The tips contained in the earlier section, "Spot Color Linear Fountain Fills with PostScript Halftone Screens," apply to both conical and square fountain fills. As with the other

Radial fountain fill with 20% edge padding

FIGURE 7-20

Center of a radial fountain fill offset 20% to the right and 20% up

FIGURE 7-21

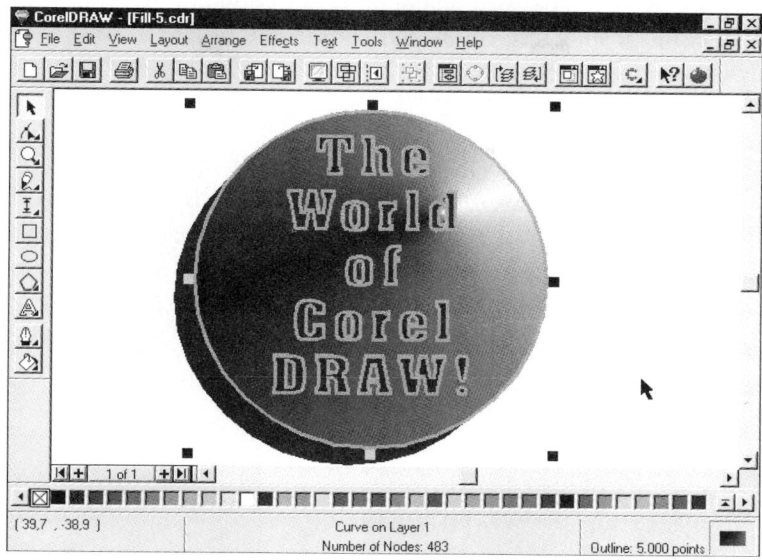

Conical fountain fill

FIGURE 7-22

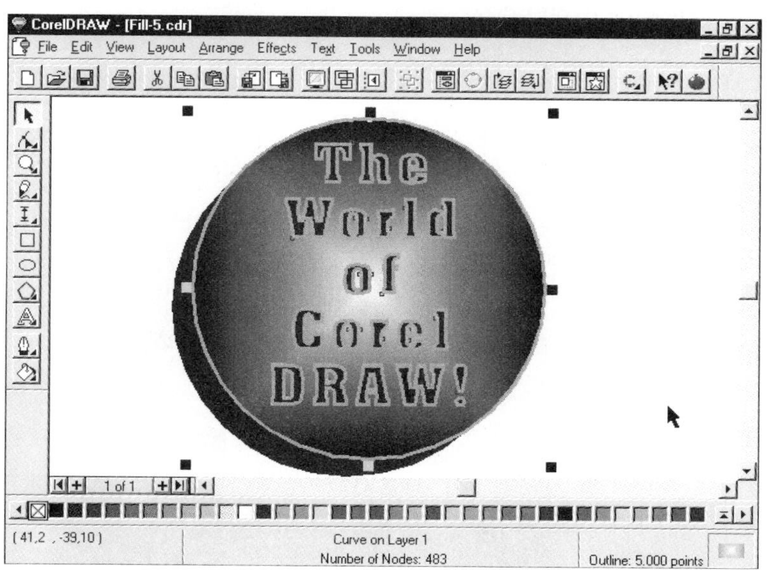

Square fountain fill

FIGURE 7-23

fountain fills, you can define conical or square fountain fills for existing objects or set defaults for objects that you haven't yet created.

Bitmap and Vector Fill Patterns

Coreldraw has two more ways to fill objects: bitmap fill and vector patterns and textures. Bitmap and vector refer to two methods of forming a graphic image in a computer. *Bitmap* images are formed by defining each point (or bit) in an image. *Vector* images are formed by defining the start, end, and characteristics of each line (or vector) in an image. Coreldraw comes with a number of bitmap and vector images that can be used to construct fill patterns. You can create your own or modify existing bitmap and vector images and then use them in fill patterns.

Bitmap and vector patterns are formed by repeating an image many times—*tiling*—so that each image is a single tile. Coreldraw provides the means of selecting existing bitmap and vector images; of sizing, editing, and offsetting both kinds of images; and of creating, importing, and coloring bitmap images.

Using Bitmap Fill Patterns

Bitmap images are the most numerous and the most easily manipulated, and Coreldraw provides greater capability for handling them. Look at bitmap fill patterns with the following exercise.

1. Fill-5.cdr should still be on your screen with the circle-text object selected.

2. Select the Fill tool and the Two-color button that looks like a checkerboard. The Two-Color Bitmap Pattern dialog box opens.
3. Click on the display box and then on the flyout window's scroll bar to scan through the 51 patterns that are included with Coreldraw. Then, select the Corel image shown here by clicking on it:

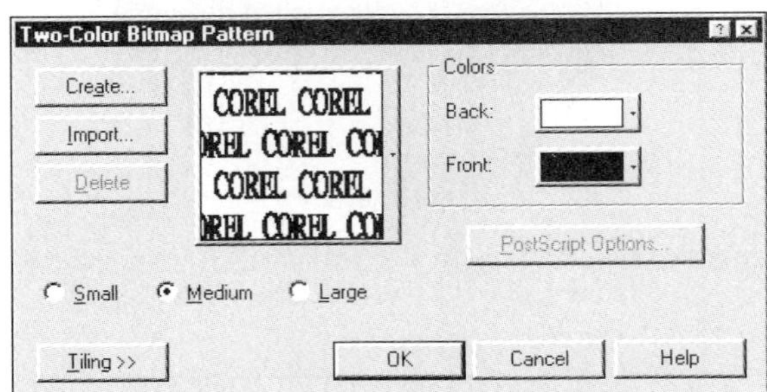

4. First click on Small, then Medium, and then Large to see the difference the three sizes make. Click on Tiling and type in your own sizes in the numeric entry boxes. The height and width do not have to be the same, but for most images you probably want them to be. The maximum size is 15 inches square. (Keep the Medium size.) Tile size is the size of each tile or image in the pattern. Different sizes work for different patterns. On some patterns, Small causes the images to look smudged, while on others, Large causes straight lines to have jagged edges. You need to pick the size that is right for the image and for what you are trying to achieve.

Clicking on either the Front or Back buttons under Colors, or the More buttons, allows you to assign a color to either the foreground (Front)—the word "Corel" in the selected pattern—or the background (Back). The default is a black foreground and white background. The Colors button opens the Color palette, and Others opens a Color dialog box that is very similar to other Color dialog boxes you have used in this chapter. You can choose between spot and process color, choose a color from a palette, specify % Tint (if you are using spot color), and specify a custom process to create a new one, or open an existing one in another file, or another named color. Also, if you are using spot color, you can select a PostScript halftone screen.

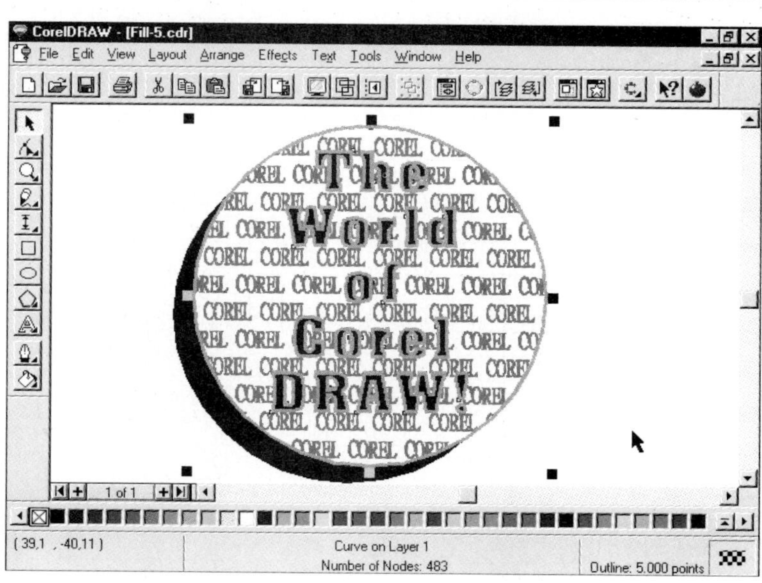

Medium-sized two-color fill pattern

FIGURE 7-24

5. Click on the Front button and then on Others. Keeping the CMYK color model, select 50-percent black (fourth button from the right in the top row of the Custom Palette) and click on OK. Keep the default white for Back, and click on OK to exit the Two-Color Bitmap Pattern dialog box. You will return to your drawing and see the bitmap pattern provide the fill for the curve object. Your screen should look like Figure 7-24.
6. Save your current drawing with the filename Fill-6.

The Import command button in the Two-Color Bitmap Pattern dialog box opens a file selection dialog box. If you select a file, the image is added to the set of images that you can access in the Two-Color Bitmap Pattern dialog box. You can offset (stagger) both the horizontal and vertical starting position of each image in the pattern, as well as offset neighboring rows or neighboring columns.

The Create button allows you to create a new bitmap image to use in constructing a fill pattern. When you click on the Create button, the Two-Color Pattern Editor opens, as shown in Figure 7-25. The Two-Color Pattern Editor provides for three different sizes of drawings: 16 pixels ("dots" on your screen) square, 32 pixels square, and 64 pixels square. The more diagonal or curve elements in your image, the larger the size you will need. From a practical standpoint you should use the smallest size possible because the larger sizes take longer to draw and take more

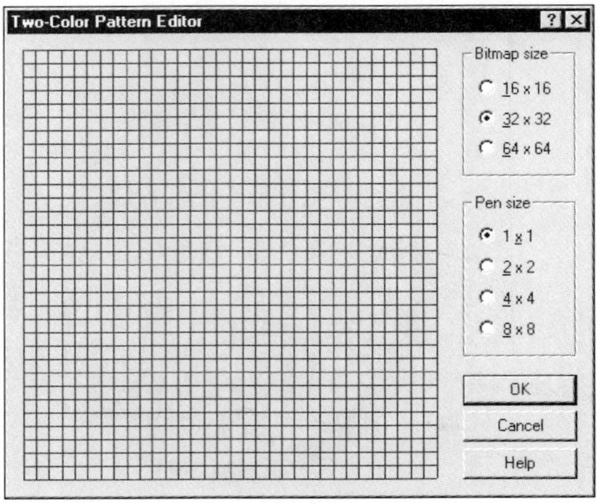

Bitmap Pattern Editor

FIGURE 7-25

room on disk. To draw, click the left mouse button to make a pixel black and the right mouse button to make a black pixel white again. If you want to erase an unfinished drawing, change the size, say, from 16 by 16 to 32 by 32. You can then change the size back, and all of the pixels will be clear. When you are done with a drawing, click on OK, and the image will be saved as one of the bitmap images that are available from the Two-Color Pattern dialog box. You can then select it to create a fill pattern.

Using Full-Color Bitmap Patterns

Coreldraw also provides full-color bitmap fill patterns. Change the fill in the curve object to a full-color pattern in the following exercise:

1. With Fill-6.cdr still on your screen, select the circle-text object. Open the Fill tool flyout and select the Full-Color fill button, shown here. The Full-Color Bitmap Pattern dialog box will open.
2. The Full-Color Bitmap Pattern dialog box lets you open bitmap files to use as fill patterns. Click on the display box to look at the patterns that are available. Select one of the patterns (the default is shown here) and click on OK. The pattern will fill the display box as shown here:

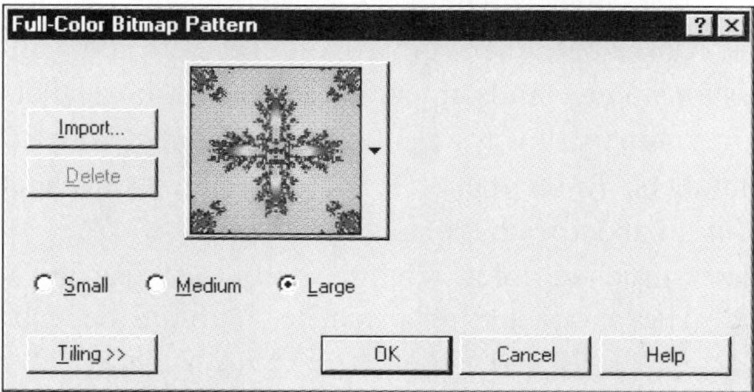

3. Click on the Tiling button, select Small, then Medium, then Large. Notice that the default tile sizes in the numeric entry boxes are not square like two-color patterns are. For now, select Large and click on OK. Your full-color filled drawing will appear, as shown in Figure 7-26.
4. Save the changed drawing with the name Fill-7.

7

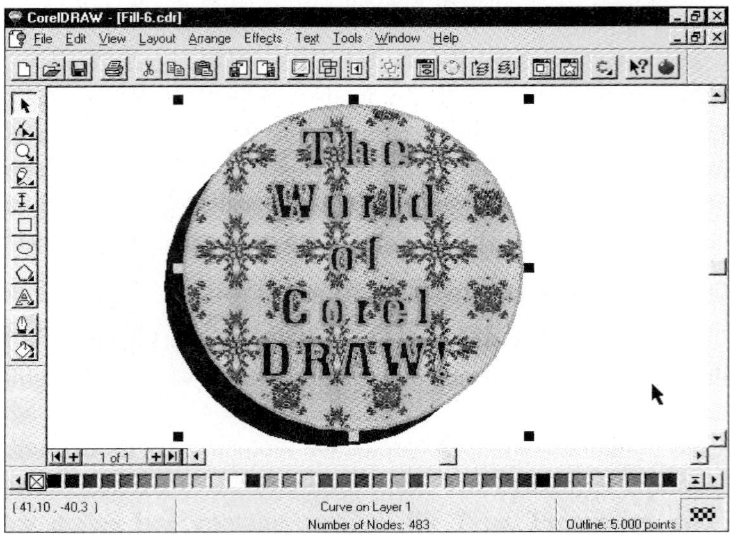

Full-Color Pattern fill

FIGURE 7-26

Using Texture Fills

You can also select from over 100 bitmap texture fills with Coreldraw. While two- and full-color fills consist of tiled patterns, textures are created with a mathematical formula. Textures for water, clouds, minerals, and others are available. Each texture can be modified in a number of ways, including by texture number. Each texture has 32,767 texture numbers. To see their effect, change the texture number, then click on the Preview button underneath the preview box.

Other parameters, such as color, brightness, contrast, density, and softness can also be modified. The parameters that can be modified depend on the texture selected.

To select a texture fill, follow these steps.

1. With Fill-7 still on the screen, select the circle-text object.

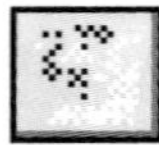

2. Open the Fill tool flyout and select the Texture Fill button that looks like clouds (shown in the margin). The Texture Fill dialog box will open, as shown in Figure 7-27.

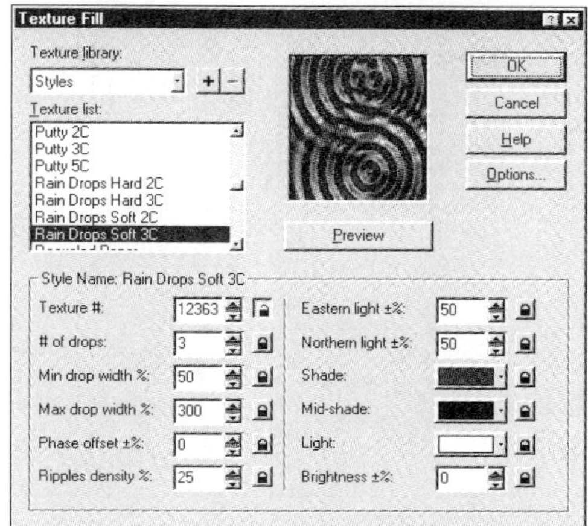

Texture Fill dialog box

FIGURE 7-27

3. Click on OK to accept the default Rain Drops Soft 3C fill. Your circle-text object will now look like Figure 7-28.

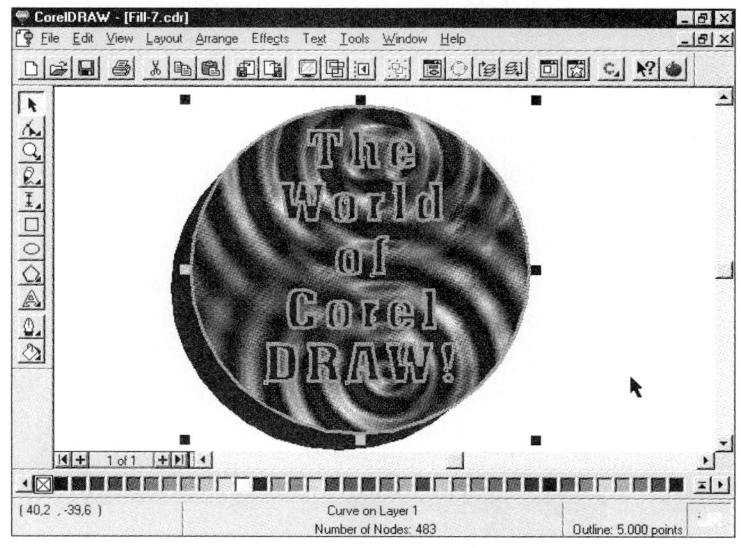

Texture fill in art

FIGURE 7-28

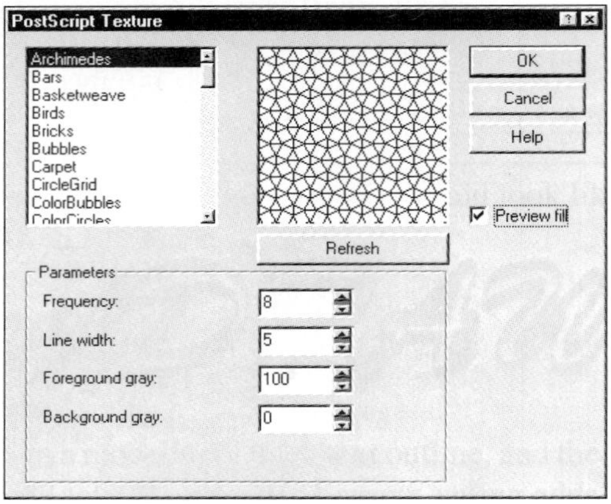

PostScript Texture dialog box

FIGURE 7-29

OTE: *Texture fills require a large amount of memory and a longer time to print. You may need to limit the size and number of texture-filled objects in your drawing because of this.*

IP: *You can also change texture parameters randomly. Select the Lock button next to the parameter you wish to modify to change it to the locked position, then click on the preview button. Each time you click on the preview button, the texture will change.*

Postscript Texture Fills

The sixth button in the bottom row of the Fill tool flyout is the PostScript Textures button (shown in the margin), which opens the dialog box shown in Figure 7-29. If you print to a PostScript printer, you can fill selected objects with a choice of 51 different PostScript textures. This number is deceptive; although only 51 basic patterns exist, you can alter the parameters for each texture to achieve wide variations in appearance.

When you assign a PostScript texture fill to an object, the Coreldraw window displays the object with a small gray "PS" pattern on a white background. The Fill designation in the status bar, however, indicates the name of the particular texture assigned. Unfortunately, you cannot view these textures until you print them.

Working with PostScript Texture fills is an adventure because of the *aleatory*, or chance, characteristics built into the mathematical formulas for the textures. Think of these textures as a way to bring more creative design elements into your drawing, even if your own drawing powers are limited.

Fill Roll-Up

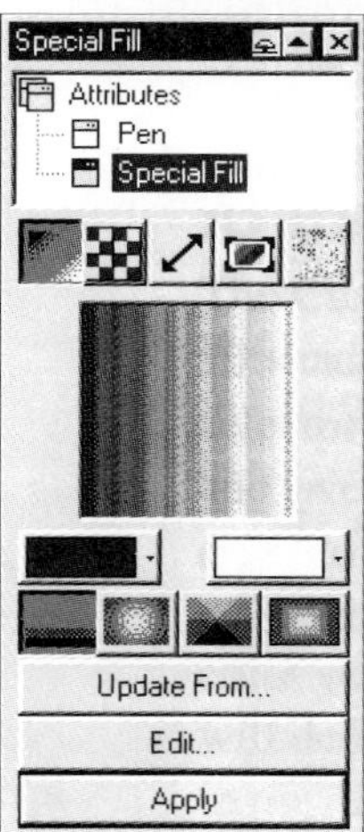

Like many other major functions, Fill Color has a roll-up window. The Fill roll-up window, shown here, is opened by clicking on the Roll-Up button, second from the left in the top row of the Fill flyout.

Like other roll-up windows, the Fill roll-up window stays open on your screen until you roll it up or close it. It provides access to the Fill Color, Fountain Fill, Two-Color Pattern, Full-Color Pattern, and Texture Fill dialog boxes. It also allows you to edit the fill of an existing object. To use the Fill roll-up, you first click on one of the five buttons at the top of the roll-up to specify the type of fill you want. Clicking the edit button, near the bottom of the roll-up, opens the dialog box for the type of fill you have selected. Also, the display area below the five fill-type buttons changes to reflect the type of fill. For Uniform Fill, this area is the current Color palette. For the other types of fill, it provides display boxes and buttons unique to those types.

Fill Tool Hints

Finally, some hints for using the Fill tool are included in this section. These by no means exhaust the many uses to which you can put the Fill tool; rather, they are tips to help you gain speed in your work or to introduce creative effects.

Copying Fill Styles

In previous chapters, you have learned how to use the Copy Properties From command in the Edit menu to copy text, Outline Pen, or outline fill properties from one object to another. You can use that same command and its associated dialog box to copy fill styles between objects, too. The following summarizes how to use this feature to best advantage.

1. Select the object or group of objects *to which* you would like to copy the fill properties of another object.
2. Select the Copy Properties From command in the Edit menu. When the Copy Properties dialog box appears, activate the Fill check box by clicking on it. If you want to copy text, Outline Pen, or Outline Color properties at the same time, activate those check boxes, too.
3. Click on OK to exit the dialog box. The pointer turns into a thick arrow to use to point to the object from which you want to copy the fill style.
4. Select the object whose style you want to copy to the selected object. The selected object redisplays with the new fill style.

The entire continuum of fill styles is available to you when you use this command. You can copy spot or process color uniform fills, PostScript halftone screens, preset shades of gray, bitmap fills, or even PostScript textures. Use this command and dialog box as a handy shortcut to defining fill properties for one or more objects.

Using Fountain Steps to Enhance Previews and Printing

You will recall that the Preferences dialog box (accessible from the Tools menu) contains many useful settings to customize the way Coreldraw displays your work. One of these settings, Preview Fountain Steps (accessed with the Display tab), applies to the use of linear, radial, conical, and square fountain fills.

Coreldraw displays a fountain fill by creating a series of concentric circles or squares that begin at the outer edge of the selection box for the object and work their way inward. You have probably noticed this process each time the preview window redraws an object containing a fountain fill. The Preview Fountain Steps setting in the Preferences dialog box lets you determine how many circles or squares Coreldraw creates to represent a fountain fill. The number ranges from 2 to 256, with 2 representing two circles with coarse outlines, and 256 representing a high number of finely drawn circles. As you can imagine, the window redraws very quickly when Preview Fountain Steps is set to a low number, and extremely slowly when the Preview Fountain Steps setting is high. Further, if you print to a device other than a PostScript printer, the number of circles you select in the Preview Fountain Steps setting represents what will actually print. You can achieve some interesting effects by varying this setting.

COREL DRAW!™ 6 in action

CATTAIL
COVE
84-In.
Double-faced entry sign.
Constructed on a concrete
base, with stone veneer.
Sign area to be sandblasted
redwood with painted and
gilded lettering & graphics.

MOGENSEN deSIGN
(818) 352-4102

PRELIMINARY
DRAFT
PLAN NO.
E3
SHEET TITLE
Entry Sign, COLOR RENDERING
PLAN NAME.
Cattail Cove Marina
DATE
6-12-92
ARCH. DEPT.
ENGR. DEPT.
SHEET NO.
01

***Cattail Cove*—William Mogensen**

William Mogensen's use of outline and fill colors has brought to life this design for a sign. You have already learned most of the techniques Mr. Mogensen used to create this design for Cattail Cove Marina. You will learn how to modify text to produce the type of effect used in this design in Chapter 10.

William Mogensen is located in Shadow Hills, California. He can be reached at (818) 352-4102, by email at william.h.mogensen@jpl.nasa.gov, and on CompuServe at 75227.3164.

Using Advanced Features of CorelDRAW! 6

In Chapter 5, you learned how to use the Pick tool to select, move, and arrange objects. In this chapter, you will use the Pick tool to transform the size or shape of selected objects.

When you transform an object with the Pick tool, you do not alter its fundamental shape; a rectangle continues to have four corners, and an ellipse remains an oval.

(This is not the case when you reshape an object using the Shape tool, which you will learn about in Chapters 9 and 10.)

The five basic transformation techniques you will learn in this chapter enable you to size, scale, mirror, rotate, and skew an object in any direction. You will also learn how to retain a copy of the original object, repeat transformations automatically, and return an object to its original format, even if you have transformed it several times.

The exercises in this chapter introduce not only the basic skills that make up the art of transformation, but also the alternative ways you can practice them. Coreldraw lets you customize the way you work when transforming objects. If you like to work interactively, you can carry out these functions using the mouse and keyboard alone. For a little extra guidance, you can look to the Status bar and rulers. And, if you need to render a technical illustration that requires absolute precision, you can select the Transform commands from the Arrange menu, which are discussed throughout this chapter.

Throughout most of this chapter, you will practice each skill using a simple text string that you create in the following section. Although you will practice on this one object, the functions you use—for size, scale and mirror, rotate, and skew—work exactly the same way in Coreldraw with multiple selected objects as with single ones. In later exercises, you can practice combining transformation operations with other skills you have learned in previous chapters.

The Transform Menu

Although most of your work will probably be done with the Pick tool, the Transform roll-up (opened with the Transform command on the Arrange menu) allows you greater precision. Use the Transform command menu to position, rotate, scale, mirror, size, or skew an object by selecting one of the commands, as shown here:

Position...	Alt+F7
Rotate...	Alt+F8
Scale and Mirror...	Alt+F9
Size...	Alt+F10
Skew...	Alt+F11

When selected, each command opens the Transform roll-up with a different set of properties for which you enter the settings for creating a specific transformation. You can then apply the measurement values to a previously selected object, or you can make them apply to a duplicate of a selected object (which will then be created). As each transformation effect is discussed in this chapter, the corresponding Transform command is also discussed.

Sizing an Object

As you discovered in Chapter 3, a rectangular selection box, made up of eight black nodes, surrounds an object when you select it. These nodes, shown in Figure 8-1, have special functions in Coreldraw—you use them to size and scale objects. When you *size* an object, you change its *aspect ratio* (the proportion of its width to its height), because you lengthen or shorten it in one direction only. When you *scale* an object, you change the object's length and width at the same time, so the aspect ratio remains the same. To size an object, you must drag one of the four middle nodes. To scale an object, you drag one of the four nodes in the corners of the selection box.

This section covers all of the available techniques for sizing objects, with exercises that will introduce you to both the interactive and menu-assisted methods for sizing and copying objects.

If you prefer to work interactively, bypassing menu commands and dialog boxes, you can size a selected object using the mouse and keyboard alone. You do not sacrifice precision when you work this way, for the Status bar assists you in setting precise values as you size an object. Practice sizing a text string interactively in the following sections.

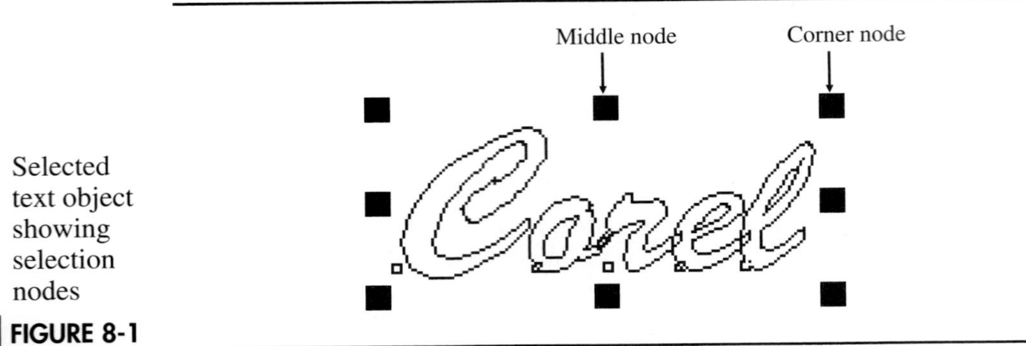

Selected text object showing selection nodes

FIGURE 8-1

Sizing Horizontally

You can size an object in either a horizontal or vertical direction. In the following exercise, you will create a text string and size it toward the right.

1. Make sure your page is in Portrait format before you begin. From the Layout menu, select Grid and Ruler Setup. In the Grid & Ruler Setup dialog box, in the Grid tab turn off the Show Grid and Snap To Grid options, and in the Ruler tab, set the vertical grid origin to 11 inches, and click on OK.
2. Make certain that Rulers in the View menu is selected (with a check mark) and that Wireframe is turned off.
3. From the Outline Pen flyout, click on the Hairline button. Click on Artistic Text, then Paragraph Text, and then OK to apply the line width to all new objects.
4. From the Fill flyout, click on No Fill (the X). Again click on Artistic Text, then Paragraph Text, and then OK to apply the fill standard to all new objects.
5. Select Character from the Text menu or press CTRL-T to open the Character Attributes dialog box. When the Text Attributes dialog box appears, select Artistic Text and Paragraph Text, then click on OK. Set the font to BrushScript BT, and size to 60 points on the Font tab. On the Alignment tab, click on the Left align button and then click on OK.

6. Select the Artistic Text tool, then click an insertion point at the 1 1/2-inch mark on the horizontal ruler and the – (minus) 6-inch mark on the vertical ruler. When the insertion point appears, type the text string, **Corel**. The text may appear to have no outline and a gray fill. The attributes you set in the Outline Pen and Fill flyouts will appear when the text object is selected with the Pick tool.
7. Open the Zoom toolbar and choose Actual Size (1:1). Use the scroll bars to move the text to where you can work with it.
8. Select the Save As command from the File menu, make sure you are in the folder where you save your drawings, and type **Corel**. Click on Save.
9. Activate the Pick tool. A selection box surrounds the text string immediately since it was the last object you drew. Your screen should resemble Figure 8-2.

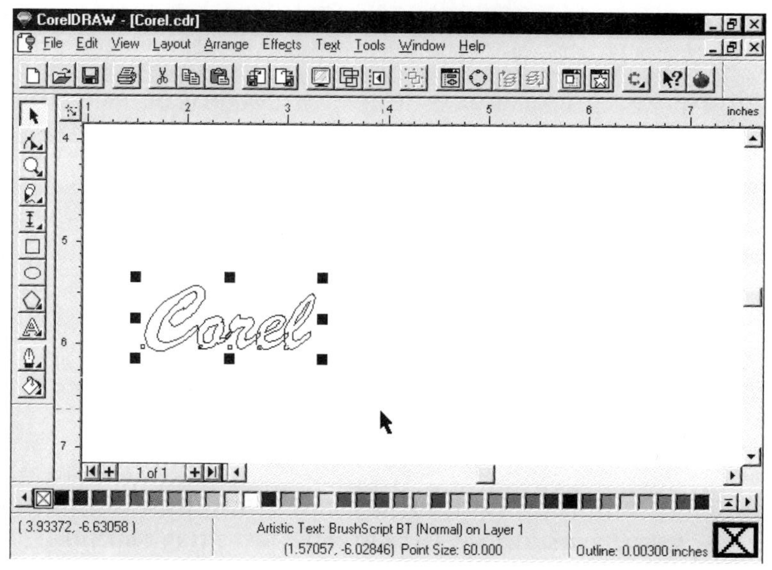

Text string ready for transformations

FIGURE 8-2

10. Position the pointer directly over the center-right node of the selection box. The mouse pointer changes to a crosshair, as shown here:

11. Depress and hold the left mouse button and drag the node to the right. The original object seems to stay in the same place, but a dashed rectangular box follows the pointer, which changes to a two-way horizontal arrow, as shown here:

12. As you drag, the Status bar displays the message "X scale:" followed by a numeric value and a percent sign. This value is the amount you are sizing the selected object, shown in increments of 1/10 of a percentage point.
13. After you have sized the object to the desired size, release the mouse button. Coreldraw redraws a horizontally-sized version of the original object, like the one shown here:

14. Select the Undo Stretch command from the Edit menu to return the text string to its original size. The original text string remains selected for the next exercise.

To size a selected object to the left instead of to the right, drag the middle node at the *left* side of the selection box. Practice sizing the text string from the left side if you wish, but select Undo Stretch after you are finished so that the original text string remains on the screen.

NOTE: *When the mouse pointer is allowed to cross a window border, the object will continue to transform until the pointer is moved back inside the window. This is called Auto-panning. If you don't like Auto-panning, you can turn it off in the Display tab on the Options dialog box, opened from the Tools menu.*

Sizing Vertically

You can also size an object in a vertical direction. The mouse pointer and Status bar information change to reflect the direction of your size.

1. Select the "Corel" text string if it is not selected already.
2. Position the mouse pointer directly over the top-middle node of the selection box. The mouse pointer changes to a crosshair.
3. Depress and hold the left mouse button and drag the node upward. The original object seems to stay in the same place, but a dashed rectangular box follows the pointer, which changes to a two-way vertical arrow, as shown here:

4. As you drag, the Status bar displays the message "Y scale:" followed by a numeric value and a percent sign. This value shows precisely how much you are sizing the selected object in increments of 1/10 of a percent.

5. After you have sized the object to the desired size, release the mouse button. Coreldraw redraws a vertically sized version of the original object.
6. Select the Undo Stretch command from the Edit menu to return the text string to its original size.

If you wish, practice sizing the text string downward in a vertical direction. When you are finished, undo your changes to the original object and then proceed with the next exercise.

Sizing in Increments of 100 Percent

In previous chapters, you saw how to use CTRL to constrain your drawing or moving operations to fixed increments or angles. The same holds true when you are sizing a selected object. To size an object in fixed increments of 100 percent, press and hold CTRL as you drag the node in the desired direction. The Status bar keeps track of the increments in which you are sizing the object. As always, remember to release the mouse button *before* you release CTRL or the object may not size in exact increments. In the following exercise, you will triple the width of the original object using CTRL.

1. Select the text string if it is not selected already.
2. Press and hold CTRL and then drag the right-middle node to the right. Notice that the dashed rectangular outline does not follow the two-way arrow pointer continuously; instead, it "snaps" outward only when you have doubled the width of the object, as shown here:

3. When the Status bar displays the message "X scale: 300.0%," release the mouse button first and then CTRL. The text string redisplays at triple its original width.

4. Select Undo Stretch from the Edit menu to revert to the original unsized object.

Retaining a Copy of the Original Object

A useful design technique is to make a copy of the original object as you size it, so that both the original and the sized objects appear on the screen. To retain a copy of the original object, just click the right mouse button once (while depressing the left button) as soon as you begin the sizing, or press the + key on the numeric keypad when the outline box appears. You can choose the technique that is most easy for you.

OTE: *Pressing the right mouse button while dragging to leave the original does not conflict with the function you assign to the right mouse button in the Options dialog box.*

You can also retain a copy of the original object when using CTRL. Try this technique now.

1. Select the text string "Corel" if it is not already selected. Position the mouse pointer over the bottom-middle node and begin to drag this marker downward.
2. As soon as the dashed outline box appears, press the + key or press and release the right mouse button once. The message "Leave Original" appears at the left side of the Status bar.
3. Press and hold CTRL and continue to drag the bottom middle node downward until the Status bar reads "Scale: 200.0%."
4. Release the mouse button and then the CTRL key. The screen displays both the original and sized object, as shown here:

5. Undo your changes to the original text string before continuing.

If the sized object does not appear in the correct proportions, you either failed to press and hold CTRL, or released CTRL before releasing the mouse button. Keep practicing until you feel comfortable with the technique, but remember to undo your changes to be ready for the next exercise.

Sizing with the Size Command

If you find the use of the mouse and keyboard controls inconvenient, you can perform all of the possible size operations using the Size roll-up, opened from the Transform flyout on the Arrange menu. The dialog box that opens when you select this command allows you to choose the direction and exact amount of sizing, and retain a copy of the original object.

Sizing an Object

Try the following exercise to become familiar with the Size dialog box.

1. Select the "Corel" text string with the Pick tool and then, from the Arrange menu, select Transform and then click on Size . The roll-up shown in Figure 8-3 appears (your horizontal and vertical values may differ). The horizontal (H) and vertical (V) controls in the center of the roll-up let you specify the direction and amount of size in increments of .01 inch (or whatever units you are using). The down arrow (in the lower half of the roll-up), when clicked, opens the Relative Position indicators. These indicators allow you to size relative to the specified anchor point. The Apply To Duplicate button determines whether you make a copy of the original object as you size it.
2. Set the numeric value for vertical (V) to 1.5 inches, using either the scroll arrow or the keyboard, and then click on Apply. The text string increases in height. Notice, however, that when you size an object using the Size roll-up instead of the mouse, the sized object is centered on the same position as the original. If you want it to appear in another location, click on the object's outline and drag it to the desired location.
3. Select the Clear Transformations command from the Arrange menu to return the object to its original size. (You can also use Undo in the Edit menu or press CTRL-Z.)

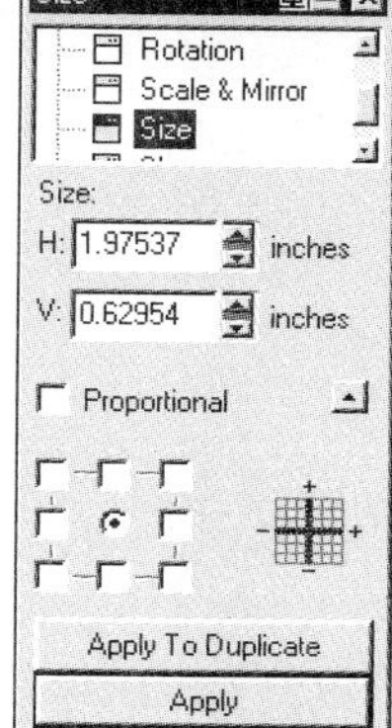

Size roll-up (after opening the Relative Position indicators)

FIGURE 8-3

4. While the "Corel" object is selected and the Size dialog box is open, set the horizontal value (H) to 2.5 inches, and then select Apply. This time, the text string increases in width.
5. Clear the current transformation by selecting the Clear Transformations command in the Arrange menu. This time, you will create a larger size duplicate while retaining the size of the original.
6. Set the vertical (V) value to 1.5 inches and then click on Apply To Duplicate to retain a copy of the original object. Coreldraw redisplays the original object against a vertically sized image about 1.5 times the size of the original.

Notice that when you use the Size dialog box for these operations, the sized object is superimposed on the original and both objects share a common point, as shown in Figure 8-4. If you want the sized object to appear above, below, or to the side of the original, first open the Relative Position drop box by clicking on the down arrow (below and to the right of the vertical scale numeric entry box) and then click on one of the eight check boxes representing the position the original object will take in relation to its duplicate. Alternatively, you can drag the sized object's outline to the desired location.

7. To erase the transformed copy of the object so that only the unaltered original remains, select Undo Duplicate from the Edit menu.

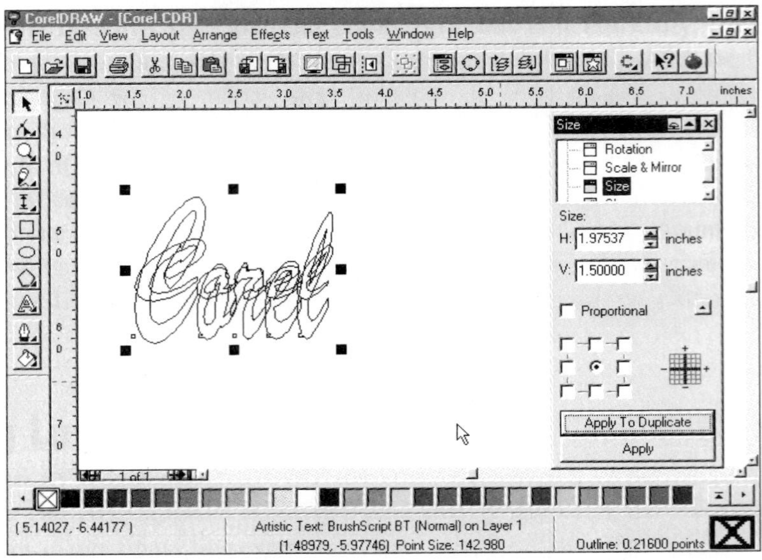

Size roll-up

FIGURE 8-4

CAUTION: *If you want to erase the copy of the original object after a transformation that leaves the original in place, use Undo Duplicate rather than Clear Transformations. If you use Clear Transformations, the transformed object on the top layer is not erased, but instead becomes an exact copy of the original. The transformation is cleared, but not the object itself. As a result, what looks like one object on the screen is actually two superimposed objects.*

Scaling an Object

As you have just seen, sizing an object involves changing its size in one direction (horizontal or vertical) only. When you *scale* an object, you change its size horizontally and vertically at the same time, thereby maintaining the same proportions and aspect ratio. You can scale an object interactively using the keyboard and mouse, or you can scale an object using Scale & Mirror on the Transform flyout found on the Arrange menu. If you prefer to work more spontaneously, you will probably favor the mouse and keyboard controls. Recall that when you size an object, you drag it by one of the *middle* nodes. Scaling an object is similar, except that you drag one of the *corner* nodes instead.

To practice scaling objects interactively, try this exercise.

1. If it is not selected already, select the "Corel" text string.
2. Position the mouse pointer directly over one of the corner nodes. You can scale from any corner but, for the sake of this exercise, use the lower-right corner marker. The pointer changes to a crosshair, just as when you prepared to size an object.
3. Drag the lower-right node diagonally downward. As you drag, the pointer changes to a four-way arrow, similar to the move arrow except that it is rotated diagonally, as shown here:

4. The original object appears to stay in the same place, but a dashed outline box follows the scaling pointer. The outline box increases or decreases in size, depending on the direction in which you drag the marker.
5. Note that the Status bar displays the message "Scale:" followed by a percentage value. This value tells you precisely how much larger or smaller you are making the object.
6. When the dashed outline box is the size you want the text string to be, release the mouse button. The selected object reappears in a scaled version.
7. Select Clear Transformations in the Arrange menu or Undo Stretch in the Edit menu to return the object to its original size.

Scaling in Increments of 100 Percent

To scale an object in increments of 100 percent of its size, all you need to do is press and hold CTRL while scaling the object. Just as when you sized objects using CTRL, the dashed outline box does not move smoothly but instead "snaps" at each 100-percent increment. Likewise, the message in the Status bar changes only when you reach the next 100-percent increment. Remember to release the mouse button *before* you release CTRL, or the increments will not be exact.

Keep in mind, too, that an object scaled to 200 percent of its original size takes up four times the area of the original object, not twice as much, because you are increasing both the height and width of the object by a factor of two.

Retaining a Copy While Scaling

To retain a copy of the object in its original location as you scale it, just click the right mouse button (while holding down the left button) as soon as you begin to scale the object or press and release the + key on the numeric keypad. The Status bar displays the message "Leave Original," just as when you leave a copy while sizing an object.

Precise Scaling with the Scale Command

If you find the use of the mouse and keyboard controls inconvenient, you can perform all of the scaling operations precisely using the Scale & Mirror roll-up on the Transform flyout of the Arrange menu. You can specify the amount of scaling desired, retain a copy of the original object, and create mirror images that appear at a diagonal to the original. Work through the following exercise to become familiar with using the Transform roll-up to scale an object.

1. With the Corel.CDR file open and in an actual size viewing magnification, select the "Corel" text string. Open the Arrange menu, click on Transform roll-up, and then select Scale & Mirror. The Scale & Mirror dialog box is displayed, as shown here:

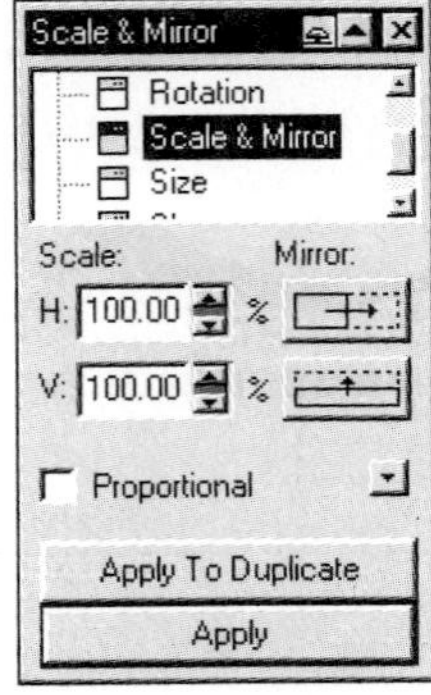

2. To scale an object, you need to set both the horizontal (H) and the vertical (V) values to the same number. Set both of these values to 150 percent, using either the scroll arrow or the keyboard.

3. Click on Apply. The text string increases in both height and width. Notice, however, that a scaled object created with the Scale & Mirror roll-up appears in the same location as the original and has the same center point. If you want the scaled object to appear elsewhere, move it to the desired location.

4. Select the Clear Transformations command from the Arrange menu to return the object to its original size.

Retaining a Copy While Using Scale & Mirror

It is easy to make a copy of the original object from the Scale & Mirror roll-up. Simply press Apply To Duplicate before you exit the dialog box.

1. Again make sure the text string "Corel" is selected and open the Scale & Mirror dialog box. This time, you will constrain the size of the image to an exact multiple of the original, as you did using CTRL and the mouse. You will also leave a copy of the original object in its original location.

2. Set the vertical and horizontal values to 200 percent and then click on Apply To Duplicate to retain a copy of the original object. Coreldraw redisplays the original object along with a scaled text string at two times the size of the original.

3. To erase the transformed copy of the object so that only the unaltered original remains, select the Undo Duplicate command from the Edit menu. If you have moved the copy of the original, the Undo Duplicate command is not available, so select the copy and press DEL to clear it.

Sizing and Scaling from the Center

In the previous sizing and scaling exercises using the mouse, the object was modified in one dimension (sizing) or two dimensions (scaling) from a fixed opposite side or sides. In other words, when you dragged the right side of the object to the right, the left side remained fixed and was in the same vertical position as was the right side of the modified object. Similarly, when you dragged the lower-right corner down and to the right, the top and left sides remained fixed and had the same horizontal and vertical positions in the modified object.

When you used the Size and Scale & Mirror options and modified an object in one or two dimensions, the opposite sides moved proportionately. That is, with the roll-up, the object was being modified from a fixed center point instead of from a fixed side or sides. When you changed the horizontal and vertical percentages, all four sides changed, leaving the same center point as the original object.

You can also size and scale an object from the center point by pressing SHIFT while dragging with the mouse. This is the same as drawing an ellipse or rectangle from the center by pressing SHIFT while dragging with the Ellipse or Rectangle tool.

Recall how you sized and scaled with the mouse originally and see how this changes when you press SHIFT:

1. The "Corel" text string should be selected on your page in an Actual Size view.
2. As you did in an earlier exercise, drag the middle node on the right side to the right several inches. Notice how the left side remains fixed. Release the mouse button and press CTRL-Z to undo the modification.
3. Press and hold SHIFT while dragging the right-middle node to the right an inch or so. Notice how the left side now moves a proportionate amount—the left and right sides are moving outward in equal amounts. Release the mouse button and press CTRL-Z to undo the modification.
4. Again, as you did before, drag the lower-right corner node down and to the right several inches. Notice how the left and top sides remain fixed. Release the mouse button and press CTRL-Z to undo the modification.
5. Press and hold SHIFT while dragging the lower-right corner node down and to the right an inch or so. Notice how the top and left sides are now moving proportionately with the bottom and right sides. Release the mouse button and press CTRL-Z to undo the modification.

Creating a Mirror Image

As you found when sizing and scaling objects, the selection box nodes are very useful and easy to use. They are also handy when creating mirror images. The

Transform roll-up, another important tool in sizing and scaling, also can be used to create mirror images with its Scale & Mirror option. You will explore both means of creating these visual effects.

Using the middle nodes on the selection box, you can create a horizontal or vertical mirror image of an object. You can choose from among several techniques the one most suited to your needs. If, for example, you choose to retain a copy of the original object, you need to use the + key or click the right mouse button. If you choose to make the size of the mirror image an exact multiple of the original, you need to use CTRL after clicking the right mouse button. You can just as easily decide not to copy the original object, or make the mirrored object a custom size. In every case, however, you will drag the *opposite* center node until it "flips" in the direction in which you want the mirror image to appear.

The following exercise assumes that you want to create a perfect horizontal mirror image of an object, like the one shown here. At the end of the exercise are suggestions for obtaining other results.

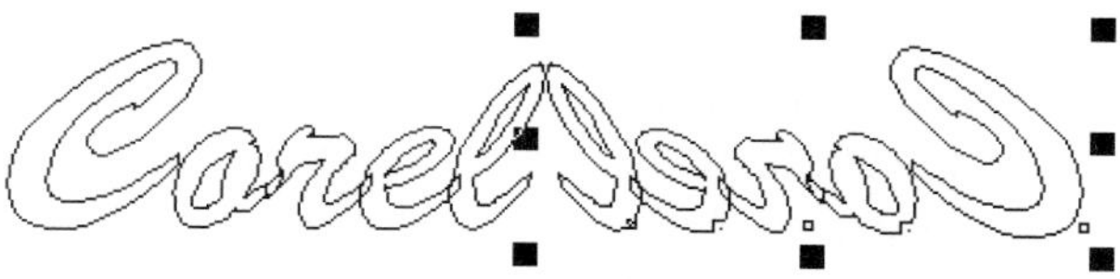

1. Select the text string "Corel" if it isn't selected already.
2. Position the mouse pointer over the left-middle node and begin to drag this node to the right.
3. As soon as the dashed outline box appears, press the + key or click the right mouse button once. The message "Leave Original" appears at the left side of the Status bar.
4. Press and hold CTRL and continue to drag the marker to the right. The CTRL key ensures that the size of the mirrored object will be an exact multiple of the original, in this case, the identical size (100 percent).
5. When the dashed outline box "snaps" beside the original object and the Status bar reads "Y scale: 100.0% (Mirrored)," as in Figure 8-5, release the mouse button and then the CTRL key. Coreldraw redraws the screen showing both the original and the mirrored object. The mirrored object is selected. If your text strings look different, select Undo Stretch and try the exercise again.

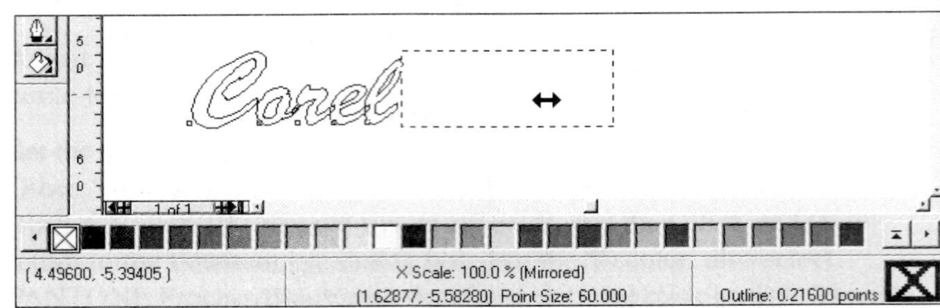

Using the mouse to mirror an object

FIGURE 8-5

6. Press CTRL-Z for Undo Stretch and to return the text string to its original unmirrored state.

You can vary this exercise to achieve different results. For example, to create a vertical mirror image that appears beneath the object, drag the upper-middle node downward. To make the mirror image double or triple the size of the original, keep sizing the mirror object using CTRL. To make the mirror image a custom size, just drag the node *without* using CTRL. If you want to create a mirror image only, without retaining the original object, do not click the right mouse button or use the + key.

The next section describes how to create a mirror image appearing at a diagonal to the original object.

Creating a Diagonal Mirror Image

Using the corner nodes on the selection box, you can create a mirror image that appears at a diagonal to the original object. You can choose from among several techniques the one that best suits your needs. If you choose to retain a copy of the original object, you need to click the right mouse button or the + key. If you choose to make the size of the mirror image an exact multiple of the original, you need to use CTRL. You can just as easily decide not to copy the original object or to make the mirrored object a custom size. In every case, however, you drag the *opposite* corner node until it "flips" in the direction in which you want the mirror image to appear.

The following exercise assumes that you are going to create a perfect diagonal mirror image of an object. In this exercise, the original object remains, but neither

the original nor the mirrored object is scaled beyond the original size. At the end of the exercise you will find suggestions for obtaining other results.

1. Select the text string "Corel," if it is not selected already.
2. Position the pointer over the node in the upper-left corner of the selection box and begin to drag the marker downward and to the right.
3. As soon as the dashed outline box appears, click the right mouse button or press the + key on your numeric keypad once to leave a copy of the original object. The message "Leave Original" appears at the left side of the Status bar.
4. Press and hold CTRL and continue dragging the node until the dashed outline box "snaps" at a diagonal to the original object and the Status bar reads "Scale: 100.0% (Mirrored)," as shown in Figure 8-6.
5. Release first the mouse button and then the CTRL key. Coreldraw redraws the screen showing both the original and the mirrored object. The mirrored object is selected. If your text strings do not appear in this way, try the exercise again.
6. Select Undo Stretch from the Edit menu or press CTRL-Z to return the object to its original unmirrored state.

8

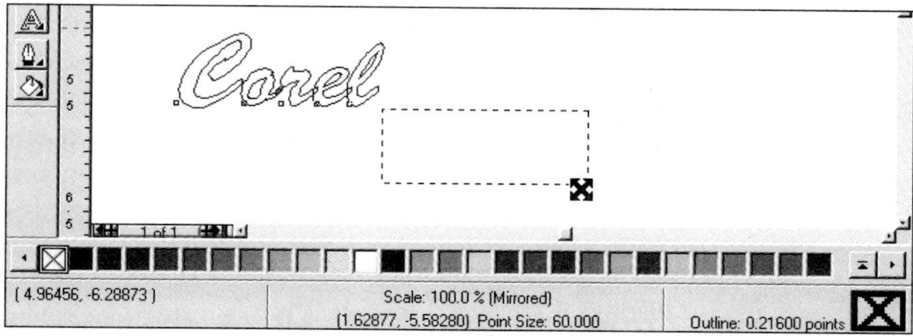

Creating a diagonal mirror image of an object while scaling

FIGURE 8-6

You can vary this exercise to achieve different results. For example, to place the mirror image at the upper-right corner of the original object, drag from the lower-left corner marker upward. To make the mirror image double or triple the size of the original, keep sizing the mirror object using CTRL. To make the mirror image a custom size, just drag the opposite node without using CTRL. If you want to create a mirror image only, without retaining the original object, do not click the right mouse button or use the + key.

Mirroring an Object with the Mirror Command

The following exercise shows you how to create a vertical or horizontal mirror image using the Scale & Mirror dialog box instead of the mouse and keyboard. When you create a mirror image, you can choose whether or not to retain a copy of the original object. You should continue working in Actual Size viewing magnification for this exercise.

1. With the text string in the Corel.CDR file selected, open the Transform roll-up and select the Scale & Mirror command.
2. In the Scale & Mirror dialog box, enter 100% in both the vertical (V) and horizontal (H) scale entry boxes. Click the vertical Mirror button. Click on Apply. The result is as shown here:

3. Select Clear Transformations from the Arrange menu to return the object to its original state.
4. This time, retaining the 100% in both scales boxes, click on the horizontal Mirror button. Click on Apply. A horizontal mirror image of the original text appears.
5. Select Clear Transformations from the Arrange menu to return the image to its original state.

If you want to merge a copy of the original object with the mirrored version, just click on Apply To Duplicate in the Scale & Mirror roll-up (remember to use Undo Duplicate to undo this operation). If you want to make the mirror image larger or smaller than the original, set the scale values accordingly. To get both a horizontal and vertical mirror image, click on both the mirror buttons.

If you want to move the mirror, you can use the Relative Position drop-down box (below and to the right of the vertical scale numeric entry box) and click on the anchor point representing the position that the mirror object will occupy relative to the original image. That is, if the center anchor point is selected, the mirror image will appear in the same spot as its original image. If an anchor point to the side of the center is selected, the mirror image will appear there.

Roll up the Transform roll-up and move it to one side.

Rotating an Object

When you click on an object once using the Pick tool, you can move, arrange, size, or scale it. In addition, the Pick tool can rotate and skew an object. *Rotating* involves turning an object in a clockwise or counterclockwise direction, at an angle that you define. When you *skew* an object, on the other hand, you slant it toward the right, left, top, or bottom in order to create distortion or three-dimensional effects.

As with sizing and scaling, you can rotate an object interactively, using the mouse and keyboard, or you can use the Rotate command on the Transform flyout on the Arrange menu. If you feel more comfortable working with roll-ups than with the mouse and keyboard, you can select the Rotate command after clicking on an object once. To rotate an object interactively, however, you must either click on a selected object a second time or double-click on an object that you have not yet selected.

Practice entering the interactive rotate/skew mode now, using the text string in the Corel.CDR file.

1. With the "Corel" text displayed at the Actual Size viewing magnification, click once on the outline of the text string. The normal selection box with its eight black nodes appears.

2. Click on the outline of the text string a second time (be sure the pointer is on the text string or you'll get other results). Coreldraw replaces the eight nodes with eight two-way arrows, as shown here:

3. You can drag any one of the corner arrows to rotate the object, but for this exercise you will work with the upper-right corner arrow.

4. Position the mouse pointer over the two-way arrow in the upper-right corner of the rotate/skew selection box. When the pointer becomes a crosshair, press and hold the mouse button and drag the mouse in a counterclockwise direction. As soon as you begin to drag, the mouse pointer changes to an arc with arrows at either end. A dashed outline box representing the text string begins to rotate in a counterclockwise direction, as shown in Figure 8-7. Notice that the Status bar displays the angle of rotation as a positive number.

5. Continue to drag the corner highlighting arrow in a counterclockwise direction until you have rotated the object more than 180 degrees. At that point, the Status bar begins to display a negative number for the angle of rotation and the number begins to decrease from 180. Use the number on the Status bar to inform yourself how far you have rotated a selected object.

6. Continue rotating the text object until the number becomes positive again. Release the mouse button when the Status bar indicates an angle of about 17 degrees. Coreldraw redisplays the object at the selected angle of rotation.

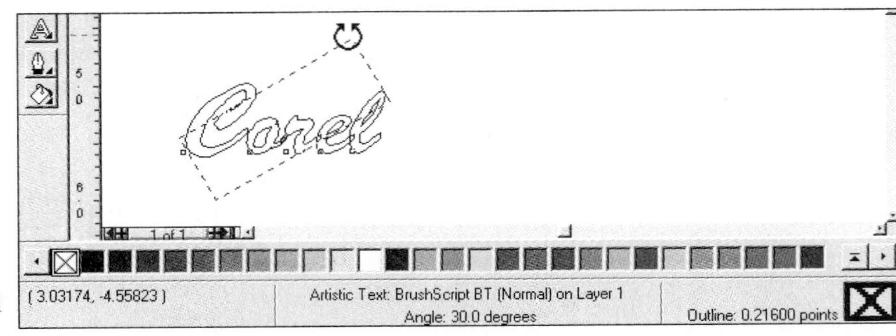

Rotating text with the Pick tool

FIGURE 8-7

7. Select Clear Transformations from the Arrange menu to return the object to its original angle.

8. The text object should again appear selected, with its normal nodes. Click on its text outline to redisplay the curved-arrow nodes. Drag the highlighting arrow in the upper-right corner again, but in a clockwise direction. The angle indicator on the Status bar displays a negative number until you rotate the text string more than 180 degrees. At that point, the number becomes positive and begins to decrease from 180 degrees downward.

9. Release the mouse button to redisplay the object at the new angle of rotation.

10. Select Clear Transformations from the Arrange menu to return the object to its original angle.

OTE: *You may sometimes rotate an object several times in succession. The angle of rotation displayed in the Status bar, however, refers to the amount of the current rotation, not to the cumulative angle.*

Rotating in Increments of 15 Degrees

As in almost every drawing or editing function of Coreldraw, you can use CTRL to constrain movement in the rotation of objects. Simply press and hold CTRL while dragging a corner arrow of the rotate/skew selection box, and the object rotates and "snaps" to successive 15-degree angles. The Status bar keeps track of the angle of rotation. As always, remember to release the mouse button before you release the CTRL key or you will not constrain the angle of rotation. You will use the constrain feature in the following exercise.

1. Double-click on the text string if it is not selected already or click once on its outline if it is selected. The two-way arrows appear to show that you are in the rotate/skew mode.

2. Position the pointer over the upper-right corner highlighting arrow until the pointer changes to a crosshair. Press and hold the CTRL key and the mouse button and drag the highlighting arrow in the desired direction. Notice that the dashed rectangular box does not follow the rotation

pointer continuously; instead, it "snaps" each time you reach an angle that is a multiple of 15 degrees.

3. When you reach the desired angle, release the mouse button first and then release the CTRL key. The object redisplays at the new angle of rotation.
4. Select Clear Transformations from the Arrange menu to return the object to its original angle.

Retaining a Copy While Rotating

If you like to experiment with design, you may find it useful to make a copy of the original object as you rotate it. Figure 8-8 illustrates one design effect you can achieve easily. This text pinwheel, suitable for desktop publishing applications, was created by rotating a text string in increments of 30 degrees and copying the original each time.

You can also retain a copy of the original object using CTRL, but that operation requires a bit more coordination. Try this technique now.

1. With the Corel.CDR file open and in an Actual Size viewing magnification, click on the text string "Corel" if it is already selected, or double-click if it is not selected. The rotate/skew highlighting arrows appear. Use the window scroll arrows to move the text object to the center of the screen. Doing this does not change the orientation of your drawing on the page.
2. Position the mouse pointer over the upper-right highlighting arrow marker and begin to drag this marker upward. As soon as the dashed outline box

Pinwheel created by rotating text

FIGURE 8-8

appears, click the right mouse button or press the + key once to leave a copy of the original.

3. Press and hold CTRL and continue dragging the arrow marker upward until the Status bar reads "Angle: 30 degrees."
4. Release the mouse button first and then the CTRL key. The screen displays both the original and the rotated object, as shown here:

5. Continue copying and rotating the text strings four more times at the same angle to create the design shown in Figure 8-8. Then, undo your changes to the original text string before going further. Use Undo or press DEL to erase the last rotation, then select the remaining objects one at a time and press DEL for each object. Instead of selecting and deleting each object, it may be easier to use Open in the File menu and again open the original Corel.CDR file.

8

Changing an Object's Rotation

Look at an object on your screen when it is in rotate/skew mode. In the center of the object is a small dot surrounded by a circle. This graphic aid appears every time you activate the rotate/skew mode and represents the center of rotation of an object. The object turns on this axis as you rotate it. If you want the object to rotate on a different axis, you can alter the center of rotation freely by dragging the center-of-rotation symbol to the desired location using the mouse. In the following exercise, you will create a simple text design that involves changing the center of a text string's rotation. You may need to zoom out during this exercise.

1. With the Corel.CDR file open and in an Actual Size viewing magnification, click on the text outline "Corel" if it is not already selected and move it to the center of the display. Click on its outlines again to access the rotate/skew mode.

2. When the rotate/skew selection box appears, position the mouse pointer over the center-of-rotation symbol until it becomes a crosshair. Drag the rotation symbol to the upper-right corner of the rotate/skew selection box, as shown here. Then release the mouse button.

3. Position the mouse pointer over any one of the corner highlighting arrows and begin dragging the arrow in a clockwise direction. As soon as the dashed outline box appears, click the right mouse button while keeping the left button depressed, or press the + key on your numeric keypad once to leave a copy of the original. Notice that because you have changed the center of rotation, the text string turns on its end rather than on its center point.
4. Press and hold CTRL and continue dragging the marker until the Status bar shows that you have rotated the text string by 90 degrees.
5. Release the mouse button first, and then the CTRL key. Both the original object and the rotated object display at 90-degree angles to one another.
6. Repeat this process two more times, until you have a text design similar to the one in Figure 8-9. To make all of the text strings behave as though they were one object, click on the Select All command in the Edit menu and group the text strings, using the Group command in the Arrange menu. Now reposition the group to the center of the display.
7. Save this figure as 4Corners.CDR.
8. Exit the document by selecting Close from the File menu.

Your new center of rotation does not have to be a highlighting arrow; you can relocate the center anywhere within the Selection box. But a corner or boundary of the selected object often proves to be a convenient "handle" when you are performing rotations.

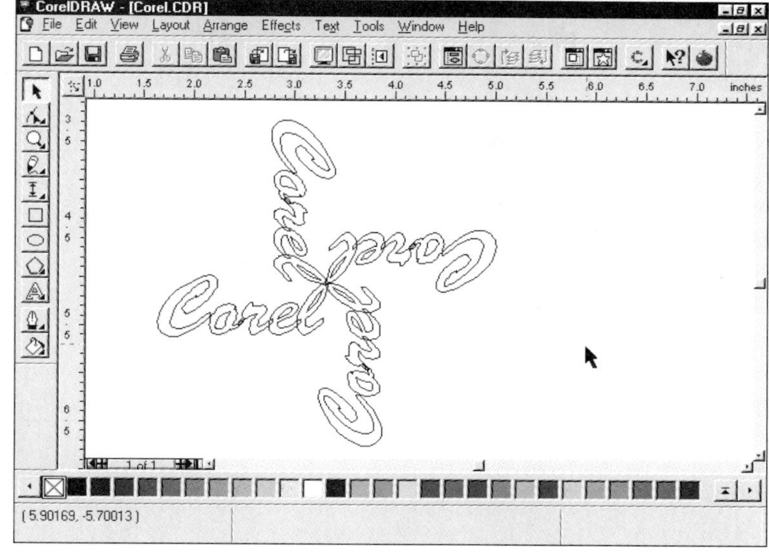

Text design created by rotating and copying an object with an altered center of rotation

FIGURE 8-9

Rotating with the Rotate Command

If you find the use of the keyboard controls inconvenient, you can perform all of the preceding rotation operations with precision using the Rotate command on the Transform flyout. You can select this command when either the normal selection box or the rotate/skew selection box is visible around a selected object. Perform the following brief exercise to familiarize yourself with the workings of the Rotate dialog box.

1. Open the Corel.CDR file and set the viewing magnification to 1:1. Place the text where you can work with it. Click once on the text string to select it.
2. Open the Arrange menu, select Transform and click on the Rotation command. The Rotate roll-up appears, as in Figure 8-10. (Your numbers may differ.)

You can enter a number in the Angle numeric entry box either by scrolling in increments of 5 degrees or by clicking on the numeric entry box and typing in a number in increments of 1/10 of a degree.

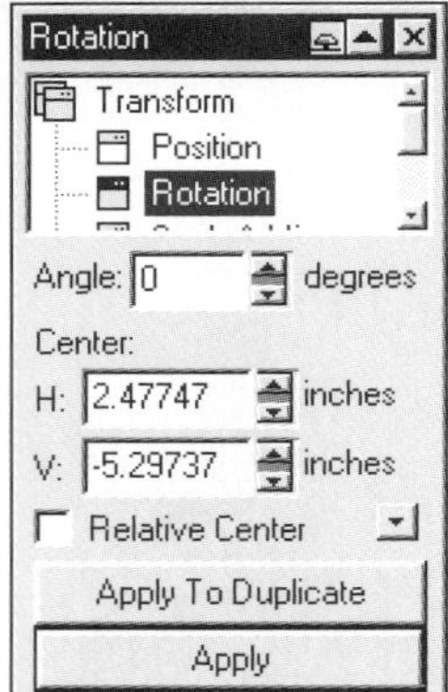

Rotation properties in the Transform roll-up

FIGURE 8-10

In addition to setting the angle of rotation, you can set the center of rotation to an absolute horizontal or vertical position, or to a relative position by clicking on the Relative Center check box.

In order to duplicate the effects created in Figure 8-9, but with the Rotate roll-up, you can set the angle and the relative center, and then click on Apply To Duplicate the required number of times.

3. Set Angle of Rotation to 30 degrees. Make sure the horizontal and vertical numeric entry boxes for Center of Rotation both contain 0. Place a check mark in the Relative Center. Click on Apply To Duplicate 5 times. Isn't this a much easier way to produce the Figure 8-8 effects!
4. When you are finished, leave the original image on the screen for the next exercise. Use Undo or press DEL to erase the last rotation, then select the remaining objects one at a time and press DEL for each object. Instead of selecting and deleting each object, it may be easier to use Open from the File menu and again open the original Corel.CDR file.

That's all there is to rotating an object at the angle and axis of your choice. You can leave a copy of the original object while rotating it, just as when you copy an

object that you are sizing or scaling. In the next section, you will practice skewing an object to achieve interesting distortion effects.

Skewing an Object

When you skew an object, you slant and distort it at a horizontal or vertical angle, thus warping its appearance. This technique can be useful for creating three-dimensional or surrealistic effects. As with the other techniques you have learned in this chapter, you can skew an object either interactively or by using the controls in the Skew dialog box.

1. With the Corel.CDR file open and in an Actual Size viewing magnification, select the "Corel" text string. Then click a second time anywhere on its outline to enter rotate/skew mode.
2. To begin skewing the object horizontally, position the mouse pointer directly over the upper-middle node and drag it to the right. The mouse pointer changes to two half-arrows pointing in opposite directions, and a dashed outline box slants to the right, the direction you are moving your mouse, as shown in Figure 8-11. The Status bar keeps track of the current angle of horizontal skew.
3. When you reach the desired skewing angle, release the mouse button. Coreldraw redisplays the object as you have skewed it, as shown here:

4. Select Clear Transformations from the Arrange menu to return the object to its original unskewed state.

8

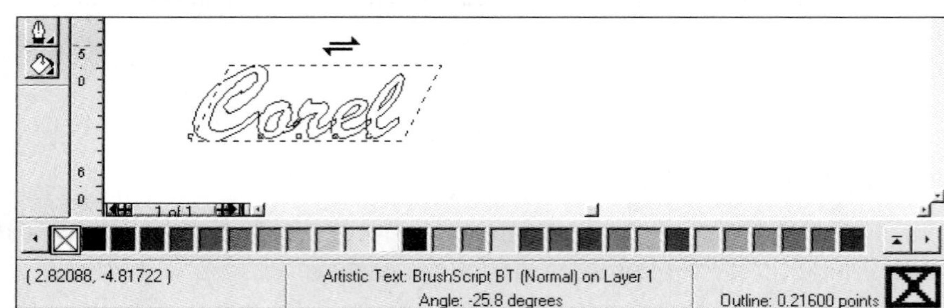

Skewing an object to the right

FIGURE 8-11

5. Practice different angles of horizontal skewing. You can skew an object greater than 85 degrees to the right or left. If you drag one of the middle highlighting arrows along the left or right *side* of the selection box, you can skew the object in a vertical direction.
6. When you feel comfortable with basic skewing operations, select Clear Transformations from the Arrange menu. Leave the text string on the screen for the next exercise.

Skewing in Increments of 15 Degrees

Once again, you can use CTRL to introduce an extra measure of precision to the interactive transformation of objects. When skewing an object, pressing and holding CTRL forces the object to skew in increments of 15 degrees. Try using this constraint feature now.

1. Select the text string "Corel" and enter the rotate/skew mode.
2. Position the mouse pointer over the upper-middle highlighting arrow, press and hold CTRL, and begin dragging the mouse to the right or left, as desired. The mouse pointer changes to the skew pointer, and the dashed outline box "snaps" in the desired direction in increments of 15 degrees.
3. When you reach the desired angle, release the mouse button first and then release the CTRL key.

4. Select Clear Transformations from the Arrange menu to return the skewed object to its original state. Leave the text string on the screen.

Retaining a Copy While Skewing

For an interesting design effect, you can skew an object and then make a copy of the original. As you will see in the following exercise, you can then position the skewed object behind the original to make it seem like a shadow.

1. Select the "Corel" text string and enter rotate/skew mode.
2. Position the mouse pointer over the upper-middle highlighting arrow and begin dragging the arrow to the right. As soon as the dashed outline box appears, click the right mouse button while depressing the left button to leave a copy of the original, or press the + key on your numeric keypad.
3. Press and hold CTRL and continue dragging the marker until the Status bar shows a skewing angle of –60 degrees.
4. Release the mouse button first and then release the CTRL key. The skewed object, which is selected automatically, appears on top of the copy of the original, as shown here:

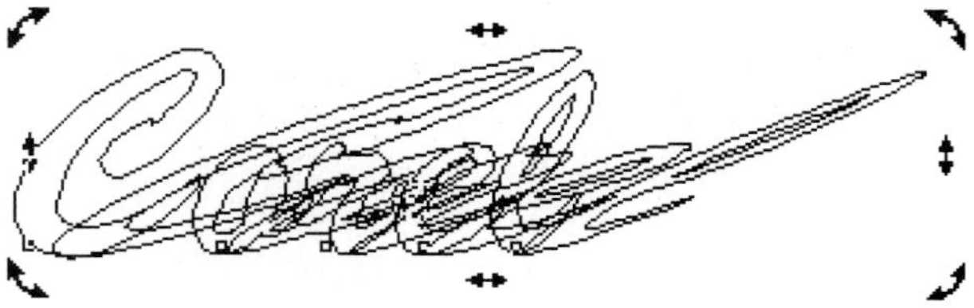

5. To place the skewed object behind the unskewed original, click on the To Back button on the toolbar.
6. Click on the Black fill option (the rightmost button on the first row) of the Fill flyout.
7. Now select the original text object. From the color palette at the bottom of the screen select a color, such as the third from the right, bottom row.

Shadow created by skewing an object

FIGURE 8-12

8. Go to the preview window by clicking on Full-Screen Preview from the View menu, or by pressing F9. Your preview should look roughly similar to Figure 8-12. From what you learned about filling objects in Chapter 7, you can refine the appearance of skewed background images to create a clearer "shadow" than this one. To turn the preview screen off, press ESC.

9. To remove the transformed copy of the object so that only the unaltered original remains, click on the copy with the Pick tool to select it and press DEL.

TIP: *Coreldraw has included the option of setting the right mouse button to toggle between the editing window and full-screen preview. If you want to do this, select the General tab in the Options dialog box on the Tools menu and select Full-Screen Preview from the Right Mouse Button Action drop-down list.*

Skewing with the Skew Command

If you find the use of keyboard and mouse controls inconvenient, you can perform all of the possible skewing operations using the Skew command on the Transform flyout in the Arrange menu. You can select this command when either the normal selection box or the rotate/skew selection box is visible around a selected object. Perform the following brief exercise to familiarize yourself with using the Skew dialog box to skew an object. The Corel.CDR image should still be on your screen.

1. If not so already, set the viewing magnification to 1:1 and click once on the text string to select it.
2. Open the Arrange menu, click on Transform, and select Skew. The Skew roll-up appears, as shown here:

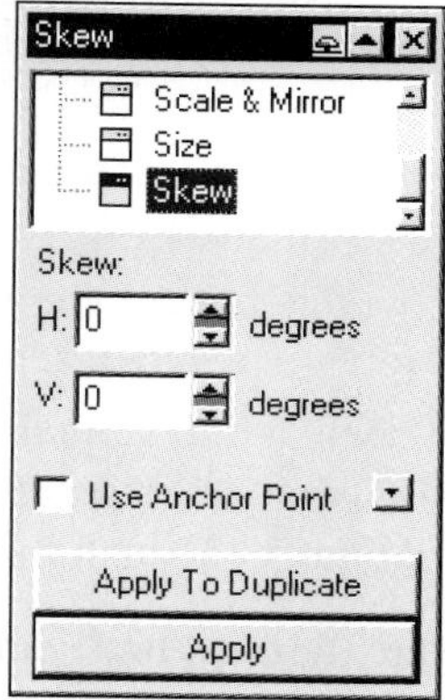

3. First, skew the text object horizontally. Enter a number in the horizontal (H) numeric entry box. You can enter a number either by scrolling in increments of 5 degrees or by clicking on the numeric entry box and typing in a number in increments of 1/10 of a degree. Only values between –75 and 75 degrees are valid.
4. If desired, click on Apply To Duplicate to make a copy of the original object as you rotate it.
5. When you are finished, select Undo Skew to return to the original object and its former angle.
6. Select the text and open the Skew dialog box once more. This time, enter a number in the vertical (V) numeric entry box. You can adjust this value in the same way that you adjusted the horizontal value in step 3. Click on Apply.
7. When you are finished, select Clear Transformations from the Arrange menu to return the original object to its former angle.

Repeating a Transformation

Coreldraw stores the most recently performed transformation in memory until you quit the current session. You can save design and drawing time by automatically repeating your most recent size, scale, rotate, or skew operation on a different object or set of objects. Just remember that the second object, the one on which you wish to repeat the transformation, must exist on the screen *before* you perform the transformation the first time. If you perform a transformation and then create another object and try to repeat that transformation on it, nothing happens. Perform the following brief exercise to see how this feature can work for you.

1. With the Corel.CDR file open and in Actual Size viewing magnification, select the Ellipse tool. Now, draw a long narrow ellipse to the right of the "Corel" text string at about the 5 1/2-inch mark on the horizontal ruler.
2. Press SPACEBAR to activate the Pick tool. Select the "Corel" text string and then start to drag the lower-right node downward and to the right. Leave a copy of the original by clicking the right mouse button or by using the + key, as described earlier in this chapter. Then, use CTRL to help you scale the text string to 200 percent. Release the mouse button and then the CTRL key.
3. Select the ellipse that you drew next to the text string. Select Repeat Stretch from the Edit menu or press the shortcut keys CTRL-R. This will create a duplicate of the ellipse and scale it to 200%, as described in step 2. If the objects extend beyond your viewing window, adjust viewing magnification to Zoom to all.
4. Select the larger text duplicate and then select No Fill from the Fill flyout menu. Your screen should be similar to Figure 8-13.
5. Select Close from the File menu to close your document. Do not save any changes to your work.

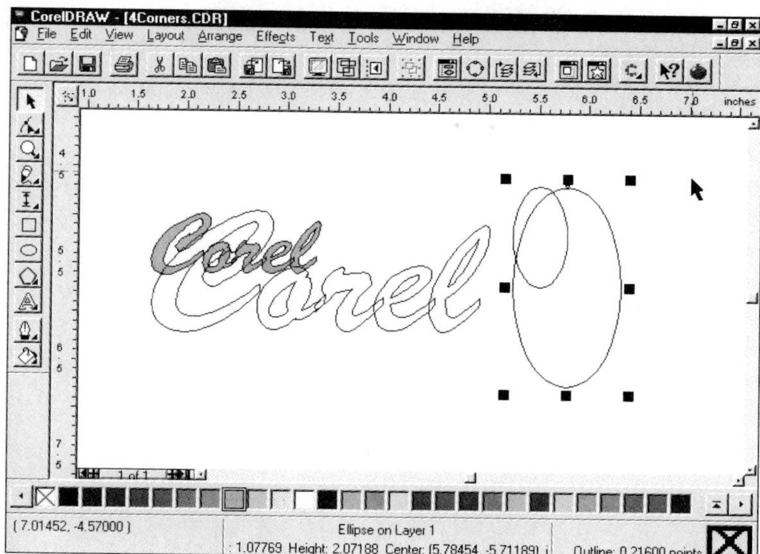

Repeating a transformation on a different object

FIGURE 8-13

You have seen how sizing, scaling, rotating, and skewing objects can lead to creative ideas for advanced designs. Continue practicing some of the techniques you have learned and see what original ideas you can come up with on your own. Chapters 13 and 14 will expand on these and other techniques and provide additional stimulation for your imagination.

Shaping Lines, Curves, Rectangles, and Ellipses

The power to reshape any object to the limits of the imagination is at the very heart of Coreldraw. Using the Shape tool, you can change any type of object into an image that can showcase your creativity.

The Shape tool flyout (the second button in the Coreldraw toolbox), shown here, contains two tools that allow you to change the underlying shape of an object: the Shape tool and the Knife. Although the Pick tool, in Transformation mode, allows you to resize, rotate, or skew an object, it leaves the fundamental shape of the object intact. When you edit an object with the Shape tool, however, it becomes something quite different from what you originally drew. With the Knife tool, you can separate an object into subpaths that can be edited singly or grouped. Using the Knife tool will be covered later in this chapter; for now, you will work with the Shape tool.

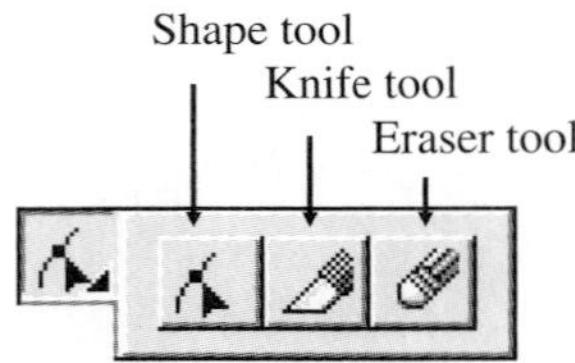

The Eraser tool, the last tool on the flyout, does not change the shape of an object. It is used to remove portions of a closed curve, rectangle, ellipse, or polygon, leaving the remaining sections as closed curves or objects.

You can apply the Shape tool to all object types: lines and curves, rectangles and squares, ellipses and circles, polygons, text, and pixel-based (bitmap) graphics. Shaping functions for text and bitmap graphics, however, are part of a broader range of editing functions that apply specifically to those object types. You will find information specifically about shaping text in Chapter 10, and about shaping curves to fit traced bitmaps in Chapter 17. This chapter covers techniques for shaping lines, curves, rectangles, ellipses, and polygons.

About the Shape Tool

The Shape tool performs several different functions, depending on the kind of object to which it is applied. You take advantage of the most powerful capabilities of the

Shape tool when you use it to edit curves, but it has specific effects on other object types as well.

When you are working with lines and curves, you can manipulate single curve points (nodes) interactively, move single or multiple curve segments, control the angle of movement, and add or delete curve points in order to exercise greater control over the degree of curvature. You can break apart or join segments of a curve and change one type of node into another. You can even convert curves to straight lines and back again.

When you apply the Shape tool to rectangles, squares, and polygons, you can round the corners of a rectangle or polygon and turn rotated, stretched, or skewed rectangles and polygons into near-ellipses and circles. When you apply the Shape tool to ellipses and circles, you can create pie-shaped wedges or arcs. If these shaping options for rectangles, polygons, and ellipses seem limited, you will be pleased to learn that you can convert any object in Coreldraw to curves—and then proceed to apply the most advanced shaping techniques to it.

Shaping Lines and Curves

You may recall that every object in Coreldraw has nodes, which appear when you first draw an object and become enlarged when you select the object with the Shape tool. Nodes on a curve (shown in Figure 9-1) are the points through which a curve passes, and each node is associated with the curve segment that immediately precedes it. Control points that appear when you select a single node with the Shape tool determine the curvature of the node and of the curve segments on either side of it. (You will learn more about control points later in this chapter.)

The Shape tool is at its most powerful when you use it to edit a curve. Ways in which you can reshape a curve include moving, adding, or deleting nodes; changing node shape; breaking nodes apart or joining them together; and manipulating the control points that define the shape of a curve segment.

Your options for shaping straight lines with the Shape tool are much more limited than for curves; lines have no angles of curvature and, therefore, no control points that you can manipulate. When you edit a line segment with the Shape tool, you can only move the nodes to stretch or diminish the length of the line segment. In the course of creating and editing a complex curve object, however, you often need to fuse curve and line segments, change curves into lines, or turn lines into curves. The Shape tool allows you to do all of these things, and so both kinds of freehand objects belong in any discussion of shaping. Converting lines to curves is covered in the section "Working with the Node Edit Roll-Up," later in this chapter.

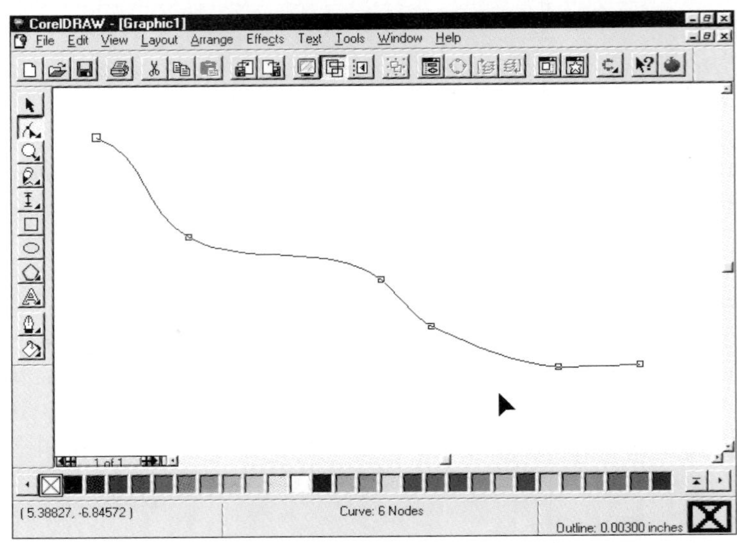

Displaying the number of nodes in a curve

FIGURE 9-1

The following sections show you how to use the Shape tool to edit specific types of objects. These sections follow the order of the drawing tools in the Coreldraw toolbox: lines and curves, rectangles, ellipses, and polygons.

Selecting Lines and Curves with the Shape tool

You must select an object with the Shape tool before you can edit it. Coreldraw allows you to select only one object with the Shape tool at a time. Although the Shape tool affects each type of object in a different way, the basic steps involved in editing are similar with all object types.

In the following exercise, you will draw a straight line and a freehand curve and then select each object in turn. To prepare for the exercise, turn off Snap To Grid and Rulers, and select Actual Size magnification.

To select an object for editing, follow these steps.

1. Select the Freehand tool and draw a straight horizontal line across the top half of the window.

2. Below the line, draw a freehand curve in a horizontal "S" shape. Select the Shape tool (shown in the margin) and small nodes appear on the curves, like this:

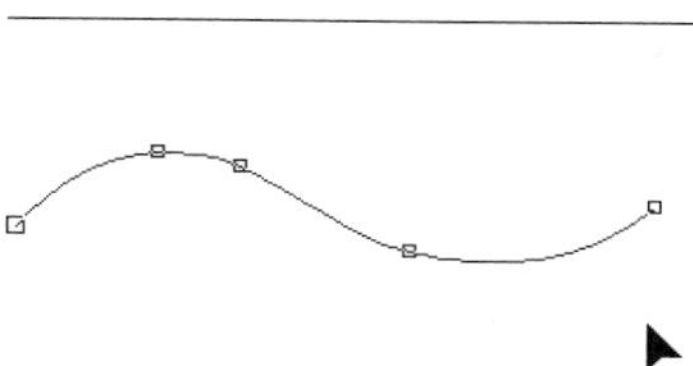

The pointer changes to an arrowhead, and the S-curve is automatically selected, because it was the last object you drew. The nodes of the S-curve increase in size, and the Status bar displays the number of the nodes in the curve. Notice that the node where you started drawing the curve is larger than the others. Often, this is the farthest to the left on lines and curves, the one at the top-left corner in rectangles, and at the topmost point on ellipses.

As you have just seen, if the object you want to work with is already selected, its nodes enlarge in size automatically as soon as you select the Shape tool and the selection box around the object disappears. The number of nodes varies, depending on the object type and (in the case of curves) the way your hand moved when you drew it. If the object you want to work with is not selected, you can click on any part of the object's outline with the pointer. In addition to the enlarged nodes, the Status bar shows the object type and information about the nodes on the object.

1. To deselect the S-curve and select the line, simply click on any point of the line with the Shape tool. Only two nodes appear on the line, one at each end. Again, the node where you started drawing is the larger. The Status bar displays the message, "Curve: 2 Nodes." (In Coreldraw, a straight line is a special type of curve.)
2. Clear the screen. Do not save your work.

IP: *Activate the Shape tool by clicking on it or by pressing F10. The pointer changes to a thick arrowhead as soon as you move it away from the toolbox and toward the page area.*

If multiple objects are selected when you activate the Shape tool, Coreldraw automatically deselects all of them, and you then must select a single object to edit with the Shape tool. If grouped objects are selected when you activate the shape tool, they also become deselected and your mouse actions have no effect. (The grouped object remains grouped when it is deselected.) The only time you can edit more than one object simultaneously with the Shape tool is when you *combine* the objects prior to selecting the Shape tool. You will see examples of editing combined objects in the "Shaping Lines and Curves" section of this chapter.

To deselect an object that you are editing with the Shape tool, either click on the outline of a different object or select another tool from the Coreldraw toolbox.

Your next step in shaping a selected line or curve is to select one or more of its nodes.

Selecting Nodes of a Line or Curve

Although you can shape only one object at a time, you can select and shape either a single node or multiple nodes. The shaping options available to you depend on whether you select one node or several. You can reshape a single curve node interactively in one of two ways: by dragging the node itself or by dragging the control points that appear when you select the node. Moving a node stretches and resizes the associated curve segment(s) but does not allow you to change the angle of curvature. Dragging the control points, on the other hand, allows you to change both the angle of curvature at the node and the shape of the associated curve segment(s). When you select multiple nodes, you can move only the nodes, not their control points; as a result, you reshape all of the selected segments in the same way.

In general, you should select single nodes when you need to fine-tune a curve, and multiple nodes when you need to move or reshape several segments in the same way without changing their angle of curvature.

The exercises in the following sections guide you through the available techniques for selecting nodes in preparation for moving or editing them. Along the way, you will become familiar with the different types of nodes that Coreldraw generates and how they indicate the shape of a particular curve.

Selecting and Deselecting Single Nodes and Identifying Node Type

When you click on a single curve node, the Status bar provides information about the type of node you have selected. The names of the three different types of nodes that Coreldraw generates when you draw lines and curves—cusp, smooth, and symmetrical—describe both the curvature at the node and, in the case of curve objects, the way you can shape the node. Straight lines contain only cusp nodes, while curves can contain all three node types.

- **Cusp nodes** Cusp nodes occur at the end point of a line or curve or at a sharp change of direction in a curve. When you edit the control points of a cusp node, you can alter the curvature of the segment that precedes the node without affecting the segment that follows it.
- **Smooth nodes** Smooth nodes occur at smooth changes of direction in a curve. When you edit a smooth node, you alter the shape and direction of both the segment preceding and the segment following the node. The curvature of the two segments remains identical in the number of degrees, however.
- **Symmetrical nodes** Symmetrical nodes occur where the segments preceding and following the node curve in identical ways. (Symmetrical nodes occur less frequently than other node types in freehand drawing, but you can change any node type to symmetrical using the Node Edit roll-up, which you will learn about in a moment.) When you edit a symmetrical node, you alter the shape and direction of the curve segments before and after the node in identical ways.

IP: *Nodes of a straight-line segment are always cusp nodes and contain no control points. They become important only when you begin adding or deleting nodes or changing a line into a curve.*

In the following exercise, you will practice selecting and deselecting single nodes.

1. Using the Freehand tool, at Actual Size (1:1) magnification and with Wireframe mode turned on, draw a curve object that looks roughly like Figure 9-2. The object should have sharp curves, gentle curves, and some in between. Don't worry if it doesn't look exactly like Figure 9-2.
2. Select the Shape tool. If the curve object was selected when you clicked on the Shape tool, it should remain selected. If your curve object is not selected, click anywhere on its outline. The Status bar indicates that this curve object contains 13 nodes (yours may be different).

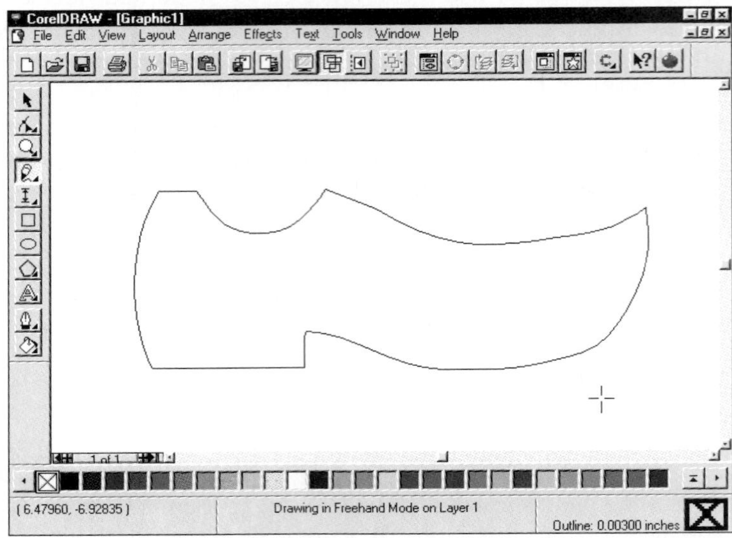

The curve object at 1:1 magnification

FIGURE 9-2

3. Click on a node at the bottom of the half circle on the selected curve object. The node becomes a black-filled square, and two control points, tiny black rectangles connected to the node by dashed lines, pop out, as shown here:

Start of curve

Selected node

Control points

(You will also see a control point extending from nodes on either side of the selected node.) The message "Selected Node: Curve Cusp" or "Curve Smooth" appears on the Status bar, depending on how you drew this curve. Which type of curve does not matter at this point.

4. Click on each node in turn to select it and deselect the previous node. Each time you select a node, control points pop out, and the Status bar

tells you what type of node you have selected. Notice that some of the nodes are cusp nodes, while others are smooth.

5. Leave this object on the screen for the next exercise.

You can always change the node type by using the Node Edit roll-up, as you will see shortly. But you can also control whether the majority of nodes you generate during the freehand drawing process are smooth or cusped. You use the Curve, Bézier settings in the Tool Properties dialog box to control what types of nodes will be created when you draw. To open the Tool Properties dialog box, point on the Freehand tool and click the right mouse button. Then select Properties from the pop-up. When the Tool Properties dialog box is displayed, select Curve, Bézier from the Tools drop-down list box. To generate mostly cusped nodes (and create more jagged curves), set the Corner Threshold option to 3 pixels or lower. To generate mostly smooth nodes and create smoother curves, set the Corner Threshold option to 8 pixels or higher.

You will become familiar with techniques for moving control points in a moment. First, finish the next section to learn how to select more than one node at a time.

Selecting and Deselecting Multiple Nodes

You select multiple nodes with the Shape tool in the same way that you select multiple objects with the Pick tool, using either SHIFT or the marquee technique. When multiple nodes are selected, you do not have control points to shape your object. You can only move the nodes as a group and reshape their associated curve segments by dragging the lines. Review the selection techniques in the following brief exercise.

1. Select the largest node (the point at which you began drawing). While pressing and holding SHIFT, select a node to the left and to the right of the first node. The nodes turn dark but display no control points, and the Status bar changes to show the total number of nodes you have selected.
2. Deselect the node farthest to the right in the selected group by holding SHIFT and clicking on the node with the Shape tool. The other nodes remain selected.

3. Deselect all of the selected nodes by releasing SHIFT and clicking on any white space. The curve object itself remains selected for further work with the Shape tool, however.

4. Select the three nodes (or whatever number your drawing has) on the bottom-left side of the object (the heel) by drawing a marquee around them, as shown here:

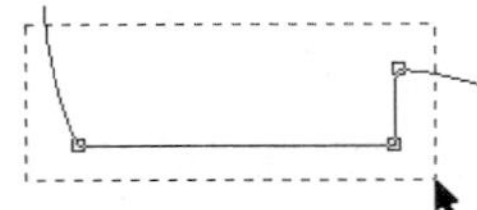

5. The selected nodes turn dark after you release the mouse button, and the Status bar tells you how many nodes you have selected.

6. Deselect one node at a time using SHIFT and the mouse button, or deselect all of the nodes by clicking on any other node or on any white space.

7. When you are finished, clear the screen. Do not save the changes.

Now that you are familiar with how to select nodes, you are ready to begin editing a curve object. You can edit a curve by moving nodes and control points interactively or by selecting options in the Node Edit roll-up.

Moving Nodes and Control Points

You can reshape a curve interactively in one of two ways: by moving one or more nodes or by manipulating the control points of a single node. You can move any number of nodes, but in order to work with control points, you can select only one node at a time.

You move nodes when your aim is to stretch, shrink, or move the curve segments on either side of a node. The angle of curvature at selected nodes doesn't change as you move them, because the control points move along with the nodes. The end result of moving nodes is a limited reshaping of the selected area of the curve object.

In general, your best strategy when reshaping curves is to move the nodes first. If just repositioning the nodes does not yield satisfactory results, you can fine-tune the shape of a curve by manipulating the control points of one or more nodes. When you drag control points to reshape a curve, you affect both the angle of curvature at the node and the shape of the curve segment on one or both sides of the node. The effects of this kind of reshaping are much more dramatic.

Try the exercises in each of the following sections to practice moving single or multiple nodes, manipulating control points, and constraining node movement to 90-degree increments.

Moving a Single Node

To move a single node, you simply select the curve and then select and drag the node in the desired direction. In the following exercise, you will draw a waveform curve, select a node, and move the node to reshape the curve.

1. To prepare for the exercise, make sure that the Snap To Grid and Rulers options are turned off. Check to see that all the settings in the Curve, Bézier Tool Properties dialog box are set at 5 pixels. (This will result in curves with a fairly even distribution of cusp and smooth nodes.) Set viewing magnification to an Actual Size (1:1) ratio.
2. Select the Freehand tool and draw a waveform curve similar to the one drawn here (don't be concerned if your curve is shaped a little differently):

3. Select the Shape tool and then select a node near the crest of one of the curves. Elongate this curve by dragging the node (not the control points) upward and to the right, as shown here:

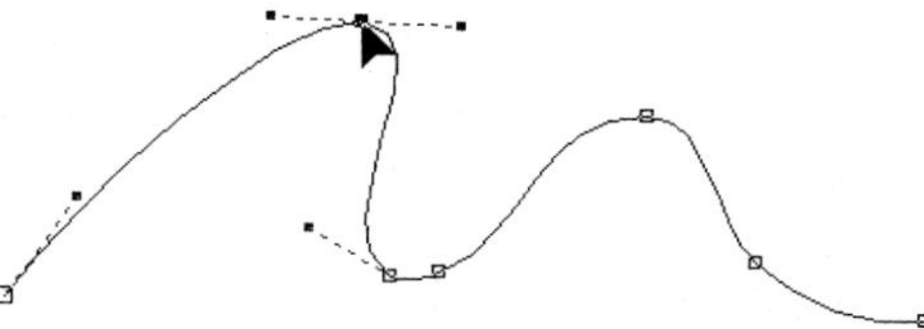

4. As you begin to move the node, the Status bar provides information about *DX* and *DY* coordinates, the distance you have traveled, and the angle of

movement relative to the starting point. Release the mouse button when you are satisfied with the stretch of your curve.

5. Select Undo Curve Edit from the Edit menu to return the curve to its original shape. Leave this curve on the screen for now. You can use it to move multiple nodes in the next exercise.

Moving Multiple Nodes

There are many cases in which you might choose to move multiple nodes instead of a single node at a time. You might move multiple adjacent nodes, for example, if you need to reposition an entire section of a curve at one time. Or you might select nonadjacent nodes and move them all in the same direction for special design effects. Whatever the case, all you need to do is select the nodes and drag them.

1. Using the mouse button and SHIFT, select one node near the beginning of your waveform curve and one near the end. Again, do not be concerned if the nodes in your curve are in different positions from the nodes in the figure. The process of freehand drawing is so complex that two people rarely produce the same results.
2. Drag one of the nodes upward and to the right. Even though the two selected nodes are separated by several others, they move at the same angle and over the same distance, as shown here:

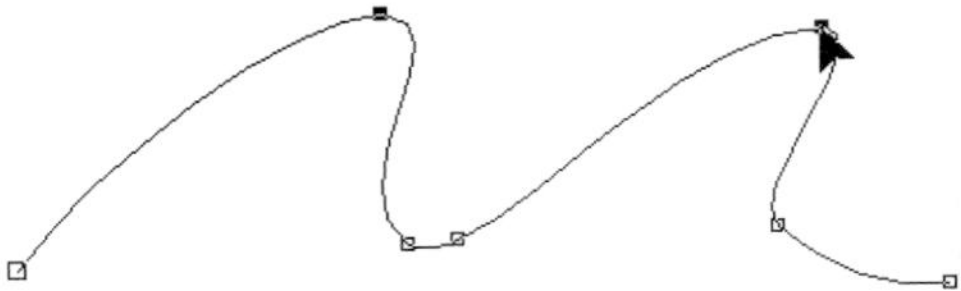

3. Release the mouse button when you are finished. Select Undo Curve Edit from the Edit menu to return the curve object to its former shape.

If you prefer to draft even the most "creative-looking" freehand curves with precision, you may wish to exercise greater control over the angle at which you move nodes. The next section will show you how to move nodes with precision.

Constraining Node Movement to 90-Degree Angles

You have the option of moving nodes and their associated curve segments in increments of 90 degrees relative to your starting point. You use the now familiar CTRL key to achieve this kind of precise movement.

1. Select the same two nodes you worked with in the preceding section, press and hold CTRL, and drag one of the nodes to the right and then up. At first, the two nodes do not seem to move at all; then they "snap" at a 90-degree angle from their starting point. The Status bar in your window reflects this precise angle of movement, as in Figure 9-3.
2. Release the mouse button when you reach the angle you desire. Select the Pick tool and press DEL to clear the curve from the screen. Do not save your changes.

What if you have moved one or more nodes every which way, but you are still not satisfied with the shape of the curve segments on either side of the node? In the next section you will fine-tune your curves by manipulating the control points of a node.

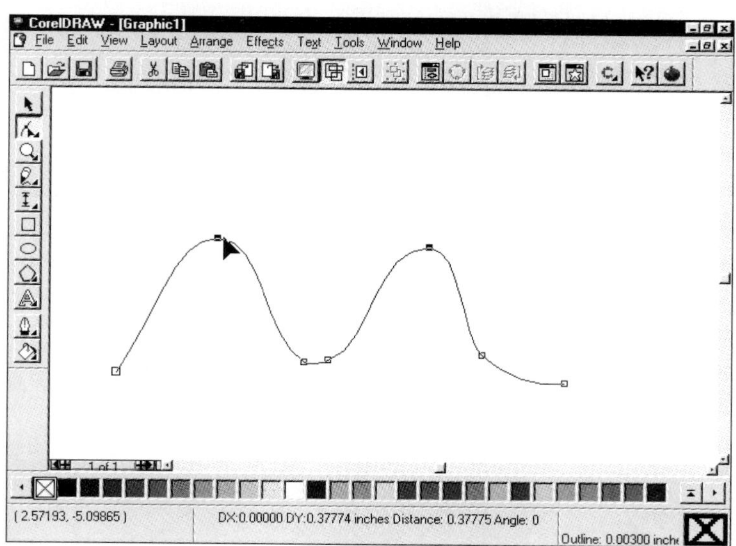

Moving nodes in 90-degree increments

FIGURE 9-3

Moving Control Points

By moving one or both control points of a node, you can control the shape of a curve segment more exactly than if you move just the node itself. The effect of moving control points varies, depending on the type of node—cusp, smooth, or symmetrical. Figures 9-4a through 9-4d illustrate this difference.

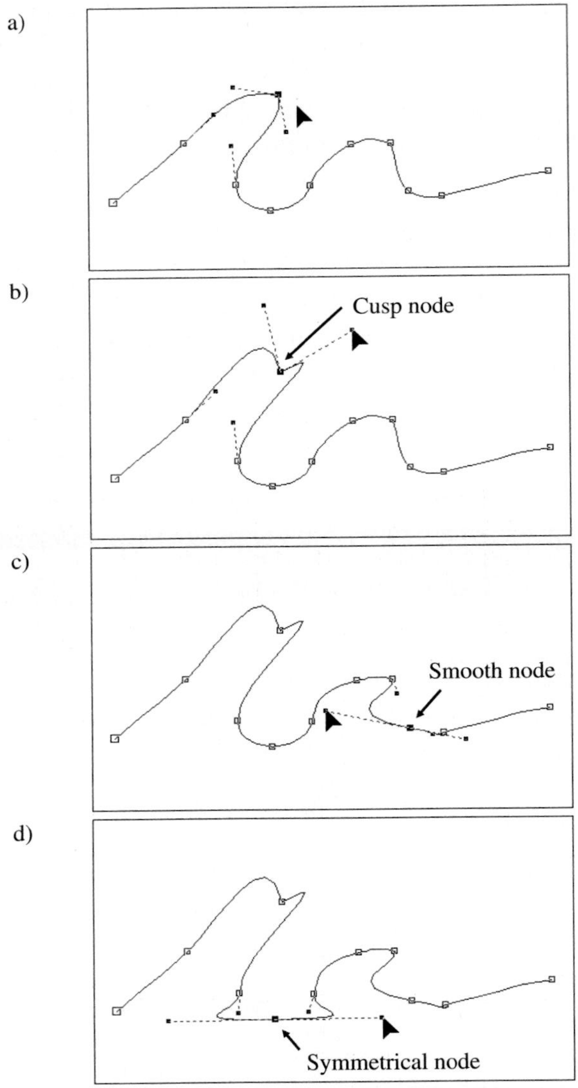

a)

b)

c)

d)

Moving control points of a cusp, smooth, and symmetrical node

FIGURE 9-4

The control points of cusp nodes are not in a straight-line relationship to one another. This means that you can move one control point and change the shape of one curve segment at a time, without affecting the other associated segment. The control points of smooth nodes, on the other hand, are in a straight line relative to one another. If you move one control point of a smooth node, you affect the curvature of both line segments at once, though not to the same degree. Finally, the control points of a symmetrical node are at an equal distance from the node. When you move one control point of a symmetrical node, the curvature of both associated curve segments changes in exactly the same way. Your waveform curve may not have a symmetrical node; because of the steadiness of hand required, symmetrical nodes rarely occur naturally in freehand drawing. You can practice moving the control points of smooth and cusp nodes, however, by following the steps in the next exercise.

1. Select the Freehand tool and in Actual Size magnification (1:1) draw a curve similar in shape to the one in Figure 9-4a. Don't be concerned if your curve has a slightly different shape. You should draw part of the curve with a steady hand and another part using more jagged movements. This will result in a more even distribution of node types.
2. With the Shape tool, select individual nodes on your waveform curve until you find a cusp node. You will know what type of node you have selected by referring to the Status bar. Do not use one of the end nodes, however; end nodes have only one control point, because only one curve segment is associated with them. If you can't find a cusp node, redraw the curve to be more jagged, and then try again. Figure 9-4a shows the waveform curve with a cusp node selected and no control points moved.
3. Drag one of the cusp node's control points outward from the node as far as you can without extending it beyond the viewing window. The farther you drag the control point outward, the more angular the curvature of the associated segment becomes. Note also that the curve segment associated with the other control point does not change.
4. Drag the other control point in any direction you choose. The angle of the second curve segment associated with the node changes, independently of the first one. If you have extended both control points independently, you will see a sharp change in curve direction at the node, as in Figure 9-4b.

5. When you have practiced this technique to your satisfaction, find and select a smooth node. Notice that the two control points of this node lie along a straight line.
6. Drag one of the control points of the smooth node outward from the node, and notice that the other control point is not affected. Now move the control point sideways. The curvature of *both* of the segments associated with the node changes. As shown in the example in Figure 9-4c, however, the two segments do not change in exactly the same way. (The curvature of your curve segments may differ from those in the example, depending on how you drew the curve and moved the control points.)
7. If your waveform curve contains a symmetrical node, select it and move one of the control points outward. Notice that when you move one control point, the opposite one moves the same amount. If you do not have a symmetrical node, observe the curvature changes in Figure 9-4d. The curvature of these segments changes by an identical angle.
8. When you have practiced with control points to your satisfaction, select the Pick tool and press DEL to delete the waveform curve from the screen.

Now you have a working knowledge of all the possible interactive techniques for moving and editing curves. It may sometimes happen, however, that even these techniques are not enough to shape your curve just as you want it. What if you are working with a cusp node and just can't make it smooth enough? Or what if you need an additional node at a certain point to enable you to fit a curve to an exact shape? For these and other node-editing tasks, you can call up the Node Edit roll-up.

Editing Nodes

Selecting a curve object and moving nodes and control points are interactive operations that you can perform without invoking a command or menu. There are times, however, when you need to *edit* the nodes themselves: to change their shape or to add nodes, delete nodes, join nodes, or break them apart. Editing nodes requires that you use the Node Edit roll-up that pops up when you double-click on a node or on the curve segment that immediately precedes it.

Working with the Node Edit Roll-Up

To call up the Node Edit roll-up, double-click on any node or on any curve or line segment with the Shape tool. The roll-up can be moved around the workspace to keep it away from your work by clicking and holding on the Title bar and dragging it to a clear area. It will remain in the window until you close it as you would any roll-up. The Node Edit roll-up tools are shown in Table 9-1.

Tool	Name	Function
	Add	Adds nodes to an object
	Delete	Removes nodes from an object
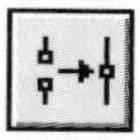	Join	Joins end nodes
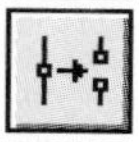	Break	Breaks a curve at a node
	Autojoin	Joins the end nodes of an open path
	To Line	Converts a curve to a line
	To Curve	Converts a line to a curve
	Cusp	Makes the selected node a cusp node
	Smooth	Makes the selected node a smooth node
	Symmetrical	Makes the selected node a symmetrical node
	Auto-Reduce	Deletes extra nodes
	Extract Subpath	Makes a separate object from a selected subpath of a larger object
	Stretch	Changes the size of an object
	Rotate	Rotates an object
	Align	Aligns nodes to guidelines

Edit Node Roll-Up Tools

TABLE 9-1

The buttons on the Node Edit roll-up allow you to add or delete selected nodes, join two nodes or break them apart, convert lines to curves and curves to lines, change the node type, or align sets of nodes on two separate subpaths. At the bottom of the Edit Node roll-up is the Elastic Mode check box. When Elastic Mode is selected, and you move multiple nodes, each node moves in proportion to its distance from the node you are moving. When Elastic Mode is not selected, each node moves the same amount. Not all options are available to you for every node, however. Some buttons appear in gray and are unavailable, depending on the number and type of node(s) you have selected. See the section pertaining to the relevant Node Edit command for more information about why particular options are not available at certain times. To select options that are available, click once on the appropriate button.

Except for Align, as soon as you select any button on the Node Edit roll-up, Coreldraw immediately applies the command to the selected node(s).

Try the exercises in each of the following sections to become familiar with using the commands in the Node Edit roll-up.

Adding a Single Node

If you have moved nodes and manipulated control points to the best of your ability but still cannot achieve the exact shape you want, consider adding one or more nodes where the curvature seems most inadequate. You can add a single node or multiple nodes, depending on how many nodes are selected, but if the node you have selected is the first node of a line or curve, you cannot add a node to it.

The following exercise illustrates the necessary steps to add a single node between two existing nodes. If not already done, set the viewing magnification to Actual Size (1:1). Make sure that the Snap To Grid is turned off for this and all of the other exercises in the "Editing Nodes" portion of this chapter.

1. Select the Freehand tool and draw a waveform curve similar to the one shown in Figure 9-5. Activate the Shape tool to select the curve for editing. Your curve may contain a different number of nodes than the one in Figure 9-5.

2. Double-click with the Shape tool on the node after (to the right of) the point at which you want to add a node. The Node Edit roll-up appears in your workspace. Click on the Title bar and drag it to a clear area, as shown in Figure 9-5.

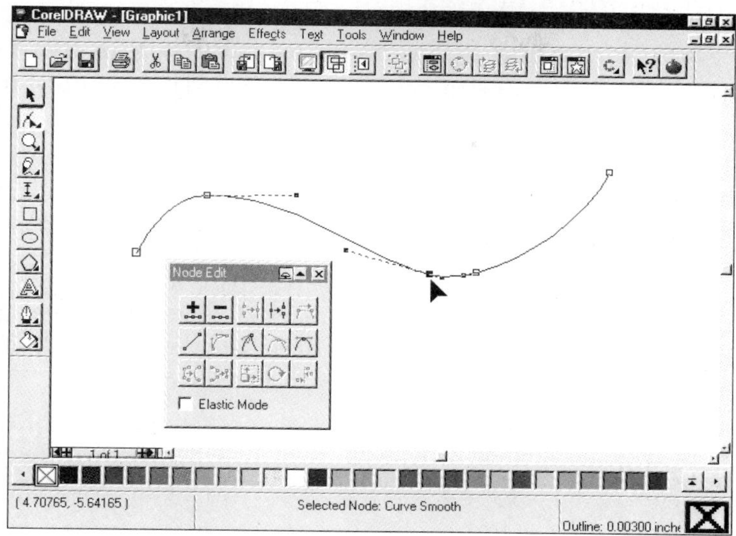

Adding a node to a curve

FIGURE 9-5

3. Select the Add (+) button on the Node Edit roll-up. A new node appears on the curve or line segment preceding (to the left of) the selected node, as shown here. Both the originally selected node and the new node are selected. If you first deselect all of the selected nodes by clicking on any white space, you can move this added node or manipulate its control points just like any other node.

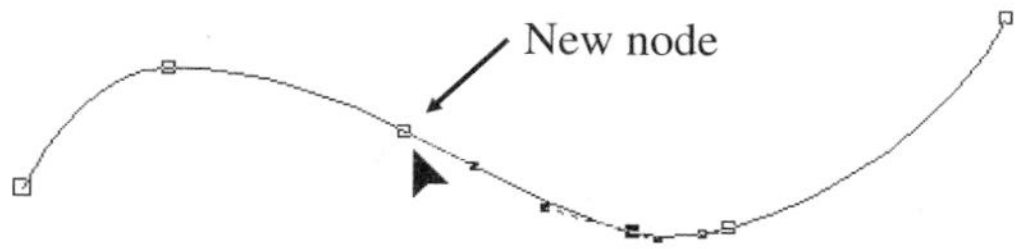

4. After clicking on any white space to deselect the selected nodes, leave the current curve on your screen for use in the next exercise.

IP: *Independent of whether the Node Edit roll-up is open, you can add a new node by clicking where you want the node with the Shape tool and pressing + on the numeric keypad.*

Adding Multiple Nodes

Perform the following brief exercise to add several nodes to a curve at one time. The technique is the same as when you add a single node, except that multiple nodes must be selected.

1. You should have a waveform curve on your screen in Actual Size magnification along with the Node Edit roll-up and the Shape tool, as you left them in the last exercise.
2. Select two or more nodes using either SHIFT or the marquee method. You will add nodes in front of each of these selected nodes. All of the squares that mark the selected nodes blacken, as shown here:

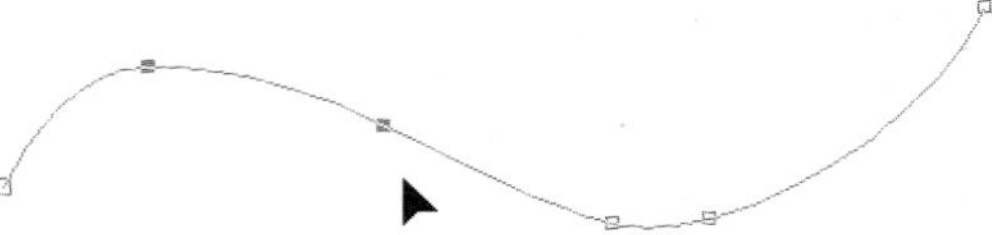

3. Click on the Add (+) button on the Node Edit roll-up. A new node appears in front of each of the selected nodes, as shown here:

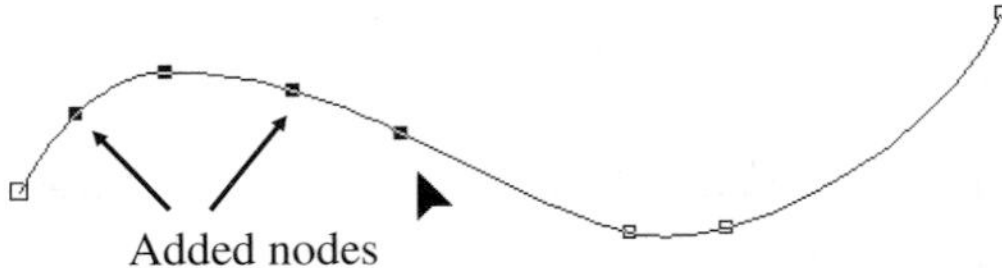

4. If you deselect all of the currently selected nodes and then select the added nodes individually, you can manipulate their control points to suit your drawing needs.
5. Again, after deselecting the nodes, leave the current curve on your screen for use in the next exercise.

The counterpart to adding nodes is deleting them. Continue with the next sections to practice deleting one or more nodes from a curve.

A New Renaissance by Georgina Curry

Georgina started out by simply sketching a female form in the pose that eventually became the angel. She then scanned the image into CorelDRAW! and manually traced it. The wings, which were added as an afterthought, were one of the hardest elements because they were an unknown. Georgina looked at books of Renaissance art to see how artists of the period drew angels. She finished the wings using variations on a feather that she had drawn for *The Huntress*, her 1993 Best of Show piece in the CorelDRAW! World Design Contest. The final touch, added on pure whimsy, was the cell phone held to the angel's ear.

The sculpted, hard-edge nature of the figure was a natural for vector-based CorelDRAW!. On the other hand, the figure remained black and white because pastel skin tones are very difficult to produce in CorelDRAW!, and because it was an angelic color in Georgina's mind. You'll notice that the only colors used are fully saturated, which are easier for CorelDRAW! and print very well on all color printers. The figure was given depth by using shadows and blends to form the armpit, the top of the breast, and the stomach. The blends were repeated until Georgina had them the way she wanted.

The gown and hair were also manually sketched and scanned into CorelDRAW!, then the Bézier tool was used to manually trace the scanned image. The gown was done in many separate segments, each with a custom fill. The gold trim is modified clip art to which a custom fill was added, giving the feeling of wrapping around the folds. An envelope was applied to constrain the gold trim to the fabric. The hair was given a shiny texture by pushing up the edge pad to 15 degrees. Also, the hair was used to separate and differentiate the wings.

The halo design is based on renaissance patterns. One-eighth of it was sketched, scanned into CorelDRAW!, and manually traced. It was then mirrored to form a quarter circle, and finally duplicated to form the full halo. Each segment is two different objects: the darker-colored apples and lines separating the weaving, and the lighter-colored leaves and center of the halo. Each object was given its own radial fill, with one darker than the other.

Georgina attended art school at Edinburgh University in Pennsylvania, majoring in commercial art and drawing. She has been a freelance artist and is currently a partner in a commercial illustration business, The Electric Easel. CorelDRAW! was one of the first computer illustration programs she tried and her award-winning *The Huntress* was the first full illustration she created. The majority of her work is now done on the computer and in CorelDRAW!, although she will often sketch the beginnings of a piece, as described above, because she finds it easier to see both detail and the overall drawing at one time.

Georgina can be reached at The Electric Easel, 10229 N. Scottsdale Road, Suite C, Scottsdale, AZ, 85253. Phone: (602), 443-8786, fax: (602) 443-8225.

The Mikado by Stephen Arscott

Stephen created *The Mikado* as an exercise for himself and for the Corel Competition. It took well over 200 hours and is as much an organizational work as it is a creative art piece. There are four files: the dragon and curtain, the woman, the man, and the text and border. Each of these files is made up of many pieces and layers. For example, just to list some of the pieces in their approximate layers, the entire figure of the woman is composed of the hand, the head with the facial features, the hair, the flowers in the hair, the umbrella, the robe in four major pieces, the flowers on the robe, the blue sash and white rope, and the umbrella handle.

The dragon was first hand sketched, then the major lines were darkened, and the image was scanned and finally traced with CorelTRACE to create the vector image that was brought into CorelDRAW!. The image at that point was a flat circle. It was colored, then five rectangles were drawn over the image and the intersection tool was used to create five separate strips. Next, the envelope tool was used to raise or lower alternating strips to fit the contour of the curtain. Finally, strips of white transparency were applied to pick up the highlights of the curtain's folds.

The design on the man's robe began as a single small square with the pattern of the left and right matching, as did the pattern on the top and bottom so that it could be replicated like tile. The square was then laid down to cover roughly all of the area that was the robe. Then the perspective tool was applied to give some depth to the appropriate areas. Next, the envelope tool was used to fit the robe to the desired contours. Finally, the colors were lightened or darkened in the appropriate areas to improve the sense of depth.

The woman's hair was just black fill in the outline, and the entire shape was accomplished by creating a single "hair" with a custom radial fill that went from black on the outside to white in the center. The hair was then copied, made various lengths, and then arranged to create the desired shapes. The flowers in the hair are actually three different pieces of clip art from the CorelDRAW! 5 collection.

Stephen created his title from a customized font, and each character, after being converted to curves, was split into "surfaces," each of which was given a custom fill and reattached to produce an extruded look. The Chinese characters, which actually say *The Mikado*, were created with Twin-Bridge, an English/Chinese computer translator that produces Chinese script. The border is a customization of a CorelDRAW! border.

Stephen attended the Ontario College of Art. After graduating, he held several positions as a commercial artist where he began using CorelDRAW! with version 1.0. In 1993, he opened his own commercial art studio called ATK Integrated Communications, Inc. He does all forms of commercial art and page layout, including using Twin-Bridge to produce a Chinese language newsletter. He has won a grand prize in both the 1993 (for page layout) and 1994 (for corporate ID) CorelDRAW! World Design Contest.

Stephen can be reached at ATK Integrated Communications, Inc., 4291 Village Centre Court, Mississauga, Ontario, Canada L4Z 1S2. Phone: (905) 896-4664, fax: (905) 896-0735.

Phalanx of Cheetahs by David Brickley

David created *Phalanx of Cheetahs* for the Intel OverDrive group to help them introduce and demonstrate the OverDrive processor chips at trade shows and on press tours. At that time, Intel offered three OverDrive processors and the idea was to create an illustration that spoke to the concept of this "add-on" speed and power. For this assignment, he created three robotic cheetahs on top of an OverDrive chip.

David started his work by going to the library where he reviewed books and pictures of cheetahs. Even though this illustration was going to be "science fiction," to be convincing, he needed to be true to a cheetah's look, posture, and manner. After drawing four or five pencil sketches of cheetahs—each sketch being more robotic—he switched on the computer and started to execute the final drawing.

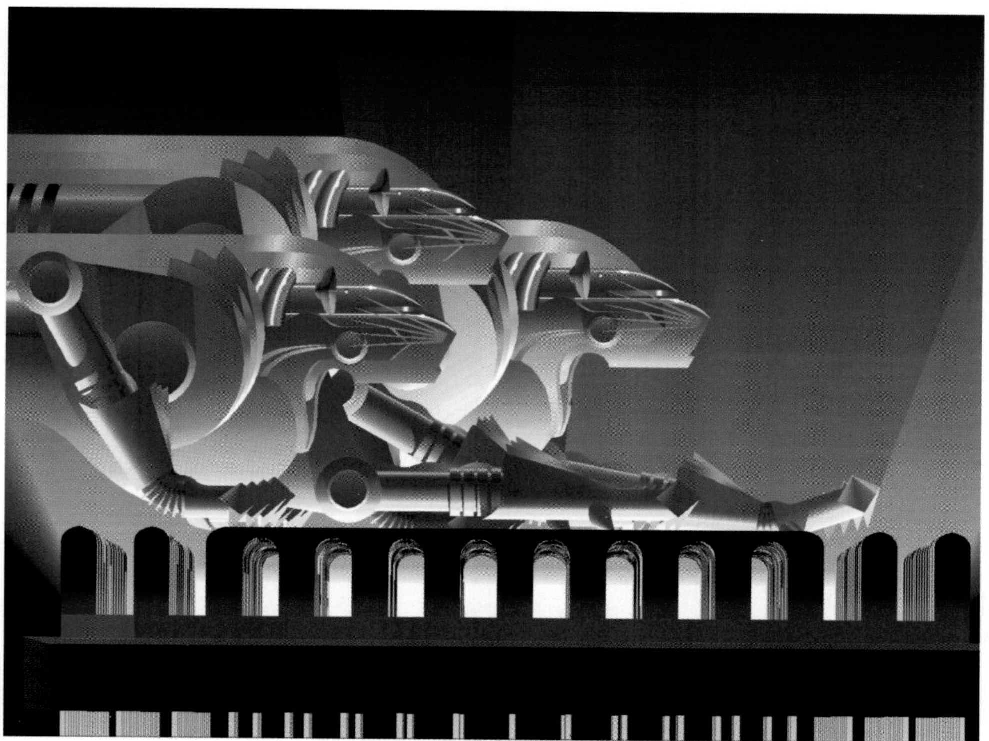

This piece was created in CorelDRAW! 4.0 and took about four long days to finish. The only special effects that were used were object blending and graded fills. The appearance of light coming up from the OverDrive chip upon which the cheetahs are standing is created by a simple "V"-shaped blend group behind the cats.

To create the visual effect of a smoky atmosphere, David added several objects behind the cheetahs that are a darker color than the atmosphere. This helps produce an effect of an object blocking light in smoke—a shadow is cast through the air. For instance, the cheetah's paw furthest to the right blocks light and casts a shadow that extends up through the atmosphere.

David has a BFA in Communications Design from the Art Center College of Design in Pasadena, California. He has been an art director for several advertising firms, a freelance art director, and for over seven years, president of his own firm, Shooting Brick Productions, Inc. His firm creates custom computer graphics for IBM compatible computer industry clients.

David can be reached at Shooting Brick Productions, Inc., 3318 NE Peerless Place, Portland, OR 97232. Phone: (503) 236-4883, fax: (503) 236-4952. David also has an excellent exhibit of his work on the Internet through a web page at:
http://www.europa.com/~brickley/index.
David can be reached on the Internet at @europa.com.
Phalanx of Cheetahs is reproduced with the permission of the artist.

Pickup Sticks by Chris Purcell

Chris was asked by Impulse Engineering to create a logo for one of their new products, Pickup Sticks. Chris began with client meetings where he learned about the product and the elements that Impulse wanted included in the logo. Among the latter were the product's and manufacturer's names, what the product does, a red Stratocaster guitar, electronic circuitry, and a sense of hot pulsating sound and energy. Chris then began with pencil sketches, which help him conceptualize what he wants to do before getting involved with the detail on the computer. Although he sometimes scans his sketches into the computer, this time Chris started from scratch in CorelDRAW!.

The first step was to create the word "PICKUP" using Helvetica Neue Condensed and then increase the thickness of the letters using the Contour roll-up. Next, Chris drew a red Stratocaster guitar using magazine pictures. At this point the guitar was just a shape with little detail. Then, the letters were combined with a surrounding black rectangle which reversed the letters and allowed the guitar to show through when the instrument was placed behind them. The areas of the guitar that showed had the necessary detail added and the custom gradation palette was used to fill various areas.

The letters were given further definition by duplicating them and using the Contour roll-up to add an outline (really a contour) on the outside of the letters. Next, the letters were given a custom fill and the light areas made a lot smaller than the dark areas to produce an effect of shiny intensity. To enhance the letters even more, the duplication process was done several times with just the bottom and top edges of the duplicates used to highlight the original outline. Finally, a metallic or reflective look was achieved by combining all the elements.

The circuit board was created by drawing four rectangular shapes, duplicating them, and flipping the duplication horizontally to produce the top circuit lines. These were then filled with a custom linear fill, duplicated again, and then flipped vertically to produce the bottom circuit lines. The net effect is one of glowing letters.

The "Impulse Engineering" and "Electric Guitar Pickups" text was added with their duplicated linear filled lines. Chris wanted to do something special with the word "Sticks," so he wrote the word with a dry marker on paper, scanned it into Corel PHOTO-PAINT where he cleaned it up a little, and then imported it into CorelDRAW!. This provided a vivid contrast to the smooth, metallic surface of the word "PICKUP."

Chris earned a BA in Illustration from Barnsfield College of Art in Luton, Bedfordshire, England. He then worked for a couple of years in an advertising agency before coming to the United States. Here, he freelanced for several years before joining Compaq Computer Corporation eight years ago. It has been interesting for him to work as a graphics designer for a computer corporation where he had all the hardware he wanted but got very impatient waiting for the software to catch up. At one point he almost had Compaq convinced to buy him an Apple Macintosh, but then CorelDRAW! showed up, enabling him to use his existing Compaq hardware. Chris has won awards in the CorelDRAW! World Design Contest in each of the years it has been run. Some of his awards include the Grand Prize for Logos in 1992 and the Best in the West in 1994.

Chris can be reached at 3702 Pineleaf Drive, Houston, TX 77068. Phone: (713) 374-4679.
Pickup Sticks is reproduced with the permission of the artist

Deleting Single and Multiple Nodes

When you draw freehand curves, it is often difficult to control mouse movement completely.

IP: *To draw with less erratic movements, you may want to try using a digital drawing tablet and pen.*

Changing the Freehand Tracking, Corner Threshold, and Auto-join settings in the Curves, Bézier Tool Properties dialog box may help, but erratic movements while you execute a curve still can produce occasional extraneous nodes. You can smooth out an uneven curve quickly and easily by deleting single or multiple extraneous nodes.

AUTION: *Always delete nodes with caution. Deleting a node at random, without checking to see if other nodes are nearby, can radically alter the shape of a curve in ways that are not always predictable. You can use the Undo command from the Edit menu to undo a node deletion if the results are not what you expected.*

Perform the following exercise to delete nodes from a curve.

1. You should still have a waveform curve on your screen in Actual Size magnification, and the Node Edit roll-up and Shape tool should be selected as you left them in the last exercise.
2. Using the Shape tool, click on a node that you want to delete, as shown here:

Keep in mind that if you delete one of the end nodes of a curve, you delete the associated curve segment as well. The next node on the curve will then become an end node. If you delete either node of a straight line, you delete the entire line in the process.

You could at this point select the Delete (-) button on the Node Edit roll-up. Coreldraw would delete the node that you selected and redraw the curve without it. The shape of your redrawn curve could be quite different from your original one; just how different it might be depends on the location of the node you selected for deletion.

IP: *As a shortcut to deleting a node, you can select a node and press* DEL *instead of invoking the Node Edit roll-up.*

You can delete multiple nodes as well as single nodes from a curve, as long as all of the nodes you want to delete are selected. To delete multiple nodes follow these steps.

1. Select additional nodes you want to delete, using either SHIFT or the marquee method; three nodes are selected here. Keep in mind that if you delete an end node, you will delete the associated curve segment along with it.

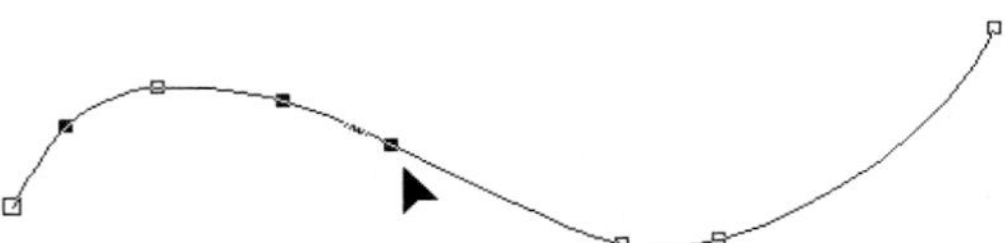

2. Select the Delete (-) button on the Node Edit roll-up. Coreldraw immediately deletes the selected nodes from the screen and redraws the curve without them, as shown here:

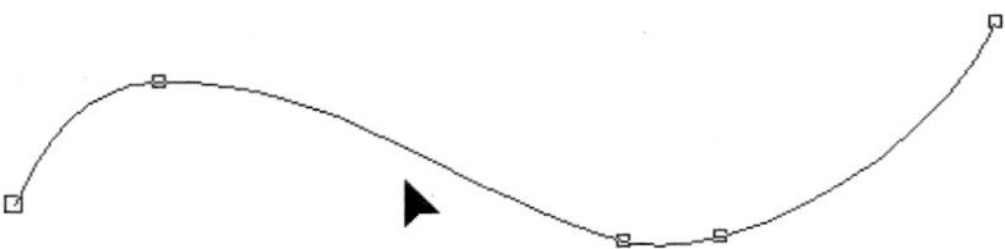

3. The shape of the curve can change subtly or dramatically between node positions; the extent of the change depends on the original positions of the selected nodes.

4. Keep the curve for the next example.

You have learned to add and delete nodes when you need to reshape a curve more than the existing nodes allow. Sometimes, though, you may want your curve to flatten to the extent that you need to replace a curve segment with a straight-line segment. You accomplish this by converting one or more curve segments to straight lines.

Converting a Single Curve Segment to a Straight-Line Segment

Coreldraw allows you to convert curve segments to line segments. Before you convert a curve to a line, you need to be able to identify whether a selected segment is a curve or a straight line. Some important guidelines to follow are:

- The shape of the *selected* node identifies the type of line segment that precedes it. A black fill in the selected node signifies a curve segment, while a hollow selected node signifies a straight-line segment.
- A curve segment has two control points; a straight-line segment has none.
- When you select the segment or its node, the Status bar indicates whether the segment is a line or curve.

9

Perform the following exercise to gain experience in converting a single curve segment into a straight-line segment.

1. Again, use the curve from the previous example. If your curve has only a couple of nodes left, add a node using the steps you recently learned so that there is a curve segment that is a good candidate for a straight line.
2. Using the Shape tool, click on a segment or node of a curve that you want to convert to a straight line, as shown here:

3. Now, select the To Line button on the Node Edit roll-up. The two control points related to the selected curve disappear, and the curve segment becomes a straight-line segment, as shown here. You can reposition, stretch, or shorten this line segment by using the Shape tool to drag the nodes at either end.

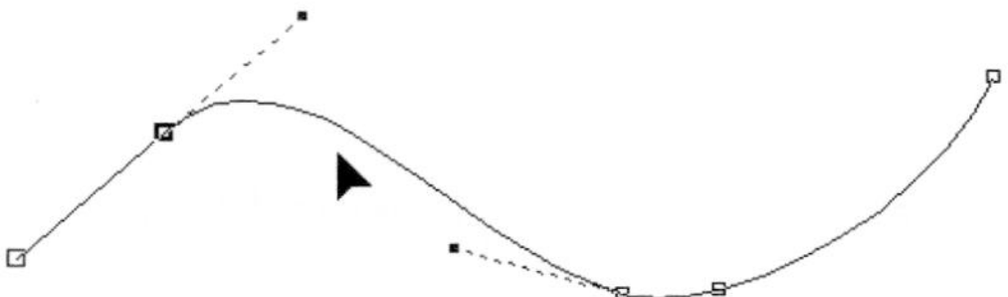

Converting Multiple Curve Segments to Straight-Line Segments

If you want a curve object in your drawing to be more angular, you can change its appearance by selecting multiple nodes or curve segments and converting them to straight lines. To convert multiple curve segments to straight-line segments, follow these steps.

1. Press ALT-BACKSPACE to undo making the curve segment a line and, if necessary, add a node so that there are at least two curve segments that are good candidates for straight lines.
2. Select the curve segments or nodes you want to convert to straight lines, using either SHIFT or the marquee technique.
3. Select the To Line button on the Node Edit roll-up. The selected curve segments convert to straight lines, and all associated control points are eliminated (straight lines do not include control points). The object becomes much more angular, as shown here. You can now reposition, stretch, or shrink any or all of the line segments by dragging the node(s).

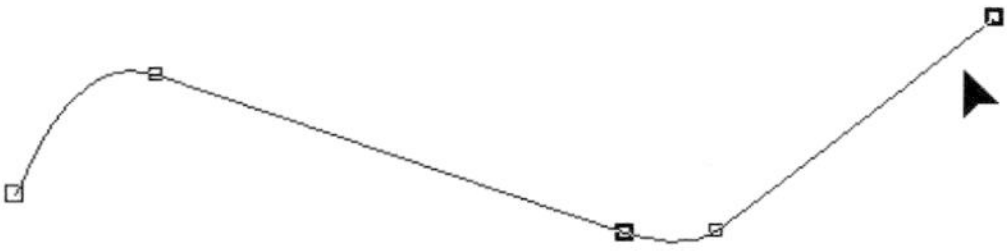

If your object consists of angular-line segments but you want to give it much smoother contours, you can convert line segments to curves. The next section shows you how.

Converting Single and Multiple Straight-Line Segments to Curve Segments

With Coreldraw, you can convert straight-line segments to curve segments through the Node Edit roll-up. Before you convert a line segment to a curve segment, you need to identify whether a selected segment is a straight line or a curve. If you are uncertain about identifying segments, review the guidelines in the previous section before you proceed. Now, try the following exercise.

1. Using the Shape tool, first deselect all nodes, then click on one of the straight-line segments you just created, or on the *end* node of a straight line. (If you select the first node of the line segment, you will not be able to convert it to a curve.) The To Curve button is now available to you.
2. Select the To Curve button on the Node Edit roll-up. Coreldraw turns the selected straight-line segment into a curve, causing two control points to appear on the line segment. These may not be visible because they are covered by the curve segment connecting the nodes. You can point on the curve segment (not on a node) and drag it out of the way to see the control points. Drag these control points to change the segments to the shape you want.

You can turn several straight-line segments into curve segments at the same time, as long as they are part of the same object. You simply select the several segments and select the To Curve button on the Node Edit roll-up. The selected straight-line segments convert to curve lines. On the surface, the segments do not appear to have changed. However, if you deselect all nodes and then select any one of the converted nodes, two control points appear. You can reshape the peaks and valleys like any other curve.

Experiment with converting all the line segments to curves, and prove to yourself that now you really are working with curves.

Another group of commands in the Node Edit roll-up allows you to change the type of single or multiple nodes. These commands—Cusp, Smooth, and Symmetrical—are the subject of the next several sections.

Cusping Single or Multiple Nodes

When you work with a cusp node, you can move either of its control points independently of the other. This makes it possible to independently control the curvature of both of the curve segments that meet at the node, without affecting the other segment.

The following exercise shows you how to turn a single smooth or symmetrical node into a cusp node.

1. Using the Shape tool and the same drawing, click on the node you want to cusp. Select any node except a cusp or end node; Coreldraw designates all end nodes as cusp nodes.
2. When the Cusp command button is enabled, click on it. The appearance of the curve does not change. However, if you manipulate the control points of this node, as shown here, you will find that you can move one control point without affecting the curve segment on the other side of the node.

   When you want a curve object to have a relatively jagged appearance, but you do not want to turn your curves into straight lines, the next best solution is to change multiple smooth or symmetrical nodes into cusp nodes. You can then shape the cusp nodes to create a more angular appearance for the affected portions of the object.
3. Save your drawing, using Save As from the File menu. Name the drawing Line; you will use it again in a later exercise.
4. Select Close, then New from the File menu and Document from the flyout to close the file and open a new document.

In the next section, you will become familiar with changing cusped or symmetrical nodes into smooth nodes.

Smoothing Single or Multiple Nodes

In the previous section, you saw that cusp nodes are desirable when you want to create a rougher, more jagged appearance for an object. When you want to make an object's curves smoother, however, you seek out the cusp nodes and turn them into smooth ones.

A smooth node can be defined as a node whose control points always lie along a straight line, like a symmetrical node, except that the control points are not equidistant from the node. A special case exists when a smooth node is located between a straight line and a curve segment, as shown here:

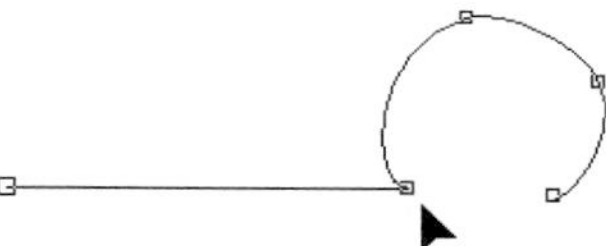

In such a case, only the side of the node toward the curve segment contains a control point, and you can only move that control point along an imaginary line that follows the extension of the straight line. This restriction maintains the smoothness at the node.

In the next exercise, you will convert a single cusp node that lies at the juncture between a straight line and curve segment into a smooth node.

1. Set viewing magnification to Actual Size (1:1), select the Freehand tool, and then draw a straight line connected to a curve segment, as shown above. Remember to click at the end of the line segment to attach the curve segment to it automatically.
2. Activate the Shape tool. Your curve object may not include the same number of nodes as the one shown above, but that is not important for the purpose of this exercise.
3. Using the Shape tool, click on the line cusp node next to the curve segment, as shown here:

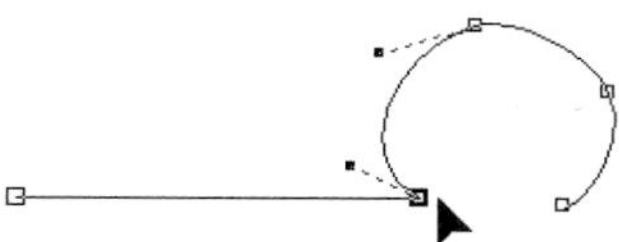

4. On the Node Edit roll-up, click on the Smooth button. The curve passing through the selected node is smoothed, like the one here, and will remain smooth when you move either the node itself or its control point. The straight-line segment does not change, of course.

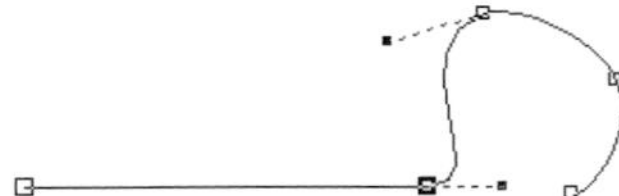

5. Select Close from the File menu to close the current document. Don't bother to save it.

To smooth multiple nodes, you simply select multiple nodes and then repeat the steps for smoothing a single node.

Go on to the next section to learn how you can turn smooth or cusp nodes into symmetrical nodes and how this affects the drawing process.

Making Single or Multiple Nodes Symmetrical

Symmetrical nodes share the same characteristics as smooth nodes, except that the control points on a symmetrical node are equidistant from the node. This means that the curvature is the same on both sides of the symmetrical node. When you move one of the control points, the other control point moves. In effect, symmetry causes the two control points to move as one.

Another important point to remember is that you cannot make a node symmetrical if it connects to a straight-line segment. The node must lie between two curve segments in order to be a symmetrical node.

Perform the following brief exercise to convert a single cusp node to a symmetrical node, using the Line.Cdr drawing with a cusp node that you created earlier. Open this drawing now.

1. Set viewing magnification to Actual Size (1:1), activate the Shape tool, and click on the curve to select it.

2. Find a cusp node that you want to make symmetrical and then click on it, as shown here:

3. Click on the Symmetrical node button. The selected node is now converted to a symmetrical node, and Coreldraw redraws the curve so that it passes through the node symmetrically, as shown here:

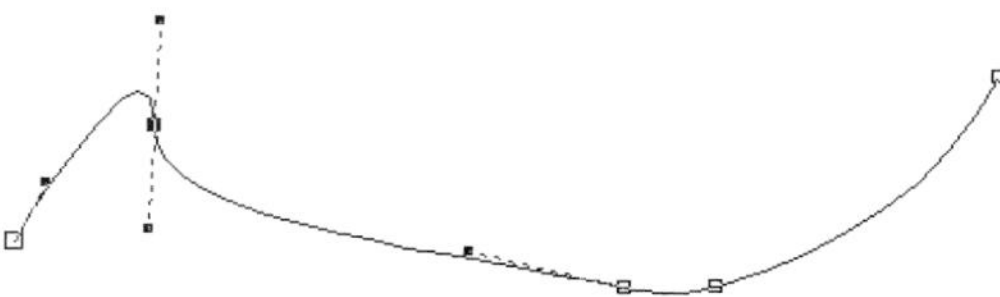

4. Move the control points of this node until you have a satisfactory understanding of how symmetrical nodes work.

Making multiple nodes symmetrical is just as easy as making single nodes symmetrical. The only difference is that you select more than one node at a time, using either SHIFT or the marquee method.

In the next sections, you will find out how to master the art of breaking nodes apart and joining them together—and why you might choose to do so.

Breaking Curves at Single or Multiple Nodes

Breaking a node involves splitting a curve at a selected node, so that two nodes appear where before there was one. Although you can move the separate sections of a broken node as though they were separate curves, Coreldraw does not regard them as separate. These split segments actually constitute different subpaths of the same curve. Breaking a node into separate subpaths gives the impression of spontaneous freehand drawing, yet it allows you to keep separate "drawing strokes" together as one object. Breaking curves at the nodes is also useful when you need to delete a portion of a curve and leave the rest of the curve intact.

OTE: *Keep in mind that you cannot break a curve at an end node, because there is no segment on the other side of the end point with which to form a separate subpath.*

When you break a node, it becomes two unconnected end nodes. You are then free to move either end node and the entire subpath to which it is connected. The two subpaths remain part of the same object, however, as you can see when you select either subpath with the Pick tool. In the following exercise, you will use the curve from the last exercise, break it at a single node, and then observe how Coreldraw handles the two resulting subpaths.

1. With the Shape tool, select a node on the curve, as shown here:

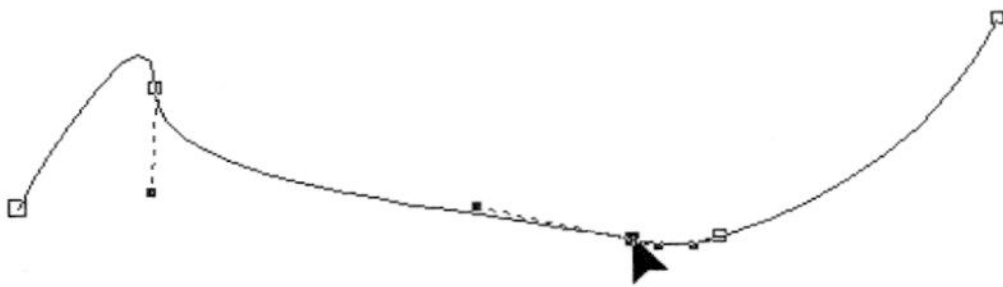

2. Click on the Break button (the second button from the right in the top row of the Node Edit roll-up). The single node splits into two nodes. Since they are close together, however, the change is not visible until you begin to move the new end nodes.
3. Move the left end point away from the subpath to the right, as shown here, and then deselect both nodes.

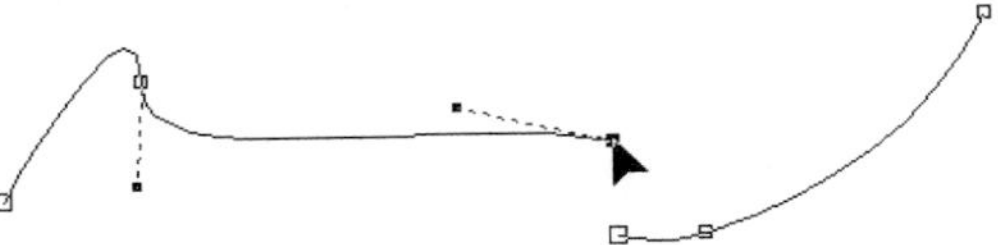

4. The object itself remains selected for editing, and the Status bar informs you that the curve now has two subpaths.
5. Press the SPACEBAR to activate the Pick tool. Notice that the Pick tool treats these two subpaths as a single curve object, even though they look like separate curves.

   There may be times when you want to make subpaths into truly separate objects, so that you can manipulate and edit them independently. As the next step shows, Coreldraw provides a means for you to turn the subpaths into independent curves.

6. To separate the two subpaths into two truly distinct objects, leave the Pick tool active and then select the Break Apart command from the Arrange menu. This command is available only when multiple subpaths of a single curve object are selected. Deselect both subpaths. Now, if you click on each subpath with the Pick tool, you will see that each segment will be separately selected.

   You can also extract a subpath from an object using the Extract Subpath button on the Edit Node roll-up. While the Break Apart command creates a separate object from each subpath, the Extract Subpath button only extracts the selected subpath, leaving the others as multiple subpaths of one object.

7. Clear the screen. You do not need to resave the Line.Cdr drawing that began this last exercise.

In this brief exercise, you have seen some applications for breaking a curve at a node. For example, you can create two separate objects from a single object, or create separate subpaths that move together as a single object.

AUTION: *If you break a closed curve object at a node, you will not be able to fill the object with a color or pattern.*

When you break a curve at multiple nodes, the result is multiple subpaths, which still remain part of the same object.

Using the Knife Tool

The Knife tool on the Shape tool flyout provides another method of separating objects into multiple subpaths. The Knife tool has the advantage of allowing you to cut a curve at any point, not just an existing node. When you cut (click on) a curve segment with the Knife tool, nodes are created at the end points of the new subpaths. Depending on how you define the Knife tool properties in the Tool Properties dialog box, the Knife tool will leave the new subpath as part of the original object or create a separate object. The Knife tool can also automatically connect the new end nodes to create a closed curve.

The reverse of breaking curves apart is joining them together. In the next section, you will find out when you can and cannot join nodes together, as well as some reasons why you might want to do so.

Joining Nodes

By now, you have probably noticed that the Join command is rarely available for selection on the Node Edit roll-up. You can join nodes only under very specific conditions.

- You can join only two nodes at a time, so only two nodes can be selected.
- The two nodes must be either end nodes of the same object or end nodes of separate subpaths of the same object.
- You cannot join an end node of an open curve to a closed object, such as an ellipse or a rectangle.

When might you want to join two nodes, then? The two chief occasions are when you want to close an open path and when you want to make a single continuous curve from the two separate paths.

CLOSING AN OPEN PATH An open path, as you will recall from your previous freehand drawing experience in Coreldraw, is a curve object with end points that do not join and which therefore cannot be filled with a color or pattern. To prevent open paths, you can set the Auto-join option in the Curve, Bézier Tool Properties dialog box to a higher number and thereby make it easier for end nodes to snap together as you draw. There are still times, however, when you might choose to join end nodes after drawing an open curve. In such cases, use the Join command in the Node Edit roll-up. The following exercise presents a situation in which you could use the Join command to make a drawing process easier.

1. Set magnification to Actual Size (1:1). Select the Freehand tool and draw a more or less oval curve, but do not finish the curve—stop drawing at a point close to where you started it, as shown here:

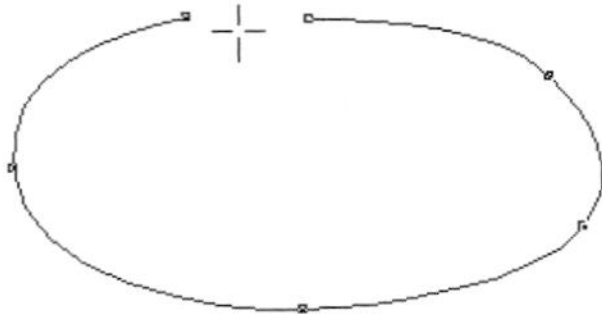

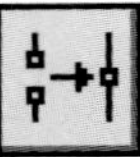

2. Click on the Shape tool to select this curve object and then select both of the end nodes, using the marquee or SHIFT key technique. You can see

that the Join command button in the Node Edit roll-up (the middle button in the top row and shown in the margin here) is now available to you.

3. Click on the Join command button in the Node Edit roll-up. Coreldraw redraws the curve as a closed path. You can then fill this path with a color or pattern, as you learned in Chapter 7.
4. Clear the screen. Do not save the drawing.

It is easy to close an open path with the Shape tool. Joining nodes from separate curves, however, is a bit trickier.

JOINING SEPARATE SUBPATHS (COMBINED OBJECTS) You can also join two end nodes if they are on two subpaths of the same curve. The two subpaths then become a single, continuous curve segment. A special case exists when you have two separate curve objects (not two subpaths of the same curve) and want to make them into a single curve. Knowing that you cannot join nodes from two separate objects, what do you do? Your best option is to combine the curves using the Pick tool and the Combine command from the Arrange menu. Even though the curves continue to look like separate objects, from the standpoint of Coreldraw they become two subpaths of a single curve. You can then join their end nodes to unite the subpaths.

1. Select Actual Size magnification and with the Freehand tool draw three separate curves, as shown here:

2. With the Pick tool, draw a marquee around all three curve segments to simultaneously select them. You can also choose Select All in the Edit menu, or double-click on the Pick tool.
3. From the Arrange menu, select Combine to make a single broken curve out of the three segments.
4. With the Shape tool, select the curve. Then select both end nodes of the first pair of end points to be joined, double-click on either of the two end nodes to open the Node Edit roll-up, if it is not already on the screen, and

click on the Join button. The result is a single continuous curve, as shown here:

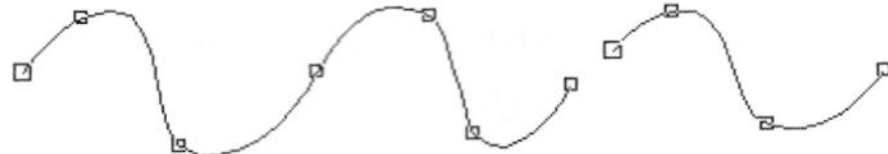

IP: *The only trick to this is to first combine the curve segments with the Pick tool and the Arrange menu before trying to join the segments with the Shape tool.*

Coreldraw joined the two selected nodes by moving each node an equal distance towards the other node and then creating a single node. You can also join two nodes by inserting a new curve segment between the selected nodes. Use this method to join two more end points.

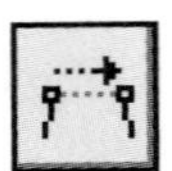

1. Select both end nodes of the remaining pair of end nodes.
2. Select the Auto-join button on the Edit Node roll-up.
3. The selected pair of end points are joined by a new curve segment, as shown here:

4. Clear the screen; do not save the changes you have made.

Going through this process is a good way to familiarize yourself with all the steps involved in both joining nodes and breaking nodes apart. Perhaps you have some new ideas for using the Join command in some of your own drawings.

Aligning Nodes

If you want two objects to share a common edge, like two pieces in a jigsaw puzzle, the Align button on the Node Edit roll-up can accomplish it for you. The two objects must first be combined with the Combine command, and you must add or delete nodes until there are the same number of nodes in each object in roughly the same location. Once you have completed aligning the two objects, you can break them apart.

Objects can be aligned vertically or horizontally, and they can literally share a common border through the alignment of their control points. If you want to superimpose one object on the other, you align them both horizontally and vertically *and* align their control points. The latter—aligning the objects all three ways—is the default alignment.

You can experiment with the Align command in the Node Edit roll-up in the following exercise.

1. At Actual Size (1:1) magnification, with the Freehand tool draw two curve objects similar to those shown here. (Wireframe should be turned on.)

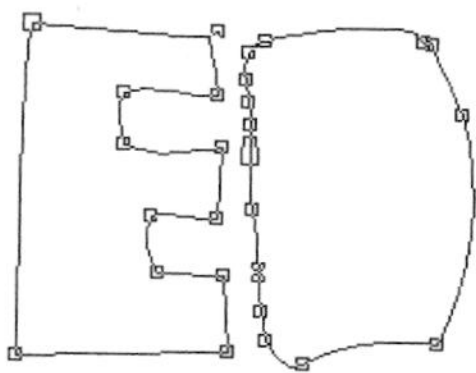

2. With the Pick tool, draw a marquee around both objects to select them. Then, from the Arrange menu, select Combine.

IP: *Use the SPACEBAR to toggle between the Pick tool and any other tool you are using at the time.*

9

3. With the Shape tool, add or delete nodes until the two objects have the same number of nodes on the "mating" side, in roughly the same position.
4. For each pair of nodes you want to align, perform these steps with the Shape tool in the order given:
   a. Select the node to be *re-aligned* (moved).
   b. Press SHIFT and select the node to *align* to (move to).
   c. Select the Align button on the Node Edit dialog box. The Node Align dialog box will open, as shown here:

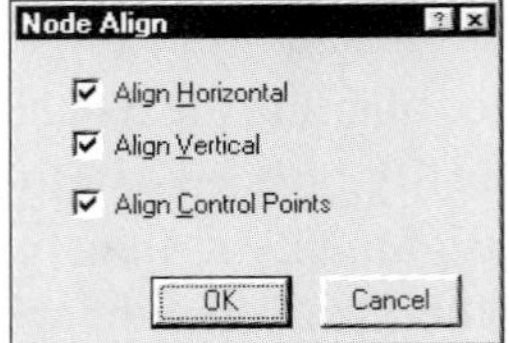

d. Click on OK to accept the default choice of all three options, which will superimpose the nodes and align the control points. You might have to tweak the control points slightly where the moved segment has reversed direction.

e. Deselect the nodes by clicking on any white space before beginning to select the next pair. When you have aligned all of the node pairs you want to align, you should have a single curve segment shared by both objects, whose shape is the same as the object to which you aligned, as shown here:

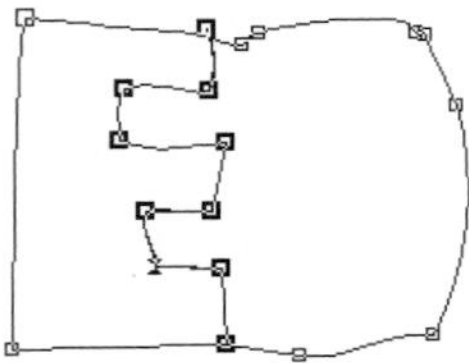

5. With the Pick tool, select the combined object and choose Break Apart from the Arrange menu.

6. Click on white space to deselect the combined object, then select and drag one of the original objects until you can see the two individual objects again. Now the two objects have a common, although mirror-image, shape on one side, as shown here:

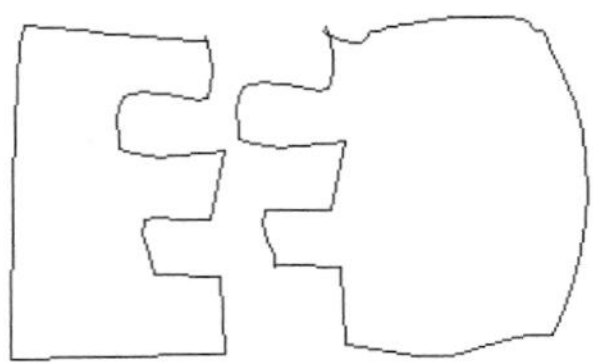

7. Delete the objects to clear the screen; do not save the changes.
8. You are finished with the Node Edit roll-up for now. Click on its Close button.

This concludes your exploration of the techniques for shaping lines and curves. In the remaining sections of this chapter, you will try your hand at shaping rectangular and elliptical objects.

Shaping Rectangles and Squares

The Shape tool has a specific function when you apply it to rectangles and squares in Coreldraw. It rounds the corners of a rectangle, thus creating a whole new shape. The Status bar keeps track of the radius of the rounded corner as you drag. You can control the degree of rounding interactively, or by using the grid if you want to be exact.

Rounding the Corners of a Rectangle

Complete the following exercise to practice rounding rectangles and squares using the Shape tool. You will begin by rounding corners interactively; later, you will use the grid to perform the same work.

1. For the beginning of this exercise, make sure that the Snap To Grid and Rulers are turned off, that Wireframe is turned on, and that you are working in Actual Size viewing magnification. Then, select the Rectangle tool and draw a rectangle of unequal length and width.
2. Activate the Shape tool and select a node at one of the corners of the rectangle. Notice that the Status bar indicates that the corner radius of this rectangle is 0.00 inches. The corner radius helps you measure the degree to which you have rounded the corners of a rectangle or square with the Shape tool.
3. Position the shaping pointer at this node and begin to drag the corner slowly toward the next nearest corner. As shown here, each of the four corner nodes separates into two separate nodes, with each node moving farther away from the original corner as you drag. The Status bar also informs you just how much of a corner radius you are creating. The

farther you drag the nodes from the corners, the more the corner radius increases:

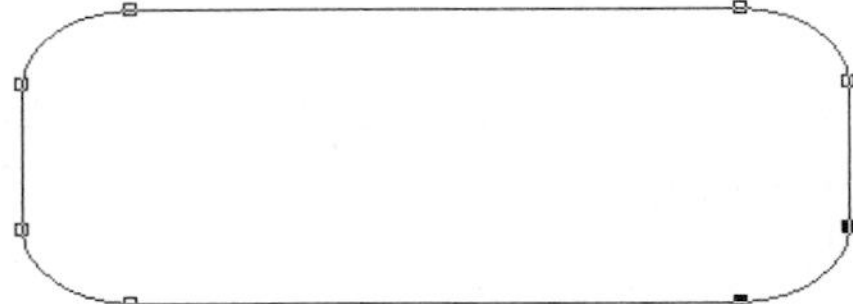

4. Continue dragging the mouse until you reach the logical limit of rounding: when the nodes from adjacent corners meet at the sides of the rectangle. At this point, your rounded rectangle has become almost an ellipse, similar to the rectangle shown here:

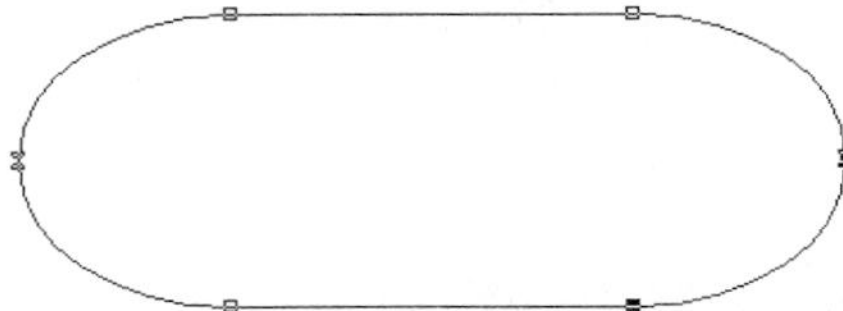

5. Begin dragging the selected node from the middle of the line back to the former corner. As you do so, the corner radius diminishes. You can return the rectangle to its original shape by dragging the nodes all the way back to the original corner.

6. Delete the rectangle from the screen, then draw a square and repeat steps 2 through 5. Notice that when you begin with a square and then round the corners to the logical limit, the square becomes a nearly perfect circle rather than an ellipse, as seen here:

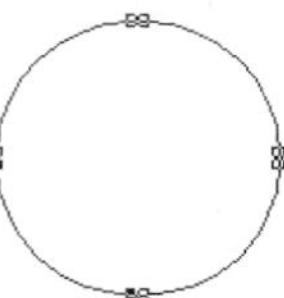

7. Press DEL to clear the screen of the square-turned-circle.

Although the Status bar information helps you round corners precisely, you can gain even greater precision using the grid and rulers. The next exercise guides you through the process of rounding corners of a rectangle or square with the help of these aids.

1. Open the Grid & Ruler Setup dialog box from the Layout menu. On the Grid tab, set both of the Frequency settings to 4 per inch, turn on Show Grid and Snap To Grid, and click on OK. Turn on Rulers.
2. Draw a rectangle 2 inches wide by 1 1/4 inches deep. Select the Shape tool and click on one of the corner nodes of the rectangle.
3. Drag this corner node away from the corner to round the rectangle. This time, the corner radius changes in precise increments of 1/4 inch because of the grid setting. The same thing happens with a square; the radius of the square also changes in increments of 1/4 inch.
4. When you have finished experimenting with the rectangle, select them and press DEL to clear the screen.

In the next section, you will see what can happen when you stretch, rotate, or skew a rectangle or square before attempting to round its corners.

Stretched, Rotated, or Skewed Rectangles and Squares

When you transform a rectangle or square by stretching, rotating, or skewing it with the Pick tool and then rounding its corners, the value of the corner radius may be distorted. The corner radius indicator on the Status bar is followed by the word "distorted" in parentheses. As Figure 9-6 shows, the final shape of such a rounded rectangle may also be distorted; in extreme cases, it can resemble a skewed flying saucer or rotated ellipse.

Practice this technique on your own and then go on to the next section, where you will find out how to turn a rectangle into a curve so that you can shape it in an infinite number of ways.

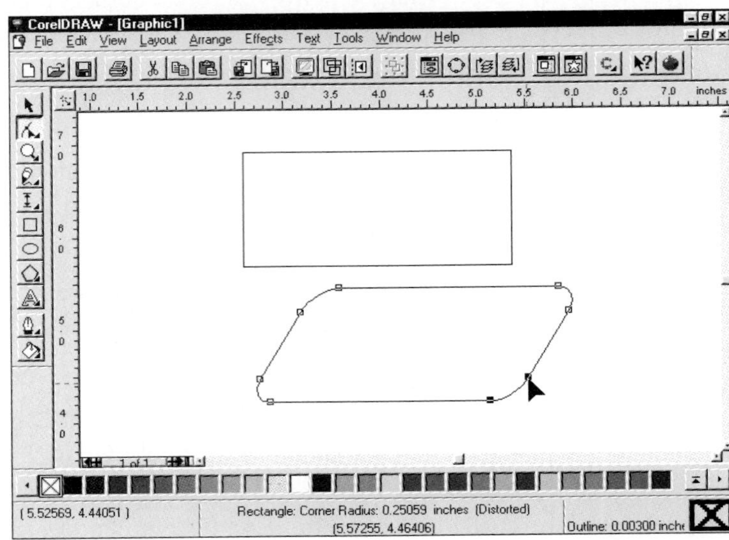

Rounding the corners of a skewed rectangle

FIGURE 9-6

Converting a Rectangle to a Curve Object

If the shaping options for rectangles or squares seem limited to you, don't worry. You can convert any rectangle or square into a curve object and, from that point onward, you can turn a formerly four-cornered object into anything at all. The technique is simple, as you will see in the following brief exercise.

1. Set magnification to Actual Size (1:1) and make sure Wireframe is turned on in preparation for this exercise.
2. Select the Rectangle tool if it is not selected already and then draw a rectangle of any size or shape.
3. Activate the Pick tool by pressing the SPACEBAR and select Convert To Curves from the Arrange menu. The Status bar message changes from "Rectangle on Layer 1" to "Curve on Layer 1." Note that the new four-cornered "curve" still has the same number of nodes as when it was a rectangle.

4. Activate the Shape tool and then select and drag one of the nodes in any direction. As the example in Figure 9-7 shows, dragging the node no longer forces the associated line/curve segment to move parallel to the other line segments.
5. Continue warping the shape of this rectangle-turned-curve in a variety of ways. For example, you could add nodes, convert line segments to curves, create symmetrical nodes, or even turn the former rectangle into a candy cane or other hybrid object.
6. The object you have been working on should be selected. If it is not, select it and then press DEL to clear the screen before going on.

Now that you have mastered the art of shaping rectangles and squares, you are ready to apply the Shape tool to ellipses and circles for some quite different effects.

Shaping Ellipses and Circles

When you shape ellipses or circles with the Shape tool, you can create either an open arc or a pie wedge. You can even shift back and forth between these two shapes as

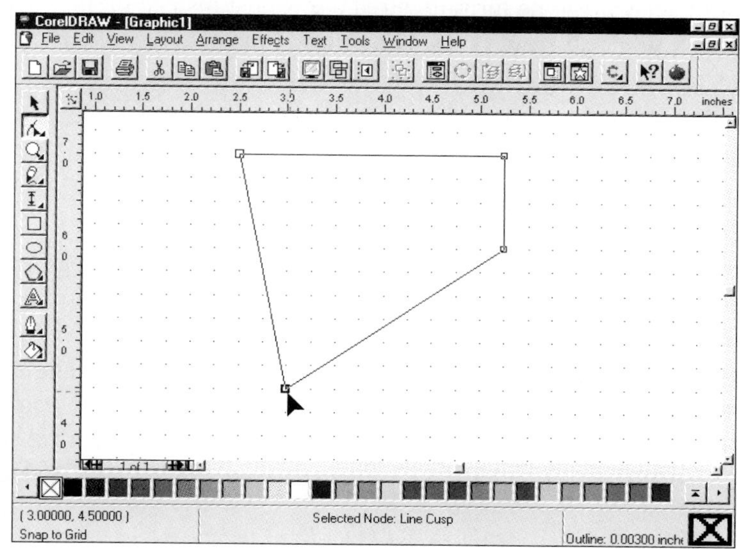

Editing a rectangle that has been converted to curves

FIGURE 9-7

you draw, depending on whether the tip of the shaping pointer lies inside or outside the ellipse or circle. You also have the option of constraining the angle of an arc or pie wedge to 15-degree increments.

Creating an Open Arc

To turn an ellipse or circle into an arc, you position the tip of the shaping pointer just *outside* of the rim at the node and then drag the node in the desired direction. Make certain that the tip of the pointer remains outside the rim of the ellipse as you drag, or you will create a wedge instead of an arc. Practice creating arcs from both ellipses and circles in the following exercise.

1. Turn off the Snap To Grid command if it is active and set the viewing magnification to Actual Size.
2. Select the Ellipse tool and, by pressing CTRL, draw a perfect circle.
3. Activate the Shape tool to select the circle automatically.
4. Position the tip of the Shape tool on the node, and then drag the node downward slowly, keeping the pointer just outside the rim of the circle, in a clockwise direction. As shown here, the single node separates into two nodes, with the second node following your pointer as you drag. If the circle seems to be turning into a pie wedge instead of an arc, the tip of your mouse pointer is inside the rim of the circle. Move it outside of the rim and the pie wedge lines will disappear.

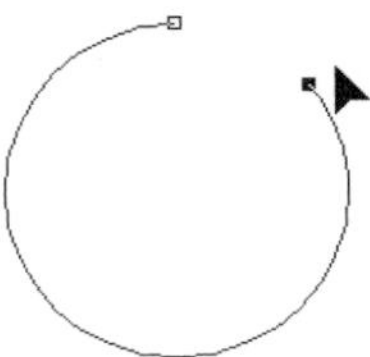

5. Note that the Status bar provides information about the angle position of the first and second nodes and about the total angle of the arc. This information is based on a 360-degree wheel, with 0 degrees at 12 o'clock, 90 degrees at 9 o'clock, 180 degrees at 6 o'clock, and 270 degrees at 3 o'clock.

6. Continue to drag the shaping pointer, but now press and hold the CTRL key as well. The angle of the arc snaps in increments of 15 degrees. Release the mouse button when your arc has the angle you want.
7. Select the Ellipse tool and again draw a perfect circle. Then repeat steps 3, 4, and 5, completing this arc at an approximate 105-degree angle.

NOTE: *If you use an ellipse instead of a circle, the "total angle" information on the Status bar is followed by the message "distorted" in parentheses. This message occurs because Coreldraw bases its calculation of an arc on a perfect circle rather than on an ellipse with different height and width. The angle assignments for arcs created from an ellipse are therefore approximate.*

8. Press the SPACEBAR to activate the Pick tool. The newly created arc is selected. Notice that the selection box, like the one shown below, is much larger than the arc itself; in fact, it seems to surround the now invisible but complete original ellipse. The purpose of this large selection box is to make it easy for you to align an arc or wedge concentrically, using the Align command in the Arrange menu.

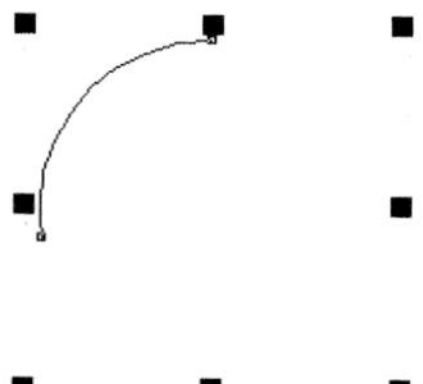

9. Select all the objects and press DEL to clear the screen before going on.

Creating a wedge shape from an ellipse is just as easy as creating an arc, as you will see in the next section.

Creating a Pie Wedge

The only difference between creating an arc and creating a pie wedge is that in the latter case, you position the tip of the shaping pointer *inside* the ellipse or circle as you drag. Perform the following exercise to see the difference for yourself.

1. Set magnification to Actual Size, select the Ellipse tool, and draw a circle. Activate the Shape tool to select it for editing.
2. Position the tip of the shaping pointer on the node and then begin dragging the node downward in a clockwise direction, keeping the pointer inside the circle. The two nodes separate as before, but this time the circle turns into a shape like a pie missing a piece, suitable for pie charts and wedges, as shown here:

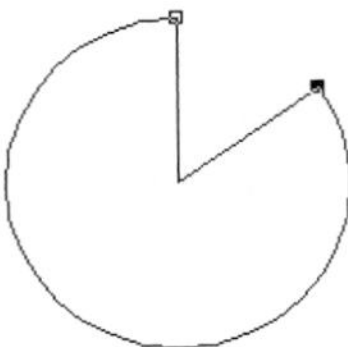

3. Press and hold CTRL and continue dragging the mouse. The angle of the wedge shape now moves in fixed increments of 15 degrees. Release the mouse button when you have obtained the desired angle.
4. Just as you did with the arc, press the SPACEBAR to activate the Pick tool. The wedge is selected. Notice the oversized selection box once more. Make sure to surround this selection box completely with the selection marquee whenever you attempt to select a wedge with a narrow total angle. You can also press the ALT key while dragging the marquee to select the entire object when only a portion of it is surrounded by the marquee.
5. Press DEL to clear the screen.

That's all there is to creating arcs and wedges from ellipses and circles. If these shaping techniques are not flexible enough for you, you can always convert the arc or wedge to a curve object, as you will see in the next section.

Converting Ellipses and Circles to Curve Objects

If the shaping options for ellipses and circles seem limited to you, don't worry. You can convert any ellipse, circle, arc, or wedge into a curve object and, from that point

onward, you can add and delete nodes, drag nodes and control points, or change node types. In the following exercise, you will create a wedge from a circle, convert the wedge to curves, and then reshape the new curve object into the body of a baby carriage.

1. Select the Ellipse tool and draw an ellipse that is wider than it is high, starting from the upper-left area of the rim and moving downward as you drag.
2. Activate the Shape tool and position the pointer on the node of the ellipse. Drag the node downward, keeping the tip of the shaping pointer inside the rim, and create a wedge with a total angle of about 240 degrees, as shown here:

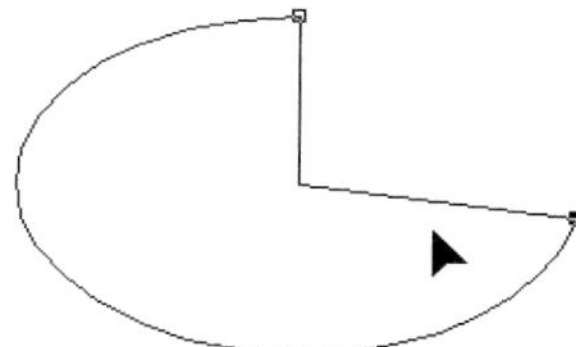

3. Press the SPACEBAR to activate the Pick tool and select the wedge, and then select Convert To Curves from the Arrange menu. Notice that because of the shape of the wedge, the new curve object has five nodes, whereas the ellipse had only one node.
4. Reactivate the Shape tool and drag the node farthest to the right upward and outward, as shown here:

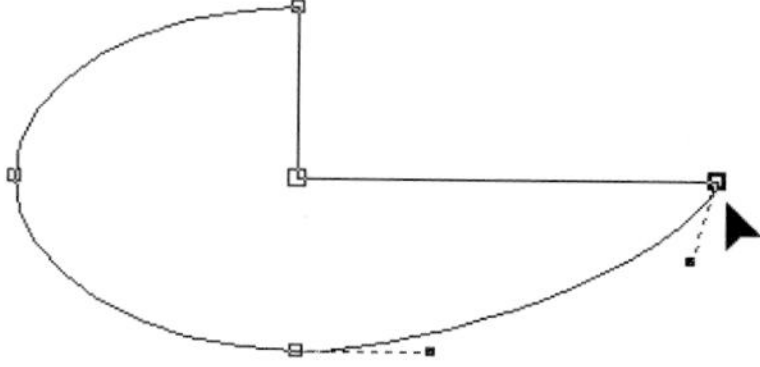

5. Since the segment next to this one is a straight line, the selected node has only one control point. Moving this node upward and outward has the effect of stretching the straight line.

9

6. The curvature of the segment associated with the node you just moved is not adequate to round out the bottom of the "carriage." To remedy this, click on the curve segment (to the left of the selected node) where you want the new node and press + on the numeric keypad. A new node appears between the previously selected node and the one below and to the left of it. It's a smooth node because of the existing curvature, and because the object originated as an ellipse.
7. Select and drag this newly added smooth node downward and to the right, until it forms a nicely rounded bottom to the "carriage" body, as shown here:

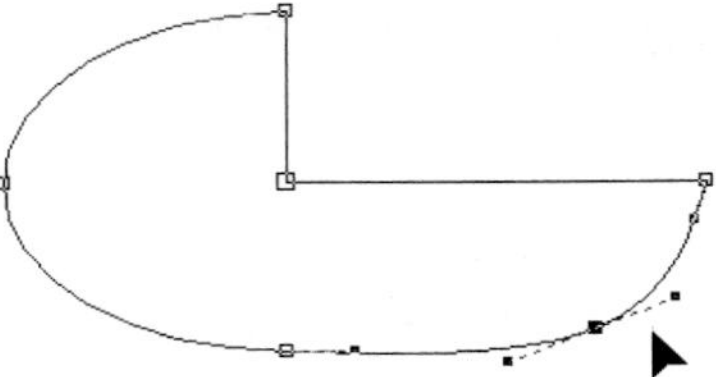

8. Clear the screen; do not save the drawing.

Perhaps the example in the preceding exercise will stimulate your imagination to create any number of complex objects from the basic objects available to you through the drawing tools. The Shape tool makes it all possible!

COREL DRAW!™ 6 in action

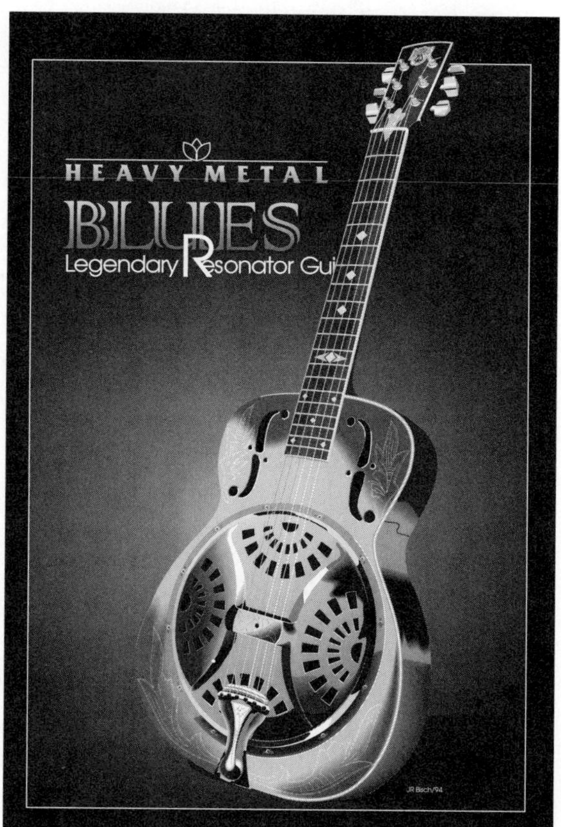

***Dobro*—Jeff Bisch**

Jeff Bisch made extensive use of Coreldraw's ability to shape lines and curves in the drawing of a dobro (a steel body guitar). As you can see, the design has a number of elements that have been repeated and modified. Mr. Bisch's use of fills added the finishing touches to create a dynamic illustration.

Jeff Bisch is located in Santa Barbara, California, and can be reached at (805) 882-1903.

Shaping and Editing Text

10

Text can be an important design element, whether you specialize in original art, graphic or industrial design, or desktop publishing. Every choice you make concerning font, style, spacing, alignment, type size, and placement can affect how your intended audience receives your work. You should have the option of editing text attributes at *any* time, not only when you first enter text on a page.

With Coreldraw, you do have that option. Using the Pick tool and the Shape tool, you can edit existing text in ways that enhance both its typographic and pictorial value. You already edited text as a graphic element in Chapters 5 and 8 by using the Pick tool to rotate, stretch, scale, skew, and reflect text strings. In this chapter, you will concentrate on editing the *typographical* text attributes (such as font and type size) of individual characters, groups of characters, and complete text strings. You will also learn to customize your text even further by converting a text string to a set of curves and then reshaping each curve. The Pick and Shape tools share these editing functions between them.

Editing Attributes for a Text String

Remember the two ways you selected attributes when you first entered a text string—the Character dialog box and the Text toolbar? You can also use each of these methods to change text attributes that already exist. Do this by clicking on the text string with the Pick tool and then selecting Character from the Text menu, or use the Text toolbar to change attributes. The changes you make will apply to every character in the text string. To change attributes for selected characters within a text string, you need to use the Shape tool, as described in the section later in this chapter entitled "Selecting and Editing Text with the Shape Tool."

In the first exercise, you will create a short text string that you can use in many different exercises throughout this chapter. Then, you will select the text string and change some of its attributes.

1. First, set your viewing magnification to actual size (1:1). Turn the Rulers, Wireframe, Show Grid, and Snap To Grid commands off for this portion of the chapter. The figures in this chapter show the status line at the bottom of the window, but you can have it at the top if you wish.

2. Open the Outline Pen tool and select No Outline as the default for Artistic and Paragraph Text. Similarly, open the Fill tool and select Black Fill as the default for Artistic and Paragraph text.
3. Select the Artistic Text tool and then place an insertion point near the upper-left corner of your viewing window. Type the following text string on three separate lines:

   Doing
   what comes
   naturally

4. Select the Pick tool and open the Text toolbar.
5. Change the text attributes to Cooper Black Italic Headline (CooperBlkItHd BT), 66 points, and center alignment.

NOTE: *While you don't have to use the fonts described here, the effects in this chapter are dependent on the particular fonts mentioned, which are available on the first CD-ROM that comes with Coreldraw. To access these fonts, open the Start menu and select Settings, Control Panel. Then select Fonts from the Control Panel; next, open the File menu and select Install New Font. In the Add Fonts dialog box, select your CD-ROM drive, and click on the Fonts directory, the TTF subdirectory, and the letter of the alphabet for the font you want; finally, select the font and click on OK to download the font. Close the Font dialog box and the Control Panel and return to Coreldraw. The fonts you will use in this chapter are: Aachen, Arial, Brush Script, Cooper Black Headline, Cooper Black Italic Headline, Franklin Gothic ITC Heavy Italic, Futura Bold Italic, Garamond ITC Bold, Park Avenue, Revue, Times New Roman, and University Roman.*

6. Because you have changed the alignment, some of the text may not appear within viewing range. If this is the case, select the Pick tool and drag the text until it fits within the viewing window, as shown in Figure 10-1.
7. Save your work in a file named Doinwhat.cdr. Leave the text on the screen for the next exercise.

You can change attributes for a text string as often as desired. However, as long as you use the Pick tool to select text, any attribute changes you make will affect the

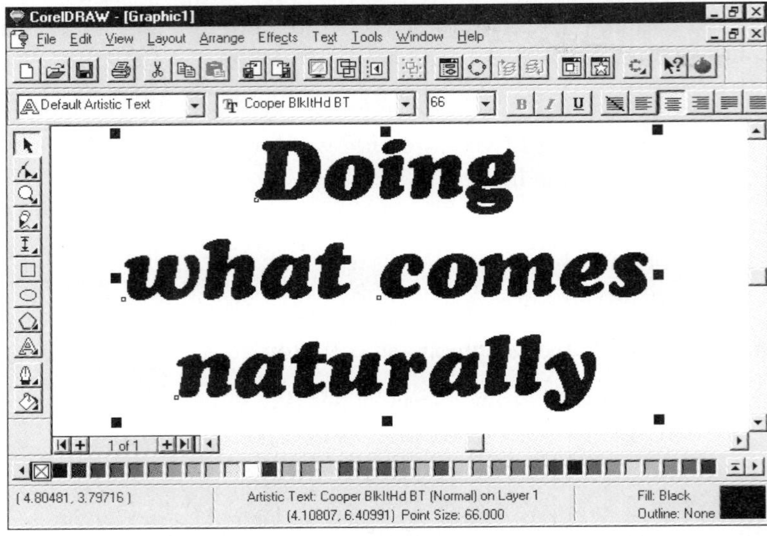

Changing font, style, justification, and type size

FIGURE 10-1

entire text string. If your work requires highly-stylized text designs, where attributes must be decided on a character-by-character basis, you need to use the Shape tool.

OTE: *You can also select and change the font, style, size, and spacing of single characters by selecting the character with the Artistic Text tool. The Artistic Text tool, though, does not allow you to change the shape of a character and is not as handy for character-by-character editing.*

Selecting and Editing Text with the Shape Tool

When the Shape tool is active, you can select any number of characters within a text string and edit their typographical attributes. Depending on how you prefer to work, you can edit attributes either interactively or by means of the Character dialog box or the Text toolbar. Some of these attributes—specifically, font, style, and type size—overlap between the dialog box and the toolbar. Or, you can move letters and adjust spacing and kerning interactively, without using menu commands, toolbars, or dialog boxes. If all these adjustments fail to give your text the desired look, you can gain more editing control by converting text to curves and then manipulating the nodes and control points.

Before you can edit text attributes on a character-by-character basis, you must first use the Shape tool to select the text string in which the characters are located. This is similar to selecting a curve object as a prerequisite to selecting one or more of its nodes. After you select a text string, you can select a specific character, multiple adjacent or nonadjacent characters, or all characters in the text string. Practice selecting different combinations of characters in the following exercise. The text from the previous exercise should still be on your screen.

1. Activate the Shape tool and, if the text is not already selected, click once on the outline of any character in the text string. As shown here, a square node appears at the base of each letter in the text string, and vertical and horizontal arrow symbols appear at the lower-left and lower-right corners of the text string, respectively:

You will become acquainted with the meaning of these symbols in a moment. For now, it is enough to recognize that this change in the text string's appearance indicates that you have selected it for editing with the Shape tool. The status line shows that you have selected all 23 characters.

2. Select a single character in the text string, the letter "n" in "naturally." Do this by clicking *once* on the *node* of this character. The status line now contains the message "1 character(s) selected," and the node at the bottom left of the letter turns black, like this:

3. Deselect the letter "n" by clicking anywhere outside the text string. Notice that the string itself remains selected.
4. Select the initial letter of each word. Click once on the node for the "D" in "Doing." Then press and hold the SHIFT key and click on the node for the initial letter of each of the other words. Check the status line to keep track of the number of characters you select.
5. To deselect these characters, either click on any white space, or press and hold SHIFT and click on each selected character node one by one.
6. Select the entire word "Doing" by lassoing its nodes with a marquee:

Your marquee does not have to surround the characters completely, as long as it surrounds the nodes. All the nodes of this word become highlighted after you release the mouse button.

7. Deselect these characters and then draw a marquee that surrounds all of the text string. All of the characters are now selected for editing.
8. Deselect all of the characters by clicking on any white space. Leave the text on the screen, with the text string selected for editing with the Shape tool, but with no individual characters selected.

You may be wondering, "Why should I bother to select all the characters with the Shape tool, when I could activate the Pick tool and change attributes for the entire text string?" You can control some attributes that way, but the Character Attributes dialog box with the Shape tool offers you three more options for altering the appearance of text. Read on to find out how those additional attributes can enhance the design of text in Coreldraw.

The Character Attributes Dialog Box

When you use the Character Attributes dialog box with the Shape tool, you can control other characteristics of selected characters besides font, style, point size, and spacing. You can tilt characters at any angle and shift them up, down, or sideways. In this section, you will learn how to access this dialog box with the Shape tool and work with each of the controls in it. As you work through the exercises, you will learn about useful applications for each type of attribute. By the end of the section, you will alter the design of the Doinwhat.cdr text string substantially.

You can access the Character Attributes dialog box either by double-clicking on a selected character node, by pressing CTRL-T, or by opening the Text menu and selecting Character. Any attributes that you alter in this dialog box apply only to the characters you have selected. Make sure, then, that you have selected all of the characters you want to edit before accessing the Character Attributes dialog box.

1. With the Shape tool active, select the node in front of the letter "n" in "naturally."
2. Access the Character Attributes dialog box in the way that is most convenient for your working habits. If you prefer to use menu commands, select Character from the Text menu. If you like using the mouse best, double-click on the selected node. When the Character Attributes dialog box is displayed, select the Alignment tab, as shown in Figure 10-2.

Take a moment to become familiar with the options available to you in this dialog box when the Shape tool is active, and with the significance of each attribute.

Reviewing the Dialog Box

The options in the Character Attributes dialog box Alignment tab, shown in Figure 10-2, allow you to control horizontal shift, vertical shift, and character angle, in addition to spacing and alignment. You are familiar with the last two attributes, but the concepts behind horizontal and vertical shifts and character angle may be new

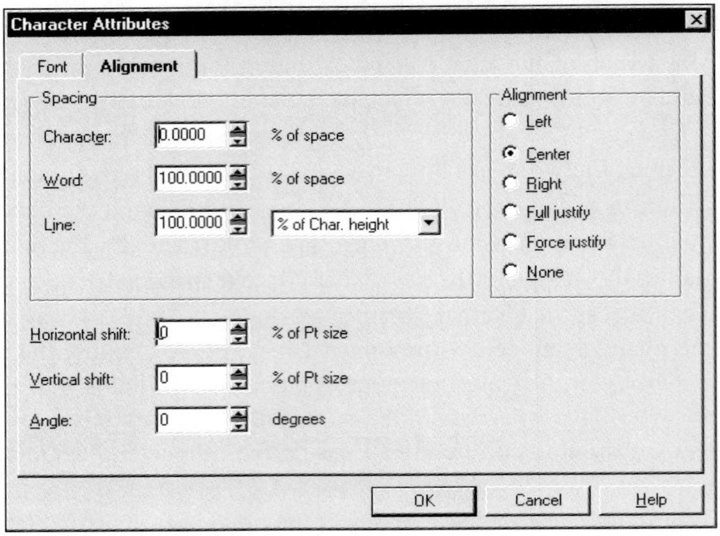

Character Attributes dialog box

FIGURE 10-2

to you. Two other effects, Superscript and Subscript, are available in the Placement drop-down list box on the Font tab of the Character Attributes dialog box. This section will explain more about these attributes.

HORIZONTAL SHIFT The Horizontal shift option controls the distance, in percentage of point size, by which selected characters shift to the right or left of their original location. This distance varies, depending on the font of the selected characters.

VERTICAL SHIFT The Vertical shift option controls the distance by which selected characters shift above or below their starting location (baseline). Coreldraw expresses this distance as a percentage of the point size of the selected characters. This distance is therefore variable, too.

CHARACTER ANGLE The Angle option allows you to tilt the selected characters in any direction and at any angle. You can turn characters upside down, sideways, or anywhere in between.

SUPERSCRIPT AND SUBSCRIPT The Superscript and Subscript options, available from the Placement drop-down list box on the Font tab, let you place selected characters above or below the rest of the text, respectively. Superscript text aligns with the imaginary line at the top of surrounding text (for example, the"2" in $E=mc^2$). Subscript text aligns with the baseline of surrounding text (for example, the "2" in H_2O).

TIP: *The values that display in the Character Attributes dialog box depend on how you open the dialog box. If you open it by double-clicking on a character, you will see the settings assigned to that character. If you open the dialog box by selecting the Character option in the Text menu (or by pressing CTRL-T), the values displayed correspond to the first character in the selected group.*

In the next five sections, you will have the opportunity to redesign text imaginatively, using many of the options in the Character Attributes dialog box.

Editing Font and Style

In the following exercise, you will assign a different font and/or style to each letter in the word "naturally." You selected the first letter of the word before entering the dialog box, so you will alter the letter "n" first of all.

1. On the Font tab, select the Aachen font in the Font list box and then select OK. Your text string redisplays on the screen, but now the letter "n" looks quite different from the surrounding letters.
2. Double-click on the character node of the "n" once more. When the dialog box appears this time, it shows the current font of the *selected* character or characters. (See the Tip in the previous section.) Press ESC or select Cancel to exit the dialog box without making a change.
3. Select each of the other letters in the word "naturally" in turn. Assign fonts and styles to them in the following order: Park Avenue normal, Franklin Gothic Heavy italic, Cooper Black Headlines normal, Revue normal, Times New Roman normal, University normal, Futura bold italic,

and Brush Script normal. When you are finished, the word "naturally" displays an interesting patchwork of fonts:

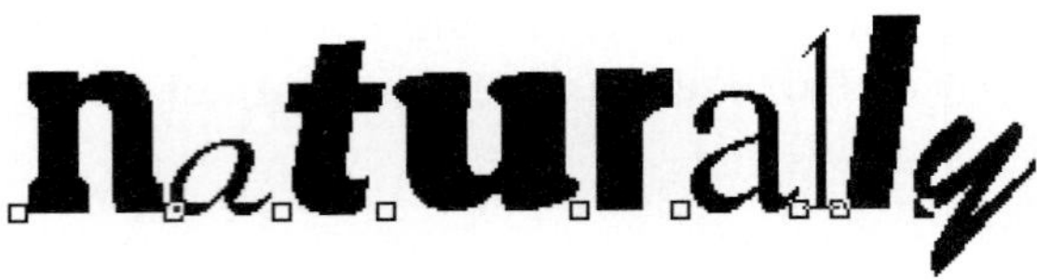

4. Save the changes you have made by pressing CTRL-S, and leave your work on the screen for the next exercise.

Go on to the next section and apply different point sizes to the letters whose fonts and styles you have already altered.

Editing Type Size

When you changed fonts for each letter in the word "naturally," you left the type sizes unaltered, yet the letters do not appear to be the same size. You have probably guessed by now that different fonts have different heights and widths for the same point size. The point size is a consistent way to measure the size of characters only *within* a given font.

In the following exercise, you will make the letters in "naturally" closer to one another in actual or physical size.

1. Using the Shape tool again, double-click on the character node of the first letter "a" in "naturally." When the Character Attributes dialog box appears, change the point size for this letter to 108 and then select OK. Even though you have substantially increased its point size, this letter only now approximates the height of its neighbors. Point size is measured from the baseline of one line to the baseline above it and is not necessarily a measure of the actual type. You may need to scroll your screen downward to see the word "naturally," since the baseline-to-baseline distance (leading) has increased.
2. In the same way, select the first letter "l" and change its type size to 72 points. (You can use the Text toolbar if you wish.)

3. Finally, select the letter "y" and change its point size to 90. Now, all of the letters seem more uniform in height and size:

4. Save your work by pressing CTRL-S, leaving the text string on screen.

To edit the word "naturally" so that it conveys a sense of a more natural state, you can shift some of the characters up or down relative to the baseline and move others sideways. In the next exercise, you will practice moving individual characters.

Horizontal and Vertical Shift

When you shift selected characters horizontally, you move them to the right or left of their starting positions, causing them to overlap with other characters on the same line. You can use this technique to convey a sense of being rushed or crowded, or simply to adjust spacing between letters precisely. When you shift characters vertically, they fall above or below the baseline, which can create a feeling of spontaneity or excitement.

In the next exercise, you will shift some of the characters in the word "naturally" to enhance the sense of spontaneity and naturalness in the text.

1. Activate the Shape tool, if it isn't already, and then double-click on the character node for the letter "n" in the word "naturally" to open the Character Attributes dialog box. In the Alignment tab, set Horizontal shift to -25 percent of the point size and then select OK. Because you set the value to a negative number, the letter shifts to the left of its original position.

2. Select the character node for the next letter "a" and set Vertical shift to 20 percent of point size. When you select OK, the position of the letter shifts above the baseline.

3. Select the following letters in turn, changing the shift settings for each. Change the Vertical shift of the "r" to -25 percent, the Vertical shift of the second "l" to 10 percent, and both the Horizontal shift and Vertical shift of the "y" to 25 percent. Notice that a negative value for Vertical shift causes the selected character, "r," to reposition itself below the baseline. The resulting text should now look like this:

4. Save your changes and leave this text on the screen.

So far, you have edited attributes for one letter at a time. In the next section, you will select a group of characters and practice positioning them as superscripts and subscripts.

Creating Superscripts and Subscripts

Perform the following exercise to create superscripts and subscripts.

1. With the Shape tool select the character nodes of all of the letters in the word "comes" except the letter "c." Double-click on the node in front of "o" to access the Character Attributes dialog box.
2. On the Font tab, click on the Placement down arrow, select Superscript, and then click on OK. The selected letters have become smaller and appear as a superscript to the letter "c," like this:

3. Select the Undo Edit Text command in the Edit menu to return the selected characters to their original position.

4. Select the same characters again and return to the Character Attributes dialog box by double-clicking on the "o" node. This time, choose Subscript in the Placement drop-down list box. When you select OK, the letters display as a subscript to the letter "c."

5. Press ALT-BACKSPACE or CTRL-Z to return the selected characters to their original position.

In the next section, you will practice tilting the characters in the word "naturally" to different angles.

Editing Character Angle

You can tilt selected characters at any angle using the Angle setting in the Alignment tab of the Character Attributes dialog box. Values between 0 and 180 degrees indicate that you are tilting the characters *above* an imaginary horizon, in a counterclockwise direction. Values between 0 and -180 degrees indicate that you are tilting the characters below an imaginary horizon, in a clockwise direction. At a 180-degree angle, the characters are upside down. Practice adjusting character angle in the following exercise.

1. Deselect any selected characters, then, with the Shape tool active, press and hold SHIFT while selecting the character nodes of the letter "n," the letter "u," and the letter "y" in the word "naturally." Double-click on one of these nodes to open the Character Attributes dialog box. Click on the Alignment tab, then set Character Angle to -15 degrees and select OK. The selected characters now appear tilted toward the right.

2. Deselect these three letters and select the letter "t," the second letter "a," and the second letter "l." Double-click on one of these nodes to access the Character Attributes dialog box. On the Alignment tab, set Character Angle

to 15 degrees and then select OK. These characters appear tilted toward the left. The word "naturally" now seems to fly off in all directions:

3. Save your changes and then select Close from the File menu to clear the screen. Open a new document by selecting New Document from the File menu.

Now that you've become familiar with the settings in the Character Attributes dialog box, no doubt you have come up with a few creative ideas of your own. When you are ready to proceed, continue through the next portion of this chapter, where you will learn some convenient ways to kern text and adjust spacing interactively.

Kerning Text Interactively

Kerning, simply defined, is the art of adjusting the space between individual pairs of letters for greater readability. There are many possible letter-pair combinations in the 26 letters of the English alphabet, but most font manufacturers provide automatic kerning for only a few hundred commonly used pairs. Occasionally you will see too much or too little space between adjacent letters. You can kern these letter pairs manually by moving one of the letters subtly to the right or left.

Using kerning as a design element can enhance the power of your message. For instance, you will draw more attention to your text when you kern letters to create special effects, such as expanded letter spacing in selected words of a magazine or newspaper headline.

The exercises in this section offer more extreme examples of kerning than you are likely to find in most text, but they will help you become familiar with the concept of kerning. Follow the steps in each exercise to learn how to kern single or multiple characters. Within the exercises is information on using constraint and alignment techniques to kern more easily and precisely.

Kerning Single Characters

The following exercise lets you practice adjusting spacing between any two text characters. As you work through the steps, you will learn how to ensure that characters align properly with the surrounding text after you move them. Before starting the exercise, adjust viewing magnification to actual size and turn on Rulers. In the Grid & Ruler Setup, turn on Show Grid, set both the Horizontal and Vertical Grid Frequency to 8 per inch, set the Horizontal grid origin to 0 inches, and set the Vertical grid origin to 11 inches. Click on OK. Retain these settings for both exercises on kerning. Select 1:1 magnification.

1. Select the Artistic Text tool and then select a text insertion point at the 1 1/2-inch mark on the horizontal ruler and the -4 1/2-inch mark on the vertical ruler.
2. Type the word **K e rning** in upper- and lowercase letters. Leave a space after the "K" and another after the "e." Press ENTER to begin a new line and type the word **T e x t** on the second line. Leave one space after the first "T," one space after the "e," and two spaces after the letter "x."
3. Select the Pick tool and set the font to Garamond bold, the type size to 72 points, and the justification to None.
4. After the text string appears, as in Figure 10-3, select the Shape tool. Since the text string was the last object you created, the Shape tool selects it automatically. A node appears next to each character in the text string; vertical and horizontal spacing control handles appear at each end of the last line of the text string.

You need to bring the letter "e" in "Kerning" much closer to the "K" and the letters "rning" closer to the "e." You do this by dragging the "e" and the "rning" with the Shape tool. Since you don't want to change the vertical positioning, you can prevent this by pressing CTRL while you drag. Make sure Snap To Grid is turned off or you will not be able to get the exact positioning described in the following steps.

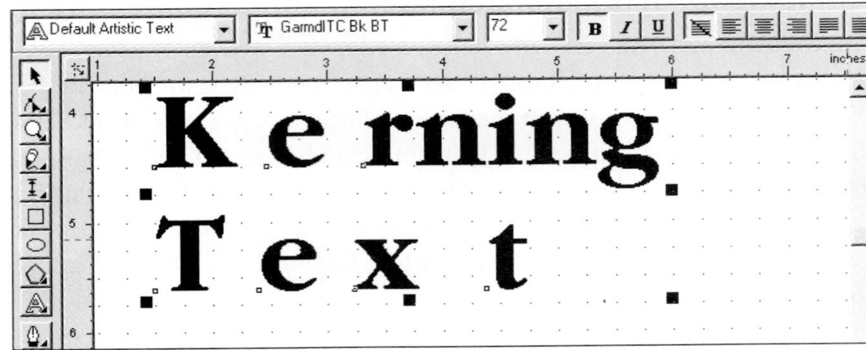

Text in need of kerning

FIGURE 10-3

IP: *You can press and hold CTRL while moving the characters, thereby constraining the text to the nearest baseline. Be sure to release the mouse button before you release CTRL to maintain proper alignment.*

1. Press and hold CTRL and then press and hold the left mouse button on the node in front of the letter "e." When you begin to move the mouse, the pointer turns into a four-headed arrow. Drag the letter to the left until its node is on the tip of the foot of the "K," as shown in the following illustration. A dashed outline of the letter follows the pointer as you drag. When you release the mouse button, the letter itself appears in this location.

2. If the "e" is not aligned as you want it, snap this letter back to its original position by selecting the Straighten Text command in the Text menu, and then repeat step 1. The Straighten Text command erases any previous kerning information, so use it only when you want to return text to its original location. If you forgot to press CTRL while dragging the "e," you

can select the Align To Baseline command, also in the Text menu. When you accidentally position a character above or below the baseline, this command forces the character to align with the baseline again. Unlike the Straighten Text command, the Align To Baseline command does not erase any previous kerning information.

3. Save your kerned text as KERN1.CDR and leave it on the screen for the next exercise.

IP: *If you require a high degree of precision in the placement of kerned text, zoom in on the character(s) you want to move.*

Kerning Multiple Characters

In practice, your most common use for moving and kerning multiple characters within a text string will be to move the remaining characters of a word closer to another letter that you have already kerned. However, you can select and reposition any group of characters, including nonadjacent characters, to another location in the same way.

1. With the KERN1.CDR file displayed in an actual-size viewing magnification and the Shape tool active, draw a marquee around the nodes of the letters "rning."
2. Press and hold CTRL, and then point on the node for the letter "r" and drag the mouse to the left until the pointer is beginning to touch the "e." All the letters in the selected group follow, as shown in the following illustration. If the selected characters do not line up with the adjoining text when you release the mouse button, review step 2 in the previous exercise. You may want to use both the Align To Baseline and Straighten Text commands. Deselect the letters "rning" when you have them in the desired location.

3. Use SHIFT to select the "e" and the second "t" in "Text." Click on the node in front of the letter "e" and drag it to the left until the pointer is on the tip of the foot (or serif) of the "T," as shown here:

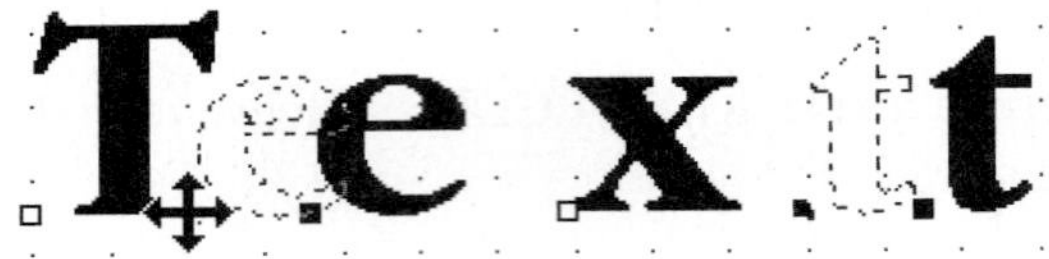

4. Both selected letters should move together across the screen without disturbing the "x." After you release the mouse button, the letters "e" and "t" will appear as shown here:

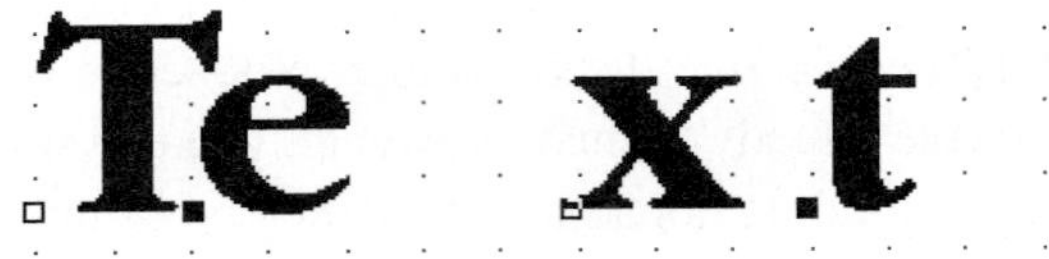

5. As you can see, the letters "x" and "t" still are not close enough to the "e." Experiment by moving these two letters on your screen until the text string appears normal.

6. Save your changes to the file by pressing CTRL-S. Close your current document and open another using the Close and New Document commands in the File menu.

Kerning is not the only text attribute that you can adjust interactively with the Shape tool. In the next section, you will learn how to adjust spacing between characters, words, and lines for an entire selected text string.

Adjusting Spacing Interactively

There are two ways to edit inter-character, inter-word, and inter-line spacing of existing text in Coreldraw. The first way, as you will recall, is to select the text string with the Pick tool and then open the Character Attributes dialog box using any of the methods discussed previously. Using the dialog box, you can numerically set the spacing you need. You enjoy the advantage of precision but experience the disadvantage of not seeing what you are doing until you are done doing it.

If you prefer to work more spontaneously, Coreldraw offers you an interactive method of spacing as well. This method involves selecting the text string with the Shape tool and then dragging one of the two stylized arrows that appear on the text string's lower boundary. Keep in mind, however, that you adjust spacing for *all* of the characters in the text string when you use this technique. To adjust spacing between two individual characters, see the previous "Kerning Single Characters" section of this chapter.

To alter inter-character spacing interactively, drag the horizontal arrow at the lower-right boundary of the text string. To alter inter-word spacing, drag the same arrow while holding down CTRL. And to alter inter-line spacing, drag the vertical arrow at the lower-left boundary of the text string.

Adjusting Inter-Character Spacing

In the following exercise, you will create a text string and adjust the inter-character spacing, observing the changes in the Coreldraw window as you work.

1. Set viewing magnification to actual size, then activate the Artistic Text tool and select an insertion point near the upper-left corner of your viewing window.
2. Type **Running out of** on the first line and **space** on the second. Click on the Pick tool and set text attributes to Arial normal, 60 points, and left aligned, using the Text toolbar. The text displays in your viewing window. If the text string is not centered in the window, select the text string and center it.
3. Select the Shape tool. Each character node appears, and stylized vertical and horizontal arrows appear at the lower-left and lower-right boundaries of the text object, as shown in Figure 10-4.
4. Position the Shape tool directly over the horizontal arrow at the lower-right boundary of the text object, until the pointer turns into a crosshair. Then, drag this arrow to the right. Notice that, as in the example in Figure 10-5, the characters do not seem to move immediately; instead, you see a dotted outline following the two-way arrow pointer. As you drag, the status line displays the information about the horizontal distance by which you are increasing the size of the text boundary.

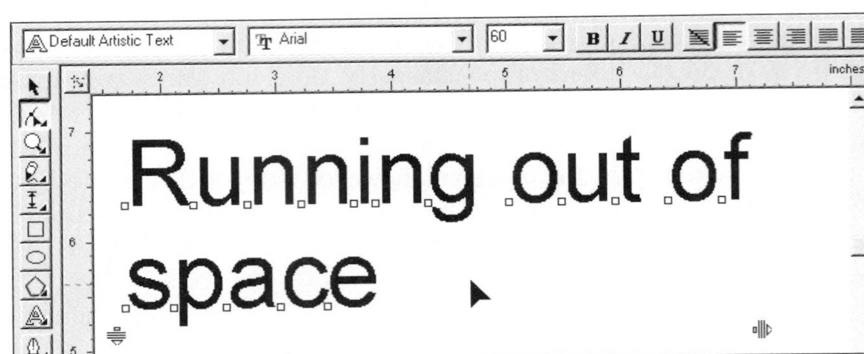

Displaying the spacing adjustment arrows

FIGURE 10-4

5. When the right boundary of the text string (represented by the dotted outline) reaches the desired point, release the mouse button. The text repositions itself to align with that boundary, and the space between each character increases proportionately, as shown here:

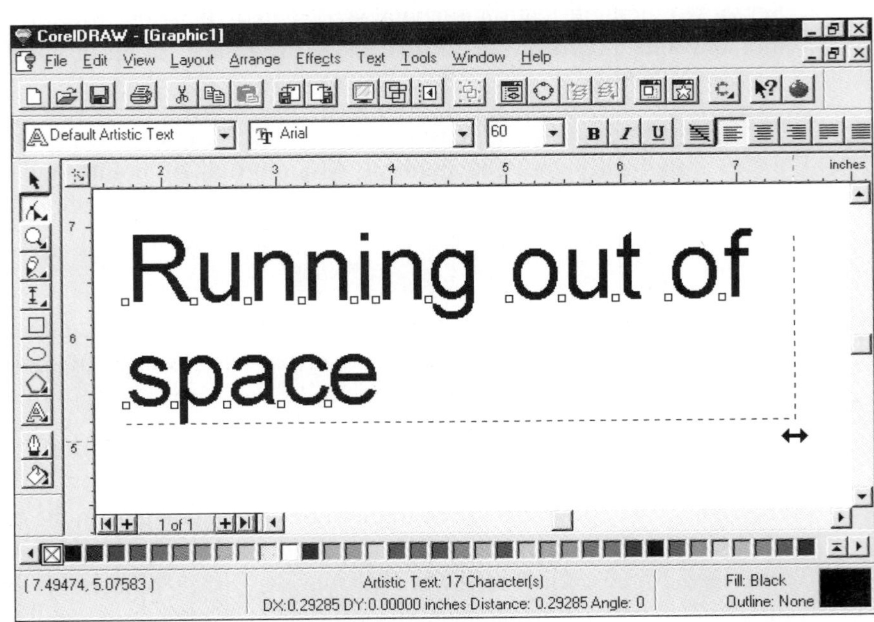

Adjusting inter-character spacing

FIGURE 10-5

Running out of

6. If you would like to know the exact inter-character spacing measurement you have obtained, select the text string with the Pick tool and access the Character Attributes dialog box. Look at the Kerning text box on the Font tab. This is a good way to check for precision.
7. Select the Undo Edit Text command from the Edit menu to return the text to its former position. Then reselect the Shape tool and *decrease* the space between characters by dragging the horizontal arrow to the left instead of the right. If you decrease the space drastically, letters may even overlap, like this:

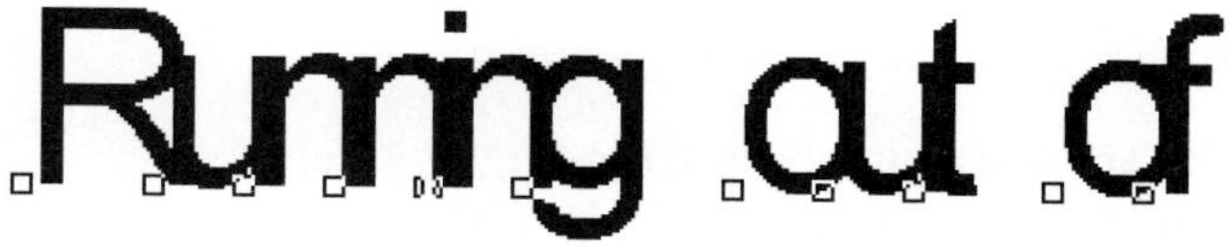

Running out of

8. Select Undo Edit Text once more to return the characters to their original positions. Leave this text on the screen for now.

Adjusting inter-character spacing is useful when you want to fit text into a defined space in a drawing, without changing the point size or other attributes. Go on to the next section to practice changing inter-word spacing independently of the spacing between characters.

Adjusting Inter-Word Spacing

Suppose that you don't need to change the spacing between letters, but your design calls for increased or decreased spacing between words. To adjust inter-word spacing interactively, you drag the same horizontal arrow that you used for inter-character spacing. The difference is that you also hold down CTRL *while* you drag. Try the following exercise, using the text string you created in the previous section.

1. With the Shape tool active and the text string selected, position the pointer over the horizontal arrow until the pointer turns into a crosshair. Then press and hold CTRL and drag the two-way arrow pointer to the right. The status line displays the horizontal distance by which you are stretching the text boundary.
2. When the outline that you are dragging has the desired width, release the mouse button first and then CTRL. (If you release CTRL first, you will adjust the inter-character rather than the inter-word spacing.) The text redisplays with increased space between each word, as shown here:

Running

3. Press CTRL-Z or select the Undo Edit Text command in the Edit menu to return the text to its original inter-word spacing.
4. Try decreasing the amount of inter-word spacing by dragging the horizontal arrow to the left instead of the right. When you are finished experimenting, select the Undo Edit Text command once more. Leave this text on the screen for the next exercise.

You can change the spacing between lines of a text string, as well as between words or characters. The next section gives you hands-on practice in editing inter-line spacing.

Adjusting Inter-Line Spacing

To edit inter-line spacing with the Shape tool, you drag the vertical arrow located at the lower left of the text boundary. Try increasing and decreasing the space between lines now, using the same text string you have been working with for the past two sections. Note that if your text string contains only one line, dragging the vertical arrow has no effect.

1. With the Shape tool active and the text string selected, position the mouse pointer directly over the vertical arrow that appears at the lower-left text boundary and drag this arrow downward. The mouse pointer turns into a two-way vertical arrow. Simultaneously, the status line displays the message "Inter-Line," followed by the vertical distance measurement, which tells you how much you have increased the size of the text boundary.
2. When you have increased the boundary by the desired size, release the mouse button. The text repositions itself to fit the new boundary. As shown next, only the spacing between lines changes, not the length or size of the text itself:

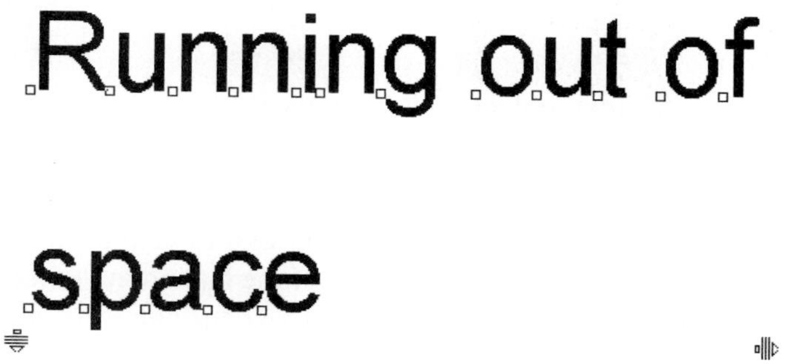

Running out of

space

3. To see the precise amount of inter-line spacing that you have added, select the Pick tool and then open the Character Attributes dialog box. Observe the Spacing amounts in the Alignment tab. When you are finished, select Undo Edit Text from the Edit menu to return the text string to its former inter-line spacing.
4. Reduce the inter-line spacing of the text string by dragging the vertical arrow upward instead of downward. When you are finished, select Undo Edit Text to return the text to its former spacing.
5. Delete all the text to clear the screen before beginning the next section.

By now, you have explored all of the possible text attributes that you can change using the Pick and Shape tools. If, however, you need to give your text an even more customized look, you have the option of converting text to a curved object and then editing its nodes.

Reshaping Characters

To give messages extra flair, you might need stylized text characters that just don't exist in standard fonts. Coreldraw can help you create such "text pictures" easily. All you have to do is select text attributes that approximate the effect you want to achieve and then convert the text string to curves. You can then reshape the text using the Pick and Shape tools.

The following exercise contains a simple step-by-step example of how to create stylized text pictures. Carry out the steps and give your own imagination a boost!

1. To prepare for this exercise, turn off Rulers, Snap To Grid, and Show Grid, and set the viewing magnification to actual size. Open the Text toolbar.
2. Select the Artistic Text tool and select an insertion point in the upper left of your working area.
3. Type **Snake** in upper- and lowercase letters and select the Pick tool. Test each of the fonts in the Fonts list box on the Text toolbar against the sample display character. The capital "S" of the Garamond font bears a fairly strong resemblance to a snake, so set text attributes to Garamond bold italic, 120 points, and left alignment, as shown in Figure 10-6.
4. Activate the Shape tool and double-click on the node for the letter "S" to open the Character Attributes dialog box.

"Snake" text: Garamond bold italic, 120 points

FIGURE 10-6

5. Your aim is to increase the size of the letter "S" and make it a *drop cap*. To achieve this, set the type size for the letter "S" to 204 points and set Vertical Shift to -20 percent of Point size. Select OK to make these changes take effect. Your text should now look like this:

Snake

6. Activate the Pick tool (or press the SPACEBAR) to select the entire text string, and then click on Convert To Curves in the Arrange menu. The text redisplays with many little nodes, indicating that it has become a curve object. If you activate the Shape tool again, the status line displays the message, "Curve: 238 nodes on 8 subpaths." This message indicates that Coreldraw now considers this text string to be one object with eight combined segments.

7. Activate the Pick tool again and select the Break Apart command in the Arrange menu. Each letter is now a separate object.

NOTE: *The spaces inside the "a," "k," and "e" fill in because the letters are formed by two objects that you just broke apart. When the two objects are combined, their common area becomes transparent, causing the space. Remember the teacup handle example in Chapter 5. If you want the spaces to reappear, select all 6 objects (3 letters and 3 holes) with the Pick tool and choose Combine from the Arrange menu.*

8. Deselect all of the letters and then click on the letter "S" with the Pick tool. Stretch the letter vertically by dragging the middle boundary markers on the upper and lower sides of the selection box. Your goal is to elongate the letter, thereby enhancing the "snake-like" appearance. You may need to scroll your screen to see all of the "S."

9. Now, select the Shape tool and manipulate the nodes of the "S" so that you achieve the general look of the following illustration. Make some areas of the "snake" narrower and others broader. You will want to

reshape and move the snake's "head," too. Make the "tail" of the snake narrower, as well.

10. You can try to match the results here exactly or develop your own creative enhancements utilizing all of the skills you have learned up to this point in the book. When you are satisfied with the appearance of the snake, save the image under the filename SNAKE.CDR.

As you can see, the possibilities for creating custom characters for text are virtually endless. If you find yourself fired up with new ideas for your own projects, experiment until you design a word picture that best enhances your message.

COREL DRAW!™ 6 in action

***Trout on the Fly*—Chris Purcell**

Chris Purcell has effectively used text as an integral design element in this illustration. Starting with a simple text string, Mr. Purcell edited the "R" in trout to create fishing line and a fly that links the graphic and text elements into a very effective design.

Chris Purcell of Houston, Texas, has won several awards in Corel's World Design Contest. He can be reached at (713) 374-4679.

Cutting, Copying, Pasting, and Object Linking and Embedding (OLE)

11

So far you have learned how to select, move, rearrange, transform, and reshape objects within a graphic. An equally important part of the editing process involves the *transfer of image information* within a graphic, between pictures, or between Coreldraw 6 and other Windows 95 applications. The editing functions that allow you to transfer image data include copying, cutting, and pasting objects and pictures; deleting or duplicating objects; and copying object properties. You access these operations using the Cut, Copy, Paste, Paste Special Delete, Duplicate, Clone, Copy Properties From, and Insert New Object options in the Edit menu.

These editing functions have many uses that will save you time and design effort. You don't have to start from scratch each time you need to duplicate an object or its properties. You can simply transfer image information, using the editing commands. You perform some of the transfer operations within a single picture; others allow you to transfer information between Coreldraw files and even between Coreldraw 6 and other Windows 95 applications.

Coreldraw allows you to transfer objects to and from the Windows Clipboard. This means that you can copy or cut and paste objects between different image files in Coreldraw, or from Coreldraw to a file in another Windows 95 application. Conversely, you can copy or cut and paste objects from files in other Windows 95 applications and paste them to the page of your choice in Coreldraw.

This chapter covers the use of the Windows Clipboard, both within Coreldraw and between Coreldraw 6 and other Windows 95 applications. It also introduces you to some additional object and style copying functions in Coreldraw that complement the use of the Windows Clipboard. You'll find out how to duplicate objects within a drawing and how to copy properties from one object to another. You'll review the difference between cutting objects from a file and deleting them permanently. Finally, you will work with object linking and embedding, usually referred to by the acronym OLE (pronounced *O'lay*). OLE provides new ways to utilize objects from different applications.

About the Windows Clipboard

If you haven't used Windows 95 applications before, you may be wondering how the Clipboard works. Think of the Windows Clipboard as a temporary storage place that can contain only one item at a time. When you select an object and then select the Copy or Cut command in the Edit menu, you send a copy of the object to the Clipboard from its original place in your drawing. You can then choose Paste from the Edit menu to send a copy of the object from the Clipboard to the desired location. The copy you sent to the Clipboard remains there until you overwrite it by copying or cutting another object, or until you exit Windows and end a session.

Windows 95 creates its own file format, called a *metafile*, out of the information that you send to the Clipboard. This standard metafile format allows you to share information between different applications that run under Windows 95. A metafile can be larger or smaller than the object you send to the Clipboard, depending on the complexity of the information you are trying to transfer. As a rule of thumb, the more complex an object is in terms of its attributes, the more memory it requires when you send it to the Clipboard.

Theoretically, all Windows applications should be able to trade information through the Clipboard. In practice, however, some types of information in objects or files transfer better than others. When you have completed the basic exercises on copying, cutting, and pasting objects within Coreldraw, turn to the section entitled "Working with Different Applications." There, you will find tips for trouble-free transfer operations through the Clipboard.

Selecting to Copy, Cut, Duplicate, Clone, or Delete

In order to duplicate, clone, or delete one or more objects, or copy or cut them to the Clipboard, you must first select the objects with the Pick tool. The Edit menu commands and their keyboard shortcuts are unavailable to you unless one or more objects are already selected.

You can select a single object, multiple objects, or all objects in a graphic for any of the Edit menu operations discussed in this chapter. To select a single object for one of the transfer operations, just click on its outline once. To select multiple objects for a transfer operation, use SHIFT or the marquee method you learned in Chapter 5. (You might also want to group the objects after you select them in order to avoid separating them from each other accidentally.) To select all of the objects in a graphic, click on the Select All command in the Edit menu.

Copying and Pasting Objects

The Copy and Paste commands in the Edit menu enable you to copy Coreldraw objects and paste them to the same file, to another file in Coreldraw, or to another Windows 95 application. When you copy an object to the Clipboard, the original object remains in position on the page. When you *paste* the object, Windows makes another copy from the copy on the Clipboard. The copy on the Clipboard remains there until you overwrite it by copying or cutting another object or group of objects, or until you exit Windows.

To practice copying objects to the Clipboard and pasting them to the same or different pictures, you will use the Arrow1.cdr file that you created in Chapter 5.

IP: *Cut, Copy, and Paste icons are available on the toolbar. For a shortcut technique, just click on them instead of using the Edit menu commands.*

Copying and Pasting Objects Within a Picture

When you copy an object to the Clipboard and then paste it to the same picture, the copy overlays the original object exactly. The copy is selected as soon as it appears on the page, however, so you can move it safely without displacing the original object.

A more convenient way to copy an object within the same picture is to use the Duplicate command. When you invoke this command, Coreldraw automatically offsets the copy of the object from the original. See the "Duplicating and Cloning Objects" section of this chapter for more details.

For the exercises in this chapter, make sure that Rulers and Status bar in the View menu are selected. Practice copying a group of objects with these instructions:

1. Open the Arrow1.cdr file and group all of the text strings in the drawing, using the Select All command in the Edit menu and then the Group command in the Arrange menu.
2. To copy the grouped objects to the Clipboard, either select the Copy command from the Edit menu, as shown in Figure 11-1, press CTRL-C, or click on the Copy icon. The pointer turns into an hourglass and a time display is shown until Coreldraw finishes copying the selected object(s) to the Clipboard.
3. Select Paste from the Edit menu, press CTRL-V, or click on the Paste icon. The screen redraws, with the pasted object selected. You will not notice anything different because the pasted object appears exactly on top of the original. (If you move the original object before pasting the copy, it will appear on the original location—not on top of the moved object.)
4. To move the pasted object away from the original, point on any outline of the selected object and drag it as desired. You can now scale, rotate, stretch, skew, or otherwise edit the pasted object.

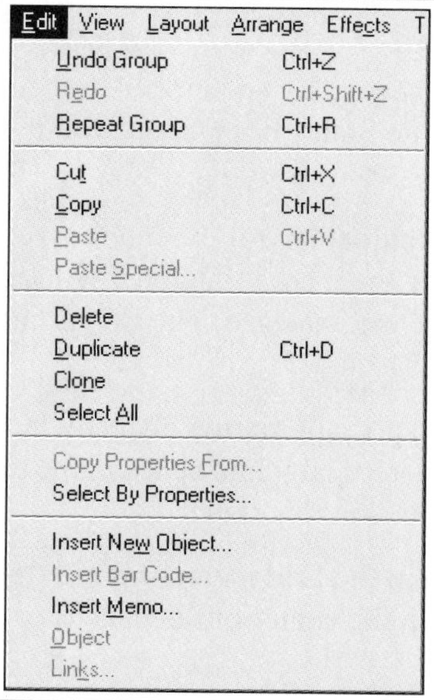

Copying an object using the Edit menu

FIGURE 11-1

5. Select Close from the File menu to clear the screen before continuing. Do not save any changes to the Arrow1.cdr document. Coreldraw will display a dialog box asking: "Leave data on clipboard for other applications?" Click on No.

Next, try copying an object to a different picture, and use it as a design enhancement there.

Copying and Pasting Between Pictures

In this exercise, you will copy the text string from the Doinwhat.cdr file created in Chapter 10 and paste it to the Kite.cdr file from Chapter 2.

1. Open the Doinwhat.cdr file and select the text string.
2. Select Copy from the Edit menu or press CTRL-C to copy the text to the Clipboard. Depending on the amount of information being copied, the pointer may temporarily turn into an hourglass, and you may get a message box telling you the status, until Coreldraw finishes copying the text string. This lets you know it's busy.
3. Close the Doinwhat.cdr file, then open the Kite.cdr file and drag all of the guidelines off the screen. Make sure Wireframe is checked (turned on) in the View menu.
4. From the Edit menu, choose Select All; then from the Arrange menu, select Group. The Status bar will tell you that there is now a group of objects.
5. Position the pointer at any of the four corner boundary markers of the group, then drag the marker diagonally inward to scale down the kite to 50 percent of its original size. The Status bar will display the change in Scale %.
6. Drag the kite so it is approximately centered horizontally and leaves about one-third of the vertical white space at the top. See Figure 11-2 to see how it's positioned at this stage.
7. Select Paste from the Edit menu or press CTRL-V. A copy of the text string will be placed in the center of the page.

Kite positioned to place copied text

FIGURE 11-2

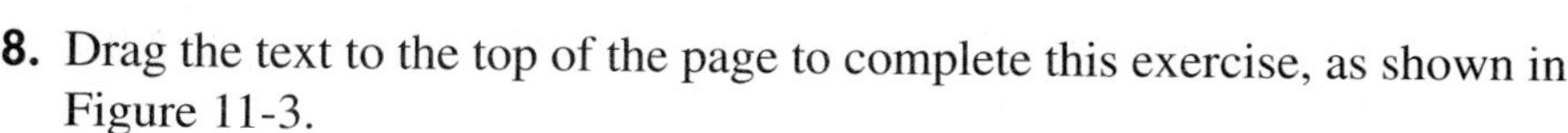

8. Drag the text to the top of the page to complete this exercise, as shown in Figure 11-3.
9. Select Save As from the File menu, type **kite2**, and select OK.

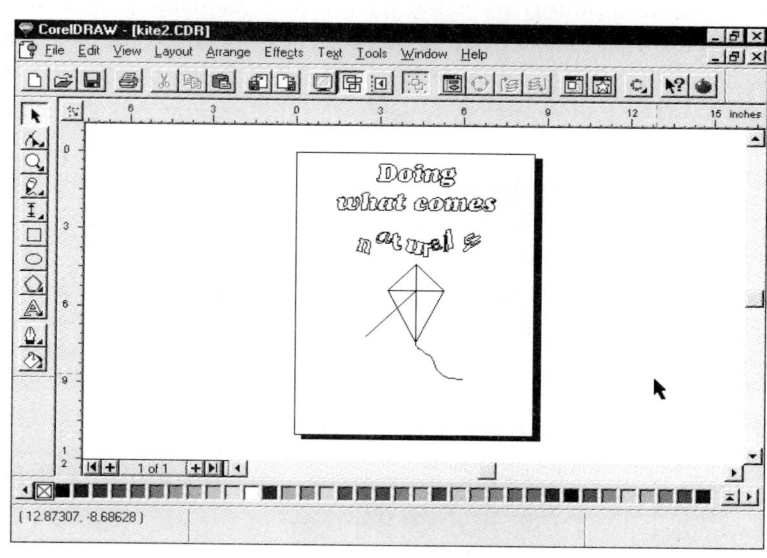

Text string copied and pasted into an existing drawing

FIGURE 11-3

As you can see from the preceding exercise, you can copy and paste existing objects and images to an illustration in progress, saving yourself work without sacrificing quality or originality. In the next sections, you will experiment with the Cut and Paste menu commands and see how their operation differs from that of Copy and Paste.

Cutting and Pasting Objects

When you select an object and then invoke the Cut command in the Edit menu, the object disappears and goes to the Clipboard. When you then select the Paste command, Windows places a copy of the cut object on the page.

The original object that you cut remains in the Clipboard until you overwrite it by cutting or copying another object, or until you end a Windows session.

Cutting and Pasting Within a Picture

There are two ways to remove an unwanted object from a picture in Coreldraw. You can either cut it to the Clipboard using the Cut command, or delete it from the program memory entirely by using the Delete command. Use the Cut command unless you are absolutely certain that you will never need the object again. If you delete an object using the Delete command, Coreldraw doesn't store a copy anywhere; unless you immediately select the Undo command, you won't be able to recover the object.

Coreldraw always pastes a cut or copied object onto the selected layer of the picture. Remember, if you want the object placed within multiple layers as it was when it was cut or copied, you must restore the original object arrangement using the commands in the Arrange menu. Otherwise, the object will be pasted onto the currently selected layer at the time it is pasted, not necessarily the layer on which it was copied.

1. Click on the kite to select it.
2. Select Cut from the Edit menu, click on the Cut icon, or press CTRL-X. The kite disappears from the drawing.
3. Select Paste from the Edit menu, click on the Paste icon, or press CTRL-V, and the kite comes back onto the drawing in the same place it was originally. (As discussed above, with multiple layers, the object

might be placed on a different layer than when it was initially cut. In that case, the object would not be *exactly* pasted to its original location.)

TIP: *Once an object has been cleared or deleted from a drawing, you can use Undo to restore it. The number of steps that can be undone depends on the Undo Levels settings on the General tab of the Options dialog box available from the Tools menu.*

Cutting and Pasting Between Pictures

Earlier in this chapter, you created a poster by combining the kite you drew in Chapter 2 with some text you created in Chapter 10. In the following exercise, you will add the word "Coreldraw," which you will cut from a drawing you create.

1. Turn off the rulers and Wireframe, and display the Text toolbar from the View menu, Toolbars option.
2. Select New Document from the File menu, then select Tile Horizontally from the Window menu. Your two open documents will be displayed as shown in Figure 11-4.

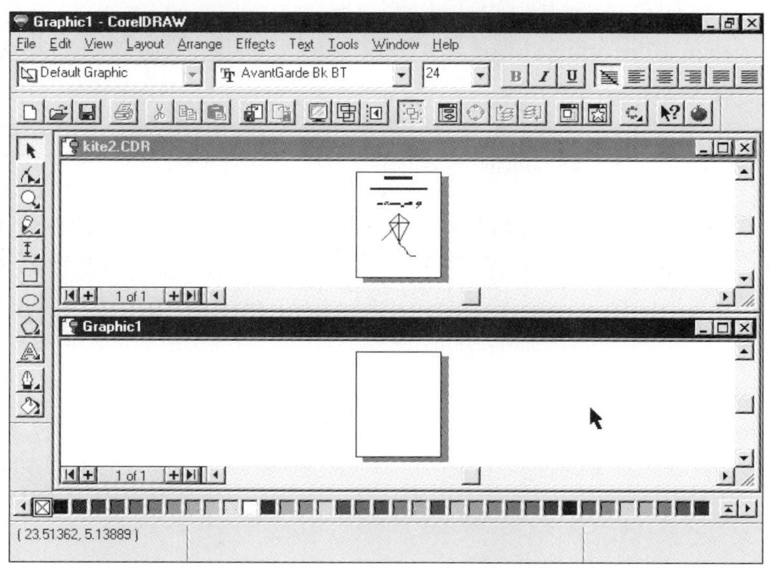

Document windows tiled horizontally

FIGURE 11-4

4. Maximize the document window you just opened, and then select Actual Size magnification.

5. Select the Text tool and place the insertion point near the center of the untitled document window. Select Times New Roman, 60-point, Italic, and select the center alignment button.

6. Using all capital letters, type **CORELDRAW!**.

7. Select the Shape tool, then select all the characters in "DRAW!". From the Text toolbar, select FreeStyle Script, 84 points. Select the Pick tool and from the Fill flyout, select Black. Then, click on any white space to deselect the text. Your text should look like this.

COREL DRAW!

8. Select Save As from the File menu and name the drawing Cd logo.

9. With the Pick tool, select the word "CorelDRAW!" and press CTRL-X , or select Cut from the Edit menu.

10. Click on the Restore button so that you can see both documents again, then click on the Maximize button on the Kite2.cdr document window.

11. Press CTRL-V or select Paste from the Edit menu. The word "CorelDRAW!" appears in the middle of the drawing.

12. Drag "CorelDRAW!" to the bottom of the poster. Then, by dragging on one of the corner boundary markers, scale it to fit in the space available, as shown in Figure 11-5.

13. Save the completed poster as Kite4.cdr.

With Coreldraw's Multi-document Interface (MDI), you can also transfer objects between documents using drag and drop while displaying two windows simultaneously, as you will see in the next exercise.

1. Select the "CORELDRAW!" text string and press DEL.

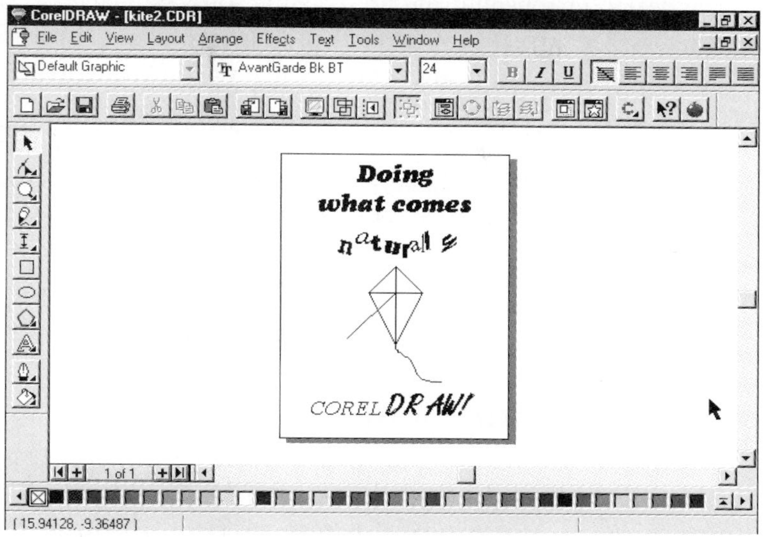

Completed poster

FIGURE 11-5

2. Select Tile Vertically from the Window menu. Your two document windows are displayed side by side.
3. Click on the Cdlogo.cdr window and press CTRL-V. A copy of the text string is pasted in the center of the page.
4. Point on the text string and drag it onto the Kite4.cdr document. Position it at the bottom of the page and release the mouse button.
5. Close both the Kite4.cdr file and the Cdlogo.cdr file without saving any changes.
6. Open a new document for the next exercise.

As you can see, Coreldraw provides more than one way to transfer objects between drawings.

Working with Different Applications

The number of software packages running under Microsoft Windows 95 is increasing almost daily. These programs include such diverse applications as word processors; desktop publishing and presentation software; database managers and form generators; and, of course, paint and illustration software. If your other favorite Windows 95 applications also support the Windows Clipboard, you should be able to transfer data back and forth between them and Coreldraw.

Features and techniques differ with every application, however; as a result, not all visual information transfers equally well between programs. There are too many Windows applications to catalog what happens to each file type as it transfers to or from Coreldraw through the Clipboard. However, the following sections should give you an idea of how the Clipboard handles graphic information that you transfer between Coreldraw and some of the most popular software.

Clipboard Memory Limits

There is a slight chance that at some point you may get an error message that says "Coreldraw Clipboard format too large to put on Clipboard." Should this happen, you can break the object into smaller groups of objects and then transfer them in several passes. You can also save the object as a new drawing, then use the Import command to move it.

In most cases, when you get the "CorelDraw Clipboard format..." message, Coreldraw will actually have copied the selected objects to the Clipboard in spite of the message. Check the Paste command in the Edit menu or the Paste icon to see if it is now available for selection. If it is, the objects have been successfully copied. If this command is not available, Coreldraw could not copy the selected object.

In general, you'll have the best chance of success when copying, cutting, and pasting Coreldraw objects that don't take advantage of too many advanced features at one time. An image that includes text, custom calligraphic outlines, PostScript fills, or Fountain fills, for example, will be more difficult to transfer to the Clipboard than an apparently complex geometrical image that contains none of these features.

Transferring Objects to Other Applications

When you copy or cut a Coreldraw object to the Clipboard, you are transferring not only the shape of an object, but also its properties. Properties include outline, outline fill, object fill, and text characteristics. Some properties do not transfer well in their original form, owing in some cases to the diversity of Windows applications and in others to the complexity of Coreldraw features.

Most problems with transferring Coreldraw objects to the Clipboard have to do with objects taking too much memory. The following tips should help you avoid Clipboard memory or Windows metafile compatibility problems.

Fountain fills and PostScript fills (both discussed in Chapter 7) are extremely memory-intensive from the standpoint of the Windows Clipboard, and they may go through unpredictable changes when transferred to another program. For example, when transferring an object containing PostScript fills, the object may be represented by blank or gray space when it is pasted into some applications and the outline may disappear.

When an object with PostScript fill is transferred through the Clipboard, you often get the outline and then either no fill, or the little "PS"s that you see on the Coreldraw screen. The PostScript fill itself is not transferred in any instance.

Text sent from Coreldraw files to the Clipboard can be sensitive also. The greater the number of letters and/or attributes in a text string, the more likely that some information will not transfer properly. The specific program to which you want to send the text may further influence the transfer of information. As a general rule, text comes in as a graphic object rather than as editable text.

On the positive side, a number of applications, such as Adobe PageMaker, can import Coreldraw-produced lines, curves, fills, Fountain fills, and text, with all of their properties, from the Clipboard without a problem.

Transferring Objects from Other Applications

When you transfer objects from your other favorite Windows applications to Coreldraw, you may not always receive exactly what you sent to the Clipboard. Sometimes this results from a limitation on what the Windows Clipboard can interpret; at other times, the apparent discrepancy is specific to the interaction between the other program and Coreldraw.

The Clipboard, for example, has difficulty transferring special text kerning or text rotation information, pattern or flood fills, pixel-by-pixel manipulations, and combined pen colors from other Windows applications to Coreldraw.

Text that you import into Coreldraw from another Windows application comes in with its defined text attributes. If you know the font, style, alignment, and other attributes you want, set these before importing the text. You can import a maximum of 4,000 ASCII text characters at a time.

Some features do not transfer well into Coreldraw. Bitmaps, for example, often don't transfer well. Text sent from other graphics applications (as opposed to word processors) often arrives in Coreldraw as curves. A fill or Fountain fill from another program may be transferred into Coreldraw as solid, or as an outline and separate fill object. Circles and ellipses may come in as connected line segments, while curves may become straight line segments. As Coreldraw, Microsoft Windows 95, and other Windows 95 applications are constantly being upgraded, however, you can expect compatibility to improve. In the remaining sections of the chapter, you will learn about special commands in the Coreldraw Edit menu that make it easy for you to copy objects or their attributes within a Coreldraw file.

Object Linking and Embedding

Object linking and embedding (OLE) is similar to copying and pasting. (In fact, copying and pasting actually embeds an object using OLE.) Linking and embedding differ in how they are linked to the original or source object, as you'll see shortly. However, with both, a connection is maintained with the source application. This enables you to merely double-click on an object in the destination application, and an *Inplace Server* containing the source application's toolbars and menus will open an editing window from which you can edit the object. If the object is linked, you will be editing the source object; if the object is embedded, you edit the destination object. (With copy and paste, the Inplace Server also opens with an editing window where you can edit the destination object.)

NOTE: *OLE's "Inplace Server" is a term for the software that opens with the source application's toolbars and menus. It is not the same as loading the source application. Rather, the source application's tools seem to appear within the Coreldraw window, for example. The Inplace Server contains an editing window with the object you are modifying. When you are finished, you return to your original program, for example Coreldraw, by clicking outside the editing window. It is all very efficient and amazingly easy to use!*

Linking

When an object is linked to its source, the object is not actually copied, but rather a dynamic link is formed. Only the original object actually exists. When you

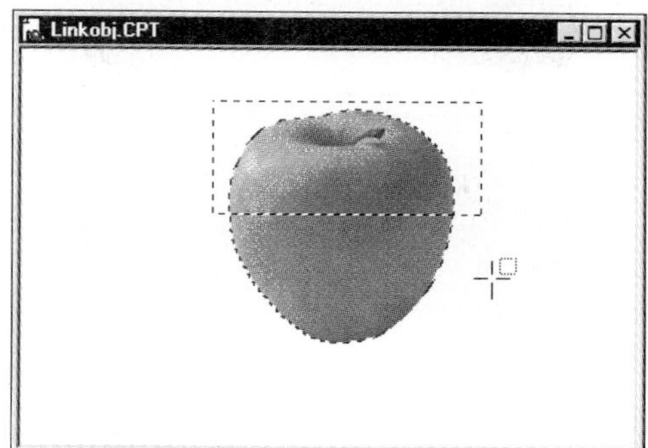

Selecting an object to link to Coreldraw

FIGURE 11-6

double-click on the destination object (the linked object), the link causes the Inplace Server to open with the source application's toolbars and menus, and the changes are made in the editing window. When you return to the destination application, an image of the changed source object will appear. To demonstrate linking, follow these steps.

IP: *An object can be linked only if the file being linked has previously been saved.*

1. Using the Start menu, open Corel PHOTO-PAINT.
2. Open a sample file from your third Coreldraw CD-ROM disk by selecting Open from the File menu, then selecting your CD ROM drive. Open the Photopnt directory, then the Objects directory. Open the file Apple.cpt, then save this file with the name Linkobj.cpt in your drawings directory.
3. Click on the Rectangle Mask Tool (the second icon from the top of the toolbox). Select some part of the picture, as shown in Figure 11-6.
4. Select Copy from the Edit menu or click on the Copy icon, and switch back to the Coreldraw window by pressing and holding ALT while pressing TAB once or twice. (You'll see the Corel balloon logo.)

5. Select Paste Special from the Edit menu to open the Paste Special dialog box shown here:

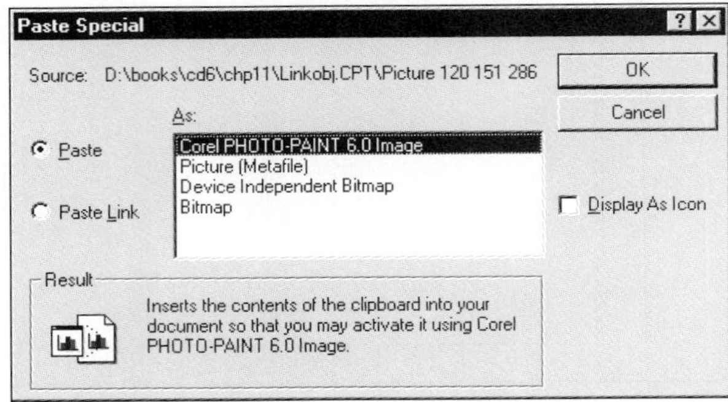

The Paste Special dialog box shows you the filename and path of the source object on the Clipboard and asks you how you want to bring it into Coreldraw. If you choose Paste, you will paste a *copy* of the object on the Clipboard (embedding), and you can modify it *without* affecting the original object. If you choose Paste Link, you will paste a *link* to the original object (no actual copy is made), and any modifications made will be made to the original.

IP: *Another way to link an object is to*
Select Insert New Object from the Edit menu
Choose Create From File
Choose Link
Type the filename or Browse and then select it
Click OK

6. Select Paste Link and then click on OK. An image of the source object is now on the page. Magnify the image by pressing F4 (or click on the Zoom to All Objects on the Zoom toolbar). You can now size and move the object, but to change its actual contents you must use the source application.

7. Double-click anywhere on the object and the Inplace Server with CorelPHOTO-PAINT's toolbars and menus will be displayed. The object will be available in the editing window, ready to be modified. When you have finished making changes, simply click outside the editing window and Coreldraw will be displayed with the changed image. You will be asked if you want to save the changes. If you don't, the changes will be lost and the original will remain untouched.

IP: *Another way to update a link is to*
Select the linked object with the Pick tool
Select Links from the Edit menu
Choose Manual or Automatic
Click on the desired action: Update the linked object now, open a window with the source object, change the source object, or break the line with the source object.

Embedding

Embedding is similar to linking, except that embedding makes a copy of the source object, and once the copy is pasted in the destination document, there is no connection between the copy and the source object. As in linking, you can double-click on the destination object and the Inplace Server will open with the source application's toolbars and menus. The difference is that you will be editing the destination copy and not the source object. To see object embedding in action, follow these steps.

1. Clear the screen by deleting all the objects, then choose Insert New Object from the Edit menu. The Insert Object dialog box appears, as you see here:

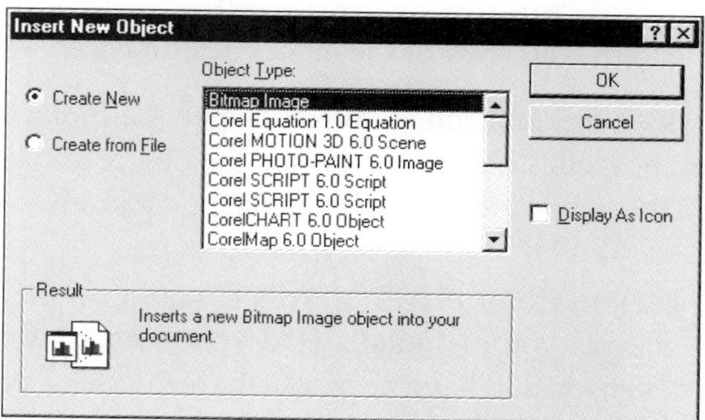

The Insert Object dialog box is very similar to the Paste Special dialog box you just used. The major difference is that Insert Object brings in objects that are not on the Clipboard. You can either go out and create a new object in some application (the Create New option) or bring in an object that is a file on your hard disk (the Create from File option). In either case, you must first select the type of object you want to bring in.

2. Select Corel PHOTO-PAINT 6.0 Image as the type of object you want to bring in, make sure Create New is selected, and then click on OK. The Create a New Image dialog box will open, asking you the size and resolution of the new picture and showing you the memory required and available to hold the picture.

3. Click on OK to accept the default dimensions, and Corel PHOTO-PAINT! will open. This new window is titled Corel PHOTO-PAINT 6.0 in Graphic1.

4. Once again, open the Linkobj.cpt file. Select an object in the picture and copy it to the Clipboard. Click on Corel PHOTO-PAINT 6.0 in Graphic1 to select it.

5. Choose Paste from the Edit menu and then click on As New Object from the submenu that opens. The object you copied will appear in the Corel PHOTO-PAINT 6.0 in Graphic1 window.

6. Choose Exit and Return to Coreldraw from the File menu and then click on Yes to update Corel PHOTO-PAINT 6.0 in Graphic1 in Coreldraw, then click No to save changes to Linkobj.cpt. Click No to remove the contents of the Clipboard. Corel PHOTO-PAINT! will close and Coreldraw will open with the copied Corel PHOTO-PAINT! object in the middle of the page.

7. Press F4 to enlarge the view of the embedded object.

8. Double-click on this embedded object to open the Inplace Server. After making changes, click anywhere outside the object to return to Coreldraw (this may take a while). Click Yes to update Coreldraw.

If you now go back to Corel PHOTO-PAINT! and open the original object, it will not have the changes you just made. Had you linked this object rather than embedded it, the changes would have been transferred.

Duplicating and Cloning Objects

As you saw earlier in the chapter, you can use the Copy and Paste commands in the Edit menu or on the toolbar to make a copy of an object within a drawing. This process can be somewhat time-consuming if you use it frequently, because you need two separate menu or toolbar commands or keyboard combinations to perform one action. A more convenient way of achieving the same end is to use the Duplicate command in the Edit menu or its keyboard shortcut, CTRL-D.

The Duplicate command causes a copy of the selected object or objects to appear at a specified *offset* from the original. In other words, the duplicate copy does not appear directly on top of the original, but at a horizontal and vertical distance from it, which you specify.

You can also use the Duplicate command alone or with the Combine command in the Arrange menu to achieve unusual logo or graphic designs, or special effects. In the next exercise, you will create and duplicate three different series of rectangles, each with a different specified offset. Then you will combine them to create the design shown in Figure 11-7.

1. Starting with a blank page, change the page format to Landscape using Page Setup on the Layout menu. Also, make sure that Rulers and Wireframe are turned on (as indicated by a check mark next to each option in the View menu).

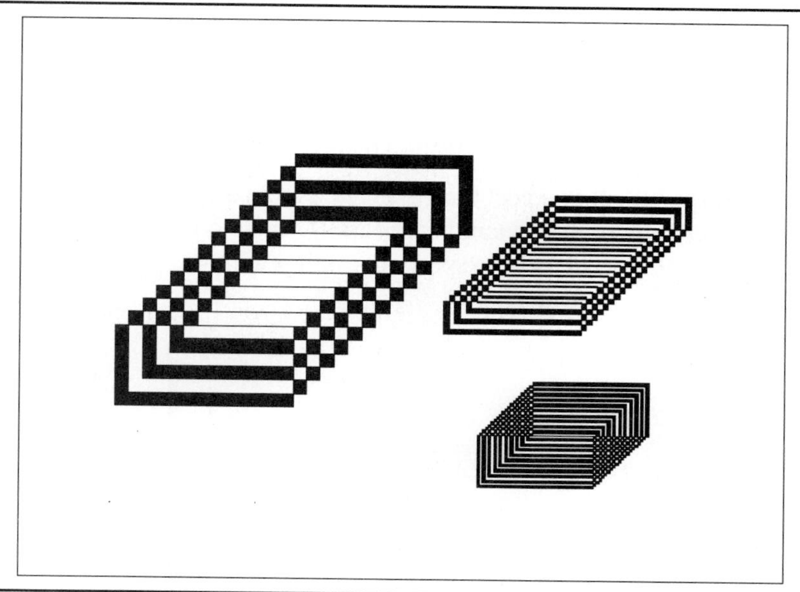

Special effects created with the Duplicate and Combine commands (with Full screen preview)

FIGURE 11-7

Place Duplicates and Clones settings

FIGURE 11-8

2. Select the Options command from the Tools menu. In the General tab, check that the Place Duplicates and Clones settings are set to the default value setting of 0.25 inch, as shown in Figure 11-8. If the values are correct, select OK and exit the dialog box. If either of these settings is different, change it to 0.25 inch.

3. Select the Rectangle tool and draw a rectangle about two-thirds of the way down the left edge of the page. The rectangle should be wider than it is high.

4. Press CTRL-D or select the Duplicate command from the Edit menu. An exact copy of the rectangle appears 1/4 inch to the right and above the original. Press CTRL-D repeatedly until you have created 14 copies of the rectangle, as shown here:

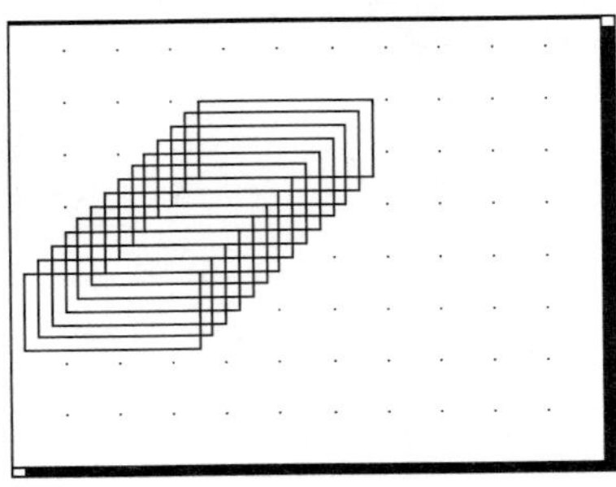

5. Change the Place Duplicates and Clones settings in the General tab of the Tools menu, Options dialog box to 0.05 inch in both the Horizontal and Vertical numeric entry boxes. Click on OK.

6. With the Rectangle tool still selected, draw another rectangle to the right and below the first series. Then, press CTRL-D 20 times in succession. This time, the duplicates appear at much shorter intervals, as shown here, giving a smoother appearance to the transitions between the series of duplicated objects.

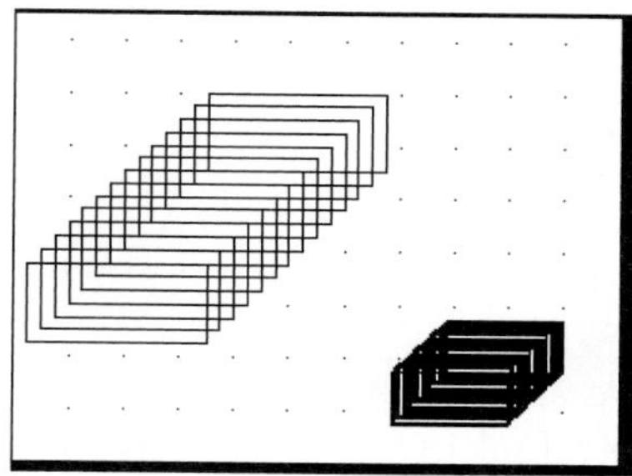

7. Refer to the Place Duplicates and Clones settings in the Preferences dialog box one more time, and change both values to –0.10 inch. The negative number indicates that the duplicates will appear below and to the left of the original object.

8. Draw a third rectangle to the right of the first rectangle and well above the second, and press CTRL-D 20 times in succession. This time, the duplicates appear to the left of and below the original object, as shown here:

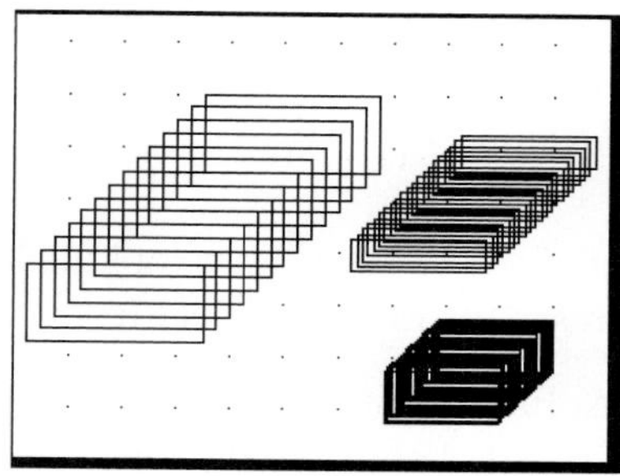

9. With the Pick tool, select each of the series of objects in turn by drawing a marquee around them, and apply the Combine command from the Arrange menu to combine the series. While each object is selected, open the Fill tool at the bottom of the toolbox and click on the black solid fill in the

bottom row of fills. You will recall from Chapter 5 that using the Combine command causes alternating objects in a group to become transparent. You won't see any change on the screen immediately.

IP: *You can also fill all the objects at one time by using Select All from the Edit menu, applying the Combine command from the Arrange menu to all the objects, and then selecting the black solid fill for all.*

10. After completing step 9, press F9 to toggle to Full screen preview. As you can see from Figure 11-7, the various offsets lead to different special effects when you combine each group of rectangles. Press ESC to return to the Normal view.
11. Save this file as Dupecomb.cdr and then close it.

The preceding exercise shows you only one potential use for the Duplicate command. You can probably think of many others that will spark your creativity and enhance your design abilities, especially since you can apply this command to multiple or grouped objects as well as single objects.

Cloning an Object

Cloning an object is the same as duplicating; however, the resulting objects can be used in different ways. A cloned object will still have a link to the original object, which is called the *master*. When you make changes to the master, those same changes will appear in the clone. The connection will remain until some change is made to the clone itself; then, the link is broken. Try this for yourself with the following steps.

1. Open a new drawing, choose the Ellipse tool, make an ellipse near the top of the page, then press SPACEBAR to select it.
2. Choose Clone in the Edit menu. You see a duplicate appear on top of the original. Move the selected object to the lower part of the page (it will be the master and is identified as the Control Ellipse on the Status bar).
3. Drag one of the sizing handles to make the master about half the original size. The clone changes to match the master.

4. Now select the clone and change its size. Then go back and change the master. The master-clone relationship has been terminated and the clone will no longer follow the master.
5. Select all the objects and delete them before proceeding.

IP: *When you delete the master object, the clone is also deleted.*

In the next section, you will see an example of another interesting Coreldraw copying technique—one that transfers properties rather than the objects themselves.

Copying an Object's Properties

Suppose that you have spent a lot of time designing an object, giving it a custom calligraphic outline, special fills, or a unique combination of text attributes. You would like to give the same set of attributes to another object, but you don't want to waste time setting up all those attributes from scratch. Coreldraw allows you to save time and enhance the design of your image by using the Copy Properties From command in the Edit menu. You can practice using this command in the following exercise.

1. From the Layout menu, Page Setup option, change the page format to Portrait and turn off both Rulers and Wireframe.
2. Adjust magnification to Actual Size (1:1), select the Text tool, click on an insertion point near the top left of the screen, and type **Corel**. Activate the Pick tool, selecting the text object, and from the Text menu, select Character. On the Font tab, set the Fonts selection to Aachen BT, Style to Bold, and Size to 96 points. On the Alignment tab, change the Spacing for Character to 40 percent and Alignment to None, Click on OK. From the Fill flyout select the Black fill.
3. Click on any white space to deselect the word "Corel."
4. Select the Text tool again and place a second insertion point below the first one. In the Text toolbar, set attributes to AvantGarde Bk BT Italic, 48 points, and left alignment. Now type **DRAW!**. Select the text with the

Text tool and from the Fill flyout select the Black fill. Your screen should look similar to Figure 11-9, after deselecting the text.

5. If DRAW! is not already selected, select the Pick tool and click on the second text string. Click on the Copy Properties From command in the Edit menu. The Copy Properties dialog box appears, as shown here:

The Copy Properties dialog box contains four options: Outline Pen, Outline Color, Fill, and Text Properties. You can choose to copy any or all of these properties

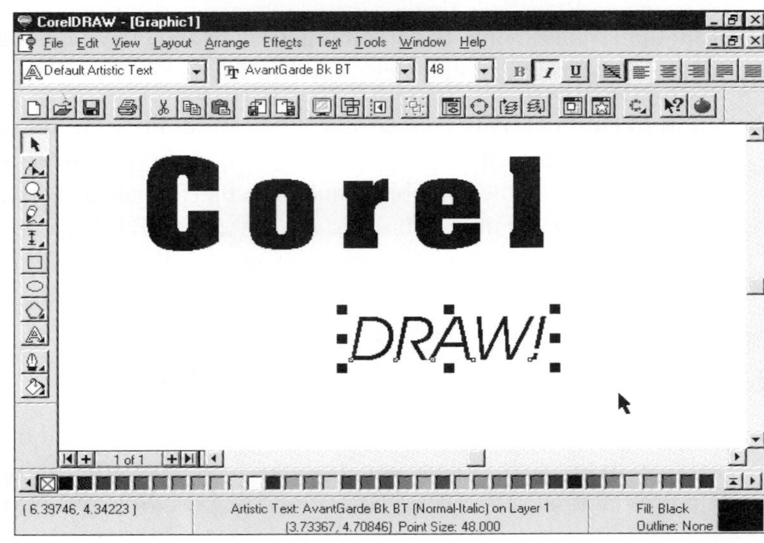

Preparing to copy properties from one text string to another

FIGURE 11-9

to the selected object. If you use the Shape tool instead of the Pick tool to select your text, the Text Properties option will be dimmed and unavailable.

6. Click on the Text Properties check box to place a check mark in it. Notice that a message at the bottom of the dialog box instructs you to select the object *from* which you want to copy the attributes.
7. Click on OK. The pointer changes to a thick arrow. This reminds you to click on the object from which you want to copy attributes.
8. Select the "Corel" text string by clicking anywhere on its outlines with the tip of the arrow. The "DRAW!" text string immediately changes to reflect the same attributes as the "Corel" text string, as shown in Figure 11-10. If you miss the outline when you click, a dialog box comes up, giving you the chance to try again.
9. Delete all the objects to clear the screen.

You have had and will have opportunities to use the Copy Properties dialog box in other chapters.

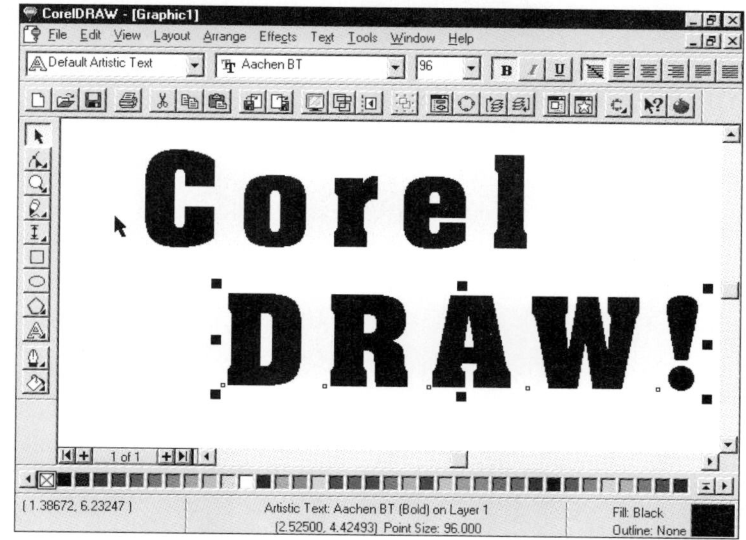

After copying text attributes for DRAW! from the Corel object

FIGURE 11-10

11

At this time, you may want to reset some of the default values, such as those in the Tools menu, Options dialog box and the General tab (Place Duplicates and Clones numeric values to .250 inch), Snap To Grid in Layout menu turned off, and Rulers in the View menu turned on.

You have experimented in this chapter with the available techniques for copying, cutting, and pasting objects and attributes within or between Coreldraw files and between Coreldraw and other applications. These techniques will help you work more efficiently with Coreldraw. In the next chapter, you will learn how to output your work to different types of printers and how to create files for both spot and process color printing.

COREL DRAW!™ 6 in action

***Eastern Tiger Swallowtail*—Gerry Wilson**

This complex design by Gerry Wilson makes extensive use of the clipart included with Coreldraw. All of the flowers and plants that make up the majority of the design are clipart. Using clipart, as Gerry did, allows you to increase your productivity with Coreldraw. The clipart included with Coreldraw can be modified using the same tools and techniques you use in your original work.

Gerry Wilson, who has won several awards in Corel's World Design Contest, lives and works in Brooklyn, NY, and can be reached at (718) 836-9181.

Printing and Processing Your Images

12

No matter how sophisticated an image may look on your computer monitor, you can judge its true quality only after it has traveled from your hard drive to the outside world. The means by which graphics travel from your computer to your intended audience is a question of output, and until recently output meant printer and paper. In today's world, however, paper is only one possible means by which your artwork can reach your audience. With the File menu Export option, your Coreldraw files can be exported in various file formats that can be used in film, videotape, CD-ROM, and 35mm slide recorders. Coreldraw offers you a choice of all these media and their associated output devices.

If print media remain your preferred end products, you can produce your images using the Print command in the File menu. Coreldraw allows you to print selected objects within an image, scale your image to any desired size, print oversize images on multiple tiled pages, print from selected layers, or print to a file that you can send to a service bureau. You can prepare color separations for both Pantone spot and process color images, add crop marks and registration marks, print in film negative format, and add file information to your printouts. With a PostScript printing device, you can also reproduce the dotted and dashed outlines and fills, custom halftone screens, and PostScript textures you learned to use in Chapter 7. Also, Coreldraw 6 now allows you to print PosScript fills on non-PostScript printers.

If you want your images produced as slides or used in presentations, you will use the Export command, not the Print command, to generate your output. Corel PRESENTS, discussed in Chapter 15, allows you to assemble the slides, charts, and drawings you've created in Coreldraw into professional presentations. If you have the appropriate equipment, you can also output onto a CD-ROM in Photo-CD format.

The first part of this chapter describes how to prepare for printing. The second part of the chapter guides you step-by-step through the printing process using the Print and Print Options dialog boxes.

Preparing To Print

Before you select the Print command, you should make certain that your printer is correctly installed to run under Windows. You may want to also adjust several default settings in Windows in order to customize printing for the special needs of Coreldraw. Two of these settings, called "Timeout settings," determine how long Windows waits before sending you messages about potential printer problems. The settings you need to review are all in the Windows Printers window.

TIP: *If you work with a PostScript printer, you should be using Windows' own printer driver or a Windows-compatible PostScript driver that came with your printer (for example, the PostScript driver for the HP4M), whichever driver is* newer.

The short sections that follow will guide you through the process of reviewing and editing your printer setup.

Printer Installation and Setup

If you have not specified the correct printer and port either when you installed Microsoft Windows or afterwards, you will not be able to print in Coreldraw. To check whether your printer is correctly installed to run under Microsoft Windows, follow these steps.

1. Click on the Start button on the Taskbar. The Start menu will open.
2. From the Start menu, choose the Settings option and then click on Printers. The Printers window appears and displays an icon for each of your installed printers. An example of a Printers window is shown next:

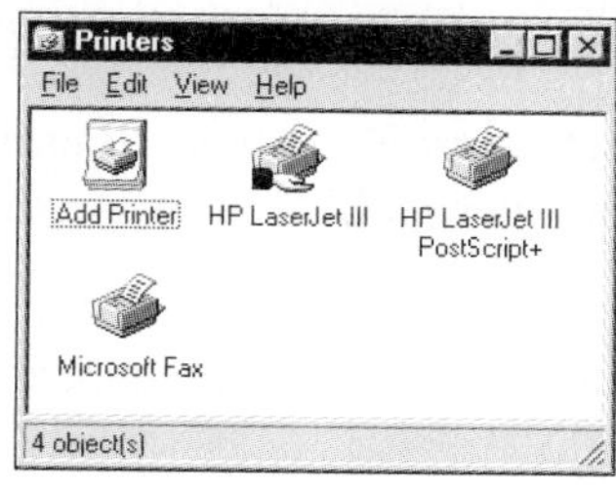

The Printers window should contain an icon for the printer you are going to use, and this printer should be set as your default printer.

3. If your printer is in the dialog box, check to see if it is set as your default by right-clicking on it with the mouse. In the popup menu that appears, Set As Default should be checked as shown next. If it isn't, click on it and then skip over step 4.

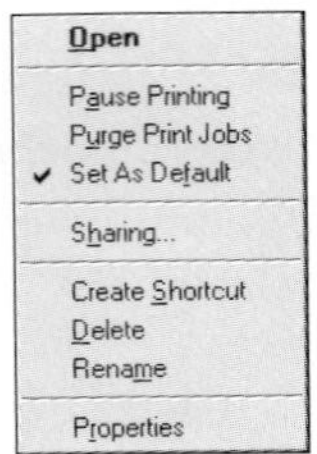

4. If your printer is missing from the Printers window, double-click on Add Printer. The Add Printer Wizard appears and leads you through the installing of your printer. You may be asked to insert one of the original Windows Install disks so that the printer's software driver can be copied to your hard disk. Repeat these steps for all the printers you will use.

Printer Timeout

After checking for correct printer installation, you should customize the Timeout settings, found in the Printers Properties Details tab for the printer you want to use. These settings define how long Windows waits before sending you messages about potential printer problems. The default Timeout settings installed with Microsoft Windows may be adequate for average Windows applications, but you should customize them to improve printing performance in Coreldraw. To edit Printer Timeout, use the following steps.

1. From the Printers window, right-click on your default Printer icon again. When the popup menu opens, click on Properties. The Properties dialog box will open.
2. Click on the Details tab. The Details tab appears as shown in Figure 12-1.

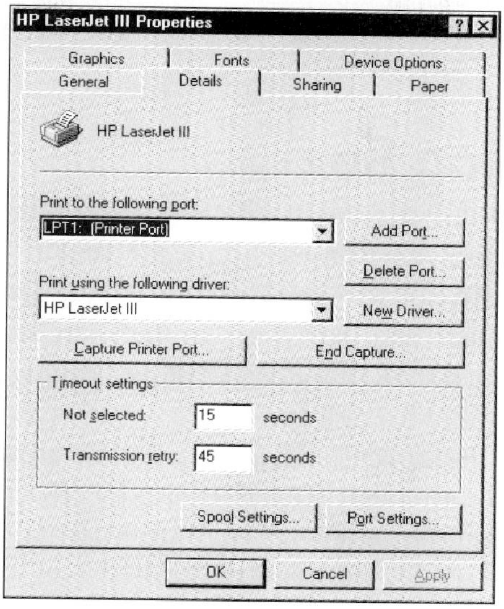

The Details tab of the printer's Properties dialog box

FIGURE 12-1

The Timeout settings section, in the lower part of the Details tab, shows two settings: Not selected and Transmission retry. The Not Selected setting determines how long Windows waits before informing you that the printer is not connected properly, not turned on, or otherwise not ready to print. Leave this setting at its default value of 15 seconds, because if the printer is not ready to perform, you want to find out as soon as possible.

3. Adjust Transmission Retry from its default value of 45 seconds to 300 seconds (equal to 5 minutes). The Transmission Retry value determines how long the printer waits to receive additional characters before a timeout error occurs. Although 45 seconds may be long enough for most software that runs under Windows, it is not always adequate for graphics applications such as Coreldraw. The output file that Coreldraw sends to your printer can contain complex information, requiring more time to transmit. If you don't change the Transmission Retry setting, the printer will halt processing before receiving all of a print job.

By verifying your printer setup and Timeout settings each time you run Coreldraw, you can prevent potential printing and communications problems before you even attempt to print.

Now that you have customized the Windows printer settings to improve printing performance in Coreldraw, you are ready to begin printing in Coreldraw.

The Print Dialog Box

To begin the process of printing in Coreldraw, you must select the Print command in the File menu. An image must be on the screen before you can select this command. So that you can practice printing using the options in the Print dialog box, import a clip art image and then use it in the exercises that follow. Each section explores one printing option or one aspect of the printing process. Start by importing a piece of clip art.

You can use any piece of clip art that you want. The piece used here, shown in Figure 12-2, is car18.cmx from the \Clipart\Transpor\Personal\ directory on the fourth CD-ROM. If you cannot see any color and you have a color monitor, turn off Wireframe in the View menu. Save this clip art as Benz.cdr in your \Drawings\ directory.

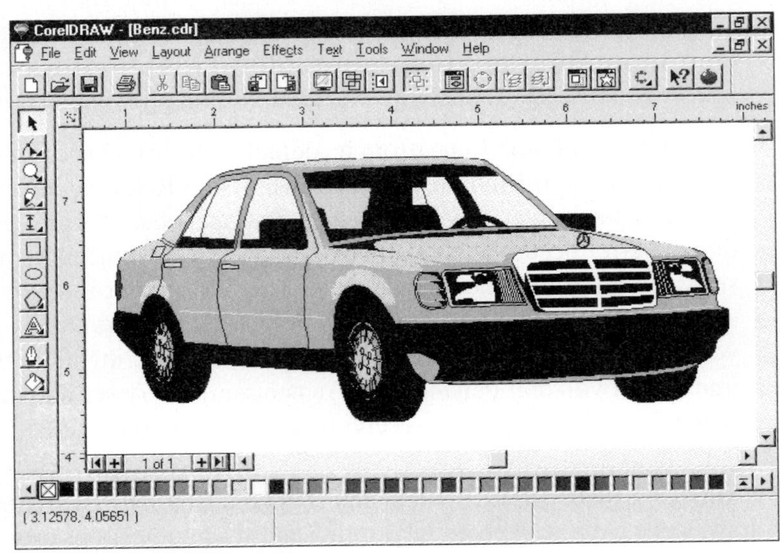

Benz.cdr used in the printing exercises

FIGURE 12-2

Selecting the Print Command

Select the Print command from the File menu. The Print dialog box appears, as shown in Figure 12-3. The Print dialog box allows you to determine what and how you want to print: All, Current Page, Selection, or a range of pages; whether you want to print to a file for a PC or a Macintosh to output; and the number of copies. You can accept the Windows default printer (which you selected above) or another printer, using the Printer Name drop-down list box. If you click on Properties, the printer's Properties dialog box opens, as shown in Figure 12-4. This is similar to the Properties dialog box you saw earlier in the chapter but without the General, Details, and Sharing tabs. From Coreldraw, the Properties dialog box opens with the Paper tab in view, where you can select paper size, page orientation, and paper source. You may have other options, depending on the printer selected. The other tabs, Graphics, Fonts, and Device Options provide settings in each of those areas, some of which are printer-dependent. Look at each of those tabs and become familiar with the options available with your default printer. When you are done with the printer's Properties dialog box, click on OK to return to the Print dialog box. If you click on the Options button you get the Print Options dialog box shown in Figure 12-5. The

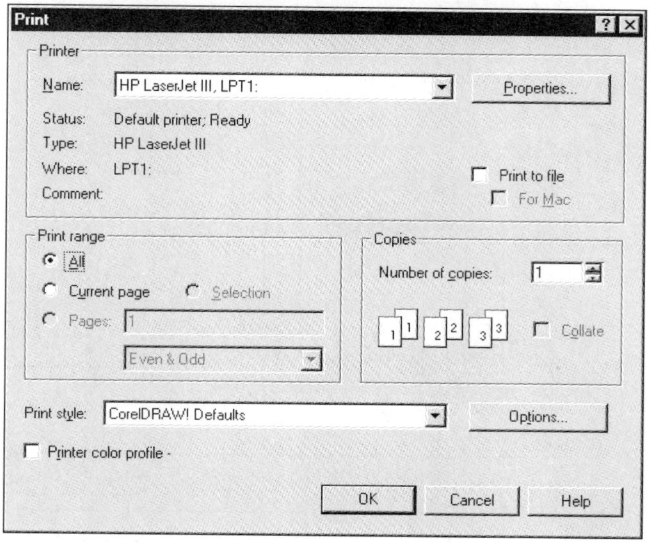

Print dialog box

FIGURE 12-3

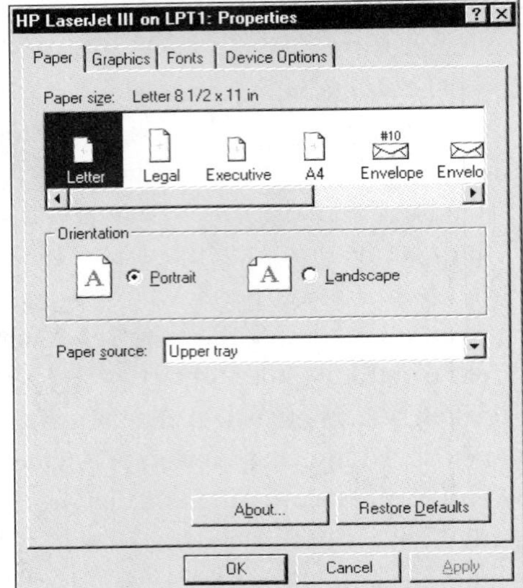

The printer's Properties dialog box, Paper tab

FIGURE 12-4

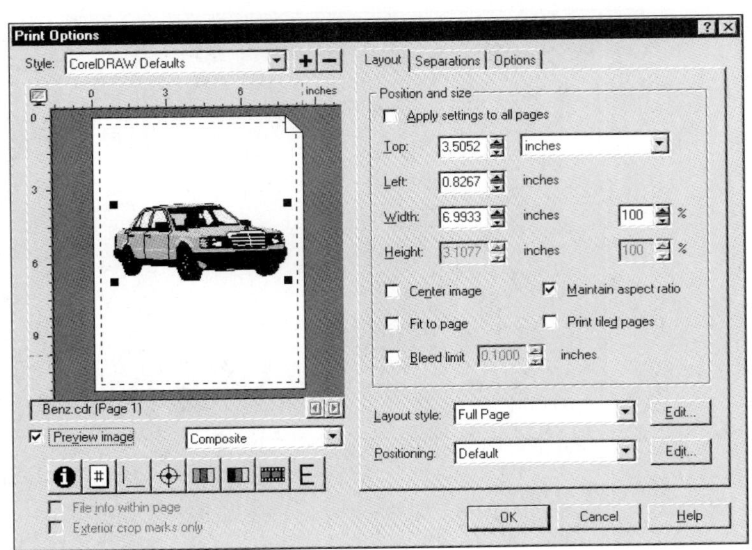

Print Options dialog box

FIGURE 12-5

Print Options dialog box allows you to preview how the printed image will look and fit on the page as well as to change the position of the image and the type of layout to be used. Also, you can specify that you want color separations, the features of those separations, and, if you are using a PostScript printer, several options for that. Finally, you can save the settings you make as a particular printing style and use that style at a later date. These features will be covered in detail later in this chapter.

The preview display box on the left, which displays the effects of the Position and Size settings when the Preview Image option is selected, can also be changed interactively by dragging any of the handles of the bounding box to the desired position. In addition, you can drag the graphic to any position on the page. These changes affect only the printed output, not the actual Coreldraw drawing. If you right-click in the preview display box, a popup menu allows you to determine if you want the preview, if it should be in color, and if you want full image drag.

Below the preview display box are a series of buttons that turn on or off various information or "printer's marks" that are helpful if the image is to be commercially printed. Exactly how these items are used will be described later in this chapter, but the purpose of the buttons is shown in Table 12-1.

Before you experiment with the printing options, select Cancel to exit the Print Options dialog box, and return to the Print dialog box.

Checking Printer Setup

Whenever you print, it is good to develop the habit of checking your printer properties before you select any print options. You do this with the Properties dialog box that you saw in Figure 12-1. It can be opened either from the File menu (Print Setup option) or from the Print dialog box (Properties button). The Properties dialog box for your printer contains controls that allow you to define the paper size, orientation, and source; how graphics and fonts are handled; and other settings peculiar to your printer. The other items in the Properties dialog box will vary according to the printer you selected in the Printers window, Print Setup in the File menu, or the Print dialog box. For example, the Properties dialog box shown in Figure 12-1 shows the controls available for a non-PostScript printer.

Some of the controls in the Properties dialog box are important because they help you avoid possible pitfalls when you attempt to print complex images. Later in this chapter you will find hints on adjusting these settings to prevent or minimize printing problems. Take a moment to explore the contents of your printer's Properties dialog box and of any nested sub-dialog boxes that are accessible by

TABLE 12-1 Print Information Buttons

Button	Purpose
i	Prints the path and filename, the current date and time, the tile and plate number, and the screen frequency. If you are printing color separations, the color name and screen angle will be printed.
#	Prints the page number.
	Prints crop marks if the Coreldraw page size is smaller than the physical paper size.
	Prints registration marks to align color separations.
	Prints a color calibration bar if you are printing color separations.
	Prints a densitometer scale if you are printing color separations.
	Prints a negative or reverse image for use with film.
E	Flips the image from left to right for use with film, so that the emulsion side of the film can be placed down.

clicking on special command buttons. When you are ready, click on Cancel in the Properties dialog box and return to the Print dialog box.

Number of Copies and Collating

In the Print dialog box, you can enter the number of copies you want printed at one time in the Number of copies numeric entry box or you can click on the arrows to increase or decrease the number in the box. This can be a number from 1 through 999. If you are printing a multiple-page document and you are printing multiple copies of it, you can choose to collate the copies or not. For example, if you have four copies of a three-page document and did not collate it, you would get four copies of page one, followed by four copies of page two, and four copies of page three. By collating, you would get four sets of the three pages in order. The diagram opposite the Collate check box will show you how your output will be paginated.

Pages to Print

With multiple-page documents, you can specify the pages to be printed in the Print dialog box by choosing to print all the pages, just the currently selected page, a range of pages, a list of pages, or just the odd or even pages in several orders. Both page ranges and page lists are entered in the text box opposite "Pages:" and can be intermixed. For example if you want to print pages 3, 5, and 7 and then pages 11 through 15, you would enter: **3,5,7,11-15** (including the commas and hyphen) in the text box.

Printing Only Selected Objects

The Print dialog box allows you to choose to print only selected objects by clicking on Selection in the Print range area. There are several reasons why you might want to do this, rather than print the entire graphic.

- You want to reduce printing time and need to check only a portion of the image.
- Your picture contains a great deal of fine detail, such as in a technical illustration, and you want to examine certain areas for accuracy.
- You have experienced printing problems and want to locate the object or objects that are causing the trouble.

Whatever your reason, you can print just the selected objects within a picture by activating the Selection check box in the Print dialog box. You must select the desired objects before you select the Print command, however, or the Selection option button will not be available. Practice printing selected objects in the Benz.cdr file now.

1. If the Print dialog box is still open on your screen, click on Cancel to exit and return to the Benz.cdr file.
2. Click anywhere in the image to select it; the Status bar tells you that you have selected a group of 39 objects. Choose the Ungroup command in the Arrange menu or press CTRL-U to ungroup all of the objects.
3. Using the Pick tool, deselect the group, then select just the hood ornament by clicking on it; it's selected if the Status bar changes to "Group of 7 objects."

4. Leave the hood ornament selected and press CTRL-P. When the Print dialog box appears, review your printer's properties, and then click on the Selection option button. If you open the Print Options dialog box by clicking on Options, the preview display box shows only the selected object—the hood ornament (which may be a black dot).
5. Select the OK command button (twice if you went in to look at the preview display box) to begin the printing process. After a short time, the image of the hood ornament should emerge from your printer. Leave the Benz.cdr image on your screen for the next exercise.

As you learn about the other options in the Print and Print Options dialog boxes, you will think of effective ways to combine one or more of them with the Selection option. Assume, for example, that you are working with a complex technical illustration and need to proof just a small area. If you activate both the Selection and Fit to page options, you can print a magnified image of the selected objects in order to proof them more easily.

Tiling a Graphic

You can choose from several different methods of sizing a graphic in Coreldraw. The most obvious method is to use rulers when creating objects. Another method involves defining a custom page size with the Layout menu Page Setup command and the Page Settings dialog box, Layout tab. You can also use the Pick tool to scale an image to the desired size after you have created it.

Posters and other applications, however, require images that are larger than any paper size available for your printer. Even if you print final versions of these images on a Linotronic or other imagesetter that has fewer restrictions on paper size, how do you obtain accurate proofs? The answer is through tiling the image. Here, tiling refers to the process of printing an oversize image in sections that fit together precisely to form the complete picture. If, for example, you create a poster that is 11 inches wide by 17 inches high and select Print tiled pages in the Print Options dialog box, the image will print on four 8 1/2-by-11-inch sheets (or on some multiple of whatever size paper you use for your printer).

In the following exercise, you will enlarge the page size for Benz.cdr, scale the image to fit the page, and print the entire image with the Print tiled pages option enabled.

1. With the Benz.cdr image still on your screen, click on the Select All command in the Edit menu to select all of the objects in the picture. Then select the Group command in the Arrange menu to keep all objects together.
2. If necessary, activate the Rulers command in the View menu and then select the Page Setup command in the Layout menu. When the Page Settings dialog box appears, click on the Landscape option button and choose Tabloid in the Paper drop-down list box. Selecting Tabloid will result in a page that is 17 inches wide by 11 inches high in Landscape format. Click on the OK command button to exit the dialog box. The rulers show you the change in page size.
3. With the Pick tool active, position the pointer at the upper-left corner boundary marker of the selected, grouped image. When the pointer turns to a crosshair, drag the mouse until you have scaled the image to fit the upper-left corner area of the page. Do the same for the lower-right corner boundary marker so your screen looks like Figure 12-6. Note that the image retains its proportions.

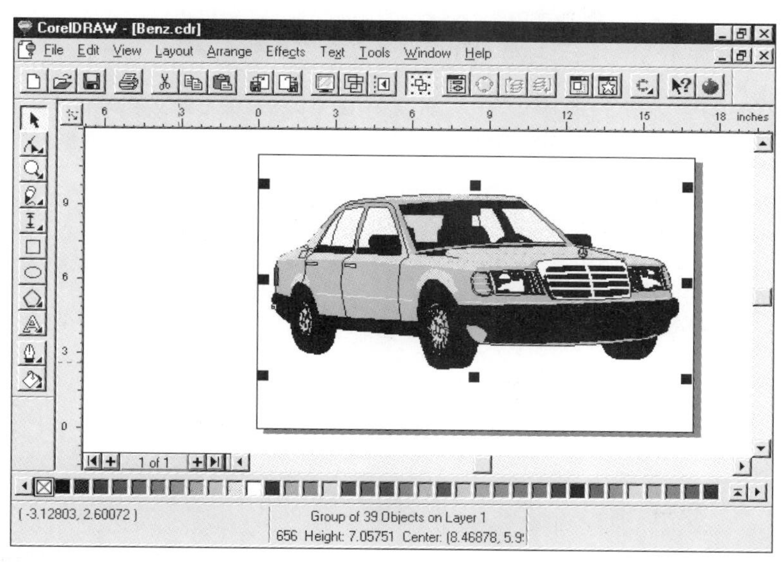

Benz.cdr on a tabloid page

FIGURE 12-6

4. Move the scaled image so that it is centered on the enlarged page (use the Align to Center Page option in the Align rollup to do this automatically) and then select the Print command from the File menu. If you get a message advising you that the printer paper orientation does not match that of the document, click on Yes to have the printer adjusted automatically.
5. When the Print dialog box appears, click on All in the Print range, make sure the Printer and other options in the Print dialog box are correctly selected, and then click on Options.
6. When the Print Options dialog box opens, you can see in the Preview box that the image is larger than the paper size (assuming that the printer is set for 8 1/2-by-11-inch paper size). Deselect any options that are currently active, except Preview Image, and then click on the Print tiled pages option to activate it. You will see the image spread over two or more pages, as in Figure 12-7.

OTE: *Depending on the algorithm your printer uses, the number of sheets used for tiling may vary.*

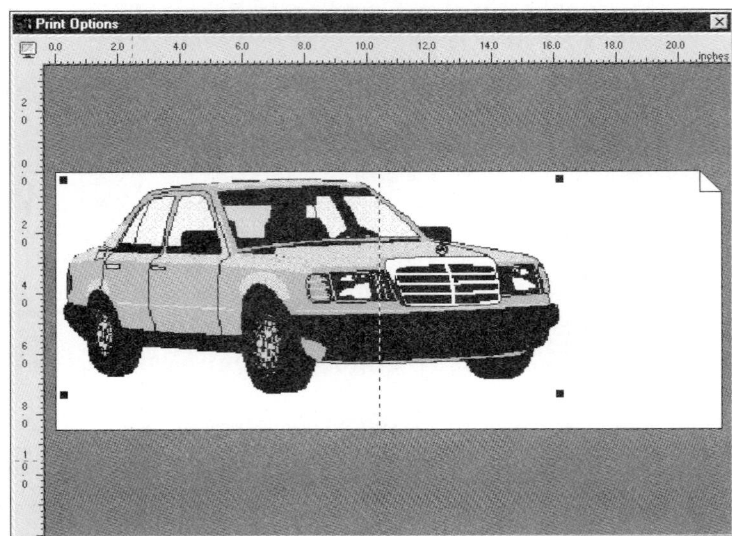

Full-screen preview of a tiled print image

FIGURE 12-7

7. To see the tiled image better, click on the Full-screen Preview icon (the monitor icon) in the upper window and then select OK twice to print. After a few moments, the image begins to print.

8. When the file has finished printing, select Close in the File menu. Do not save the changes you have made to the picture. From the View menu, turn off the Rulers command and in the Layout menu, Page Setup command, return to letter-size paper. Then select Benz.cdr from the list of recent files in the File menu to reopen this file in its original state. Leave Benz.cdr on the screen for the next exercise.

Since most printers do not print to the edge of the page, you may need to use scissors or a matte knife to cut and paste the tiled pieces together exactly. Still, this method gives you a fairly exact representation of your image as it will print on a printer that handles a larger format. To assist you in fitting the tiles together, you can adjust the tile overlap either in inches or percent of the page.

Scaling an Image

There is a difference in Coreldraw between scaling an image on the screen with the Pick tool and defining a scaling value in the Print Options dialog box. When you scale an image visually in Coreldraw itself, you are altering its actual dimensions. When you adjust the values in the scale numeric entry boxes or the preview window in the Print Options dialog box, however, you change only the way the file prints, not its actual size.

Perform the following exercise to print the Benz.cdr file at a reduced size using the scale numeric entry boxes.

1. With the Benz.cdr file on the screen, click on any outline within the image. As the Status bar informs you, the entire image is grouped.

2. Select the Print command from the File menu. (If asked, click on Yes to automatically reorient the printer to the drawing.) When the Print dialog box appears, make sure All is set for the Print range, and then click on Options.

3. When the Print Options dialog box opens, deselect Print tiled pages on the Layout tab if it is still selected, and any other options except Preview Image and Maintain aspect ratio. Opposite Width and Height on the right of the Print Options dialog box are, first, two numeric entry boxes that are in the units you are currently using (inches in Figure 12-6); then, to the

right of these boxes, there are two additional numeric entry boxes for entering percentages. This second pair of boxes is used to scale the image for printing. The current values in the scale numeric entry boxes should be 100 percent (actual size). When Maintain aspect ratio is checked, the Height units and scale numeric entry boxes are dim, since they will automatically change as you change the width to keep the aspect ratio of width to height the same. Therefore, to scale the image for printing and maintain the aspect ratio, you only need to change the scale factor for Width.

4. Using the bottom scroll arrow in the Width scale numeric entry box, scroll to 10 percent, as shown here:

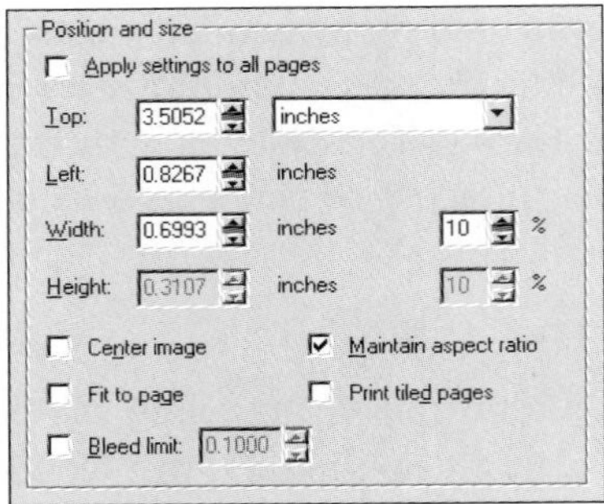

5. Depending on your printer, you may not be able to print as small as 10 percent. If this is the case, increase the scale until your printer accepts the image.

6. Click on OK twice to begin the printing process. Again, depending on your printer, the image will probably print centered on your page, but it may be slightly offset.

7. Leave the current image on the screen for further work.

You have seen how you can reduce the scale of an image to 10 percent of original size. The lower limit is 1 percent of original size. You can also increase the scale of an image beyond 1,500 percent of original size. If you expand the scale of an image beyond the dimensions of the page, however, remember to activate the Tile option as well.

Fitting an Image to the Page

Like the Scale option, the Fit to Page option in the Print Option dialog box does not affect the actual size of the graphic. When you select this option, Coreldraw automatically calculates how much it must increase the scale of the graphic or selected object(s) in order to make it fill the entire page. In the following exercise, you will combine the Fit to page option with the Selected Objects option you learned about previously.

1. Click anywhere within the Benz.cdr image; since the entire image is grouped, you select all objects automatically.
2. Click on the Ungroup button in the toolbar and then click on any white space to deselect all objects. Select several objects—like the grill, hood ornament, and headlights—by clicking on them. You can see what you have selected by choosing Preview Selected Only from the View menu and then pressing F9 (Full-screen Preview). It should look like this:

3. When you are done looking at the Full-screen Preview, press ESC.
4. With the objects selected, choose the Print command in the File menu. When the Print dialog box appears, click on the Selection option button and then on the Options button.
5. In the Print Options dialog box, deselect any options, except Preview Image, that are currently active, click on the Fit to page option to activate it, and then click on OK twice to begin printing. After a few moments, the grill, headlights, and ornament appear on the paper, filling the entire sheet. 12

OTE: *When the Fit to page option is selected, the Centered option is also automatically enabled.*

6. Leave the Benz.cdr image on the screen for the next exercise.

Next you will experiment with printing an image to a file.

Printing to a File

There are two common reasons why you might choose to print an image to a file:

- You are creating files to send to a service bureau for output on a Linotronic or other imagesetter.
- Your printer is busy and you prefer to copy the print information directly to the printer at a later time.

To print to a file, you select the Print to file option in the Print dialog box and name the output file in the Print to File dialog box that opens. Printer output files created in applications that run under Windows differ depending on the printer you have selected, but all files use the extension .PRN. The printing parameters included in the file are those that you set for the currently selected printer in the Print, Print Options, and printer Properties dialog boxes.

The following exercise assumes that you are going to send an output file to a service bureau for use on a PostScript imagesetter. In order to do this, you do not need to have a PostScript printer, but you must have a PostScript printer driver installed in Windows. If you do not have a PostScript driver installed, use the Add Printer icon in the Printers window. You can either use one of the PostScript drivers that came with Windows (the service bureau can tell you which), or the service bureau will provide you with the correct drivers for their equipment (make sure it works with Windows 95). Refer to the discussion under "Checking Printer Setup" earlier in this chapter for assistance in loading a new driver. Once you have the PostScript driver set up, practice printing the Benz.cdr image to a file with the following exercise.

1. With the Benz.cdr file on the screen, deselect all objects in the image, choose Select All from the Edit menu, then Group from the Arrange menu.
2. Press CTRL-P, and when the Print dialog box displays, click on All for the Print range if it isn't already selected, choose the printer you want to use, and then click on Print to file.

3. If you are going to print on a printer or imagesetter controlled by a Macintosh computer, select the For Mac option. Without this selection, the print files you produce will not work on a Macintosh.
4. Click on Options and, in the Print Options dialog box, turn off Fit to page (the two scale numeric entry boxes should automatically return to 100%) and click on OK.
5. Select OK again; the Print To File dialog box will appear, as shown next. This dialog box looks like and operates similarly to the Save File As dialog box.

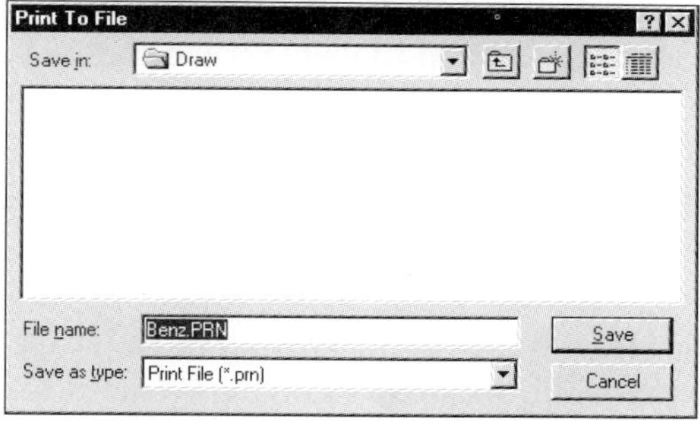

6. If the filename Benz is not already in the File name text box, type it, and then select Save. Coreldraw adds the file extension .PRN automatically to designate this as a printer output file.
7. Make the changes you need in the dialog box and click on OK to begin the process of printing to a file.
8. When printing is complete, select Close to clear the image from the screen without saving any changes.

When printing an image to a file, you can combine several options. For example, if you are creating color separations for commercial printing, you might choose to activate the Print as Separations and Print to file options at the same time.

Using Print Options

The Print Options dialog box, accessed through the Options command button in the Print dialog box, has not only the options that have been described above and that you saw in Figure 12-5, but two additional tabs with settings for creating color separations and for other features. The next sections introduce you to advanced print options, including those that are in the Separations and Options tabs as well as those that are in the Print Options dialog box itself and in the Layout tab. Since you may use some of these options in combination, the sections are ordered according to task, rather than according to their appearance in the Print Options dialog box.

Printing File Information with a Graphic

If you are like most illustrators and designers, you probably revise a graphic several times, renaming it with each revision so that you can choose the best version later. You are therefore familiar with the bewilderment of viewing multiple printouts of the same graphic and not knowing which sheet represents which version.

Coreldraw provides a convenient solution to this common frustration. By activating the file information option, you can print the path, filename, date and time of printing, and other information with your image. This information appears in 6-point Courier outside the top and bottom margins of your page, not on your graphic (unless you select the File info within page option). You select the file information option by clicking the leftmost button (with the "i" in it) under the preview display box. If you activate the file information option without the within page option, choose a page size in the Page Settings dialog box that is smaller than the actual paper size you are printing on. This step is necessary because the file information is visible only if you reduce page size below the size of the paper in your printer tray. If you are using 8 1/2-by-11-inch paper, for example, you must use the Page Settings dialog box to define a custom page size of smaller dimensions and then fit the graphic within that page. You can practice defining a custom 7-by-9-inch page size and printing file information in the following exercise. You'll start by loading another Coreldraw clip art file, which you will use for the rest of the chapter.

1. Start a new graphic, turn Rulers on and import the Tocan.cmx file, which is in the \Clipart\Bird\ directory on the fourth CD-ROM. The toucan will appear, as shown in Figure 12-8. (Note the difference in spelling between Tocan, the filename, and toucan, the actual bird name.) Save this file as Tocan.cdr.
2. Select the Page Setup command in the Layout menu. Select Custom in the paper size drop-down list box, and define a page 7 inches wide and 9

\Clipart\Bird\Tocan.cmx image as it first appears

FIGURE 12-8

inches high. Then click on OK to exit the dialog box. The toucan is now larger than your page.

3. Click on the toucan to select it. Then, from the Arrange menu, choose Transform, Scale & Mirror. Enter 80% in both the horizontal and vertical scale factors, and click on Apply. The toucan is reduced so it fits on the page, as you can see in Figure 12-9. Save this image as Tocan.cdr.

4. Press CTRL-P to open the Print dialog box. Make sure that the Printer and other settings are what you want. Then, if Print to file is still selected, click on it to deselect it and click on the Options command button. In the Print Options dialog box, click on the file information button on the left under the preview display box and make sure that Fit to page is not selected in the Layout tab. Click on OK twice to begin printing. After a few moments, the image emerges from your printer. The path and filename, date and time of printing, and other information appear just beyond the bottom boundary of the custom page, and the word Composite (meaning the print is a composite of all the colors) is printed at the top of the page, as shown in Figure 12-10.

5. Leave this image on the screen for subsequent exercises.

Tocan.cdr image scaled to fit a 7-by-9-inch page

FIGURE 12-9

Tocan.cdr printed with file information

FIGURE 12-10

Since Coreldraw generates object-oriented art, you can scale your images without distortion. It is therefore convenient to change page size so that you can print file information for your own use. Another common use for the file information option is in conjunction with the Print as Separations, Crop Marks, and Registration Marks options, which are discussed next.

Color Separations, Crop Marks, and Registration Marks

When you specified outline fill and object fill colors in Chapter 7, you learned about the differences between spot color and process color in the commercial printing process. If you plan to send output files to a PostScript imagesetter, you can reduce your commercial printing expenses by generating color separations on paper or in a file. Doing this reduces the number of intermediary steps that commercial printers must perform to prepare your images for printing.

Put simply, color separation is the process of separating the colors that you specify for an entire image into the primary component colors. When you generate color separations using the process color system (CMYK), the output is four separate sheets, one each for the cyan, magenta, yellow, and black color components of the image. The commercial printer uses the four sheets to create separate overlays for each color, in preparation for making printing plates.

When you generate color separations using the spot color system, the output is one sheet for each color specified in the image, and the commercial printer creates overlays for each color. This process becomes very expensive as the number of spot colors in an image increases, so it is a good idea to use the process color system if you plan to have more than three colors in a given image.

When you generate color separations using the Print Separations option in the Separations tab of the Print Options dialog box, it is also important to include crop marks and registration marks. You can see examples of these marks in Figure 12-11. Crop marks are small horizontal and vertical lines printed at each corner of the image to show the exact boundaries of the image. A commercial printer uses crop marks to trim the piece to its finished size. Registration marks, two of which appear at each corner of an image, are crossed lines over a circle. Registration marks assist the commercial printer in aligning color separation overlays exactly; if misalignment were to occur, the final printed product would display a host of color distortions. When you activate the file information option, Coreldraw prints the color for the page together with the halftone screen angle and frequency on the top and the filename, date, and time on the bottom.

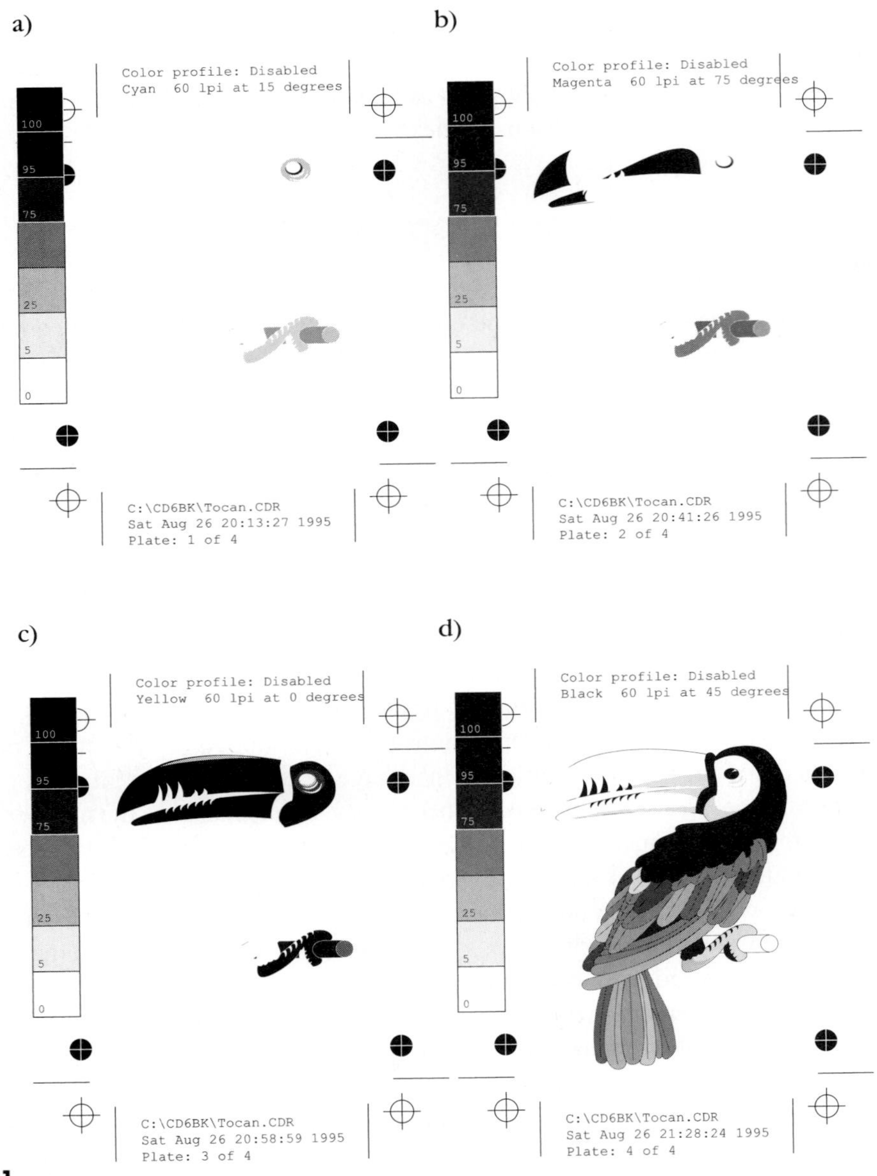

a)

Color profile: Disabled
Cyan 60 lpi at 15 degrees

100
95
75
25
5
0

C:\CD6BK\Tocan.CDR
Sat Aug 26 20:13:27 1995
Plate: 1 of 4

b)

Color profile: Disabled
Magenta 60 lpi at 75 degrees

100
95
75
25
5
0

C:\CD6BK\Tocan.CDR
Sat Aug 26 20:41:26 1995
Plate: 2 of 4

c)

Color profile: Disabled
Yellow 60 lpi at 0 degrees

100
95
75
25
5
0

C:\CD6BK\Tocan.CDR
Sat Aug 26 20:58:59 1995
Plate: 3 of 4

d)

Color profile: Disabled
Black 60 lpi at 45 degrees

100
95
75
25
5
0

C:\CD6BK\Tocan.CDR
Sat Aug 26 21:28:24 1995
Plate: 4 of 4

Process color separations for the toucan

FIGURE 12-11

Two other options are available in the buttons under the preview display box: color calibration bars and densitometer scales. Selecting color calibration bars prints a bar of colors on the page. Densitometer scales are used to check the accuracy of the printer used to print the separations. The densitometer strip on each separation page contains precise tints of the ink color for that page. These can be checked against standard reference values to determine the accuracy and consistency of the printer.

CAUTION: *Just as with file information, you can see crop marks and registration marks from your printer only if you define a custom page size that is smaller than the size of the paper you are using, unless you select the Within page option. The exception to this rule is if you are printing to Linotronic or other imagesetting equipment.*

In the following exercise, you will generate color separations for the toucan on your screen using the Print Separations, Crop Marks, Registration Marks, Calibration Bar, Densitometer Scale, and file information options. If you send files to a PostScript imagesetter, you may perform this exercise as well with the Print to file option activated.

1. With the Tocan.cdr image still on the screen, turn on Preview Selected Only in the View menu. Select the image and, from the Arrange menu, choose Ungroup. Click in any white area to deselect the ungrouped object. Then, select various objects in turn, pressing F9 to see just that object on the preview screen, magnifying portions of the image if necessary for more accurate selection. When you select a color object, open the Uniform Fill dialog box and check the process color values that have been specified.
2. After you have observed the fill colors of various objects, choose Select All from the Edit menu and then Group from the Arrange menu to regroup the bird. Then select the Print command in the File menu. When the Print dialog box appears, click on Options and the Separations tab. Finally, activate the Print separations option.
3. Click on those buttons that are not already on, among the first six under the preview display box, to print file information, page number, crop marks, registrations marks, color calibration bars, and densitometer scales. Your dialog box should now look like Figure 12-12.

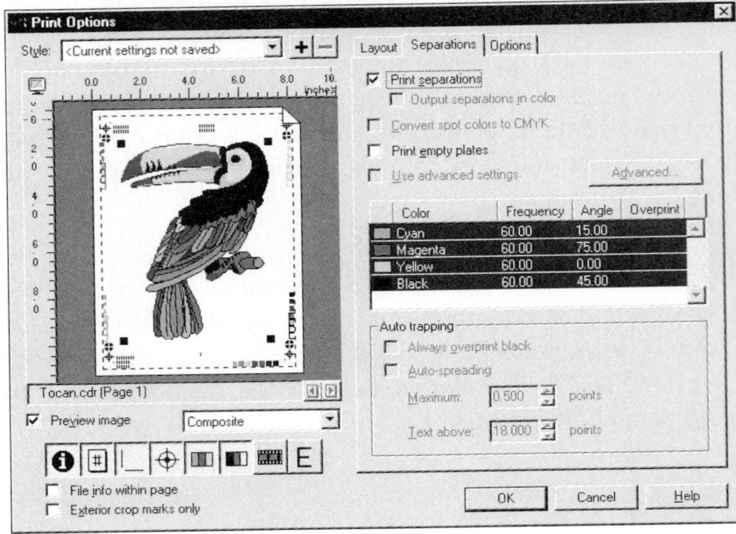

Print Options dialog box with the Separations tab active

FIGURE 12-12

In the Separations tab is a list box containing the names of the four process colors. (If you were preparing to print an image using the spot color method, you would see specific color names here instead.) By default, all of the colors are selected and a separate sheet will print for each of them. You can deselect any or all of them by clicking on the color and then reselect them by clicking on the color again. For this exercise, leave all of the colors selected. For future reference, you can choose to print separations for either one color or a few colors at a time. To do so, just click on the color or colors in the list box that you do not want printed.

Above the Colors list box are five check boxes: Print separations, Output separations in color, Convert spot colors to CMYK, Print empty plates, and Use advanced settings. If you have a color printer, you can select Output separations in color to print your separations in color. Convert spot colors to CMYK converts spot colors in your drawing to CMYK values. When the output for your drawing is to be process color, you should use only CMYK colors. Print empty plates prints a page for a particular color even if it is blank. Use advanced settings, which is only available with a PostScript printer, to specify custom halftone screen angles and line frequencies in the Advanced Separations Settings dialog box, shown in Figure 12-13 and opened by clicking on the Advanced button.

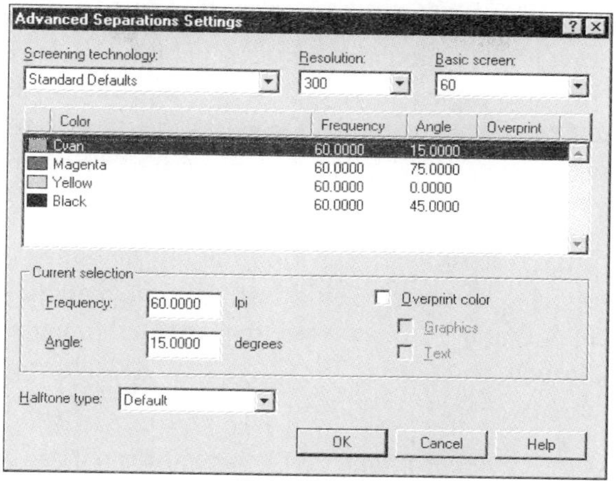

Advanced Separations Settings dialog box

FIGURE 12-13

Below the Colors list box in the Separations tab are two check boxes related to Auto trapping. Trapping is the process of adjusting colors that print on top of each other. Normally, when objects with a fill overlap, the bottom object is knocked out. This means that the part of the object being overlapped doesn't print, which prevents colors from interfering with each other when printed. When one of any two overlapping objects has a black value of 95% or higher, checking Always overprint black makes that object print without a knockout of the object beneath it. Auto-spreading is used to minimize registration errors that can occur during printing. These errors show up as white spaces around colored objects. To minimize this problem, the lighter object is made larger or spread. The overlap created makes press registration less critical. When the lighter object is on top, it is made larger; this is called a spread. When the lighter object is on the bottom, the knockout is made smaller; this is a choke. Trapping can become very complicated in any but simple graphics.

In the Advanced Screening dialog box, there are screen angles and frequency values for each of the colors you are printing. Do not alter these values unless you are very experienced in color printing and know exactly what you are doing. These angles and frequencies are preset to ensure the best possible color alignment and registration.

12

IP: *When sending output to a service bureau, inquire whether your screen settings should be adjusted for a specific imagesetter.*

1. Click on OK to save the Separations settings and exit the dialog box; then click on OK once more. If you are printing directly to your own printer, Coreldraw now begins printing the separations. In several minutes, four sheets of paper appear. The first shows the color values for cyan, the second for magenta, the third for yellow, and the fourth for black. As shown in Figure 12-12, each sheet also contains crop marks, registration marks, filename and date information, and color and screen information.
2. If you chose to print to a file, the Print to File dialog box appears after you have exited the Options dialog box and clicked on OK in the Print dialog box. When you are prompted to name the output file, type **colorsep**, and select OK; Coreldraw adds the extension .PRN automatically.
3. Leave the Tocan.cdr image on the screen for the next exercise.

CAUTION: *If you fill objects with any PostScript halftone screen pattern other than the default pattern, your custom settings will have no effect when you print color separations for the objects, because Coreldraw uses the halftone screen function to calculate color separation angles. This limitation applies only to the objects for which you print color separations. If you require separations for only a few objects, you are free to assign PostScript halftone screen patterns to any remaining objects. If you assign non-default PostScript halftone screens to objects for which you must print color separations, your screen assignments have no effect.*

Keep in mind that you can combine any number of options when you specify color separations. For example, you can tile separations for an oversize image, include file information, make selected objects fit a custom page size exactly, or scale the selected image for printing. If you are sure that the current image is in your final version, you can also print it in film negative format, as you will do in the next section.

Creating an .EPS File

If you take your work to a service bureau, they may request an .EPS file. The normal Coreldraw print file is a .PRN file, so you must use the Export command to create an .EPS file. Use the following instructions to do that:

1. With the object, like the toucan, that you want to print on the screen, choose Export from the File menu to open the Export dialog box.
2. Type the filename in the File name text box, and in the Save as type drop-down list box, select Encapsulated PostScript (EPS), like this:

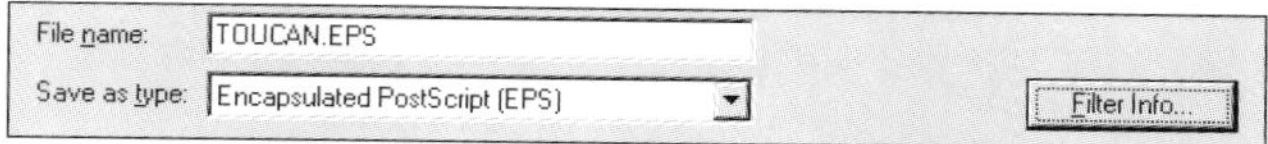

3. Click on Export, and the EPS Export dialog box will open. Under most circumstances you want to accept the defaults. Click on OK to actually write the file on disk.

The one drawback to using this kind of file for output is that you have none of the benefit of any of the features of the Print Options dialog box. You cannot get color separations or any of the printer's marks or any special sizing or scaling.

Film Negative Format

In commercial black and white or color printing, the transfer of the image or of color separations to film negatives is one of the last steps to occur before the printing plates are made. Think of the difference between a snapshot and the negative from which it was produced: colors in the negative appear inverted and backward. You can do the same thing in Coreldraw when you activate the right two buttons under the preview display box in the Print Options dialog box. The button second from the right (see Table 12-1 earlier in this chapter) creates a negative image in which white portions of the original image fill with black and dark areas in the original image become light. The rightmost button flips the image horizontally, including the file information and registration marks. This flipping of the image allows the printer to place the emulsion side of the film down during the plate-making process.

Creating a negative and flipped image can save you money, but only if you are certain that the color separations in the image (if any) are in final form and will not need any further color correction or screen-angle adjustments. If you intend to send a film negative file to a service bureau for output on a high-resolution imagesetter, ask the bureau management whether they can produce your file in film negative format automatically. Many imagesetters can print your color separation file as a film negative just by flipping a switch. This might be preferable if your aim is to achieve a higher output resolution than that provided by your own 300 or 600-dpi laser printer.

In the following exercise, you will print one color separation screen for the Tocan.cdr file in film negative format. You can print this screen directly onto paper or create a file to send to a service bureau. Steps are provided so that you can print the film negative format to your printer and to a file.

1. With the Tocan.cdr file open, click on the Print command in the File menu. (If you printed to a file in the previous exercise and want to do that again, make sure that the Print to File option is still active.)
2. Open the Print Options dialog box, click on the Separations tab and make sure that the print options that you used in the previous exercise—Print separations and the file information, crop marks, registration marks, color calibration bars, and densitometer scale buttons—are still active. Then, click on the print negative and emulsion side down buttons.
3. You do not need to print out all four color separation sheets to see how the Print Negative option works, so click on the Cyan, Magenta, and Yellow bars to turn them off, leaving only the Black to print. Click on OK to exit the Print Options dialog box and click on OK once more to begin printing.

If you are printing directly to your printer, the color separation now begins to print. In a few moments, the color separation sheet for black appears in film negative format, as shown in Figure 12-14. The image in the figure shows only the graphic and its file information, but your output sheet is covered with toner all the way to the edges of the printable page area. If you elected to print to a file, the Print to File dialog box appears, prompting you to enter a filename.

4. If you are printing to a file, type **neg-blk** in the File Name text box and then click on OK to generate your file. When you finish printing, leave the image on the screen.

You need not limit yourself to printing in film negative format when you are working with a spot or process color image. You can also use this printing option with black-and-white images.

Color separation sheet for black printed in film negative format

FIGURE 12-14

Fountain Fill Steps

You can use the Options tab of the Print Options dialog box to control the number of steps used to create a fountain fill on both PostScript and non-PostScript printers. The steps are numbered from 2 through 2,000 or higher, depending on your printer. You may want to change the number of fountain steps for either of two reasons: to increase the smoothness of the fill and get rid of banding or to increase the speed of printing. You increase the number of steps to increase the smoothness of the fill, and you decrease the number of steps to speed up printing. The "normal" number of fountain steps depends on the resolution of your printer. For a 300-dpi laser printer, the normal value is 64, while for a 600-dpi laser printer or a 1,270-dpi imagesetter it is 128. A value below 25, while fast to print, produces obvious banding. On the other end, at around 100 for a 300-dpi laser printer, you can add fountain steps without any gain in the smoothness of the image, but with a decided increase in print time.

IP: *Try out a series of values for fountain fill steps to see which are correct for your output device. Low-resolution (300 dpi) printers support only a limited number of steps.*

Flatness Setting for PostScript

The Set flatness to setting in the PostScript Preferences of the Options tab in the Print Options dialog box, which is active only for PostScript printers, allows you to reduce the complexity of the curves in a drawing and thereby improve the likelihood of being able to print the drawing and also reduce the printing time. As you increase the Set flatness to setting, curves become less smooth with more straight ("flat") segments and, therefore, less attractive in some applications.

Level 1 PostScript printers have upper limits on the number of curve segments they can handle, and they check for this limit. When a print image exceeds this limit, the image won't be printed. The normal Flatness setting is 1. If you are having problems printing a complex image, increase the Flatness setting in increments of 3 or 4 until you can print. By about 10, the curves are obviously less smooth. Selecting Auto increase flatness increases the flatness value by 2 until the object prints or the flatness value exceeds the starting value by 10. You can choose values from 0.2 to 100. Settings below 1 increase the curvature (decrease the flatness).

Screen Frequency for PostScript

The default screen frequency can be selected for a halftone screen in the PostScript Options dialog box. As you may recall from Chapter 7, you can access this dialog box whenever you assign a spot color to an outline or object fill. The frequency of the default screen pattern determines how fine the halftone resolution will appear on the printed page. Each type of PostScript printer has a default screen frequency, with the most common being 60 lines per inch for 300-dpi printers and 90 to 200 lines per inch for high-resolution imagesetters. The Default setting for Screen frequency in the Options tab of the Print Options dialog box is based on your printer with a 300-dpi printer having a screen frequency of 60. In most cases, it is best to let the printer you are using determine the screen frequency and therefore use the Default setting.

You can override the Default setting, however, by clicking on the down arrow on the right and either selecting the desired value from the drop-down list or entering the desired value. Thereafter, all of the objects in your image will have the custom screen frequency. The most common reasons for altering this value are as follows.

- You want to create special effects, such as the fill patterns, that result from altering the halftone screen settings, as discussed in Chapter 7.

- You experience visible banding effects while printing objects with fountain fills and want the color transitions to occur more smoothly.
- You are sending output files to a service bureau whose imagesetters are capable of variable resolutions and halftone frequencies.

In the first two cases, you would decrease the default screen frequency for the selected printer, while in the third case, you should ask the service bureau what screen frequency is best. If you have a 300-dpi PostScript printer, perform the following brief exercise to compare how reducing the default screen frequency alters the appearance of your output.

1. With the Tocan.cdr image open, click on the Print command in the File menu. The Print dialog box appears.
2. Open the Print Options dialog box and make sure that the Print separations option is activated in the Separations tab. Click on Cyan, Magenta, and Yellow to turn them off, and then click on Use advanced settings and on the Advanced button to open the Advanced Separations Settings dialog box you saw in Figure 12-13.
3. Change the value in the Black Frequency numeric entry box to 30 lpi (lines per inch). This setting will cause only the color separation for the color black to print at a different screen frequency.
4. Click on OK to exit the Advanced Separations Settings dialog box and click on OK again to exit the Print Options dialog box. Click on OK one more time to begin printing. After a few moments, the color separation sheet appears. If you compare this output sheet with the one produced in the "Color Separations, Crop Marks, and Registration Marks" section, you will not notice a big difference, but if you look closely you will see that the dot pattern of the 30-lines-per-inch screen printout appears coarser.
5. Select New from the File menu to clear the screen of the Tocan.cdr file. Do not save any changes to the image.

If you alter the default screen frequency in order to proof an image, be sure to change the frequency back to Default before sending the final output file to a service bureau. Otherwise, your image will not appear to have a much higher resolution than what your printer could offer.

OTE: *If you assign custom PostScript halftone screen patterns to an object while drawing, any changes you make to the default screen frequency at printing time will have no effect on the screen frequency of that object.*

Creating Special Effects

13

The Effects menu is used to produce dramatic effects in your work. In this chapter, you will explore the Coreldraw special effects found on the Effects menu. For instance, one special effect is the Add Perspective feature. It allows you to create depth in text or graphics by stretching the borders of an object. The object seems to fade away into the distance. You can create a simple 3-D effect or a more complex version, such as that seen here:

FADING AWAY

With the Envelope feature, you can cause text within the envelope to conform to any shape you make the envelope. In Coreldraw an *envelope* is a box that surrounds text or graphics. You can pull the envelope in different directions, distorting the shape as you might with putty. Any object within the envelope will follow the shape of the envelope, as seen here:

HAVE THAT BLOATED FEELING?

Another special effect is the Blend feature, which allows you to blend one object into another, as shown here:

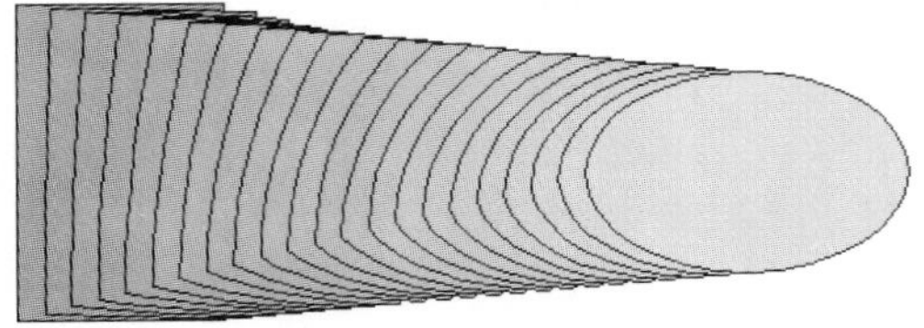

You define the beginning and ending objects, and Coreldraw fills in the blend steps.

The Extrude feature gives depth to objects. An example of an extruded object is shown here:

Contour allows you to create a blended type of effect with a single graphic or text object. You can display this effect inside or outside an object, or centered, as shown here:

Another feature in the Effects menu is PowerLine. This feature allows you to draw a line of varying width and darkness. It differs from the Pencil tool in that the object created with PowerLine is a graphic having its own fill, outline, and nib attributes. An example is shown here (this was created from the letter "H"):

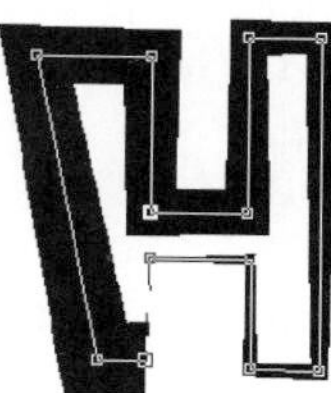

A Lens feature is used to simulate placing a lens over an object, with the lens acting as a transparent window, a magnifier, a color filter (by filtering, adding, or inverting colors), a brightener, or other special effect. An example of a magnifier lens is shown here:

The Bitmap Color Mask allows you to hide or show colors in an imported bitmap. When you hide a color, that area of the bitmap becomes transparent so objects behind it become visible.

The final feature in the Effects menu is PowerClip, which allows you to place one object, or group or objects, into another. One object becomes a container and the other the contained item. In this example, a bird was placed in an ellipse:

As you can see, the Effects menu contains many powerful and dramatic drawing effects. You will explore these special effects beginning with the Envelope feature.

Using an Envelope

An envelope is a bounding box with eight handles that surround the text or graphic. You pull the handles to reshape the object within the envelope.

The Envelope roll-up, shown in Figure 13-1, contains the options for applying and editing envelopes.

With the Envelope roll-up, you can add a new envelope to a selected object. You may either apply the first envelope to an object or apply a second envelope over an object shared by the first envelope.

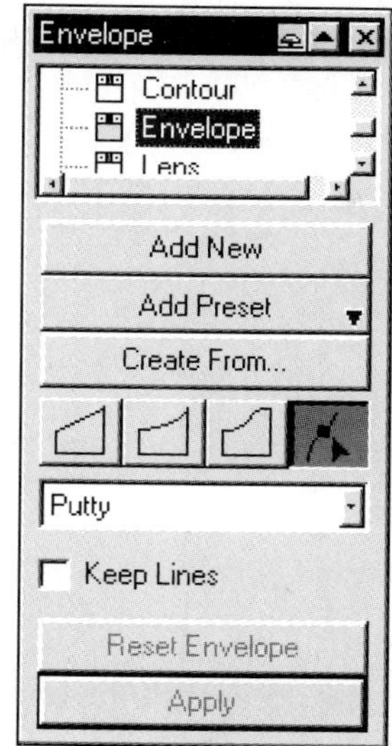

Envelope roll-up

FIGURE 13-1

With the Add Preset button, you can select from a predefined group of envelope shapes, as shown here:

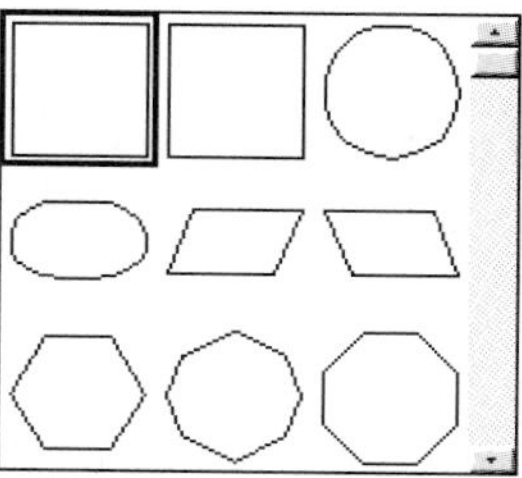

With the Create From button, you can also create an envelope from an existing object to place around a new object. You may select one of four editing modes that determine how the envelope can be reshaped, as shown here:

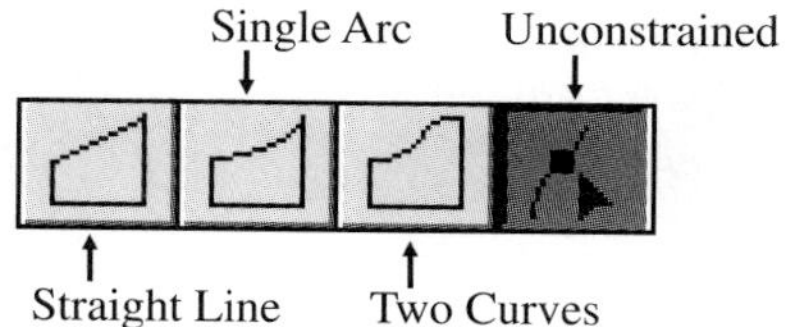

The first three modes allow you to change the shape of a side of the envelope in a specific way. The first one allows you to pull the side in a straight line, the second in a curved line, the third in a line with two curves. The fourth envelope editing mode is unconstrained. It allows you to pull in any direction, and to change a line to a curve.

As you move the handles, the envelope changes shape. When you tell Coreldraw to apply the editing changes, the contents of the envelope are reshaped to conform to the new shape, as you will see shortly.

Below the editing modes is a drop-down list box containing four mapping options. These options control how an object will be fitted to the envelope:

- *Horizontal* Maps the object to fit the horizontal dimensions of the envelope.
- *Original* Maps the object's boundary box (selected handles) to the envelope's shape. It produces an exaggerated effect.
- *Putty* Maps only the corners of the object's boundary box to the envelope's corners.
- *Vertical* Maps the object to fit the vertical dimensions on the envelope.

You will now create and duplicate some text to use for the first three editing modes.

Creating and Duplicating Text

To prepare for the first exercise, you need to create a piece of text and then duplicate it twice.

1. Set the view to Actual Size (1:1). Click on the Text tool and then click on the screen, at about the middle left.
2. Type **Happy Birthday** and select the text by dragging on it. Open the Text toolbar, if it's not displayed, and change the type size to 36 points and the font to Cooper Md BT. With the Pick tool, center the text on the screen. Now you will copy the text twice so that there are three copies, one for each of the first three editing modes.

3. Press CTRL-D twice to duplicate two copies. The three copies will be stacked on top of each other, as shown here:

Now you will move them apart.

1. Select the top copy (the last copy created) and drag it towards the top of the screen. Select the bottom copy and drag it towards the bottom of the screen. Center the text objects horizontally on the screen.
2. Space the three text objects so that you can easily work with each one. Figure 13-2 shows an example of the screen with the three copies rearranged.

Now you are ready to work with the first envelope editing mode.

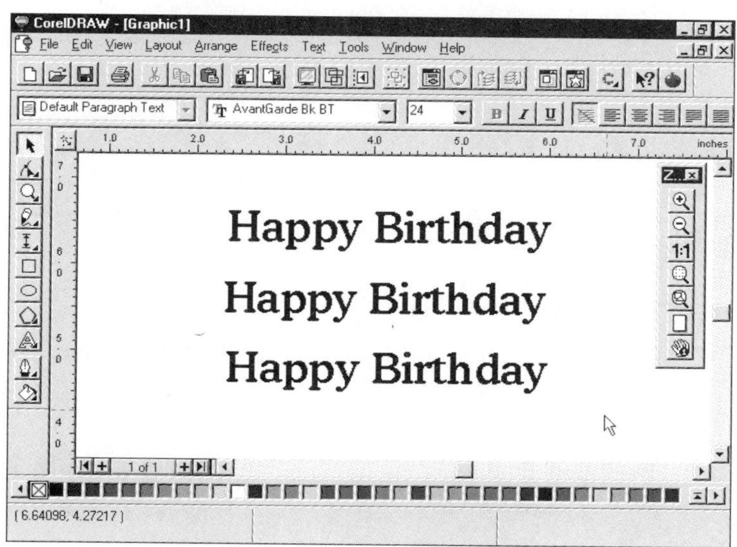

Text to be used for illustrating envelopes

FIGURE 13-2

13

Straight Line Envelope

The Straight Line editing mode allows you to pull envelope handles in a straight line. You can move one control point at a time.

As in all of the first three editing modes, the handles can be moved only in a restricted way: handles located in the center of the sides move left or right; handles located in the top and bottom center move up or down; corner handles move up or down or left or right.

The easiest way to understand the feature is to try it out. Follow these steps.

1. If the top text object is not selected, select it by clicking on it so that the selection box surrounds it.
2. Open the Envelope roll-up from the Effects menu.
3. Choose the first editing mode, Straight Line.

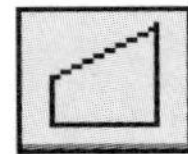

4. Click on Add New.

   The envelope will appear on the screen, surrounding the selected text. You can see the eight handles. Also, the Shape tool is selected, and the pointer turns into a shaping arrow.

5. Pull the top-middle handle up, as shown here:

6. Pull the bottom-center handle up as well.
7. Click on Apply to have the text conform to the envelope, as shown here:

You can see how the text conforms to the new straight line. Next you will see how the Single Arc editing mode differs.

Single Arc Envelope

The Single Arc editing mode allows you to create an arc by pulling the handles up, down, right, or left. Handles can be pulled only one at a time and, as with the Straight Line mode, they can be moved only in a restricted way: handles located in the center of the sides move left or right; handles located in the top and bottom center move up and down; corner handles move up or down or left or right.

Follow these steps to try it out.

1. Click on the Pick tool, then select the second text copy by clicking on it so a selection box surrounds it.
2. From the Envelope roll-up, choose the second option, the Single Arc.

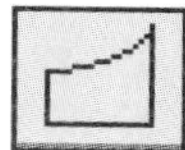

3. Click on Add New.
4. Pull the top-middle handle up.
5. Pull the bottom-middle handle up.
6. Click on Apply.

The text will conform to the Single Arc envelope, as shown here:

You can see how the Straight Line and Single Arc editing modes differ. Now try out the third editing mode.

Two Curves Envelope

The third choice allows you to create two curves by pulling one of the eight handles. You can move only one handle at a time, and the same restrictions apply as in the Straight Line and Single Arc modes.

Follow these steps to try the Two Curves editing mode.

1. Click on the Pick tool and click on the third text object so it is selected.
2. From the Envelope roll-up, choose the third button, Two Curves.

3. Click on Add New. The envelope will surround the third text object.
4. Pull the top-middle handle up. Then pull the bottom-middle handle up.
5. Click on Apply. The text will conform to the Two Curves envelope, as shown here:

You can see how two curves are created out of the line, shaping the text in an entirely different way. These three envelope editing modes have an additional feature that can be used to constrain the shapes.

Using CTRL and SHIFT with Envelopes

You can use CTRL or SHIFT with the three editing modes to produce surprising results. Three effects can take place:

- If you hold down CTRL while you drag on a handle, the opposite handle will move in the same direction.
- If you hold down SHIFT while you drag on a handle, the opposite handle will move in the opposite direction.

- Finally, if you hold both SHIFT and CTRL while dragging a handle, all four corners or sides will move in opposite directions.

You can use these keys with any of the first three Envelope options. Try the CTRL method now with the first text object on your screen. The Two Curves Envelope button should still be selected.

1. Click on the top text image with the Shape tool so that the envelope and handles appear on the screen. Now experiment for a moment.
2. From the Envelope roll-up, click on Add New to get an envelope around the text. Note that it is not the right one. The previous envelope correctly reflected its shape.
3. Click on Reset Envelope to restore the previous envelope.
4. Press CTRL while dragging the top-middle handle down.
5. Click on Apply. The text should be changed, as shown here:

You can see two immediate effects: First, the top and bottom sides move in the same direction. You expected that. Second, and unexpectedly, the lines are *not* being shaped according to the Straight Line edit mode that was earlier applied to this particular text object. Instead, the lines are being shaped according to the Two Curves edit mode, the last mode applied. Whenever you apply a new editing mode to any envelope on the screen, all new edits will be assigned the new mode as well. If you need to change the shape of an object while retaining the original edit mode, simply reselect that mode before making your changes.

Now you will try the SHIFT method with the second text object.

1. Click on the middle text object so that the envelope and handles appear on the screen.
2. From the Envelope roll-up, select the Single Arc option.

3. Press SHIFT while dragging the top-right handle out to the right. The left and right sides will move in opposite directions, as shown here:

4. Click on Apply; you'll see an interesting effect.

The SHIFT-CTRL method is just as easy.

1. Click on the bottom text object to select it.
2. From the Envelope roll-up, select the Two Curves option.
3. Press SHIFT-CTRL while dragging the top-right handle to the right. The top and bottom and both sides all move in opposite directions, as shown here:

4. Click on Apply.

These techniques are particularly useful when you are changing the shape of drawings located in circles or rectangles and you want one or all of the dimensions to be altered to the same degree.

Now you will explore the fourth envelope editing mode.

Unconstrained Envelope

The Unconstrained editing mode is the most dynamic of the four modes. The handles can be moved in any direction, and they contain control points that can be used to

fine-tune and bend the objects even more dynamically. Unlike the first three Envelope options, the Unconstrained mode lets you select several handles and move them as a unit. To experiment with this, first clear the screen of its contents, then follow these steps.

1. Select the Text tool and click on the middle left of the screen.
2. Type **Not Constrained**. Select the text and change the type size to 48 points and the font to Bookman.
3. From the Envelope roll-up, choose the fourth envelope button, Unconstrained.

4. Click on Add New.

   You will see the text object surrounded by the envelope and its handles.
5. Pull the top-middle handle or node up and then the bottom-middle node down, as shown in the following illustration:

You can see that a pair of control points appeared first on the top-middle and then on the bottom-middle nodes. These control points, like Shape tool control points, allow you to alter the shape by exaggerating and bending the curve.

6. Place the pointer on the left control point of the bottom-middle node and pull it down. (To experiment with it, move it down and then back up so that you will see what happens with the handle.)

7. Click on the top-middle node to select it. Place the pointer on the right control point of the top-middle node and pull it up, as shown here:

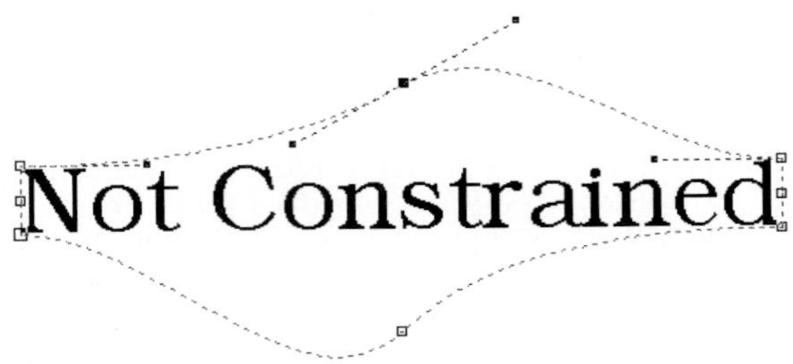

8. Click on Apply. Now, suppose you want the last letters to curve up at the end.
9. Click first on the bottom-middle node, press and hold SHIFT, and then click on the bottom-right node. Release SHIFT. Now you can move all selected nodes together.
10. Drag the bottom-middle node down, as shown here:

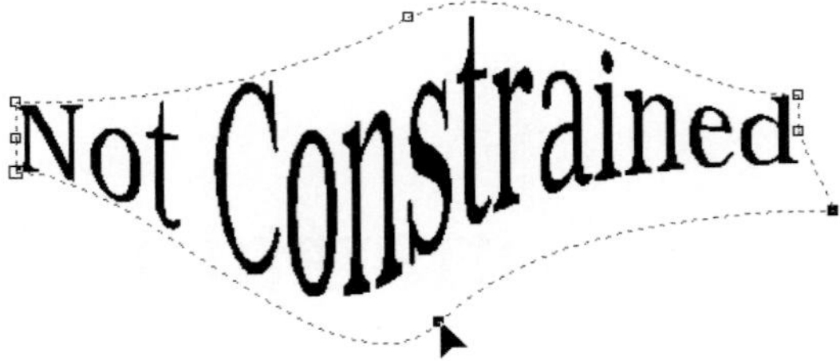

11. Click on Apply for another interesting effect.

One way that you can use the Unconstrained edit mode is to modify text to conform to a shape, for example, text within a circle or oval. First you create the circle, oval, or whatever shape you want as a border and then move the text with its envelope within the border. Next, you manually move the control points of the text so that they correspond with the border shape. Then, if you don't want the border to appear, you can delete it.

Continue to experiment until you are comfortable with the Unconstrained edit mode. Then you can move on to more Envelope features.

Adding a New Envelope

Sometimes you may want to use more than one of the editing modes on an object. Adding a new envelope allows you to do this. You apply an envelope and shape the object with it. Then you add a new envelope, which replaces the first envelope while retaining its shape. With the new envelope, you select a new editing mode and change the shape again. To try this out, clear the screen and follow these steps.

1. Select the Text tool and click on the middle left of the screen.
2. Type **New Envelope**, select the text and set the type size to 48 points, and select the Futura Md BT font.
3. From the Envelope roll-up, attach an envelope by selecting the Straight Line editing mode and then Add New.
4. Click on the top-left handle and drag it up.
5. Click on the bottom-right handle and drag it down, as shown here:

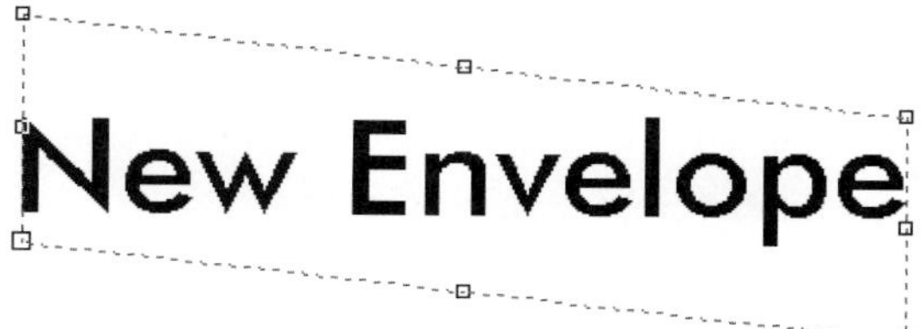

6. Click on Apply.

Now you will apply a new envelope and change the shape using another editing mode on top of the Straight Line editing mode.

1. From the Envelope roll-up, select the Two Curves editing mode. Click on Add New.

2. Now drag the lower-right handle down, as shown here:

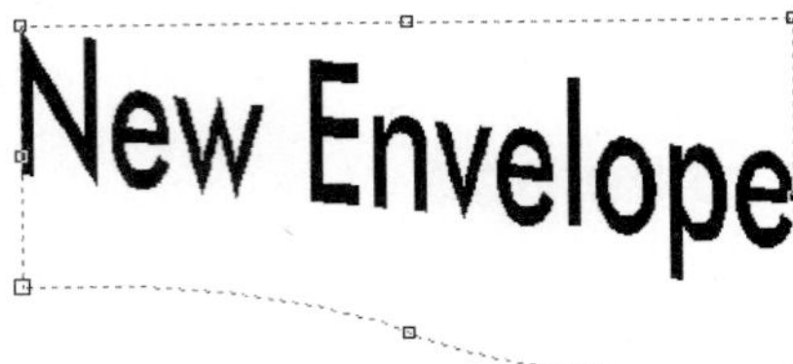

3. Click on Apply.

Notice that the text is limited by the original envelope's shape. The text adopts a new image within the constraints of both envelopes.

IP: *One way that a new envelope can be used is with certain fonts that do not bend or reshape themselves exactly as you want. You can form the basic shape with one of the first three edit modes and then apply the Unconstrained edit mode to fine-tune the text. In this way, you can manually form the letters with more precision than you might get with the font alone.*

4. Remove the previous envelopes by clicking on Clear Transformations from the Arrange menu. If the envelope remains on your screen, selecting the Pick tool will remove it.

Now you can copy an envelope to a new object.

Create From

The Create From command allows you to copy the envelope and its current shape to a new object. The new object does not need its own envelope. However, the copied-from object must be a Single Curve object, having nodes and control points. To try out this feature, you will first create a new object.

1. Click on the Ellipse tool. Draw a circle below the text, using the CTRL key. (If necessary click on No fill in the Color palette.)

2. Specify the Two Curves editing mode and select Add New. Using the Shape tool, pull the top-middle node down and the bottom-middle node up. Click on Apply.
3. Select the text again with the Pick tool.
4. Select Create From in the Envelope roll-up.

   The pointer will turn into a thick arrow. You will move the arrow to the source of the envelope, which is the circle.
5. Move the arrow to the circle, and click on it.
6. Click on Apply.

The destination object—that is, the text—will be reshaped with the new tool to match the ellipse, as shown in Figure 13-3.

Sometimes you might want to start over again. Clearing an envelope allows you to do that.

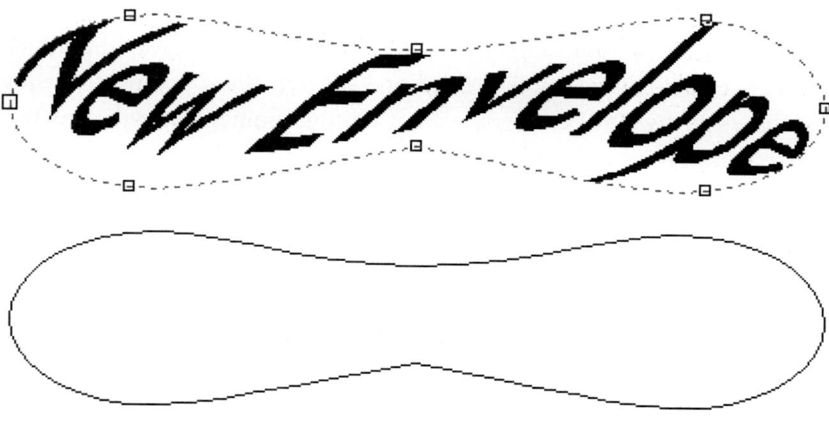

Using Create From to reshape a second object, in this case, text, into an ellipse

FIGURE 13-3

Clearing an Envelope

The Clear Envelope command on the Effects menu (not on the roll-up) removes the current envelope and all shape changes that occurred with it. The Clear Envelope command appears on the Effects menu when you have opened the Envelope roll-up. If you have applied more than one envelope, only the most recent one will be removed.

To clear the last envelope from the current text object, select Clear Envelope from the Effects menu. The drawing will be returned to the previous Straight Line edit mode. However, if you have applied a perspective (perspectives are discussed shortly) to the object after applying the most recent envelope, the perspective must be removed before you can clear the envelope.

NOTE: *The Clear Transformations command, found on the Arrange menu, removes all envelopes, restoring the drawing to its original shape. If you have applied perspectives, they will also be removed and the original shape restored. You use Clear Envelope to remove the last envelope applied and Clear Transformations to remove all envelopes.*

Creating Perspective Effects

Perspective gives an object a sense of depth, as if the object were moving away from you. This effect can be applied from one- or two-point perspective views. Figure 13-4 shows the two kinds of perspective. The one-point perspective, on the top, gives the effect of moving away from you in a straight line. The two-point perspective, on the bottom, distorts the view so that the object is moving away and being twisted in the process.

Using One- or Two-Point Perspective

You apply perspective in much the same way that you change the shape of an envelope. A perspective bounding box with handles surrounds the object. You can drag the handles to shorten or lengthen the object, giving the perspective you want. Follow these steps to try it out.

Examples of one-point and two-point perspectives

FIGURE 13-4

1. Close the Envelope roll-up by clicking on its Close button and then clear the screen. Select Full Page view.
2. If the rulers are not showing, click on Rulers in the View menu to display them. If the zero points are not set to the lower-left corner, pull the ruler's zero points to the lower-left corner of the page. Place a horizontal guideline at 9 inches and a vertical guideline at 1 inch.
3. Select the Text tool and click at the intersection of the guidelines, just below the horizontal guideline.
4. Type **Moving Away**, select the text, set the type size to 60 points and the font to Times New Roman Normal.
5. Select Add Perspective from the Effects menu.

An envelope will surround the text, and the pointer will change to the Shape tool. When you place the pointer on the handles, it will change to a crosshair. You move the handles according to the coordinates, which tell the location of the pointer. The coordinates are shown in the upper-left corner of the Status bar.

You will now change the shape of the text object. To change to one-point perspective, drag the handle either up, down, right, or left (that is, vertically or horizontally). In the following instructions and in the next several exercises, you will see sets of coordinates. These are meant as guidelines and are approximate. The coordinates are in inches and always have the horizontal displacement before the vertical.

1. Place the pointer on the bottom-right handle and drag it vertically, straight down, until the coordinates are approximately 5.7 and 7.5.
2. Drag the bottom-left handle vertically, straight down, until the coordinates are approximately 1.0 and 6.0, as in Figure 13-5. This is an example of a one-point perspective.

Now you will alter the shape to add the two-point perspective. You do this by dragging the handles either toward or away from the center of the object. If you drag toward the object, the shape is pushed under; if you drag away from the object, the shape is pulled out toward you.

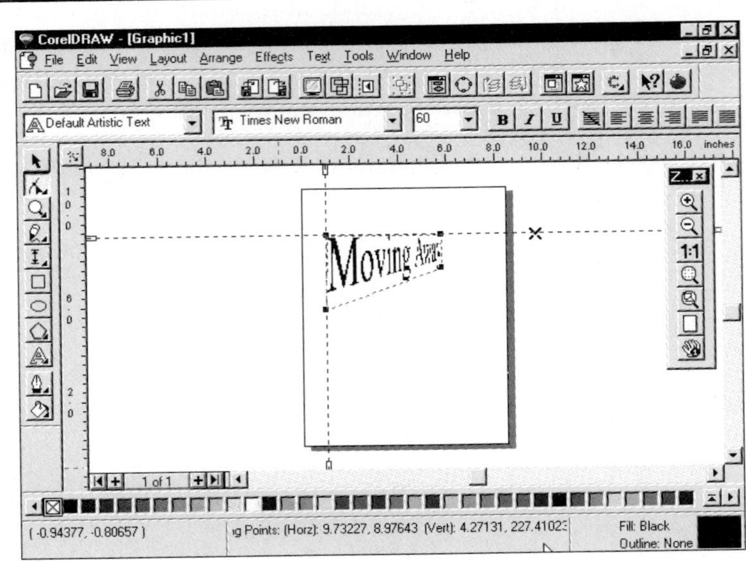

One-point perspective created by dragging the handles straight down

FIGURE 13-5

3. Drag the handles as close as possible to the following coordinates, as shown in Figure 13-6.

   Upper-right corner: 6.9, 9.0
   Lower-right corner: 6.6, 8.0
   Lower-left corner: 2.0, 6.5

You should see two X symbols, known as *vanishing points*, which you will learn about next. One X may be hidden beneath the bottom of the screen. Scroll up to see it.

Using the Vanishing Point

In Figure 13-6, just off the page on the right, is the horizontal vanishing point. On the bottom of the page is the vertical vanishing point. Each of these points is marked with an X.

You can change the perspective by moving the vanishing point itself. By moving the vanishing point toward the object, the edge closest to the point becomes shorter; the edge becomes longer when the point is moved away from the edge.

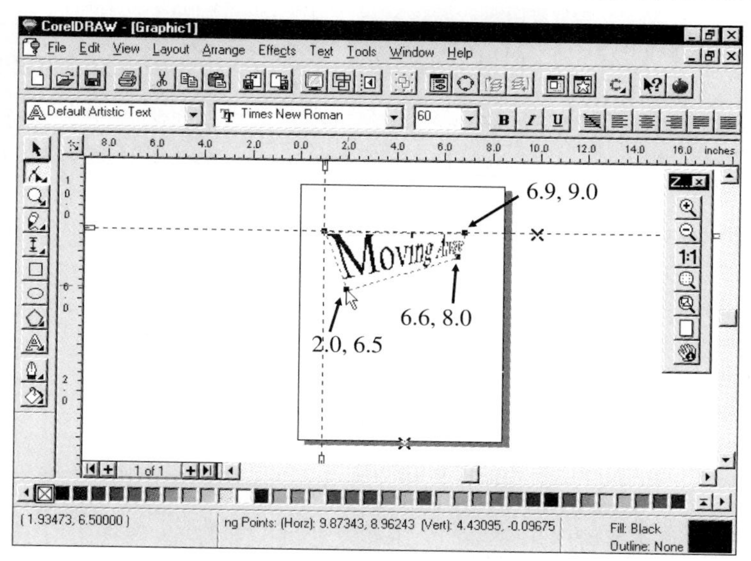

Two-point perspective created by dragging the handles diagonally toward or away from the center of the object

FIGURE 13-6

When you move the vanishing point parallel to the object, the far side will remain stationary, while the side nearest the point moves in the direction you drag the vanishing point.

Take a moment now to play with the vanishing point. When you are satisfied, you can explore some of the other perspective features. Before proceeding to the next section, restore the vanishing points to their original locations.

Adding a New Perspective

You can add a new perspective to an object on top of one that already exists. This allows you to change the perspective, within the limits of the perspective already applied. To see how this is done, follow these steps.

1. Select Add Perspective from the Effects menu. A new, second bounding box will be applied to the object. Now you will change the perspective again.
2. Drag the handles to the following coordinates, or close to them, as shown in Figure 13-7.

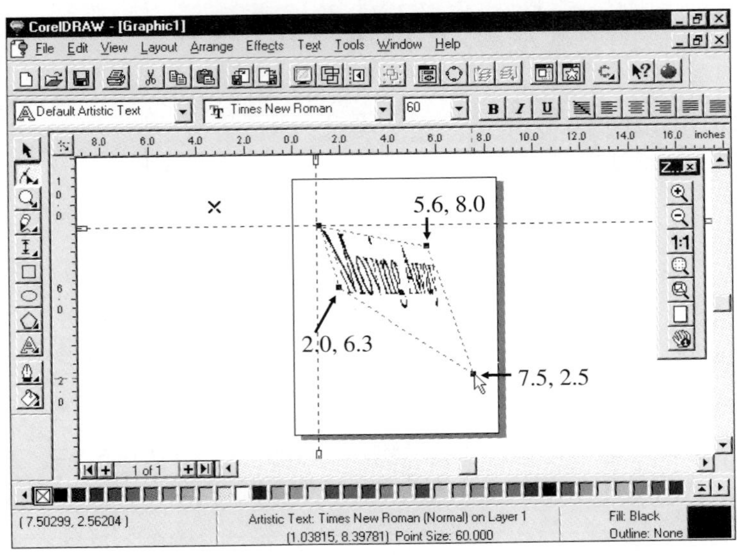

Changing the shape with Add New Perspective

FIGURE 13-7

Upper-right handle: 5.6, 8.0
Lower-left handle: 2.0, 6.3
Lower-right handle: 7.5, 2.5

Now you will apply this perspective to a new object.

Copy Perspective From

When you select the Copy Perspective From command, you use the shape of one object to change the perspective of another one. First, you will create a form to which the perspective will be applied.

1. Select the Ellipse tool and draw a perfect circle (by holding down CTRL) under the text object.
2. From the Copy command on the Effects menu, select Perspective From on the flyout. The thick arrow will appear.
3. Move the tip of the arrow to the outline of the text object and click on it. The circle will be redrawn with the new perspective.
4. Use the Pick tool to drag the circle over the text object. (It doesn't matter if the reshaped circle isn't the same size as the text.)
5. Click on No fill (the X) on the Fill flyout if necessary.

The result should look like Figure 13-8. (It may differ because of the work you did with the vanishing point.)

Clearing a Perspective

Clear Perspective, similar to Clear Envelope, removes the most recent perspective applied to an object. The Clear Perspective option appears when you have chosen Add Perspective. If you've applied more than one perspective, only the last one is removed.

If you've applied an envelope over a perspective, you must first remove the envelope before the perspective can be removed. Before you remove the envelope, be sure to duplicate the object in order to retain the shape you have created with the envelope. Then you can restore the shape by using the Copy Envelope From command after the perspective is removed.

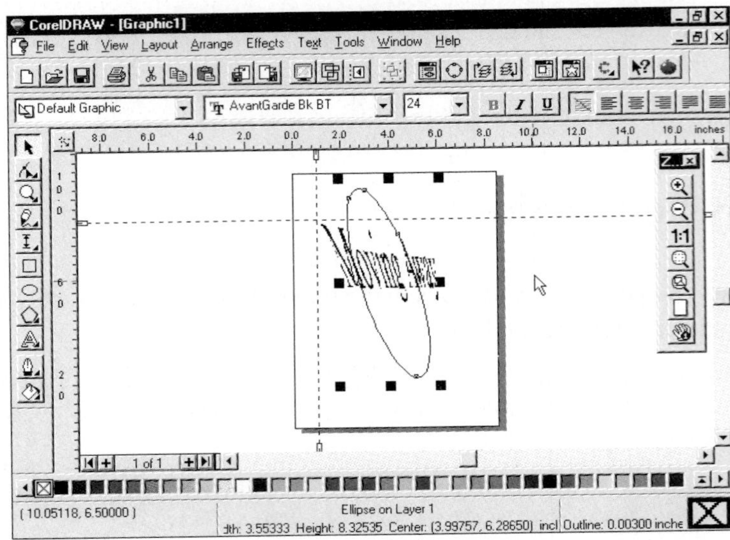

The circle reshaped with a copied perspective

FIGURE 13-8

Notice that Clear Transformations in the Arrange menu will clear all perspectives and envelopes from an object at once. This is used when you want to restore an object to its original shape.

Now remove the perspective from the current object by following these steps.

1. Select the text and ellipse with the Pick tool.
2. Select Clear Perspective from the Effects menu. The shape will be changed.
3. Select Clear Transformations from the Arrange menu. See the change again.
4. Clear the screen by deleting all the objects, then remove the guidelines by dragging them back to the rulers.

Blending Objects

The Blend command causes one object to be blended into another by a number of connecting images. For example, you can turn a square into a circle with 20

intermediate images. You can also use this feature to create highlights and airbrush effects. The images can be of different colors, line weights, fills, and so on.

Before the objects are blended, you must fill them and place them where you want them on the screen. And, of course, first you must create the objects to be blended.

1. Set the magnification to Actual Size (1:1). Select the Text tool and click on the upper-left area of the screen.
2. Type **Happy**, select the text by dragging on it, and set the type size to 48 points and the font to Revue BT, Normal.
3. While the text object is still selected, click on the yellow box in the palette at the bottom of your screen as the fill for the word "Happy."
4. With the text still selected, click on the lower-center area of the screen.
5. Type **Birthday**, select the text by dragging on it, and set the type size to 72 points and the font to Revue BT.
6. Click on navy blue in the palette at the bottom of your screen for the word "Birthday."
7. Move both objects where you can see them on the screen: "Happy" in the upper-left corner, and "Birthday" in the lower-right corner.

Now you are ready to blend the two objects.

Blending Two Objects

Blending is done with the Blend roll-up. To blend the objects, you must first select the two objects. Then you simply open the Blend roll-up, tell Coreldraw how many intermediate steps you want created between the two objects, and click on Apply. A new object will be created for each step you specify.

1. From the Edit menu, choose Select All. You must be careful that both objects are selected. If they are not, you will not be able to use the Blend command.
2. When both objects are selected, select Blend from the Effects menu. The Blend roll-up, shown in Figure 13-9, will appear.

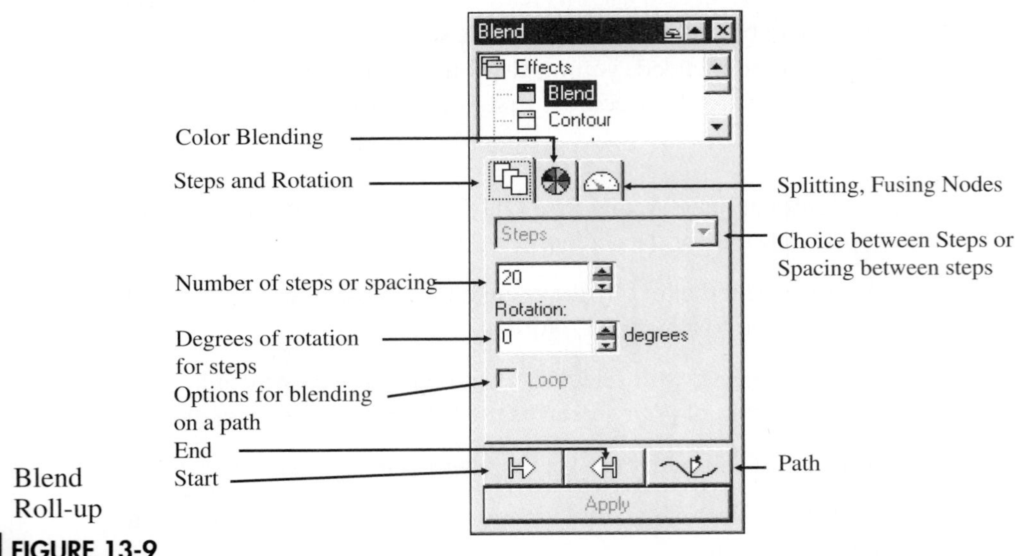

Blend Roll-up

FIGURE 13-9

The menu contains three main modes, represented by the tabs below the Function list box at the top of the roll. The first tab displays the Steps and Rotation controls. The second tab displays color blending properties, and the third tab provides controls for splitting and fusing blends.

The Steps and Rotation controls, on your screen now, are used to control how many steps you want in the blend and what degree of rotation will occur between the two objects. The Loop check box controls where the center of rotation is to be. You'll see its effects shortly. At the bottom of the menu are three controls. The two arrows allow you to select the start (the right-pointing arrow) and end (the left-pointing arrow) objects. The rightmost button is used to manage the blend path.

You now tell Coreldraw the number of intermediate steps between the two objects. The default is 20 steps. You will indicate the degree of rotation and whether to map matching nodes in a minute.

1. Type in **10** steps and accept the 0 degrees of rotation. Click on Apply. You will see the two objects blended on the screen, as in Figure 13-10.

Next you will see what the rotation can do.

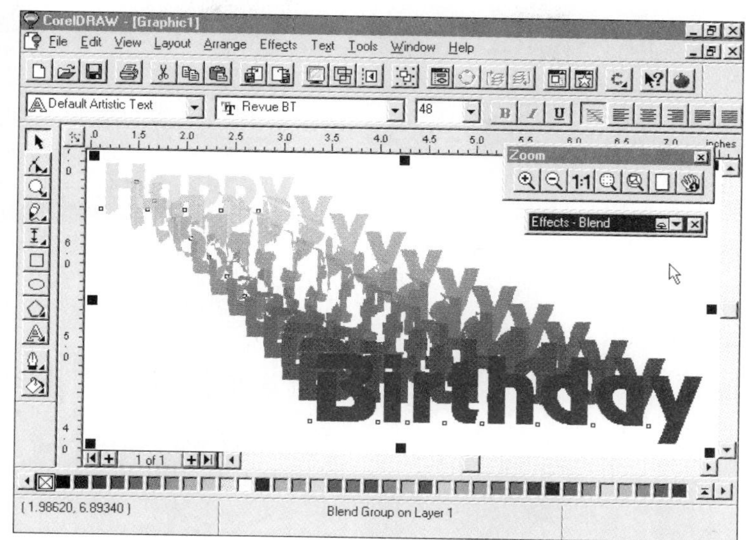

Blending "Happy" into "Birthday" with no rotation

FIGURE 13-10

Rotating the Blended Objects

You can cause the blended objects to be rotated by putting a degree of rotation in the Blend roll-up. You cause the intervening steps to be rotated counterclockwise if a positive number is entered, clockwise if a negative number is entered.

The Blend roll-up allows you to specify the degrees of rotation to be used in the intervening steps. Let's see how this is used.

1. Change the degree of rotation to 95.0 in the Blend roll-up. Click on Loop and click on Apply.

TIP: *Clicking on the Loop option makes the blend rotate around a center point midway between the beginning and the ending objects' centers of rotation. If Loop is not selected, the blend will rotate around the object's own center of rotation. Experiment to see the differences.*

The effects of blending will appear on the screen, as shown in Figure 13-11. Now try out clockwise rotation with these steps.

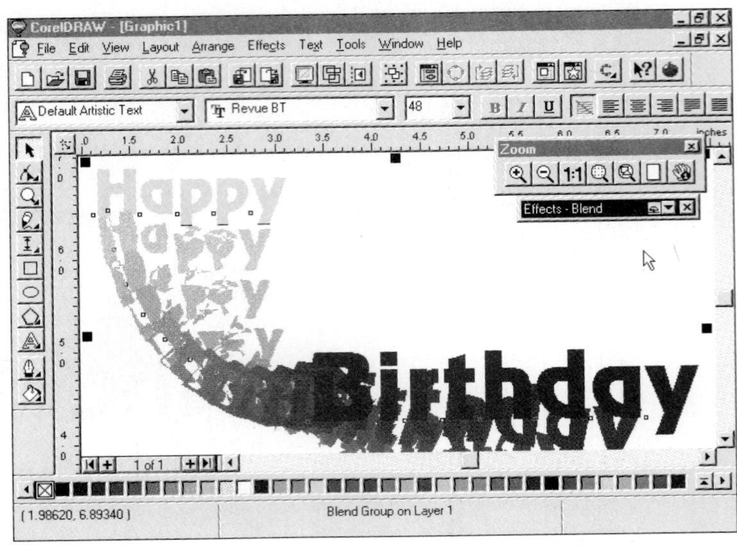

"Happy" blended into "Birthday" with 95 degrees of rotation

FIGURE 13-11

1. In the Blend roll-up, type **–90.0** for the degree of rotation and click on Loop to deselect it. Click on Apply. The results look something like Figure 13-12.
2. To experiment, select Loop and then click on Apply.

One other rotation feature, discussed next, can be used to create interesting effects.

Mapping Matching Nodes

By varying the beginning nodes of both of the objects, you can create some unexpected results. The nodes identify where the blend is to begin and end. You will try two different ways of identifying the nodes.

1. Clear the screen and switch to full page view.
2. Select the Rectangle tool and create four different-sized rectangles on your screen, as in Figure 13-13. Make sure that all four rectangles are unfilled. Click on the X in the lower-left corner of your screen for no fill.

"Happy" and "Birthday" blended with -90 degrees of rotation

FIGURE 13-12

3. Press SPACEBAR for the Pick tool and marquee-select the two rectangles on the left.

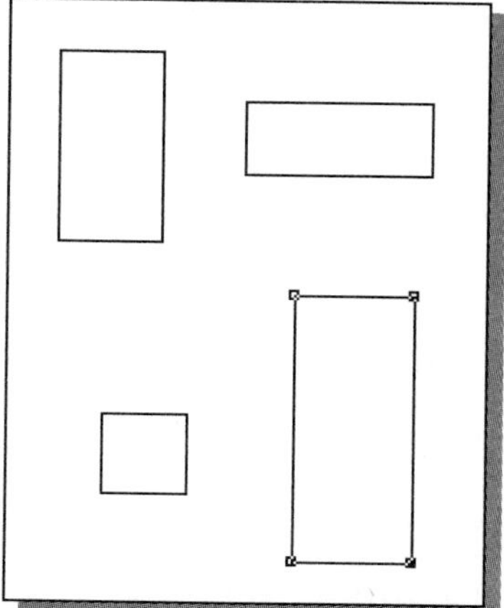

Placement of rectangles on the page

FIGURE 13-13

4. In the Blend roll-up, enter 20 Blend steps and 90 (positive) degrees of rotation, and select Loop. Click on the Splitting and Fusing tab (third tab from the left) and then on the Map Nodes button. When you move the pointer off the roll-up onto the page, it will become a curved arrow and one of the selected objects will have nodes displayed on each corner, as shown here:

   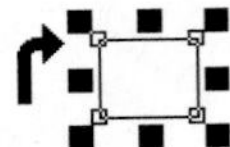

5. Select the upper-left corner node by moving the arrow to that node and clicking on it. The second object's nodes will be displayed.
6. Select its upper-left corner node by moving the arrow to that node and clicking on it.
7. Click on Apply in the Blend roll-up.

   You will now see one result of mapping matching nodes.
8. Marquee-select the second two objects.
9. Click on Map Nodes on the Splitting and Fusing tab in the Blend roll-up.
10. With the arrow, click on the lower-right node of the first object (the one with the corner nodes selected).
11. Click on the upper-left node of the second object and click on Apply in the Blend roll-up. The blend will occur, as in Figure 13-14.

You can continue to experiment with Map Nodes, adding a different degree of rotation if you want to see its effects. When you are finished, you can look at another major feature found on the Effects menu, the Extrude command.

12. Clear the screen and close the Blend roll-up.

Extruding Objects

Extruded objects appear to have a 3-D look. You can use the Extrude feature on text, closed shapes, or open paths. The results can be very dramatic.

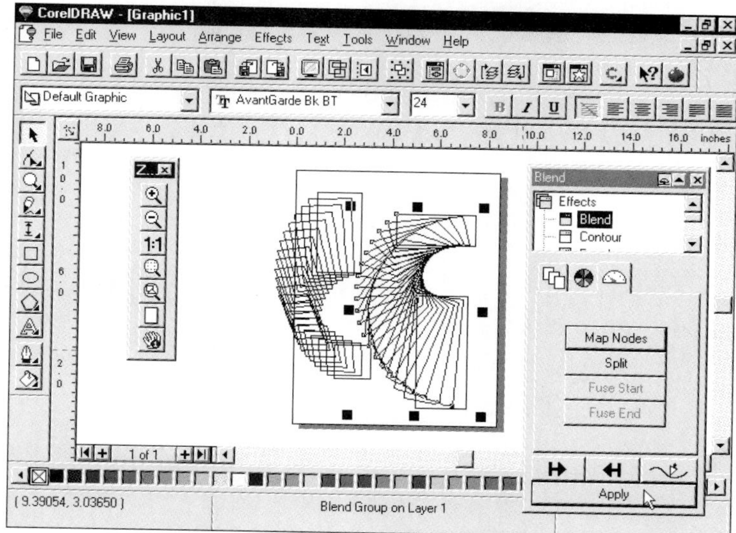

Blends with two types of Map Nodes

FIGURE 13-14

There are three ingredients to the Extrude feature that affect the results: the depth and direction of the extrusion, the spatial alignment of the extruded object, and the shading and coloring of the extruded object. Each of these will be investigated separately. First, create the objects to be extruded with the following steps.

1. Click on the Text tool and click in the upper-left corner of the page.
2. Type **T**, select the letter, then select CentSchbook BT, Normal and enter 120 points for the size.
3. Click on purple from the Color palette on the bottom of the screen. From the Outline Pen flyout, click on the Hairline button.
4. Click on Duplicate from the Edit menu or press CTRL-D to create a copy of the "T." Repeat it to make a second copy.
5. With the Pick tool, select each of the copies and drag one to the upper-right corner of the page, one to the upper-left corner, the other to the lower-left corner.
6. Click on the Freehand tool and draw a wavy line in the lower-right part of the page. Your screen should look something like Figure 13-15.

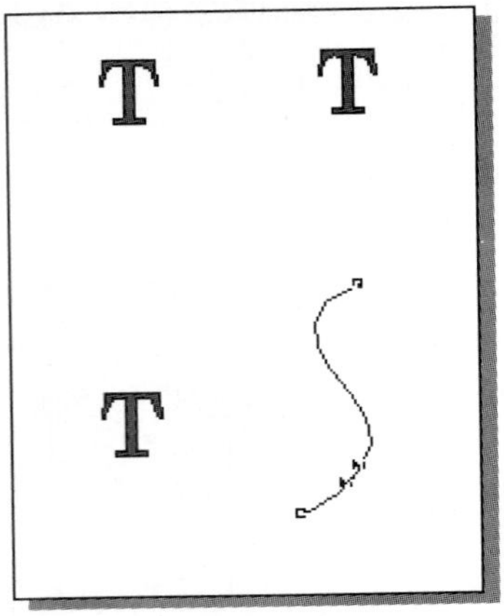

Placement of objects for experimenting with the Extrude command

FIGURE 13-15

Now you are ready to experiment with extruding.

Extrude Roll-up

Extruding is controlled by the Extrude roll-up, shown in Figure 13-16, which you open from the Effects menu.

The Type and Depth mode is one of five modes that the Extrude roll-up can be in. These modes, which are activated by the five tabs on the upper part of the roll-up, perform the following functions:

- Presets provide predefined extrusion properties that you can apply to an object.
- Type and Depth allows you to determine the depth of the extrusion, the location of the vanishing point, whether the vanishing point is in front of or behind the object, and whether the extrusion is in a perspective or orthogonal (parallel) view.
- Rotation allows you to rotate the extruded object in any of three dimensions.
- Light Source allows you to determine the location of the light source and its intensity to provide shading effects.

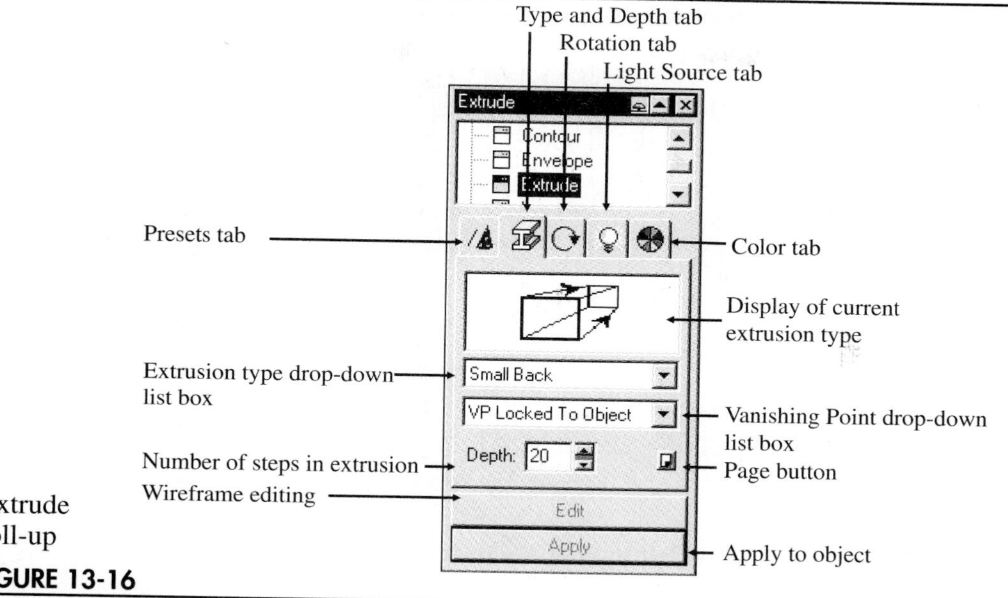

Extrude roll-up

FIGURE 13-16

- Color allows you to determine if the extruded object will use the same coloring as the original object, or whether the extruded portion and its shading should be different (and what those different colors should be).

Selecting these modes significantly changes the options available in the Extrude roll-up, as you will see in the following sections.

Extrusion Presets

The Extrusion Preset mode presents you with a selection of preset extrusions that you can apply to an object. To explore this feature, follow these steps.

1. Select the topmost left "T" with the Pick tool.
2. From the Effects menu, select Extrude if the Extrude roll-up is not already open.
3. Select the Presets tab (the first tab on the left).

The roll-up shown here will be displayed (your display may show a different Preset option):

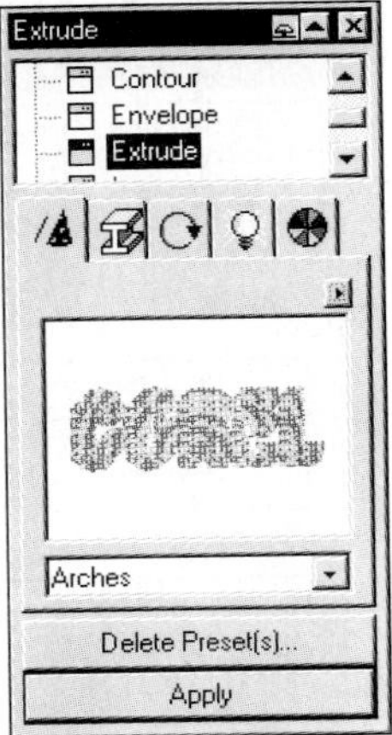

4. Click on the Preset Extrusion drop-down list box and choose Extrude06.
5. Click on Apply. The "T" should look like this:

6. From the Effects menu, choose Clear Extrude.

You may want to experiment some more with the preset extrusions. If you do, clear the effects before continuing with the next extrusion mode.

Type and Depth

Type and Depth is the default mode for the Extrude roll-up—the window automatically opens in this mode. If you are in another mode and want to return to this mode, you can do so by clicking on the Type and Depth tab, the second tab from the left on the Extrude roll-up.

Examine the Extrude roll-up now by following these instructions.

1. With the Pick tool, click on the topmost left "T" to select it.
2. On the Extrude roll-up click on the Type and Depth tab.

Perspective and Parallel Extrusions

You normally see an extrusion in a perspective view—it gets smaller as it extends away from you. Therefore, a perspective-type of extrusion is often what you'll want to use. The alternative extrusion is the Parallel view, or *orthogonal*, meaning that the lines forming the extrusion will be parallel to each other. The choices for extrusion types are shown here:

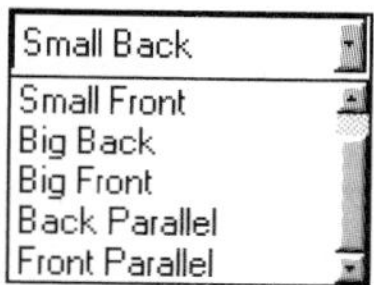

The first four extrusions are perspective types, where you are looking from front to back or back to front. If you select the Back Parallel or Front Parallel type, the extrusion will be parallel. See this for yourself with this exercise.

1. Select Back Parallel type if it is not already selected. Click on Apply in the Extrude roll-up. The wireframe behind the "T" on the right is filled in to form a short extrusion, which does not grow narrower as it extends toward the center of the page—it is in a parallel view with a centered vanishing point, as you can see here:

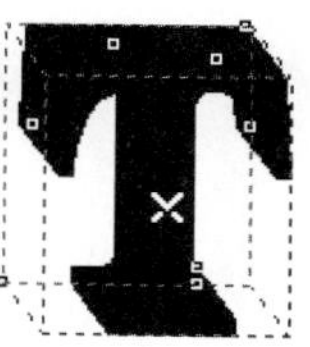

2. Click on the right "T." From the Extrusion type drop-down list box, choose Small Back. Click on Apply. An extrusion is created behind the "T," narrowing as it extends toward the center of the page—it is very obviously in perspective.

3. Click on the black color fill on the Color Palette on the bottom of the screen to clearly distinguish the letter from its extrusion, as shown here:

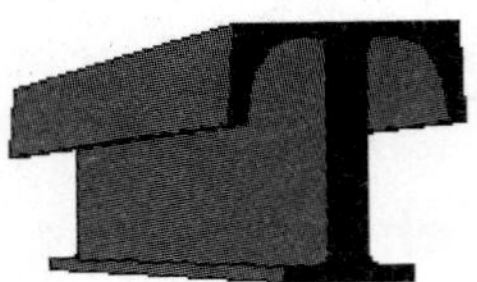

Vanishing Point Options

The vanishing point is represented by a small X, seen when an extrusion is being created. This marks the point to which the extrusion will extend given the current settings. You can use the vanishing point to modify the extrusion by dragging it from one location to another, or by moving the object and assigning the vanishing point a fixed location. The choices on the Vanishing Point options list (on the Type and Depth tab) give you several alternatives for working with vanishing points. The options have these meanings:

- *VP Locked to Object* Locks the vanishing point in position relative to the object. As you move the object, the vanishing point moves with it.
- *VP Locked to Page* Locks the vanishing point in one location on the page. As you move the object, the vanishing point remains locked in place.
- *Copy VP From* Copies a vanishing point from one object for use with another. You will have two vanishing points in one location, each tied to a different object.
- *Shared Vanishing Point* Allows objects in a group to share one vanishing point.

Changing the Depth

The Depth counter is available only if you are working with an extrusion in perspective, and it determines how far toward the vanishing point the extrusion extends. You can think of this counter number as the percentage of the distance between the object and the vanishing point that is occupied by the extrusion. The Depth counter can go from 1 to 99. A value of 99 makes the extrusion extend all the way to the vanishing point, and a value of 1 creates no extrusion. A value of 0 or a negative number is not a valid entry.

Now you will reuse the "T" on the right, keeping the Small Back type.

1. Click on the up arrow of the Depth counter to increase the depth to 70. (You can also drag across the Depth setting and type in **70**.)
2. When the depth is at 70, click on Apply. A new, more elongated extrusion will appear, as shown here:

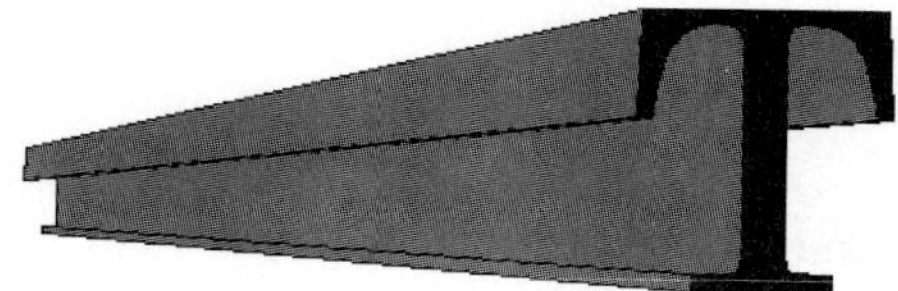

You can also affect the depth and direction of the extrusion by working directly with the vanishing point, as you'll see next.

Moving the Vanishing Point

You can move the vanishing point on the page in two ways: by adjusting the horizontal and vertical counters in the Extrude roll-up, or by clicking on Edit and dragging the X that indicates the vanishing point. Try both techniques.

1. Use the "T" on the right. Set the depth to 40, and keep the extrusion type Small Back.
2. Click on the Page icon beneath and to the right of the Depth numeric entry box to display the Vanishing Point options, as shown here:

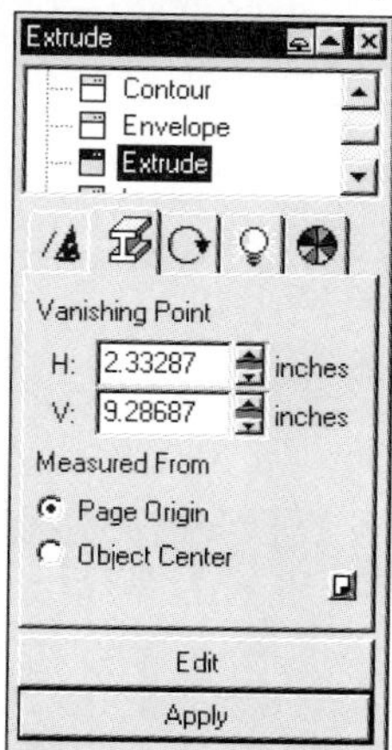

You can set the horizontal and vertical locations by typing an absolute number into the counters. You select how these numbers are to be measured by clicking either the Page Origin or Object Center option.

3. Change the horizontal and vertical counters for the vanishing point so they both have a value of 6.5. You can do this either by clicking on the up arrows or by dragging across the numbers and typing the new value. Keep the Page Origin default and click on Apply. Click on Edit to see the vanishing point.

By moving the vanishing point, you've made the extrusion shift to follow it, as you can see here. If you rotate the vanishing point around the object, the extrusion will also rotate. If you move the vanishing point away from the object, the extrusion will extend out following the vanishing point (although the depth value doesn't change—it is a percentage, so it merely rescales the extrusion).

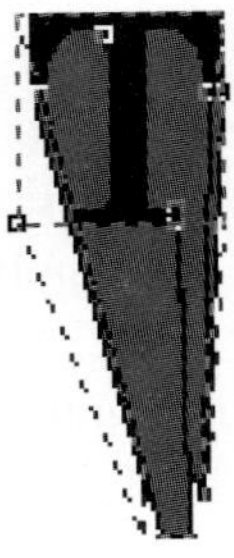

4. Drag the vanishing point to the upper-right corner of the page. (Click on Edit if the vanishing point is not currently displayed.)
5. Click on Apply to complete the extrusion.

Again, the extrusion will follow, as shown here:

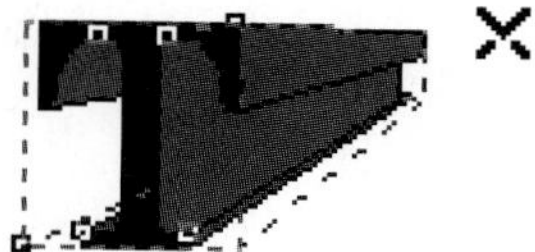

Clearing an Extrusion

If you have an extrusion that you want to remove without getting rid of the original object, you cannot just press DEL, which would get rid of everything, including the object. You must use the Clear Extrude option in the Effects menu.

1. Select the extruded "T" on the right, then select Clear Extrude from the Effects menu. The extrusion is removed, leaving the original selected object.
2. Press DEL to remove that letter and to get ready for the next exercise.
3. Click on the extruded "T" on the left. Press DEL, and the entire object and extrusion are removed from the page.

To prepare for the next exercise on 3-D Rotation, follow these steps.

4. Click on the remaining "T" to select it.
5. Click on the Page button on the Type and Depth tab to return to the Type and Depth options.
6. Select Small Back extrusion type and set the depth to 70. Click on Apply.
7. Click on a black color from the Color palette to distinguish the letter from its extrusion.

Now you are ready to proceed with the next mode.

3-D Rotation

The third mode in which you can place the Extrude roll-up is 3-D Rotation. You change to this mode by clicking on the Rotation tab (the third tab from the left) on the Extrude roll-up. Try that now, and the Extrude roll-up will change to include the 3-D rotator that you see here:

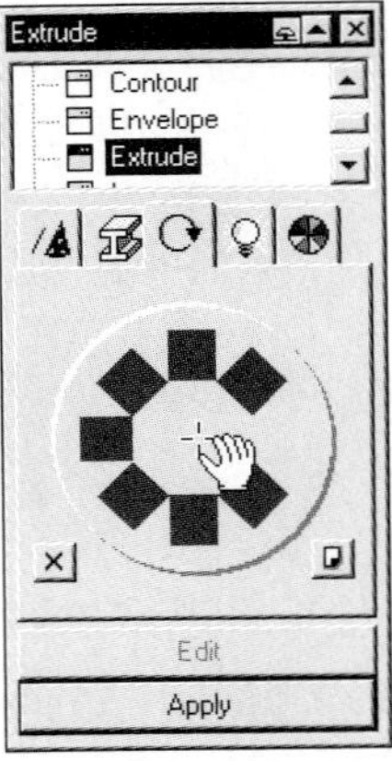

When it approaches the 3-D rotator, the pointer changes to a hand holding a crosshair, and in the center of the roll-up is a graphic of the Corel logo. You set the rotation of the selected object by dragging the pointer, and the Corel logo rotates so you can judge the amount of rotation to apply. Where you place the pointer when you press the mouse button establishes the anchor for the rotation. As you drag the mouse, a yellow line is displayed linking the anchor point to the pointer and showing the angle of rotation. In the lower-left corner of the roll-up is an X button that allows you to clear the current rotation. The 3-D rotation does not change the vanishing point, only the object and its extrusion. Try the rotation tool now with this exercise.

1. Click on the Edit button, then point on the center of the rotation circle and drag up, towards the top of the screen. The Corel logo representing the extrusion will rotate upward—the face of the extrusion moves up, while the other end of the extrusion moves down, as you can see here:

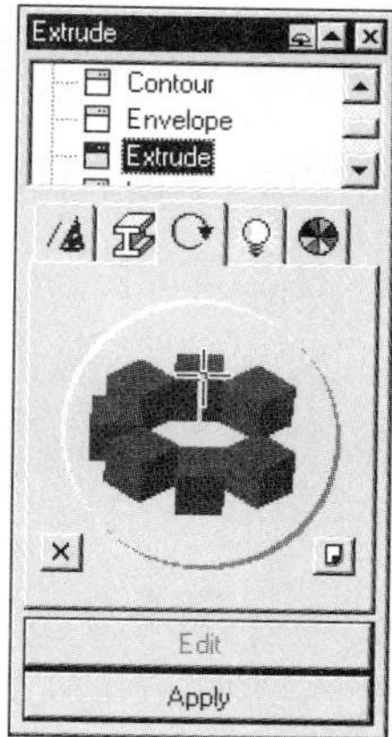

2. Click on Apply to fill in the wireframe and complete the rotation.
3. Click on the X, then click on Apply to remove the rotation and return the extrusion to its original position.
4. Experiment with the Rotation tool to see the effects of rotating the object in various directions. Click on the X after each experiment to return the extrusion to its original position.
5. When you are through, click on X and then Apply.

With the Rotation tool, you can look at the extruded object from literally any angle.

IP: *By clicking on the Page button on the Extrude roll-up you can enter the rotation value directly in the Angle spinner on the second page of the Rotation tab. This allows for finer control over the extrusion.*

Shading and Coloring

You will remember that we originally set the color of the letter "T" to purple. Then, when the extrusion was produced, it was also purple, making the extrusion difficult to see. So you then placed a black fill in the letter so that the extrusion would be seen more clearly.

Altering the shading and coloring can also affect the contrast between the object and the extrusion. See now how you can change this, using the remaining "T" selected.

1. Click on the Color tab (the fifth from the left) to place the Extrude roll-up in coloring mode. The roll-up's appearance will change, as you can see here:

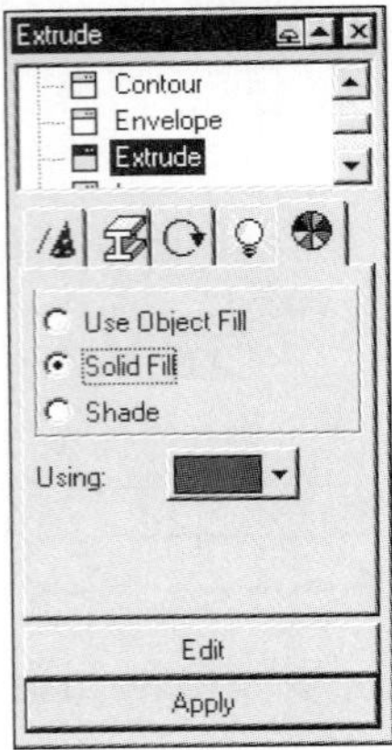

The Use Object Fill option fills the extrusion with the same color as the selected object. Solid Fill allows you to use different fills for the object and the extrusion, and Shade allows you to create a graduated fill. The current coloring scheme is Solid Fill, where the object and the extrusion fills are determined separately. In other words, the object's fill color is not used as the color for the extrusion.

2. Click on Use Object Fill to make the extrusion's color the same as the objects.
3. Click on Apply.

The extruded object now has no clear differentiation, as shown in the following illustration. (Deselect the "T" to see it more clearly by clicking anywhere else on the screen, then select it again for the next step.)

4. Change it back by clicking on Solid Fill and then click on the Using color button. The current Color palette will open. Click on the second gray from the right in the second row, then click on Apply.

This two-color scheme is nice, but you can improve on it with shading. When you select the Shade option, you can specify a range between two colors or shades for the extrusion. You will get a linear fountain fill along the extrusion, with the From color nearest to the original object, and the To color at the vanishing point.

1. Click on Shade to give the extrusion a shaded fill.
2. Click on the From color button and select the same gray you chose above. Then click on the To color button and choose the second gray from the right in the top row of the palette. Click on Apply. The extrusion changes to this:

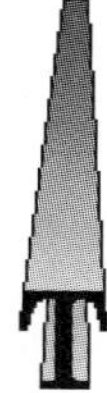

To give your extrusion even more life, you can put a spotlight on it and change the location of that light.

3. Click on the Lighting tab (the fourth button from the left) of the Extrude roll-up. The Extrude roll-up changes once more, this time to include a device for setting up to three light sources (the three light bulb buttons on the left of the roll-up), a display box for placing the light sources, a slider to control intensity, and an On/Off switch for full color ranges:

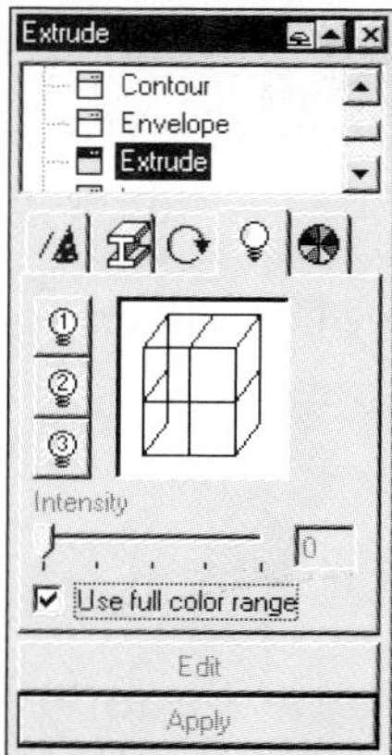

4. Click the first light bulb to turn the first light source on. Then drag the light source (represented by the circle-1) to the upper-left corner of the front surface of the wireframe. Next, drag the Intensity control to about 85.
5. Click on Apply. The extrusion will be redrawn like the following (your extrusion may differ depending on how you set it):

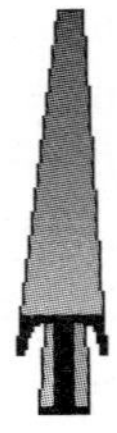

OTE: *The differences between the extruded "T" with and without lighting may appear slight. The shape of the object and the shading applied affect the final appearance of the object.*

Experiment with placing the light source and using multiple light sources. When you are done, you will experiment briefly with how an open path can be used in a creative way with extrusions.

Applying Extrusions to Open Paths

Open paths can be used to create some dramatic effects with extrusions. In this case, you will create a ribbon from your wavy line.

1. Click on the wavy line to select it.
2. Click on the Color tab on the Extrude roll-up. Then click on Shade, if it isn't already selected. Make the From color gray, and the To color black. Click on Apply. Your wavy line will change to a shaded ribbon, like this:

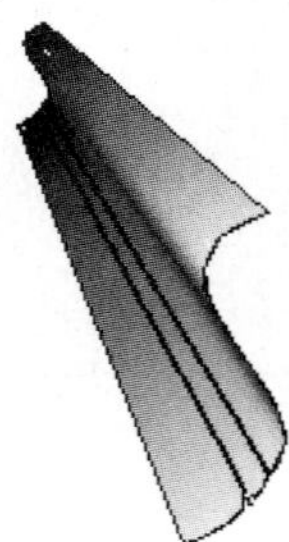

3. Clear the screen and close the Extrude roll-up before continuing.

Now you will work with contours.

Using Contours

Contours add concentric outlines, either inward toward the center of an object or outward away from the edge of it. Contours can be made to look like blending, but for a single object. They cannot be applied to groups of objects, bitmap objects, or OLE objects.

Follow these steps to get an understanding of what contours can do for you.

1. Using the Ellipse tool, create three circles, each filled with black. With the Text tool, type **L**. Select the "L" by dragging on it. Set the "L" to 120 points and Futura Md BT, bold-italic. Your screen should look similar to Figure 13-17.
2. With the Pick tool, select the first circle on the upper left.
3. From the Effects menu select Contour. The Contour tab of the roll-up looks like this:

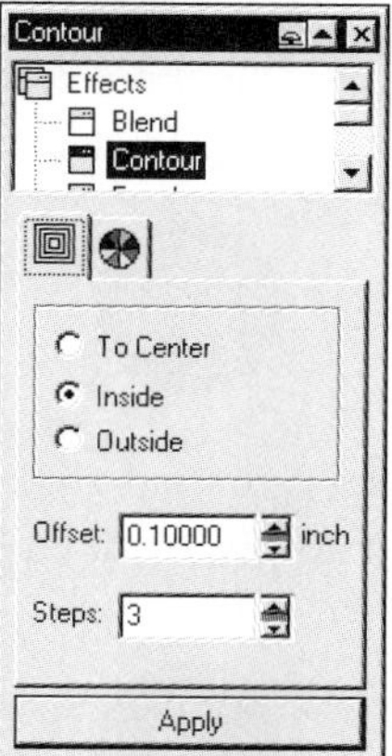

You have a choice of where the contour is to be applied: toward the center of the object, from the edges inward (not necessarily to the center, depending on the number of steps and the Offset), and from the edge of the object outward. Offset is used to define the thickness of each layer of the contour, and Step defines the number of layers you want in the contour. You can define the outline and fill colors or patterns from the Color tab as well.

13

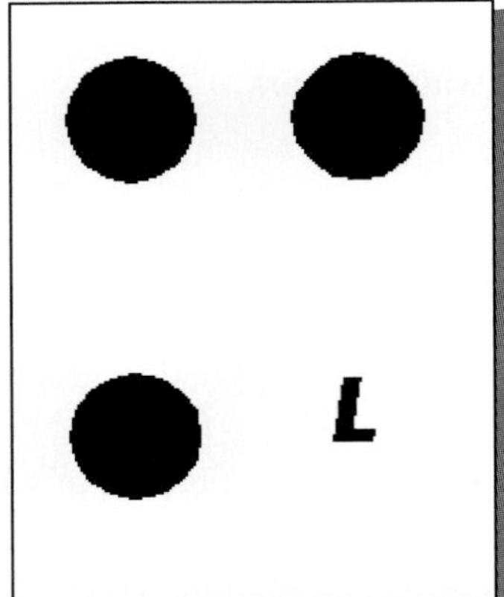

Objects set up to experiment with Contours

FIGURE 13-17

In some of the following illustrations, the object being displayed is not selected (it does not have a bounding box around it) in order to show it more clearly. Your screen will have the object selected.

1. Click on To Center and set Offset to .3 inch. Select the Color tab and, from the Outline Pen flyout, select black. From the Fill flyout, select light blue. Click on Apply. Your selected circle will look like this:

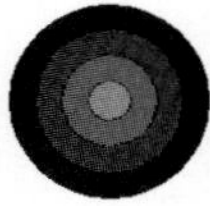

2. Select the next circle to the right and click on Inside. Set Offset to .2 inch, set Step to 3, and click on Apply. Your circle looks like this:

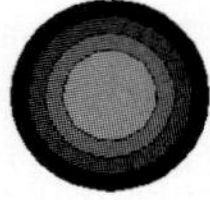

3. Select the third circle, click on Outside, keep Offset at .2 inch, keep Step at 3, and click on Apply.

4. Click on the "L" to select it. Click on Apply to see how the contour setting affects text. Figure 13-18 shows the results.

A fuzzy-edged blend effect is achieved by turning off the Outline Pen. The concentric outlines then blend into each other.

5. On the Outline Pen flyout from the toolbox, click on the X to turn off the outline. The black outlines are removed and the colors blend more readily.

TIP: *To edit an individual contour, first select the contoured object and then select Separate from the Arrange menu. Hold down* CTRL *and click on a contour node. A bounding box surrounds a single contour, and the Status bar refers to it as "Child Curve." You can then edit the contour by resizing, rotating, or changing the fill or outline.*

To prepare for the next section, clear the screen and close the Contour roll-up. Another feature, PowerLine, is discussed next.

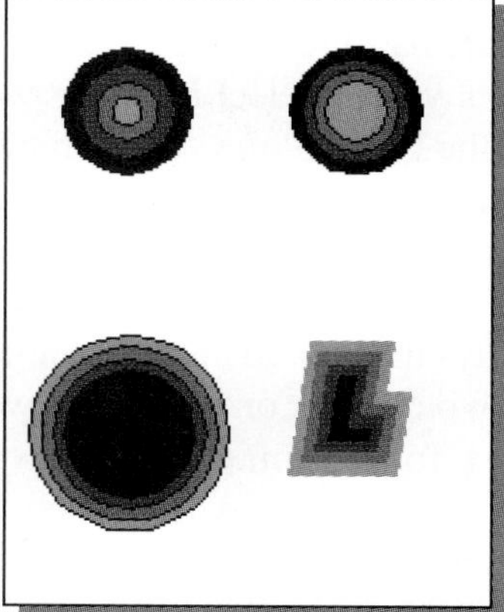

Results of contouring

FIGURE 13-18

Using PowerLines

The PowerLine feature gives you a tool to create graphic lines. The lines resemble those drawn by hand, of varying width and darkness, such as you get with calligraphic pens or paintbrushes. Since the line contains both outline and fill, it can be treated as a graphic. Coreldraw comes with 24 preset PowerLines (including None and Custom), and you can create your own and then save them.

To get the PowerLines, you select PowerLine from the Effects menu. It looks like this with the Preset tab selected:

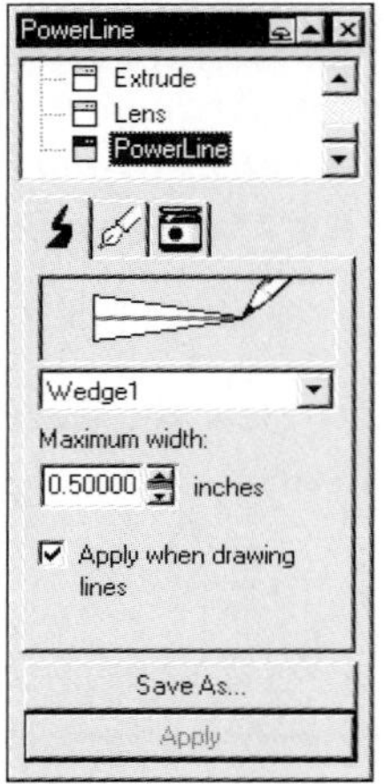

The PowerLine feature has three modes or controls: The first, the Preset tab seen in the illustration, allows you to select preset PowerLines for your own use. The second, represented by the Pen tab (the second tab from the left), allows you to set the angle, ratio, and intensity controls for the PowerLine in use. The third, represented by the Ink tab (the third tab from the left), allows you to control the Pen leakiness, spread, ink flow, and scale of the PowerLine.

The Preset tab displays the PowerLines available for your use. To see the whole list of PowerLines, you would click on the drop-down list box down arrow. Beneath the list box is a setting for maximum width, which defines the thickness the PowerLines may be. Clicking on the Apply when drawing lines check box allows you to apply the PowerLine settings to new lines you expect to create. You can save your own unique PowerLines to the preset list by clicking on the Save As command button.

To begin with, you will use a circle to experiment with the effects available with this new feature.

Applying PowerLines to an Object

You can apply PowerLines to existing objects. Follow these steps to see how you can create intriguing effects with an ordinary circle.

1. With the Ellipse tool, draw a circle. Fill it with 30-percent black (the eighth color from the left at the bottom of your screen). From the Outline Pen flyout, set the width to 2 points by clicking on the button next to the Hairline button.
2. Select PowerLine from the Effects menu, if it is not already on your screen.
3. Choose Wedge 1 as the type of PowerLine and leave the maximum width at .5 inch. Click on Apply. Your circle looks like this:

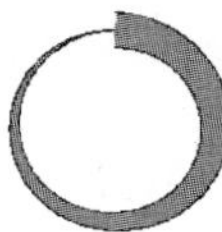

4. Click on the Ink tab (the third icon from the left) for applying speed, spread, and ink flow. The roll-up looks like this:

5. You use the Pen leakiness setting to control the line sharpness on curves. The higher the number, the greater the "skid" around the curves. Use Ink spread to control smoothness and width. The higher the number, the smoother the line. A high number would be more like a paintbrush, while a lower number would be more like an ink pen. Use Ink flow to control

the darkness of the line and how much ink flows as you draw the line. A high number lets more ink flow, while a lower number restricts the ink flow. Finally, use Scale with Image to resize the PowerLine as the values change.

6. Set Pen leakiness to 20, Ink spread to 50, and Ink flow to 50. Click on Apply. The circle looks like the following:

Varying the Nib

You can also vary the nib shape of the line by selecting the Pen tab (the second tab from the left). The resulting roll-up looks like this:

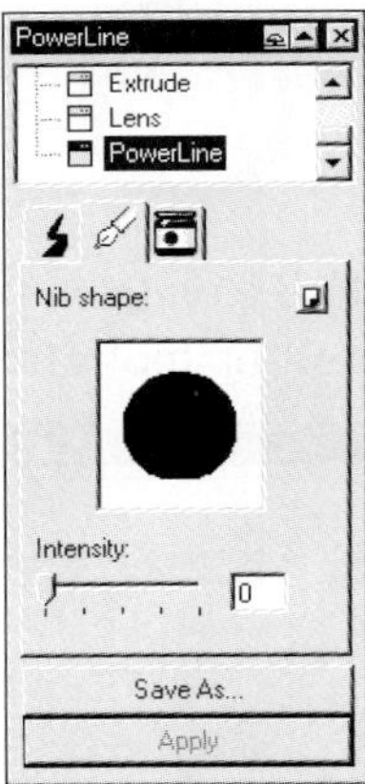

With this roll-up you can vary the nib shape, angle, and intensity. The display box contains a circle representing the nib shape. You can change it by placing the pointer on the display. As you drag the pointer, the nib shape and angle change. Beneath the display box is the slide control or numeric entry box for Intensity settings. This determines how strongly the nib is being pressed. At the top of the tab is a Page icon, which displays controls for entering absolute values for the nib shape angle, ratio, and intensity, as you've done previously using the Pen roll-up.

Follow these steps to experiment with the nib shapes.

1. Click on the Pen tab.

2. Set Intensity to 75.

3. Click on the Page button and set the angle to 14 degrees and the nib ratio to 50. Click on Apply. The circle now looks like this:

4. Clear the screen before proceeding.

Once you have a shape, you can pull it in different directions using pressure lines.

Using Pressure Lines

For more interesting effects, you can create your own pressure lines, and you can use the Shape tool to edit a pressure line.

1. Click on the Preset tab on the PowerLine roll-up. From the drop-down list box, select Pressure. Increase Max Width to 1.00 inch. Select the Freehand tool and draw a large squiggly line as shown here, and click the No fill button on the Color palette.

2. Select the Shape tool. Double-click on a pressure line node. A Node Edit dialog box will appear. Click on Edit Width. The dialog box appears as shown here:

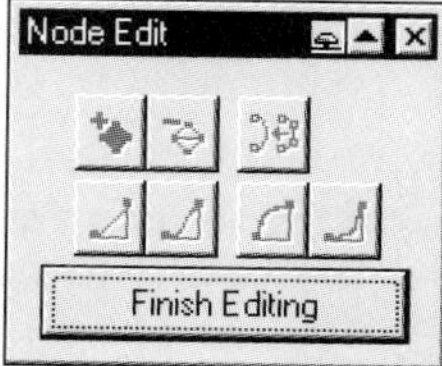

Two nodes on a straight line appear on each node of the line. You pull them along the line to broaden the line or make it more narrow.

3. With the Shape tool, move the upper nodes right and left away from the line to broaden it; move the lower nodes to the center to narrow the line, as shown here:

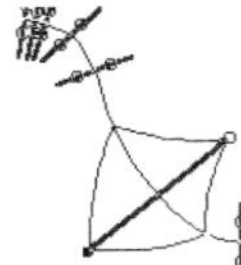

4. Select black fill from the Fill tool; the line will be filled in.
5. Click on the Finish Editing button on the Node Edit dialog box.
6. Using the Shape tool, shape the line however you wish by dragging the nodes.

One example is shown in Figure 13-19.

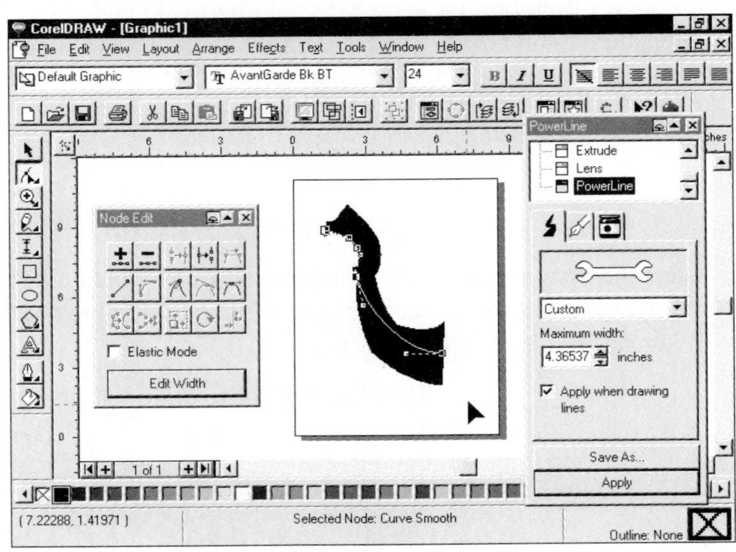

Results of shaping pressure PowerLines

FIGURE 13-19

Now you will explore the Lens effect, but before proceeding, clear the screen and close the PowerLine roll-up and Node Edit dialog box.

Using Lens

The Lens feature can be used to achieve several interesting effects. You can place a "lens" over an object to make the object seem transparent where the lens is placed; to magnify a portion of the object; to filter out or add colors; to produce complementary, inverted, or negative colors; or to produce grayscale or infrared images.

A simple example is the easiest way to show the effects produced by the Lens feature. Follow these steps.

1. Pull the ruler zero points to the upper-left corner of the page. Then pull two horizontal guidelines to –2 and –10 inches.
2. From the File menu, import Cougar.cmx from the fourth CD-ROM disk in the \Clipart\Animal\ directory path. (If you do not have this available, use any clipart you have.) Save the image as **Cougar.cdr**. Drag the image off the page to the side. You are going to place a black rectangle beneath it.
3. With the Rectangle tool, draw a rectangle within the ruler lines and the page borders. Fill the rectangle with black, as shown in Figure 13-20.
4. Select the clipart with the Pick tool and drag it into the center of the rectangle. From the Arrange menu, select Order and then To Front from the flyout to place the clipart on top of the rectangle.
5. Using the Ellipse tool together with CTRL, draw a perfect circle around the clipart image. When you release the Ellipse tool, the circle will disappear into the black background.
6. From the Color palette on the bottom of the screen, click on the bright red color. The clipart will be hidden behind the red circle, as shown in Figure 13-21.

Now you will experiment with some of the Lens effects. The circle will become the lens through which you can see the clipart image beneath. Variations in images are created by selecting alternative lens types.

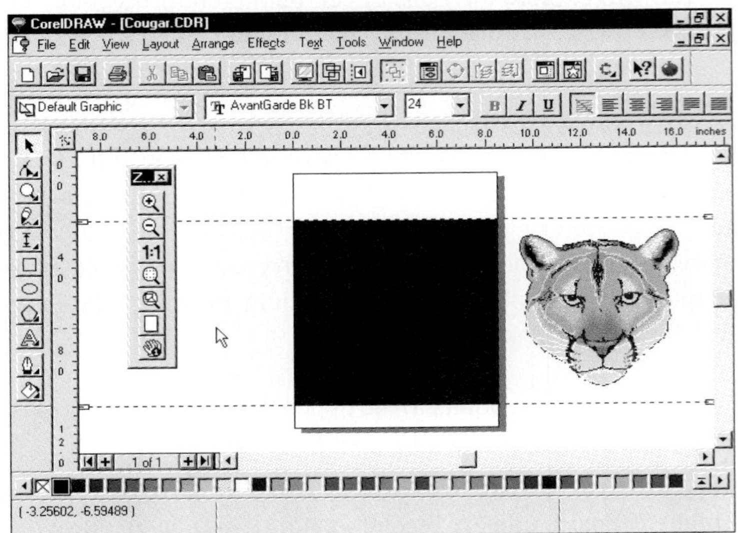

Black rectangle with clipart

FIGURE 13-20

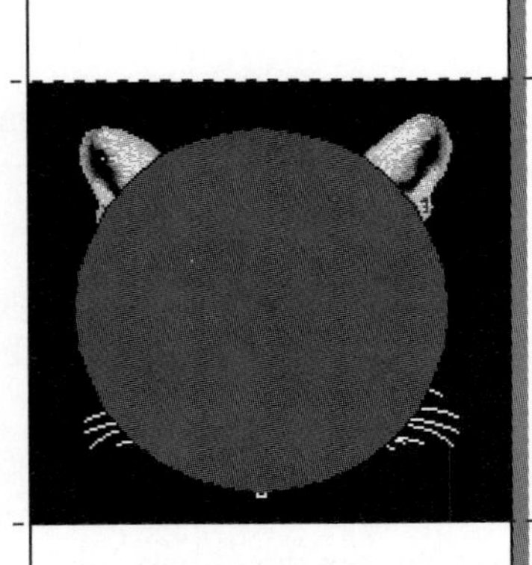

Circle drawn around clipart with Ellipse tool

FIGURE 13-21

7. From the Effects menu select Lens. It looks like this:

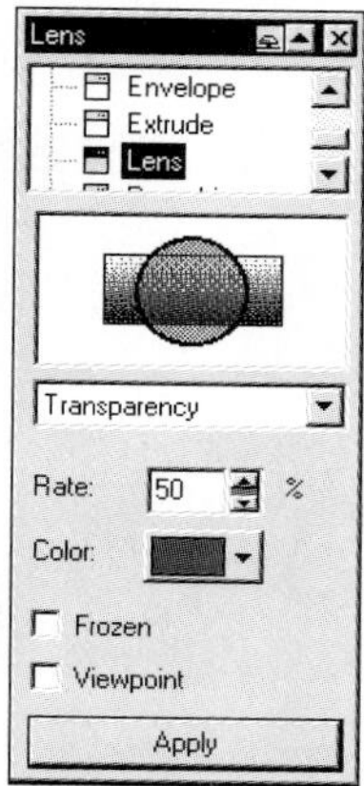

Transparency is the default lens type. In the display box, you can see a lens-type display that shows the effects produced by the selected lens type. Below the display is a drop-down list of 11 lens types and None. You will use several of the lens types to illustrate their effects. Beneath the list is the Rate of transparency. The Rate percentage sets the clarity of the lens: 100% would appear as clear glass, and 0% would completely obscure the clipart image. Each lens type has its own setting. The Frozen checkbox groups the contents of the lens with the lens itself so that as you move the lens the contents moves with it. The Viewpoint checkbox allows you to define the center of the area that will be displayed in the lens. Now you will see the effects of the Transparency type.

1. Choose Transparency, set the Rate at 80%, then click on Apply to see the image of the cougar through the red-tinted lens, as shown in Figure 13-22.
2. From the drop-down list, select Magnify and set the Amount to 3x. Click on Apply. The results are shown here:

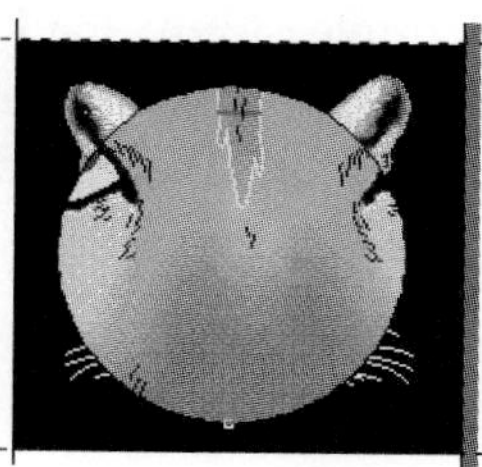

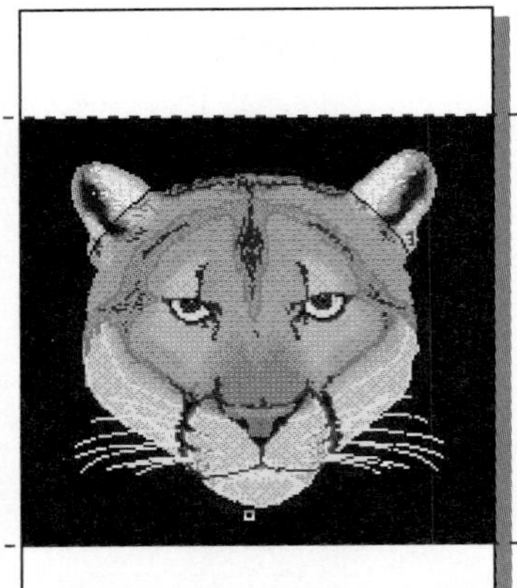

Clipart seen through a red-tinted transparent lens

FIGURE 13-22

3. From the type list, select Invert and click on Apply. The image now looks like this:

4. Finally, from the drop-down list, select Heat Map and click on Apply. You'll see another interesting result.
5. Set the Palette Rotation to 25% and click on Apply to see how that works.
6. You now have seen an example of how the Lens effect works. Experiment with the other lens types to see how they can be used as well. Next you'll look at a feature that's new with Coreldraw 6, the Bitmap Color Mask.
7. Close the Lens roll-up, and close Cougar.cdr.

Using the Bitmap Color Mask

The Bitmap Color Mask effect allows you to hide selected colors of an imported bitmap, such as you would create in Corel PHOTO-PAINT. This allows the object behind the bitmap to be displayed. Selecting Bitmap Color Mask from the Effects menu displays the Bitmap Color Mask roll-up, shown in Figure 13-23.

At the top of the roll-up is the Eyedropper button. Selecting the Eyedropper and clicking on the imported bitmap selects a color to be hidden as shown. You select whether a color should be hidden or shown using the drop-down list box. The list box allows you to define up to ten colors to be hidden or displayed. The Tolerance slider is used to determine how close a color in the bitmap has to be to the selected color in order to be included.

In the next exercise, you will create an object that will be displayed behind the selected colors in an imported bitmap.

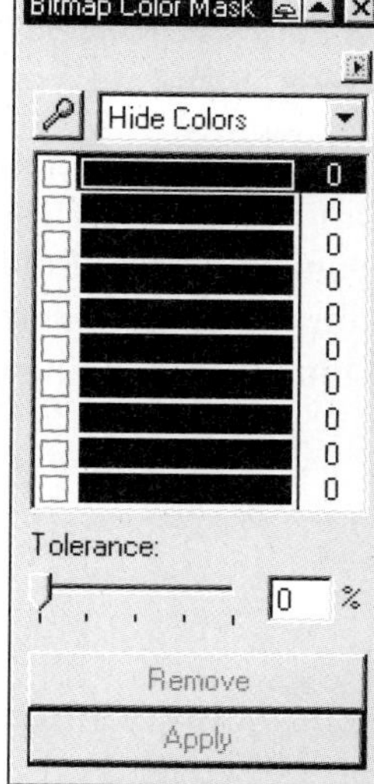

Bitmap Color Mask roll-up

FIGURE 13-23

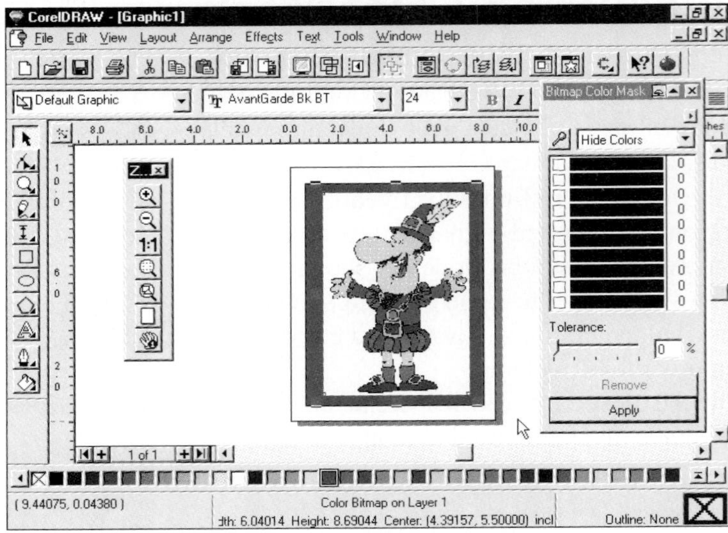

Actor1 bitmap

FIGURE 13-24

1. With the Rectangle tool draw a rectangle that is almost as large as the page. Select red from the color palette at the bottom of the screen for a fill color.
2. From the File menu, import Actor1 from the fourth CD-ROM disk in the \Clipart_Bitmaps\Cartoons\ folder. (If you do not have this available, use any bitmap graphic you may have.) Enlarge the bitmap to fill the page. Figure 13-24 shows the imported bitmap. (Most or all of the red rectangle is hidden behind the bitmap, depending on how large your rectangle is.)
3. Click on the Eyedropper to select it, then click on the actor's face to select the skin color. The first color bar in the display box displays the selected color.
4. Click on Apply.
5. The rectangle behind the bitmap will show through the selected color areas of the bitmap, as shown here:

6. Select Show Colors from the drop-down list box, then click on Apply, and only the selected color areas of the bitmap will be displayed.
7. Clear the screen and close the open roll-ups before continuing.

The final effect on the Effects menu is PowerClip, which you will work with in the next section.

Using PowerClip

PowerClip places one object within another. You use this to create one image out of two, where one object is the designated container and the other is the contents of the container. You may have multiple layers of PowerClips where one completed image becomes the contents for another.

The following rules apply:

- Containers can be closed path objects, grouped objects, or artistic text.
- Contents can be closed path objects, grouped objects, artistic text, or bitmap images.
- Both containers and contents may contain uniform, fountain, or no fills; two-color patterns; full-color patterns; or textures.
- You may use PowerClips with other Effects menu features, such as Blend, Extrusion, or Transform options.
- You can copy a PowerClip with the Copy command in the Edit menu to create both a new container and its contents. If you create a new container object and use the Copy PowerClip in the Effects menu, the newly created container is filled with the contents of the copied PowerClip.
- You can clone a PowerClip using the Clone command on the Edit menu.
- You may group PowerClips and then ungroup them.

Follow these steps to experiment with this fun feature. You will create a rectangle within which a bull will be placed.

1. Import the clipart Bullt.cmx from the fourth CD-ROM, in the \Clipart \Animal\ folder. Use any clipart if this is not available to you. Save this as Bullt.cdr.

2. Select the bull with the Pick tool and reduce its size to about 1/4 of the page and place it in the lower-right quadrant of the page.
3. Select the Rectangle tool and draw a rectangle (no Fill), about 1/4 the size of the page. With the Pick tool, place it in the upper-left quadrant of the page, as seen in Figure 13-25.
4. With the rectangle selected, select the Extrude Roll-up from the Effects menu and click on the Type and Depth tab, the second from the left. Choose Small Back from the Type list and change the Depth setting to 40. Pull the vanishing point slightly to the right and click on Apply. This is the container for the bull.
5. Select the bull with the Pick tool and choose PowerClip from the Effects menu. A flyout menu will appear, as shown here:

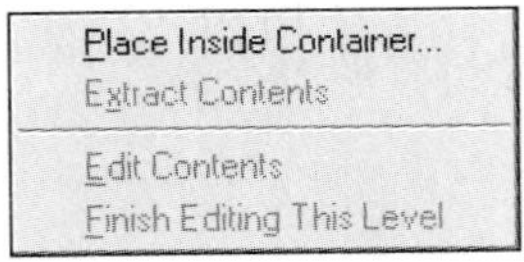

6. Choose the Place Inside Container command. The pointer will turn into a thick arrow. Move the arrow to the box and click on a line of it. The bull will be placed in the box, as seen here:

You can see from the flyout that you can also extract the contents from a container, edit the PowerClip, or halt editing.

When you are finished, leave Coreldraw without saving your test files. They can easily be created again.

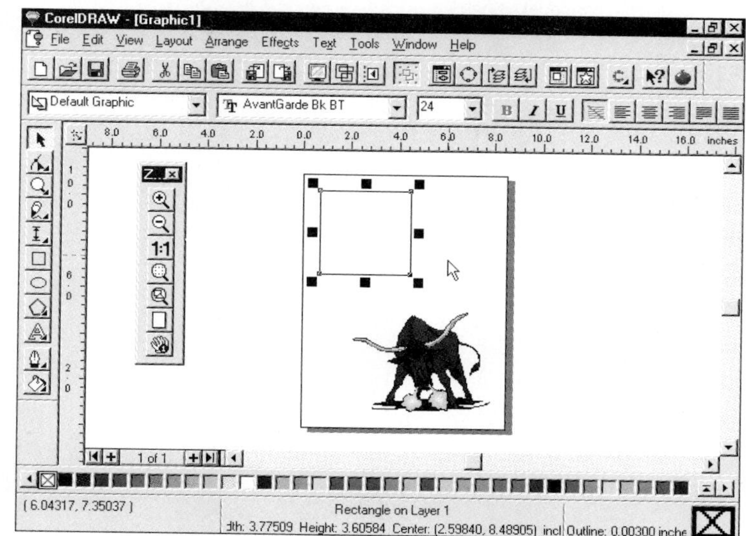

Container and contents for the PowerClip effect

FIGURE 13-25

Combining Coreldraw Features

14

The previous chapters in this book concentrated on teaching you a specific set of skills. The exercises throughout the book built on skills you had already learned as you mastered new ones.

This chapter, however, takes a different approach. It assumes that you have mastered all of the basic skills in Coreldraw and are ready to explore applications that combine many different techniques. In this chapter you will find ideas, and perhaps some of these ideas will inspire you in your own work. However, you will not find a comprehensive catalog of every possible technique or special effect of which Coreldraw is capable. The three major exercises that make up this chapter feature text that is manipulated in various ways, amply demonstrating Coreldraw's magnificent ability to turn text into word pictures.

Each of the three main sections in this chapter contains one exercise in designing a graphic. The title of the section describes the type of graphic; the introduction to each exercise briefly describes the main Coreldraw techniques that help you create the graphic. If you need to review certain techniques, you can refer back to the chapter or chapters that first introduced these skills. You will also learn how to customize how Coreldraw works and how to automate Coreldraw functions. Bon voyage!

Integrating Clipart and Line Art

In the following exercise, you will design a poster that integrates clipart images with line art—in this case, text. You can use this exercise to review text editing, size and scale, and outline and fill techniques (Chapters 4, 6, 7, 8, 10, and 13). Since the poster format is 20 inches by 15 inches, you also can brush up on the page setup, printing, and tiling skills you learned in Chapter 12. The end result of your exercise should look similar to Figure 14-1.

Creating the Headline

To begin building the poster, create the 3-dimensional headline by following these steps:

1. Starting with a blank page, turn on the Rulers and turn off Wireframe view from the View menu. Also, make sure the Snap To options (Grid,

Classic Car
Auto Auction
April 10th, 11am
Paine Field, Everett
Admission: $10
Sponsored By The Lynnwood Rotary
Cars may be previewed April 9th, 8am - 5 pm
For Information
Call: 555-1234

Completed poster

FIGURE 14-1

Guidelines, and Objects) from the Layout menu are turned off for this exercise.

2. Select Page Setup from the Layout menu, select Custom from the Paper drop-down list box, verify that Landscape is selected, enter 20 inches for the Width and 15 for the height, and click on OK.
3. Set the zero points for the rulers to the upper-left corner of the page by dragging the rulers' zero points to the upper-left corner of the page.
4. Save and name the planned image. Select Save As from the File menu, select the folder where you are saving your Coreldraw files, and type **Auction** in the File Name text box. Then press ENTER or click on the Save button to save the file and return to the Coreldraw screen.
5. Select the Text tool and place the insertion point at –2 inches vertically and 10 inches horizontally. Open the Text toolbar, select Bookman (BookmanITC Lt BT), Bold-Italic, 150 points, and centered alignment.
6. Type **Classic Car**, press ENTER, and continue typing **Auto Auction**.
7. Click on the Pick tool to select the text, then open the Character dialog box from the Text menu, click on the Alignment tab, then enter 35 in the

Character Spacing and 80 in the Line Spacing spinners, and click on OK. The text spreads out horizontally and moves together vertically. Click on the Save button on the toolbar.

8. If your Status bar does not say Outline: None, Fill: Black (shows black in the color swatch), open the Fill flyout and click on the Black fill button, and then open the Outline Pen flyout and click on the X (no fill).
9. With the text selected, select Transform from the Arrange menu, then select Position from the flyout. The Position roll-up will be displayed. Set both the Horizontal and Vertical Position spinners to 0.1 inch, and click on Apply To Duplicate. This creates a copy of the text offset by 1/10 inch from the original. The duplicate of your text will be selected.
10. Open the Fill flyout and click on the White fill button (this is the second button from the right in the top row). The text disappears from the screen and all you can see are the nodes.
11. On the Position roll-up, select Apply To Duplicate once more. On the Fill flyout, click on the Black fill button. Your headline should now look like this (don't worry at the moment if your text is not perfectly centered). Close the Position roll-up.

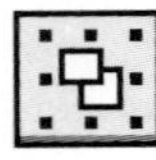

12. Choose Select All from the Edit menu and then click on the Group button on the toolbar. If your text is not properly centered, center it now and then press CTRL-S to save the changes you have made to the file.

Entering Remaining Text

The remaining text can be entered quickly with these instructions.

1. With the Artistic text tool, place an insertion point at 14 inches horizontal and –6 inches vertical. Then, from the Text toolbar, select ZapfHumnst, Bold, 96 points, and Centered alignment.
2. Type **April 10th, 11am** and press ENTER, then type **Paine Field, Everett**, press ENTER, and finally type **Admission: $10**.
3. Click the Text tool at 10 inches horizontal and –11 inches vertical. From the Text toolbar select ZapfCalligr BT, Bold, 72 points, and Centered. Then type **Sponsored By The Lynnwood Rotary** and press ENTER.
4. Reduce the point size in the Text toolbar to 60, and type **Cars may be previewed April 9th, 8am - 5pm** and press ENTER; then type **For Information,** press ENTER, and finally type **Call: 555-1234**. When you are done, select the Pick tool and click on any white space to deselect all the text. Your page should look like Figure 14-2. Click on the Save button to save your work.

Classic Car
Auto Auction
April 10th, 11am
Paine Field, Everett
Admission: $10
Sponsored By The Lynnwood Rotary
Cars may be previewed April 9th, 8am -5 pm
For Information
Call: 555-1234

Completed text for auction poster

FIGURE 14-2

Adding Clipart

The final step in building the poster is to add the clipart. Three pieces will be added, one in the hole at center-left and the other two in the bottom-left and bottom-right corners. Your clipart is on the fourth Coreldraw CD-ROM. Add the clipart now with these instructions.

1. If not already done, click on the Pick tool and then click in any white space to deselect the text string.
2. Select Import from the File menu and select All Files in the Files of type drop-down list box. In the Look in drop-down list box, select your CD-ROM drive, then select the \Clipart\Transpor\Personal\ path in the list box below, and then double-click on the file named car074.cmx. (If this piece of clipart is not available to you, use any piece of clipart you have.) The car will come into the center of your poster. Drag it to the left, resize it as necessary, and drag it into the hole that should perfectly fit it, as shown in Figure 14-3.

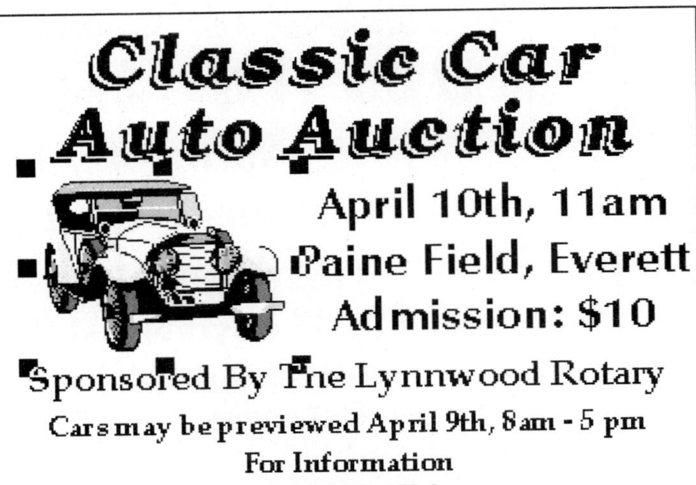

First piece of clipart in place

FIGURE 14-3

3. Select Import from the File menu again, make sure you are in the same folder as in step 2, and double-click on Oldcar2.cmx. Drag the second car to the lower-left corner, and resize it to fit the space available.
4. Use the Zoom tool to magnify the lower-left corner of the poster. Include enough of the text around the second car to give yourself a frame of reference.
5. Resize the car so that it fits in the space available for it, like this:

6. Press CTRL-S to save the poster, return the poster to Zoom To Page view, and then click on any white space to deselect the second car.

7. Again select Import from the File menu or click on the Import button on the toolbar, make sure you are in the same folder as in step 2, and double-click on car077.cmx. Drag this third car to the lower-right corner.
8. Use the Zoom tool and magnify the lower-right corner of the poster. Include some of the text for a frame of reference.
9. Resize the car so that it fits in the space. Since the car is a little boxy for the space, drag one of the middle sizing handles to elongate the car, like this:

10. Return to Zoom To Page view, deselect the third car, and save the poster. Select Full-Screen Preview from the View menu to look at the finished poster. What you see should look like Figure 14-1.
11. Press SPACEBAR or click the right mouse button to return to the Editable Preview window and select Close from the File menu or click on the Close button to clear the screen. Click on the New button on the toolbar to create a new page for the next exercise.

You may choose to print this oversize poster on your own printer. If you do, be sure to activate the Print tiled pages option on the Print Options dialog box. Your poster will print on four separate sheets, each containing one quarter of the graphic. If your printer does not have enough memory to print this graphic at 20 by 15 inches, select Fit to page in the Print Options dialog box.

To add to your Coreldraw drawing gallery, continue with the next exercise. There, you will create a color design that takes advantage of Coreldraw features that fit text to a path and mirror images.

Fitting Text to a Path

If you have followed this book from the first chapter onward, you have learned nearly every available Coreldraw drawing technique. One important (and very creative) technique remains: fitting text to a path using the Fit Text to Path command from the Text menu. You can cause a text string to follow the outline of *any* object, be it a circle or ellipse, a rectangle or square, a polygon, a line, a curve, a complex curved object, or even another letter that has been converted to curves.

Once you have fitted text to an object, you can delete that object without causing the text to lose its newly acquired shape. If you edit text attributes later, however, the text may change its alignment. You can remedy this simply by fitting text to the same path again. You can also make the curve object transparent by selecting no outline or fill color.

Fit Text to Path Roll-Up

You open the Fit Text to Path roll-up by selecting Fit Text to Path from the Text menu or by pressing CTRL-F. There are actually two Fit Text to Path roll-ups: one for fitting

text to an open line or curve, the other for fitting text to a closed rectangle or ellipse. The roll-up for fitting text to an open line or curve is shown on the left in the following illustration; the roll-up for fitting text to a closed rectangle or ellipse is shown on the right. Which roll-up appears is determined by the objects you have selected.

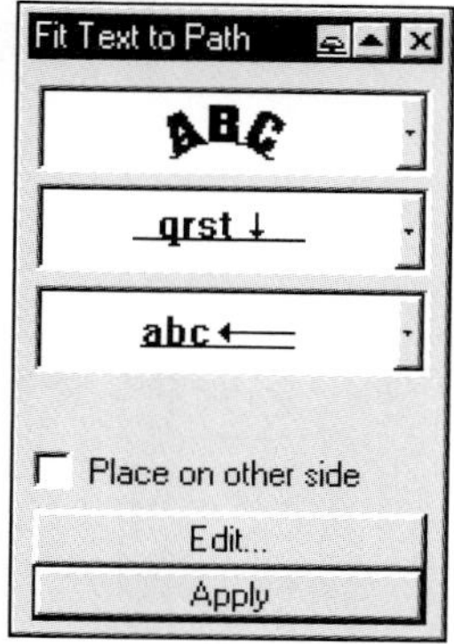

The two roll-ups share two drop-down list boxes. The list box at the top of the roll-up lets you determine the orientation of the text, while the second list box lets you select where the text will sit: above, below, or on the path of the object and its distance from it. Also, both roll-ups have a check box for moving the text to the opposite side of the path. The difference in the two roll-ups is in how to align the text on the object. For an open object, you have a drop-down list of alignment possibilities, whereas closed objects have a four-sided button to set their alignment. Each of these elements will be discussed in the next several sections. Figure 14-4 shows several examples of fitting text to a path that will be referred to in these sections.

Orientation of the Text

The orientation of the text is its degree of rotation, or skew, as it follows the path it is fitted to. There are four options for orientation in the top drop-down list, shown here. Most of the examples in Figure 14-4 show the first (default) orientation; in this orientation, the letters rotate to follow the path. Figure 14-4f shows the second orientation, and Figure 14-4c shows the fourth orientation.

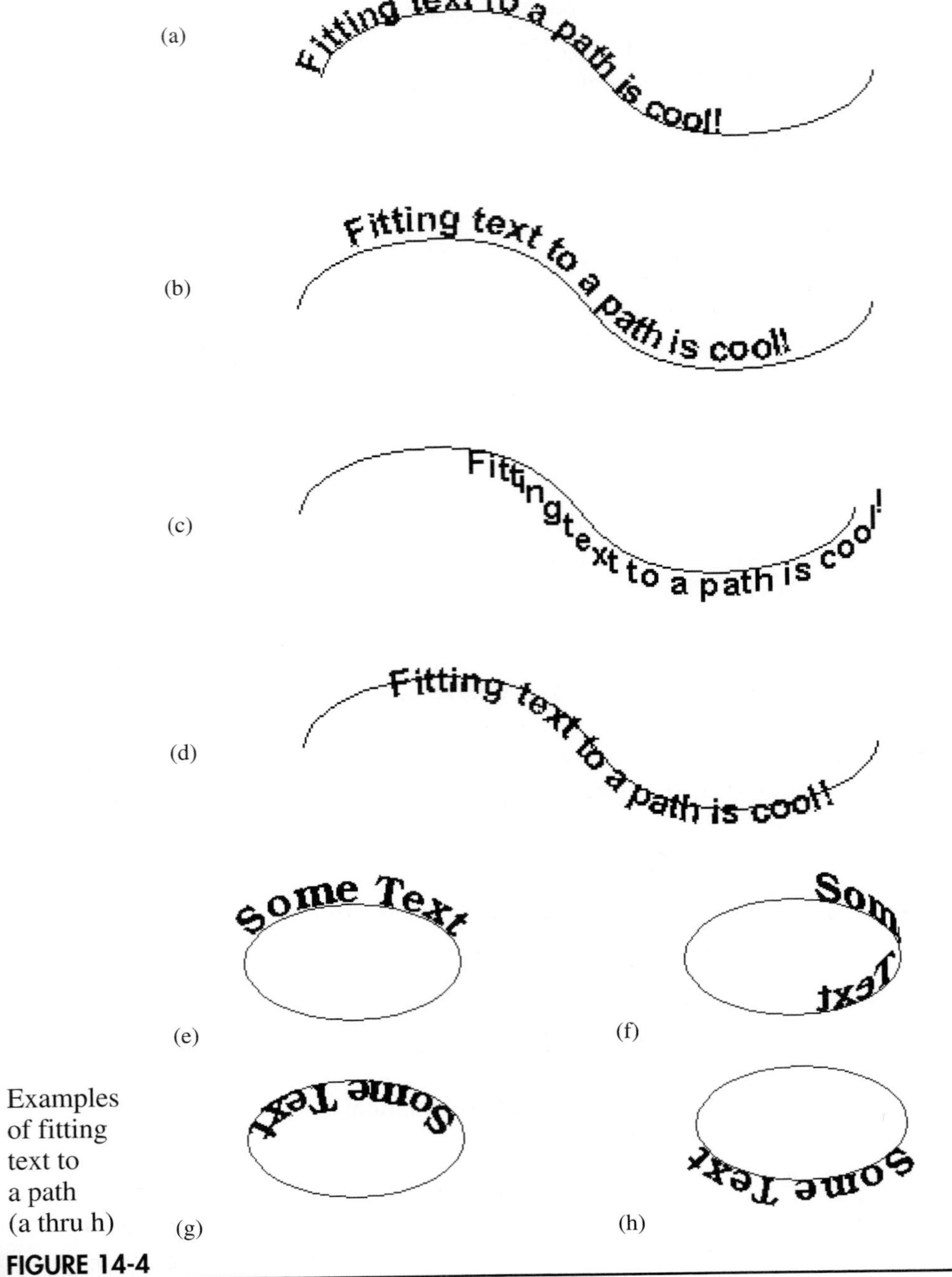

Examples of fitting text to a path (a thru h)

FIGURE 14-4

Distance of the Text from the Path

The second drop-down list box, shown here, offers five alternative settings for the distance of the text from its path. (Not all five choices are always available.)

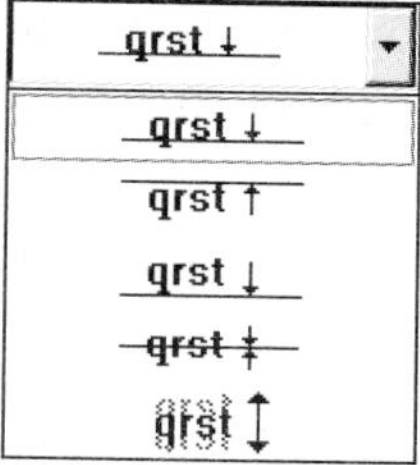

Figure 14-4a, f, g, and h show the first alternative, in which the text sits right on the path (the baseline of the text is on the path, and the descenders are beneath it). Figure 14-4c shows the second alternative, in which the text sits underneath the path. Figure 14-4d shows the fourth alternative, in which the line runs through the text. Figures 14-4b and e shows the fifth alternative: the text can be pulled away from the path either with the mouse or with the Fit Text To Path Offsets dialog box, opened with the Edit button on the roll-up, as shown next.

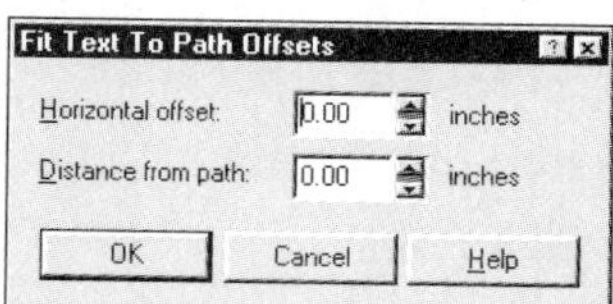

Aligning the Text on the Path

For open paths, the third drop-down list box on the roll-up provides three alternatives for aligning text on a path. Figure 14-4a shows the first alternative, in which the text is aligned with the left end of the path. Figures 14-4b and d show the second alternative, in which the text is centered on the path; while Figure 14-4c shows the third alternative, with the text aligned to the right end of the path.

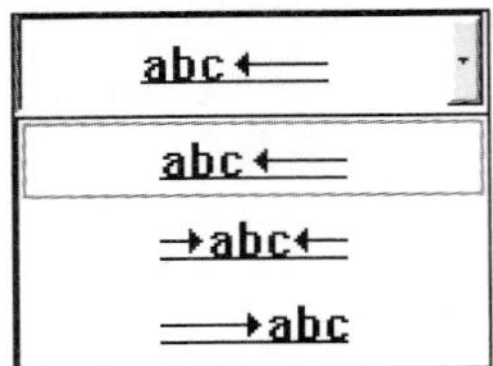

For closed-path rectangles and ellipses, the text is aligned to the middle of one of four sides by clicking on the corresponding side of the four-sided button that is displayed (shown here). The text itself is rotated as it is moved to the right, as shown in Figures 14-4f and h. If you want to flip the text to the other side of the path, click on the Place on other side check box in the Fit Text to Path roll-up. Figure 14-4g shows the result of having this box checked, while Figure 14-4h shows the result of having the bottom side selected but not the Place on other side check box.

Using Fit Text to Path

In the following exercise, you will design a stylized "rainbow" image that consists of a series of scaled and aligned wedges. You will then fit the word "Rainbow" to a curve, combine the text string with a background object to create a mask, and overlay the transparent letters on the rainbow colors. The result is shown later in Figure 14-7.

1. Starting with the new document you opened in the last exercise, select Page Setup from the Layout menu. In the Page Settings dialog box, select Letter from the Paper drop-down list box and select the Landscape option button, then click on OK. This results in a page that is 11 inches wide and 8 1/2 inches high.

2. Turn on Rulers and Wireframe view. Open the Grid & Ruler Setup dialog box and make sure Inches is selected for the Horizontal and Vertical Units and the Horizontal and Vertical Origin are set to 0-inches on the Ruler tab. Select the Grid tab, confirm that Snap To Grid is selected, and both Horizontal and Vertical Grid Frequency are set to 8 per inch. Click on OK.

3. Set new outline and fill defaults so that all of the objects you draw will be standardized. First, open the Outline Pen flyout and then click on the X (for no outline) button (the leftmost button on the second row). The Outline Pen defaults dialog box appears. Click on Artistic Text and accept the

checked Graphic, so that both are selected. Click on OK to set no outline as the new default for Graphic and Artistic Text objects.

4. Click on the Fill tool and then on the Black fill button. The Uniform Fill defaults dialog box appears. Click on Artistic Text and accept the checked Graphic so that both are selected. Click on OK to define a default fill color of black for all new Graphic and Artistic Text objects.

5. Activate the Ellipse tool, then position the pointer at the 3 1/4-inch mark on the horizontal ruler and the 2-inch mark on the vertical ruler. Press and hold CTRL-SHIFT and drag the mouse down until the Status bar shows a diameter of 3 inches. As you may recall from Chapter 3, the use of CTRL and SHIFT together results in a circle drawn from the center outward. When you release the mouse button, the circle appears with the node at the top.

OTE: *If you drag the mouse upwards, the node of the circle will be placed at the bottom (6 o'clock), rather than the top (12 o'clock) of the circle.*

6. Create a 90-degree wedge from this circle, as you learned to do in Chapter 9. Activate the Shape tool and position the pointer at the node of the circle. To turn the circle into a pie wedge, press and hold CTRL and drag the node in a counterclockwise direction until you reach the 9 o'clock position (90 degrees on the Status bar). (Hold the tip of the Shaping pointer *inside* the rim of the circle as you drag, or you will see an open arc instead of a wedge.) Release the mouse button when you reach the 9 o'clock position. The wedge appears, as shown here:

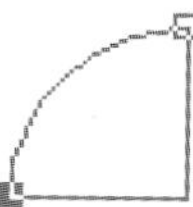

7. Click on the Pick tool to select the wedge automatically. Notice that the selection box is much larger than the wedge, as shown here. Coreldraw continues to treat the wedge as though it were a full circle.

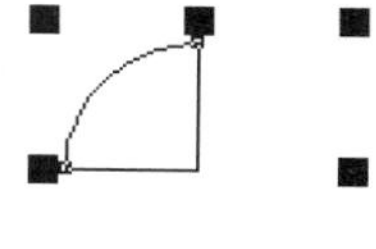

8. With the wedge still selected, open the Scale & Mirror Transform roll-up from the Arrange menu. Click on the horizontal mirror button and then on Apply. The curve of the wedge now faces upward and to the right.

9. To scale the wedge and leave a copy of the original, position the pointer at the node in the upper-right corner and scale the wedge upward and to the right, until the Status bar value reaches approximately 117 percent. When you reach the desired point, continue to hold the mouse button, but press the + key on the numeric keypad to leave a copy of the original. Then release the mouse button. The original wedge remains in position and a scaled version overlays it, like this:

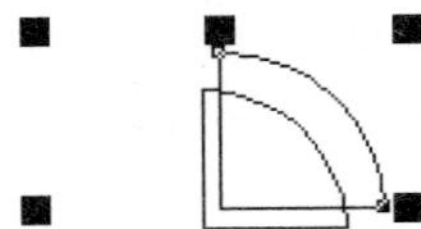

10. Press CTRL-R (the Repeat key combination) five times to create five additional wedges, each larger than the previous one. Your screen should show a total of seven wedges, resembling Figure 14-5.

11. Next, align the wedges so that they form one-half of a rainbow. Double click on the Pick tool to select all seven wedges, and then select Align & Distribute from the Arrange menu. When the Align & Distribute roll-up appears, click on the Tack button (the leftmost button on the upper-right corner of the roll-up) to set the pin up mode. Click on both the Horizontally Center and Vertically Center buttons, select Center of Page in the Align To drop-down list box, and then click on Apply. The roll-up closes and the wedges realign with a common corner point in the center of the page, as you can see here:

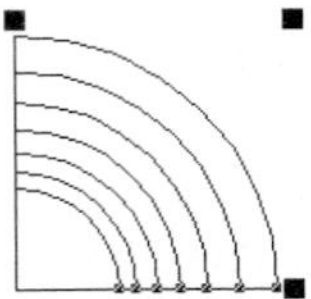

12. With the seven wedges still selected, select Order from the Arrange menu and then Reverse Order on the flyout. You will not see a visible change at this point, but you have positioned the larger wedges in the back and the smaller wedges in the front. When you turn on the preview window later

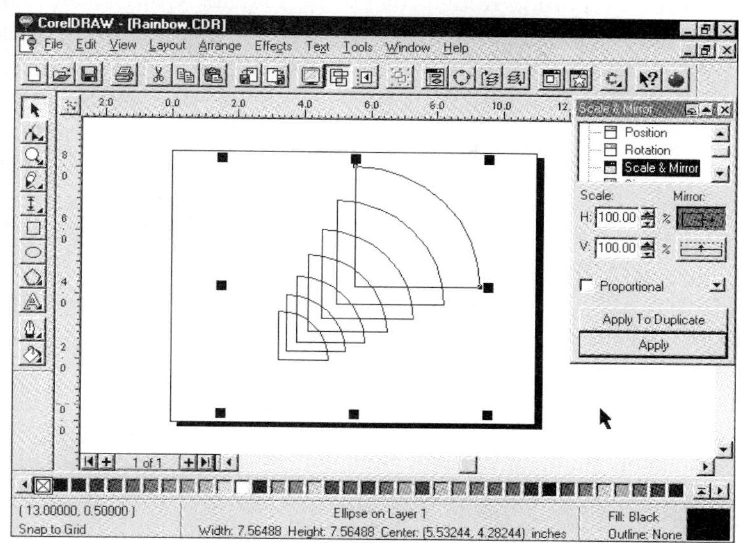

FIGURE 14-5 Series of scaled wedges created using the Repeat key combination

in the exercise and begin to assign fill colors to the wedges, you will see each wedge as a ribbon-like band.

13. Select Save As from the File menu. When the Save Drawing dialog box appears, select the path to the folder where you are saving your drawings, type **Rainbow**, and then press ENTER or click on Save.

14. To design the other half of the rainbow, you create a horizontal mirror image of the currently selected image. In the Scale & Mirror roll-up, select the Mirror horizontally button and click on Apply to Duplicate. The mirror image of the seven wedges appears and fits tightly against the original group of wedges, as shown here:

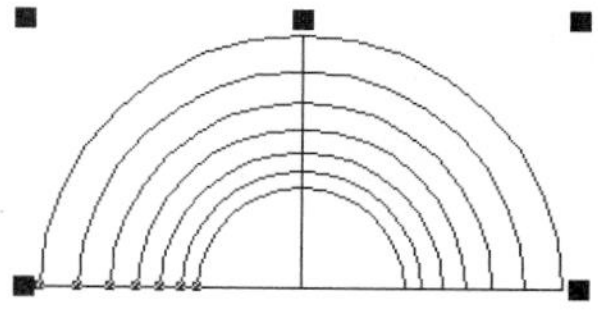

15. You can now begin to assign fill colors to the wedges of the "rainbow." First select Preview Selected Only from the View menu.

16. Deselect all of the wedges by clicking on any white space. Then, select both the largest wedge on the left half of the "rainbow" and the smallest wedge on the right half. To select both of them, click on the first curve outline, then, while holding down SHIFT, click on the second curve outline. The editing window looks as though all of the wedges were selected, because the selection box of the largest wedge surrounds all of the objects. However, the Status bar shows that two objects are selected, and the preview window, reached by pressing F9, also shows you that only two wedges are selected, as you can see here:

17. Close the preview window by pressing SPACEBAR or clicking the right mouse button. Then, with the two wedges still selected, click on red in the palette at the bottom of the screen. Turn off Preview Selected Only from the View menu and press F9 again to see the color. Press SPACEBAR again to close the preview window.

18. Deselect the previous wedges. Then select the second-largest wedge on the left half of the "rainbow" and the second-smallest wedge on the right half; then select orange fill from the palette at the bottom of the screen.

19. Continue in the same way with the next five pairs of wedges. Assign colors as follows: third pair, yellow; fourth pair, green; fifth pair, baby blue; sixth pair, blue; seventh pair, purple. Check your colors by pressing F9, then return to Editable Preview view. When you are finished, press F9. The two halves of the rainbow show an opposite sequence of colors, as you can see by the black-and-white representation here:

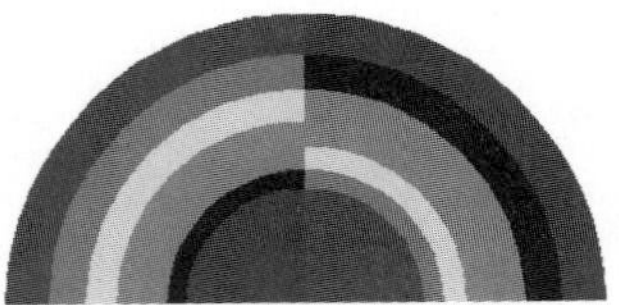

20. Press SPACEBAR to return to your drawing, double click on the Pick tool to select all 14 wedges, and then click on the Group button on the toolbar. This prevents you from accidentally moving or editing an individual wedge apart from the group.

21. Now you are ready to prepare the text that will eventually overlay the rainbow as a transparent mask. First, select the Ellipse tool and position the pointer at the 2 1/2-inch mark on the horizontal ruler and the 7 1/2-inch mark on the vertical ruler. Press and hold CTRL and drag the mouse downward and to the right to draw a circle 6 inches in diameter. The circle overlays most of the "rainbow" for now, but you will delete it when it has served its purpose.

22. Select the Text tool and place an insertion point in any white space on the page. Type **Rainbow**, then click on the Pick tool. Open the Character Attributes dialog box, select the Font tab, and set text attributes to Aachen bold, 120 points. Click on the Alignment tab, then set Character spacing to 10 percent and Alignment to None. Click on OK.

23. Press and hold SHIFT and select the circle you just drew. Then press CTRL-F or select Fit Text to Path from the Text menu.

24. When the Fit Text to Path roll-up opens, make sure that all of the defaults in the roll-up are set: rotated text orientation (the first option on the first drop-down list), text sitting on the path (the first option on the second drop-down list), the top quadrant on the four-sided button, and Place on other side not checked. After verifying these settings, click on Apply. In a few seconds, the text appears right side up, but on the circle. Drag the circle and text down until the text is centered in the rainbow, as shown in Figure 14-6.

25. Deselect the text to leave only the circle selected and then press DEL to delete the circle. The text retains its new shape.

26. Click again on the outline of the text string to select it, then fill the text with white by clicking on the white button in the color palette.

27. Create a rectangle that will become the background of the mask. Select the Rectangle tool and draw a rectangle that completely covers the "rainbow."

28. Press the SPACEBAR to select the rectangle automatically. Give the rectangle a white fill by clicking on the white button on the color palette.

29. Move the rectangle to a clear area of the page, then select the text string and move it on top of the rectangle.

30. To center the text on the rectangle, select both objects, click on Align & Distribute in the Arrange menu (if you closed the Align & Distribute 14

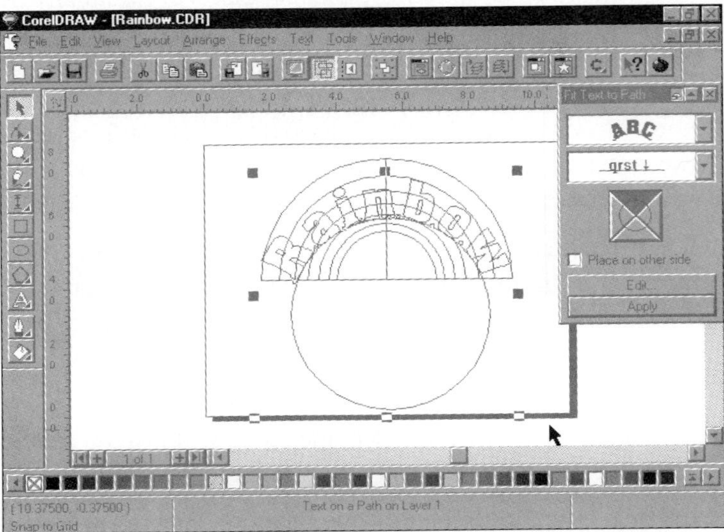

Fitting text to a circle

FIGURE 14-6

roll-up), and select the Horizontally Center option button in the Align & Distribute roll-up. Deselect any other options that are selected. Click on OK to leave the Align & Distribute roll-up and redisplay the newly aligned objects.

31. With the text and rectangle both selected, select Combine from the Arrange menu. When the two objects combine, their common area, the text, becomes transparent "holes" in the white rectangle.
32. Move the newly combined object back over the grouped rainbow wedges so that the rectangle and the word "Rainbow" completely overlay the wedges.
33. Double-click on the Pick tool and then press F9 for Full-Screen Preview. With the white rectangle invisible against the page, all you can see are the rainbow colors behind the transparent text string, as shown in Figure 14-7.
34. Return to the Editable Preview window and select both the combined object and the wedges and apply the Group command from the Arrange menu or click on the Group button on the toolbar.
35. Press CTRL-S to save the changes to your work, then select Close from the File menu to clear your screen.

Rainbow colors appearing as fill through the mask object

FIGURE 14-7

The main emphases in this last exercise have been on fitting text to a path, working with color effects, creating a mask, aligning objects, repeating operations, and creating mirror images. In the next and final sample application, you can achieve 3-D effects using fountain and contrasting fills, outlines, and repeated scaling.

Achieving Special Effects with Text and Graphics

The "FAX" image in Figure 14-8 has a vibrant, 3-D look; the graphic represents the power of facsimile to quite literally "broadcast" to the world. Several special effects techniques contribute to the dynamic quality of the image:

- Text fitted to a curve
- Text objects with drop shadows (shadows placed behind and offset from the original)
- A "globe" with an off-center radial fountain fill
- Repeated duplication and expansion of a text string
- Judicious use of contrasting fills
- Inclusion of a backdrop that makes the image seem to burst beyond its boundaries

You already have practiced the basic skills that make all of these special effects possible. In the exercise that follows, you will re-create this image using the Leave Original and Repeat keys, fountain fill and node editing techniques, and the Duplicate, Fit Text to Path, Group, and Page Setup commands. For a review of shadow and fountain fill techniques, see Chapter 7.

1. Open a new document by clicking on the New button on the toolbar, then select Page Setup from the Layout menu. When the Page Setup dialog box appears, make sure that Landscape and Letter are still selected and then click on OK.
2. To prepare the Coreldraw screen for the exercise, activate Snap To Grid from the Layout menu, select Grid and Ruler Setup, and set both Horizontal and Vertical Grid Frequency to 8 per inch on the Grid tab, then click on OK. From the View menu, activate Rulers and Wireframe view as well. Drag the rulers' zero points to the upper-left corner of the page.

Fax illustration using fountain fill, drop shadows, and a background frame to enhance 3-D effects

FIGURE 14-8

3. Change the default outline to a hairline by opening the Outline Pen flyout and then clicking on the Hairline button on the second row of the flyout (the button with two arrows pointing at each other). When the Outline Pen defaults dialog box appears, click on Artistic Text, accept the checked Graphic, and then click on OK.

4. Change the default outline color to black by opening the Outline Pen flyout and clicking on the Black button on the first row of the flyout. The Outline Pen defaults dialog box appears; select Artistic Text, accept the checked Graphic, and click on OK, as you did in step 3.

5. Save your document by selecting Save As from the File menu. Name the file **Faxworld**. As you work through the rest of this exercise, save your work often using the Save button on the toolbar or by pressing CTRL-S.

6. Create a small circle to which you will fit text. To do this, select the Ellipse tool and position the crosshair pointer in the center of the page at 5.5 inches horizontally and – 4.25 inches vertically. Press and hold SHIFT and CTRL and draw a perfect circle 0.75 inch in diameter.

7. Now enter the text that you will fit to this circle. Select the Text tool and place an insertion point about an inch above the circle. The exact location does not matter, because when you invoke the Fit Text to Path command later, the text will snap to the circle no matter where it is. Type **FAX** in all-capital letters. Select the Pick tool and open the Character Attributes dialog box by pressing CTRL-T. On the Font tab, set text attributes to Franklin Gothic Heavy (FrnkGothITC Hv BT), Normal, 30.0 points. Click on the Alignment tab, select None for the Alignment, and click on OK.

8. With the text still selected, hold down SHIFT and select the circle. With both objects selected, press CTRL-F or select Fit Text to Path from the Arrange menu. Accept the defaults and click on Apply. The text wraps around the outside of the circle, centering itself at the top. Use the Zoom tool to magnify the image. The result is shown in Figure 14-9.

9. Select the Pick tool and click on any white space to deselect the text string and circle, then select the circle and press DEL to delete it. The text remains curved, even though the circle is no longer there.

10. Double-click on the text string to enter rotate/skew mode, press and hold the CTRL key, and rotate the text by 45 degrees in a clockwise direction, so that it looks like this:

11. Switch to Zoom To Page view and move the text to the lower-left corner of the page, approximately 1/2 inch from the bottom-left page edge.

12. Now you are ready to begin creating a text pattern. Turn off Snap To Grid and, with the Pick tool still selected, position the pointer at the upper-right corner node of the text object and begin to drag it up and to the right. As soon as the dotted outline box appears, press and release + on the numeric keypad (to leave a copy of the original). Continue scaling the text until

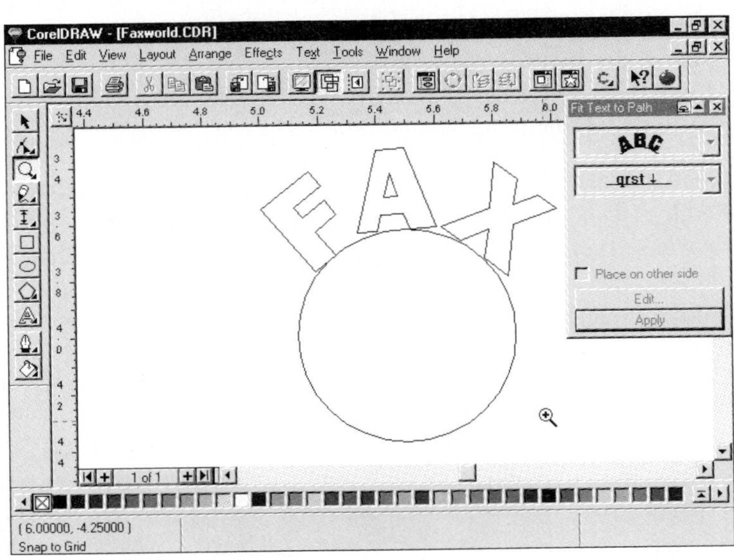

Magnified view of text fitted to a small circle

FIGURE 14-9

the Status bar indicates a value of approximately 129 percent. Then, release the left mouse button. A larger scaled version of the text string appears on top of and offset from the original.

13. Press CTRL-R, the Repeat key, ten times to repeat the scaling and duplication of the text. Ten scaled replicas of the text string overlay one another, each one larger than the previous one. The last text string exceeds the boundaries of the page, as shown in Figure 14-10.

14. Leaving the most recently created text string selected, select Options from the Tools menu. Make certain that the Place duplicates and clones values are both at 0.25 inch on the General tab and then click on OK. These values determine the placement of a duplicate object relative to the original.

15. Press CTRL-D to create an exact duplicate of the top text string, offset 1/4 inch above and to the right of the original. The duplicate is selected as soon as it appears.

16. Double click on the Pick tool and then press F9 for the Preview window. All of the text strings appear with black fills. Press SPACEBAR again to return to the Editable Preview window and then click on the Group button on the toolbar to group all of the text strings. Next, select a white fill by clicking on the white button on the color palette and turn off Wireframe view. The text strings redisplay with a fill of white, making it easier to distinguish them from one another.

17. With all text strings still selected, click on the Outline Pen tool and then on the Outline Pen Roll-up button (the third from the left in the top row) to open the Pen roll-up. Click on the Edit button to display the Outline Pen dialog box. Change the Width setting to 0.1 inch, turn on Scale With Image, click on OK, and then on Apply. Close the Outline Pen roll-up. The text strings redisplay with a medium outline of uniform width.

18. Ungroup and deselect all text strings and then select only the last text string you created (the top). Click on the Fill tool and then on the Fountain Fill button (the first button in the second row) to open the Fountain Fill dialog box. Choose a linear fountain fill and an angle of 45 degrees. For the From color, select white. Similarly, for the To color, select black. Click on OK again to make this fill pattern take effect.

19. Now create a drop-shadow effect. Press Tab to select the text string in the layer just below the text string with the fountain fill. Assign a fill of black

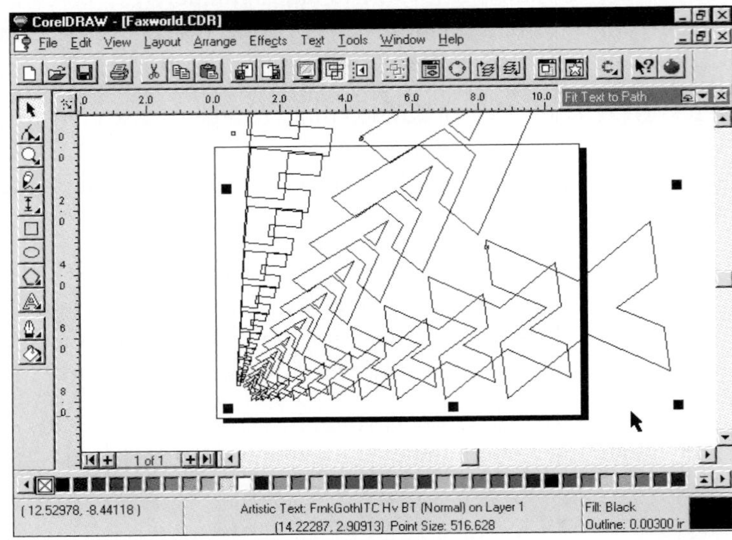

Scaled and repeated text strings exceeding the page boundaries

FIGURE 14-10

to this object by clicking on the black button on the far left of the palette at the bottom of your screen. Press F4 to switch to Zoom To All Objects view to see your whole work. Figure 14-11 shows the result of your selection.

20. Continue pressing Tab to select each text string in the reverse order from which it was created. Fill the text strings in the following sequence, starting with the largest text string after the drop shadow: 90-percent black, 80-percent black, 70-percent black, 60-percent black, 50-percent black, 40-percent black, 30-percent black, 20-percent black, and 10-percent black. Fill one more text string with 10-percent black and the remaining (smallest) text strings with white. You can quickly apply these shades by using the Color palette at the bottom of the screen, beginning with the second black from the left. The resulting gradation of fills and the drop shadow make the repeated text strings seem to leap out of the screen, as shown in Figure 14-12.

21. To group all text strings so that you cannot separate them accidentally, double-click on the Pick tool and then on the Group button. Move the group upward and away from the left side of the page. You will bring the group back later, but for now you need room to create more objects.

22. Switch to Zoom To Page view, select Snap to Grid from the Layout menu, then select the Ellipse tool and position the pointer 4 1/2 inches from the top of the page and 3/4 inch from the left margin. Press and hold CTRL and draw a circle 3 inches in diameter, starting from the upper-left area of the rim. Use the Status bar as a guide.
23. Turn the circle into a 3-D globe by giving it a radial fountain fill. To do this, click on the Pick tool to select the circle automatically, then select the Fill tool and then the Fountain Fill button. When the Fountain Fill dialog box appears, select a radial fountain fill, but leave the other settings unchanged. Click on OK to have the fountain fill take effect. The globe reappears with a white highlight in the center and the fill gradually darkening toward the rim.
24. Prepare to create an off-center highlight so that the light source seems to be coming from above and to the right of the globe. Select the Freehand tool and draw a short straight line segment above and to the right of the globe. Select both the line segment and the globe, and select Combine from the Arrange menu to combine these into one object. Whenever the window redraws from now on, Coreldraw extends the first stage of the fountain fill as far as the line segment, as shown in Figure 14-13. This

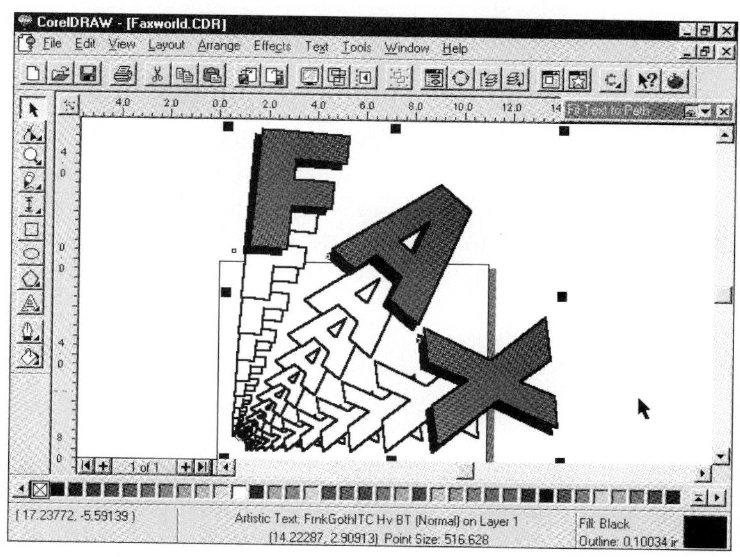

Drop-shadow effect using duplicated text and black fill

FIGURE 14-11

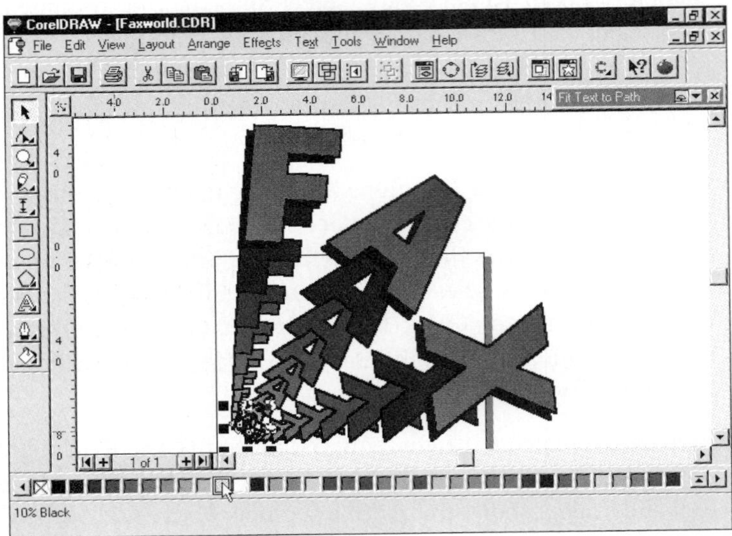

Gradation of fills, leading to 3-D effect

FIGURE 14-12

means that you can control the placement of the highlight on the globe by moving the nodes of the line segment with the Shape tool.

25. If you wish to change the placement of the highlight on the globe, activate the Shape tool and move the uppermost node of the line segment in a clockwise or counterclockwise direction. You can move either or both nodes; experiment until you find the placement you want.

26. Now make the line segment invisible. Click on the Pick tool to select the combined object automatically, and then click on the Outline Pen tool and again on the White Outline Color button in the first row of the flyout. The line segment seems to disappear from the screen, but you can still use it to manipulate the highlight on the globe.

IP: *The line you created will still be visible in Wireframe view.*

27. Create a rectangle that will form a backdrop for the rest of the image. Click on the Rectangle tool and begin a rectangle at the 1-inch mark on the horizontal ruler and the –1 1/2-inch mark on the vertical ruler. Extend

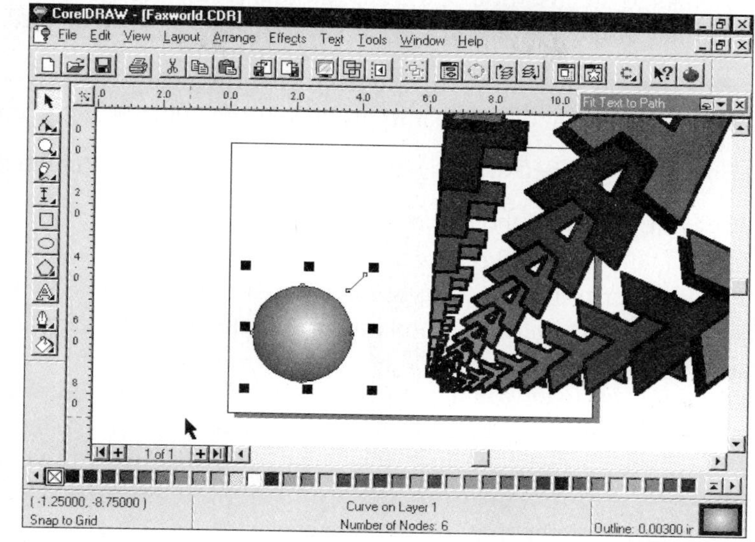

Changing the center of a fountain fill by combining a line segment with a globe

FIGURE 14-13

the rectangle downward and to the right until you reach the 7 1/2-inch mark on the horizontal ruler and the –7 1/4-inch mark on the vertical ruler. Then release the mouse button.

28. Click on the Pick tool to select the rectangle automatically, select Order from the Arrange menu, and then select To Back. The globe appears as the top layer (yes, the line reappears, but it will be obscured again in a moment).

29. With the Fill tool, assign a fill of 20-percent black to the rectangle.

30. Select the "FAX" grouped text strings and move them on top of the globe, so that they seem to be emerging directly from the highlight. To make certain that the text strings are the top-layer object, click on the To Front button on the toolbar. This also hides the line segment that you used as a "handle" to change the center of the globe's fountain fill, as shown in Figure 14-14.

31. Press F4 to switch to Zoom To All view to see all of the text strings. With the grouped text object still selected, scale the text strings down until the Status bar displays a value of approximately 42 percent. Return to Zoom To Page view by pressing SHIFT-F4 and select Full Screen Preview.

Thanks to the insertion of the background rectangle, the text strings still seem to thrust outward in 3-D, as shown earlier in Figure 14-8.

32. Press F9 and click on Select All from the Edit menu. Then click on the Group button on the toolbar to group all of the objects in the image.

33. Save your finished drawing by clicking on the Save button on the toolbar.

34. Select Close from the File menu to clear the screen.

If you have performed all three of the exercises in this chapter, you are well on the way to understanding how to combine many different Coreldraw features, tricks, and techniques. Perhaps these exercises have stimulated you to create your own original designs, or given you new ideas for embellishing existing ones. Whatever your field, your work in this tutorial has given you the tools to create more effective illustrations, documents, presentations, and designs. Coreldraw makes it all possible!

In the remaining sections of this chapter, you will learn how to automate Coreldraw's functions and how to customize Coreldraw's menus and toolbars.

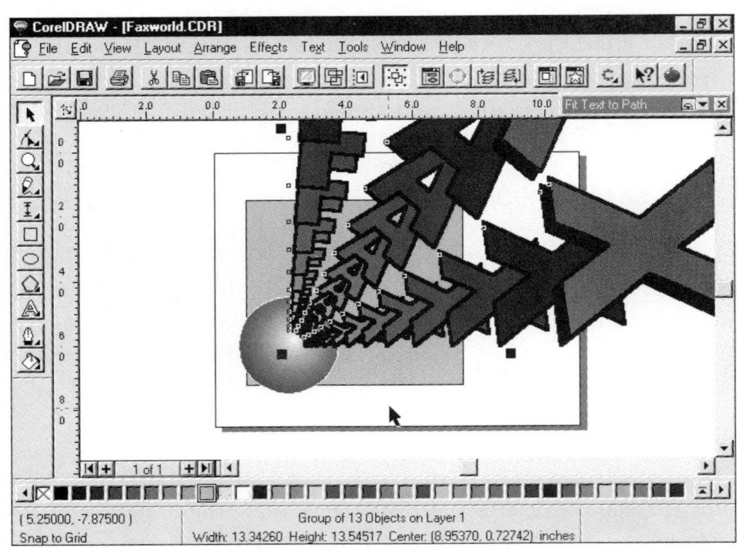

Grouped text strings overlaid on the globe highlight for 3-D effect

FIGURE 14-14

Using Corel SCRIPT

As you've seen in the exercises in this chapter, creating complex drawings can often require repeating a series of steps as different objects are selected. Even creating a new document can require you to select a number of options from the various Coreldraw menus before you can begin drawing. With CorelDRAW! 6, you now have a powerful tool to simplify repetitive actions. Corel SCRIPT is a standalone program that allows you to create a file, known as a *script*, containing a series of actions that you can execute at one time by running the script file.

OTE: *Corel SCRIPT can only be used with CorelDRAW! 6 and Corel PHOTO-PAINT.*

A Corel SCRIPT file can contain both *application commands* and *intrinsic statements*. Application commands are Corel SCRIPT equivalents of Coreldraw menu commands. For example, the Corel SCRIPT command FileOpen performs the same function as the Open command from the File menu in Coreldraw. Intrinsic commands are unique to Corel SCRIPT and control the flow of the script, display dialog boxes or information, and retrieve information from your computer. For example, IF, THEN, and ELSE are intrinsic statements used to control the flow of a script. The IF statement sets up a test, as in IF a drawing is open. The THEN statement defines the action to be taken when the IF statement is true. The ELSE statement defines the action to be taken when the IF statement is false.

This might be implemented in a script designed to create a new document if there is no open document, but not to create a document if one is already open. In this case, the IF statement would define the test (is there an open document), the THEN statement would skip to the next step if a document is open, and the ELSE statement would create a new document if one isn't open. The ELSE statement would use the application command FileNew to create the new document.

Corel SCRIPT files are plain text files that can be opened in Windows 95 Notepad or a word processor as well as Corel SCRIPT. However, word processors can add formatting that would prevent the script from functioning properly. When the script is run, Corel SCRIPT *compiles*, or interprets, the text into commands that are understood by Coreldraw.

Corel SCRIPT can be opened from both the Windows 95 Start menu (in the Corel Applications program group) and from within Coreldraw itself. In Coreldraw, open the Tools menu, select Scripts, and then select Corel SCRIPT Editor. The Corel SCRIPT application window shown in Figure 14-15 will be displayed.

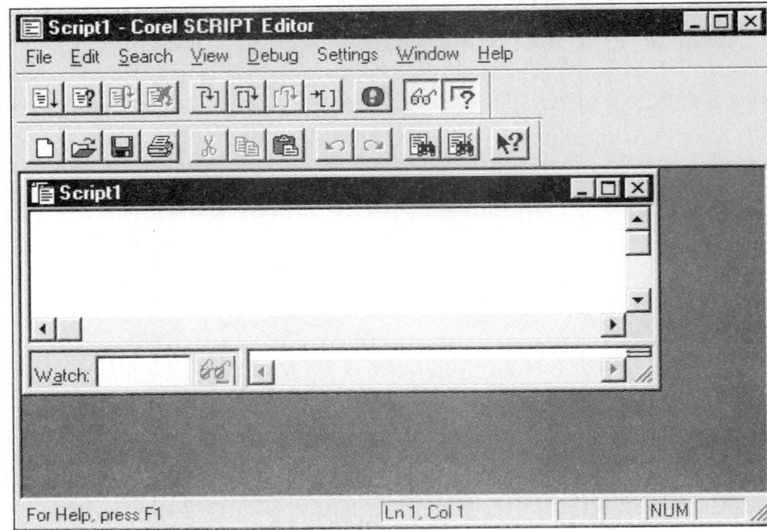

Corel SCRIPT application window

FIGURE 14-15

As you can see, the Corel SCRIPT application window contains many of the same features as the Coreldraw application window. You can also have multiple scripts open at one time. On the Corel SCRIPT menu bar, the File, Edit, View, Window, and Help menus contain options similar to the same Coreldraw menus. The Debug menu contains commands that help you find errors in a script and the Settings menu allows you to customize Corel SCRIPT features.

There are two toolbars in the Corel SCRIPT window: the Standard Toolbar and the Debug Toolbar. The Standard Toolbar (the lower toolbar) contains some of the same buttons as the Coreldraw Standard Toolbar, which you have used throughout this book. The four buttons that are new are Undo, Redo, Find, and Replace, shown here:

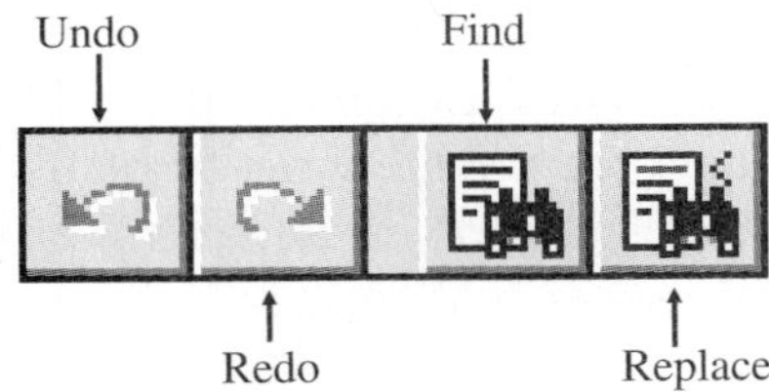

The Undo and Redo buttons function in the same manner as the Undo and Redo commands on the Edit menu in Coreldraw. The Find and Replace buttons function in the same manner as the Find and Replace commands in Coreldraw's Text menu.

The Debug Toolbar also helps find errors in a script. The tools and their functions are explained in the following table:

Button	Name	Function
	Run	Runs the selected script
	Check Syntax	Checks for errors in spelling or commands in the selected script
	Restart	Resets all variables and starts from the first line of the script
	Reset	Resets all variables and returns to the first line of the script
	Step Into	Executes the current line of the script, then stops
	Step Over	Skips the current line
	Step Out	Skips the remainder of the current line
	Run to Cursor	Executes the script until it reaches the current cursor location
	Toggle Breakpoint	Sets a point where the script will stop for debugging
	Toggle Watch Window	Opens or closes a window that displays the value of a variable
	Toggle Compiler Output Window	Opens or closes a window to displays the output of the script

Corel SCRIPT Dialog Editor

You can also create custom dialog boxes to display information or get input from the user. For example, if your script needs the name of a file to open, the script can display a custom dialog box where you will enter the name of the file to open. When you close the dialog box, the information will be used by the script to open the named file. Custom dialog boxes are created with the Corel SCRIPT Dialog Editor, shown in Figure 14-16, that is opened from the Corel SCRIPT Edit menu.

The commands in the File, Edit, View, Arrange, Window, and Helps menus are similar to the menu commands you have used throughout this book. The Control menu contains objects, such as drop-down list boxes and option buttons, that you can add to your Custom dialog box. These same objects are displayed on the toolbars that make up most of the Corel SCRIPT Dialog Editor window.

IP: *Point on each button to see an explanation of its function in the Status bar.*

To create a new dialog box, you can click on the control's button, the click in the dialog box displayed in the script window to place the control. You then enter the information relating to the object.

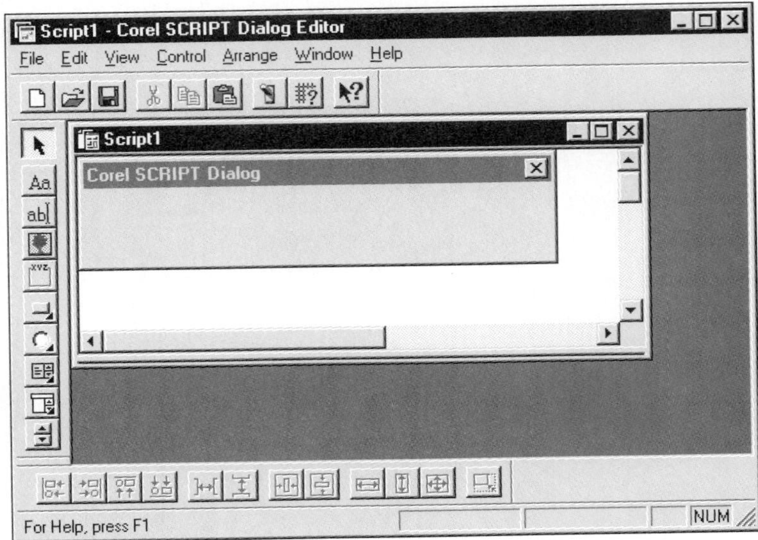

FIGURE 14-16 Corel SCRIPT Dialog Editor

A number of sample scripts are included with your Coreldraw package in the \Corel\Scripts\ folder. These scripts demonstrate how to use both Corel SCRIPT and Corel SCRIPT Dialog Editor to customize Coreldraw to suit your working habits and preferences.

There is still another way that you can customize Coreldraw to suit yourself. You can customize keyboard shortcuts, menu commands, color palettes, roll-ups, and toolbars using the Customize dialog box.

Using the Customize Dialog Box

The Customize dialog box is opened by selecting Customize from the Tools menu. The Customize dialog box shown in Figure 14-17 will be displayed. Select each tab to look at its contents as you read through the following sections.

KEYBOARD SHORTCUTS Using the Customize dialog box is very easy. On the Keyboard tab, shown in Figure 14-17, new keyboard shortcuts are created by first selecting the command from the Commands display box, then clicking in the Press new shortcut key text box, and pressing the shortcut key combination you want to assign to the command. If there is a conflict with an existing shortcut, it will be

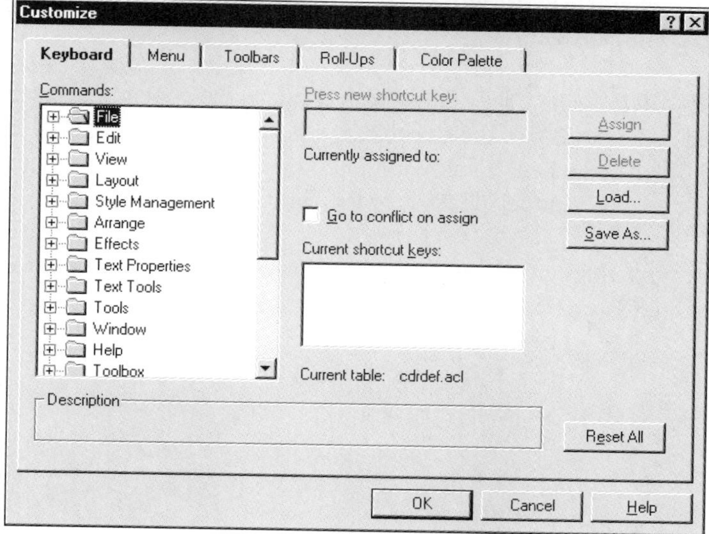

Customize dialog box

FIGURE 14-17

displayed. You can then replace or keep the existing keyboard shortcut. You can save your new shortcuts as a file so you can load them at any time. This means you can keep several shortcut files tailored to specific types of work and load the shortcut files as needed.

MENU COMMANDS Commands can be added or removed from any Coreldraw menu using the Menu tab. You can even add a new menu containing your most frequently used commands. The Commands list box contains all the possible commands and the Menu list box displays the commands currently included on each menu. You add commands by selecting the command you want to add from the Commands list box, then selecting the menu and placing it in the menu where you want to add the command. Clicking on the Add button adds the command to the selected menu. Commands are removed by first selecting the command from the Menu list box and clicking on the Remove button.

TOOLBARS Toolbars are customized by simply dragging tool buttons to or from a toolbar. The tool buttons are grouped by function in the Command Categories list box. Selecting a category displays the associated tool buttons in the Buttons display box. Dragging a tool button from the Buttons display box onto a toolbar adds the button in the location it is dragged to.

ROLL-UPS Roll-ups are customized in much the same way as menus. There are two list boxes displaying the Left aligned roll-ups and the Right aligned roll-ups. The source and destination roll-ups are determined by clicking on either the Move>> or <<Move command button.

COLOR PALETTE The Color Palette tab controls the appearance of the Color palette displayed at the bottom of the Coreldraw screen. You can have a 3-D effect and large or small color swatches, display a "no color" well, set the number of rows for the Color palette, and set the function of the right mouse button.

In the next chapter, you will be introduced to another complete application that is part of the CorelDRAW! 6 package: Corel PRESENTS.

COREL DRAW!™ 6 in action

***1921 T Bucket*—Reed Fisher**

Reed Fisher has won many awards for his renderings of cars. This illustration shows Reed's attention to detail, so important to drawings of this type. Notice how the chrome firewall behind the engine reflects the rear of the engine, and how the windshield subdues the colors behind it.

Reed Fisher works in San Clemente, California, and can be reached at (714) 498-0634.

Using Corel PRESENTS

15

Corel PRESENTS is a new module in the Coreldraw family. It replaces several modules in previous versions of Coreldraw, including CorelCHART, CorelSHOW, and CorelMOVE. The purpose of Corel PRESENTS is to provide all of the features necessary to prepare and deliver a presentation, whether it be on the computer screen, projected, or printed. With Corel PRESENTS, you can create or import text, both vector and bitmapped graphics, traditional charts, animation, sound, and video clips to produce a series of slides. In this chapter you'll be introduced to Corel PRESENTS and be led through the creation of a presentation.

Starting a New Presentation

When you first start Corel PRESENTS, the New Presentation window, shown in Figure 15-1, is displayed. This allows you to create a new presentation in one of

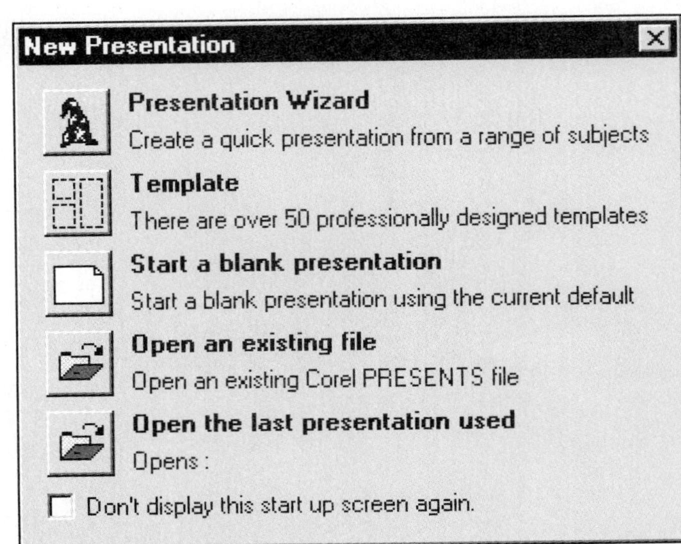

New Presentation window

FIGURE 15-1

three ways or to open an existing presentation in one of two ways. If you are starting a new presentation, the question is which alternative to choose. Delay that answer for a short while and look at the alternatives, beginning with the Presentation Wizard.

Beginning with the Presentation Wizard

If you do not have Corel PRESENTS on your screen, start it now, and when the New Presentation window opens click on Presentation Wizard. If you or someone else has turned off the New Presentation window (by selecting the Don't display this start up screen again), open the File menu, choose New, and select From Wizard. In either case, the initial Presentation Wizard dialog box opens, as shown in Figure 15-2.

Click on Next. The second Presentation Wizard dialog box lists several different types of presentations from which you can choose one to serve as a model for the one you wish to create. For this exercise, choose New Product, then click on Finish. Corel PRESENTS opens with the 15-slide presentation "dummy" called Newprod.cpr that you can see in Figure 15-3. Using this dummy presentation, you

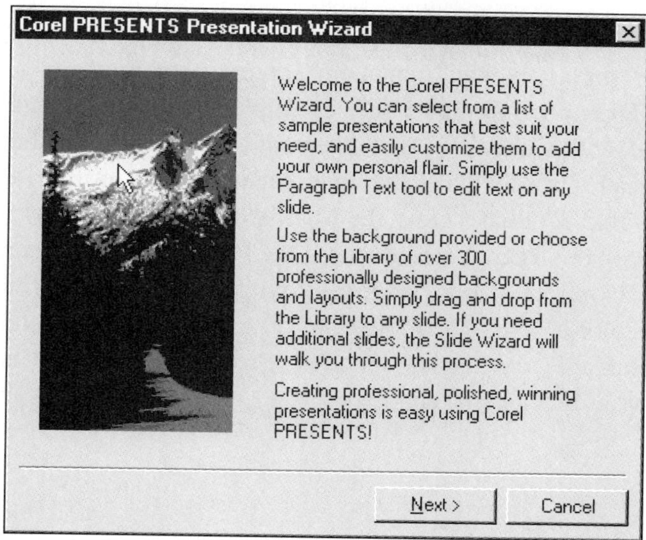

Initial Presentation Wizard dialog box

FIGURE 15-2

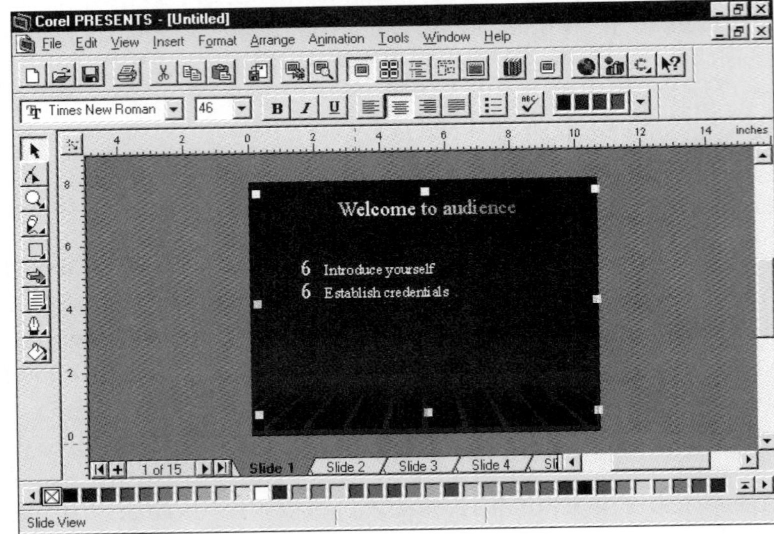

Corel PRESENTS with the Newprod.cpr dummy presentation

FIGURE 15-3

can go through and add your own titles, text, and graphics following the suggested pattern of the dummy presentation.

Corel PRESENTS Environment

Use the presentation that is on your screen to take a quick look at the Corel PRESENTS environment. First of all, you'll notice that there are many similarities with Coreldraw. The leftmost eight buttons on the Standard toolbar (at the top in Figure 15-3) are the same, the remaining tools are described in Table 15-1. The Text toolbar (below the Standard toolbar in Figure 15-3) has buttons that you probably recognized through the Bullets button. The next button (ABC with a checkmark) is for checking your spelling and the final buttons are for assigning color to text. The toolbox has the ellipse and polygon tools on a flyout from the rectangle tool and has added the geometric shapes tool and flyout to create two and three-dimensional shapes.

Icon	Name	Purpose
	Run presentation	Runs through all the slides in the presentation
	Preview slide	Opens a full-screen preview of the slide
	Slide view	Displays one slide on the screen and allows editing
	Slide Sorter view	Displays all of the slides in the presentation and allows you to rearrange them
	Outline view	Displays all of the slides in outline format with text indented from the slide titles
	Master layout view	Displays the current master layout for the slide being edited
	Background view	Displays the background for the slide being edited
	Libraries	Displays the backgrounds and master layouts that are available
	Insert slides	Allows inserting one or more slides before or after the current slide
	Insert a map	Allows inserting a map created with Map server
	Insert a chart	Allows inserting a chart created with Chart server

Unique buttons on the Corel PRESENTS Standard toolbar

TABLE 15-1

Corel PRESENTS Views

Among the most important aspects of using Corel PRESENTS are the views that are available. These views allow you to work on parts of the presentation and/or to perform various tasks. As you can see in Table 15-1, you can select a view to use through the buttons on the Standard toolbar. You can also use the View menu, which is shown next, and has the added benefit of alternative Master layouts and Speaker Notes, Handout, and Animation views.

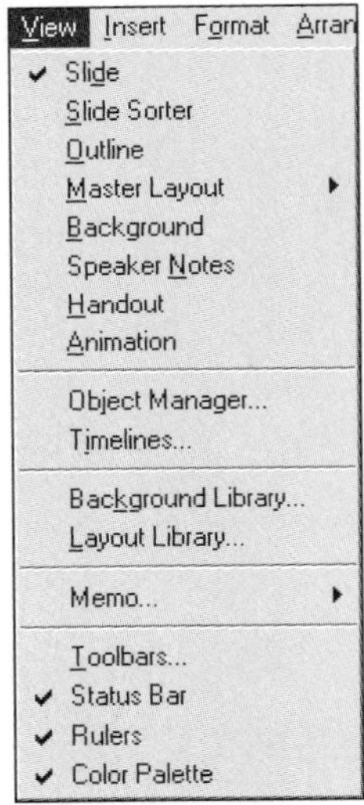

- **Slide** view is the initial view, shown in Figure 15-3, and is where you add the text and graphics to an individual slide.
- **Slide Sorter** view, which you see in Figure 15-4, gives you an overview of the presentation and allows you to rearrange the slides and make global changes.
- **Outline** view, which is shown in Figure 15-5, lets you look at and work on all of the text at one time and control the hierarchy of the points. You can also drag and drop text from any OLE2 enabled word processing application, or type directly in this view.
- **Master Layout** view is actually four separate views, Title Slide Master, Slide Master, Handout, and Speaker Notes, as you can see in Figure 15-6. Each of the master layouts allows you to establish a layout with one or

more text areas containing a particular text format, bullet style, and case style (leading caps, all caps, or no caps), which you can apply to any slide using the Layout library.

- **Background** view lets you edit the background of the current slide by creating or importing graphics.
- **Speaker Notes** view displays a page on which you can show one or more slides and enter notes for the speaker.
- **Handout** view also displays a page on which you can show one or more slides and enter information you want to hand out to the audience.
- **Animation** view brings up the animation toolbar that allows you to play an animation or video clip contained on a slide and adjust the timing of it.

Corel PRESENTS Pop-Up Menus

Pop-up menus opened with the right mouse button are very important in Corel PRESENTS, and there are some functions you can find only in pop-up menus. Two of the more important pop-up menus are the Slide pop-up, shown next on the left,

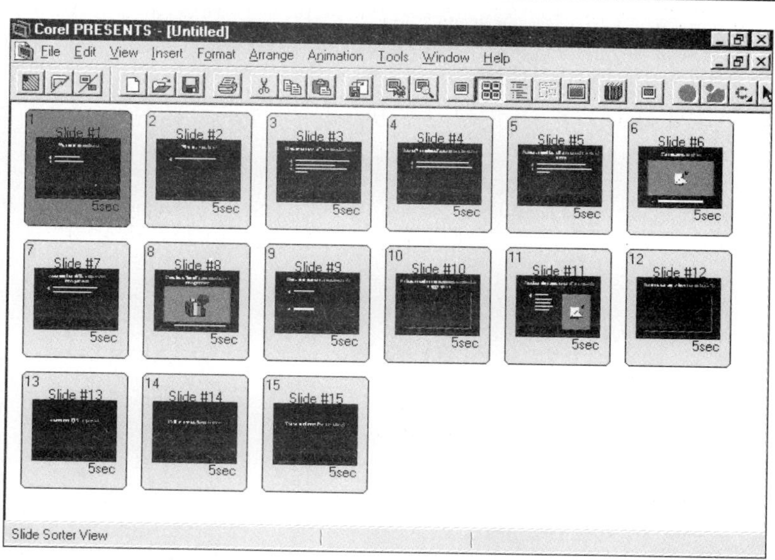

Slide Sorter view

FIGURE 15-4

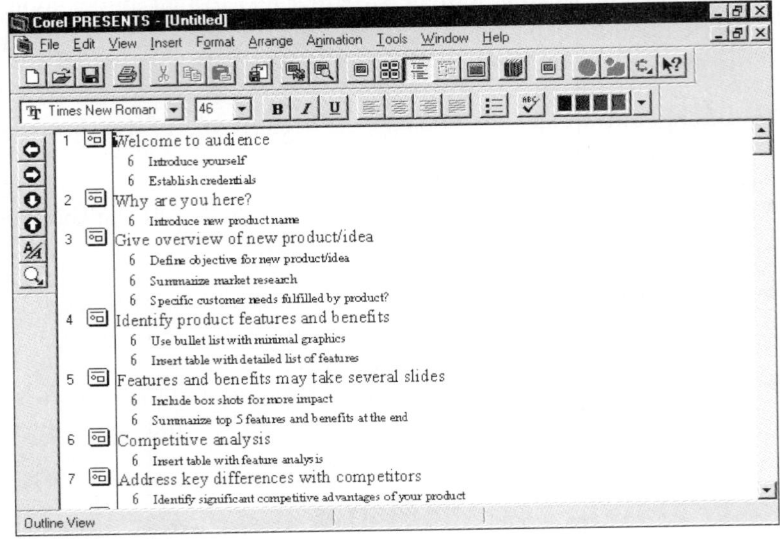

Outline view

FIGURE 15-5

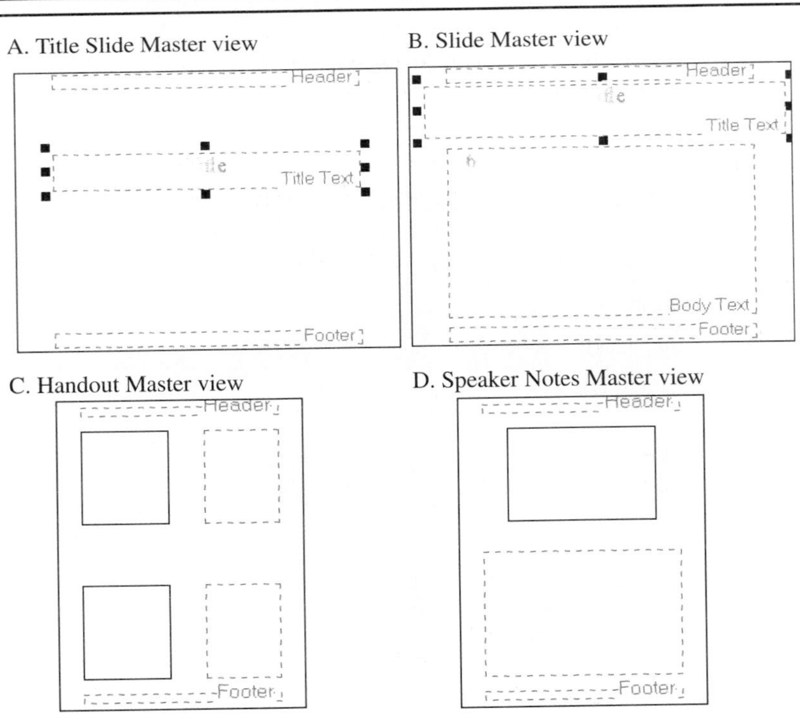

Master views

FIGURE 15-6

and the Object pop-up, shown on the right. Both of these pop-up menus provide options that relate to the item you clicked on and allow you to open the Properties dialog box for that item.

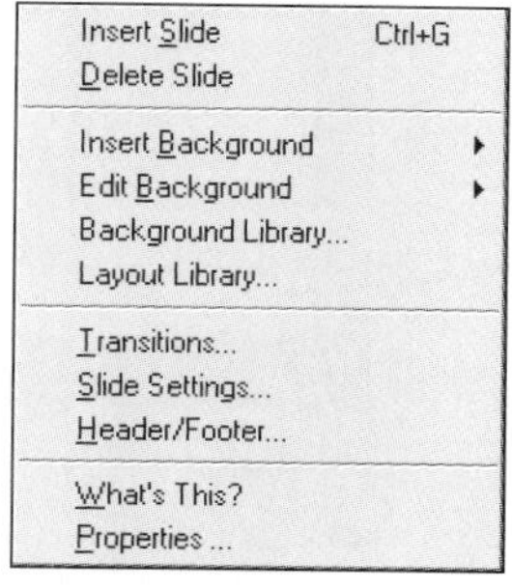

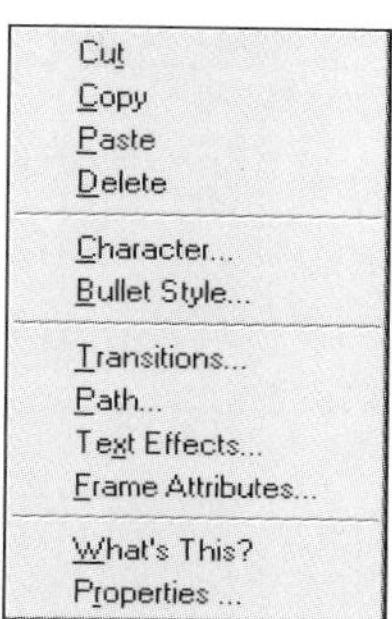

IP: *If you don't quickly see how to do something in the toolbar or regular menus, try right-clicking on the object you want to do something to.*

The Slide Properties dialog box, shown in Figure 15-7, controls the transitions used in opening the slide, allows you to name the slide and determine how much of it to show, and asks whether there is a header and/or footer (and if so, what they will contain). The Object Properties dialog box, which you can see in Figure 15-8, controls the transition effects for the selected object as well as text blocks within the object, the path taken by the transition effects among the objects on the slide, and the attributes assigned to the object.

NOTE: *The Object Properties Attributes tab allows you to determine if you want to override or replace an attribute on an individual slide—such as the font, style, or size of a text object—with that same attribute on the corresponding master layout.*

Libraries

The Libraries, which you can open from the Standard toolbar or the View menu (Background Library or Layout Library), has two tabs that contain backgrounds you can use in the presentation (shown in Figure 15-9) and layouts for text and graphics (shown in Figure 15-10). As you are creating a presentation, you can apply a

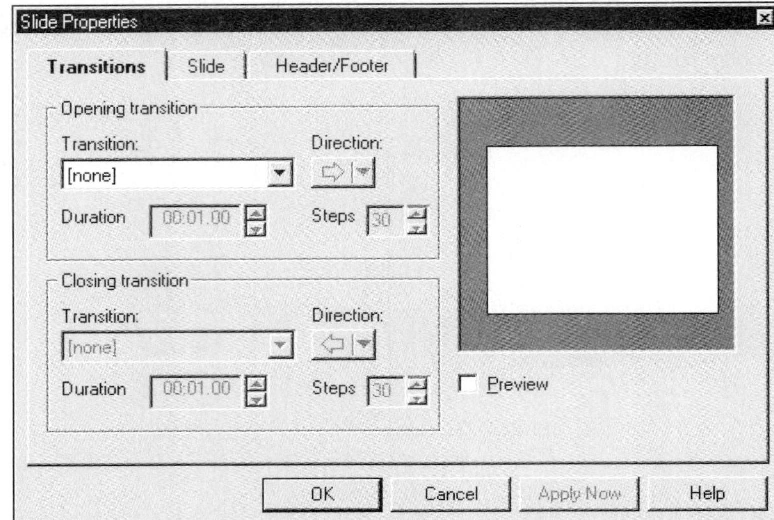

Slide Properties dialog box

FIGURE 15-7

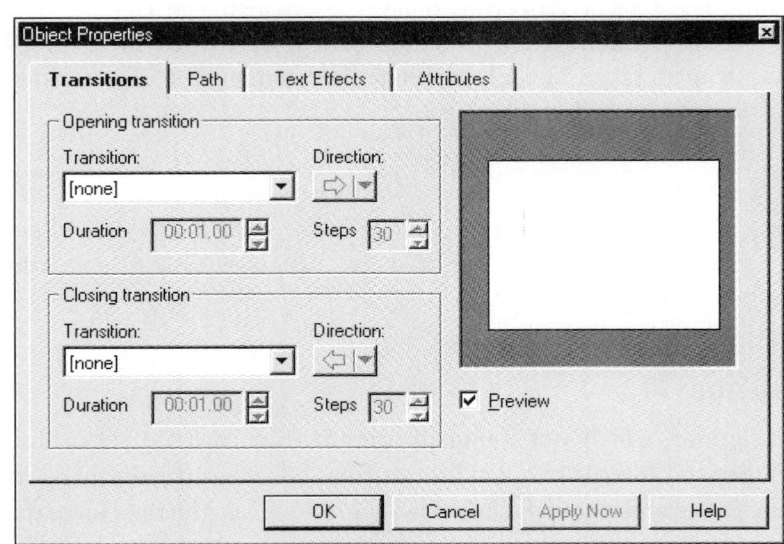

Object Properties dialog box

FIGURE 15-8

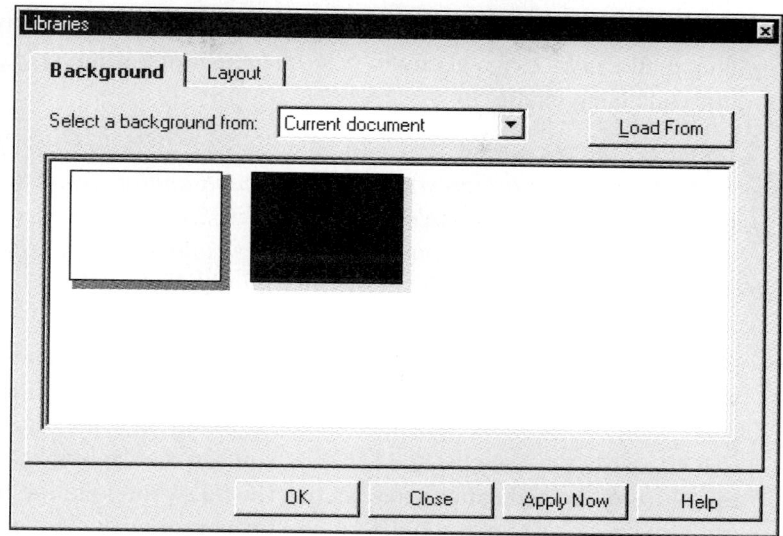

Background Library

FIGURE 15-9

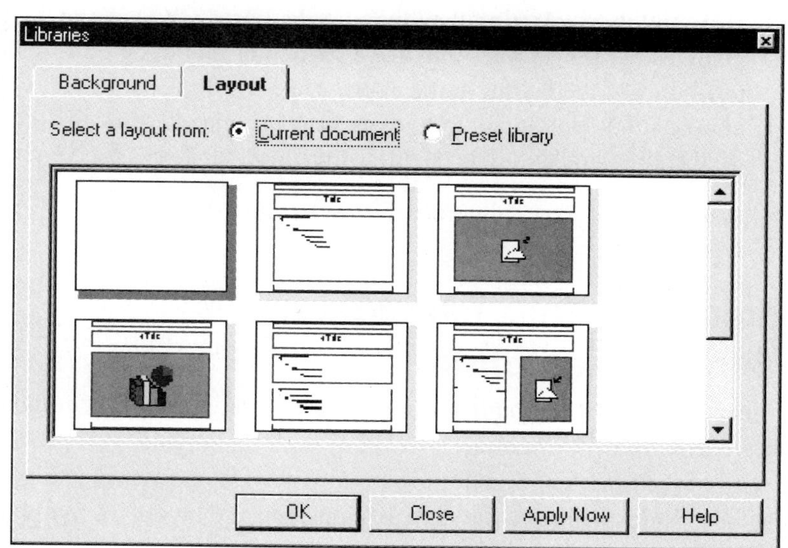

Layout Library

FIGURE 15-10

background and/or a layout to the active slide by opening the Libraries, selecting a background and/or layout, and clicking on Apply Now. Once you apply a background and/or layout to a slide, all new slides get that same background and layout until you change them.

TIP: *If you want to apply a new background and/or layout to a group of already created slides, select the slides in Slide Sorter view, select the background or layout from the Libraries, and click on Apply Now or double-click on the thumbnail in the Libraries dialog box.*

- A *background* is a pattern, color, graphic, text, or a combination of these four elements, that is applied to the selected slides in a presentation. A background is created or changed in Background view and once created will appear in the Background Library. You can then apply it to any slide by selecting the slide and then selecting the background in the library. You can also attach a sound or audio clip to a background and have it played for each slide that uses the background.
- A *layout* is a set of one or more predefined areas or blocks that can contain text, graphics, charts, maps, or other OLE objects. Text areas can contain a particular text format, bullet style, and case style (leading caps, all caps, or no caps). You can apply a layout to any slide by selecting the slide and then selecting the layout in the library. You can make global changes to all the slides that use a particular layout by editing the attributes of the layout in the appropriate Master Layout view. If you choose a layout with a chart, map, or OLE object, you can double-click on the slide and create or identify the chart, map, or OLE object you want.
- A *template* is a combination of a background and a layout.

Beginning with a Template or a Blank Presentation

The other choices for beginning a new presentation are with a template or with a blank presentation. If you choose to begin with a template, you get a single slide with the background and layout of the template you choose. If you add additional slides, those slides will have the same background and layout (or template) until you

change it. If you start with a blank presentation, then you will use the current default background and layout. You will do this in a minute.

So, which way is the best way to start a new presentation? It depends on what you want to do and how much time you have. If you want a presentation to have exactly *your* look, then beginning with a blank presentation is the best way for you. If you are in a hurry and are comfortable with the look of one of the "canned" presentations offered by the New Presentation Wizard, then the Wizard is the best way for you. The template option is somewhere in between the Wizard and a blank presentation.

The best way to determine which way is best for you is to try each of the options on a real presentation and you can then see for yourself which way is best under specific circumstances. In the next section, you will have the opportunity to build a presentation from scratch and you will be able to see both the flexibility and effort that that takes. Since both the Wizard and the template approaches simply eliminate steps you have to perform in the blank presentation approach, you will be able to go through the Wizard and template approaches on your own.

Creating a Presentation from Scratch

When you start with a blank presentation, the steps that you can perform to create a presentation are as follows:

- Define slide properties
- Select or prepare and add a background
- Select or prepare and add a layout
- Add, format, and position text
- Change the master layout
- Add additional slides
- Prepare, add, and edit graphics
- Prepare and add charts
- Prepare and add animation
- Add sound and/or video
- Edit and spell check text in Outline view

- Add slide and object transitions
- Organize the slides in Slide Sorter view
- Create speaker notes
- Create an audience handout
- Run the presentation

Of course, many of these steps are optional as are many of the embellishments within each step. A presentation can be as simple as a few slides with text only to as complex as a grand product announcement with sound and animation. In the remaining sections of this chapter, follow along as a presentation is created using many of the features of Corel PRESENTS.

Defining Slide Properties

A presentation can be given in many mediums and each has its default size and other characteristics. For example, the Corel PRESENTS default is a computer screen presentation that is 6.67 inches by 5 inches in Landscape orientation, and has fairly small margins. Some of the alternatives that are available in Corel PRESENTS are as follows:

- Standard letter-size paper—8.5 inches by 11 inches, Portrait orientation
- 35-mm slide—11 inches by 7.33 inches, Landscape orientation
- Computer screen—6.67 inches by 5 inches, Landscape orientation
- Overhead projection—10 inches by 7.5 inches, Landscape orientation

Corel PRESENTS also has many other paper sizes, including European sizes, and if you don't see the size you want, you can use Custom and set the size to anything you want. Your first task after opening a blank presentation is determining how you are going to deliver the presentation and then setting the size and other properties accordingly. You do this through the Page Setup dialog box shown in Figure 15-11. Once set, the orientation, paper type, size, and margins are applied to the entire presentation. Other properties, such as a header and/or footer can be applied to the entire presentation as well as changed on individual slides.

Begin the creation of a new presentation now and define the properties with the following steps (the presentation described in the following steps and sections is a

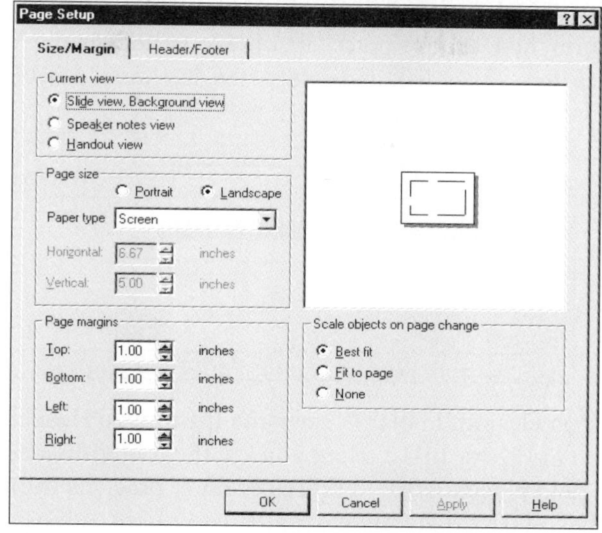

Page Setup dialog box

FIGURE 15-11

proposal for a maritime museum; you can use the steps to create a presentation for anything that suites your needs or fancy):

IP: *You can undo many mistakes by pressing CTRL-Z, or by opening the Edit menu and choosing Undo if you take one of these actions immediately after making the mistake.*

1. If you haven't already, open a new blank presentation either by starting Corel PRESENTS and selecting Start a blank presentation in the New Presentation dialog box or, if Corel PRESENTS is already open, by selecting New from the File menu and Document from the submenu that opens.
2. Open the File menu and select Page Setup to open the Page Setup dialog box that you saw above.
3. Make sure Slide view, Background view is selected for the Current view, and that Landscape and Screen are selected for the Page size.
4. Drag across the Top margin number, type **.5**, and press TAB twice. Repeat this process to set the margins for the left and right margins at .5 inch. (The bottom margin is left at 1.00 to leave room for a footer.)

5. Accept the default Best fit for the Scale objects on page change setting.
6. Click on the Header/Footer tab, click on Slides in the View area, open the Footer drop-down list, and select ";Slide 1;*date*" as you see here:

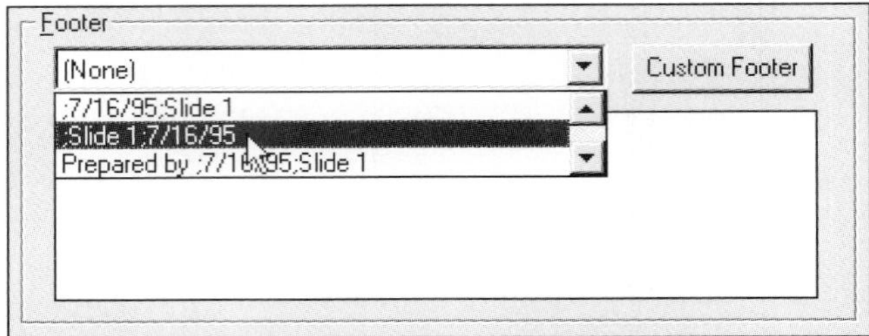

7. Click on Custom Footer to open the Customize Header/Footer dialog box shown in Figure 15-12. Here you see the footer divided into three sections with field placeholders in braces or curly brackets for the user name, slide number, and date in the left, center, and right sections respectively. The placeholders, which can be typed or created by clicking on the appropriate macro button, will be replaced by actual values on the slide. The center section also has the word "Slide" that will be literally repeated on each slide. Anything you type will literally appear in the section of the header or footer in which you type it, unless it is a placeholder. The placeholders you can use are as follows:

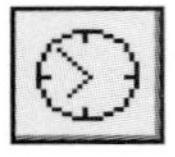

- **{date}** to print the current date and/or time (click on the clock icon in the Macros area to select the date/time format you want to use)

- **{userorganization}** to print the organization name that has been entered in the User Info tab of the Options dialog box, which is opened from the Tools menu, Options command (click on the factory icon in the Macros area to add this to the header or footer)

- **{slides}** to print the total number of slides (click on the two-page icon in the Macros area to add this to the header or footer)

- **{slidenum}** to print the number of the current slide (click on the single-page icon in the Macros area to add this to the header or footer)

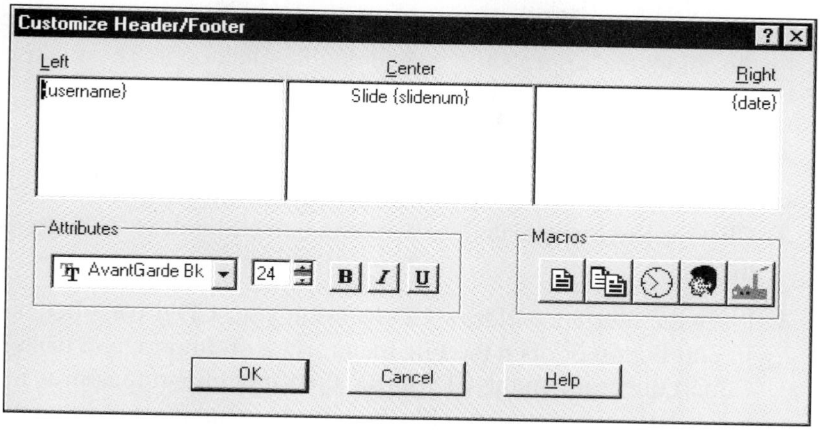

Customize Header/Footer dialog box

FIGURE 15-12

- **{username}** to print the user name that has been entered in the User Info tab of the Preferences dialog box, which is opened from the Tools menu, Options command (click on the head icon in the Macros area to add this to the header or footer)

8. Drag across the {username} placeholder in the left section and type **Maritime Museum** to add this text to the footer. Then drag across the type size in the Attributes area, type **18**; click on B to make it bold; if Italic is on, click on it to turn it off; and click on OK twice to close first the Customize dialog box and then the Page Setup dialog box. When you return to Slide view, you'll see the footer at the bottom of the slide.

Adding a Background

A presentation can be created on a blank or white background and be perfectly adequate for many uses. As a matter of fact, if you are preparing a printed presentation, a plain or white background is preferable because it is easier to read in black and white. If your presentation is either on a computer screen or a projected image, then you may want to consider a fancier background. In Corel PRESENTS, a background can be many things. It can be a simple colored background; a fountain, texture, or uniform fill; any sort of pattern; or it can be or contain a graphic. For this example, choose a solid color and add a graphic to it, with these steps.

1. Click on the Libraries button in the Standard toolbar and click on the drop-down arrow to open the list box. Click on Group01.cpb. Pick one of the colors that appeals to you and double-click on it. The one used here is the light blue in the fifth row.
2. Click on OK to close the dialog box. You will see the background on your slide.

3. Click on the Background view button in the Standard toolbar to switch to that view.
4. Place the fourth Coreldraw CD-ROM in your CD drive, click on the Import button or open the File menu, click on Import, and from the Clipart directory on the CD, select a piece of clipart to appear in the lower-left corner of each slide that gives a graphic representation of your subject. A sailing ship (Eagle_.cmx) was chosen here. Click on Import after choosing the clipart you want to use.

5. Size your clipart image so it is very small and then move it to the lower-left corner of the page, as you can see in Figure 15-13. This completes the background. Click on the Slide view button in the Standard toolbar to return to that view.

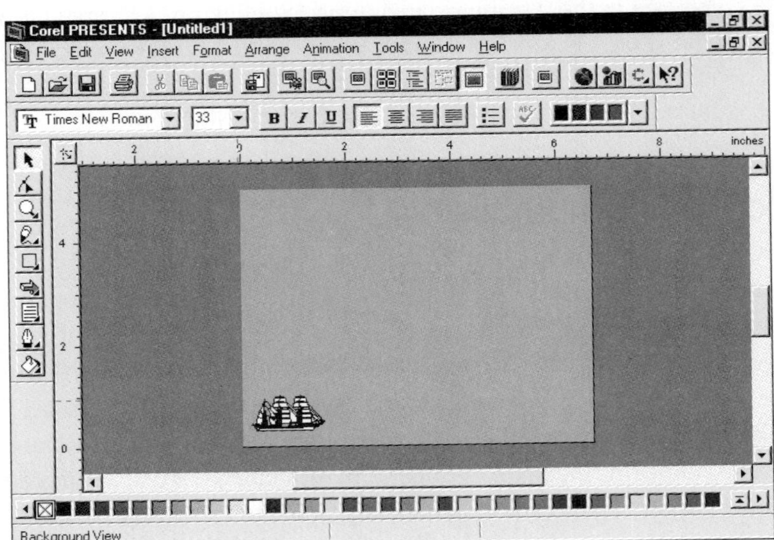

Background with a graphic in the corner

FIGURE 15-13

Adding a Layout

A layout divides a slide into areas that will be used for various purposes, such as titles, bulleted lists, and graphics. Like backgrounds, there's a library of layouts from which you can choose, and once chosen, you can edit them in the Master layout views. Add a layout to the presentation you have started with the following steps.

1. Click on Libraries in the Standard toolbar, click on the Layout tab, and click on Preset library.
2. Double-click on the title layout in the upper-left corner, as shown in Figure 15-14, and click on OK to close the Libraries dialog box. The layout will appear on your slide in Slide view.
3. Drag the smaller Title Text area above the larger one and then drag them both down, as shown in Figure 15-15.
4. Drag the title areas up or down to position them so they look good on the page.

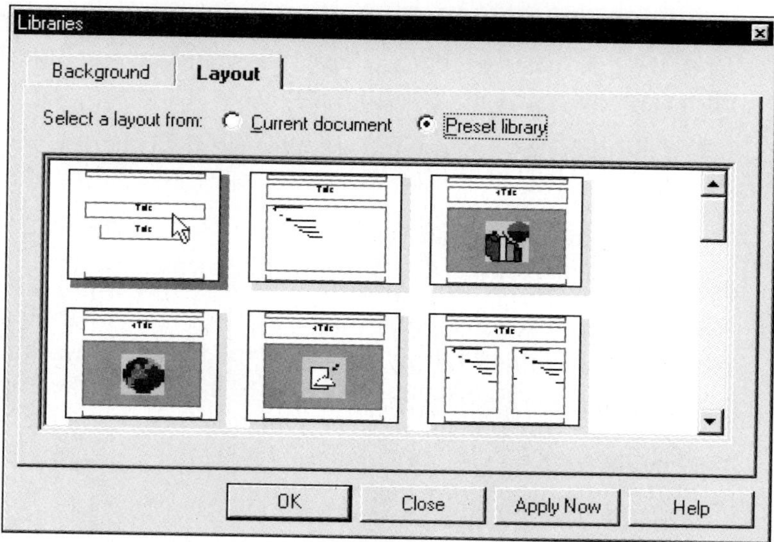

Selecting the layout

FIGURE 15-14

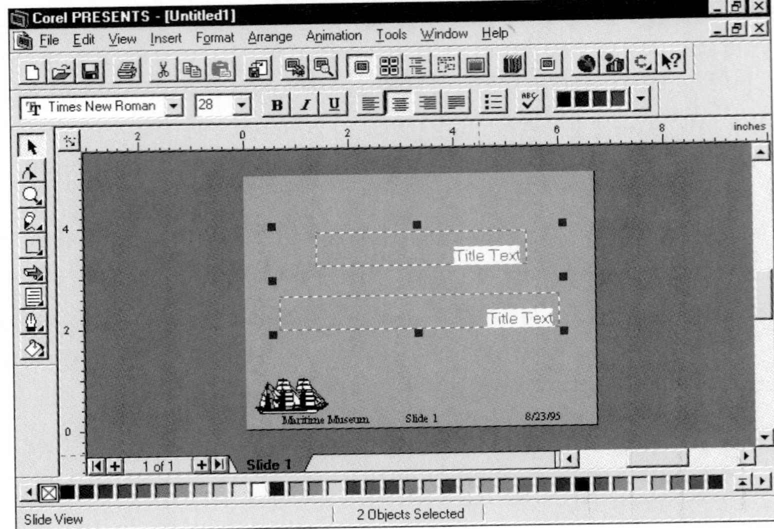

Rearranged title layout

FIGURE 15-15

Saving and Opening a Presentation

Based on the adage "save early and often," this is a good time to do that for this presentation. Use the following steps for that purpose.

1. Open the File menu and choose Save. Since this the first time the file has been saved, the Save as dialog box will open.
2. Select the directory you want to use, type the filename you want to use, and click on Save.
3. If you want to take a break and leave Corel PRESENTS for a bit, click on the close button or select Exit from the File menu.
4. When you are ready to return to Corel PRESENTS, restart it in your normal way and reopen the presentation you have been working on by clicking on Open the last presentation used in the New Presentation dialog box, or by clicking on the presentation filename at the bottom of the File menu.

15

Adding and Formatting Text

The principle component of any presentation is the text on the slides. Corel PRESENTS gives you the tools of a word processor to enter and format text. Try that next.

OTE: *Like Coreldraw, Corel PRESENTS has both an Artistic text tool for freeform text* outside of the text boxes *and a Paragraph text tool for title and body text. Bullets can only be applied to Paragraph text.*

1. Select the Paragraph text tool, and click in the top Title Text box, which should be the smaller of the two boxes.

IP: *A shortcut to select the Paragraph text tool is to double-click with the Pick tool in a text box.*

2. Type **A Proposal for**. When you are done typing, press and hold SHIFT, and press HOME to select the three words.
3. From the font drop-down list box, choose Arial MT Black; select 30 points for the type size, and click on center alignment if it isn't already selected.
4. Again with the Paragraph text tool, click in the bottom Title Text box, and type **A Maritime Museum** and select the three words.
5. Choose Arial MT Black, 32 points, and center alignment. When you are done, select the Pick tool, click outside the text boxes, and your slide should look like Figure 15-16.
6. Save your presentation.

Adding Additional Slides

Corel PRESENTS allows you to add one or several slides at a time, and in either case you can make use of the Insert Slides Wizard to apply the

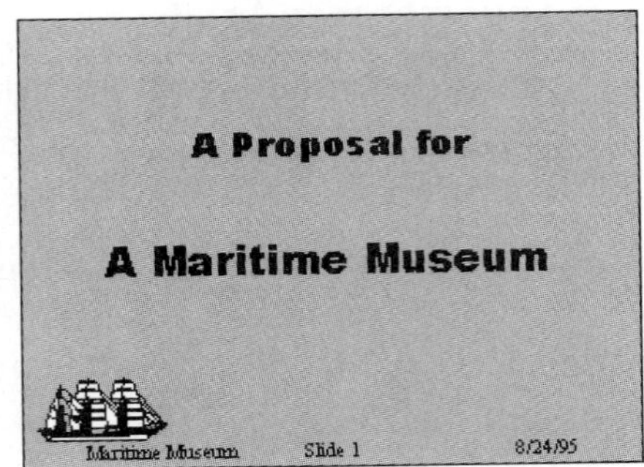

Completed title text

FIGURE 15-16

background and layout that you want. Add four new slides now and see how the Insert Slides Wizard works.

1. Click on the Insert Slides button in the Standard toolbar. The Insert Slides Wizard opens as shown in Figure 15-17.
2. Change the number of slides to 4, make sure After current slide is selected, and click on Next. The Select a Layout dialog box opens.

OTE: *If you click on Finish, you'll get four slides with the exact same background and layout as your first slide.*

3. Click on Preset library, select the second layout in the top row with the smaller and larger text areas (with a title text block at the top and larger body text block below), and click on Next. The Select a Background dialog box opens.
4. Select the background with the graphic in the bottom-left corner and click on Finish. The four new slides will be added to your presentation, so you now have five slides, as you can see by the tabs at the bottom of the window in Figure 15-18.

OTE: *Your footer did not appear on these new slides because, as a default, headers and footers are not displayed. If you want them to appear, right-click on the slide outside of a text box, select Properties, open the Slide tab, and click on Show Header and/or Show Footer.*

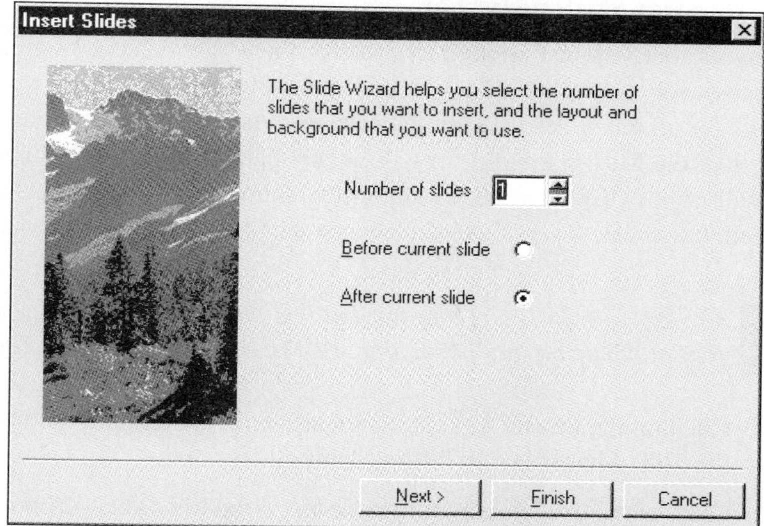

Insert Slide Wizard

FIGURE 15-17

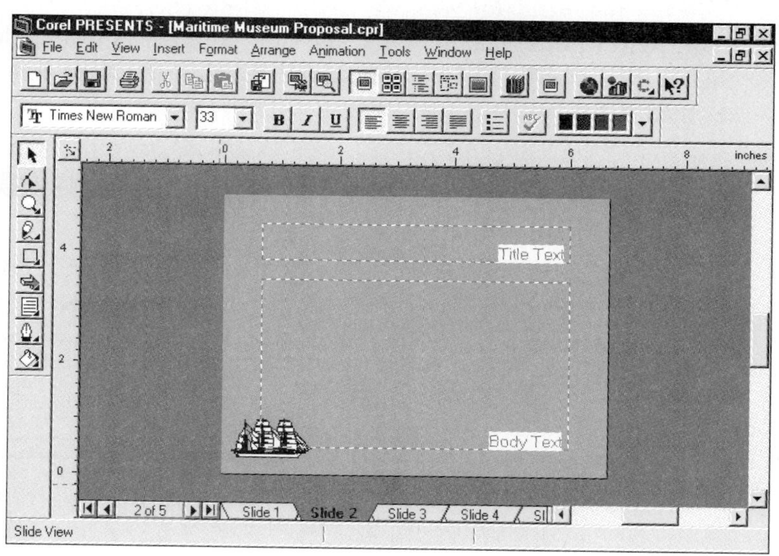

Four new slides added

FIGURE 15-18

Changing the Master Layout

The layout that you just applied to your four new slides has a number of default attributes, such as font size and type, and style of bullet. If you want to change these defaults for all the slides that use the particular layout, then you need to make the changes in the Master Layout view. You can make these changes at any time and they will affect all related slides unless the slides have directly had the attribute changed. Use the next set of steps to change the Master Layout for your new slides.

OTE: *If you change an attribute on an individual slide, you disconnect that attribute on that particular slide from the Master Slide layout.*

1. Click on the Master Layout view button in the Standard toolbar to open the Slide Master layout for your new slides.
2. Click in the Title Text block and select Arial MT Black, 28 points, and center alignment.
3. Click in the body text block and select Arial, 20 points, bold, left aligned, and click on the Bulleted List button if it isn't already selected.
4. Right-click in the body text block and select Bullet Style from the pop-up menu.
5. In the Select Bullet dialog box, make sure WingDings is the selected font, change the font Size to 18 points, and then select the large diamond you see next. Click on OK.

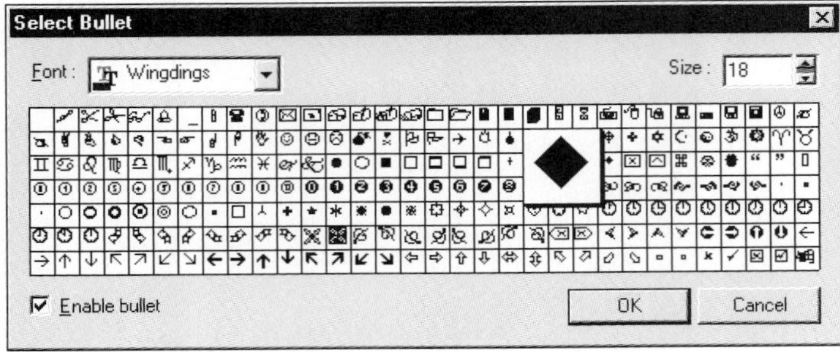

6. Double-click on the second body text line (Level two) to place the paragraph insertion point there, then right-click on that line and again open the Select Bullet dialog box. Make sure that WingDings and 18 points are selected, click on the filled in square seven characters to the left of the diamond you chose above, and click on OK. (You will not be using body text levels three through six, so you don't need to reformat them.)
7. Click on the Slide view button and then save your presentation.

Adding Bulleted Text

Much of the text in most presentations is in bulleted lists. Add some bulleted text on your new slides with the following steps (you can use any text you want, the text below is only an example).

1. Click on the Slide 2 tab if it isn't already selected. Then, with the Paragraph text tool, click in the Title Text block at the top of the slide and type **Reasons for a Museum.**

OTE: *If you don't use the Paragraph text tool, you will not see your text in Outline view.*

2. With the Paragraph text tool, click in the lower text block and type the following paragraphs, pressing ENTER at the end of each line and pressing TAB in front of each of the last three lines:

   Lots of ships need restoration
   Many people are interested
   It complements the harbor
   It will draw many tourists
   It looks financially feasible:
      Fees will support it
      A pier is available
      Grants can be requested

   When you are done, your slide should look like the one in Figure 15-19.
3. Click on Slide 3 and then save your presentation.

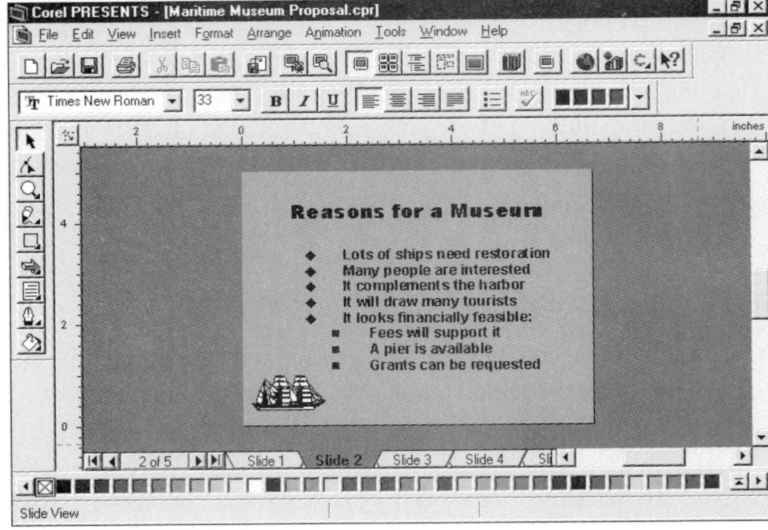

The entry of bulleted text

FIGURE 15-19

Adding and Editing Graphics

Like Coreldraw, the word "graphics" in Corel PRESENTS covers many different objects. The ship in the corner is a clipart graphic. A Coreldraw image that you import is a graphic, and an object that you draw with the tools available in Corel PRESENTS is a graphic. Use both of the latter two methods with these steps (since the current graphic on the background and the body text block conflict with the graphic to be added, remove these on Slide 3 only):

1. Open the Libraries and in the Background tab select the colored background without the sailing ship in the corner and click on OK.
2. Back in Slide 3, click in the Body Text block to select it and press DEL.
3. With the Paragraph text tool, click in the Title Text block and type **Proposed Logo**. With the Pick tool, click outside the text block.
4. Click on the Import button or open the File menu, choose Import, and select a Coreldraw graphic to import. The piece used here is a professionally drawn logo by Cindy Turner of Turner and de Vries, Ltd (see the Corel In Action page in this chapter) and looks like Figure 15-20 when it is imported.

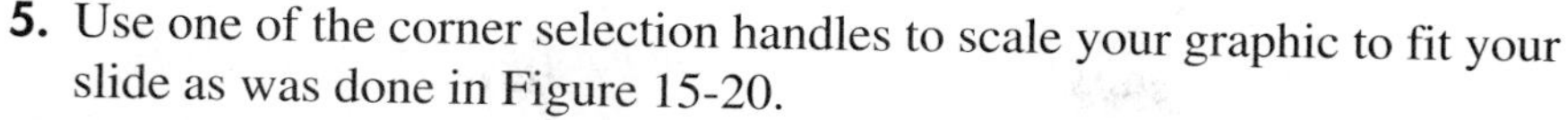

5. Use one of the corner selection handles to scale your graphic to fit your slide as was done in Figure 15-20.
6. Save your work and click on Slide 4 to open it.
7. Open the Geometric Shapes flyout and select the 3D star on the far-right of the top row. With it, drag a small star in the lower-right corner to balance the sailing ship in the lower left. Select the Pick tool and click on bright blue in the palette at the bottom of the screen.

OTE: *All of the geometric shapes are fully editable. You can ungroup them, use the shape tool to edit them, and select different colors for different segments.*

8. Save your presentation.

Many of the drawing functions that you have in Coreldraw are available directly in Corel PRESENTS.

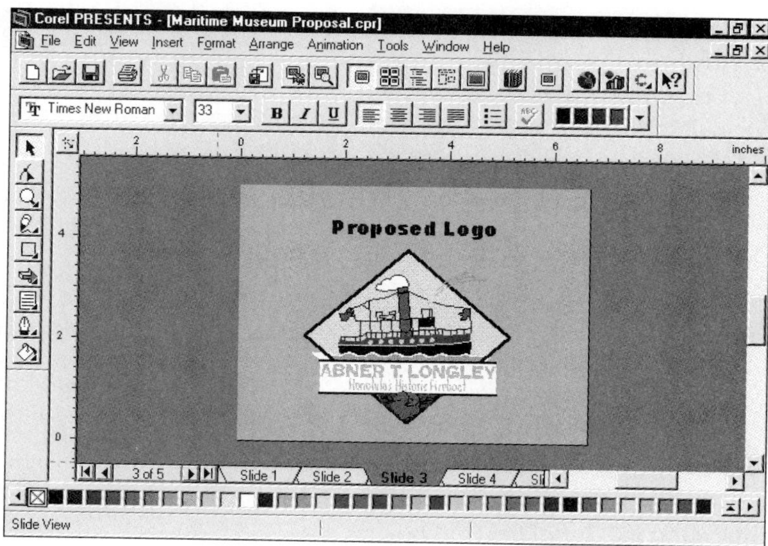

Graphic placed on a slide

FIGURE 15-20

***Abner T. Longley*—Cindy Turner**

The *Abner T. Longley* is an example of the kind of quick logo or emblem that can be done with Coreldraw. In this case, the *Abner T. Longley* was used on T-shirts, cups, and other objects to promote the historic fireboat. In a presentation, like the one in this chapter, you want quick and effective art, not a masterpiece, that helps get your message across. The *Abner T. Longley* is a good example of that kind of piece.

Cindy Turner is a partner in Turner & de Vries Ltd. in Kailua, Hawaii. She can be reached at (808) 261-2179.

Preparing and Adding a Chart

Many presentations require the graphical display of numerical information, which in Corel PRESENTS is called a *chart*. Corel PRESENTS allows you to create and incorporate many different types of charts. For this presentation, you want to include a stacked vertical bar chart of receipts. See how with the following instructions. (Slide 4 should be on your screen.)

1. With the Paragraph text tool, click in the Title Text block and type **Projected Receipts**. The font should be Arial MT Black, 28 points, and centered.

2. With the Pick tool click on the Body Text block, delete it, and then click on the Insert a Chart button in the Standard toolbar. The mouse pointer turns into a special crosshair.
3. Define the area that will be occupied by the chart by dragging a rectangle that covers the upper part of the body text block so that it is just above the masts on the ship. When you release the mouse button after defining the rectangular area, the Chart Type dialog box will open, as shown in Figure 15-21.

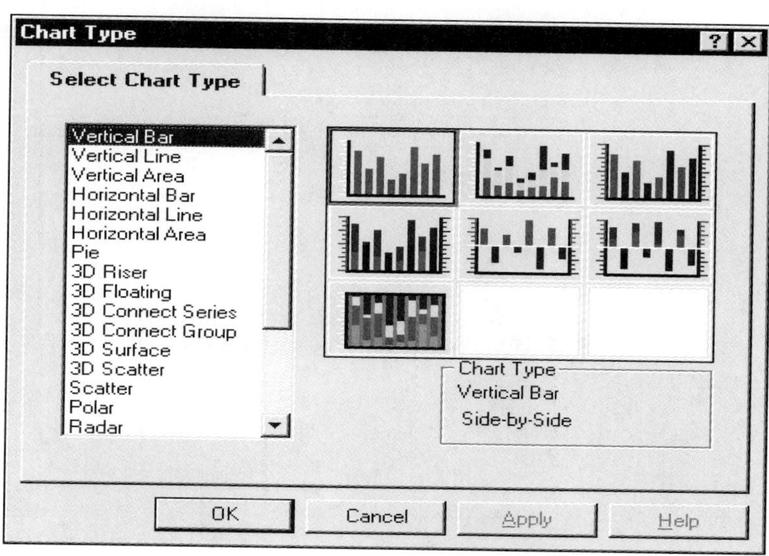

Selecting a chart type

FIGURE 15-21

4. Click on Vertical Bar in the list on the left, click on the stacked bar chart in the middle of the top row of examples, and click on OK. A chart will appear on your slide. The Chart Server will open and display your chart, like that shown in Figure 15-22.

NOTE: *If your chart did not come in the size you described in Step 3, it is because you are sizing OLE objects (which a chart is) to a "best fit," which is the default. You can change this by opening the Tools menu, choosing Options, and then in the General tab, turning off (no checkmark) Insert OLE objects using best fit.*

5. Click on the Chart Data icon just above the toolbox or select Data from the Chart menu to switch from chart view to Chart Data view.

6. Type the information shown in the table in Figure 15-23 (click in the cell, then begin typing—the new text replaces the dummy text—the numbers are unchanged from the dummy text) and click on OK. You will be returned to the Chart Server.

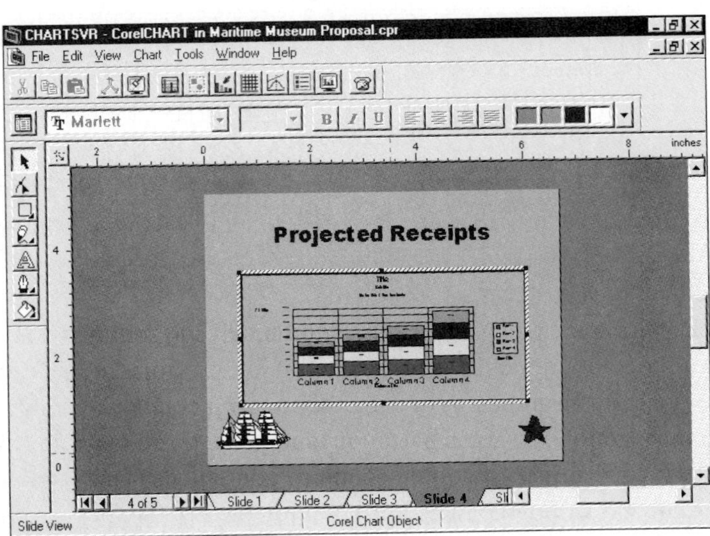

Chart Server chart creation tool

FIGURE 15-22

Chart Data

File Edit

A1

	A	B	C	D	E	F	G
1		Year 1	Year 2	Year 3	Year 4		
2	Members	30	35	40	50		
3	Locals	25	30	35	45		
4	Groups	20	25	30	40		
5	Tourists	15	20	25	35		
6							
7							
8							
9							

OK Cancel Help

Chart Data table for the bar chart

FIGURE 15-23

IP: *You can import data into the Chart Data table using the File menu Import command.*

7. With the Artistic text tool, select the various chart titles and change them as follows:

   Title - **Maritime Museum**, Subtitle - **Annual Revenue**, Note - (delete it), Y1 Title (on the left) - **Thousands**, Column Title or Groups Title (on the bottom) - **Years after opening**, Row Title or Series Title (under the legend on the right) - **Sources**.

IP: *If you can't easily see the titles on the screen, open the Chart menu and choose Format Chart to open the dialog box shown in Figure 15-24. Here you can turn the titles on and off and change their content.*

8. Click on the on the slide outside of the chart and you will be returned to the Corel PRESENTS normal window.

9. Click on the Preview Slide button in the Standard toolbar and you'll see your chart a little better, as you can see in Figure 15-25.

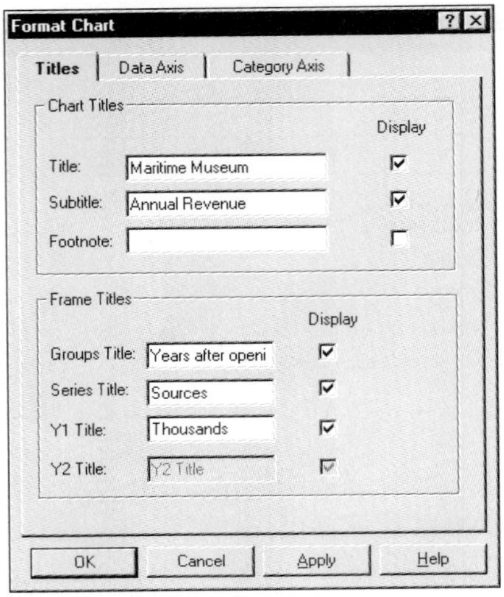

Format Chart
Titles
Data Axis
Category Axis
Chart Titles
Display
Title:
Maritime Museum
Subtitle:
Annual Revenue
Footnote:
Frame Titles
Display
Groups Title:
Years after openi
Series Title:
Sources
Y1 Title:
Thousands
Y2 Title:
Y2 Title
OK
Cancel
Apply
Help

Entering chart titles

FIGURE 15-24

Projected Receipts
Maritime Museum
Annual Revenue
Thousands
Year 1
Year 2
Year 3
Year 4
Sources

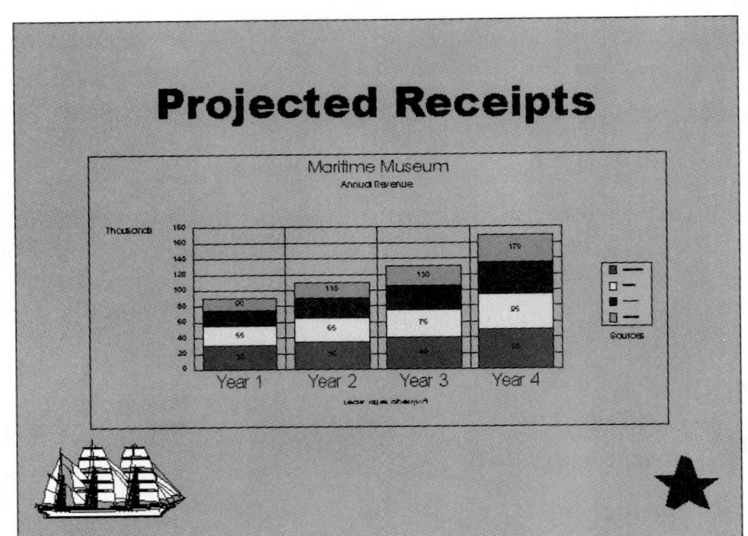

Full-screen preview of your chart slide

FIGURE 15-25

10. Press ESC or wait a minute, and you will again see the normal Corel PRESENTS windows.

11. Save your presentation.

OTE: *If you want a chart to be the full size of a slide, press F4 or select Fit Object to Slide in the Arrange menu. You will not see any background when you do this.*

Preparing and Adding Animation

Animation adds motion to your presentation by playing back a series of images in sequence. This helps keep your audience's attention. There are many forms of animation that you can use in Corel PRESENTS, from simple animation of objects on a slide to adding animated characters. Here you will take the sailing ship that you have had on the background and, after bringing it to the slide layer, move it across the slide. Use these steps.

1. Click on Slide 5 and then click on the lower Body Text block to select it. Drag the bottom border of the text block up above the sailing ship, like this:

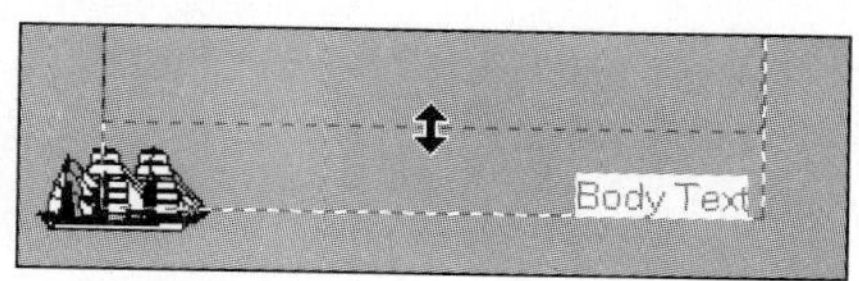

2. With the Paragraph text tool, click in the Title Text block and type **Fund Raising Steps**. Your formatting should be the same as the titles on the other charts.

3. With the Paragraph text tool type into the Body Text box the following list. When you are done, your slide should look like that shown in Figure 15-26.

Write grant requests
Begin corporate campaign
Begin membership drive
Begin "Sell a board" campaign
Continue selling cruises
Continue selling T-shirts

4. Open the Background view and copy the sailing ship to the Clipboard (select it, then click on the Copy button). Reopen the Slide view, open the Libraries, click on a background without the ship, and click on OK.
5. In the Slide view, paste the sailing ship on the left side of the slide, approximately where it is in the background.
6. Right-click on the sailing ship and choose Properties. The Object properties dialog box will open.
7. Click on the Path tab, scroll the list box up, and select Across Right. This will cause the ship to move across the slide. Click on the Preview check box and you will see the ship move across the screen.
8. Click on OK to close the dialog box and then save the presentation.

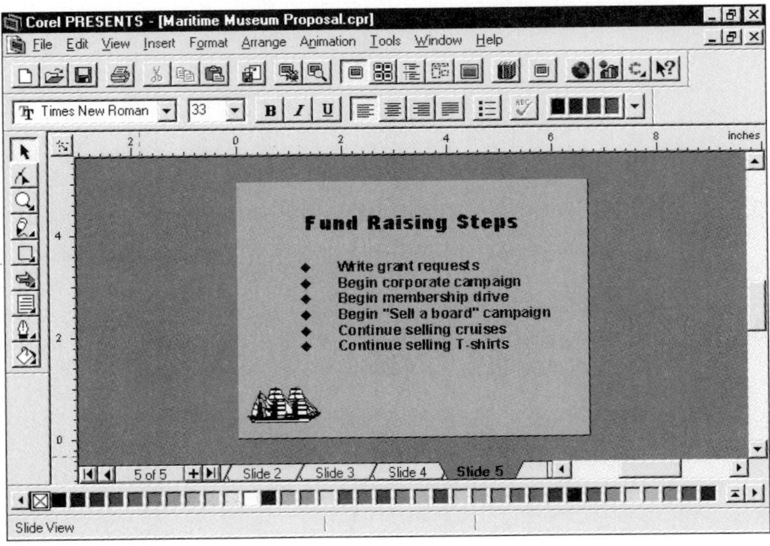

Text on Slide 5

FIGURE 15-26

Adding Sound

Sound is another technique to get the attention of your audience. Corel PRESENTS gives you the capability of adding sound to your slides. The sound can be a sound effect, a music clip, or a voice narration, and it can be an existing .WAV file or you can record it from an audio CD or a microphone. Of course, you must have the audio equipment (a sound board and speakers) to be able to use sound in Corel PRESENTS. If you have the necessary equipment, add sound to your last chart with these steps.

1. With Slide 5 still your active slide, open the File menu and choose Import. The Import dialog box will open.
2. Open the Files of type drop-down list box and choose Windows Waveform (WAV).
3. Open the \Windows\Media folder and choose Chimes.wav, as you can see in Figure 15-27.
4. Click on Import. The sound will be attached to Slide 5 and you will hear it when Slide 5 is opened.
5. Click on the Preview Slide button in the toolbar. Slide 5 will fill the screen, you will hear the sound you attached to it, and you will see the sailing ship move across the screen.

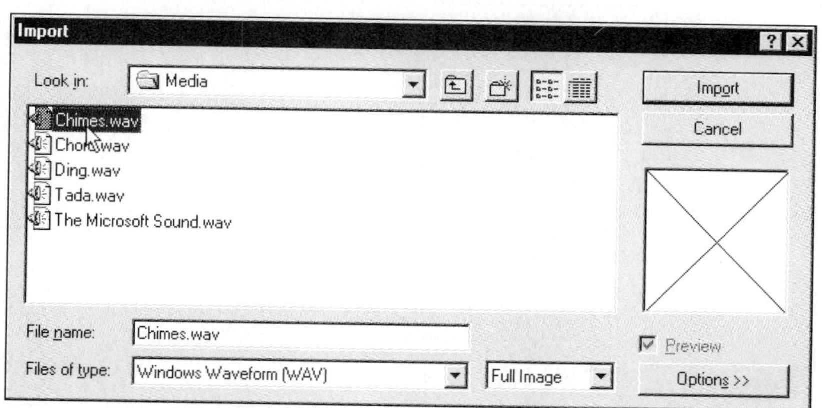

Importing a sound

FIGURE 15-27

Using Outline View

The Outline view lets you look at and edit all the text on the slides together without the graphics. This allows you to concentrate on the text and get it just right. You can enter text directly in Outline view, or drag and drop a word processing document or text file from any OLE2 enabled application. This a quick way to build a presentation. Look at your existing slides in Outline view next.

1. Click on the Outline view button in the Standard toolbar. You will see an outline with all your text appearing, as shown in Figure 15-28.
2. If your text is too small to read, click on the Zoom tool to open the flyout, and then click on the Zoom-in tool with the + sign.

3. Initially the Outline view displays the font you selected for the slide. If that is not good for reading in Outline view, you can turn it off just for the Outline view with the Show formatting tool that you see on the left.

4. To move indented items in the outline to the next higher level, click on the Promote tool (left-pointing arrow), or, to reverse the process, click on the Demote tool.

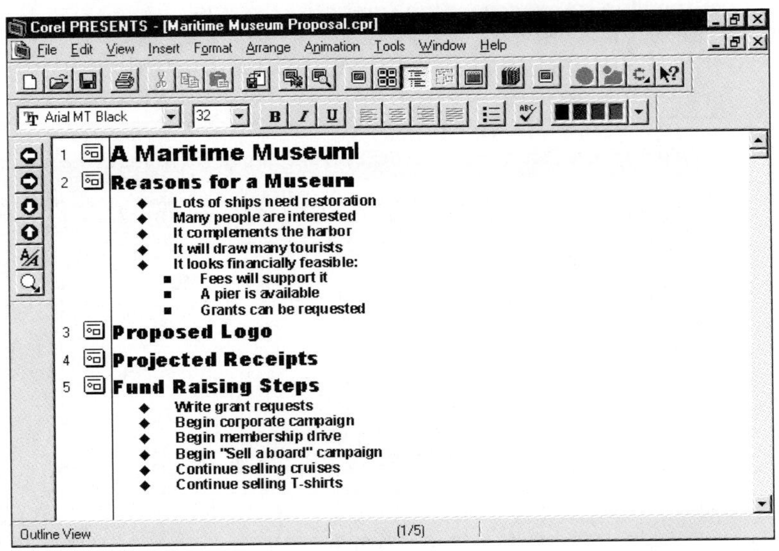

Outline view

FIGURE 15-28

5. Read through your text and make any necessary changes.

6. Click on the Spell Check button in the Formatting toolbar. If the Spell Checker finds an error, the Spell Checker dialog box will open, as shown Figure 15-29. When the Spell Checker is done, it will tell you.
7. When you are done checking the spelling, click on Slide view once again.

Using Slide Sorter View

While it is great to see the detail of each slide, sometimes it is necessary to see as many of your slides as possible at one time to organize them and figure out which to use. Corel PRESENTS provides such a view in the Slide Sorter view shown in Figure 15-30. In Slide Sorter view, you can rearrange slides by dragging them around and you establish the transitions between slides and objects on slides. Work with the Slide Sorter view next.

IP: *While in Slide Sorter view you can use Select All from the Edit menu and have your changes apply to all slides.*

1. Click on the Slide Sorter view button in the Standard toolbar. The Slide Sorter view will appear, as shown in Figure 15-30.
2. Click on Slide 3, and drag it to the end of the presentation (after Slide 5). The slides rearrange and what used to be Slide 3 becomes Slide 5 and old slides 4 and 5 become 3 and 4, as you can see in Figure 15-31.

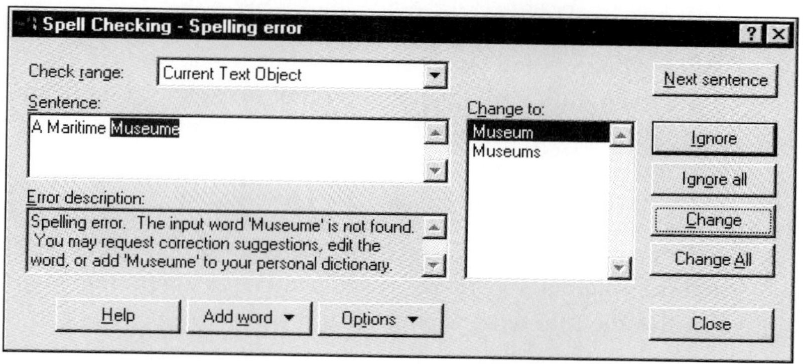

Spell checker

FIGURE 15-29

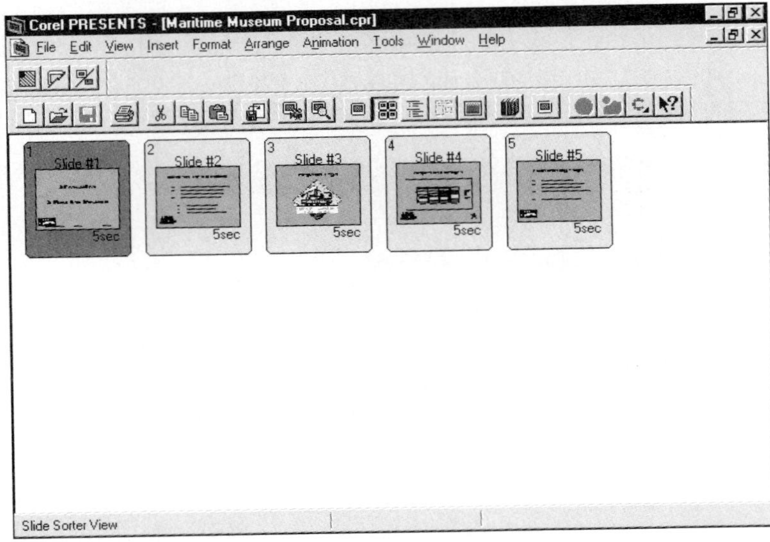

Slide Sorter view

FIGURE 15-30

3. If you wish, you can remove the 35-mm slide frames by clicking on the Show/Hide Jacket button on the right in the Slide Sorter tool bar. The view then looks like this:

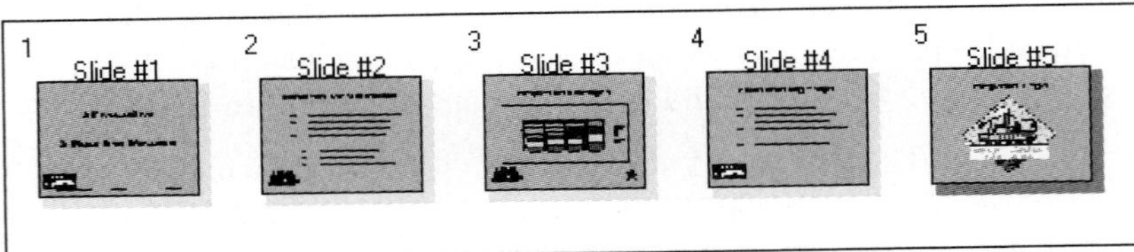

4. The Show/Hide Slide button in the middle of the Slide Sorter toolbar allows you to turn individual slides on or off so they do not appear when you run the presentation and an "X" appears across the slide in Slide and Slide Sorter views. You can use this to tailor a presentation to a particular audience without creating a separate presentation.

5. The Transition button on left in the Slide Sorter toolbar opens the Slide Properties dialog box where you can add an opening transition to the slide. See the following section on transitions.

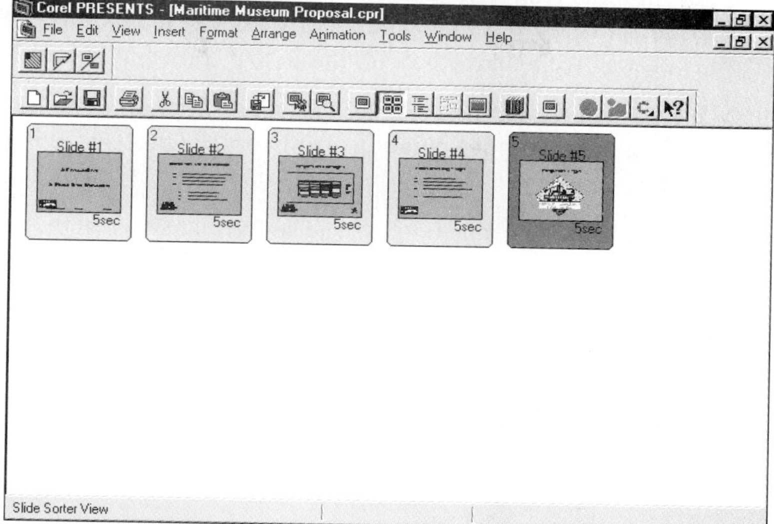

Slide 3 moved to the end

FIGURE 15-31

Adding Transitions

A *transition* is a dynamic effect such as a "fade" or "wipe" which can be applied to the entire slide or to individual objects on a slide, including text. Corel PRESENTS provides many types of transitions, including Clock, Iris, Pond Ripple, Radar Screen, Rain, and Shutters. You can apply opening transitions to a slide, and both opening and closing transitions to any object. Try both slide and object transitions next.

1. Return to Slide view for Slide 1, right-click on an open area of the first slide, and select Transitions from the pop-up menu. The Slide Properties dialog box will open, as you saw in Figure 15-7.
2. Open the drop-down Transition list for the Opening transitions and select Wipe Across.
3. Open the Direction box and select the downward pointing arrow. Make sure the duration is 1 seconds (the duration is displayed in minutes:seconds.hundreths) and the Steps are 30.
4. Click on OK to close the dialog box. If you would like to see the transitions played out full screen, click on the Preview slide button in the Standard toolbar.

5. Click on Slide two, right-click on the bulleted text, and choose Properties. The Object Properties dialog box will open. Click on the Text Effects tab and you will see a dialog box similar to that shown in Figure 15-32.
6. Make sure the Grouping is Paragraph, select Straight In in the Opening Transition, use the right-pointing arrow for the Direction, and set the Duration to 5.
7. Leave the Closing Transition at none so the text stays on the screen. Click on Preview to see your work and then click on OK.
8. Save your presentation.

Creating Speaker Notes

Depending on the presentation, you may want to prepare some speaker notes to go along with the slides. Corel PRESENTS has the facilities to do this and include a

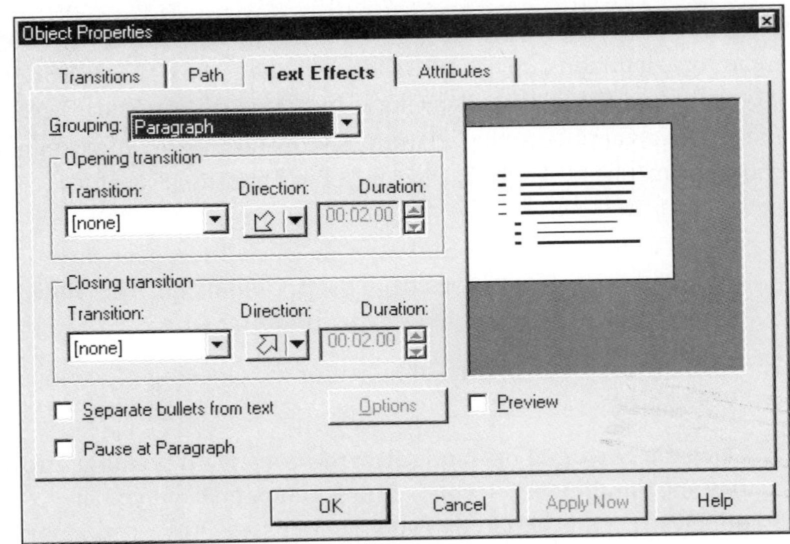

Object Properties Text Effects

FIGURE 15-32

miniature representation (thumbnail) of the slide on it. Prepare a set of speaker's notes now with the following steps:

1. Open the View menu and choose Speaker Notes. The Speaker Notes view will open, as you can see in Figure 15-33.
2. Open the Libraries, click on the Layout tab and the Preset library, and double-click on the speaker notes layout that you want to use. Click on OK to return to the speaker notes.
3. Select the Paragraph text tool and type the notes that you want in the text boxes on your layout.
4. When you are ready, click on the Print button in the Standard toolbar to print the notes.

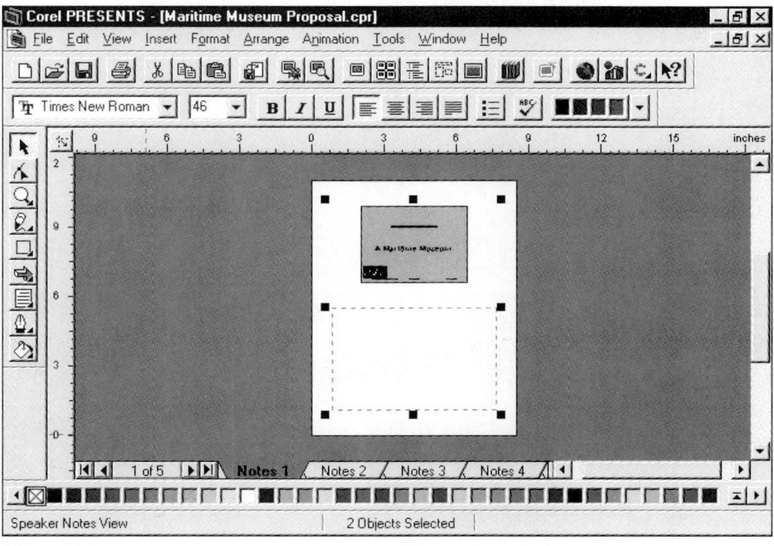

Speaker Notes view

FIGURE 15-33

Creating an Audience Handout

Like speaker notes, an audience handout is an optional item that you can use if you wish. Corel PRESENTS provides several optional layouts for this. Create an audience handout next.

1. Open the View menu and choose Handout. The Handout view will open as you can see in Figure 15-34.
2. If you want to change the layout, open the Libraries, click on the Layout tab, click on Preset library, double-click on the layout that you want to use, and click on OK to return to the handout.
3. Type the notes that you want to use in the text frame on the right of each slide image.
4. When you are ready, click on the Print button in the Standard toolbar to print the notes.
5. Save your work.

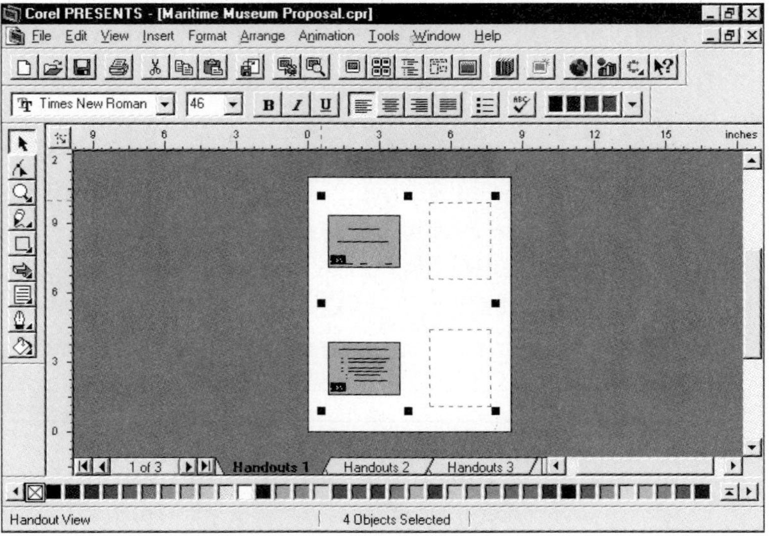

Handout view

FIGURE 15-34

Running a Presentation

There are many ways to use or run a presentation. You can print the presentation and use it that way. You can create either 35-mm or overhead slides and project them. You can run the presentation on your computer screen, or you can project the computer screen image onto a large screen. Here, try printing it and then running it on your computer screen.

1. Return to the Slide view and click on the Print button in the Standard toolbar. Your presentation will be printed.
2. When printing is done, click on the Run Presentation button in the Standard toolbar. Your first slide will open on your screen using your opening transition.
3. Press ENTER, click the right mouse button, press SPACEBAR, or press RIGHT ARROW. The first slide will close and the second slide will appear using its text opening transition.

TIP: *While you are running a presentation, you can use the left mouse button as a marking pen to annotate a slide. If you click on the pen in the lower right of the screen, you can change the color and thickness of the pen, and if you press DEL you will clear the annotation.*

4. From there on, use ENTER or one of the other techniques to go from slide to slide. When you are done, press ESC to return to Slide view.
5. Save your presentation one last time.

This chapter has given you a good introduction to Corel PRESENTS that will allow you to easily build your own presentations. At the same time, there are many additional facets of Corel PRESENTS that you should explore on your own by browsing through the menus and dialog boxes in the various views.

Introducing Corel PHOTO-PAINT

16

Corel PHOTO-PAINT is a multifaceted paint and animation program. It allows you to create bitmap images with an extensive toolkit of drawing tools, to enhance and retouch scanned photos, and to create and edit movies. You can include the resulting images in Corel PRESENTS, Coreldraw graphics, CorelVENTURA documents, or in other applications.

Getting Started with Corel PHOTO-PAINT

To start Corel PHOTO-PAINT, first bring up Windows, open the Corel Applications folder, and then double-click on Corel PHOTO-PAINT 6.

Corel PHOTO-PAINT 6

After a short time, you will see the screen displayed in Figure 16-1 (maximized).

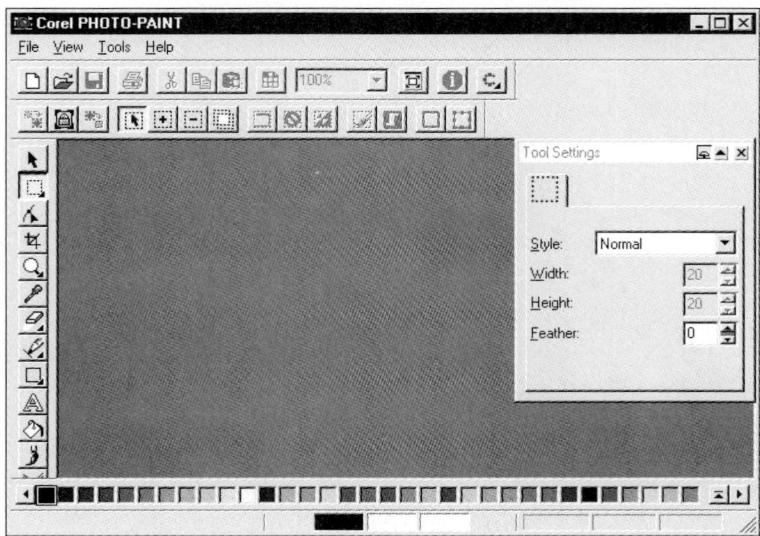

Initial Corel PHOTO-PAINT 6 screen

FIGURE 16-1

At this point, you can either open an existing picture on disk or create a new one. If you want to create a new image, select the File menu and choose New; confirm or change the defaults in the Create a New Image dialog box, shown in Figure 16-2, and a blank window will open where you can create the picture.

If you want to open an existing picture, select File Open and identify the file you want. Once you've loaded a picture into Corel PHOTO-PAINT, your screen will look something like Figure 16-3. In this case, a sample file has been opened called Apple.cpt, from the \Photopnt\Samples\ folder either in the \Corel folder on your hard disk or on the CD-ROM.

Corel PHOTO-PAINT Screen Elements

The Corel PHOTO-PAINT window contains many features to help you create pictures or retouch photos.

At the top of the screen is the Title bar. On the right are the Maximize and Minimize buttons, which allow you to resize or restore the Corel PHOTO-PAINT window.

The Menu bar, which is discussed shortly, is beneath the Title bar. Beneath the Menu bar are toolbars. Two toolbars, the Standard toolbar and the Mask/Object toolbar, are shown in Figures 16-1 and 16-3. Below the toolbars is the Corel PHOTO-PAINT work area, where you can create or open a picture or movie. The

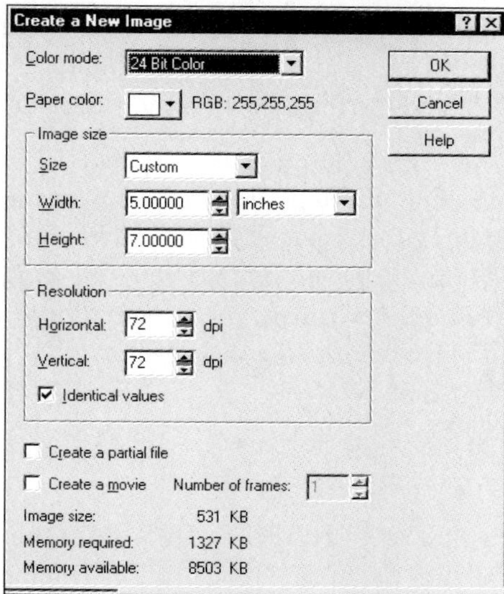

Verify setting for creating a new image

FIGURE 16-2

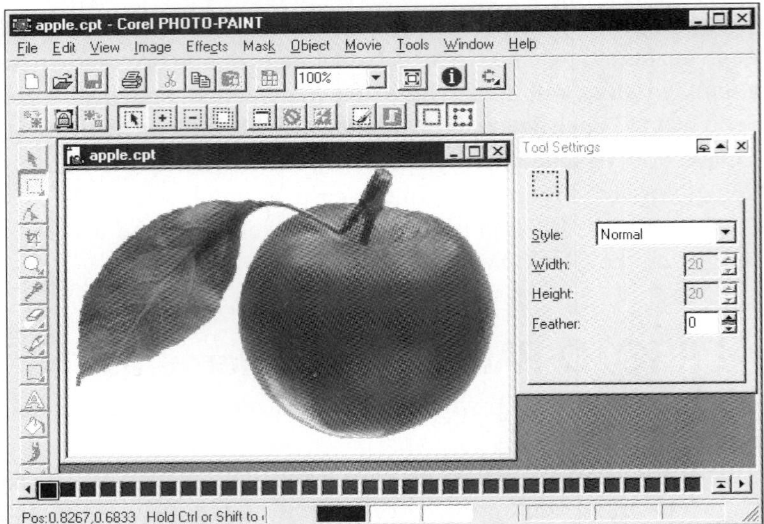

Opening an existing picture file

FIGURE 16-3

Tool Settings roll-up, on the right, is open and ready to be used immediately. The Color Palette, a bar of small squares of color, is below the work area. Arrows on the left and right of the Color Palette allow you to scroll back and forth along the colors and patterns. Beneath it is the Status bar, which displays messages and pointer coordinates. In the middle are three larger color swatches. The first is the paint color, which is what a brush would paint with, for example. The second color is the paper color for new images, and the third color is the fill color.

IP: *If you click on the Color Palette with the left mouse button, it will reset the paint color. If you click on it with the right mouse button, the fill color will be reset. If you hold down* CTRL *and click on the Color Palette with the left mouse button, it will reset the paper color. If you double-click on one of the three color swatches, a dialog box will be displayed so that you can change the color or its characteristics.*

The Menu Bar

When you first bring up Corel PHOTO-PAINT, the Menu bar contains only 4 menus. When you open a picture (such as Apple.cpt), the Menu bar expands to 11 menus. Open each of them in turn as they are discussed in the following paragraphs.

FILE MENU The File menu contains the normal file-handling and printing features. In addition, you can open a new picture from the Clipboard or choose Select Partial Area of a partially loaded picture to open a section of the image which you can select from a grid that overlays the image. You can undo changes by using Revert to bring up a previously saved image. You can also acquire images by selecting a source device, such as a scanner, with the Acquire Image command. The Send command allows you to send a picture to another computer using Microsoft Exchange. You can also reopen the last four images previously opened. Finally, from the File menu, you can exit Corel PHOTO-PAINT.

EDIT MENU The Edit menu offers the standard editing features like Undo, Cut, Copy, Paste, and Clear. Undo List keeps track of the actions done to an image, and to undo one or more of them, you select the actions and then click on Undo. You can Clear Clipboard to get more memory space. You can also save an interim image at a certain point in your design process using the Checkpoint command; you can then try out various enhancement features and return safely to your saved image with the Restore to Checkpoint command. The Copy To File and Paste From File commands allow you to copy to and from external files.

VIEW MENU The View menu manages the screen display of images. You can zoom in and out of pictures—display a 100% increase, return to the Actual Size 1:1 view, or Zoom To Fit the screen. You can select which toolbars to display; selectively hide or show eight roll-up menus, the Ruler, or the Status bar; and select from up to 10 Color palettes. You can set up a grid pattern and then use it to place precise masks and objects, using the Snap to Grid feature to be more accurate. When an image contains more colors than your screen can display, the Screen Dithering option improves the onscreen appearance of the image by optimizing color transitions. Color Correction improves the linearity of the monitor. Full-Screen Preview shows only the active picture (clicking anywhere on the screen then removes it), and Maximize Work Area removes the menus, Title bar, and the Windows Taskbar from the screen to give you more work room (click the right mouse button to get a menu which allows you to return to normal view).

IMAGE MENU The Image menu allows you to add special effects to a picture or scanned photo. The Resample command allows you to change the size and/or resolution of an image, while Paper Size lets you increase or decrease the total number of pixels while changing the placement of the subject relative to the background. Duplicate copies the image. Calculations allows you to combine two channels to create a new image. Flip allows you to flip an image horizontally or vertically, and Rotate displays options to rotate an image in degrees clockwise or counterclockwise. The Convert To command converts to another color—for example, 16 Color or 256 Color to RGB Color or CMYK Color. You can use the Split Channels To command to separate an image into color component channels that you can edit; then, you can recombine the image with the Combine Channels command. The Color Table displays each color in a 16 or 256-color image so you can edit one or a block of colors; you can redisplay your image using colors from a variety of color tables. Crop provides a submenu with two options for cropping: To Mask creates a new image from a mask, and Border Color crops or removes a selected color. Deskew allows you to "unskew" an image that may be slightly skewed when it is opened. Preserve Image will prevent an underlying image from being changed when you are creating masks and objects. Finally, the Info option displays measurements and technical details about an image.

EFFECTS MENU The Effects menu allows you to select and apply special effects filters to pictures or masked areas. The Effects filters only work with colors such as Grayscale or 24 or 32-bit color such as RGB or CMYK. If you are working with paletted colors, such as 16 Color or 256 Color, you will need to convert them to one of the other color types first. Later in this chapter you will see how these filters can enhance an image.

MASK MENU A mask is a defined area of an image that can be used to either confine changes to that area or protect an area. You can use either the area defined by the mask or, when inverted, the area excluded by the mask to be the area changed. The Mask menu, along with the Color Mask roll-up, provides options for creating, applying, and working with masks.

OBJECT MENU The Object menu allows you to manipulate selections, or *objects*, that are extracted from an existing image. The Object features will provide unlimited opportunities for you to create composite images from multiple sources or to isolate portions of your images.

MOVIE MENU The Movie menu provides options for creating and manipulating a video clip or movie presentation. You can insert, move, and delete frames, and maintain control over the viewing of the movie by rewinding or fast forwarding, either rapidly or frame by frame.

TOOLS MENU The Tools menu allows you to adjust certain default settings with its Options command. For example, you can determine certain startup defaults, identify third-party plug-in filters, set advanced color defaults, and set defaults for working with a Pen. The Customize command allows you to assign shortcut keys to the menu, to vary the menu responses, to assign icons to the toolbar, and to vary the appearance of the Color palette and mouse button. With Roll-Up Groups, you can either Customize Roll-Ups to determine the alignment of roll-ups or open Roll-Up Groups, such as the Objects/Channels roll-up. Task Progress allows you to check and then change the priority for printing queued documents. Scripts allows you to run or create macros. The Color Manager provides two options for Run Color Wizard to guide you through creating profiles for your scanner, monitor, and printer, or to Select Color Profile. MultiMedia Manager provides options for managing and working with your multimedia files (it takes the place of the previous version of Mosaic).

WINDOW MENU The Window menu contains the standard arrangement and activation commands. Also, from the Window menu, you can refresh the screen.

HELP MENU Finally, the last main menu provides help for Corel PHOTO-PAINT. By clicking on Help Topics you will find an overview of the product, beginning How Tos, and a Reference and Glossary to get you started. The Index provides a detailed list of subjects from which you can choose. Find allows you to search for specific words, but will take some time as it builds a database of words and phrases.

The Roll-Up Menus

The eight roll-up menus, shown in Figure 16-4, can be displayed by selecting Roll-ups from the View menu. The roll-ups are Channels, Color, Color Mask, Navigator, Nibs, Objects, Recorder, and Tool Settings. They stay on the screen and can be rolled up or down like the roll-ups in Coreldraw.

NOTE: *On the Title bar of the roll-ups are three buttons: Auto-Close, which is a toggle that switches between closing the roll-up automatically as soon as it is used and leaving it open on the screen (think of it as a tack—when it is down or pushed in, the roll-up remains on the screen); Roll-up, another toggle, which rolls up the roll-up or opens it; and Close, which removes the roll-up from the screen.*

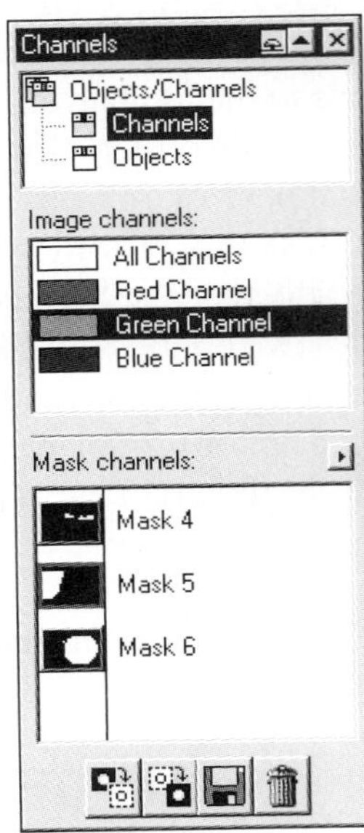

a. Channels roll-up

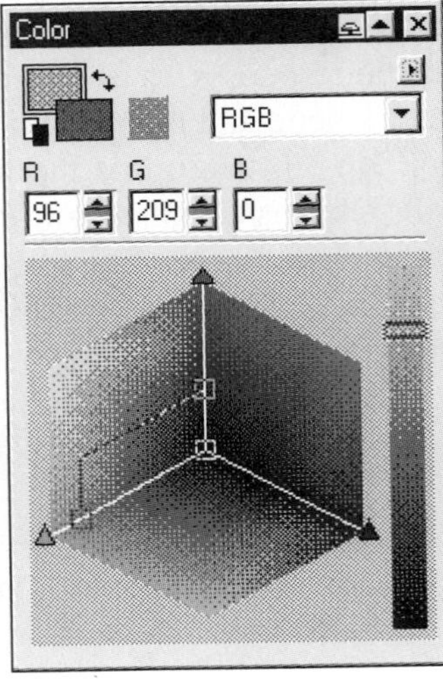

b. Color roll-up

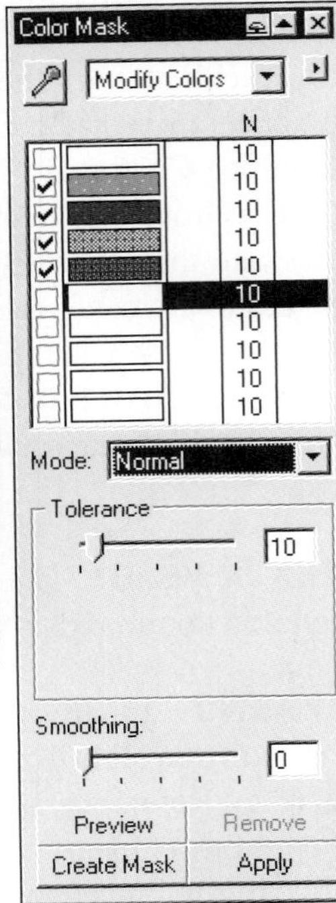

c. Color Mask roll-up

d. Navigator roll-up

e. Nibs roll-up

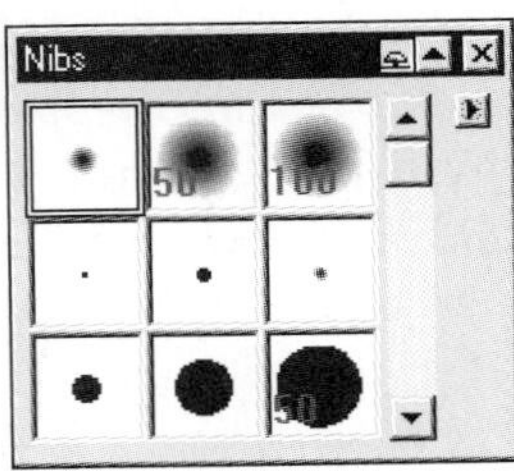

f. Objects roll-up

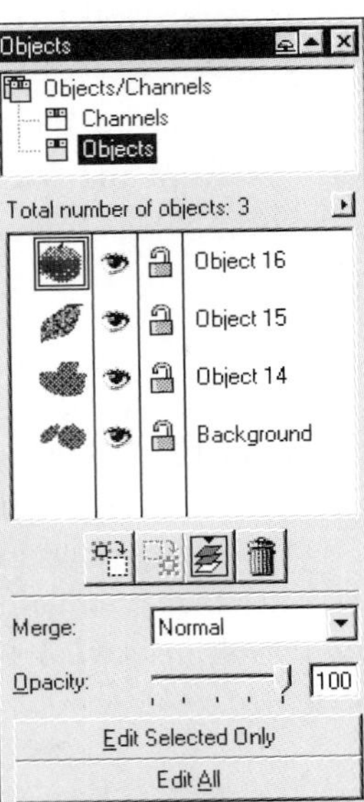

Roll-Up menus

FIGURE 16-4

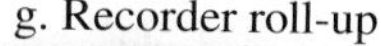

g. Recorder roll-up

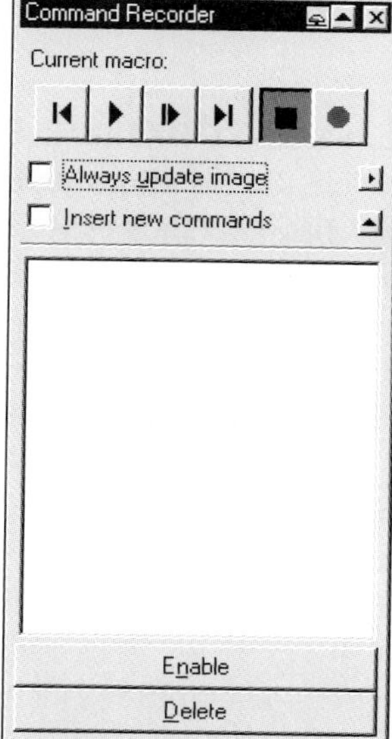

h. Tool Settings roll-up

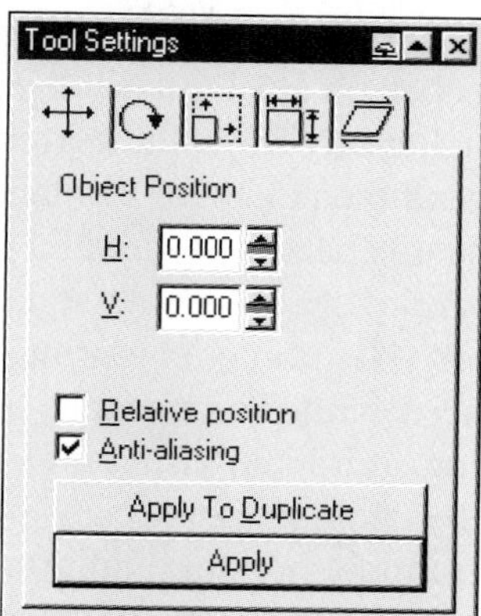

Roll-Up menus (*continued*)

FIGURE 16-4

CHANNELS ROLL-UP The Channels roll-up displays functions for either the Channels or Objects roll-ups, depending on which name is selected at the top of the roll-up. When you select Channels from the View menu (or click on its name on the roll-up), the Channels roll-up is displayed, an example of which is shown in Figure 16-4a. It performs two functions. You can separate images into color elements or channels, such as RGB into Red, Green, and Blue channels. You click on the channel name and it will be displayed in the image window. In this way you can isolate an image channel and apply special effects to it alone. The choices displayed in the Image Channels will differ depending on the color type of the image. For example, in Figure 16-4a, the image is RGB color.

The second function stores masks in channels. You can create several masks, storing them in mask channels, and, since only one mask can be active at one time, you can switch back and forth between them as you want. The first of the four buttons on the bottom of the Mask channels display is Channel to Mask, which places the selected mask channel on the displayed image. The second button, Save Mask to New Channel, adds the active mask to the Mask Channels. The third button, Save to Current Channel, updates the selected channel with changes made to an image, and the fourth button, Delete Current Channel, deletes the selected channel. When you click on Objects from the Roll-ups option of the View menu (or click on its name on the roll-up), the Objects roll-up is opened. It is described below and displayed in Figure 4f.

IP: *When you create and save a .cpt file, any mask channels associated with it are saved also. Saving a file to a different format will cause the masks to be lost.*

COLOR ROLL-UP The Color roll-up, shown for RGB Color in Figure 16-4b, allows you to select paint and paper colors for creating outlines and special effects. By selecting a color type from the drop-down list box (such as RGB, HSB, or Palette), you can click on a color to set the paint or paper. The small squares in the upper left of the dialog box show the current paint and paper colors. If you select one of the squares and then click on a color, the selected square will show the color. Another small square appears on the right when the color selected is out of the printer's color range. A third set of smaller squares to the left of the paint and paper boxes shows the colors your printer can print. If you click on it, the paint and paper colors will be replaced with the printable colors. A submenu containing several options for displaying additional visual information, such as the color name or mixing area, is opened by clicking on the right-pointing arrow on the upper right of the roll-up. As you select more options, additional options appear on the submenu. You can create colors by using the color model as displayed in Figure 16-4b, or by selecting colors by name, mixing them, or selecting them from a Color palette.

COLOR MASK ROLL-UP The Color Mask roll-up, shown in Figure 16-4c, allows you to either modify or protect colors by choosing one of these options from the drop-down list box at the top of the roll-up. The colors are set by clicking on the check box in the row. When you click on the eyedropper button, the pointer turns into an eyedropper that allows you to pull color from the image and insert it into one of the checked rows. (Right-click off the eyedropper button to deselect the eyedropper.) The Mode of mask (Normal, Hue, Saturation, Brightness, or HSB) can be chosen from the drop-down list box beneath the check box display. To define the color range to be included in the color mask, you can expand or restrict the Tolerance by moving the slider to the right or left. A readout of the Tolerance level is displayed on the right. A submenu can be opened by clicking on the right-pointing arrow on the right top of the roll-up. It provides options to open, save, or reset a color mask, or to edit color. Use the Color Mask roll-up to mask the whole image, rather than a selected part of it, as with the toolbox color-sensitive mask tools.

AUTION: *The Color Mask roll-up cannot be used with palleted colors such as 16 or 256 Color or Black and White.*

NAVIGATOR ROLL-UP The Navigator roll-up, shown in Figure 16-4d, allows you to zoom in and out of the picture display. You click on a command on the roll-up and the results are reflected in the screen image. Using the buttons on the bottom of the roll-up, you can display the image to the left at Zoom 100% of its size, Zoom to fit, Zoom to 1:1—its actual size, or Zoom In and Zoom Out to increase or decrease the size of the image by smaller amounts. By using the grabber in the display on the roll-up, you can identify the specific area of the image to be enlarged, and then return it to its actual size.

NIBS ROLL-UP The Nibs roll-up, shown in Figure 16-4e, allows you to choose a size and shape of nib to use while painting or drawing. Click on the scroll bar to see the many choices available. The right-pointing arrow on the upper right of the roll-up displays a submenu with additional options.

OBJECTS ROLL-UP As described above, the Objects roll-up displays either channels or objects depending on which choice is selected from the View menu (or chosen from the top of the roll-up). The Objects roll-up, shown in Figure 16-4f, gives you certain choices about the objects in your image. You can see the total number of objects and, below that, four columns containing one row for each object. The first column shows a thumbnail image of the object; the second, an eye, which when clicked on is a toggle to display or hide the object; the third column is a lock, which is a toggle to allow the object to be modified (unlocked) or not (locked); and finally, the fourth column names the object. The Background, also considered an object, will always be shown whether there are other objects or not. Click on an object to select it, click on the eye or the lock to work the toggles. The small arrow to the right of the object count shows a submenu with options for displaying the potential icon sizes: Small, Medium, or Large. At the bottom of the columns are four buttons: Create Mask from Object (to Mask), Create Object from Mask (from Mask), Combine Objects, and Delete Objects. In addition, you can adjust the opacity of an object and select 1 of 20 Merge modes to control how colors blend with the paper color to create a special effect.

TIP: *Objects are displayed in their stacking order—that is, by the way they are stacked on the background, which is always on the bottom. The top of the stacked objects will be on top of the list of objects. To reorder the objects in the column (or change their order in the stack), place the pointer on the name/number of the object and drag it to the position desired.*

RECORDER ROLL-UP The Command Recorder roll-up (listed as Recorder on the View menu), shown in Figure 16-4g, records Corel PHOTO-PAINT commands, keystrokes, mouse actions, and other actions so that you can automate a frequently used procedure or sequence of actions. You can save these recorded commands and play them back as needed in future Corel PHOTO-PAINT sessions. The buttons on the top provide options to advance or rewind the script. They are Rewind, Play, Step Forward, Fast Forward, Stop, and Record. Always update image causes the image to reflect the current position of the script. Insert new commands allows you to record new commands within a recorded script. Enable allows you to play a selected group of commands, and Delete removes them. The small right-pointing arrow under the Record button displays a submenu with options for creating a new script, or opening or saving one.

TOOL SETTINGS ROLL-UP The Tool Settings roll-up, shown in Figure 16-4h, controls the characteristics of the tool selected (the Object Picker tool in the figure). So, the appearance of the Tool Settings roll-up will vary depending on the tool selected. For most tools, double-clicking on its icon in the toolbox will cause the Tool Settings roll-up to be displayed. For instance, by double-clicking on the Paint tool, the Tools Settings roll-up changes to accommodate the characteristics of that tool. It allows you to control width, shape, nib, texture, color variation, or thickness, plus many other brush attributes. (For others, select Tool Settings from the View, Roll-ups menu.) Many tools have a number of preset styles that can be used to create special effects. For example, the Paint tool allows you to use a spray can, airbrush, calligraphy, felt tip pen, and many other tools that you will learn about later in the chapter.

Toolbars

Below the Menu bar, Corel PHOTO-PAINT provides a collection of commonly used features on a number of *toolbars*. The toolbars that appear can be selected from the View, Toolbars menu. As with the toolbars you've already used in other Corel applications, the buttons that appear on the toolbars change depending on the current task. To see what each button does, simply point on a button and its name will appear in a pop-up label and its function will appear in the Status bar. The buttons that appear on the first toolbar when Corel PHOTO-PAINT opens are shown here:

The first four buttons in the default toolbar perform the same functions as selecting the New, Open, Save, and Print commands in the File menu. The next three buttons perform the same functions as the Cut, Copy, and Paste commands in the Edit menu. The next button, which looks like a grid, is used to select a different partial area of an image that was loaded as a partial file.

IP: *If your system has a limited amount of RAM, editing partial files can speed your work and avoid draining system resources.*

The Zoom drop-down list box, the next item on the toolbar, allows you to magnify or shrink your view of an image. The third button from the right maximizes the work area by hiding the Title bar, Menu bar, and Windows Taskbar. The second button from the right displays Image Information, such as the picture's name, width, height, memory size, and so on. Finally, the last button, Application Launcher, provides a quick way to transfer to Coreldraw and back.

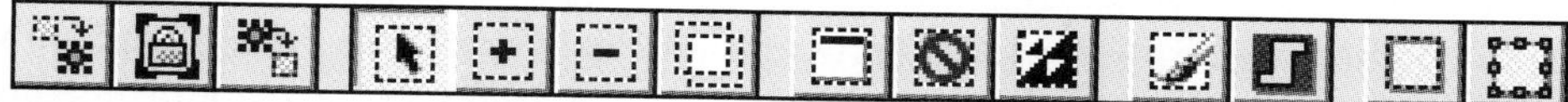

The second toolbar, also displayed when the program is first loaded, contains 14 buttons. The first three allow you to create an object from a mask (Create Object), preserve images (Preserve Image) so changes don't alter the original image, and create a mask (Create Mask) from an object. The next four buttons are used to work with masks: Normal creates a mask defining a single area that is replaced when you create another mask; Add to Mask creates additional masks as you define more areas; Subtract From Mask shrinks a mask by removing an area from it as you create additional masks; and XOR Mask creates a mask by excluding the area overlayed by two or more defined areas. The next three buttons deal with masks: All masks the whole picture, None removes all masks, and Invert inverts the mask so that the selected masked area becomes protected.. The next two buttons, Paint On Mask and Overlay Mask, are often used together to create special effects. Paint On Mask allows you to adjust the transparency of a mask so that you can control the amount of color or effect that will be applied. When the Paint On Mask is applied, it changes the image to shades of gray—the blacker the image, the more protected the mask from changes and the whiter, the less protected. The Overlay Mask overlays the image with a colored filter (by default, tinted red) through which you can see a mask's details. When used with the Paint On Mask, which obscures the detail of the mask, the details can be seen. Finally, Show Mask Marquee and Show Object Marquee turn the marquees on masks or objects on or off.

Corel PHOTO-PAINT Tools

The Corel PHOTO-PAINT toolbox either is in its default location on the left edge of the screen or appears as a floating window that you can move around on the screen. You can choose to display or hide the toolbox, by using the View, Toolbar submenu and then clicking on the Toolbox option. To make it a floating toolbox, click and drag the edge of the toolbox into the work area.

Tools within the toolbox are arranged according to function. There are 14 tools shown on the toolbox, as you can see in Figure 16-5.

Many buttons represent groups of tools; these can be identified by a small black triangle in the lower-right corner of the tool button. When you click on a button with a triangle and momentarily hesitate, a flyout menu displays the tools in the group. If you choose to float the toolbox, drag the toolbox away from the edge of the screen, as shown in Figure 16-6. You can return it to its original place by double-clicking on the Title bar.

The tools within the toolbox can be selected by clicking on a tool button or, in the case of group tools, by dragging the cursor on a flyout menu until the tool you want is highlighted. To see what a particular tool does, point on the tool and view its name on the pop-up label, and its function on the Status bar. Most tools have a Tool Settings roll-up associated with them. By double-clicking on a tool icon, you

Object Picker
Rectangle Mask
Path Node Edit
Crop
Zoom
Eyedropper
Eraser
Line
Rectangle
Text
Fill
Paint
Effect
Clone

The Corel PHOTO-PAINT toolbox

FIGURE 16-5

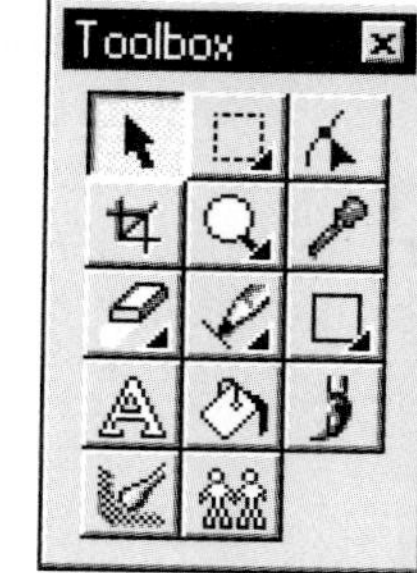

The floating Corel PHOTO-PAINT toolbox

FIGURE 16-6

can open its roll-up and adjust settings for that particular tool (with some tools, a second roll-up opens, or none). Settings are saved until you next change them. A brief summary of each of the tool groups is provided in the following sections.

OBJECT PICKER TOOL The Object Picker tool is used to select an object. Once selected, an object can be moved, cut, copied, pasted, stretched, rotated, or otherwise manipulated. When you double-click on the icon, an Objects roll-up is displayed.

MASK TOOLS The Mask tools create masks in various shapes and different color configurations. There are two types of masking tools: regular masks, which define an area based on shape; and color-sensitive masks, which define an area based on color. The masks themselves do not differ in the way they are used—it is just in defining the masks that the tools differ. The regular Mask tools are the Rectangle Mask, Circle Mask, Mask Brush, or Freehand Mask tools. The color-sensitive Mask tools are Lasso Mask, Magic Wand Mask, or the Color Mask roll-up. (The Mask Transform tool moves a marquee around a mask, so it is a different type of tool, as described below.) The Rectangle Mask tools opens a submenu with these options:

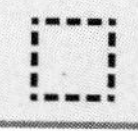

The Rectangle Mask tool defines a rectangular mask by dragging a rectangle around the shape to be masked. Hold CTRL to confine the shape to a square. Hold SHIFT to alter the mask shape from the center.

The Circle Mask tool defines a circular mask by dragging a circle around the shape to be masked. Hold CTRL to confine the shape to a circle. Hold SHIFT to alter the oval shape from the center.

The Freehand Mask tool defines an irregularly shaped mask by clicking to set anchor points or by dragging the tool freehand. Double-click to end the drawing of, or to set, the mask.

The Lasso Mask tool defines a colored area to be masked by "drawing" the area with a lasso or clicking to set anchor points. Double-click on a mask to set it. It will shrink until the mask surrounds the desired color. When you double-click on the icon, a Tools Settings roll-up is displayed.

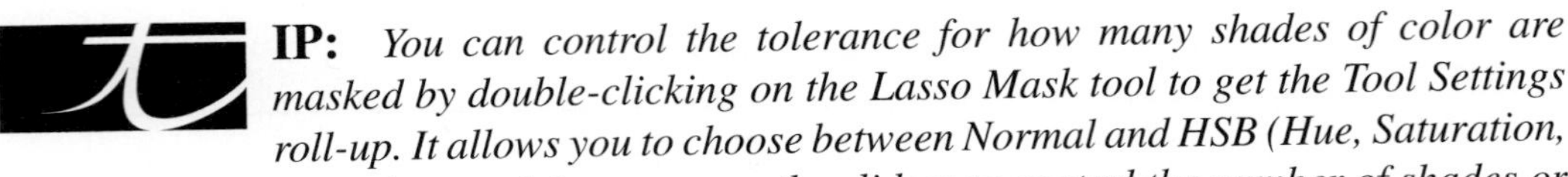

IP: *You can control the tolerance for how many shades of color are masked by double-clicking on the Lasso Mask tool to get the Tool Settings roll-up. It allows you to choose between Normal and HSB (Hue, Saturation, Brightness) colors and then to move the sliders to control the number of shades or intensity. Click on Anti-aliasing to smooth the edges.*

The Magic Wand Mask tool defines and selects objects with similar colors. Click in the image on the color you want. The areas with a similar color will be masked. When you double-click on the icon, a Tool Settings roll-up is displayed.

The Mask Brush tool defines a mask by brushing over it. Hold CTRL to confine the brush to vertical or horizontal directions. When you double-click on the icon, a Tool Settings roll-up is displayed.

The Mask Transform tool moves the marquee surrounding the mask to a different place. The image is unchanged. When you double-click on the icon, a Tool Settings roll-up is displayed.

IP: *To move a mask (the marquee plus its contents), click inside the marquee and drag with any mask tool. If you press* ALT *before dragging, the contents will be copied and the duplicate can be dragged.*

PATH NODE EDIT TOOL The Path Node Edit tool allows you to define a path and select nodes from a path to be edited with the Tool Settings roll-up by dragging a rectangle around the nodes. You can precisely change the shape of a mask by converting it to a path and manipulating the nodes. You can also use paths to create special effects with brush strokes (Stroke Path Function).When you double-click on the icon, a Tool Settings roll-up is displayed.

CROP TOOL The Crop tool allows you to select an area of an image to be cropped. You draw a rectangular shape around the area you want to crop, which can be moved or sized by dragging on the handles of the bounding box. Double-click within the box to delete all but the area within the rectangle. When you double-click on the icon, a Tool Settings roll-up is displayed.

ZOOM TOOLS Two Zoom tools are used to manipulate the display of the picture in some way. For instance, with the Zoom tool, you can zoom in (click) or out (right-click) of an area. Use the Hand tool to move the image. When you double-click on the icon, a Tool Settings roll-up is displayed.

EYEDROPPER TOOL The Eyedropper tool picks up a color from a picture so the same shade can be applied elsewhere by the next tool selected. The Eyedropper is used to refine or apply hand retouching (for instance, painting with a brush after choosing a color with the Eyedropper) to only parts of a picture. (Filters are usually used to manipulate entire selected areas of a picture.) When you double-click on the icon, a Color roll-up is displayed.

ERASER TOOLS Three Eraser tools are used to undo a mistake. The Local Undo tool reverses your last action, the Eraser tool erases portions of an image, and the Color Replacer tool applies the paper color to the image color. When you double-click on the icon, a Tool Settings roll-up is displayed.

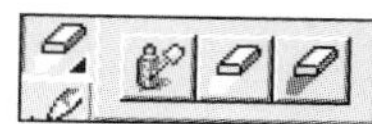

LINE, CURVE, PEN TOOLS The Line tools create lines, curves, and irregularly shaped lines with the Line tool, Curve tool, and Pen tool. To draw a straight line, click on the Line tool and click on where you want the line to begin. Move the pointer to where you want the line to end and click to anchor the line and continue, or double-click to terminate the line. When you draw a curve, you can simply draw the line freehand. Then, when you release the mouse button, it changes from the Curve tool to the Shape tool and displays nodes on the curve, allowing you to pull and drag nodes to create the curve you want more precisely. The Pen tool can be used to draw lines freehand and, together with the Tool Settings roll-up, can be used to create calligraphic and other special effects. When you hold CTRL while drawing with the Line or Curve tools, the line or curve is confined horizontally or vertically. When you double-click on the icon, a Tool Settings roll-up is displayed that allows you to alter the nib, size of the line, and other line attributes.

RECTANGLE, ELLIPSE, POLYGON TOOLS These hollow or filled shape tools let you quickly create many common shapes used in drawing your own images (unfilled): rectangles, ellipses, and polygons. When you double-click on the icon, a Tool Settings roll-up is displayed.

TEXT TOOL The Text tool allows you to type text onto your image. Double-clicking on the Text tool opens the Tool Settings roll-up where you can set the text formatting attributes, including font and size, bold, italic, alignment of text, and so on.

FILL TOOL Double-clicking on the Fill tool opens the Tool Settings roll-up, which allows setting various fill colors and patterns. On the top of the roll-up is a set of four buttons: Uniform Fill, Fountain Fill, Bitmap Fill, and Texture Fill. To open the individual fill dialog boxes, click on the Fill button, and then click on the Edit command button.

PAINT TOOL The Paint tool is the bread and butter of the Corel PHOTO-PAINT program. It allows you to add to a picture (or delete from it) color or texture. When you double-click on the icon, a Tool Settings roll-up is displayed.

EFFECT TOOL The Effect tool allows you to add special effects to the paint. You can use or create preset filters to smudge, smear, brighten, tint, or apply other effects. When you double-click on the icon, a Tool Settings roll-up is displayed.

CLONE TOOL The last icon on the toolbox is for the Clone tool. (This icon may be hidden by the Color Palette; simply drag the palette to one side to see the icon.) The Clone tool duplicates painting or drawing strokes elsewhere within a picture, or applies them to a duplicate of a picture. As you draw, a clone is produced. When you double-click on the icon, a Tool Settings roll-up is displayed.

This section has provided a brief introduction to Corel PHOTO-PAINT's many tools and their capabilities. To really appreciate the power and versatility of Corel PHOTO-PAINT, you have to apply the magic these tools offer to on-screen images. The remainder of this chapter is dedicated to showing how some of the more exciting features of this program work.

16

Using Corel PHOTO-PAINT Features

The two major tacks that you can take with Corel PHOTO-PAINT are to modify existing images and to create new ones. The next section will start out with one of the existing sample files provided by Corel PHOTO-PAINT. Using this file, we will explore various ways you can manipulate the image by selecting segments to create masks and objects. The next logical step—enhancing your images through one or more filters or the retouching tools—makes it possible to transform existing pictures with amazing effects. Finally, you will see how to create your own images.

Making an Object

Before you can create objects from images, you have to define a mask. Corel PHOTO-PAINT provides a collection of tools to solve the different problems you might face in defining a mask with just the right detail. The masking tools are contained in the flyout associated with the second tool in the toolbox, as shown here:

In order to put the masking tools to use, an image has to be present in the painting area. We will use a sample file of the apple shown in Figure 16-3.

1. Select the File Open command. In the Open an Image dialog box, use the Look In drop-down list box to locate your Corel PHOTO-PAINT files. These can be found either on the CD-ROM or your hard disk in the \Corel\Photopnt\Sample folder.
2. When you locate the correct folder, select the Apple.cpt file. You can also use any bitmap file (.pcx, .tif, .bmp) you have available.

The image appears on your screen in a window.

3. Maximize the window as shown in Figure 16-7.
4. Click on the Rectangle Mask Tool, the second tool down in the toolbox. Point on each tool in the flyout and read its function displayed on the

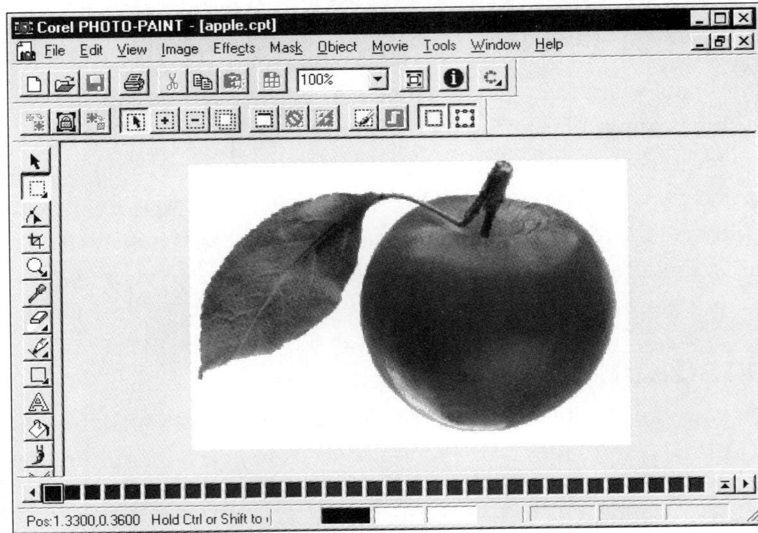

Maximized sample file prepared for masking

FIGURE 16-7

Status bar. As you can see, Corel PHOTO-PAINT offers a number of ways for you to select a portion of the image for masking. In this example, you want to isolate the apple.

5. Click on the Freehand Mask tool—the third tool from the left end. Since the apple is an irregular shape, this tool allows the highest degree of flexibility in defining the object. Notice how the Freehand Mask Tool icon now becomes the tool that appears in the toolbox and that the mouse pointer turns into a crosshair with the freehand shape in the upper right of the crosshair when you move the pointer into the image area.
6. Click and drag the crosshair around the apple, being careful not to catch any more of the leaf than a section of the stem. Don't be too concerned about how much white space is between the apple and the marquee. Complete the selection by dragging the crosshair back to the starting point. Double-click to end the selection. The area around your selection is now surrounded by a marquee. Your screen should now look similar to Figure 16-8.

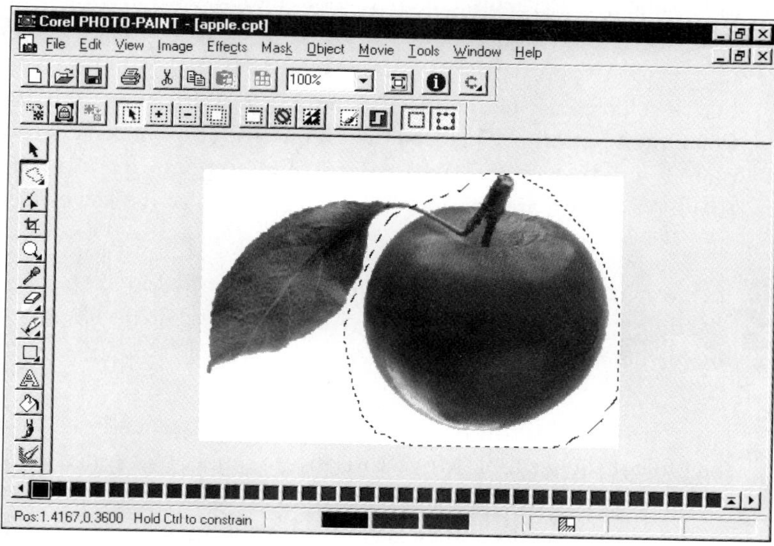

Image with mask

FIGURE 16-8

7. Now, to convert the selected area to an object, select Create from Mask from the Object menu or click on the Create Object icon on the toolbar. Eight handles will appear around the marqueed area of the picture.

You have created your first simple object—a copy of the apple without the leaf. Now you can manipulate the object by performing actions (probably familiar to you) such as moving, sizing, rotating, and skewing, and a few others described in the following section.

Working with Objects

You can create multiple objects from one image; cut, copy, or drag and drop objects into other images and applications; and order them as layers. In the following example, we will extract our selection, manipulate it, and save it for use later in the chapter.

To gain more working room so you can work with two images, the paper size should first be increased.

1. Select the Image menu and choose the Paper Size command. In the Paper Size dialog box, change the units of measure to Pixels and the Width dimension to approximately 800. Make sure the Maintain Aspect check box is selected so the height is increased proportionately and that the Placement option is Centered. Click on OK. (You may be warned that the picture will be a partial file.) After a few moments, the new paper size fills the painting area and the image redisplays in the lower-right corner.

IP: *If you select Automatic view resize in the Tools, Options dialog box, the image will be automatically resized so that you do not need to scroll the image when you resize the paper.*

2. Use the vertical scroll bar to center the image vertically and then select the Object Picker tool. Move a duplicate object by right-clicking the area within the eight handles and dragging the object to the left of the original image but within the image window. Position the object in an area where it doesn't overlap the original image. When you release the mouse button a pop-up menu will display; select Copy Here. If you deactivate the object marquee (by clicking on the Show Object Marquee, which acts as a toggle to activate/deactivate the visible object marquee), your screen should look similar to Figure 16-9.

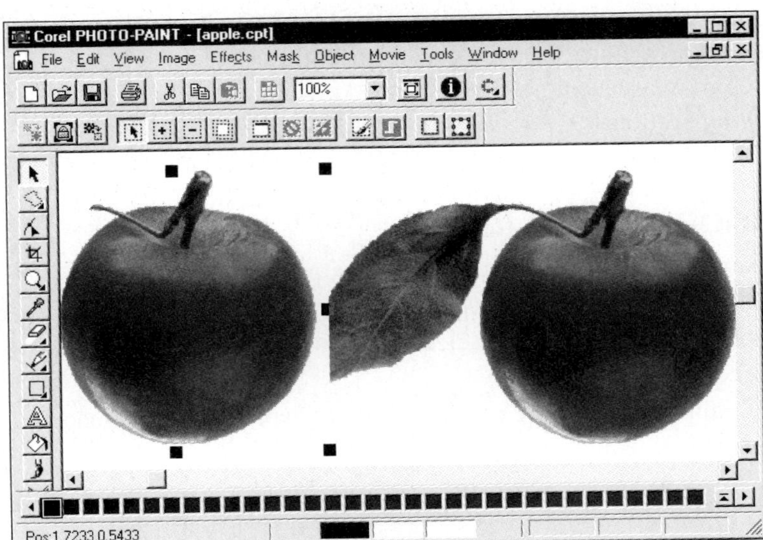

Screen after duplicating and moving an object

FIGURE 16-9

3. Experiment with moving, sizing, rotating, and skewing the apple. See Chapters 5 and 8 if you need to review these features. When you are through, return the object to something close to Figure 16-9, even if you have to reload the image from the disk and reselect the object.

4. To see what type of image this is, click on the Info icon. You will see that it is 256 Color. Click OK to remove the information from the screen. You'll need to convert the image to another color type since paletted colors, such as 16 Color and 256 Color, cannot use the special effects filters. From the Image menu, select Convert To and choose RGB Color (24 Bit) from the submenu. If you were to click on Info again, you would see that the image has been converted to 24 Bit Color.

5. Select the object if it isn't already selected. Then open the Objects roll-up by choosing it from the View, Roll-ups menu. Adjust the Opacity slider to see what effect it has on the object. (Opacity is not available for paletted colors, such as 16 Color and 256 Color.)

6. With the object still selected, open the Object menu to see what other options are available to you. Again choose some of the commands, such as Flip and Rotate, and observe their effects. If you change the object so drastically you cannot get it back to the appearance of a normal apple, close the window and start fresh with a new copy of the Apple.cpt file.

7. With the object still selected, click on the Copy button (or choose Copy from the Edit menu or press CTRL-C). Doing this copies the object to the Clipboard, from where you can paste it into a new window. You can now close all open files. Choose No when prompted to save and click Yes when asked to leave the Clipboard for other applications.

8. Click on the New button at the left end of the toolbar or choose New from the File menu. Accept the default settings in the Create a New Image dialog box by clicking on OK.

9. Click on the Paste button or choose Paste and then As New Object from the Edit menu. Maximize the drawing window so your object looks like Figure 16-10.

10. Click on the Save button and save the file as AppleObj in your Drawings folder. Notice that the default file extension is .cpt, identifying it as a Corel PHOTO-PAINT file. Click on OK. The object you saved is now an independent bitmap taken from the Apple.cpt file.

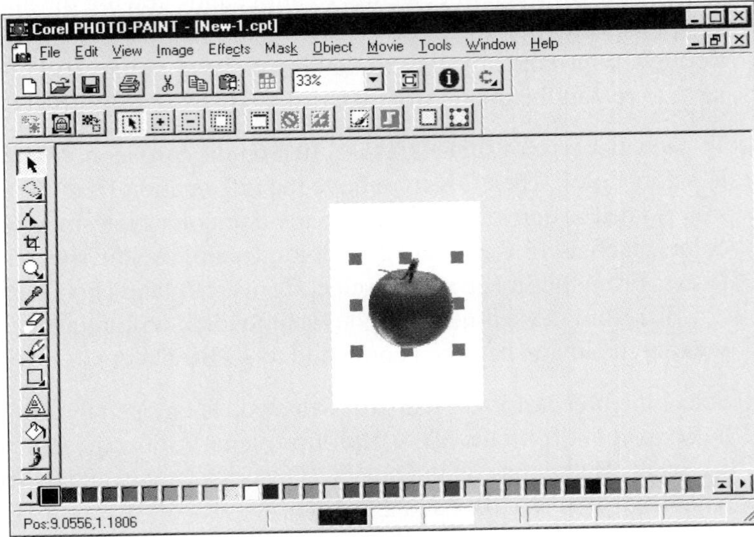

New object created from Clipboard copy

FIGURE 16-10

11. Click on Close in the File menu to remove the image from your screen. In the next exercise, you'll go back to the original apple.

Masks and Filters

Masks have two functions, in general. They can act like a protective film over an area of your image or they can define an area to be modified. You can protect or modify colors either inside or outside of the defined area. Masks can protect or modify specific colors or they can protect according to the degree of transparency you assign them. As discussed earlier, the second tool group in the toolbox contains the Mask tools.

Try a mask tool with these instructions.

1. Again open the Apple.cpt sample file. Maximize its window. In this example, it will be all right to use the default paper size.
2. Click on the Mask tool and open its flyout. Choose the Lasso Mask tool (looks like a rope—fourth from the left) and, as before, encircle the apple to isolate it from its leaf. Double-click to end the drawing.

3. From the Image menu, select Convert To and select CMYK Color (32 Bit) from the submenu.
4. Select the Effects menu and choose the 2-D Effects option. In the submenu that appears, choose the Tile option. Accept the default settings in the Tile dialog box and click on OK. The apple mask changes into multiple smaller images of itself within the confines of the mask, as shown in Figure 16-11.

 **OTE:** *A similar dialog box, with appropriate varying options, appears with many of the Effects menu filters. Use it to define the specific settings for a filter.*

5. Save the image (using a new filename), if you want, and close the file.

By default, the mask applies the effects of the tiling within its boundaries and protects colors to the area outside the boundaries. By choosing Invert from the Mask menu, you can cause the tiling to affect only the area outside the mask. By opening the Color Mask roll-up from the View menu, you can protect or modify individual

Image using Tiled filter for a special effect

FIGURE 16-11

colors. You can adjust the degree of transparency to vary the opacity of effects applied to the masked area using Paint On Mask.

The tiling effect that was applied to the mask was one of the filters provided by Corel PHOTO-PAINT. The following section describes the filters in more detail.

Filters

Filters can create professional results and can be used in creative, complex ways. They also provide an easy way to enhance images and to try out various special effects. As demonstrated in the previous example, filters are easy to apply; they are just as easy to remove: simply choose the Edit menu Undo command. Their ease of use and no-fuss removal make filters the predominant way to professionally strengthen your images.

NOTE: *In addition to the ample number of filters provided by Corel PHOTO-PAINT, you can use third-party filters such as Adobe and Kai's Power Tools plug-in filters. Using the Tools, Options dialog box (Filters tab), you can insert plug-in filters and add them to your Effects menu.*

Corel PHOTO-PAINT filters are grouped in the Effects menu. Most filters have associated dialog boxes that allow you to adjust their respective settings. You can preview a filter that changes one of the views to show what the result of your choices will be, reset the image to its original state, try another setting or another effect—all from one dialog box, such as seen in Figure 16-12. In addition, some of the dialog boxes contain thumbnails of the alternative choices for a filter in addition to the two views of the image to which you are applying an effect. For example, in the Color Hue filter, thumbnails are displayed of choices such as More red, More green, and More blue. You can combine these to create a different effect.

The best way to see a filter's effect is to open an image and use the preview box in the filter's dialog box to display the results of different settings. The following section briefly describes each filter within the ten Effects menu groups.

2-D Effects Filters

Band Pass balances shading or highlights in an image by letting you adjust the frequencies of sharp and smooth areas.

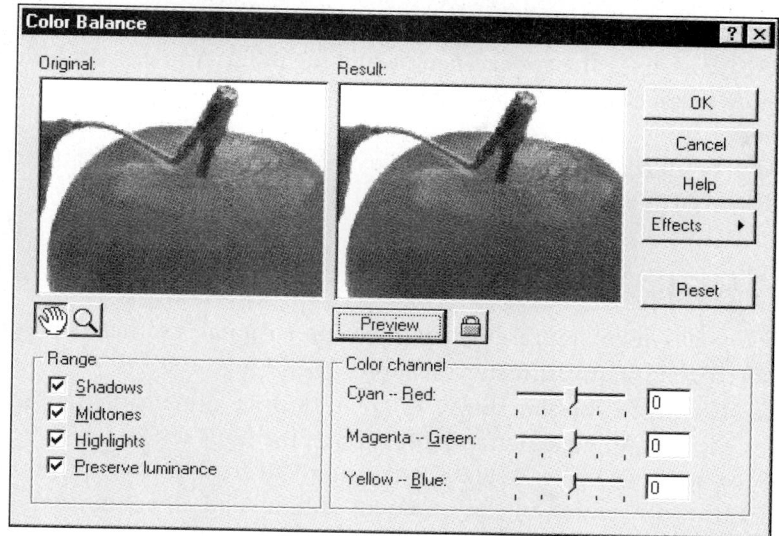

Filters dialog box from Effects menu

FIGURE 16-12

Displace changes an image relative to another image or displacement map. It uses color values to display the image either horizontally or vertically.

Edge Detect creates an outline or textured effect. You can adjust the edge sensitivity and color of the fill.

Offset moves an image based on the vertical and horizontal values set in the dialog box. A space is created in the gap where the image was moved, which can be filled with a color or part of the image.

Pixelate creates block-like segments of an image in a rectangular or circular pattern. You can adjust width, height, and opacity of the blocks.

Puzzle creates a puzzle-like appearance out of an image.

Ripple gives a wave-like appearance to an image. You can set the period, amplitude, and orientation of the wave effect.

Shear distorts the image by making it conform to a curve or wave that you can define.

Swirl rotates an image around its center. You can set the angle of rotation.

Tile creates multiple images of the original image within its boundaries. You can adjust the width and height of the multiple image (see Figure 16-11), which determines how many images will be displayed.

Trace Contour uses lines to outline the edges of an image while reducing the number of colors drastically.

User Defined allows you to define your own effect by entering values into a matrix.

Wet Paint gives the appearance of running paint. You can control the effect by changing the degree of wetness and the percentage of the depth of the object that is affected.

Wind produces a windblown effect by creating thin lines in the image. The effect is adjusted by the opacity and strength of the pseudo-wind.

3-D Effects

3D Rotate provides a representative three-dimensional box that displays the vertical and horizontal rotation effects you apply.

Emboss gives you the ability to create a three-dimensional appearance to an image. You can set the color and direction of the light source.

Glass applies a "sheet of glass" over a masked area. You can set the shape, width, bevel, refraction angles, opacity, amount of light, and other appropriate settings.

Map to Object adjustably wraps the image around an object.

Mesh Warp covers an image with an adjustable mesh whose intersections can be dragged to alter the appearance of the image.

Page Curl curls the corners of the page over the image. You can set the corner to be curled, whether the curl is vertical or horizontal, and whether you can see through the curl (transparent vs. opaque).

Perspective allows you to distort an image by dragging on corner control points.

Pinch/Punch compresses and expands an image in a three-dimensional way.

The Boss, which requires a mask first, makes an image look three-dimensional by dropping or slanting the edges around a mask. Use the Invert on the mask to push the image into the page.

Whirlpool create a fluid effect, which can be like fountains or a whirlpool (rings), or smudged.

Zigzag creates a distorted image by producing curves and angles from the center out.

Adjust Filters

Blur provides several levels of blurring, from merely softening to Gaussian blur.

Color Hue adjusts the color hues in the image, allowing more red, green, blue, magenta, yellow, or cyan to be added to an image in the shadows, midtones, or highlights, and preserves luminance. The Step slider increases the color intensity.

Color Tone adjusts the color tone to be darker or lighter, to saturate or desaturate, and to have more or less contrast. The Step slider controls the extent of the tone adjustment.

Noise adds noise and blurring to an image—speckles and colored dots overlaying the image. You can control the noise by choosing from More spike, More Gaussian, More uniform, Diffuse, Minimum, Medium, Maximum, Jaggy despeckle, and Remove noise.

Sharpness provides thumbnail choices for Unsharp mask, Adaptive unsharp, Sharpen, Directional sharpen, and Find edges. You can increase or decrease the effects of the filter with the Percentage and Background sliders.

Artistic Filters

Alchemy provides a great variety of brush stokes that can be applied to an image. You can choose between many brush stroke types, how a stroke is to be applied (random, orderly, painted, horizontally, or vertically), color characteristics, size of brush, angle, brightness, and transparency.

Canvas allows you to place a pattern over an image to serve as a background or to create a filtering effect. You can create certain effects by setting transparency and embossing levels.

Glass Block gives a distorted appearance of viewing an image through several thicknesses of blocks of glass. You can adjust the glass block width and height.

Impressionism creates an oil painting, with an impressionist-style effect. By adjusting the horizontal and vertical scatter, you can set the degree of the effect.

Smoked Glass gives an appearance of looking through tinted glass. You can adjust the amount of tint and its percentage. The tint color used is the paint color.

Terrazzo "dissects" the image and puts it back together according to varying patterns, which you can choose by clicking on Symmetry. You can play with feathering and opacity, and use color modes with dizzying effects.

Vignette creates an oval spotlight on an image that shades off gradually into the surrounding area. Adjustments can be made to the offset, fade, and color of the vignette.

Blur Filters

Directional Smooth determines from which direction to apply the greatest amount of smoothing.

Gaussian Blur blurs the image. The amount of haze or blur can be controlled with the Radius slider.

Jaggy Despeckle diffuses colors and removes jagged edges from bitmaps by changing the dot height and width values.

Low Pass blurs an image by graying its edges, resulting in an image with reduced highlights and color. The intensity of haze or blurring can be controlled by adjusting the Percentage and Radius sliders.

Motion Blur creates the illusion of movement. You can set the speed (or amount of blur) and the direction of the motion.

Smooth tones harshness with minimal loss of detail.

Soften smoothes and tones harshness. It also softens transitions between shadows and lighter areas.

Color Adjust Filters

Brightness and Contrast Intensity allows you to modify the relative lightness or darkness of an image.

Color Balance changes the blend of cyan or red, magenta or green, and yellow or blue in the image, depending on the color type.

Deinterlace produces a smoother image by removing even or odd scan lines.

Desaturate converts the colors in an image to shades of gray and black without changing the color mode to Grayscale. It reduces the saturation level of colors in the image.

Equalize redistributes shades of colors, making the darker colors black, the lighter colors white, and stretching those in between. This is useful for color images that will be color separated and printed using a high-resolution imagesetter.

Gamma provides a means to adjust the midtones of an image without affecting the darker (shadow) and highlighted areas.

Hue/Saturation/Lightness provides control over the degree of color ("colorness") of a selection without affecting its brightness. When changing the hue, you are shifting the color around an imaginary color wheel, with red at 0 and 360 degrees and the other colors in a rainbow sequence in between. Saturation is a measure of how intense you want a particular color.

Level Threshold darkens segments of an image. Values below the threshold will darken the image while those above remain unaltered.

Replace Colors allows you to replace colors in an image with others. You control the colors by setting Hue, Saturation, Lighting, and Range (color tolerance) values.

Tone Map provides an interactive means of creating and saving color corrections. All colors (using the RGB color model) can be modified, or each color channel can be individually changed.

Color Transform Filters

Bit Planes provides a sort of metallic look with bright colors. It is used to show tonal changes (color gradiants) in an image.

Halftone produces colored halftone dots from the color image. You can control the size of the dots with the Max Radius slider and the color mixture with the Cyan, Magenta, and Yellow sliders.

Invert flips colors; a white background becomes black, yellows become blues, and so forth.

Posterize reduces the overall number of colors and creates areas of solid colors and grays from gradations.

Psychedelic randomly applies colors to an image to produce a chaotic explosion of colors.

Solarize allows you to select levels of an image to be reversed, as in a photo negative.

Noise Filters

Add noise provides a granular effect to an image. Choose from a heavy and larger grain size (Gaussian), a thinner and lighter colored grain (Spike), or moderate grainy appearance (Uniform).

Diffuse scatters colors to create a smoother, but somewhat blurred, look.

Dust & Scratch filters out image noise—dust and scratch marks in an image.

Maximum lightens an image by decreasing the number of colors present. Adjustments are made by increasing or decreasing the radius of pixel values affected and the percentage of the effect to be applied.

Median removes noise from images that have a grainy appearance.

Minimum darkens an image by decreasing the number of colors present. Adjustments are made by increasing or decreasing the radius of pixel values affected and the percentage of the effect to be applied.

Remove noise softens edges in scanned images by comparing each pixel to those surrounding it. The maximum variance from the average value can be adjusted.

Render Filters

3-D Stereo Noise adds noise to the image, creating a 3-D image similar to the "Magic Eye" image. The image must be simple for best results.

Julia Set Explorer 2.0 allows you to add fractal designs to your image. You can select from a large list of preset fractals, or design your own.

Lens Flare provides a spot of light with reflections as if photographed from a choice of three lens types: 50-300mm zoom, 35mm prime, and 105mm prime. You can adjust the brightness of the light with the Brightness slider.

Lighting Effects provides one or more light sources. You can select a preset Light Type from the drop-down list box, or you can vary the settings yourself for color, intensity, aperture, exposure, direction, and elevation.

Sharpen Filters

Adaptive Unsharp highlights details along edges without affecting other areas of the image or selection.

Directional Sharpen determines from which direction to apply the greatest amount of sharpening.

Find Edges accentuates edges along boundaries of areas of different colors and shades.

High Pass strips away the shading, color, and low-frequency detail to reveal the highlights and luminous areas of an image.

Sharpen brings out detail and sharpens edges.

Unsharp Mask highlights details along edges and sharpens smooth areas of the image.

Retouching Images

Another of the features designed for use on existing images allows you to correct any imperfections and enhance the image's overall appearance. The majority of the tools that are used to retouch images combine colors by tinting, blending, smearing, and smudging. These tools are all located in the Effects tool group (second tool from the bottom of the toolbox). Additional tools that are commonly used are those in the Local Undo group and the Eyedropper. In the following example, you will retouch the apple that you isolated earlier.

1. Close the Apple.pcx image and open AppleObj.cpt to display the apple you earlier separated from its attached leaf. Your image should look something like Figure 16-13.

As you probably already noticed when you removed the leaf, the leaf's stem was abruptly cut off. Let's see what you can do to enhance the image.

2. Maximize the size of the image.
3. Select Zoom from the View menu and choose 200% from the submenu. You can experiment with other magnifications to see which one you are most comfortable working with.
4. Select the Freehand Mask tool and draw around the part of the stem to be erased, as shown here:

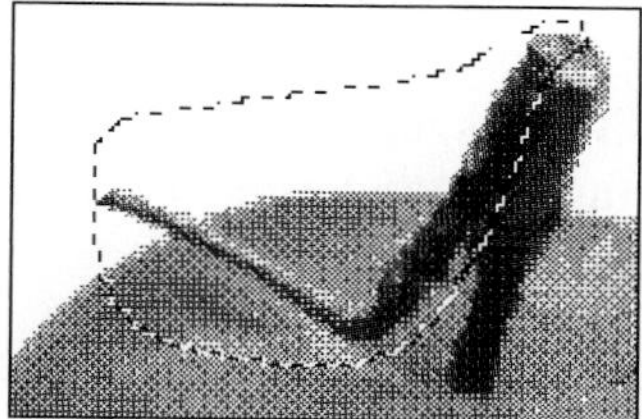

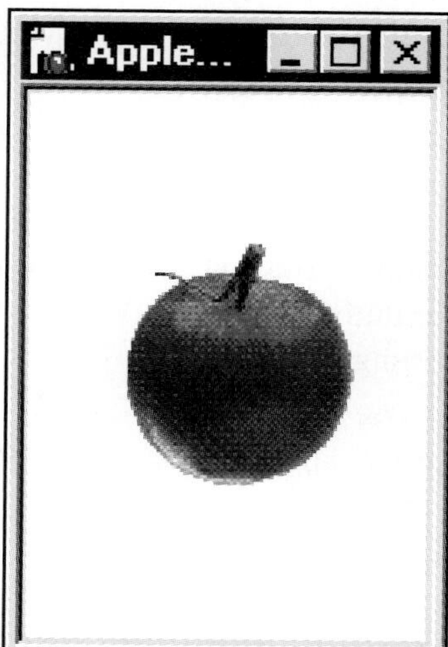

Saved AppleObj.cpt image

FIGURE 16-13

5. Double-click on the Paint tool to open its Tool Settings roll-up. On the first tab you are given a choice of a tool to paint with, for example, a spray can, air brush, pencil, pen, or marker. Click on the icon that looks like a pencil. The type will be set to 2B. Set the Size to 8. Fold up the Tool Settings roll-up.

6. From the Eraser tool group in the toolbox, click on the Eraser tool in the middle of the flyout. Carefully drag the pointer, in the shape of a small rectangle, over the portion of the leaf's stem that extends beyond the apple. Do not be concerned if you erase a piece of the apple. You can undo the action now or retouch it later. You might want to select Checkpoint from the Edit menu to save your work to this point. This will allow you to try a few different retouch techniques and safely return to the image with the stem removed.

7. Click on the Eyedropper tool and click the eyedropper-shaped mouse pointer in the red color next to the leaf's stem. This picks up the local color so you can use it to disguise the dark color of the stem. Check the paint color in the Status bar (the leftmost color) to make sure you picked up the color you want to use.

8. Click on the Paint Brush tool and drag the mouse pointer across the leaf stem in the area where you picked up the red color. Continue covering the leaf's stem with red, moving toward the apple's stem. Depending on how well you want to exactly match the adjacent coloring, you might want to pick up the lighter shades near the apple's stem and use them to disguise the leaf stem.

9. At this point, you have a much better looking apple. You can accomplish similar results by using the Effects tools to smear, blend, smudge, and tint. Choose Restore to Checkpoint from the Edit menu to try some of these other techniques. You can also work on the base of the apple's stem to provide a more uniform shading. When you are through, your image could look something like Figure 16-14.

OTE: *Another technique is to use the Clone tool (normal Clone) to clone opposite sides of the stem over the stem to hide it. Then use the blend tool to blend them together.*

16

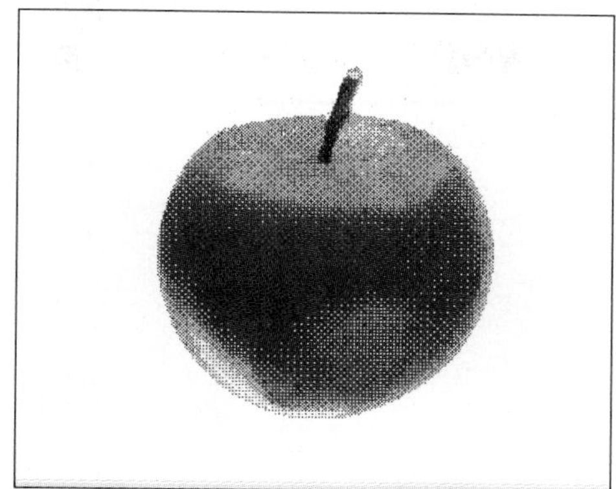

Apple with stem modified

FIGURE 16-14

10. If you are connected to a printer, choose Print from the File menu and click on the Options command button. In the Layout tab, size and position the image to your liking, and then click on OK to return to the Print dialog box. Click on OK.

11. Present the printed apple to your favorite teacher!

Drawing Tools

Up to this point you have been using Corel PHOTO-PAINT to work on existing images. The second facet of Corel PHOTO-PAINT provides the ability to create your own images with an assortment of drawing tools. The Paint, Line, Fill, and Clone tool groups include the majority of tools you will need to draw your own pictures. You are probably familiar with the basics of using these tools from Coreldraw and other painting applications, like Windows' Paintbrush. There is an infinite variety of drawing possibilities that exist—too extensive to cover here—and you are encouraged to fine-tune your artistic talents by trying out the available tools as you desire and as time allows.

This introduction only touches on the numerous capabilities found in Corel PHOTO-PAINT. The program contains many more surprises. Continue to experiment with it, and you will be impressed with its capabilities.

CORELDRAW!™ 6 in action

Warped—Tim Gorski

Warped was created using the Meshwarp filter in Corel PHOTO-PAINT. It shows the kind of fun that you can have with the many filters in PHOTO-PAINT.

Tim Gorski, who has won awards for his work in Corel PHOTO-PAINT, lives in Fort Lauderdale, Florida, and can be reached at (305) 463-7618.

Tracing Bitmap Images and Text

17

Bitmap images contain no objects for you to select; they consist entirely of a fixed number of tiny dots or *pixels*. If you enlarge or reduce the size of the bitmap without converting it to a Coreldraw object, distortion or unsightly compression of the pixels results. The solution is to trace the bitmap in Coreldraw or Corel OCR-TRACE and turn it into an object-oriented drawing.

You can then change the shape and color of the object's outline and the color of its fill, edit it normally, and print it, all without distortion. The Coreldraw package offers you three different methods for tracing an imported bitmap. The most sophisticated of these is Corel OCR-TRACE, a separate program included with Coreldraw. You will be amazed at the speed and accuracy with which this product can turn even the most complex bitmap into a finished curve object ready for editing. Corel OCR-TRACE will be discussed later in this chapter in the section "Tracing with Corel OCR-TRACE."

In Coreldraw itself, you can choose between manual tracing and the semiautomatic Autotrace feature. These methods are slower than Corel OCR-TRACE and require more work on the part of the user, but they offer you a high degree of control over the curves that result from your tracing. They are discussed in the early sections of this chapter.

Creating a Bitmap Image

Coreldraw treats a bitmap image as a unique object type, separate from other object types such as rectangles, ellipses, polygons, curves, and text. Unlike all of the other object types, bitmaps must be created outside of Coreldraw.

There are several ways to secure a bitmap image for importing into Coreldraw. The easiest method is to import a bitmap clipart file or Photo CD image from a CD-ROM. The next easiest method is to scan an existing image, such as a photograph. Alternatively, you can sketch a drawing by hand and then scan the image in one of the supported bitmap file types (such as .PCX or .TIF). Finally, you can create your own original pixel-based images with Corel PHOTO-PAINT.

Once the bitmap image is available, you are ready to import it into Coreldraw.

Importing a Bitmap Image

Coreldraw accepts many bitmap file formats for import: .TIF, .BMP, and .PCX, to name a few. The .TIF format is one that most scanners support, and is the format used for the bitmap clipart included with your Coreldraw software. If the bitmap you want to import is in a format that Corel doesn't support, you can convert it to a .TIF file using an image conversion program, such as Inset Graphics' Hijaak or U-Lead Systems' ImagePals.

To import a bitmap, you use the Import command from the File menu and select the appropriate bitmap file format in the Import dialog box.

The standard Coreldraw package includes a number of bitmap files in the \Images\ folder on the third CD-ROM. In the following exercise, you will see how to import one of the sample bitmap files.

1. Starting with a blank Coreldraw document, make sure that Rulers and Wireframe are turned off.
2. Select Page Setup from the Layout menu and make certain that the page is set for Portrait and that the page size is Letter. Click on OK to save these settings. On the Layout menu, none of the Snap To options should be checked.
3. Select Import from the File menu. The Import dialog box appears.
4. Open the Files of type drop-down list box and select TIFF Bitmap (.TIF).
5. In the Look in drop-down list box, specify the drive and the folder that contains the Coreldraw sample .TIF files. This is the \Images\ folder on the third CD-ROM.
6. Double-click on the Cartoons folder to open it, then select Dogh5.tif. Click on Import to open the bitmap in Coreldraw. You may use a different bitmap file if you do not have this file available.

After a few seconds, the image appears, centered on the page and surrounded by a selection box. The Status bar displays the message "Color Bitmap on Layer 1" (or "Monochrome Bitmap on Layer 1" for a black and white .TIF file).

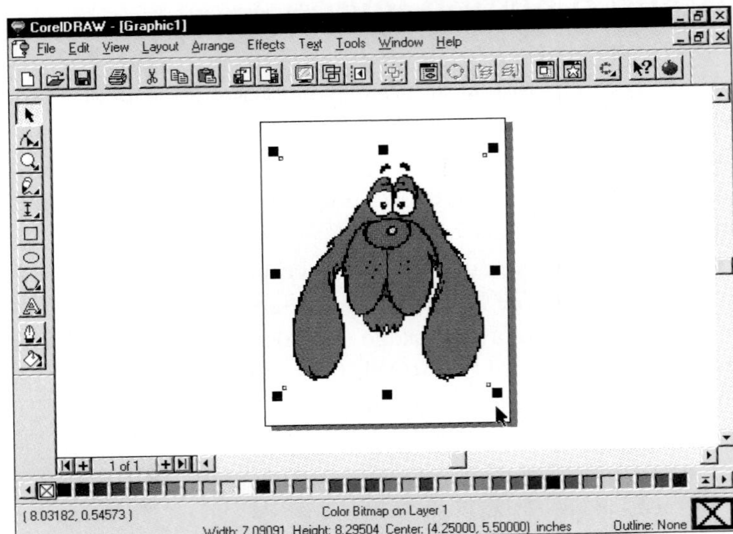

Bitmap image imported for tracing

FIGURE 17-1

7. Select the Pick tool, then press the SHIFT key and enlarge the bitmap by dragging any of the corner selection boxes outward, as shown in Figure 17-1. You can see how bitmaps become "jagged" when they are enlarged.

8. Select Save As from the File menu. When the Save Drawing dialog box appears, change the folder to the one in which you save your Coreldraw drawings. Type a name—for example, **autotrace**—in the File name text box, and then click on Save.

Autotracing an Imported Bitmap

As mentioned earlier, Coreldraw lets you turn an imported bitmap image into a resolution-independent curve object by tracing the image. You can trace a bitmap image either semiautomatically, using the Autotrace feature, or manually. You can also use the fully automatic Corel OCR-TRACE program described later in this chapter. Manual tracing is a good choice if you desire total control over the appearance and placement of the outline curves. If you find it cumbersome to use the mouse for tracing long paths manually, however, use the Autotrace feature instead. You have less control over the results, but you will spend less time manipulating the mouse.

IP: *Using a stylus and graphics tablet such as one from Wacom, Kurta, or CalComp gives you more natural control over curves and hand movements.*

The Autotrace feature becomes available to you only when the bitmap object is selected. Autotrace is semiautomatic in the sense that the software draws the actual curves for you, but you must define a number of parameters before tracing begins. You control the shape of the outline pen, the color of the outline fill, the interior fill of the object, and the smoothness of the curves.

In the following exercise, you will use Autotrace to trace portions of the autotrace.cdr image that you imported earlier as a .TIF file.

1. With the image you will use still on the screen, press F4 to select Zoom to All Objects view. To establish the Outline Pen properties for the traced object, you must first deselect the bitmap.
2. Deselect the object, then click on the Outline tool and then on the hairline button on the second row of the flyout. This will result in hairline curves of a very fine width. Click on OK in the Outline Pen defaults dialog box to apply this default to all graphic objects.
3. With the object still deselected, click on the Fill tool and then on the X (the no fill button) on the flyout. Again, accept this as the default for all graphic objects.
4. Next, you need to change the properties of the Freehand tool. Select the Freehand tool and, while pointing on the Freehand tool, click the right mouse button. Select Properties from the popup. When the Tool Properties dialog box is displayed, make sure Curve, Bézier is selected in the Tools drop-down list box. On the General tab, adjust the settings as follows: Freehand tracking, 5 pixels; Autotrace tracking, 5 pixels; Corner threshold, 8 pixels; Straight line threshold, 3 pixels; and Auto-join, 10 pixels. These settings will result in smoother curves, smooth (rather than cusp) nodes, curves rather than straight line segments, and curve segments that snap together when they are as far as 10 pixels apart. Click on OK to make these settings take effect.

5. Turn on Preview Selected Only from the View menu.

Now you are ready to begin Autotracing. Select the bitmap with the Pick tool and then select the Freehand tool. Notice that the pointer looks different (as shown on the left): instead of being a perfectly symmetrical crosshair, it has a wand-like extension on the right. This is the Autotrace pointer. It appears only when you activate the Pencil tool with a bitmap object selected.

OTE: *You can use either the Freehand or Bézier tool to Autotrace bitmaps. These exercises use the Freehand tool since it is the default Pencil tool.*

6. Position the wand of the Autotrace pointer to the left of the bitmap and click once. After a moment, a closed curve object appears, completely enclosing the contours of the bitmap. Press SHIFT-F9 to switch to wireframe view while the curve is still selected, and you see the traced line similar to Figure 17-2. Press SHIFT-F9 again to return to full color mode.
7. Position the tip of the Autotrace pointer inside one of the dog's eyes and click. A closed curve object quickly appears. (If you are using a different bitmap, click inside any closed region.)

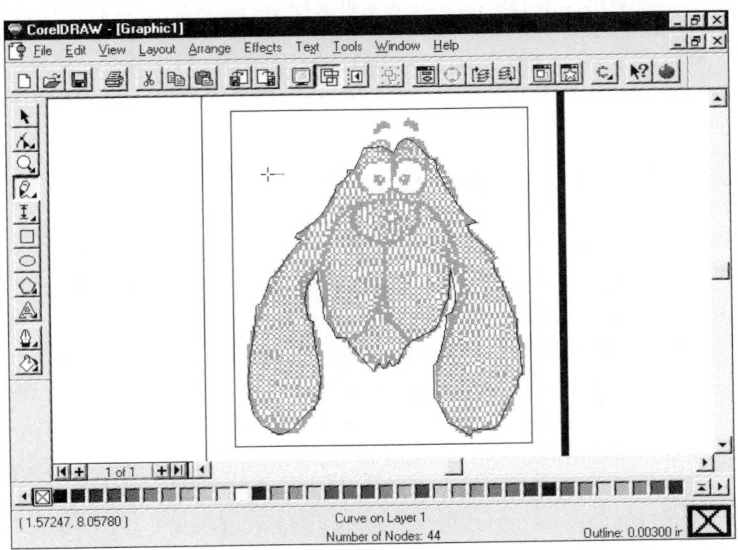

Autotraced curve—wireframe view

FIGURE 17-2

8. Create more Autotrace curves in the same way.
9. Select the Pick tool and click on the bitmap somewhere other than where you were tracing. Press DEL to remove the bitmap and see your handiwork. Autotrace produces a rough approximation of your bitmap object, as you can see in Figure 17-3.
10. Save your changes to the image by pressing CTRL-S.
11. Select Close from the File menu to clear the screen, then select New and then Document from the flyout to open a new document.

TIP: *If you have trouble selecting a region that results in the curve you need, try pointing at the desired region using the tip of the wand on the Autotrace pointer instead of its center point. You will find that you can aim the wand more accurately when you are working in a magnified view.*

As you saw in the previous exercise, the results of the Autotrace feature depend on your choice of the area to outline and on exactly how you position the Autotrace pointer. Even if you use Autotrace to trace the same area twice, Coreldraw may

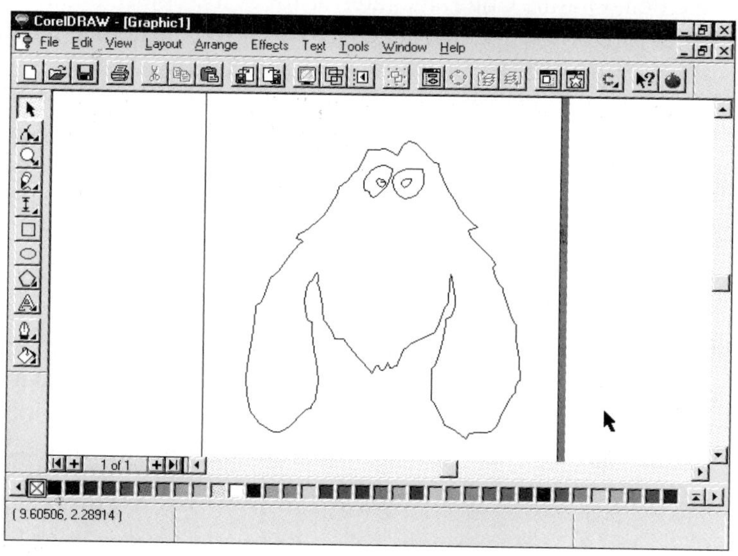

Result of Autotracing part of a bitmap

FIGURE 17-3

change the number and positions of the nodes each time. The path that an Autotrace curve takes can sometimes seem to be quite unpredictable, especially if there are not clear separations between light and dark areas or between areas of different color. With practice, you will gain skill in positioning the Autotrace pointer for the best possible results.

Tracing Manually

You don't have to be a superb drafter to trace a bitmap with precision in Coreldraw. By magnifying the areas you trace and adjusting the Curve settings in the Tools Properties dialog box, you can trace swiftly and still achieve accurate results. To trace a bitmap manually, you deselect the bitmap just before you activate the Freehand tool. This action prevents the Freehand tool from becoming the Autotrace pointer.

Manual tracing is faster and easier than Autotracing if the imported bitmap contains multiple subjects with no abrupt changes in brightness levels or colors from one pixel to the next. Most commercial clipart fits this description. Using the manual method avoids the problem of Autotrace curves that extend beyond the subject with which you are working. As a result, you usually need to do less editing after your initial manual tracing than after using AutoTrace.

Just as when you use the Autotrace feature, you can define the default shape of the Outline Pen, Outline Color, the interior fill of the object, and the smoothness of the curves before you begin tracing. In the following exercise, you can manually trace portions of your .TIF file.

1. Once again, import a .TIF file as you did earlier. You can use the Dogh5.tif used earlier in this chapter, or you may use a different image.
2. When the bitmap object appears, press F4 to Zoom to All Objects. Also, make sure Snap To Grid, Rulers, and Wireframe are turned off, and Preview Selected Only is turned on.
3. The default for the Outline Pen tool should still be hairline (this should be displayed on your Status bar). If not, deselect the object and click on the Outline Pen tool and then on the hairline button on the second row of the flyout. Accept this setting as the default for all graphic objects.

4. The default for the Fill tool should still be None (again, this should be displayed on your Status bar). If not, deselect the object and click on the Fill tool and again on the X button on the flyout to change the object fill color to None. This prevents any closed paths that you trace from filling with an opaque color and obscuring other traced areas that lie beneath. (You can edit the fill colors of individual objects later.) Again, accept this as the default and then reselect the bitmap.
5. Next, you need to change the properties of the Freehand tool. Point on the Freehand tool and click the right mouse button. Select Properties from the popup. When the Tool Properties dialog box is displayed, make sure Curve, Bézier is selected in the Tools drop-down list box. On the General tab, adjust the settings as follows: Freehand tracking, 1 pixel; Autotrace tracking, 5 pixels; Corner threshold, 10 pixels; Straight line threshold, 1 pixels; and Auto-join, 10 pixels. These settings will result in curves that closely follow the movements of your mouse. You will generate smooth (rather than cusp) nodes, curves rather than straight line segments, and curve segments that snap together when they are as far as 10 pixels apart. These settings promote ease of editing should you need to smooth out the traced curves later. Click on OK to save these settings.
6. Deselect the bitmap object and activate the Freehand tool. (If you see the Autotrace pointer instead of the regular Freehand pointer, you haven't deselected the bitmap.) Position the Freehand pointer anywhere along the outline of a closed area, then depress and hold the mouse button, trace all the way around, and end the curve at the starting point. Should you make any errors, you can erase portions of the curve by pressing the SHIFT key as you drag the mouse backward (before you release the mouse button).

TIP: *For even smoother curves, trace in a series of small joined segments, placing a node every time the angle of the curve changes. This "connect-the-dots" approach avoids the jaggedness that can occur when you try to trace large areas with a single sweep of the mouse.*

7. Zoom in and trace more of the picture with the Freehand tool. You can trace the outline of small details in the bitmap as open curves and use Autotrace as well as manual, all in the same picture.

8. In order to do some Autotracing in your bitmap, select the Pick tool and select the entire bitmap object. Remember that unless the bitmap is selected, you cannot enter Autotrace mode.
9. Select the Freehand tool again with the bitmap selected. Position the Autotrace pointer inside one of the small detail areas of your bitmap and click to trace a curve around this tiny area automatically.
10. Using Autotrace, trace a few more small details of your picture. When you have finished, your screen should look roughly similar to the way it looked in the previous section, "Autotracing an Imported Bitmap." Save the image at this point under the filename **mytrace**.
11. Select the Pick tool and click on the bitmap somewhere other than where you were tracing to select the entire bitmap. Press DEL to remove the bitmap and see your handiwork. Your screen should show the curve objects, as you see in Figure 17-4.
12. Save your changes by pressing CTRL-S, and then select Exit from the File menu.

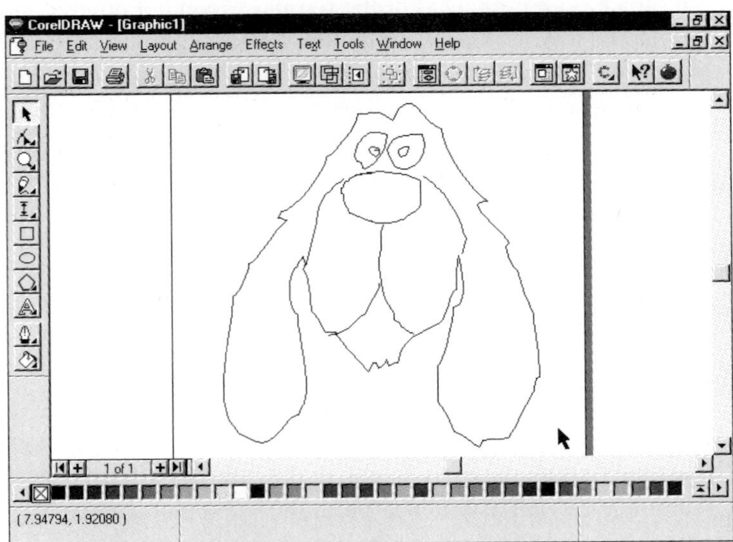

Combining Autotracing with manual tracing

FIGURE 17-4

As you have just seen, it is possible and sometimes even preferable to combine both the manual and Autotrace methods when tracing complex bitmap images. Manual tracing is best for obtaining exact control over the placement of curves in bitmaps that contain several subjects close together, as is the case with most clipart. The Autotrace method is useful for tracing small closed regions, like the details of the bitmap in the previous exercises. The Autotrace method is also more convenient to use when the bitmap image has a single, clearly defined subject with sharp contours and/or clear delineation between light and dark areas and between colors.

Whether you use the Autotrace feature, manual tracing, or a combination of both methods, you can always edit the curve objects you create.

Tracing With Corel OCR-TRACE

A third method of tracing bitmap images is available to you—one that is more rapid, sophisticated, and efficient than either the manual or the Autotrace method. The Corel OCR-TRACE tracing program allows you to trace bitmaps automatically at high speeds and save them in any vector format available in Coreldraw. You can choose from six methods of tracing bitmap graphics, and you can customize tracing parameters to suit your needs. You can also convert bitmap text to editable text using Corel OCR-TRACE's OCR (Optical Character Recognition) functions. (Bitmap text is really a graphic, not text that can be edited in a word processor or using Coreldraw's text functions. Corel OCR-TRACE converts the bitmap text into a text file that you can edit.) You can even trace a bitmap image and convert text from the same file. When you are finished tracing a bitmap graphic, you can edit the resulting object-oriented image in any drawing program that can read the vector file format you choose, including Coreldraw.

The following sections provide instructions for preparing to use Corel OCR-TRACE, for selecting and tracing bitmaps and text, and for customizing and editing tracing parameters.

Preparing to Use Corel OCR-TRACE

Corel OCR-TRACE is installed in the same folder and program group where you installed Coreldraw. Before you begin using Corel OCR-TRACE for the first time, check the amount of free space available on your hard drive. When you trace bitmaps using Corel OCR-TRACE, temporary files are generated on your hard drive. If you trace large bitmaps, or more than one bitmap during a session, you are almost certain to require several megabytes of hard drive space for these temporary files. You should have at least 5MB of space free, and 10MB is recommended.

Loading Corel OCR-TRACE

Unless you have over 8MB of memory, do not run any other Windows 95 applications in the background while you are running Corel OCR-TRACE. This means that you should exit Coreldraw while running Corel OCR-TRACE—not just switch out of it. Corel OCR-TRACE requires a large amount of memory to work efficiently. If you run other applications concurrently, Corel OCR-TRACE may not run or may function very slowly.

To load Corel OCR-TRACE, open the Windows 95 Start menu and select Corel OCR-TRACE 6 from the Corel Graphics flyout. The opening screen appears and is then replaced by the Main window, shown in Figure 17-5. (The Trace toolbar has been dragged from below the toolbox for clarity.)

Like Coreldraw, Corel OCR-TRACE has a multiple document interface. The document window is split into two halves, with the original image to be traced on the left and the traced image on the right. (When you open Corel OCR-TRACE, the document window is not opened automatically. When the image to be traced is loaded, it is placed in the left window, and when you complete the tracing you will see it on the right, as shown in Figure 17-6.) Like most other Coreldraw applications, Corel OCR-TRACE has a Text toolbar and Standard toolbar across the top of the window, a toolbox down the left side, and a Status bar across the bottom.

If you maximize the document window, as shown in Figure 17-7, the original is displayed on the left, the traced image is in the upper window on the right, and the bottom-right window is used for editing text that you trace using Corel OCR-TRACE's OCR functions.

When a file is opened, Corel OCR-TRACE contains nine menus: File, Edit, View, Image, OCR-Trace, Text, Tools, Window, and Help. Many of the functions on the menus are familiar to you from using Coreldraw. The File menu provides the normal file options as well as Acquire, which allows you to scan an image directly into Corel OCR-TRACE if you have a scanner. The Edit menu provides the normal edit functions. The View menu functions are similar to Coreldraw with the addition of Layout, which lets you select either Vertical or Horizontal orientation. The Image menu lets you invert the colors of the bitmap and convert a color bitmap to black and white; in addition, you can flip and rotate the image.

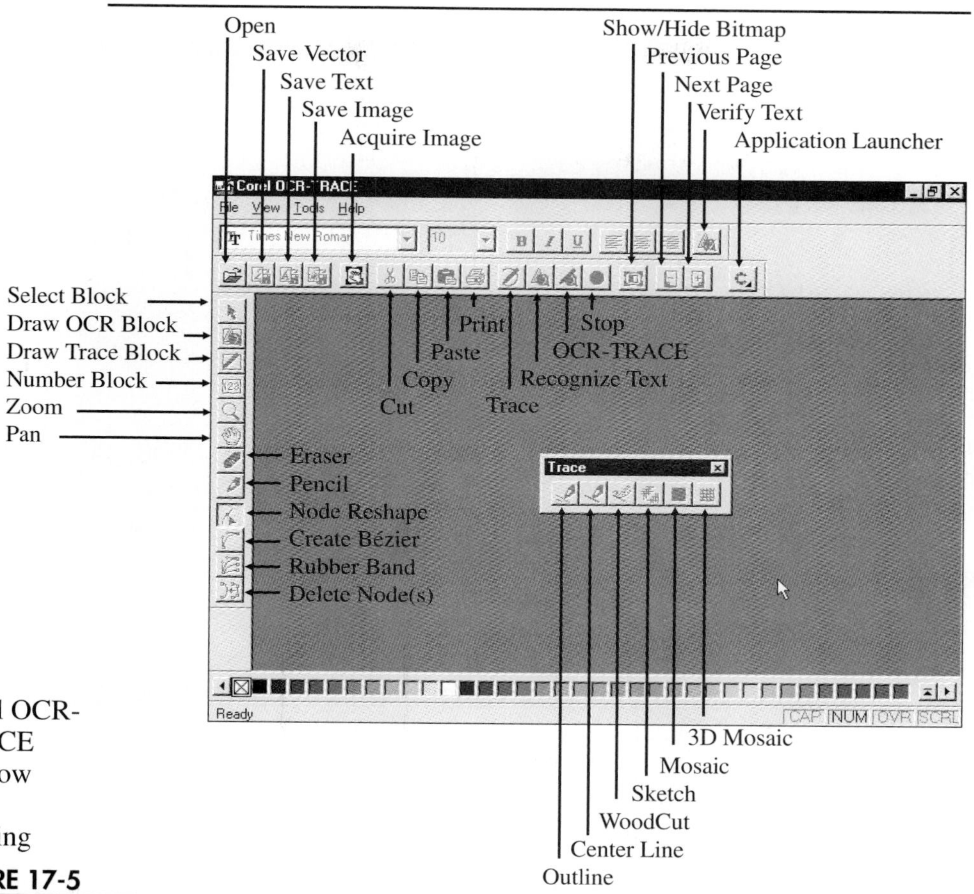

Corel OCR-TRACE window upon opening

FIGURE 17-5

The OCR-Trace menu provides access to the six different tracing methods for graphics (Outline, Center Line, WoodCut, Sketch, Mosaic, and 3D Mosaic), as well as the OCR functions. The Perform OCR command is used when you are converting a file that contains only text. If the file contains a graphic and text, you would use the Perform OCR-Trace command. With Perform OCR-Trace, both the graphic and the text will be traced. The OCR-Trace menu also opens a very extensive'tabbed dialog box of options for adjusting the properties of the tracing method you select. A tabbed dialog box for changing the OCR properties is also opened from the OCR-Trace menu. The Text menu allows you to set character and paragraph properties, as well as find and replace text. The Tools menu contains the Options command and opens the

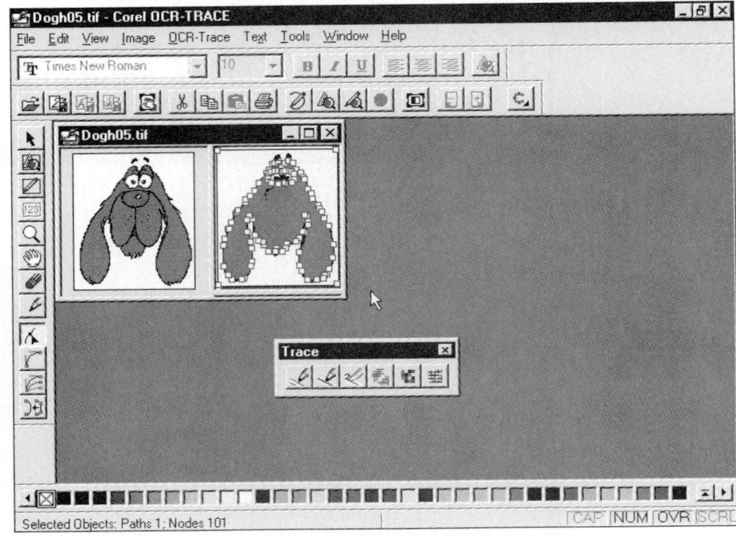

Corel OCR-TRACE screen with document window open

FIGURE 17-6

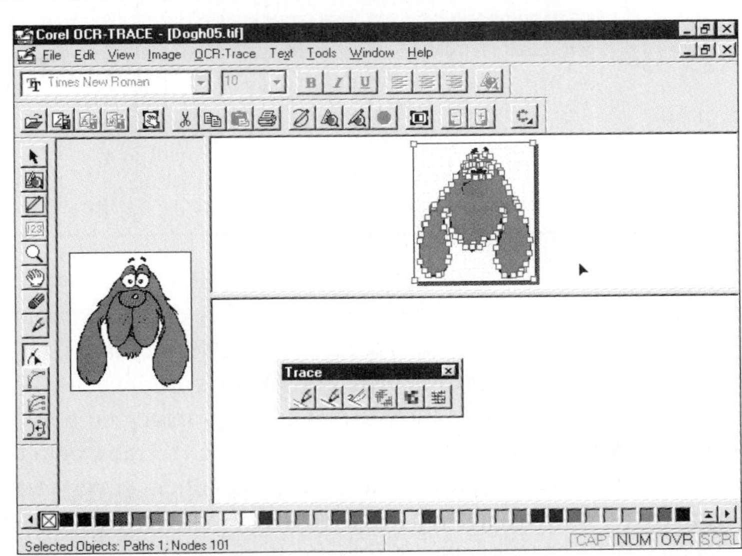

Corel OCR-TRACE screen with document window maximized

FIGURE 17-7

Page Manager, Layer Manager, and Color Manager. The Window and Help menus are similar to their Coreldraw counterparts.

Opening Files to Trace

You open files in Corel OCR-TRACE by selecting Open from the File menu, by clicking on the Open button on the ribbon bar, or by using the Acquire command from the File menu to scan an image directly into Corel OCR-TRACE. In the first two cases, the standard Open Files dialog box appears.

Tracing a Bitmap with Corel TRACE

Tracing a bitmap graphic involves several steps, as follows.

1. Use one of the two methods to display the Open dialog box and then specify the source folder of the file you want to trace, using the Look in drop-down list box, if necessary.
2. Select a file to trace by clicking on its name in the Files list box. Then click Open.
3. Edit the tracing options, if desired, by selecting Trace Settings from the OCR-Trace menu.
4. Select one of the tracing methods from the Perform Trace flyout from the OCR-Trace menu or click on one of the buttons on the Trace toolbar to begin tracing the selected file.

In the following exercise, you will use Corel OCR-TRACE to *batch trace* (trace one after the other) two bitmap graphics.

1. Click on Open and change to the drive and folder where your bitmap files are located. This exercise will use two files from the third Corel CD-ROM, but you can use any two bitmap files you may have.
2. Select the first bitmap file from the list in the Files list box (Dogh5.tif in this case). Click on Open.

3. Once the first bitmap file is opened, select Page Manager from the Tools menu. The Page Manager dialog box shown here will be displayed.

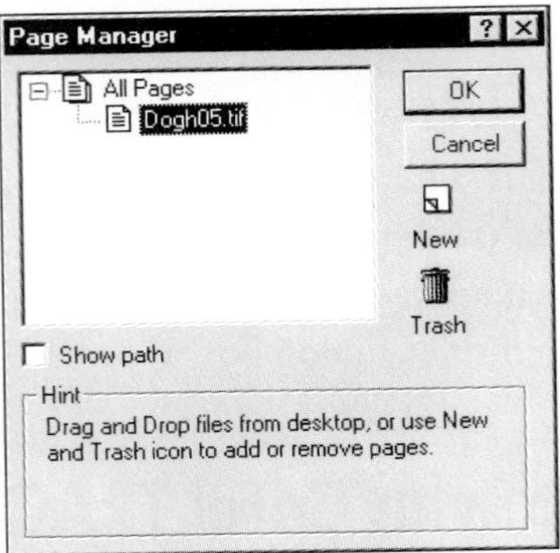

4. Click on the New button. The Import dialog box will be displayed. Select the second bitmap file to be traced, then click on Import. In this case, Actor1.tif. The new page will be displayed in the Page Manger display box. Click on OK.

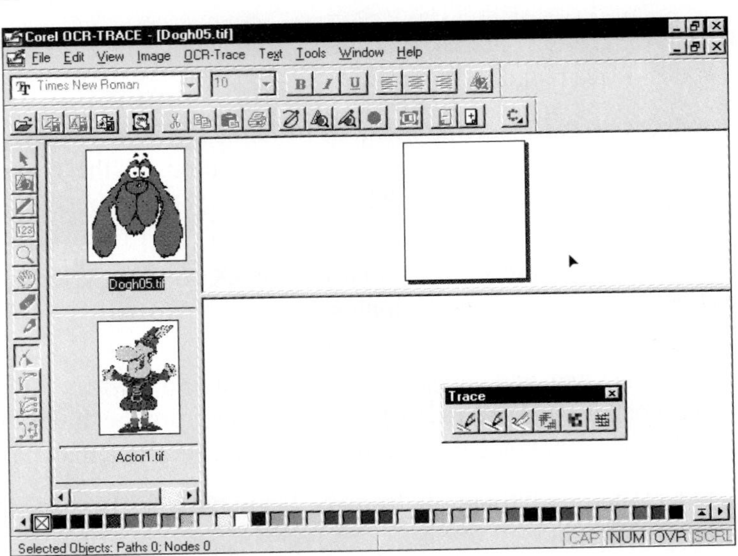

Two bitmaps to be traced

FIGURE 17-8

5. Maximize the OCR-TRACE document window so that you can see both bitmaps on the left side of the document window, as shown in Figure 17-8.

NOTE: *By opening the second file using Page Manager you created a multipage document with two pages. When you save your traced images, they will be saved as a single document. If you don't want to create a multipage document, open each file separately. You can also open a multipage document in Coreldraw and then separate the pages into individual files.*

For this exercise, you will trace the two bitmaps using the Outline method. The Outline method is best for tracing bitmaps with thick lines, many fills, and a hand-sketched look. The Center Line method, on the other hand, is best for architectural or technical illustrations that have thin lines of fairly uniform thickness and no fill colors. See the next section of this chapter for more details on the differences between the Outline and Center Line methods of tracing.

6. Select Perform Trace from the OCR-Trace menu, then By Outline from the flyout. The Outline Trace Multiple Pages dialog box will open. Notice that each page icon in front of the filename now has a checkmark on it. This indicates that the page will be traced. You can deselect or select a page by clicking on its page icon.

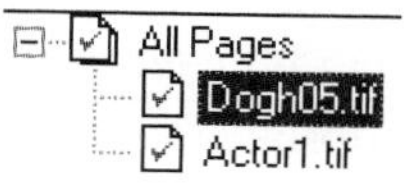

7. Click on OK on the Outline Trace Multiple Pages dialog box to begin tracing the two sample files. After a few seconds, the top window on the right side of the screen contains the traced image of one of the bitmaps. To see the other traced image, select the bitmap on the left side of the screen (you can click on either the filename or image to select it).
8. Select Save from the File menu, then Vector from the flyout. When the Export Vector dialog box opens, you can select which pages to save as a single file. Each page with a checkmark will be included in the file. Both pages should be checked.
9. Click on OK. When the Save Vector dialog box is displayed, select Corel Presentation Exchange 6.0 (CMX) from the Save as type drop-down list box. The Corel Presentation Exchange 6.0 format supports multipage

documents, unlike some of the other formats. Name the file **Traces** and click on Save. The file will be saved as Traces.cmx.

OTE: *Corel Presentation Exchange 6.0 (CMX) files can be readily imported into Coreldraw. If you are planning to work with the images in another application, you should be sure to select a file format that will work with that application. You should also save each trace as a separate file.*

The preceding exercise gave you a glimpse of what Corel OCR-TRACE can do. In the next section, you will learn more about how you can customize the options that determine the smoothness, fineness, and clarity of the curves during the tracing process.

Customizing Your Tracing Options

In Coreldraw, you modified the properties of the Freehand tool when using Autotrace in order to produce smoother curves while tracing. You can also modify the properties associated with any of the OCR-TRACE tracing methods to define your own custom tracing properties.

To modify any tracing properties, select Trace Settings from the OCR-Trace menu. The Trace Settings dialog box shown in Figure 17-9 will be displayed. Each tab of the dialog box contains the properties you can modify for that tracing method. The following sections will describe how each tracing method works. As you read about each method, select the appropriate tab of the Trace Setting dialog box to view the properties that can be modified for that method. You can also try out each method on your bitmap files by selecting the appropriate method from the Perform Trace flyout on the OCR-Trace menu.

Outline Tracing

When you select Outline as the tracing method, Corel CR-TRACE seeks out the *outlines* of areas and traces around them. Every color becomes a closed object, which is then filled with black or white, a color, or a gray shade to match the original bitmap as closely as possible. This method is most appropriate when the images that you trace contain many filled objects or have lines of variable thickness.

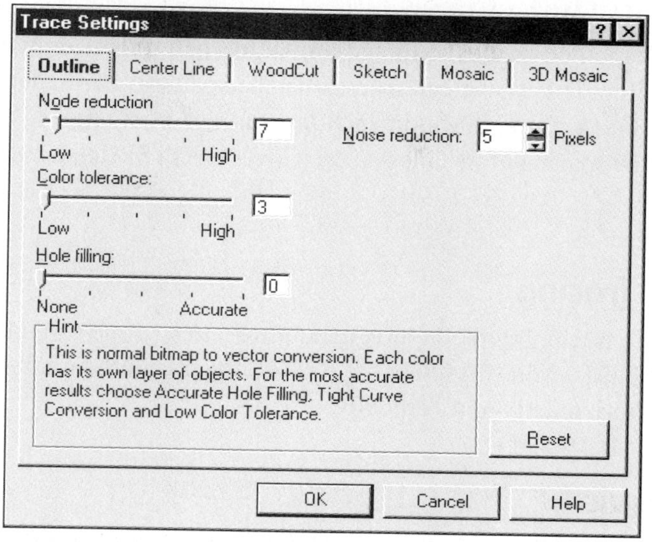

Trace Setting dialog box

FIGURE 17-9

Center Line Tracing

When you select Center Line as the tracing method, Corel OCR-TRACE seeks out the *center* point of lines in a bitmap and traces down the middle of those lines. No attempt is made to close paths or fill them. The resulting accuracy and attention to fine detail makes this tracing method the best choice for scanned images of technical or architectural drawings. Center Line is also appropriate for tracing drawings in which line thickness is fairly uniform.

WoodCut Tracing

When WoodCut is selected as the tracing method, Corel OCR-TRACE creates a series of parallel closed curves within the outline of the traced bitmap. This produces an effect similar to a wood block print. The thickness of the objects will vary, with the maximum thickness determined by the value in the Sample width spinner on the WoodCut tab of the Trace Setting dialog box.

Sketch Tracing

The Sketch method creates an image similar to a pen and ink drawing, where a series of parallel lines is used to create a cross-hatched pattern. The image is built by having several layers, with the lines on each layer at different angles. You can adjust the angle and the spacing of the lines on each layer on the Sketch tab of the Trace Setting dialog box.

Mosaic Tracing

The Mosaic tracing method converts a bitmap to a group of rectangles, circles, or diamond shapes. You can select the type of object and the number of objects to be tiled both horizontally and vertically.

3D Mosaic

A 3D Mosaic tracing is similar to the Mosaic method. The difference between 3D Mosaic and Mosaic is that with 3D Mosaic, the objects that are created will have a three-dimensional appearance.

Optical Character Recognition

When a page of text is scanned, the resulting file is actually a bitmap graphic, not a text file that can be imported into Coreldraw or a word processor and edited. With Corel OCR-TRACE's OCR functions, you can convert the bitmap text into a text file that can be edited and imported into Coreldraw as you would with a text file created in a word processor.

Corel OCR-TRACE can convert text in five languages (English, French, German, Spanish, and Swedish), recognize multiple columns and tables, and recognize both serif (such as Times New Roman) and sans serif (such as Arial) fonts from typeset, dot-matrix, and faxed documents. A spell checker is included for each language. Corel OCR-TRACE will even work with documents that have been scanned at an angle. (If the page was tilted when it was scanned.)

To explore the power of Corel OCR-TRACE, you must first acquire or create a bitmap file containing text. Corel OCR-TRACE can differentiate between text and a graphic in the same file, so you can use any bitmap file that contains text. If you have a scanner, you can scan any printed page to create a file. If you don't have a scanner, and you don't have a bitmap text file available, you can create one in Coreldraw. If you need to create a new bitmap text file follow these steps.

1. Open Coreldraw with a new, blank document.
2. With the Paragraph tool, create a short paragraph on the page. Click on the Pick tool to select the paragraph.
3. Select Export from the File menu, then select TIFF Bitmap (.TIF) from the Save as type drop-down list box in the Export Files dialog box.
4. Click on the Selected only check box, if it is not already selected.
5. Name the file **ocrtext** and click on the Export button. The Bitmap Export dialog box will be displayed.
6. In the Bitmap Export dialog box, select FAX Fine (200x100) from the Resolution drop-down list box. Click on OK.
7. Exit Coreldraw.

NOTE: *With Corel OCR-TRACE, bitmap text has to have a resolution of at least 200 dpi. If you are using a scanner, you should scan at a resolution of 200 or 300 dpi. The higher the resolution the larger the file will be. If you are working with a faxed document that was transmitted at fine resolution (200x100 dpi), it will be converted to 200x200 dpi.*

Now you are ready to work with Corel OCR-TRACE's OCR functions.

Recognizing Bitmap Text

Working with bitmap text involves the same basic steps you have already used to trace bitmap graphics. In the following exercise, you will convert your bitmap text file into a regular text file that can be edited in Coreldraw or any word processor.

1. In Corel OCR-TRACE 6, select Open from the File menu, then select your bitmap text file from the Files list box. Click on Open.

2. Select Perform OCR from the OCR-Trace menu. If the resolution of your bitmap file is less than 200 dpi, Corel OCR-TRACE will display a dialog box informing you that better results will be obtained with a higher resolution. Click on OK if this dialog box is displayed.

   After a few moments, your converted text will be displayed.

3. Select Save from the File menu, then Text from the flyout. In the Save Text dialog box, select the folder you want to save the text to, select Text (.txt) from the Save as type drop-down list box, then name the file **newtext** and click on Save.

OCR Properties

You can adjust the properties of the OCR function using the OCR Setting dialog box, shown in Figure 17-10, opened from the OCR-Trace menu. The Language tab allows you to select the language of the bitmap text, check the spelling, select a character to be inserted where Corel OCR-TRACE doesn't recognize a character, and set the Confidence level of the conversion. When Corel OCR-TRACE converts

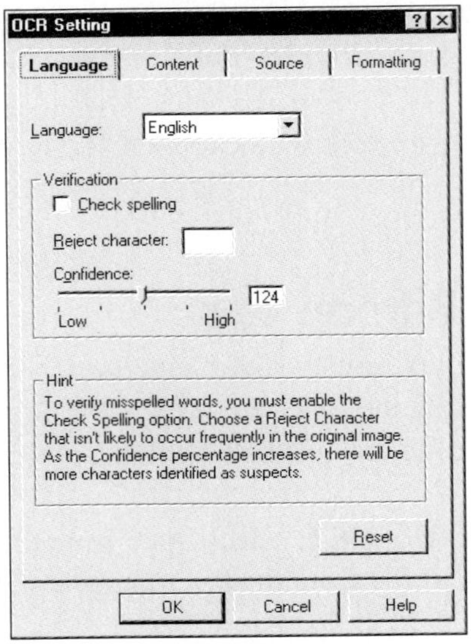

OCR Setting dialog box

FIGURE 17-10

a bitmap text file, some characters will be unrecognized (reject characters) and others will be suspect. That is, Corel OCR-TRACE will be unsure if the conversion is correct. The Confidence level setting determines the point at which Corel OCR-TRACE will consider a character to be suspect. A lower setting results in fewer characters being suspect, while higher settings will result in more characters being suspect. Experience with the different types of bitmap text you use will help you determine the appropriate Confidence level setting.

The Content tab properties select what type of text or text and graphics you will be converting. Corel OCR-TRACE can work with single or multiple column text, tables, and text and graphics in the same file. The Source tab allows you to select the source of the text (Normal, Dot Matrix, or Fax), the orientation of the text, and allows you to deskew text that was scanned at an angle. You can also rotate the text from Landscape to Portrait orientation. With the Formatting tab, you can select to keep or ignore the formatting of the bitmap text. You can also select individual font formats to keep or ignore.

Corel OCR-TRACE is a powerful part of the complete CorelDRAW! 6 package. With these tools, you will find little in the fields of computer graphics and desktop publishing that you cannot accomplish.

COREL DRAW!™ 6 in action

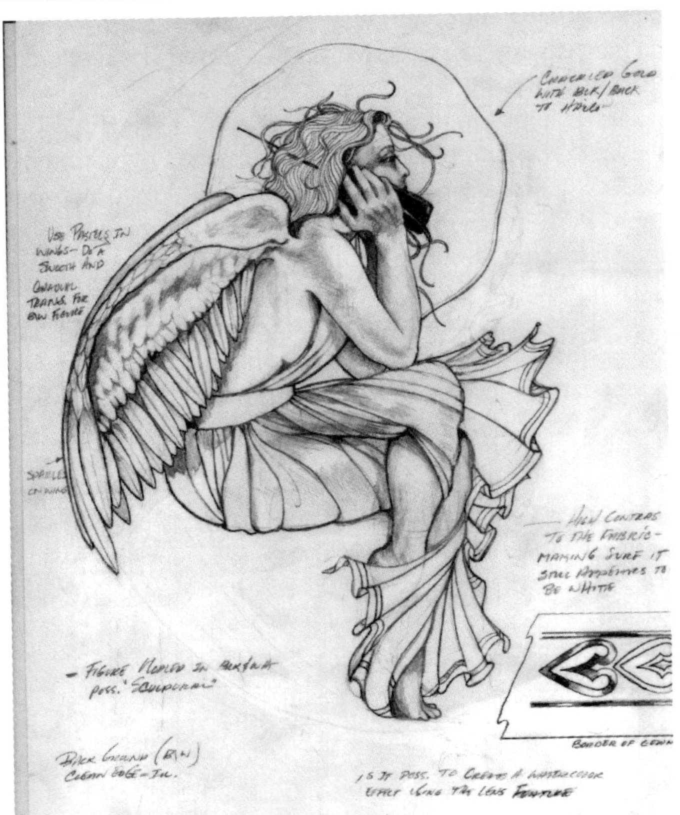

***A New Renaissance* — Georgina Curry**

You may already be familiar with Georgina Curry's work. Her illustration, *The Huntress*, won Best of Show in the fourth Corel World Design Contest. To create *A New Renaissance* (included in the color section), Georgina began with a pencil sketch that was then scanned. The border on the girl's dress was also traced and then repeated and modified to match the folds of the fabric.

Georgina Curry, of the Electric Easel in Scottsdale, Arizona, can be reached at (602) 443-8786.

Introducing CorelDREAM 3D

18

CorelDREAM 3D is a sophisticated three-dimensional modeling and rendering tool. It allows you to create objects, place those objects in scenes, and then view those scenes from many different angles, with the light source coming from different positions. Finally CorelDREAM 3D will render a scene into a 2D bitmap image that you can print or bring into another product. This chapter will introduce you to CorelDREAM 3D and guide you through the creation of objects and a scene, and the rendering of that scene into a reproducible image. The discussion here assumes that you are following along on your computer, so if it is not already running, start your computer and load CorelDREAM 3D.

CorelDREAM 3D Environment

When you first start CorelDREAM 3D, it will look similar to Figure 18-1. While there are some similarities to Coreldraw and other Corel products, there are many differences. In the following sections you'll take a quick tour of the CorelDREAM 3D environment, where you'll be introduced to the features and see many of those differences. Following this tour, you'll use many of the features to create objects and scenes, and in the process see how the features work.

CorelDREAM 3D Windows

The first thing you probably notice in CorelDREAM 3D are the four windows that are open within the CorelDREAM 3D window. The purpose and use of these windows are as follows:

- **Perspective** window is where you view and manipulate objects to create a scene. When you want to create an object, the Perspective window turns into the Modeling window which you'll use and learn about very shortly.

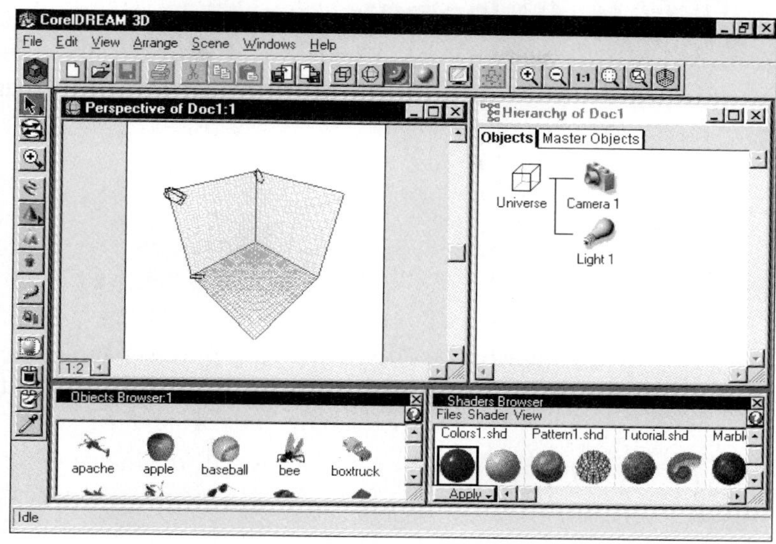

CorelDREAM 3D window

FIGURE 18-1

- **Hierarchy** window helps you keep track of the pieces that make up objects and the objects that make up scenes.
- **Objects Browser** window provides ready-made 3D objects that you can drag onto your Perspective window.
- **Shaders Browser** window provides colors, patterns, textures, and shading that you can use to render objects in a scene.

All four of these windows are initially opened when you start CorelDREAM 3D, but you can close them if you wish and work in just one window. There is one additional window that is not initially open, the Shader Editor, that allows you to modify seven attributes of how an object looks, including color, shininess, and reflection.

All but the Objects Browser window can be reopened from the Windows menu if you decide to close them and then find they are needed. The Objects Browser is opened with the Browse 3D Clipart option in the File menu.

CorelDREAM 3D Toolbars

CorelDREAM 3D has two toolbars, Standard and Zoom. Both of these have a number of buttons with which you are by now familiar. The unique buttons are as follows:

Icon	Name	Purpose
	Display Planes	Allows you to turn on and off the various planes as well as the objects in the Perspective window
	Bounding Box Quality	Sets the view of the image in the Perspective window to be only the bounding box around the object
	Wireframe Quality	Sets the view of the image in the Perspective window to be a wireframe representing the object
	Preview Quality	Sets the view of the image in the Perspective window to be preview quality
	Better Preview Quality	Sets the view of the image in the Perspective windows to be better than preview quality
	Zoom to Working Box	Zooms in or out so all of the three walls of the perspective working box are displayed

The four View Quality buttons give you increasingly more detail on your objects, but at the expense of the time that it takes to redraw them. Normally you leave them on Preview quality unless you are only working with the bounding box or its projection on one of the walls, then you can use one of the faster views. If you are working on the final color and texture of an object, then you will want to be in Better Preview Quality.

CorelDREAM 3D Toolbox

The tools in CorelDREAM 3D's toolbox differ depending on whether you are working in a Perspective window or in a Modeling window. The tools that are available in the Perspective window are as follows:

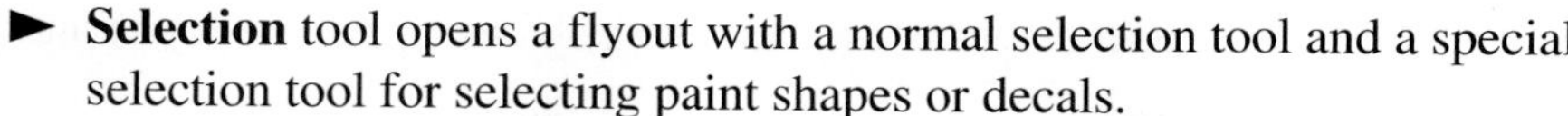

- **Selection** tool opens a flyout with a normal selection tool and a special selection tool for selecting paint shapes or decals.

- **Rotation** tool opens a flyout with a virtual trackball for rotating 3D objects around any of the three axes and a one-axis rotation tool for rotating the 2D projection of a 3D object on one of the walls of the working box.

- **Zoom** tool opens a flyout with a zoom in, a zoom out, and a hand tool. The zoom in and zoom out tools are as in other Corel products, and the hand tool is similar to a panning tool for moving the working box around in the Perspective window.

- **Free Form** tool is used to open the Modeling window, in which a new object can be created.
- **Basic Shapes** tool opens a flyout, which is used to create some or all of an object using a cone, a cube, a cylinder, an icosahedron (a 20-sided solid), or a sphere.

- **3D-Text** tool is used to enter three-dimensional text.

- **Modeling Wizard** tool leads you through the creation of an object.

- **Create Light** tool is used to add a new light source to the scene.

- **Create Camera** tool is used to view the scene from a different position or under different circumstances.

- **Render Area** tool is used to look at just a selected area of a scene and see how it will look when it is completed.

- **Paint Shape** tool opens a flyout that allows you to add a rectangular, polygonal, or oval form-fitting decal to an object.

- **3D Paint Brush** tool opens the Brushes dialog box that allows you to select a paint brush or an eraser with a number of characteristics that you can select.

- **Shader Eye Dropper** tool is used to pick a shader up off an object and place it in the Shader Editor window.

The following tools are uniquely available in the Modeling window:

- **Bézier tool** allows you to draw Bézier lines and curves. All freehand drawing in CorelDREAM 3D is done with the Bézier tool.
- **Point Editing** tool opens a flyout that allows you to convert nodes or points from corner points to curve points and vice versa, delete points, and add points along a curve.

- **Rectangle** tool opens a flyout that allows you to draw a rectangle, a rounded corners rectangle, an oval, and a polygon.

- **2D Text** tool allows you to enter normal text into the Modeling window and have it converted to 3D text when it is brought over to the Perspective window.

Creating a Scene in CorelDREAM 3D

Creating a scene in CorelDREAM 3D requires the following steps.

- Create simple objects
- Combine the simple objects into complex objects
- Arrange the complex objects into a scene
- Use the Shader Browser to apply color, shading, and textures to the objects
- Position lights and cameras on the scene
- Render and view the scene

Like creating many things, creating a CorelDREAM 3D scene is an iterative process that goes back and forth among the above steps. In the remaining sections of this chapter, though, you'll work through each of the steps in order.

Creating Objects

CorelDREAM 3D comes with a library of objects that you can drag off the Objects Browser and directly use or modify and use in your scenes. No matter how extensive this library is, you will probably find that you need to create some objects yourself. Most objects that you create are actually a number of simpler or more basic objects that have been combined. Therefore, begin by creating several simple objects. There are three ways to create geometrical objects (using the Free Form, Simple Shape, or Modeling Wizard tool) and two ways to add text objects (the 3D Text tool in the Perspective window and the 2D Text tool in the Modeling window). Try each of these techniques.

Creating Free Form Objects

The Free Form tool opens the Modeling window, in which you can create a 2D object and then convert it to 3D. Do that with the following instructions.

1. Close the Objects Browser and Shaders Browser windows.

2. Click on the Free Form tool. The mouse pointer turns into a crosshair.
3. Click the crosshair in the center of the blue base plane in the Perspective window. The Perspective window turns into the Modeling window, as shown in Figure 18-2. Only the look of the window tells you that you are in the modeling window.
4 Type **Wall** for the name of your first object, and click on OK to close the Set Name dialog box.

You have created an empty object called a Wall. Even though you can't see it in the Modeling window, you can see it in the list of objects in the Hierarchy window, as shown in Figure 18-3. The default view of the Modeling window is still a 3D perspective view with the active drawing plane being a right-facing vertical plane. You know which plane is active because it is light blue, while the inactive planes are gray. You can use the modeling tools (the Bézier tool, the Node Editing tool, the

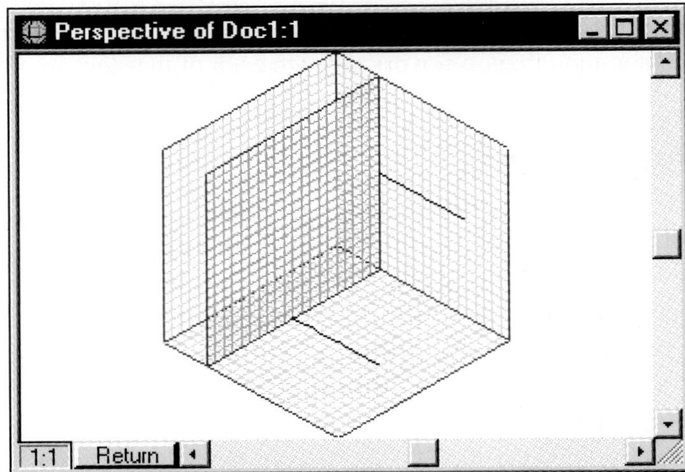

Modeling window for creating free form objects

FIGURE 18-2

Rectangle tool, and the 2D Text tool) to create 3D objects in the Perspective window, but it is much easier to first draw a 2D cross section of the object and "extrude" it into 3D.

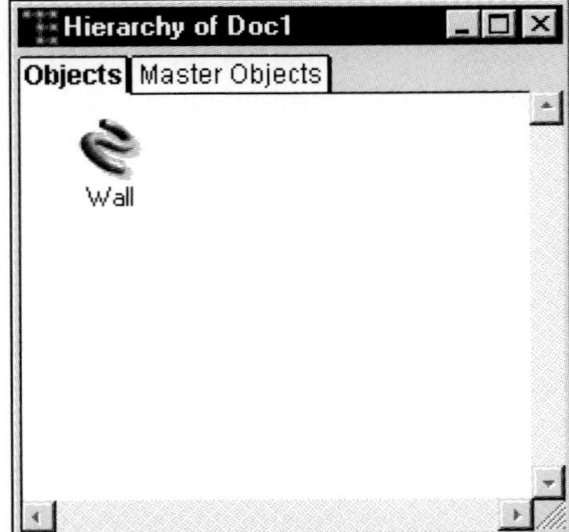

Hierarchy window showing the first object you will create

FIGURE 18-3

TIP: *You can change which plane you want to draw on by simply clicking on the plane you want to use. Also, you can determine which planes are displayed by clicking on the corresponding plane in the Display Planes tool on the far left of the toolbar.*

2D DRAWING To do a 2D drawing, you want to take the active plane and work on it head-on. You can do that by changing the view from the reference perspective to just the drawing plane. Do that next with these steps.

1. Open the View menu and choose Type, Drawing Plane. Maximize the Perspective window. You will be looking at the drawing plane head-on.

2. Click twice on the Zoom-in button in the tool*bar* (not the tool*box*) and then use the Panning Hand tool or the scroll bars to move the grid as shown in Figure 18-4.
3. Open the View menu again and choose Grid. Click on the Snap to check box of the Grid dialog box that opens, as shown next. This causes the lines you draw to precisely conform to the grid that is on your screen. Click on OK.

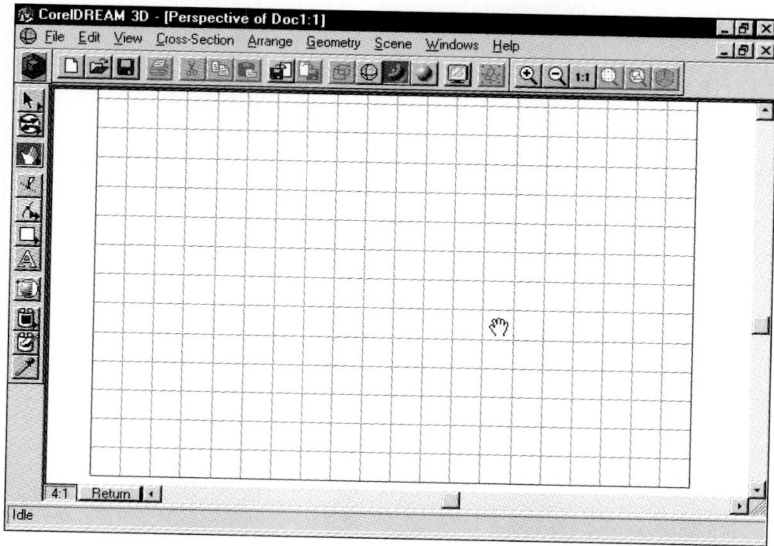

Drawing grid properly aligned

FIGURE 18-4

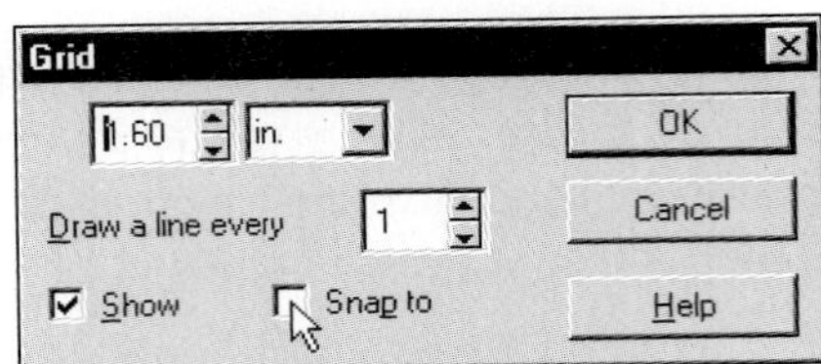

4. Use the Bézier tool to click on the grid intersections shown in Figure 18-5. As you have seen in Coreldraw, the lines will be filled in for you. Begin in the lower left and proceed clockwise. Finish by clicking on your original point to close the shape. If you have a closed object, it will fill with the default red color.

NOTE: *If you make a mistake before finishing the shape, press* DEL *for each line segment you want to remove and redraw. If you want to make a change after completing the shape, use the Selection tool to first click on and then drag a node. (You can tell a node is selected because it will be filled in black.) If you drag a line instead of a node, the entire object will move.*

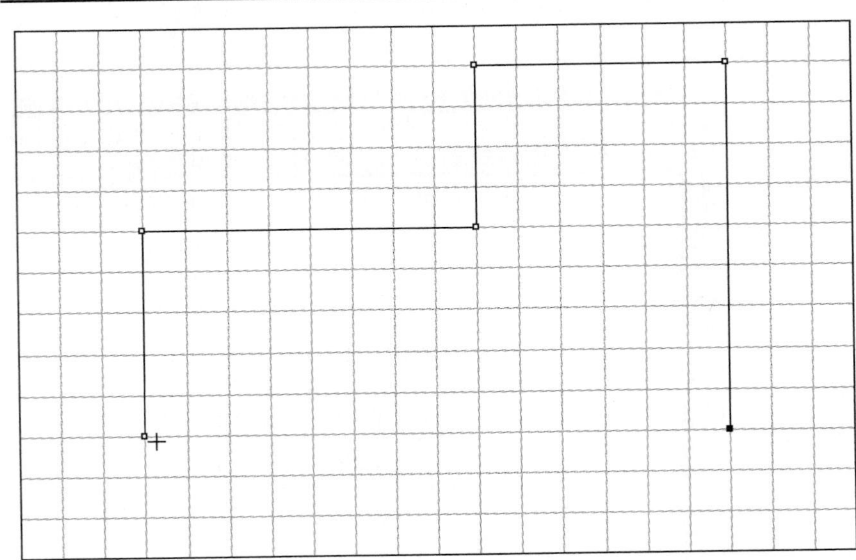

2D drawing on one plane

FIGURE 18-5

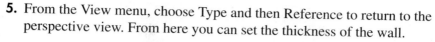

5. From the View menu, choose Type and then Reference to return to the perspective view. From here you can set the thickness of the wall.
6. Click on Zoom Out in the toolbar so that the image on your screen looks like that shown in Figure 18-6.
7. With the Selection tool, click on the Sweep Path description line on the right wall and pointed to in Figure 18-6. The line will become selected with a node at either end.
8. Drag the right node of the line to the left to shorten it to one grid space, as shown in Figure 18-7. You have now completed the wall and are ready to return to the Perspective window.

9. Click on the Return button in the lower left of the of the Modeling window. You'll be returned to the Perspective window, where your wall is probably a black and red blob on the ground plane of the working box. For now, don't worry about this. Later you will come back and work with your wall in the Perspective window.
10. Open the File menu and choose Save. In the Save dialog box, select the folder you want to use and type **Wall** for the filename. Choose Close and then New, both from the File menu, to open a clean working box.

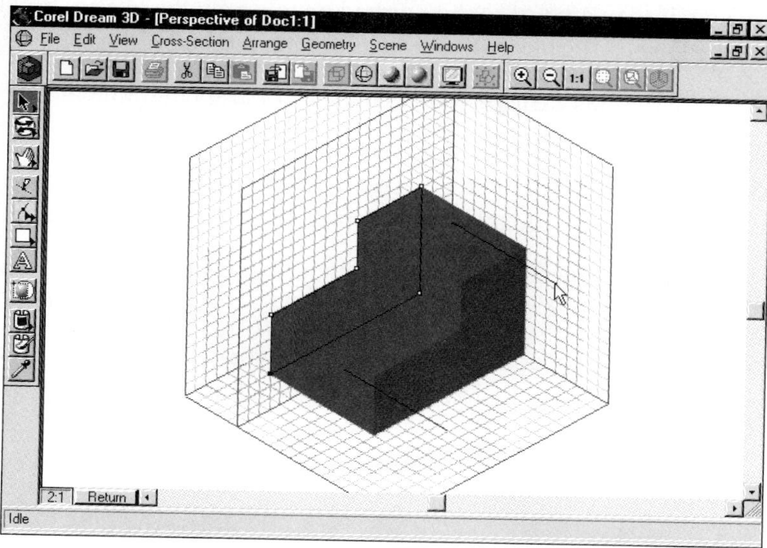

Extruded image of "Wall" showing the Sweep Path description line to shorten

FIGURE 18-6

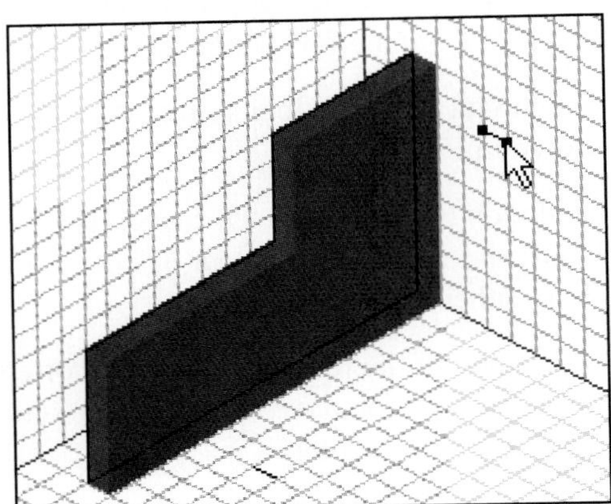

Narrowing the thickness of the wall

FIGURE 18-7

Placing Basic Shapes

The Basic Shapes flyout allows you to place one or more basic shapes in the Perspective window. Once there, you can change them and combine them to make more complex objects. Place several basic shapes with these steps.

1. Click on 1:1 in the Zoom toolbar to enlarge the perspective working box and, if they are not already turned on, click on the left and right walls in the Display Planes tool on the left of the toolbar.

2. Open the Basic Shape flyout and select the sphere. The mouse pointer turns into a crosshair.

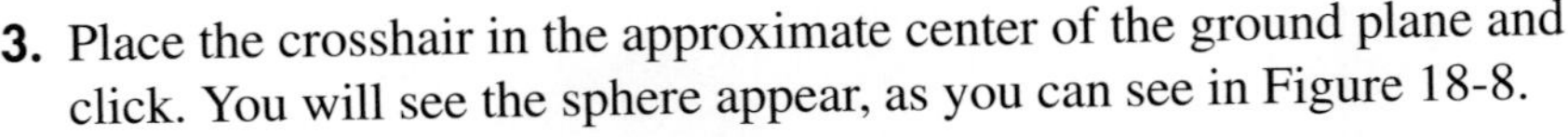

3. Place the crosshair in the approximate center of the ground plane and click. You will see the sphere appear, as you can see in Figure 18-8.

4. Again open the Basic Shape flyout, select the cylinder, and click the crosshair above the sphere.
5. One final time, open the Basic Shape flyout, select the cone, and click this time above the cylinder. You now have all the pieces to make a rocket, as shown in Figure 18-9.

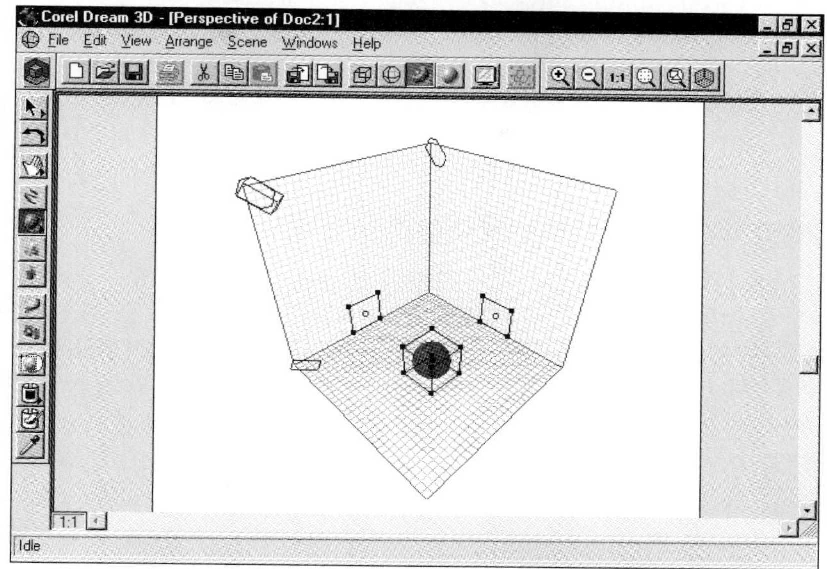

Sphere placement in the working box

FIGURE 18-8

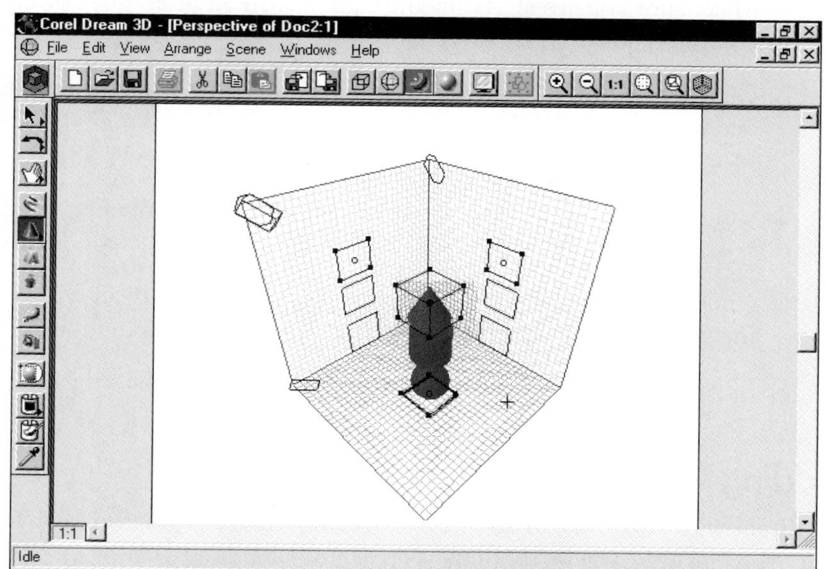

Three basic shapes to make a rocket

FIGURE 18-9

Don't worry if your three basic shapes do not line up like those in Figure 18-9. It is very hard to "eyeball" where to place something in 3D space. Later you'll come back and see how to do this very easily.

6. Save this work with the name **Rocket**, close the file, and open a new one.

Using the Modeling Wizard

Both the Free Hand tool and the Basic Shapes tool produce fairly simple objects. They can be combined in many ways to produce more complex shapes, but CorelDREAM 3D has another tool, the Modeling Wizard, that you can use directly to produce more complex shapes. Try that next with the following instructions.

OTE: *The Modeling Wizard is just a guided tour of the freeform modeler and everything that is produced in the wizard can be created by hand in the modeler. Also, you can edit an object created by the wizard in the freeform modeler.*

1. Make sure you are at 1:1 magnification with all three sides of the working box turned on.
2. Click on the Modeling Wizard in the toolbox and click the crosshair that appears on the center of the ground plane of the working box. The Modeling Wizard dialog box appears, like that in Figure 18-10.
3. Click on the Lathe Object and then on Next. The Lathe Objects dialog box will open.
4. Click on Vase profile and then click on done. Your object will appear in the working box, which after zooming in, will look like Figure 18-11.
5. Save this object as **Vase**, close the file, and open a new file.

Adding Text in the Modeling Window

The final way that you can add new objects to your working box is by adding 3D text. You can do this directly in the Perspective window, or you can add 2D text in the Modeling window and have it extruded into 3D text when you return to the

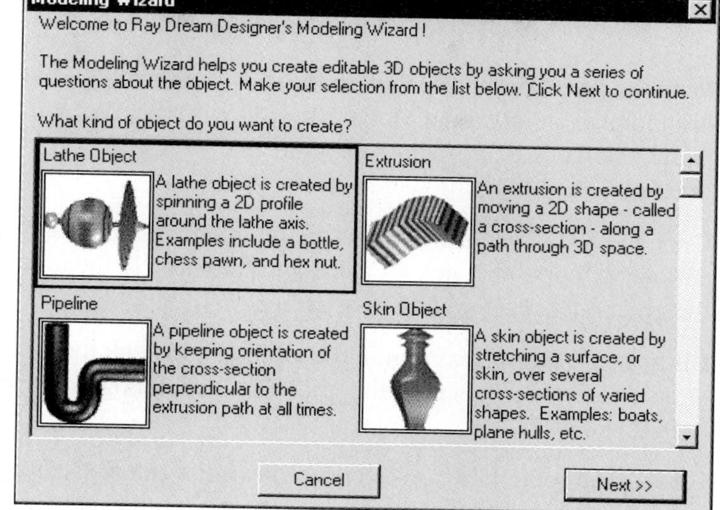

Modeling Wizard dialog box

FIGURE 18-10

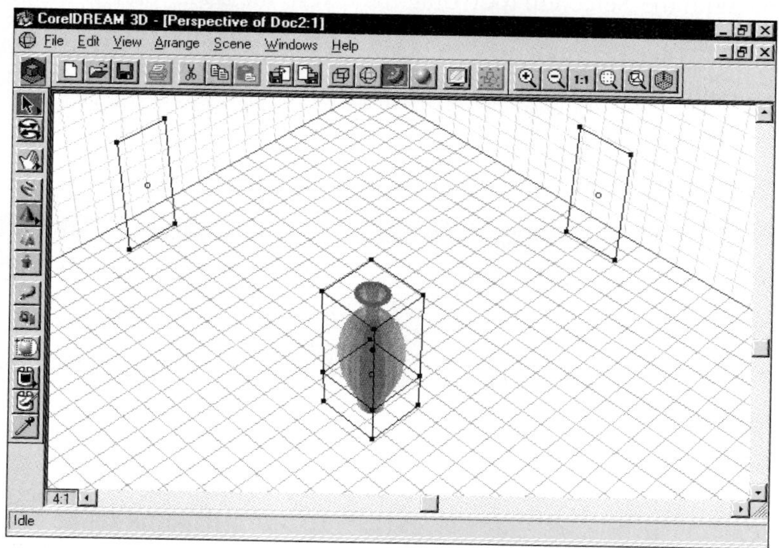

Final object created with the Modeling Wizard

FIGURE 18-11

Perspective window. Try adding text in the Modeling window with the following exercise.

1. With the Free Form tool, click in the middle of the Perspective window ground plane to open the Modeling window. Type **Text 1** as the object name, click OK to close the Set Name dialog box, and, if it isn't already, maximize the Modeling window.
2. Open the View menu, choose Type, and then Drawing Plane to get the 2D surface to work on. Click on the Zoom In button in the toolbar and align the grid so it is centered on your screen.

3. Click on the Draw Text tool in the toolbox and click the resulting I-beam mouse pointer anywhere in the grid. The Text dialog box opens, as shown in Figure 18-12.
4. Change the font in the top-left drop-down list box to Century Schoolbook (or any font you like), make it bold, 48-points, and center alignment.
5. Click in the text box at the bottom of the Text dialog box, type **BOOST YOUR**, and click on OK. The words appear on the grid, going off both sides.
6. With the Selection tool, drag the text to the upper part of the grid.
7. With the Text tool, again click on the grid; leave the default settings of 72 points, Arial, Plain; type **POWER** and click on OK.

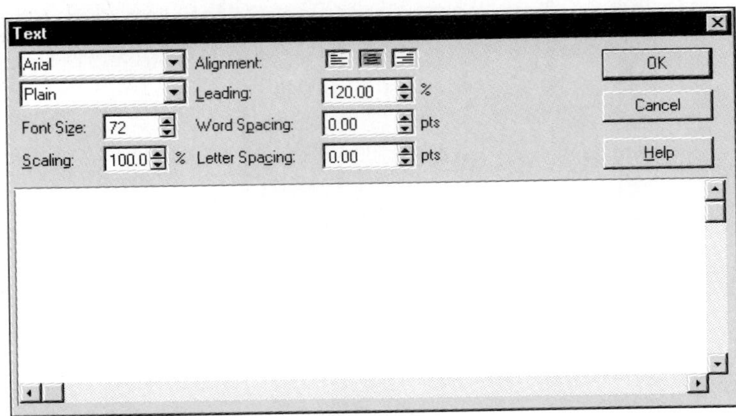

Modeling Text dialog box

FIGURE 18-12

8. With the Selection tool, drag the two lines of text so they look like this:

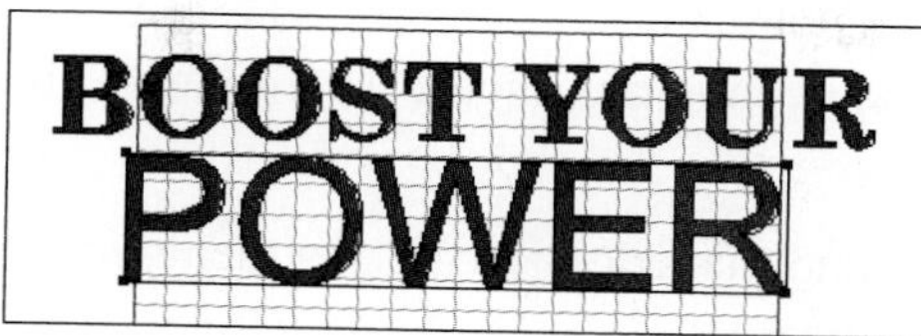

9. If you see that you've made a mistake, use the Text tool to click on the text that needs to be changed, and the Text dialog box will reopen.

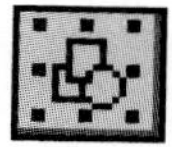

10. When you are happy with the text, press and hold SHIFT while clicking on both pieces, and then select Group from the Arrange menu or click on the Group button in the toolbar.

11. From the View menu, return the Type to Reference. After a moment, you'll see your text extruded into 3D, like you can see in Figure 18-13.

You saw earlier how you can shorten the Sweep Path description lines to reduce the thickness of the extrusion, but you can also, of course, lengthen it. Another feature of the Modeling window, and a good reason to create text there, is that you can extrude the text in several ways, including making it fit an envelope.

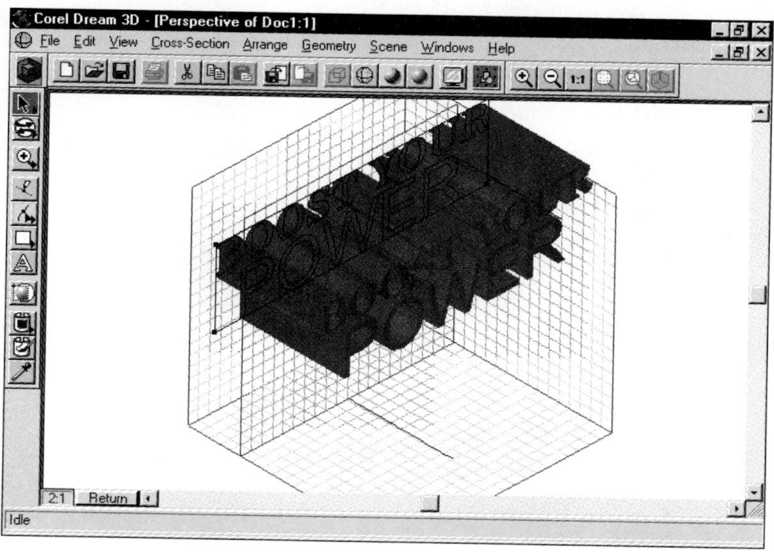

Extruded text

FIGURE 18-13

12. Open the Geometry menu and choose Extrusion Envelope, Symmetrical. Four Scaling Envelope lines will be added to the existing Sweep Path description lines, as shown in Figure 18-14 before the extruded text is redrawn.
13. Click on the ground plane to select it and then click on the envelope line furthest to left. Since you selected Symmetrical, if you move this envelope line, all four envelope lines will move with it.
14. Drag the left or back node to the right toward the center line, about two-thirds of the distance to the center. When you release the mouse button, the other envelope lines will move symmetrically and then the text will redraw, as you can see in Figure 18-15. The effect is that the text is flying out at you.
15. Click on Return in the bottom left of the Modeling window to transfer the text to the Perspective window.
16. Click on the Zoom In tool and turn on the two side walls of the working box so your text image looks like Figure 18-16.
17. Save your work as **Text.**

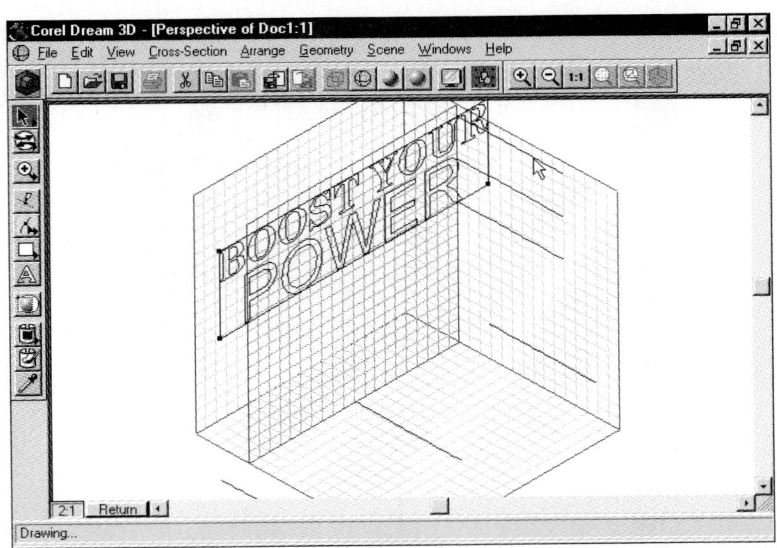

Scaling Envelope lines

FIGURE 18-14

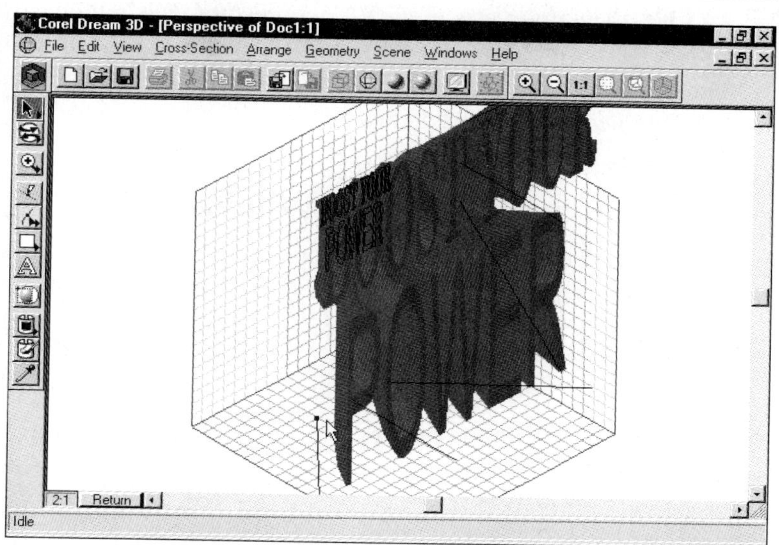

Envelope line moved to cause the text to jump out

FIGURE 18-15

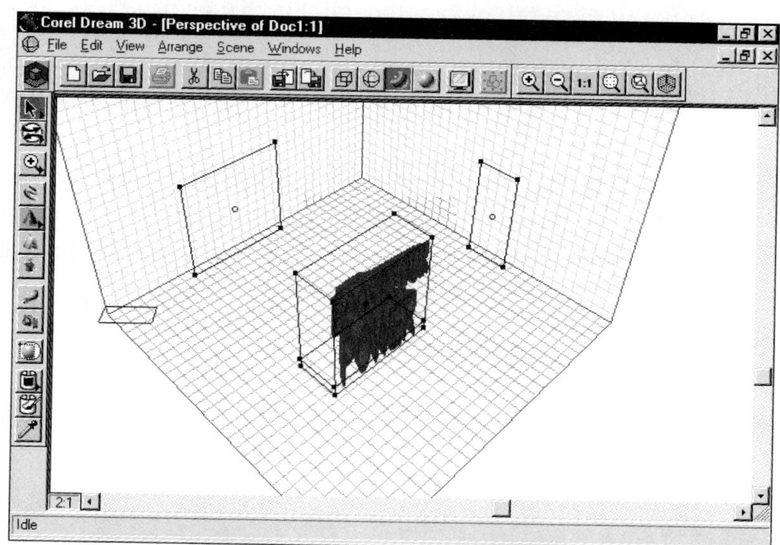

Text back in the Perspective window

FIGURE 18-16

OTE: *The point size in the Modeling window is not consistent with the point size in the Perspective window. (72 points in the Modeling window is much smaller than 72 points in the Perspective window.) You have to scale up the Modeling window text to compensate.*

Adding Text in the Perspective Window

Adding text in the Perspective window is considerably easier than in the Modeling window, but you also have a lot less flexibility. See for yourself with these steps (the text and Perspective window from the previous exercise should still be on your screen).

1. Click on the Text tool in the toolbox, and click it in the lower part of the ground plane. The Perspective window changes into a text entry window as shown in Figure 18-17.
2. Click on Bevel On Front Face and on the middle (curved in) bevel type. Accept the other defaults.
3. Click in the text area at the bottom, type **GET ROCKETS!**, and click on Return at the bottom left of the window.
4. Click on the Zoom Out button and most of your text becomes visible. It does not fit the working box though. Fix that next.
5. With the Selection tool, right-click on the new text, and select Edit in Active Window. The Perspective window text box opens again with the text you entered.
6. Click between the words "Get" and "Rockets," remove the space, and press ENTER to force "Rockets" to a new line. Click on Return to reopen the normal Perspective window. The text is now a little closer match to the size of the working box, as you can see in Figure 18-18.
7. Once again, save your work.

You can see how very different 72 points in the Perspective window is from 72 points in the Modeling window. This is just a quirk of CorelDREAM 3D that you must work around.

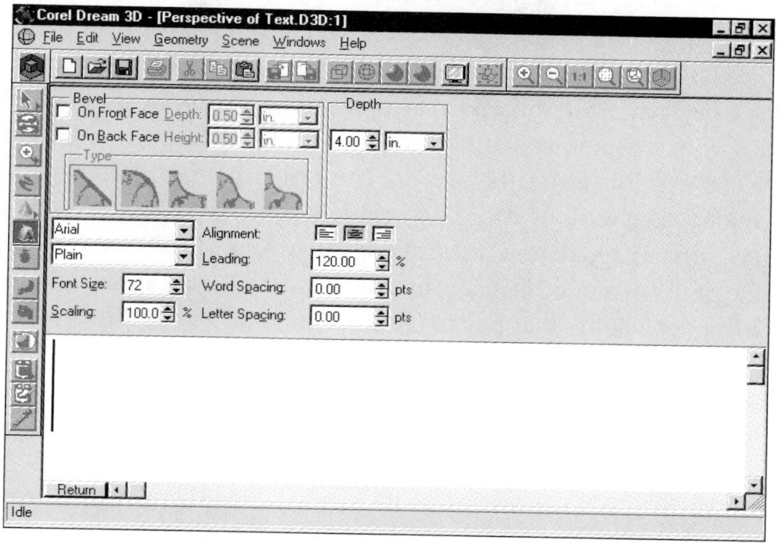

Perspective window text box

FIGURE 18-17

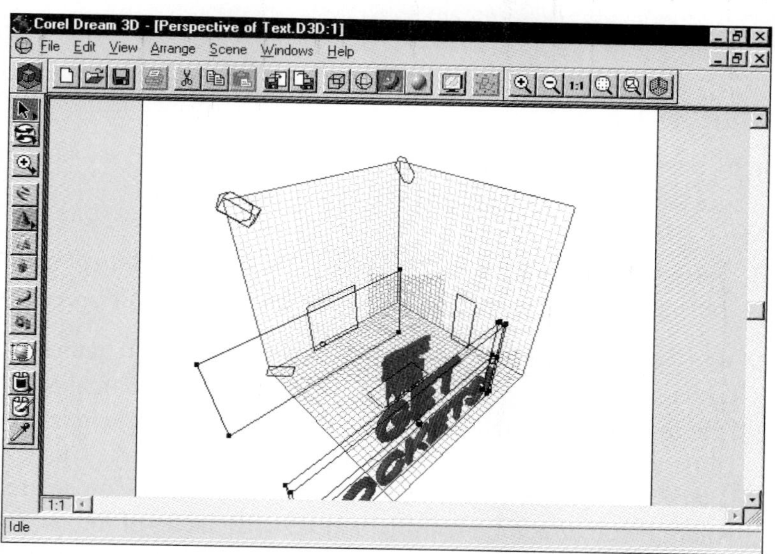

New text in the Perspective window

FIGURE 18-18

Positioning and Combining Objects

In the previous sections of this chapter, you have created several objects that you now need to position and combine to make more complex objects and create a scene. Moving objects in 3D space is very difficult because you are doing it using a 2D display, your monitor, and a 2D instrument, your mouse. CorelDREAM 3D has a couple of ways to make this easier. The principal way is to give you three 2D projections—the walls of your working box—which you can manipulate in 2D space and have that manipulation translated back to your 3D object. For example, if you drag the projection of a 3D image up one of the walls, you know that you are moving the object "up" along that plane. On the other hand, if you move the object itself "up," there is no certain definition of what you did. CorelDREAM 3D helps you even here: if you drag the object itself, the object will move parallel to the working (blue) plane. In other words, if the working plane is the floor (which is the default), when you drag the object it will stay at a constant "height" above the floor. If you hold down ALT, you can then drag the object along the plane perpendicular to the working plane—by default this is the vertical or Z axis.

IP: *Whenever possible, position an object by moving the projections of the object and not the object itself.*

Positioning Text

Begin by positioning the text objects you created above and see how this works for you. (Your two text objects should still be on your screen.)

1. With the Selection tool, click on the "Boost Your Power" text. The text object as well as its projection on the three walls will become selected.

2. Drag the right wall projection of the selected text up and to the left as shown in Figure 18-19. If you hesitate for just a moment after pressing the mouse button and before you begin to move the object, you will get a little identification tag, like the one shown on the left. This tells you the name of the object you have clicked on. If you click on an area with multiple objects, the identification tag will list all of the objects and you can select the one you want to work with by clicking on it in the tag. The selected object has a check mark beside it.

3. With the One Axis Rotation tool, drag the left side of the floor projection of the "Boost..." text 45-degrees clockwise, like this:

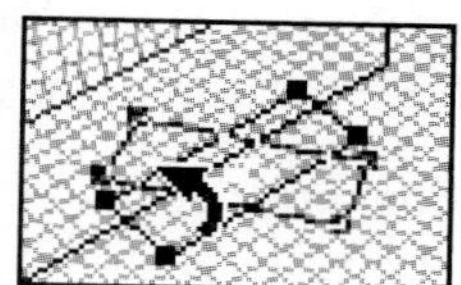

OTE: *The rotation takes place about a small circle in the center of the projection called a hot point, You can drag the hot point from its default centered position to change the center of rotation.*

AUTION: *It is easy to mistakenly drag the hot point and therefore cause problems. If you do that, use Center Hot Point in the Arrange menu to return the hot point to its default position.*

4. With the Selection tool, click on "Get Rockets!" Drag the projection on the left wall up and to the right, so it is about one-third of the way into the projection of the other text and equally spread across the ground plane.

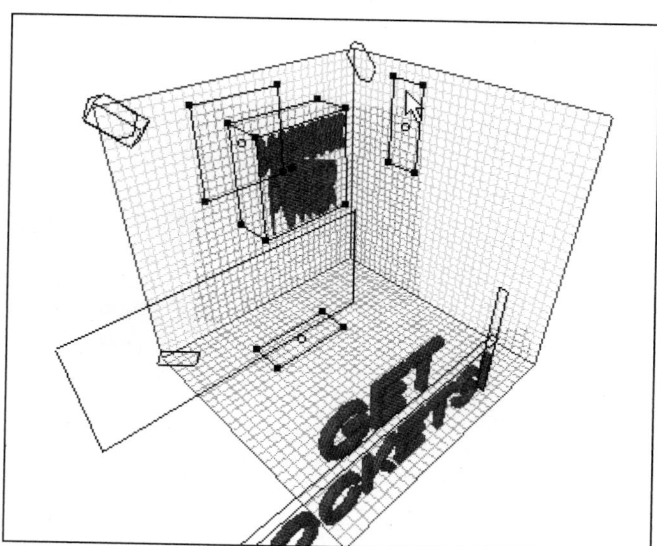

Moving the "Boost Your Power" text

FIGURE 18-19

5. Again with the Selection tool, drag the "Get Rockets!" projection on the ground plane "back," or to the left, so it is roughly under the first piece of text. If necessary, click on the first piece of text and drag its projection on the left wall up so it is above the second piece.
6. With the One Axis Rotation tool, rotate clockwise the floor projection of "Get Rockets!" so it is parallel to the upper piece of text. Finally, use the Selection tool to align the two text pieces as shown in Figure 18-20.
7. Save your work and close your text file.

Duplicating and Combining the Wall

To create a four-sided enclosure with the wall that you built earlier in the book, you need to duplicate it, move the pieces into the proper position, and then combine the pieces. Try that next.

1. Open the Wall.d3d file that you saved earlier. After the object is loaded, turn on the three walls if they are not already on, zoom in, and position the working box so you can easily see the object as well as its projection on the walls.

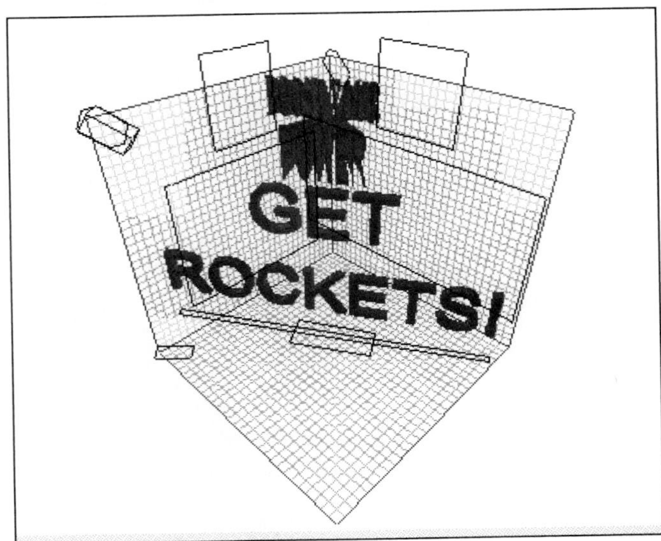

Text in its final position

FIGURE 18-20

2. Right-click on the object and select Duplicate from the pop-up menu (you could have also chosen Duplicate from the Edit menu). A second object is created, but it occupies the exact same space as the first object and so, from the Perspective window, you cannot tell that you have two objects.

3. Open the Windows menu and click on Hierarchy of Wall.d3d to open that window, as you can see in Figure 18-21. Here you have two free form objects, both named Wall.

4. Click on the upper free form object's name (Wall), and in the dialog box that opens, type the name **Wall 1**, like this:

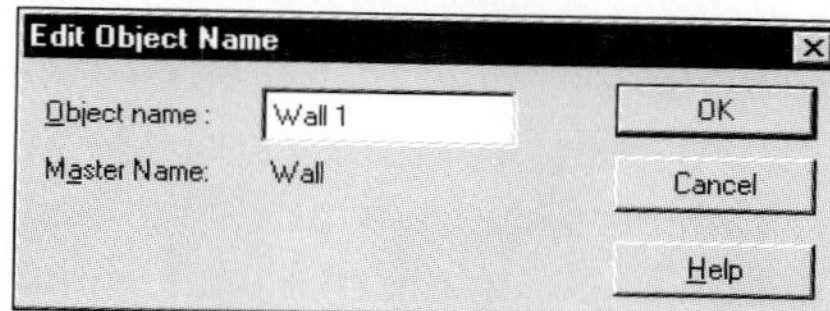

5. Click on OK and then, in a similar fashion, name the second wall **Wall 2**. Minimize the Hierarchy window, and then maximize the Perspective window. With the walls separately named, you can now use the name tags to identify which you are working with.

√Wall 1 XY
Wall 2 XY

6. With the One Axis Rotation tool, click on the floor projection of the two walls so the name tag appears, and then select Wall 1. Then hold down SHIFT and drag that part of the floor projection to the left of the hot point clockwise 90 degrees.

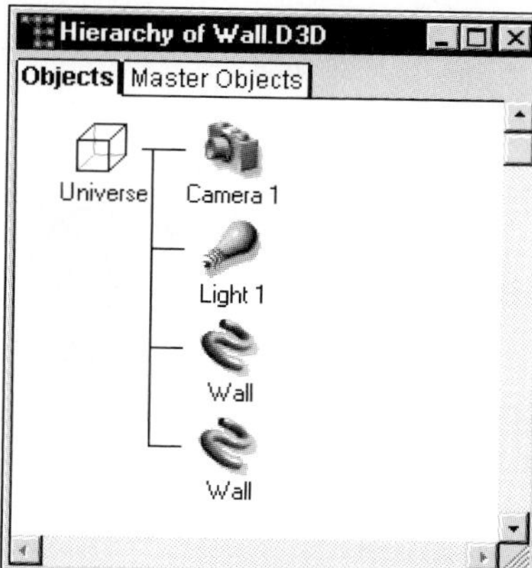

Hierarchy window with two Walls

FIGURE 18-21

IP: *When you hold down the* SHIFT *key, you constrain the rotation, by default, to 30-degree increments. You can change this rotational constraint in the Perspective section of the Preferences dialog box, opened by choosing Preferences in the File menu.*

7. With Selection tool, drag Wall 1 itself so that it is at the right end of Wall 2—so their taller sides join, as shown in Figure 18-22. You can use the projections to help you align the sides.

OTE: *When you drag an object in the Perspective window, it will remain parallel to the currently active plane, in this case the floor or ground plane.*

8. Hold down SHIFT while you select Wall 2, and then click on the Group/Ungroup button to group the two wall segments.
9. Using the steps above, duplicate and position the wall segments to create an enclosed area like that shown in Figure 18-23.

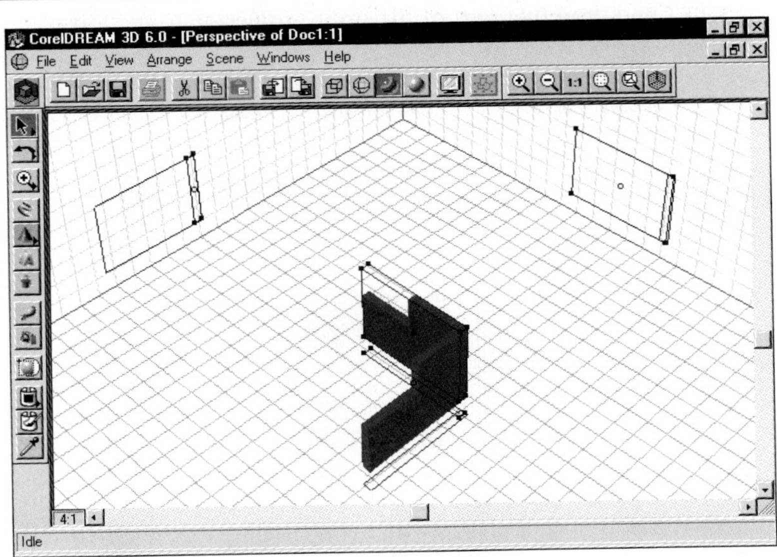

Joining of two wall segments

FIGURE 18-22

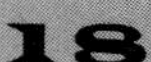

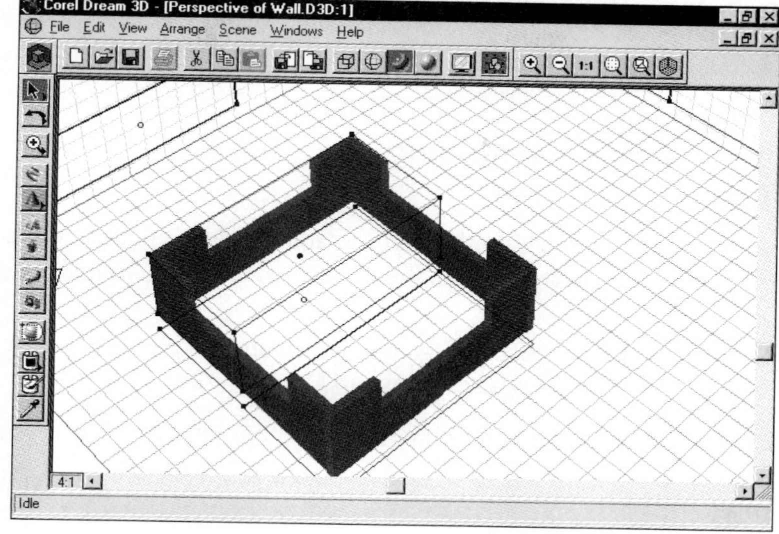

Final enclosure made of the wall segments

FIGURE 18-23

10. Open your Hierarchy window, click on the plus signs to open the groups, and look at the structure you have created. Give the groups different names. One possible structure and set of names are shown here in Figure 18-24.
11. Save and close your file.

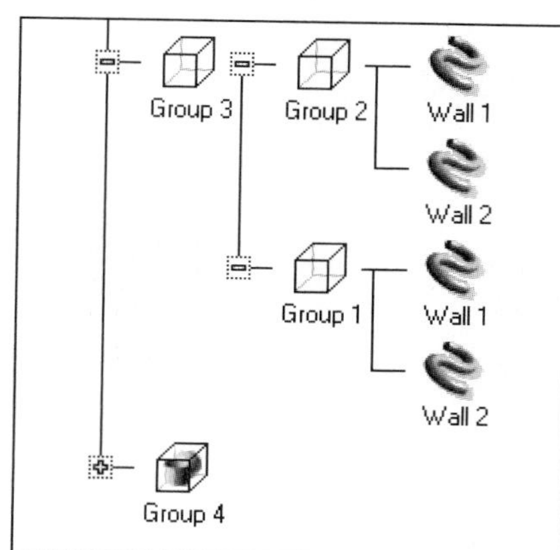

Hierarchy of wall structure

FIGURE 18-24

OTE: *Leaving the groups in the Hierarchy window open, as you see for Group 3 in Figure 18-24, ungroups the objects just as if you had clicked on the Group/Ungroup button.*

Positioning and Combining the Rocket Assembly

The rocket assembly is currently three separate objects, a cone, a cylinder, and a sphere. In this section, you'll align them and then join them to make a rocket.

1. Open the file Rocket.d3d, zoom in, turn on the sides if necessary, and align the working box, as shown in Figure 18-25.
2. While holding SHIFT, select the cone and the cylinder to jointly select them.
3. From the Arrange menu, select Align Objects. The Alignment dialog box will open.

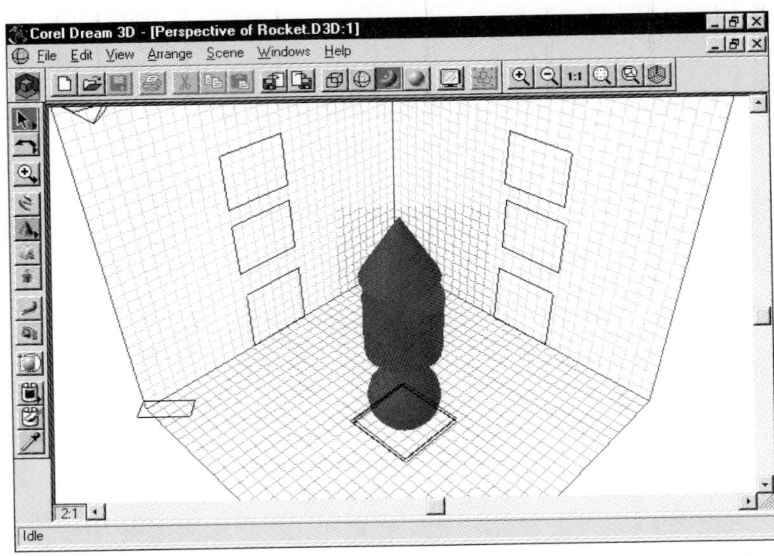

The rocket assembly correctly positioned

FIGURE 18-25

4. If your dialog box shows only the X axis, click on the key or small right-pointing arrow in the lower-right corner to expand the dialog box to include the Y and Z axes, like this:

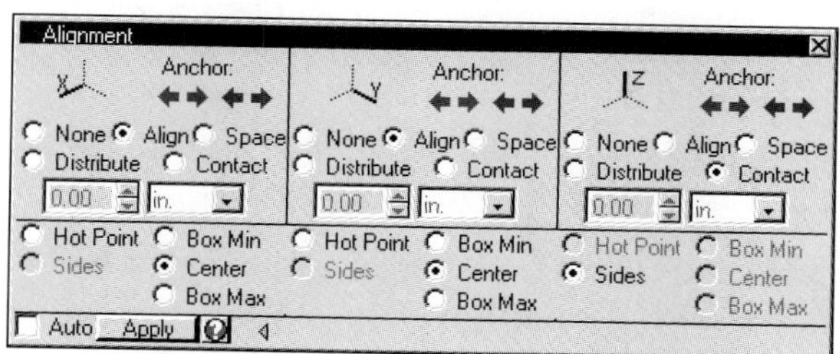

5. For the X and Y axes, choose Align and Center. For the Z axis, choose Contact and Sides. Click on Apply and close the dialog box.
6. Click on the Group/Ungroup button to group the two segments. Then, by dragging the projection on the right wall, drag the grouped segment up to approximately double the distance between the group and the sphere. Your result should look like that shown in Figure 18-26.
7. While holding SHIFT, select the sphere and again open the Alignment dialog box. Keep the X and Y axes aligned center, but make the Z axis have no (None) alignment. Click on Apply and close the dialog box.

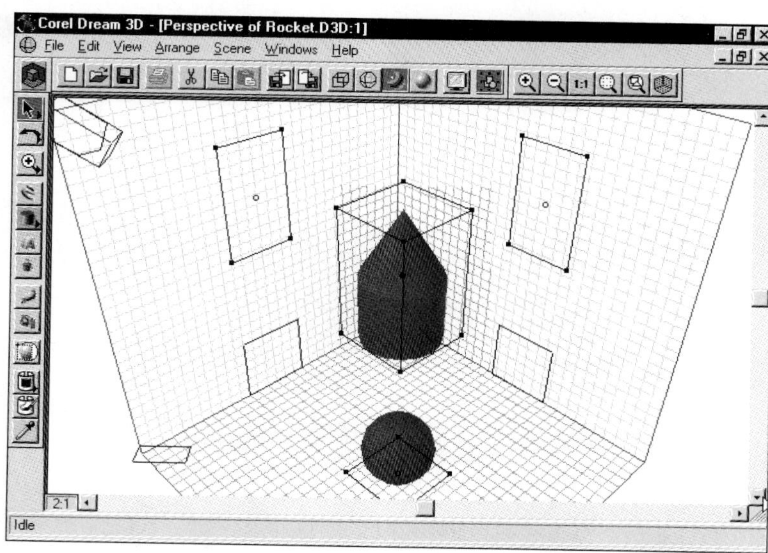

The cone and cylinder aligned

FIGURE 18-26

8. Add another cylindrical basic shape as you did originally, align it and the sphere on the X and Y axes, and then lower the cylinder so only half of the sphere is visible. Group the sphere and the lower cylinder.
9. Add a third cylinder and drag it so it is roughly between the upper group of two objects and the lower group. SHIFT select the two groups and the third cylinder, open the Alignment dialog box, align the X and Y axes on the center, and align the Z axis to contact sides.
10. Click on apply and close the dialog box. The results will look like Figure 18-27.
11. With all three segments selected, click on Group/Ungroup and save the file.

Precise Positioning of Objects

Positioning objects by dragging them is great for gross alignment within the working box, but for really precise positioning, dragging will never do it. The Alignment dialog box you just used is good when you are trying to align two objects in relation to each other, but it will not help you position an object in space. For that, you need to use the Object Properties dialog box shown in Figure 18-28. Open this dialog box

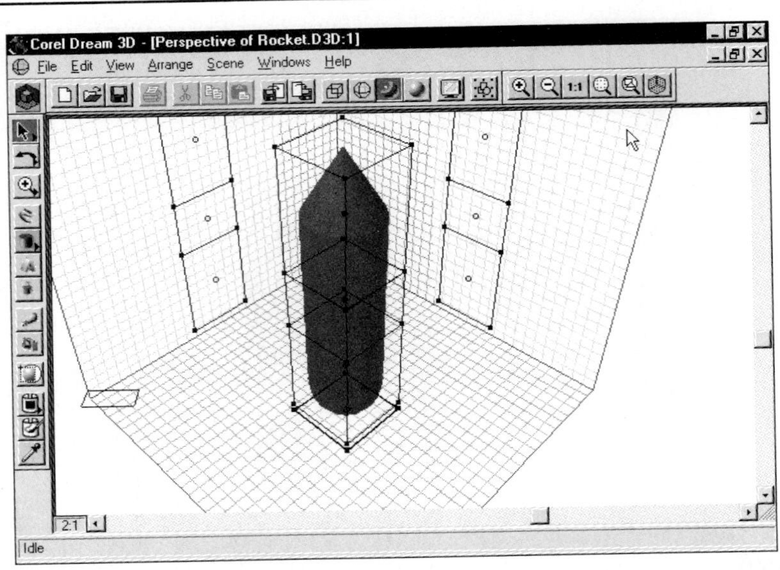

The finished "rocket"

FIGURE 18-27

and try out its controls with the following steps (your rocket should still be on your screen).

1. Right-click on the rocket, and select Properties from the pop-up menu that appears. The Object Properties dialog box for your rocket will appear. Don't be concerned if the values in your dialog box are different from those shown in Figure 18-28.
2. Change the name of your rocket from "Group 3" to **Rocket**. Then absolutely center your rocket in the working box universe by changing the X, Y, and Z coordinates in the top of the dialog box to 0 and clicking on Apply.
3. If your Yaw, Pitch, and Roll are not 0, make them so and then save the file so that you can always return to this position, shown in Figure 18-29a.

IP: *You can quickly return to an absolute centered position by choosing Align on Universe from the Arrange menu.*

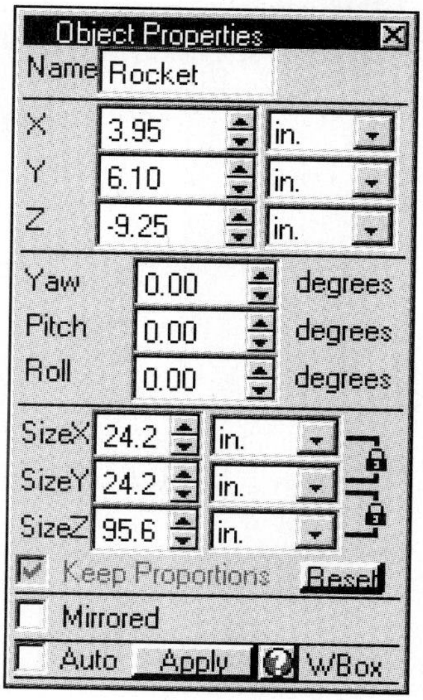

FIGURE 18-28 Object Properties dialog box

4. Start out by seeing what yaw, pitch, and roll are in relation to your working box. Type **45** in the Yaw spinner, make sure Pitch and Roll are 0, and press ENTER or click on Apply. Your rocket will rotate about the vertical (Z) axis by 45 degrees, as you see in Figure 18-29b.

5. Return the Yaw spinner to 0 and make the Pitch spinner **45**. You'll see the image shown in Figure 18-29c. Return Pitch to 0 and make the Roll **45**, and you'll see Figure 18-29d.

TIP: *The three axes are: X extending to the left, Y extending to the right, and Z extending vertically. The three motions are: Yaw rotating about the Z axis, Pitch rotating about the X axis, and Roll rotating about the Y axis. The plus direction is counterclockwise. The negative direction is clockwise. See Figure 18-30.*

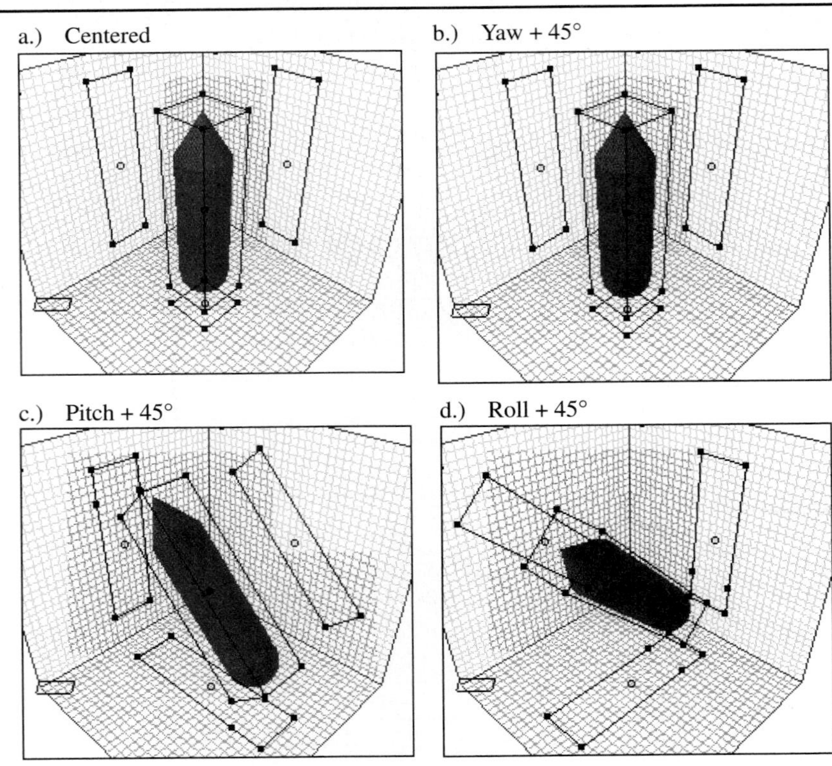

Types of rotational movement

FIGURE 18-29

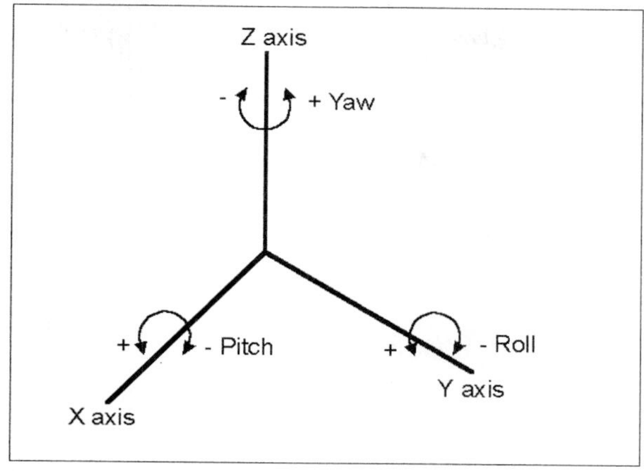

Rotational movement about the axes

FIGURE 18-30

Notice how in the above rotations, the bottom swung up when the top (nose) swung down. This is because the rocket is rotating about the hot point in its center. If you wanted the rocket to rotate on its base, then you would drag the hot point down to where you want the rotation.

6. Return Roll to 0, click on Apply, and drag the projection of the hot point on the right wall down to the base of the object.
7. Change Roll to 45 and click on Apply. The rocket now rotates from the base as you can see here:

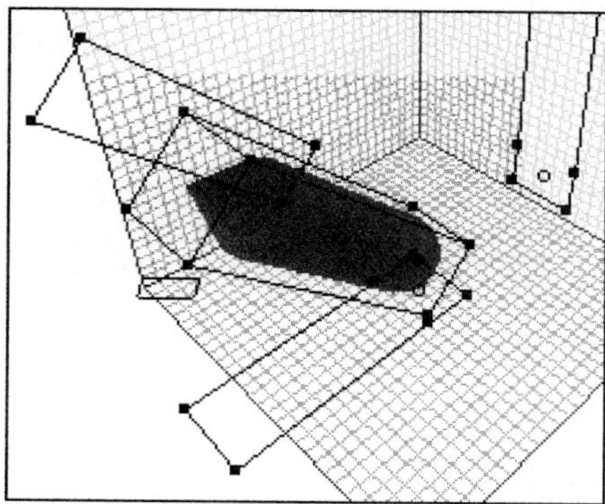

8. Return Roll to 0, click on Apply, and choose Center Hot Point in the Arrange menu.

By combining positional movement from the X, Y, and Z spinners at the top of the dialog box, with rotational movement, you can make your rocket fly as shown in Figure 18-31. The Objects Properties dialog box allows you to scale your rocket, so you can increase the length (the Z size) and have the other sides automatically change to maintain the same proportions. Finally, you can have the rocket pointing down instead of up by clicking on Mirrored. If you tried increasing the size, click on Restore, turn off Mirrored, click on Apply, and close the Object Properties dialog box.

Using the Virtual Trackball

As great as the precise positioning of the Object Properties dialog box is, many people just want to put their hands into the monitor and move the object around. CorelDREAM 3D gives you this capability in the Virtual Trackball, which allows you to rotate your object (rocket in this case) on any axis or combination of axes in a 3D space.

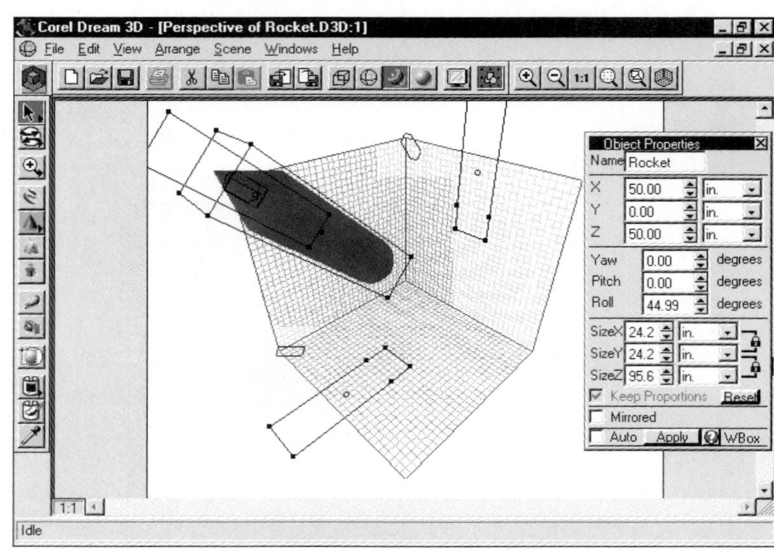

Combining positional movement with rotational movement

FIGURE 18-31

1. With your rocket centered in its universe (if it isn't, choose Align On Universe from the Arrange menu), click on the Virtual Trackball and then click on your rocket. A circle will appear about the object to remind you that you are rotating the object in 3D space.
2. Move the rotational pointer to the rocket and press and hold the mouse button down while you rotate the rocket in any plane. One such rotation is shown here:

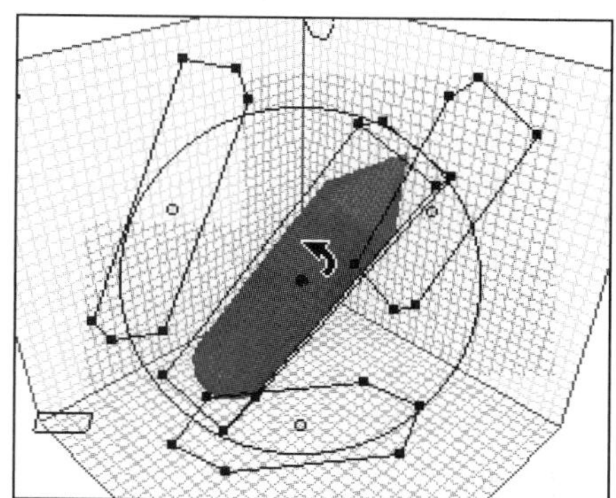

3. When you have exercised this very powerful capability all you want, return the rocket to its centered position by choosing Align On Universe from the Arrange menu.

NOTE: *The Virtual Trackball is a very valuable tool, but it can also move your object in such a way that you are no longer sure what you are looking at and are not sure which way to turn it to correct it. In such cases, use the Arrange menu's Align On Universe to get back to your starting position.*

Applying Shaders

The objects you have created so far have a good geometric form, but they lack the color, texture, and other surface properties to give them a realistic look. The application of surface properties in CorelDREAM 3D is done with *shaders*, which allow you to determine the color, shininess, bumpiness, transparency, reflectivity, and refraction. You can either apply a ready-made shader from the Shaders Browser, or you can create your own with the Shader Editor. You'll do both in this section.

Using the Shaders Browser

The Shaders Browser is like a palette, but it contains far more than different colors. It is a palette of all the surface properties mentioned above. In the Shaders Browser, the surface properties have already been combined to produce some standard looks. Try these on your rocket with the following steps (your rocket should still be on your screen).

1. Turn off the floor and two walls of your working box, and then open the Shaders Browser window from the Windows menu. Arrange your windows so that your screen looks like Figure 18-32.
2. In the Hierarchy window, click on the plus sign to the left of the Rocket group and again on the plus sign next to Group 1 and Group 2. This opens up the segments of the rocket and ungroups them, allowing you to treat the segments separately.
3. Scroll the Shaders Browser horizontally so you can see Metals1.shd and then drag the silver-colored sphere to each of the cylindrical segments. Click on the Better Preview Quality button in the toolbar to see the results (look in the Status bar to see when the shading is complete). Depending

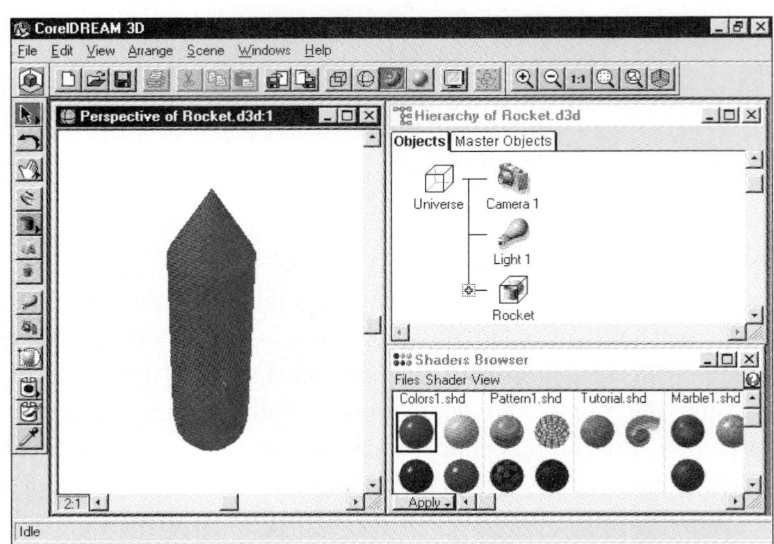

Windows set up for applying shaders

FIGURE 18-32

on the resolution and the number of colors at which you are running your display, this will look more or less metal-like.

4. Select the spiral shape on the right in the Tutorial.shd of the Shaders Browser, select the Perspective window, select the Paint Oval Shading Shape tool, and drag it down and across the top cylinder. The results at 640x480 and 256 colors (translated into 256 shades of gray) are shown in Figure 18-33.

The Paint Shading Shape tools are like appliers of decals, with the decals coming from the Shaders Browser.

Using the Shader Editor

The Shaders Browser has a lot of interesting shaders, but often you'll find that you want something a little different. For that purpose, CorelDREAM 3D has included the Shader Editor, where you can construct a custom shader with exactly the surface properties that you want. See how this works on your rocket.

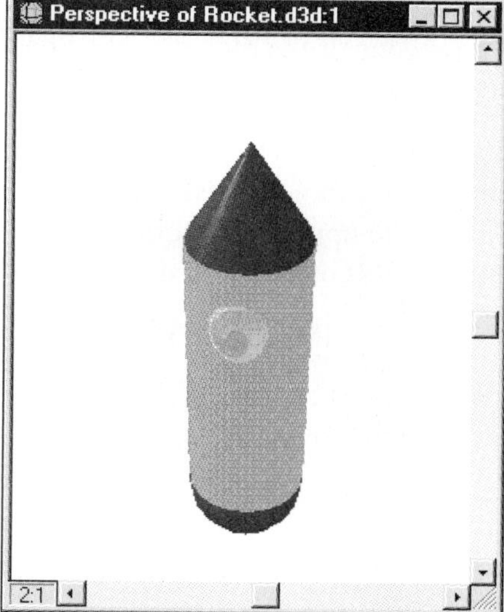

The metallic rocket body with a "decal" applied

FIGURE 18-33

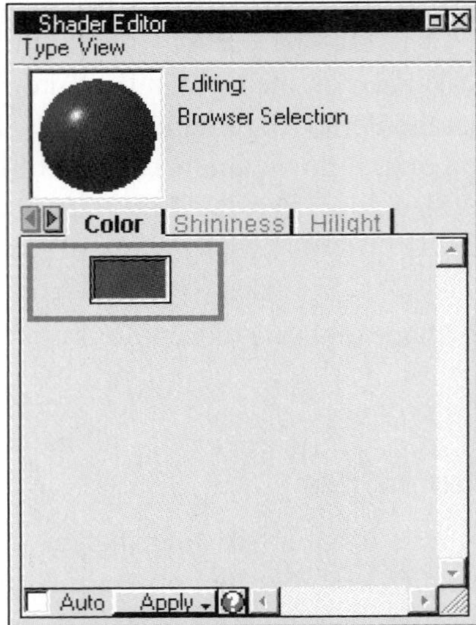

Shader Editor

FIGURE 18-34

1. The first thing you want to do is create and apply a shiny white surface to the nose of the rocket. To do that, double-click on the red color sphere in the Colors1.shd section of the Shaders Browser. The Shader Editor dialog box will open, similar to the one shown in Figure 18-34.
2. Click on the nose cone of the rocket so the Shader Editor reflects the current properties of that surface.
3. Double-click on the color swatch to open the Color Editor shown next. In the Color Editor, you can use the sliders to choose a color or you can use the color wheel in the upper-right corner to open a Color palette. You can also select either the RGB or the CMYK color model.

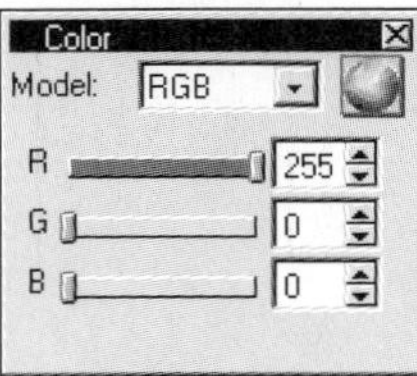

4. White is the presence of all colors, so drag the green (G) and blue (B) sliders all the way to the right so all three colors are 255. The color swatch will change to white. Close the Color Editor.
5. Click on the Shininess tab and increase it to 100-percent. Do the same thing for Highlight. If you click on the right-pointing arrow to the left of the Color tab, you'll see that there are other tabs. These should be set to 0. Click on Apply. (Your display quality should be set to Better Preview Quality.)
6. Select the sphere at the bottom of the rocket and double-click on the color swatch to open the Color Editor. Use the sliders or the Color palette to select a color that you associate with a rocket's exhaust.
7. Save your rocket with a different name, but leave it open. Close the Color dialog box, the Shader Editor, and the Shaders Browser.

On your own, apply surface properties to the other objects you created.

Positioning Lights and Cameras

In all of your work in CorelDREAM 3D so far, you have viewed your work from a "camera," or viewing point, that is in the upper foreground of your working box, using a single light source in the upper left. The position of the lighting is very important because it produces the shadows that give you the 3D effect. Also, the positioning of the view point or camera is important because the view you get in 3D space is very different from different angles. CorelDREAM 3D allows you to add both additional lights (lighting sources) and cameras (viewing locations). Do that with your rocket.

1. Maximize the Perspective window, turn on the walls, and align your image so that it is centered and you can see the upper-left corner, as shown in Figure 18-35. The object in the upper-left corner is your sole lighting source (hold down the mouse pointer on it to see its name—Light 1 3D; the 3D means you have the object itself, not a projection). If you look at your rocket, its shadows are consistent with this lighting source. (If you didn't save your file immediately above, do so now so you can easily return to this image.)

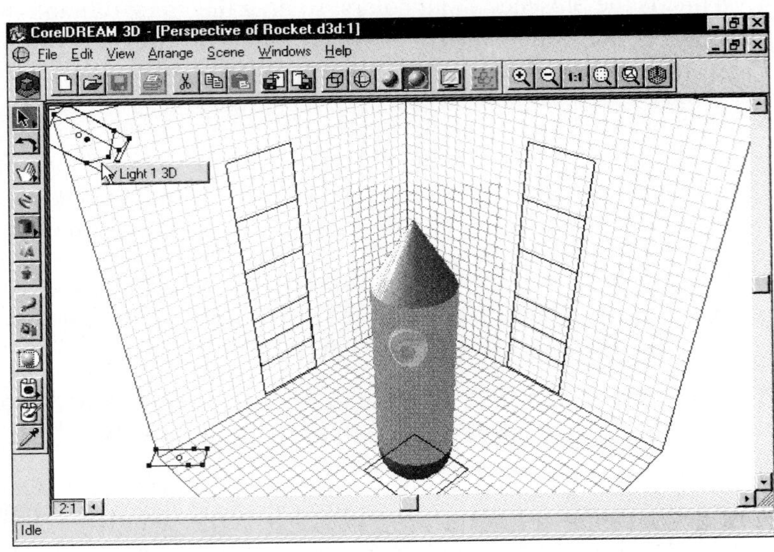

Window aligned to show Light 1 and its shadows

FIGURE 18-35

OTE: *A lighting source is like any other 3D object in your working box in that it takes up 3D space and has projections on each of the walls that you can move to change the lighting source.*

2. With the Selection tool, drag the projection on the floor or ground plane of Light 1 until it is in the floor corner closest to you. Then use the One Axis Rotation tool to rotate the floor projection of Light 1 counter-clockwise so the light is pointing on the "front" of the rocket. Compare the shadows on your rocket, like those in Figure 18-36, with those before you moved the light shown in Figure 18-35. (The square in the middle of the rocket is a projection of Light 1.)
3. Return Light 1 to its original position (probably the easiest way to do this is to close the current file *without* saving it, and then reopen the same file).

4. Click on the Create Light tool in the toolbox and click the resulting crosshair in the far upper right (opposite the position of Light 1).
5. Click on the Selection tool, hold down SHIFT while clicking on the nose cone of the rocket to select both it and your new light, and then from the Arrange menu choose Point At. If you have Better Preview Quality

selected, you'll see the effects of the new light on the nose cone are like those in Figure 18-37.

NOTE: *If your light did not come in as shown in Figure 18-37, that is just one of the hazards of working in 3D space—it's very hard to know where to place the original point. After placement, you can drag the floor and wall projections to better position the light.*

6. With the new light selected, open the Scene menu and select Light Settings. The Lighting Parameters dialog box will open, as shown in Figure 18-38. Here, you can set all of the characteristics of your light. Try the various controls and observe the effects on the sample window in the dialog box. When you have the light the way you want it, close the dialog box.

7. Select the Create Camera tool and position it about two-thirds of the way up the front-left wall. Using the Selection tool, with the camera still selected, hold down SHIFT, select the top cylinder of the rocket, and then choose Point At from the Arrange menu.

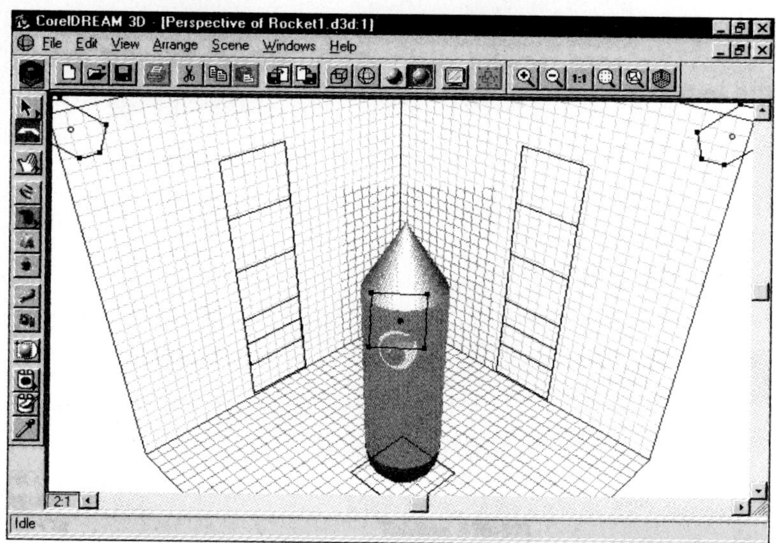

Light 1 moved closest to the observer

FIGURE 18-36

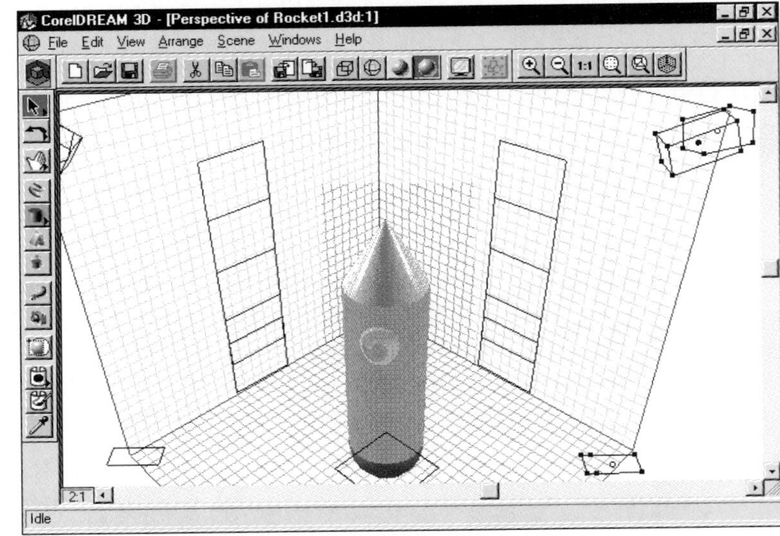

Effects of the new light coming from the right

FIGURE 18-37

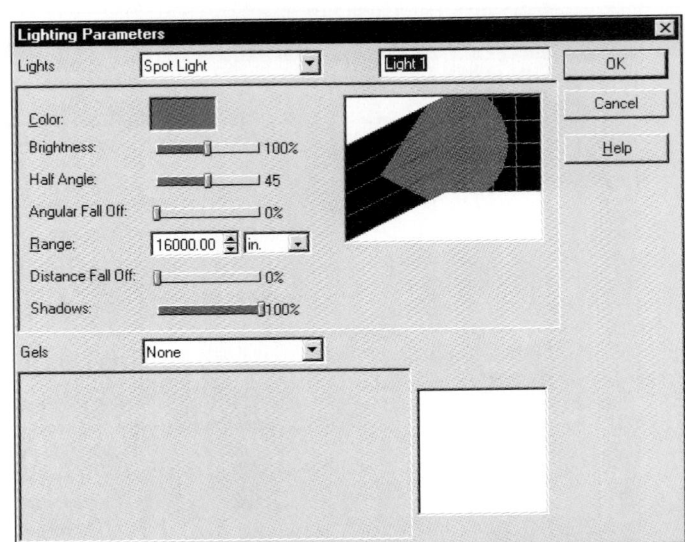

Lighting Parameters dialog box

FIGURE 18-38

8. From the Scene menu, select Camera Settings to open the dialog box shown next.

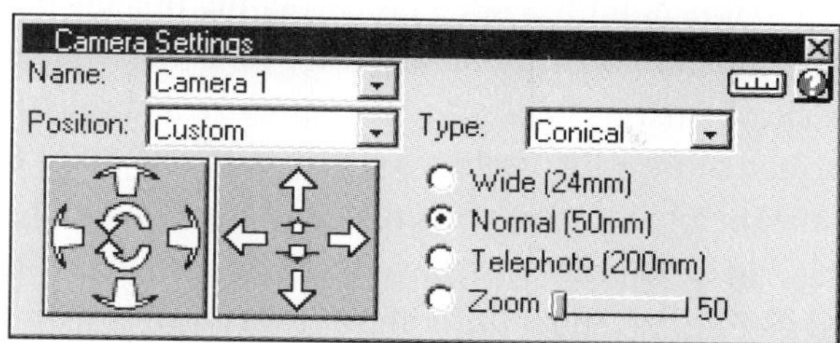

9. Open the Name drop-down list box and select Camera 2. As soon as you do, you'll get a new view of your rocket, representing what that camera sees. One example is shown in Figure 18-39. Your view may be very different, depending on where you placed your camera.
10. Add another camera on the opposite wall and then, with the Camera Settings dialog box, try out the various controls, switching from camera to camera. If you want, add a third new camera and position it so you have the views you want of your rocket. If desired, add more lights.
11. When you are done with your camera placement and setting, save your work under a new name.

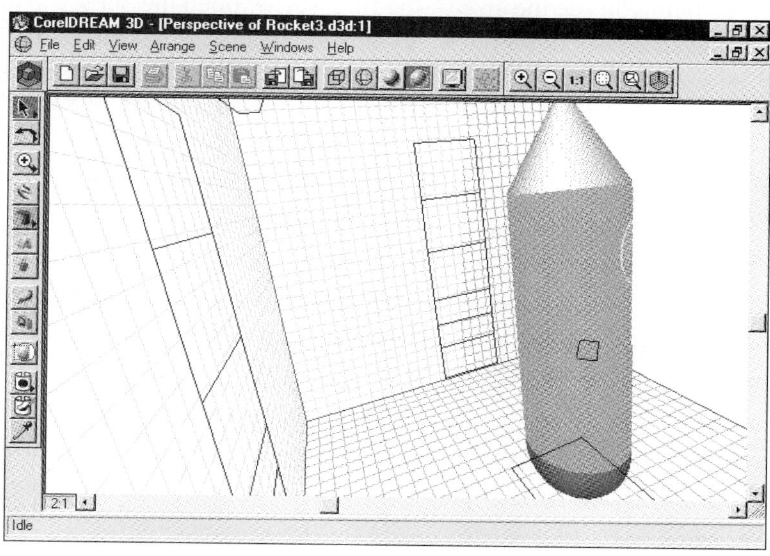

View from Camera 2

FIGURE 18-39

Preparing and Rendering a Scene

All of your work up to this point has been preparing the objects that you will use in your scene and nothing has been done on the scene itself; that is left to your imagination—it is simply using steps you have already learned to create, position, and prepare the surface of the objects that you will use. The point of CorelDREAM 3D, though, is to take the objects that you create, arrange them into a scene, add the appropriate lighting, check various viewing angles, and finally, when you are ready, to "snap" a finished picture, to render the completed scene into a bitmap image. After all the preparatory work, the final steps are anticlimactic. All that remains is to make the settings that will control the rendering, check the final view, render the scene in all its final glory, save the bitmap, and then print it. Run those steps to complete the chapter.

1. From your camera work that you did above, pick a view you want to use in the final scene. Remember that you can use the camera controls to get the exact angle you want.

IP: *Remember to go to 1:1 magnification when you are doing your final viewing so you will see how your final scene will be printed.*

2. To help you see the size of the final scene, open the View menu and choose Production Frame. A black rectangle will appear on the screen showing you the area that will be included, as you can see in Figure 18-40.

IP: *If you have the production frame displayed while you are working with the camera settings, you can get a good idea of how the settings are affecting the final view.*

3. From the Scene menu, choose Render Setup Final. The Artwork Settings dialog box will open, as shown in Figure 18-41. This is where you set the size of the production frame and the resolution to use.

IP: *The larger the production frame and the higher the resolution, the longer it will take to render and print and the larger the output file size.*

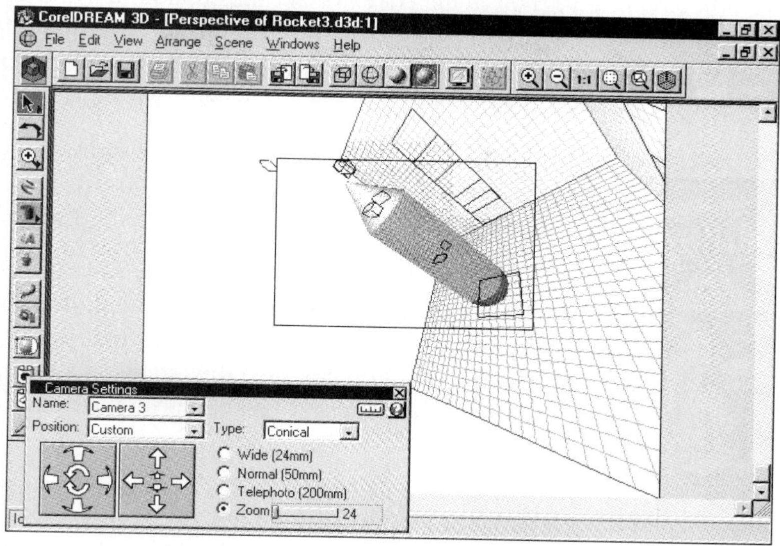

Adjusting the view within the production frame

FIGURE 18-40

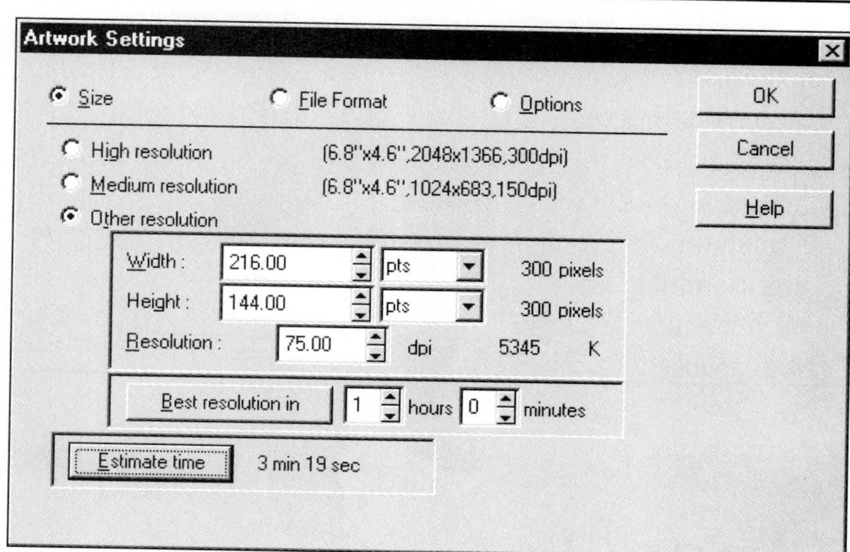

Artwork Settings dialog box

FIGURE 18-41

4. Click on File Format in the Artwork Settings dialog box and select the file format for the bitmap image that will be produced. You should pick a format that will allow you to do what you want to do with the image. TIFF is a convenient format.

5. Next click on Options. Here, you can determine the camera you want to use and the surface features you want enabled. In most instances the defaults should serve your needs. When you are satisfied with the settings, click on OK.

6. Open the Scene menu again, and click on Render Final. In a short time, the Imaging window will appear with the final image of your scene, as you can see in Figure 18-42. You can save this image in a bitmap format (such as .TIF, .PCX, or .BMP), and/or you can print the image. When you have done that, you're done!

This chapter has given you a good introduction to CorelDREAM 3D, but there is much more in this very powerful product that you should explore on your own.

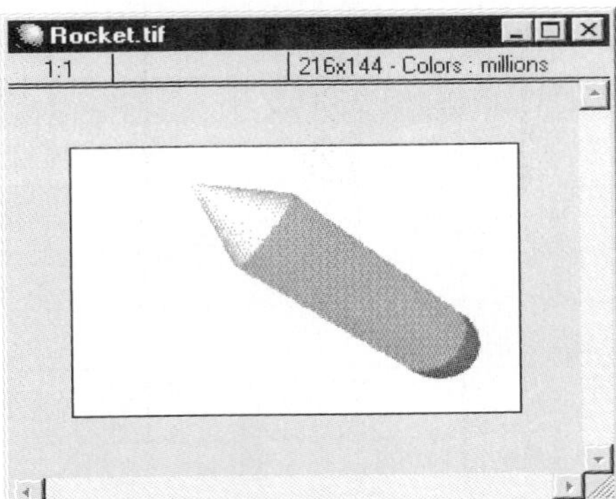

Final Rendered image

FIGURE 18-42

COREL DRAW!™ 6

in action

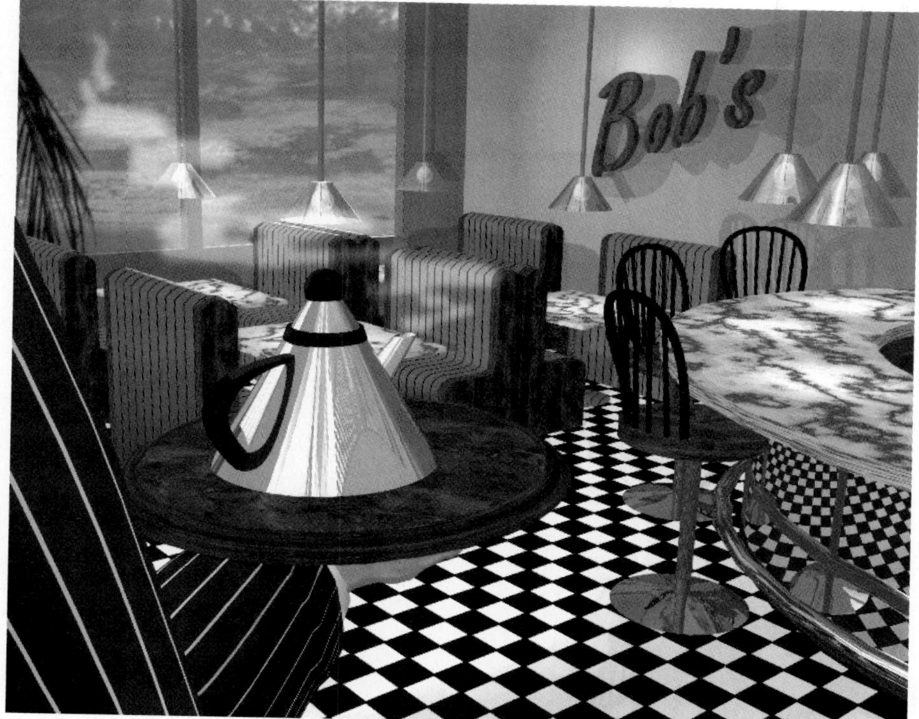

Bob's Caf—Robert Boutin

Robert Boutin used CorelDREAM 3D to create *Bob's Caf.* You can see many of CorelDREAM 3D's features in the piece including 3D text and 3D shapes.

Robert Boutin works for Corel Corporation in Ottawa and was the in-house award winner for 1995 in Corel's World Design Contest. Bob can be reached through Corel at (613) 727-8200.

A

B

C

D

E

H

I

J

K

L

M

N

O

P

Q

R

S

T

U

V

W

Z

The NEW CLASSICS

ORACLE DBA HANDBOOK

by Kevin Loney

Every DBA can learn to manage a networked Oracle database efficiently and effectively with this comprehensive guide.

Price: $34.95 U.S.A.
Available Now
ISBN: 0-07-881182-1
Pages: 704, paperback

TUNING ORACLE

by Michael J. Corey, Michael Abbey and Daniel J. Dechichio, Jr.

Learn to customize Oracle for optimal performance and productivity with this focused guide.

Price: $29.95 U.S.A.
Available Now
ISBN: 0-07-881181-3
Pages: 336, paperback

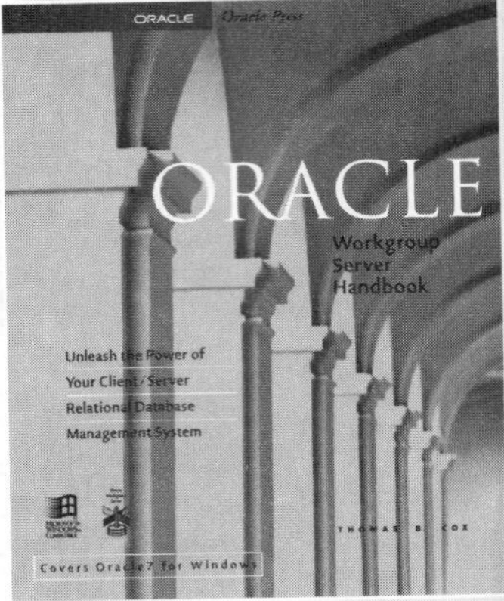

ORACLE WORKGROUP SERVER HANDBOOK

by Thomas B. Cox

Take full advantage of the power and flexibility of the new Oracle Workgroup Server and Oracle7 for Windows with this comprehensive handbook.

Covers Oracle7 for Windows

Price: $27.95 U.S.A.
Available Now
ISBN: 0-07-881186-4
Pages: 320, paperback

ORACLE: A BEGINNER'S GUIDE

by Michael Abbey and Michael J. Corey

For easy-to-understand, comprehensive information about Oracle RDBMS products, this is the one book every user needs.

Price: $29.95 U.S.A.
Available Now
ISBN: 0-07-882122-3
Pages: 560, paperback

ORACLE® *Oracle Press*™

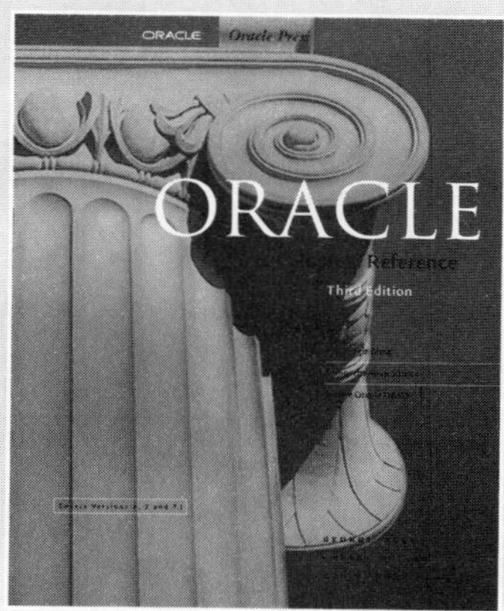

ORACLE: THE COMPLETE REFERENCE

Third Edition

by George Koch
and Kevin Loney

Get true encyclopedic coverage of Oracle with this book. Authoritative and absolutely up-to-the-minute.

Price: $34.95 U.S.A.
Available Now
ISBN: 0-07-882097-9
Pages: 1104, paperback

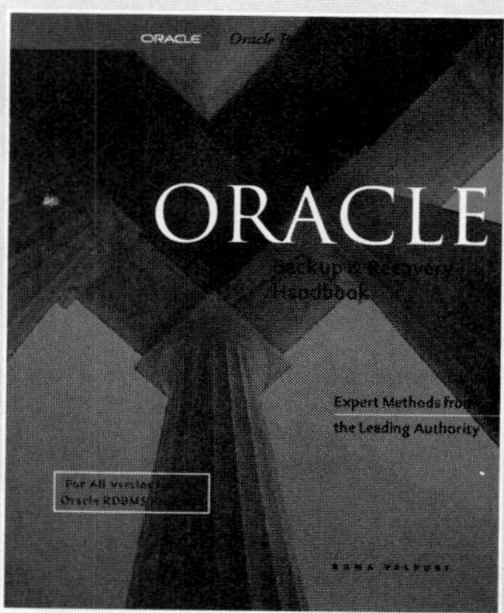

ORACLE BACKUP AND RECOVERY HANDBOOK

by Rama Velpuri

Keep your database running smoothly and prepare for the possibility of system failure with this comprehensive resource and guide.

Price: $29.95 U.S.A.
Available Now
ISBN: 0-07-882106-1
Pages: 400, paperback

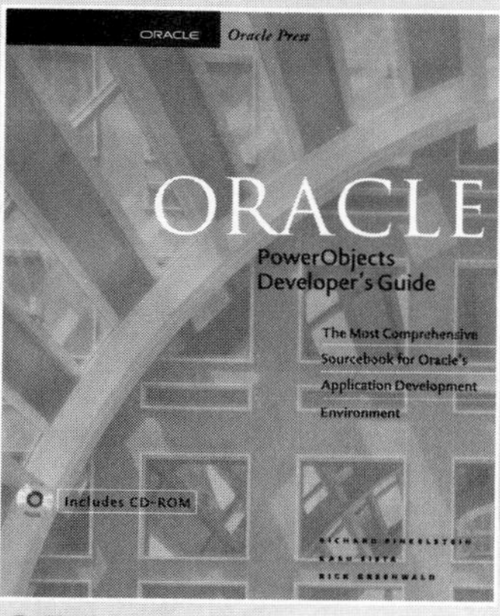

ORACLE POWER OBJECTS DEVELOPER'S GUIDE

by Richard Finkelstein,
Kasu Sista, and Rick Greenwald

Integrate the flexibility and power of Oracle Power Objects into your applications development with this results-oriented handbook.

Price: $39.95 U.S.A.
Includes One CD-ROM
Available September, 1995
ISBN: 0-07-882163-0
Pages: 656, paperback

ORACLE POWER OBJECTS HANDBOOK

by Bruce Kolste
and David Petersen

This is the only book available on Oracle's new single/multi-user database product.

Price: $29.95 U.S.A.
Available August, 1995
ISBN: 0-07-882089-8
Pages: 512, paperback

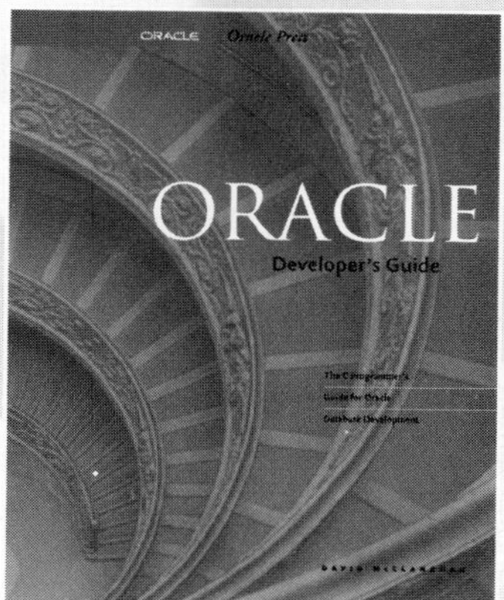

ORACLE DEVELOPER'S GUIDE

by David McClanahan

Learn to develop a database that is fast, powerful, and secure with this comprehensive guide.

Price: $29.95 U.S.A.
Available November, 1995
ISBN: 0-07-882087-1
Pages: 608, paperback

BC640SL

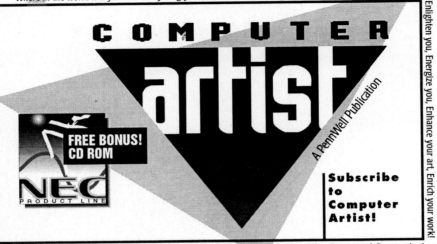

SURF THE NET WITHOUT GETTING WET!

From the safety and comfort of an easy chair, see what has fascinated millions and held the world spellbound. Now the elusive postings on the Internet are available to every reader—no computer necessary! The one and only INTERNET INSIDER uncovers surprising and sordid details direct from reputable sources on the Net—from the clever, amusing, and often shocking to the touching, sentimental, or sad.

FIND BIZARRE, STRANGE, AND TITILLATING STUFF THAT WILL MAKE HEARTS POUND...

INTERNET INSIDER HAS IT ALL

INTERNET INSIDER

by Ruffin Prevost
$14.95 U.S.A.
ISBN: 0-07-882084-7

"MORE EXCITING THAN CHOCOLATE ICE CREAM... MORE INFORMATIVE THAN THE 7 O'CLOCK NEWS."

SEE WHAT'S FASCINATING MILLIONS OF PEOPLE WORLDWIDE...

The INTERNET YELLOW PAGES Second Edition
by Harley Hahn and Rick Stout
$29.95 U.S.A.
ISBN: 0-07-882098-7

Schildt's WINDOWS 95 PROGRAMMING in C and C++
by Herbert Schildt
$29.95 U.S.A.
ISBN: 0-07-882081-2

THAT'S EDUTAINMENT! A Parent's Guide to Educational Software
by Eric Brown
Includes one CD-ROM
$29.95 U.S.A.
ISBN: 0-07-882083-9

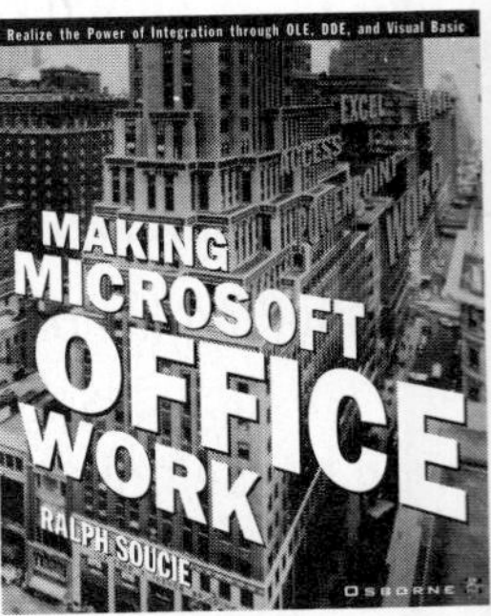

Making MICROSOFT OFFICE Work
by Ralph Soucie
$24.95 U.S.A.
ISBN: 0-07-881188-0

BC640SL